THE 9 COMPETENCIES AND THE PRACTICE BEHAVIORS [illegible] NCE

Competency 5: Engage in Policy Practice	
A. Identify social policy at the local, state, and federal level that impacts well-being, service delivery, and access to social services	1, 2, 3, 4, [illegible] 11, 12, 13, 14, 15, 16
B. Assess how social welfare and economic policies impact the delivery of and access to social services	1, 2, 3, 4, 5, 6, 7, 8, 9, 10, 11, 12, 13, 14, 15, 16
C. Apply critical thinking to analyze, formulate, and advocate policies that advance human rights and social, economic, and environmental justice	1, 2, 3, 4, 5, 6, 7, 8, 9, 10, 11, 12, 13, 14, 15, 16

Competency 6: Engage With Individuals, Families, Groups, Organizations, and Communities	3, 6, 8, 11, 13, 15
A. Apply knowledge of human behavior and the social environment, person-in-environment, and other multidisciplinary theoretical frameworks to engage with clients and constituencies	3, 6, 8, 11, 13, 15
B. Use empathy, reflection, and interpersonal skills to effectively engage diverse clients and constituencies	

Competency 7: Assess Individuals, Families, Groups, Organizations, and Communities	3-16
A. Collect and organize data, and apply critical thinking to interpret information from clients and constituencies	3, 4, 5, 6, 7, 8, 9, 10, 11, 12, 13, 14, 15, 16
B. Apply knowledge of human behavior and the social environment, person-in-environment, and other multidisciplinary theoretical frameworks in the analysis of assessment data from clients and constituencies	
C. Develop mutually agreed-on intervention goals and objectives based on the critical assessment of strengths, needs, and challenges within clients and constituencies	
D. Select appropriate intervention strategies based on the assessment, research knowledge, and values and preferences of clients and constituencies	

Competency 8: Intervene With Individuals, Families, Groups, Organizations, and Communities	1-16
A. Critically choose and implement interventions to achieve practice goals and enhance capacities of clients and constituencies	3, 4, 5, 6, 7, 8, 9, 10, 11, 12, 13, 14, 15, 16
B. Apply knowledge of human behavior and the social environment, person-in-environment, and other multidisciplinary theoretical frameworks in interventions with clients and constituencies	3, 6, 8, 11, 13, 15
C. Use inter-professional collaboration as appropriate to achieve beneficial practice outcomes	1, 2, 3
D. Negotiate, mediate, and advocate with and on behalf of diverse clients and constituencies	1, 2, 3, 4, 5, 6, 7, 8, 9, 10, 11, 12, 13, 14, 15, 16
E. Facilitate effective transitions and endings that advance mutually agreed-on goals	

Competency 9: Evaluate Practice With Individuals, Families, Groups, Organizations, and Communities	
A. Select and use appropriate methods for evaluation of outcomes	
B. Apply knowledge of human behavior and the social environment, person-in-environment, and other multidisciplinary theoretical frameworks in the evaluation of outcomes	
C. Critically analyze, monitor, and evaluate intervention and program processes and outcomes	
D. Apply evaluation findings to improve practice effectiveness at the micro, mezzo, and macro levels	

Social Welfare Policy in a Changing World

Shannon R. Lane
Yeshiva University

Elizabeth S. Palley
Adelphi University

Corey S. Shdaimah
University of Maryland, Baltimore

Los Angeles | London | New Delhi
Singapore | Washington DC | Melbourne

FOR INFORMATION

SAGE Publications, Inc.
2455 Teller Road
Thousand Oaks, California 91320
E-mail: order@sagepub.com

SAGE Publications Ltd.
1 Oliver's Yard
55 City Road
London EC1Y 1SP
United Kingdom

SAGE Publications India Pvt. Ltd.
B 1/I 1 Mohan Cooperative Industrial Area
Mathura Road, New Delhi 110 044
India

SAGE Publications Asia-Pacific Pte. Ltd.
18 Cross Street #10-10/11/12
China Square Central
Singapore 048423

Acquisitions Editor: Joshua Perigo
Content Development Editor: Alissa Nance
Production Editor: Astha Jaiswal
Copy Editor: Deanna Noga
Typesetter: C&M Digitals (P) Ltd.
Proofreader: Heather Kerrigan
Indexer: Celia McCoy
Cover Designer: Janet Kiesel
Marketing Manager: Zina Craft

Library of Congress Cataloging-in-Publication Data

Names: Lane, Shannon R., author. | Palley, Elizabeth S., author. | Shdaimah, Corey S., author.

Title: Social welfare policy in a changing world / Shannon R. Lane, Adelphi University, Elizabeth S. Palley, Adelphi University, Corey S. Shdaimah, University of Maryland, Baltimore, MD, USA.

Description: Thousand Oaks : SAGE Publishing, 2019. | Includes bibliographical references and index.

Identifiers: LCCN 2019030479 | ISBN 9781544316185 (paperback) | ISBN 9781544316161 (epub) | ISBN 9781544316178 (epub) | ISBN 9781544316192 (pdf)

Subjects: LCSH: Social policy. | Public welfare.

Classification: LCC HN18.3 .L36 2019 | DDC 306—dc23
LC record available at https://lccn.loc.gov/2019030479

Printed in the United States of America

This book is printed on acid-free paper.

19 20 21 22 23 10 9 8 7 6 5 4 3 2 1

BRIEF CONTENTS

DETAILED CONTENTS

PREFACE

The three of us have taught policy courses to BSW and MSW students in several different schools for many years. Students often come into their social work education with a drive for social justice and a calling to help people. Their enthusiasm can be tested by required social work policy courses, which some students feel are disconnected from the social work practice they've imagined. We wrote this book so that we could have the text we have always wanted for our classes in which the link between policy and practice is clear. While we want our students to know the historical foundations of our profession, to understand the policy process, to have the theoretical knowledge to assess the policies they find, and to have a basic understanding of critical subject matter, we also want them to feel connected to the material. We want students to know what policies affect people, including themselves, and community! We have designed this book with both BSW and MSW students in mind—it often answers specific questions that those students have asked us throughout our academic careers.

The world is changing very quickly. We started thinking about this book after the 2016 elections, when it was clear that the political world had shifted in ways that would affect policy, including the election of President Trump on the Republican ticket and power changes in many states, but it was too early to tell what all the effects would be. As we continued to write, the 2018 midterm elections changed control of the House of Representatives to the Democrats and brought more women and people of color into elected office, while also reinforcing conservative power structures in many states. As this book goes to press with the 2020 elections just around the corner, we know that policies will continue to change at a rapid rate. We hope that students will have both the curiosity about what is happening in the policy world and the tools to research and stay informed about policies in the areas that are important to them. The title, *Social Welfare Policy in a Changing World,* seemed appropriate for the times.

OUR VISION

We have three goals for *Social Welfare Policy in a Changing World*. First, we want students to understand the importance of policy. We believe that once students see the many ways that policy affects every aspect of their lives and the lives of people and communities, they will no longer perceive a disconnect between policy and practice. As students read through this book, particularly the vignettes that start each chapter, we hope they will start to see the handprints that policy decisions make all around them.

Second, once they see how much policy decisions matter in their lives, we hope they will develop curiosity about those policies. We hope they will want to learn which policies provide services and benefits clients need and which are harmful to communities. We hope students will use the information in this book and the analysis here as models for the questions that they can ask about policies and policy proposals.

Third, we hope students will see the many ways in which they can influence policy decisions. We want students to feel that they have the power to create change and feel compelled to use their power in collaboration with allies and with those around them.

HOW OUR BOOK ENGAGES STUDENTS

Social Welfare Policy in a Changing World and the online supplemental materials have been designed to engage BSW and MSW students. Each chapter starts with a vignette to allow students to place the policies they are going to examine in the context of people they might meet in their practice and a set of reflection questions that help set the stage for the chapter. At the end of the chapter, students can return to the vignette to see how their answers to the questions have changed as their understanding of the subject matter has grown. Each chapter has interactive activities that ask students to reflect on what they are reading, do more research, or think about ways they could advocate to address the problem at hand. The online materials have interactive activities, many of which connect with online resources. These activities are designed to work in a face-to-face or online class, to make them accessible to social work students no matter what form their classroom takes. We want to introduce students to the language that is used in the policy process, so key terms are bolded in each chapter and defined both in the chapter and in the glossary.

CONTENT, ORGANIZATION, AND LANGUAGE

The first three chapters provide the foundation for the rest of the book, and we recommend the reader start with those. The first chapter puts social policy and the social work profession within a historical context, and highlights the ways in which social work values and ethics inform social work within policy arenas. The second chapter reviews the policy process, using specific social work examples to take students beyond high school civics to a deeper understanding of the complexities and nuances of the policy process, and the multiple places where their intervention can be effective in influencing policy. The third chapter provides examples of theories that students can use to analyze policy along with a beginning framework they can use to apply theories to a policy.

The remainder of this book is divided by content area, which allows faculty to assign all thirteen content chapters, or choose the ones that are more relevant for their goals. These content chapters include many areas that you might expect to see in a social work policy book, including education, health, immigration, housing and homelessness, child welfare, work and employment, and policy related to people with disabilities and older adults. It also includes chapters on child care and early childhood education, criminal justice, higher education, families, and the environment. While many of these are rarely found in social work policy texts, they are key policy areas of social work practice and therefore critical for social work students to understand.

In this book we pay close attention to language. We generally use what is called person-first language, which centers on the person rather than a particular facet of their identity or character trait. One exception to that is when people themselves have asked to be identified in a particular way. This may be because they want to lay claim to an identity or to change public perception. That means that descriptions of groups can be controversial and can change over time. There can also be disagreement among members of identity groups about how they want to be referred to. In this book, we have chosen to adhere most closely with how groups want to self-identify and, in some cases, we explicitly discuss the evolution of how groups have been identified over time. In a similar vein, we recognize that racial and ethnic categories can be controversial and they have been used for rhetorical purposes across the political spectrum. In acknowledgment of the political nature of how we categorize racial and ethnic groups, we explicitly share that we have chosen to use follow the guidelines for using grammatical conventions related to racial and ethnic demographic characteristics adopted by the Columbia School of Journalism (Perlman, n.d.)[1]

[1]Perlman, M. (n.d.). Black and white: Why capitalization matters. Columbia Journalism Review. Retrieved from https://www.cjr.org/analysis/language_corner_1.php

You might also notice that we do not have a chapter that focuses specifically on race, poverty, gender, or sexual orientation. These are often linked with oppression and discrimination in discussions of social policy. Because we believe that these issues are so integral to the policies we discuss, we have instead woven them into every chapter in the book.

Angela Conley, BSW, a county commissioner in Hennepin County, Minnesota, says,

> A lot of our elected officials have law backgrounds, public policy backgrounds. There's something to be said about the public servant with a social work background. It's ultimately rooted in humanity, sometimes love, and rooted in the need to see people uplifted. That's what we're elected to do.

We hope that you will leave this book with a clear understanding of how the love of social justice and commitment to helping people that brought you to social work can combine with your newfound knowledge about the policy process. This combination will allow you to make the world better for clients and communities.

Instructor Resources

SAGE edge for instructors supports your teaching by making it easy to integrate quality content and create a rich learning environment for students with:

- **a password-protected site** for complete and protected access to all text-specific instructor resources;
- **test banks** that provide a diverse range of ready-to-use options that save you time. You can also easily edit any question and/or insert your own personalized questions;
- **editable, chapter-specific PowerPoint® slides** that offer complete flexibility for creating a multimedia presentation for your course;
- **lecture notes** that summarize key concepts by chapter to help you prepare for lectures and class discussions;
- **chapter-specific discussion questions** help launch engaging classroom interaction while reinforcing important content;
- **chapter activities** for individual or group projects provide lively and stimulating ideas for use in and out of class reinforce active learning
- **multimedia content** featuring third party videos that bring concepts to life; and
- **sample course syllabi** for semester and quarter courses that provide suggested models for structuring your courses.

SAGE edge for students enhances learning, it's easy to use, and offers:

- an **open-access site** that makes it easy for students to maximize their study time, anywhere, anytime;
- **multimedia content** featuring third party videos that bring concepts to life;
- **eFlashcards** that strengthen understanding of key terms and concepts; and
- **eQuizzes** that allow students to practice and assess how much they've learned and where they need to focus their attention.

Access the instructor and student sites at edge.sagepub.com/lane.

ACKNOWLEDGMENTS

Thank you to Nathan Davidson, Alissa Nance, Joshua Perigo, and the rest of the team at Sage for your wisdom, enthusiasm, and advice throughout this process.

Thank you to the reviewers and substantive experts for your time, effort, and insights, which improved the book tremendously: Joan Davitt, Justin Hodge, Linda Houser, Jan Johnson, Sylvester Amara Lamin, Vicki Lens, Linda Long, Natalie Matthews, Victoria Osborne, Beverly C. Sealey, W. Patrick Sullivan, Carolyn J. Tice, and Alex Vitale. As we always assure our students, no one can be an expert in all areas of policy. We are grateful to these social workers and members of allied professions who shared their wisdom, although of course all mistakes are our own.

We want to particularly thank the Graduate Assistants who worked with us as we wrote this book, including Ivana Alexander, Laurie Rodriguez, Francis Furmanek, Adilene Garcia, and Jonas Rosen. You will see their contributions highlighted throughout. Thank you especially to Jennifer Dull who co-authored the education chapter and who drafted all our learning objectives. Thank you for bringing your enthusiasm, expertise, and perspectives to this work.

SHANNON'S ACKNOWLEDGMENTS

Thank you to my co-authors Corey and Elizabeth for your hard work and incredible knowledge that has informed this book. Thank you to my colleagues in social work education, faculty, staff, and particularly students. Your passion for the profession, questions, and commitment to social justice helped inspire and direct this book. I am particularly grateful to my teachers and mentors in the policy world, particularly Senator Tom Daschle, Kelly Fado, John Tropman, and Tanya Rhodes Smith. The late Nancy A. Humphreys, founder of the Humphreys Institute for Political Social Work at the University of Connecticut, has influenced my teaching and research profoundly, and I am forever grateful.

Thank you to my friends and family who have been supportive, willing to talk through policy questions and ideas, provided child care, and kept me energized and enthused, especially to Sheila Lane, Cara Lane-Toomey, and Jennifer McClendon; Jim Geraghty, Aileen Miller, Allison Yezril, and company; and Laura Bartok, Mae Flexer, Ellen Graham, Natalie Matthews, and Political Institute colleagues. Thanks to the Jewish Community Center of Greater New Haven staff, teachers, and families for providing a great place to write while simultaneously educating and caring for my children. To my husband Michael Kapralos, thanks for encouraging me to write and choosing your moment for appendicitis when I needed inspiration to write about health policy. To my daughters Kathleen and Caroline, thanks for entertaining yourselves while I wrote, your amazing laughs, and reminding me every day that your future is worth the work it takes to change policy.

ELIZABETH'S ACKNOWLEDGMENTS

Thank you to my co-authors Corey and Shannon for all your hard work and support throughout the book writing process. Thank you to my husband, Alex Vitale, who helped provide not only substantive expertise about criminal justice but also for being a supportive spouse. Thank you to my mother who has always been willing to read and edit anything I give her with amazing speed and also for being an incredibly supportive, loving parent. Thanks to my father for helping keep me grounded and reminding me to put one foot in front of the other when things become stressful. Thanks to my daughters, Amelia and Charlotte Vitale, for not only reminding me that I need to help make the world a better place for them but also for your newly burgeoning interest in social justice issues from homelessness, to climate change, to animal rights, to women's rights. You are amazing and make everything worthwhile.

COREY'S ACKNOWLEDGMENTS

Mentors and colleagues Jim Baumohl, Joan Davitt, Michael Reisch, Haksoon Ahn, Amanda Lehning, Jennifer Swanberg, and Sandy Schram engaged me in critical conversations about policies, policy change, and U.S. social welfare history over many years in the classroom, hallways, at meetings, in transit, and over meals. Inspiring activist social workers include colleagues Adam Schneider and Jeff Singer, and my earliest and most recent community organizer collaborators David Koppisch and Amanda DeStefano, respectively. All these—and many others profiled in this book—show how social work academics, researchers, organizers, and activists can contribute what they do well to make the world a better place, and they keep me hopeful. I thank Ivana Alexander and Jonas Rosen for their research assistance and in particular for their fascination and outrage, which confirmed why it was important that we write this book. Shannon and Elizabeth remind me that the best collegiality is where constructive criticism and kindness coexist. Our different perspectives and shared vision made this text more complete and, we hope, more accessible.

I am always learning from my family. Amichai, Cliel, Elad, and Sagi do not hesitate to correct me when I am wrong and keep me open and humble to new ideas, challenges, and perspectives. I love that our household is full of passion and caring and that you all live your ideals and don't just discuss them.

ABOUT THE AUTHORS

Shannon R. Lane, LMSW, PhD, is Associate Professor at the Wurzweiler School of Social Work at Yeshiva University. She began her political career as a staff member for U.S. Senate Democratic Leader Tom Daschle while an undergraduate at The George Washington University. She received her MSW from the University of Michigan and returned to Capitol Hill to work for Senators Daschle, Pryor, and Nelson. Since 2004, she has been affiliated with the Nancy A. Humphreys Institute for Political Social Work at the University of Connecticut School of Social Work. She has worked with the Humphreys Institute to coordinate the Campaign School for Social Workers, which has trained more than 1,200 social work students and professionals from around the country to run for political office and hold leadership positions in political settings. She earned her PhD in Social Work from the University of Connecticut and has taught social work policy, macro practice, and research at Yeshiva University, Sacred Heart University, Adelphi University, and the University of Connecticut. Shannon researches strategies to increase the political involvement of social workers and underserved populations and has won national awards for her research on effective teaching of policy and voter engagement. She serves on the editorial board of the *Journal of Social Policy and Research*, is a member of the Council on the Role and Status of Women in Social Work Education with the Council on Social Work Education, and serves as Deputy Registrar of Voters for her town. She and Suzanne Pritzker, PhD, authored *Political Social Work: Using Power to Create Social Change* in 2018 (Springer Publishing).

Elizabeth S. Palley, JD, MSW, PhD, is Professor and Director of the Doctoral Program at the Adelphi University School of Social Work where she teaches social policy to BSW, MSW, and PhD students. She received her JD and MSW from the University of Maryland School of Social Work and her PhD from the Heller School at Brandeis University. She began her career working as a lawyer advocating on behalf of children with special education needs and families with lead poisoned children. Following her experience as a lawyer, she returned to school to pursue a PhD. Her research since that time has focused primarily on policy implementation and the challenges that implementers, often social workers, face as well as the unintended consequences of social policy on those it is designed to help. She has written extensively about special education, child care policy, and pregnancy discrimination in both peer-reviewed journals and op-eds and is an editor of the *Journal of Policy Practice and Research*. In 2009, she had a Fulbright to South Korea where she taught at Yonsei University in their Social Welfare doctoral program. In 2014, she wrote *In Our Hands: The Struggle for U.S. Child Care Policy* (NYU Press) with co-author, Corey Shdaimah.

Corey S. Shdaimah, LLM, PhD, is the Daniel Thursz Distinguished Professor of Social Justice and Academic Coordinator for the MSW/JD and MSW/MPP dual degrees at the University of Maryland School of Social Work. She holds law degrees from Tel Aviv University and University of Pennsylvania and a PhD from Bryn Mawr College Graduate School of Social Work and Social Research. Her work focuses on how policies unfold on the ground, with a special interest in how people charged with implementing policy work in and around policies that they believe are unjust or inefficient. She is also interested in how people who are targeted by policies work around them. In the past 10 years she has focused on prostitution policy, including prostitution diversion programs that target street-based sex work, dependency court reforms, and child care policy (often with Elizabeth). Because Corey is interested in learning from people who are most affected by policy but least often heard, her research methods almost always include participatory components ranging from input in research design, engaged qualitative techniques including ethnographic research and photovoice, and work with community groups about how and where to disseminate knowledge that will be of practical as well as academic use. Corey is the author and co-author of many articles, three books including *Change Research: A Case Study on Collaborative Methods for Social Workers and Advocates* (with Sanford Schram and Roland Stahl, Columbia University Press), and co-editor (with Katie Hail-Jares and Chrysanthi Leon) of *Challenging Perspectives on Street-Based Sex Work* (Temple University Press).

SOCIAL WORK

A Value-Based Profession in Historical Context

LEARNING OBJECTIVES

1.1: Summarize social work's values, ethics, and early history

1.2: Review social welfare policy throughout the various eras of U.S. history

1.3: Discuss the current policy context and its potential effect on social welfare policy

If you are reading this textbook you are probably a BSW or MSW student in a required policy class. If you are like the majority of your peers around the country, you are probably planning a career of what many refer to as a *clinical* social work practice (Council on Social Work Education, 2015). This means that you intend to focus on enhancing the well-being of individuals, families, and communities through practices and interventions that bring out the best in them or help them cope with difficult circumstances through therapy, counseling, or case management. If you are like the remaining minority of social work students, you are focused on what many refer to as *macro* practice, which means that you intend to bring about changes in programs, systems, or broader society using methods such as community organizing, policy practice, or administration. These two groups of students typically come into required policy classes with different hopes, concerns, and expectations. What you and your peers share is the choice to carry out your mission within the framework of social work, a value-based profession that is governed by a Code of Ethics. Your new professional Code of Ethics requires that you attend to the interactions that occur between the individual and society to provide the best possible services for clients and communities. While this may be challenging, we hope that this book helps you embrace this as central to your identity as a social worker and that it will be a source of professional pride.

Policy literacy, analysis, and advocacy have been a part of social work practice from its inception. This chapter examines the roots of social welfare policy, including historical markers such as the English Poor Laws and the New Deal, and how they have influenced social policy in the United States. It describes the debates between early social workers from the Charity Organization Societies and Settlement Houses, the foundational movements of the modern social work profession, to which we can trace tensions in our current professional practices. It highlights the time periods and events that are most critical to U.S. social policy from the post-Civil War period until the Trump administration. All this lays the framework for the policies discussed in this text. For each time period, we briefly describe major political, economic, and social milestones with a parallel description of the social work profession's status, challenges, and progress. This chapter also highlights significant contributions to social policy and the policy process in the United States that were made by social workers. Last, this chapter introduces the values of the profession, using the National Association of Social Workers' (NASW) Code of Ethics (2017) as a basis, with a focus on the six core values of the profession and Ethical Standard 6: *Social workers' ethical responsibilities to the broader society.*

Vignette: Clinical and Macro Social Workers as Partners in Change

Read the NASW Code of Ethics. Based on what you know from the media or your personal, work, or volunteer experiences, think about the following questions as you read the vignette. When you finish the vignette, answer the questions below.

1. How do Shellie and Julian's responses differ?
2. How does each response comply with or contradict the NASW Code of Ethics?
3. Propose two examples of how Shellie and Julian might work together in an integrated response.
4. What role might race, class, gender, and other aspects of identity play in this vignette?

Julian is a school-based social worker. He works with Gene, who has been struggling both academically and with his behavior in school. Julian can see that Gene and his family are distressed, and they have sought his assistance in helping Gene acclimate to school. He has helped them secure assessments, an individualized education plan, counseling, and home-based resources. Julian's advocacy efforts, even when successful, are often met with resistance and bureaucratic hurdles. Moreover, Gene is one of many children in Julian's school who face similar challenges. Julian does not have enough time to help all the children in need, and also finds the help he can provide under current laws, school district policies, and available resources is not what it should be. Although he does not know the names of all the policies and directives that impact his work with Gene, Julian knows that they include the Individuals with Disabilities Education Act (IDEA). Julian also knows that testing in the schools, required by IDEA and state government requirements, have changed teachers' and school administrators' ability and willingness to assist children on his caseload, including whether or not they will work with him to retain students with disabilities.

Julian has begun talking with Shellie, a friend from his BSW program who works for a nonprofit disability rights organization. Shellie told him that her organization has been challenging policies that affect children like Gene. For example, they have been tracking the relationship between school testing scores and disciplinary action for children with behavioral disabilities. For the past few months, Shellie has been expressing her frustration with Julian because she claims that his work focuses too much on helping Gene and his family adapt to what she sees as a broken system. It feels to Julian that Shellie doesn't value the importance of the help that he provides to Gene and his family in a time of need. While he finds her work praiseworthy in the abstract, he thinks it is cruel to leave Gene and his other clients "high and dry" while they await policy changes that may never come.

POLICY PRACTICE AND ME: A SOCIAL WORK PERSPECTIVE

Before you get too deep into this book, it will be helpful to think about the values and ethics of the social work profession and how they relate to your own values and ethics. This is a good time to reflect on the history of the profession you have chosen and some of the trailblazers who founded the profession.

Social Work Values and Ethics[1]

The profession of social work is anchored in values. Codes of ethics around the world require social workers to work for individual and societal change, regardless of their practice focus (British Association of Social Workers, 2002; Canadian Association of Social Workers, 2004; IFSW, 2004; NASW, 2017). The preamble to the NASW Code of Ethics (2017) states:

> Social workers are sensitive to cultural and ethnic diversity and strive to end discrimination, oppression, poverty, and other forms of social injustice. These activities may be in the form of direct practice, community organizing, supervision, consultation, administration, advocacy, social and political action, policy development and implementation, education, and research and evaluation. Social workers seek to enhance the capacity of people to address their own needs. Social workers also seek to promote the responsiveness of organizations, communities, and other social institutions to individuals' needs and social problems.

Likewise, the Educational Policy and Accreditation Standards (Council on Social Work Education, 2015) that govern U.S. social work education require that students master core competencies to engage diversity and difference in practice (competency 2); advance human rights

[1]This section, the sections on social work history, and a portion of the section on social work practice were adapted from Shdaimah & McCoyd, 2012.

and social, economic, and environmental justice (competency 3); and engage in policy practice (competency 5). Most professional social work codes of ethics integrate policy-level and individual change efforts. The NASW Code of Ethics (2017) encourages social workers to assess the need for, and strive to achieve, individual and system level change (ethical standard 6). It does not divvy up this work among different professionals but asks that all social workers, whatever their mode of practice, engage in such activities.

Sarah Banks (2010) argues that integrity, also an obligation explicitly noted in most social work codes of ethics, include an awareness "of the totality of the aims, values and rules of the profession, ensuring that their actions are consistent with these norms" (p. 2172). This means that social workers who act with the required integrity must address situations and social forces that give rise to practice environments that are in conflict with social work values. To the extent that these are systemic, ethical social workers should not be content to find the *least bad* ways to resolve dilemmas but should instead actively engage in public dialogue to change the climate so that all social workers can serve all clients in anti-oppressive ways (cf. Strier & Binyamin, 2014).

The social work values of social justice, human worth and dignity, and the centrality of human relationships promote equity and fairness. Individual level practice is important, but insufficient on its own because individual distress is connected to, and affected by, social forces, such as unemployment, discrimination, famine, and war. To work only at the individual level of change may provide temporary relief, but does not address systemic factors that impact clients and others who are or may be in the future in similar situations (Cloward & Piven, 1971/1993; Dempsey, 2008). The individual focus, in fact, may perpetuate injustice (Becker, 2005) and intensify individual distress through victim blaming (Ryan, 1976). Knowledge of policies and their implications for vulnerable populations is also necessary so that well-intentioned social workers do not unwittingly perpetuate harms, as evidenced by workers in state agencies who have at times stigmatized and punished low-income families (Martin, 2012). Similarly, social policy advocacy that remains at the societal level abandons the individual to her circumstances (Shdaimah, Stahl, & Schram, 2009). Structural change alone can take time: Leaving individuals in distress while awaiting social change is callous. Therefore, social workers must be committed to using all the skills and tools at our disposal to work on both.

Charity Organization Societies (COS): Charity Organization Societies, a movement of early social workers that believed in assessing and meeting social needs through systematized and verifiable process. Generally, COS viewed individual misfortune as due to character flaws or poor choices.

Settlement House Movement (SHM): A movement that originated in England and was adopted in many U.S. urban areas with large immigrant populations. Early settlement house workers lived and worked together with people in the communities that they served as partners. It saw poverty and other problems as rooted primarily in systemic problems rather than individual failure.

Social Work History

Many trace the beginnings of U.S. social work to the **Charity Organization Societies (COS)**, which are identified with Mary Richmond and "scientific philanthropy" and to the **Settlement House Movement (SHM)**, which is identified with Jane Addams and a grassroots social advocacy (Brieland, 1990; Ehrenreich, 1985; Reamer, 1998). It often appears that these two types of practice were in direct opposition, in part due to the polarization that grew as social work developed and professionalized (Ehrenreich, 1985). The COS-grounded perspective viewed individual misfortune as generally due to character flaws or poor choices. The SHM-grounded perspective viewed human misfortune as a result of social structures and institutions that constrain individuals.

The historic split between clinical practice and policy practice was not nearly as polarized as many have made it out to be. Both Richmond and Addams, despite their different foci, saw interplay between individual choices and the social context (Addams, 1911; Richmond, 1917). Direct contact with her Hull House neighbors led Addams and her Chicago settlement house colleagues to craft integrated clinical and macro responses to poverty, ill health, and childcare needs (Knight, 2005). Purposely situated in the community it served, Hull House used research to collect individual experiences to understand them within the broader social system. The settlement house workers used surveys, which later became a basis for sociological research, to convince fellow citizens and policymakers of needed changes in areas as diverse as public sanitation and child labor practices (Zimbalist, 1977). Likewise, Richmond (1901) was committed to "a scientific practice of philanthropy." She developed schema of concentric circles to show the levels of influence and targets for intervention including individuals, families, communities, policies, and societal contexts. Social work's scientific investigation led to comprehensive investigation and understanding of problems. Addams and the Hull House residents, and Richmond, acted in individual and policy arenas because they saw the individual and the society as connected and brought both perspectives to problems they tackled.

Social work has continued to respect the influences of both individuals and social structures, seeing them as inextricably connected. A hallmark of social work practice and ethics has been an ongoing thread in the history of social work calling for a need to connect policy to practice (Adams, 2004; Zubrzycki & McArthur, 2004), practice at multiple levels (Breckenridge & James, 2010), and the use of critical ethical reflective practice (Lay & McGuire, 2010). The focus of this text is the United States, but similar conversations about the importance of incorporating macro practice has been heard in other places such as Israel (Weiss Gal, 2008), Great Britain (Reamer & Shardlow, 2009; Stepney, 2009) and Australia (Giles et al., 2007; McDonald & Marsten, 2008; Shankar, Martin, & McDonald, 2009). Calls for integrated practice have been frequent (Hugman, 2009; Johnson, 1999; Specht & Courtney, 1994), but not all that effective. This may reflect the difficulty of implementing integrated practice on the ground rather than a rejection of such arguments. In the next chapter, we provide an in-depth discussion of the key concepts and practices that can help social workers identify and integrate policy into their own practices.

A BRIEF HISTORY OF U.S. SOCIAL WELFARE POLICY

Michael Katz (2013) famously noted that a dominant thread in U.S. social welfare policy is its preoccupation with sorting those categorized as "deserving poor" from people categorized as "undeserving poor." People seen as undeserving are considered responsible for their plight, often through poor decision making such as an unwillingness or inability to take advantage of opportunities that are presumed to exist. People seen as deserving are those who have tried and failed, through no fault of their own, to meet their own needs. We purposely use quotation marks here, because the brief history that we provide below suggests that groups of people most often fall into these categories as a result of their demographic characteristics (i.e., race, gender, ethnicity) and the source of their need (i.e., poverty, desertion, job loss).

Pre-colonial (Including Elizabethan Poor Laws)

The roots of U.S. public assistance are in England. The English welfare system is often traced to the 1601 **Elizabethan Poor Laws** (the Statute of 43 Elizabeth), which are the beginnings of public responsibility for people who were unable to meet their own needs. Kurzman (1970) sees these laws as part of a shift that reflected (1) a secular view of assistance rather than (only) a religious obligation, (2) the recognition of unemployment as a condition requiring assistance rather than (only) disapproval, and (3) a role for national government in assistance. Established by Queen Elizabeth in the wake of widespread unemployment and famine, these laws set up a system of local government relief. They required localities to collect taxes to support those deemed worthy of assistance and required the election of two local "Overseers of the Poor" in each jurisdiction to administer the relief. Some of those requiring assistance, such as older adults and people with

Elizabethan Poor Laws: Legislation enacted in England in 1601 that was seen as the beginnings of public responsibility for people who were unable to meet their own needs

Outdoor relief: Assistance that allowed people to remain in their own homes (in contrast, see **indoor relief**)

Indoor relief: The provision of assistance requiring removal of individuals from their own residence into public institutions such as orphanages, hospitals, or almshouses (in contrast, see **outdoor relief**)

Principle of less eligibility: The idea that any assistance should either be so meager, or contingent upon under conditions so onerous, as to make it undesirable in comparison to any other options for sustenance

disabilities, received what was called **outdoor relief** (i.e., assistance that allowed them to remain in their own homes; Bloy, 2002). Others were provided with **indoor relief**; this included people who were sent to orphanages or hospitals, as well as those considered able-bodied, sometimes called *sturdy beggars* or *idle beggars* who were forced to live in almshouses and perform labor. Children whose parents were unable to support them were apprenticed out, and their parents lost the right to direct their care and upbringing (Hansan, 2011). Those considered able to work who refused could be fined or jailed.

Due to concerns about families migrating to receive assistance, the 1662 Law of Resettlement and Removal allowed localities to expel dependent nonresident individuals or families. The **principle of less eligibility** informed both the original design and subsequent changes to poor relief. According to this principle, any assistance should either be so insufficient or so difficult to get that getting assistance would be the least desirable option for sustenance. Such provisions would lead individuals to seek aid only in the direst of circumstances and would support a capitalist system based on profit made from the exploitation of wage labor.

While the Elizabethan Poor Laws changed over the centuries, its chief features remained the same. These features, many of which continue through history into our current policy, include (1) demonstration of acceptable need; (2) worthiness of recipients; (3) local discretion in administration; (4) making assistance contingent upon submission to authority or imposition of conditions; and (5) the principle of less eligibility.

Colonial Times Until the Civil War

Welfare state: The helping functions that governments provide for the social welfare of its populace

Overseers of the poor: Officials who were tasked with administering and supervising aid to people in poverty in England beginning in the 16th century, a practice that was transplanted to parts of the colonial U.S.

Although some colonists drew on continental religious traditions, most came from England and therefore localities instituted poor laws following the traditions described above. As with the Elizabethan Poor Laws, the U.S. **welfare state** (the helping functions that governments provide individuals and communities for social welfare) was narrowly conceived as helping people from within the community, and only in dire circumstances. Care for older adults and those who were widowed, unemployed, or ill were often combined. Like their British predecessors, early U.S. social welfare policy was intertwined with punishment, rehabilitation, and socialization to community norms. Colonial and early U.S. social welfare policies were administered by local **overseers of the poor**, who viewed assistance through a moral lens and attempted to distinguish between those who deserved aid and those who did not (Day, 2006). Like their English counterparts, they were authorized to levy taxes from the local communities to fund the aid.

Most early American assistance was administered in group settings such as workhouses or almshouses, the first of which was established in Boston in 1662 (Huey, 2001). Some shared sites with prisons. Anyone considered able to work performed difficult and unpleasant labor in exchange for aid according to the principle of less eligibility. Indoor relief were designed to inculcate recipients with the dominant Protestant capitalist values of hard work, frugality, and self-sufficiency (Weber, 1992/1830). In rural areas where congregate care was not feasible, care of those in need was contracted out, sometimes through a process of bidding, which often led to abuse (Hansan, 2011). Although early social welfare policy may be seen as punitive, stingy, and stigmatizing, it also met important needs. In the early years of the Republic, social upheaval and change left individuals and families vulnerable to changes in the economy, illness, and injury. Like today, individuals and families relied on assistance temporarily when in need, which is contrary to the image of continuous or inherent *dependence* that is so often depicted. Using a feminist lens, historian Ruth Wallis Herndon (2012) illustrates the ways almshouses served women as a source of community and sustenance for their families as a result of very limited choices (Baylson, 2017[2]).

[2]Drawing on the work of Eva Rosen and Sudhir Vanketesh (2008) and Carisa Showden, Mira Baylson describes such decision making as "bounded agency," which she defines as "the exertion of power or action to solve immediate problems or choose between alternatives even though the solution or choice is "not necessarily optimal or desirable in the abstract."

As the U.S. population grew and social institutions developed, different types of welfare functions were separated; for example, designated orphanages would separate children who had lost their parents from other categories of "needy" people. The poor conditions of workhouses and the increasing cost of indoor relief for a growing population also led to shifts in assistance. These combined with forces such as immigration, urbanization, industrialization, changes wrought by the Civil War, and changing racial dynamics. All of these factors led to changes in social welfare policy in the mid-1800s. In the next section we explore policies that were designed to respond to these changes.

REFLECTION

WOMEN AND POVERTY THEN AND NOW

Read the following article, which is linked at edge.sagepub.com/lane

Herndon, R. W. (2012). Poor women and the Boston almshouse in the early republic. *Journal of the Early Republic, 32*(3), 349–381. doi:10.1353/jer.2012.0064

Choose one of the four women whom Herndon profiles and put yourself in her place.

1. Write a brief journal entry in which you reflect on
   a. Your feelings about your situation
   b. Your hopes for the future
   c. Your concerns about the future
   d. The advantages and disadvantages of seeking assistance at the Boston almshouse
2. Thinking as a person living in your own time, how might your situation be different from the woman whom you chose and why?

Civil War and Reconstruction

The U.S. Civil War was waged from 1861 to 1865. The Union Army fought the Confederate Army, representing 11 states that tried to secede from the United States ending the uneasy compromise that allowed the existence of slavery at the discretion of individual states. By the end of the Civil War, 620,000 lives were lost, the majority by disease (National Park Service, n.d.). In the period immediately following the war, between 1865 and 1870, three significant amendments were made to the U.S. Constitution. The Thirteenth Amendment abolished slavery. The Fourteenth Amendment granted citizenship to all those born in and naturalized in the United States, effectively granting citizenship to formerly enslaved African Americans. The Fifteenth Amendment prohibited states from withholding the right to vote from men due to their race (women, regardless of race, were not afforded the Constitutional right to vote until 1920).

The Civil War resulted in the freedom of four million formerly enslaved people as well as the dislocation of white and black populations and destruction of many cities in the South. The U.S. Bureau of Refugees, Freedmen, and Abandoned Lands (generally called the Freedmen's Bureau) was established by the federal government to oversee the social and economic rebuilding of the South. This Bureau was operated by the U.S. War Department in multiple arenas to improve the lives, business, and social and economic relations of African Americans and poor whites in the aftermath of the economic destruction of the Civil War (National Archives, 2016).

A review of the Bureau's records shows that African Americans fought hard to realize the new rights accorded to them under the federal law. There were many successes, including the election of African Americans to local, state, and federal government, but there were also challenges. This approximately decade-long period following the Civil War was referred to as **Reconstruction**. Formerly enslaved people and advocates wanted to build different social,

Reconstruction: Approximately decade-long period following the Civil War during which the defeated Southern states were rebuilt under supervision of the federal government

Black Codes: A series of laws and regulations enacted in the post-Civil War South to curtail social, economic, and civil rights of African Americans

political, and economic structures, while many whites in the South sought to restore or recreate the relations of power and privilege that existed prior to the war. Local and state legislatures enacted policies to curtail social, economic, and civil rights of African Americans known as the **Black Codes**. Although these were initially reversed by the federal government, once Reconstruction ended in 1877, Southern states and local government regained and maintained a firm hold on power through segregation, voter suppression, and preferential treatment for whites. Oppressive economic arrangements such as sharecropping, which replicated conditions of slavery, kept some poor whites and many African Americans working the fields of white landowners for little compensation. Similarly, convict leasing allowed for the forced labor of people arrested as vagrants or convicts (Cohen, 1991). Illegal tactics of intimidation and violence were also widespread. It was not until the civil rights movement a century later that these systems of oppression began to be dismantled. Reconstruction was not only hampered by former supporters of the Confederacy, but also by the federal administrative apparatus of recovery. Reconstruction was run by the federal government, and there was much animosity between these Northern administrators and many of the white citizens of the South. On top of the devastation to the economy and the loss of homes, farms, and livelihoods that made recovery difficult, there were accusations of mismanagement and corruption.

The involvement of so many U.S. soldiers and the collateral effect of the Civil War on their families also led to what many historians consider to be one of the most progressive and generous social safety net programs of its time. Federal pensions were provided to veterans and dependents of Union soldiers killed in the war. While federal benefits did not extend to Confederate soldiers and their families, former Confederate states often provided similar assistance. Initially pensions were provided only for veterans who sustained injuries in the Civil War. In 1890, eligibility expanded to include veterans who became unable to perform manual labor regardless of whether the source of their disability was war-related so long as they had served at least 90 days (Skocpol, 1992). Over time, the military pension system was used as a form of pension when age itself made veterans and their dependents eligible for disability benefits that were paid well into the 20th century (Orloff, 1998). Many view the Civil War pension system as groundwork for later U.S. social welfare provision.

Gilded Age

The Gilded Age, as its name suggests, is characterized by a thin patina of wealth covering a much darker reality.[3] Although a small portion of the U.S. population enjoyed great wealth, the overwhelming majority of Americans lived with great hardship and uncertainty. The vagaries of a capitalist industrial system where profits were made from the hard labor of the masses or through speculative investments shook the economy that was unchecked by oversight, regulation, or government protections. The great accumulation of wealth from the building of railroads, mining, and industry often relied on a large, low-paid labor force. Many of these low-wage workers were immigrants fleeing violence and famine in their countries of origin and desperate for work. They performed dangerous and backbreaking tasks during long hours, often in conditions that lead to poor health, disability, and occupational and environmental hazards. Some factory owners and mine operators ran what was called a *company town* so that workers were beholden to their employers for housing, food, public safety, and their children's education.

In many cases, employers held monopolies or near-monopolies. This meant that they faced no competition, leaving workers and the consumers to whom they sold their products and services

[3]This moniker is based on the title of a novel by Mark Twain and Charles Dudley Weaver. "Neither writer had a clue that their title would become the brand of an American era that extended from the end of the Civil War into the opening years of the twentieth century. The co-authors adapted *The Gilded Age* from a familiar line in Shakespeare's play *King John*: 'To gild refined gold, to paint the lily.' . . . Extending the point, the bright shine of gilding can and does hide a base metal that lies beneath" (Martin & Tichi, 2016).

with no leverage to negotiate wages or prices. Photo 1.1 depicts the difficulty faced by workers who were squeezed between meager wages and high costs, in this case by the Pullman Company.

Politics were marked by corruption and systems of patronage, whereby politicians garnered votes by using their power to reward supporters. The patronage system itself was legal, and federal, state, and local politicians of the day, including President Andrew Jackson, used it openly (Riordan, 1995). The right to vote was among the few means of leverage and power that immigrants held. Patronage systems (New York's Tammany Hall was one of the most infamous) were therefore mutually beneficial for many elected officials and the immigrant groups or neighborhoods where they lived. They were one of the few avenues that populations marginalized by discrimination could use to gain access to employment opportunities and services, particularly at the local level. The patronage system was curbed by the Pendleton Act of 1883, which led to the creation of a federal civil service system based on merit rather than favors to supporters; similar state legislation followed. While legislation could not entirely eliminate favoritism, it helped build a civil service system made up of workers who had knowledge and expertise that did not change with political winds.

Chicago Labor Newspaper, July 7, 1984

PHOTO 1.1 The Condition of Laboring Man at Pullman

DISCUSSION

THE IMPACT OF GROWING INEQUALITY

Socioeconomic inequality in the United States has grown over the past decades. Discuss the following:

1. What are some potential negative and positive consequences of wealth or income inequality?
2. What impact might these have on people's future opportunities in education, jobs, housing, or in other arenas?
3. How do large socioeconomic differences affect relationships between groups in broader society?
4. How might the balance of power evolve and change as inequality grows? As it shrinks?

One concept that came to prominence in this time period, used to justify inequality, oppression, and control, was Social Darwinism. **Social Darwinism** was an adaption of Charles Darwin's theory of evolution, which states that species evolve over time through a natural process in response to changes in climate, predators, disasters, food supply, and so on (Darwin, 1869). According to Darwin, organisms and species that are best suited to environmental conditions become dominant through survival and reproduction. Although there is no evidence that Darwin intended for his theory to be used for social purposes and many important flaws exist in such application, Social Darwinists such as Herbert Spencer sought

Social Darwinism: An adaption of Charles Darwin's theory of evolution, Social Darwinsists championed techniques such as sterilization to curb social ills. This discredited theory was not grounded in evidence and led to unethical policies such as eugenics.

to use evolutionary principles to manipulate the social environment (Degler, 1991). Social Darwinism led to state-sanctioned sterilization and justification of now-scientifically discredited racist and classist policies. Social Darwinism was embraced by many different groups for different reasons, including xenophobia, self-interested greed, and misguided desire to improve the population. The eugenics movement was supported by so-called social progressives and the conservatives of the day.

Progressive Era

The Progressive Era, from approximately 1890 to 1920, was a time of increased political activism. The United States was changing rapidly with industrialization, which led to social and economic transformation. Progressives were unified in their concern for problems associated with industrialization, including urbanization, political corruption, alcoholism, and immigration, and they sought government-based remedies. They advocated for prohibition, women's voting rights, worker protections, and child labor laws. This is the period also associated with the birth of social work as a profession.

Urbanization: A shift from a primarily rural, farming society to one in which the majority of the population resided in cities

Urbanization describes a shift in the United States from a primarily rural, farming society to one in which most of the population resided in cities (Boyer, 1992). Two streams of population fed the growing cities. The first came from within the country. The other was immigrants from other countries, many also from rural areas in their countries of origin. Seeking a better life through the promise of employment and opportunity, both groups left behind the ability to sustain themselves in times of need with food from family farms and stable social networks. Urban life was characterized by close quarters, poor sanitation, and overcrowding. The dire conditions in the tenements of New York were documented by Jacob Riis (1890) in his famous photojournalistic series *How the Other Half Lives*. Riis described multiple families cramped into poorly ventilated and structurally unsound tenements with little access to light or water. Riis was a **muckraker**, a term used to describe Progressive Era journalists who exposed poor conditions and corruption, often through shocking description, to inspire reform. Another muckraker was Upton Sinclair (2012/1906), whose popular book *The Jungle* graphically depicted the dangerous working conditions in Chicago meatpacking plants and the plight of those who worked in them.

Muckrakers: Progressive Era journalists who exposed poor conditions and corruption, often through shocking description, to bring attention to them and inspire reform

Immigrants were the target of much controversy. After 1870, nearly 25 million people emigrated primarily from Europe, with smaller waves from China. The influx of immigrants with different languages and cultural practices were seen by many as a threat to "American" identity and unity; others saw immigrants as a resource for growth and a social asset (Addams, 1909; Foner, 2002). Reformers of this era sought to Americanize immigrants, often in ways that disparaged existing cultural and religious practices, diet, and language. These reformers set about "teaching" immigrants how to cook and keep house, and provided children with care and education with the explicit goal of acculturating their families. The first federal law passed to regulate immigration was the Chinese Exclusion Act of 1875. While all immigrant populations faced discrimination and prejudice, xenophobia was particularly virulent toward Asian immigrants, the majority of whom came from China through California to build railroads and work in the gold mines (Kristofer, 2003).

The Gilded Age and Progressive Era were important times for the profession of social work, described briefly above. Originating in England in the mid-19th century, COS systematized and coordinated the provision of assistance. This was in part a result of the rise of a growing faith in science as an objective way to discover truth to solve problems. It also coincided with professionalization. The COS developed principles designed to identify those deserving of aid and provide relief together with moral instruction (Waugh, 2001). In this manner, the COS tried to control the behavior of both the givers and receivers of aid (McFadden, 2014). The

COS was contested by some contemporaries as harsh and judgmental. Many of the criteria they used to determine fault and deservingness would be viewed today as clearly rooted in racist, chauvinist, and anti-immigrant prejudice. However, the COS and its scientific case management system had many benefits and is a precursor to modern social work in its attention to documenting client needs and progress, home visiting, and coordination among agencies to make the best use of resources. Others argued that it represented not elitist and moralistic views of poor people, but rather recognition of the complex nature of poverty that required concerted, thoughtful, and informed effort (Waugh, 2001). While the COS focused on the idea of scientific charity (Lane & Jacob, 1973), members of the Settlement House Movement (SHM) lived among the people they served, purposely forming bonds of community (Chen, 2013). Working with local community members, settlement house workers promoted health, education, and daycare. Settlement house workers were engaged in broader political advocacy, particularly around child work regulations and public health.

Largely comprised of a philanthropic, female workforce, foremothers of the social work profession were not always respected. Research, political activism, and commitment to social arrangements that promote human flourishing began largely as charitable efforts. As their work became systemized, early social workers sought recognition as professionals. In 1915, Abraham Flexner, who had recently published an influential report on medicine as a profession, told the National Conference of Charities and Correction that social work did not meet the criteria of professionalism (although he admitted at the outset of his speech that he knew little about social work and could be convinced otherwise). This was a blow to the young profession that led to self-reflection and pursuit of professionalism along criteria laid out by Flexner. These included establishing educational requirements and efforts to develop a distinct body of knowledge. These efforts were contested, and many saw the pursuit of professional recognition as a distraction from the value base of the profession (Specht & Courtney, 1994). Others claimed that to accomplish our value-based mission, social work must enjoy recognition and respect. Similar debates continue today.

Great Depression

In 1929, the United States was in the throes of the **Great Depression**, the seeds of which had been sown by economic and trade policies, increased availability of credit to consumers and companies, and environmental effects that decimated agriculture (Jansson, 2012). In response to the losses of 13 million to 15 million jobs and countless homes and the closures of banks, factories, and businesses, nonprofit agencies attempted to meet the need. Overwhelmed by the enormity of need, by 1932 about one third of these agencies had closed (Trattner, 1999). Governmental response was slow and insufficient under the administration of President Herbert Hoover. In 1930, he approved $45 million to feed livestock, but refused to allow any money to go to starving farmers. He also vetoed a public works program that would spend $2.9 billion to put people back to work and kick-start the economy. Social workers played a role during this time in organizing and testifying at legislative hearings about unemployment, poverty, and hunger.

Great Depression: A period of widespread economic hardship that lasted approximately 10 years beginning with the stock market crash of 1929

The election of Franklin Roosevelt to the presidency in 1932 provided an opportunity for the enactment of federal relief programs collectively known as the **New Deal**. It also brought to national power social workers such as Frances Perkins, the first female Cabinet secretary who served as Secretary of Labor throughout Roosevelt's three-term presidency. Collectively, New Deal programs provided relief to some 20 million Americans at a price tag of approximately $4 billion, but left substantial numbers of people without jobs or in jobs paying substandard wages. These programs were also discriminatory—African Americans and women

New Deal: A set of federal relief programs enacted by President Franklin Roosevelt in 1932 in response to the Great Depression

Department of the Interior. War Relocation Authority

PHOTO 1.2 San Francisco, California. With Baggage Stacked, Residents of Japanese Ancestry Await Bus

were ineligible for many benefits or considered only after white men were provided assistance.

Many of the New Deal programs ended by 1934, but they paved the way for the creation of the Social Security Act, passed by Congress in 1935 with significant input from Hopkins, Perkins, and Wilbur J. Cohen (profiled in Chapter 9). The Social Security Act was one of the few permanent results of this time period, and provided assistance for older adults (through the Old Age Insurance program—what most people think of when they think of Social Security) and people with disabilities (Social Security Disability Insurance). As with other programs of the era, African Americans were discriminated against. The Social Security Act deliberately excluded domestic and agricultural workers, the majority of whom were African Americans, from Old Age Insurance (Brown, 1999). You can read more about components of the Social Security Act in Chapters 9 and 10.

The onset of World War II in 1941 ushered in economic benefits for many, bringing the country close to full employment (Trattner, 1999). After the need for African Americans in the labor force led to race riots and overt discrimination (Trattner, 1999), this time period also brought Executive Order 8802 (1941), which was designed to eliminate discrimination based on race, creed, or national origin in government or defense industries. World War II was also the impetus for two racist decisions by the U.S. government. First, President Roosevelt issued Executive Order 9066, which resulted in the incarceration of 120,000 Japanese, two thirds of whom were U.S. citizens born in the United States, by the time the program ended in 1946 (see Photo 1.2). Social workers were an integral part of this process.

> Social workers vetted, registered, counseled, and tagged all Nikkei [Japanese] families, along with their accompanying luggage, at the many Wartime Civilian Control Administration (WCCA) stations. . . . Social workers also staffed administrative offices within the relocation camps and the regional War Relocation Authority (WRA) resettlement centers . . . in various parts of the nation. (Park, 2008, p. 448)

The Supreme Court upheld the constitutionality of this order in *Korematsu v. United States* (1944).

The second public issue about which social workers have been relatively silent was President Harry Truman's 1945 decision to use the atomic bomb against Japan. This resulted in killing more than 200,000 people in Hiroshima and Nagasaki, with lifelong effects on the survivors such as miscarriages, stillbirths, and various types of cancer (Southard, 2015). The use of the atomic bomb was followed quickly by the end of World War II, the return of soldiers, and a renewed focus at home on the economy. Government funding for the war efforts is generally credited with improving the U.S. economy and the boom period that followed helped keep attention away from the consequences of internment camps and the atomic bomb.

Post-World War II Boom

Throughout the New Deal era and after World War II, social workers such as Bertha Capen Reynolds and Mary Van Kleeck came to be viewed as threatening if they espoused radical views (Reisch & Andrews, 2001). Addams was labeled "subversive" by Illinois and New York State Legislative committees. Reynolds lost her position as Dean of the Smith College School of Social Work in 1938 because of her radical political beliefs. These were the most well-known of countless individuals, social workers, union members, faculty, students, and more who were targeted by state legislatures, Congress, and other groups. Their membership in unions or other political organizations was seen as disloyal to the United States or as unpatriotic during the buildup to what would become the Cold War.

The post-World War II time period, roughly 1945–1960, is often characterized by **McCarthyism**, a term that describes both the anti-Communist panic stoked by Wisconsin Senator Joseph McCarthy and a general "atmosphere of personal recrimination and political oppression" (Reisch & Andrews, 2001, p. 90). Fear of change, fear of the Soviet government and Soviet allies and the related push for military spending and concern that labor and civil rights activism was harmful to the country were driving forces. In 1947, President Truman formally banned Communists or anyone sympathizing with Communists from serving in government positions. This ban resulted in thousands of anonymous reports attacking those who were seen as Communists or in any way questioning the United States or those in power.

McCarthyism: The anti-Communist panic stoked by Wisconsin Senator Joseph McCarthy that cost the jobs of thousands of suspected Communists or Communist sympathizers and the persecution of many more

During this period, the social work profession turned to focus on techniques and work with individuals rather than social action or social justice (Specht & Courtney, 1994). The profession also held back from activism in the civil rights movement, which was expanding after the 1954 *Brown v. Board of Education* decision by the Supreme Court and the Montgomery Bus Boycott, despite criticism by Whitney Young and others (Trattner, 1999). During the next era, referred to as the Great Society, many social workers began to re-engage with social action.

Great Society

The Great Society lasted from 1960, when John F. Kennedy was elected president, through the end of Lyndon Johnson's presidency in 1968. John F. Kennedy had many ideas for addressing poverty and improving the lives of U.S. citizens. During his administration, the federal government gave money to state welfare departments to encourage them to hire social workers in an effort to reduce the Aid to Families with Dependent Children (AFDC) rolls (O'Connor, 2004). He also worked to get the Community Mental Health Act of 1963 passed to provide federal money toward the construction of outpatient and preventative mental health centers, although the implementation of this after his death was flawed (Jansson, 2012). After Kennedy's assassination in 1963, Vice President Johnson assumed the presidency, and shepherded many significant pieces of legislation originally conceived by Kennedy through Congress. This period is called the Great Society Era because it expanded the federal government's role in addressing social issues such as poverty, civil rights, hunger, health care, public school aid, and tax reform.

The civil rights movement was well underway when President Johnson entered office. Reverend Martin Luther King, Jr., attracted worldwide media attention in 1955 with his peaceful protest in Birmingham, Alabama. The protest and violent police response were widely televised. It captured the public's attention because it graphically exposed unjust treatment of blacks in America. Frustrated by economic desperation, millions of black citizens united to express disapproval of the institutions that oppressed them. Riots broke out in the streets of every major city across the United States. Many social workers who had previously shied away from social reform were forced to face the unpleasant reality that reform was necessary (Trattner, 1999).

The Civil Rights Act of 1964 provided equal access to public accommodations, withheld federal funding from segregated schools, and prevented federal contractors from discriminating in employment decisions. In response to massive protests, he also supported the Civil Rights Act of 1965, which was designed to eliminate discrimination related to voting rights such as literacy or other screening tests that had been used in the South to disenfranchise black voters (Jansson, 2012).

Despite concerns raised by opponents who believed that welfare creates dependence, Johnson declared a War on Poverty, and supported several programs designed during the Kennedy administration including the Economic Opportunity Act and the Food Stamps Act of 1964. The Economic Opportunity Act provided funding for Job Corps to train conservation workers, provided loans for small businesses and farmers, and created a domestic Peace Corps (O'Connor, 2004). While Kennedy's vision of national health insurance failed, Johnson, working with Chairman of the House Ways and Means Committee Wilbur Mills, helped create Medicare to help older adults pay for health care and Medicaid to address the medical needs of those living in poverty (Jansson, 2012; Trattner, 1999). You can read more about these programs in Chapters 10 and 11. Another major legislative accomplishment of the Johnson administration that had been sought by Kennedy was a law designed to equalize educational funding by providing federal assistance to public schools with high percentages of low-income children. The Elementary and Secondary Education Act (ESEA), passed in 1965, was most recently reauthorized as the Every Student Succeeds Act (2015). Though it was clear that many changes were still necessary, the Vietnam War squandered whatever funds would have been available to make those changes. Johnson refused to increase taxes to cover both the Great Society programs and war expenses and chose to support the war. The United States spent 25 times more on the war in Vietnam than it spent trying to eliminate poverty (Chafe, 1986).

Much of the social work literature during this turbulent period examined the profession's core values and explored the relationship between social workers' personal values and their professional practice (Reamer, 1998). The exploration of these topics eventually led to the National Association of Social Workers' (NASW) adoption of its first Code of Ethics in 1960. Because of the expansion of social welfare programs, more social workers were needed to fill positions created by these programs. To increase the number of social workers in the field, the NASW opened full membership to individuals with baccalaureate degrees, although some believed that recognition of the BSW deprofessionalized social work (Stuart, 2013). Similarly, the popularity of the doctorate in social work (DSW) increased and many social workers opted for DSW degrees over traditional PhDs. The number of social work doctoral programs grew significantly, with 20 new programs beginning from 1965 to 1975 (Crow & Kindelsperger, 1975). Schools of social work recruited students from disadvantaged areas and revised curricula to include more content on group work, community organization, public administration, and social policy. Social workers began to view casework as ineffective during this period, moving away from individual therapy and toward advocacy and reform. The NASW changed its bylaws to declare social workers' dual obligation to use individual social work methods and social action to prevent and alleviate distress (Trattner, 2009). Politically oriented community action reemerged along with social workers' increased involvement in the political process. The Great Society Era served as a call to action for social workers and shattered the complacency of precious decades. Many changes made during this time continue to have a significant impact on the social work profession today.

Reagan Era

The Great Society is often characterized by a wider understanding of social problems such as poverty and racism and efforts to address them using government resources. In contrast, the Reagan Era can be viewed as a rejection of such efforts (Slessarov, 1988). Some people attribute this shift to the economic recession that began with the oil crises of 1973 and 1974, ending a sense of optimism engendered by an extended period of economic growth (Krieger, 1987). Named for Ronald Reagan, who served as U.S. President from 1981 to 1989, this historical period is often seen as an important turning point in the ideas about the proper role of government, (re)distribution of wealth, and social responsibility.

According to Krieger (1987), efforts to use economic policy to harmonize class interests were replaced by a desire to use government policy to support business interests. Often referred to as **Reaganomics** this was characterized by a belief that regulatory and tax policies favorable to businesses stimulate economic growth, also known as *supply-side* economics. A second feature of Reaganomics is a lack of business regulation characteristic of laissez-faire capitalism that leaves the market to its own devices. Proponents of Reaganomics believed that benefits that accrue to people in higher income brackets would ultimately benefit society by creating more economic opportunities, jobs, and wealth among those who would spend it. Critics of such policies often refer to them as *trickle-down* economics, suggesting that they create a windfall for the wealthy and very few benefits actually reach those at the bottom of the economic ladder.

Reaganomics: Named for Ronald Reagan, the belief that regulatory and tax policies favorable to businesses stimulate economic growth, also known as "supply-side" economics

Ronald Reagan ran for president as an outsider during a time of economic crisis. He took a strong position that "government is not the solution to our problem, government is the problem" (Reagan, 1981). Ronald Reagan and other neoconservatives famously used language and framing tactics to distinguish between types of government benefits. As Mimi Abramovitz (1983) explains, while government benefits come in many forms, all are the product of rules and regulations that can advantage and disadvantage different groups. U.S. benefits to lower-income and middle-income populations were (and continue to be) largely in the form of cash or in-kind benefits. Because of this, they are often visible as budget expenditures. Ronald Reagan targeted such benefits, framing them as handouts and a drag on the economy. He used now-disproven images of the fictitious welfare queen to depict low-income beneficiaries as undeserving recipients of society's largesse (Schram, 1995). At the same time, many of the government benefits received by the wealthy were *increased*, although these benefits remained invisible because they occurred in the form of tax expenditures or credits, so the money for them was never collected by the government. These include reduced taxes on various forms of income that do not come from wages (i.e., investment income such as interest and capital gains). Rhetorical devices that framed the restructuring of U.S. fiscal policy played on class-based conflicts of interest. Differentiation between welfare for individuals in lower income brackets in contrast to welfare for individuals in higher income brackets reflected the belief in the wealthy as primary drivers of the economy as compared to workers and consumers. These policies are largely seen as the beginning of the U.S. economic divide that has continued to grow.

Another trend that traces its beginnings to the mid-1980s was the use of legislative and administrative strategies for what is called **devolution**, shifting responsibility for funding and a source from higher to lower levels of government (i.e., from federal to state or state to local) (Demone & Gibleman, 1984). Proponents of such shifts pointed to the ability of localities to better identify and tailor responses to the needs and desires of their citizens. Opponents pointed to a lack of oversight and greater inequality when states and counties with different economic capacity relied solely on local resources of funding. According to Demone and Gibelman (1984), many state and private agencies that relied on public funding for social welfare services responded by cutting staff and programs, increasing caseloads, and increasing the use of volunteers. In response to shrinking social services, some private sector individuals, companies, nonprofit organizations, and state and local governments helped fill budget gaps. During George H.W. Bush's presidency (1989–1993), initiatives by religious nonprofit organizations were encouraged under the White House Office of Faith-Based and Community Initiatives. Such efforts raised concerns regarding the separation

Devolution: Shifting authority and responsibility from higher to lower levels of government (e.g., from federal to state or state to local)

National Institutes of Health

PHOTO 1.3 The AIDS Memorial Quilt was created with the goals of memorializing those who have died of AIDS-related causes and helping people understand the impact of the disease.

of religion and state. It is important to note that the call to end so-called big government was not uniform across sectors. In contrast to the shrinking role of the federal government in providing social benefits such as income support and education, defense spending during this time increased, including funding for the Strategic Defense Initiative, popularly known as **Star Wars** (Piven & Cloward, 1982).

Star Wars: The popular name for funding for the Strategic Defense Initiative, part of an increase in overall defense spending during a time of decreased spending on social programs

George H.W. Bush, who followed Ronald Reagan as president, held similar economic positions to his predecessor. However, he espoused some socially liberal policies. His greatest accomplishments were signing the Americans with Disabilities Act into law in 1990 and shepherding significant amendments to the Clean Air Act in 1990. In addition to economic changes, prominent social concerns in the 1980s and 1990s included the beginning of the HIV/AIDS epidemic. Initially nicknamed "gay cancer" and considered a problem for only gay men, the stigmatizing of those with the disease and the ascription of moral failing led to huge public protests by groups such as ACT UP and the creation of the AIDS quilt as seen in Photo 1.3 (Madsen, 2012; The Names Project Foundation, 2018). Such activism ultimately resulted in government recognition of HIV/AIDS as a health crisis worthy of government attention. Public investment turned what had been a leading cause of death among young men in the early 1990s into a disease that today can be controlled and suppressed with medication (Centers for Disease Control and prevention, 1998). The organizing that occurred within communities affected by this disease helped fuel and strengthen the civil rights movement for people who identify as lesbian, gay, bisexual, transgender, queer, and with other sexual orientations or gender identities (LGBTQ+).

The 1980s social welfare retrenchment also marked a growing rift within the social work profession between advocacy and direct practice, sometimes called the micro-macro divide. This was, in part, due to growing conservatism in government and a push toward social work professional recognition through licensure and federal funding mechanisms that focused on individual behavioral health (Stuart, 2013). The pendulum swing toward activism during the 1960s and 1970s had now swung back, and social work practice again primarily focused on addressing individual suffering. This is reflected in current educational and practice trends. One prominent example of successful social work policy practice that is also grounded in a focus on changing individual behavior with the goal of policy change is the Human Service Employees Registration and Voter Education fund (Human SERVE), founded in 1983 by Richard Cloward and Frances Fox Piven (Columbia University Archives, n.d.). The movement to register voters when they interact with human services agencies engaged thousands of social workers and social work students in voter registration and was considered to be a prominent driver of the National Voter Registration Act of 1993 (also called the Motor Voter law) (Lane, Humphreys, Graham, Matthews & Moriarty, 2007). This law requires that states offer opportunities for eligible voters to register when they obtain or renew driver's licenses and when they apply for public benefits such as food stamps or disability benefits. The work of Human SERVE engaged social workers who used organizing and legislative advocacy tools as well as social workers who served individual clients through case management and service provision. This is an example of how individual and policy-focused social work can work together.

ADVOCACY

SOCIAL WORKERS AND POLICY ACTION

Pick from the list below of influential social workers or select another social worker whom you have identified. Conduct your own research to answer the following questions.

1. During which time period was this person influential?
2. What is he or she known for?
3. Did this person have a BSW, MSW, DSW, or PhD in social work? If not, why is he or she identified with social work?
4. How was this person able to influence policy?
5. What can you as a future social worker learn from this person to help inform your practice?

Edith Abbott
Jane Addams
Lucy Burns
Susan Davis
Ron Dellums
Dorothy Height
Harry Hopkins
Nancy A. Humphreys
Barbara Lee
Josephine Shaw Lowell
Barbara Mikulski
Alice Paul
Frances Perkins
Jeanette Rankin
Mary Ellen Richmond
Eunice Kennedy Shriver
Ed Towns
Whitney Young, Jr.

Neoliberal Era

Bill Clinton followed George H.W. Bush as president from 1993 to 2001. Clinton is largely remembered for co-opting Reagan's ideas of individualism, welfare reform, a strong focus on law and order, and bringing the Democratic Party toward the center of the ideological spectrum (Riley, 2017). President Richard Nixon coined the term **The War on Drugs** and began the process of federalizing drug crimes (which had until that point been considered state criminal policy) to gain the support of Southern states by adding a new federal method to control African Americans (Vitale, 2017). Reagan is often given credit for tough on crime policies because he supported Congressional action to expand federal control over drug crimes with mandatory minimum sentencing and the forfeiture of cash and real estate for drug offenses (Alexander, 2012). Clinton was instrumental in further expanding the War on Drugs by calling for increased funding for federal and state prisons, providing federal funds to expand police departments, and creating federal three strikes provisions (Vitale, 2017). He took this position to show that being tough on crime was not a Republican issue. Alex Vitale (2017) and Michelle Alexander (2010/2012) document continued disproportionate use of drug policing in poor nonwhite communities, noting that, even today, "most street-level drug policing is discriminatory and ineffective" (Vitale, 2017, p. 139).

The War on Drugs: Coined by Richard Nixon, this term refers to a set of policies enacted and implemented through the Clinton administration

In 1993, one of Clinton's first acts as president was to sign the Family and Medical Leave Act into law. While a landmark in providing family leave at the federal level, it guarantees only unpaid leave for 12 weeks for parents to care for newborns and sick parents, spouses, or children, and it covers less than 60% of American workers (U.S. Department of Labor, 2013). In comparison to policies of other industrialized countries it is meager (Palley & Shdaimah, 2014). In 1993, Clinton signed the North American Free Trade Agreement (NAFTA), designed to eliminate tariffs between the United States, Mexico, and Canada (Office of the United States Trade Representative, n.d.). NAFTA critics claim that it caused many Manufacturing jobs to relocate to Mexico. Clinton also unsuccessfully tried to create a single-payer health care system, but his administration was unable to get the support of potential allies such as the American Medical Association who feared that it would lead to lower salaries for doctors or the pharmaceutical industry. In 1994, Republicans gained both houses of Congress based in part on House Speaker Newt Gingrich's **Contract with America**, the goal of which was to further reduce taxes and limit access to public assistance, particularly to single mothers receiving AFDC (Jannson, 2009).

Contract with America: Developed by Newt Gingrich, this outlined a vision of reducing taxes and limiting government

Clinton also oversaw the passage of the Personal Responsibility and Work Reconciliation Act (PRWORA, 1996), sometimes called *welfare reform*. PRWORA amended the Social Security Act to shift federal income assistance (at the time under the program called Aid to Families with Dependent Children) from a federal right for all eligible parents with children under 18 years old to Temporary Assistance for Needy Families (TANF). This block grant program gave money to states to create programs that require parents to work to receive benefits. Benefits were capped at 5 years at most (with some states offering as little as 12 months of benefits over an individual's lifetime). The ideology behind PROWRA suggests that poor parents, particularly mothers, needed to be forced to increase their personal responsibility by working for benefits. This contrasts with earlier Democratic ideas that government had a responsibility to ensure that basic needs of children were met and that children needed the supervision of their mothers. It played on Reagan's portrayal that beneficiaries were getting rich from government benefits even though this was not possible (Khazan, 2014). Clinton strongly supported this ideologically conservative bill, although he vetoed two earlier versions, at least in part, to force Congress to include child care supports along with work requirements (Palley & Shdaimah, 2014). In response the debates around PROWRA, social work educators came together in 1997 to create the organization Influencing State Policy, now called Influencing Social Policy, to increase social work's impact on policy (Influencing Social Policy, n.d.).

President Clinton was also responsible for signing the repeal of the Glass-Steagall Act, a Depression-era law that had separated commercial and investment banking. This repeal has been blamed for the 2008 financial crisis (Cirilli, 2014).

Post-9/11 America

George W. Bush, son of George H.W. Bush, served as president for two terms after Clinton (2001–2009). He was president during the domestic terror acts in New York City and Washington, DC, on September 11, 2001. His response to that, including the authorization to use military force in the Middle East, is a significant part of his legacy. He oversaw the beginning of both the wars in Iraq and Afghanistan. Bush's domestic policy is notable for the PATRIOT Act, which gave the federal government expanded powers to spy on citizens and residents of the United States, and No Child Left Behind, which led to an increased focus on testing and standardization in U.S. education. He also supported and signed a $400 billion tax cut into law, which some have suggested was responsible for turning the Clinton-era budget surplus into a deficit. He unsuccessfully tried to privatize Social Security, but his efforts were defeated, in part as a result of a downturn in the stock market (Gregg, 2017). At the end of his term, Congress passed the Troubled Asset Relief Program (TARP), which was designed to stabilize the national economy by providing federal money to ensure that stock brokerage firms and banks did not go under (Nelson, 2017). Despite NAFTA and other free trade agreements, Congress enacted and the president supported and signed a bill providing $190 billion of subsidies to farmers in 2002 (CNN.com, 2002).

When Barack Obama, the first black president in American history, was inaugurated in 2009, the U.S. economy was facing another potential major depression. Housing prices were falling rapidly, and the official unemployment rate was near 10%. The Obama administration is largely credited with stabilizing the economy by supporting and expanding Bush's Troubled Asset Relief Program. This was perceived by many citizens as a bailout for wealthy bankers and corporate executives (Nelson, 2017). During the Obama presidency, No Child Left Behind was repealed and replaced with Race to the Top, an initiative that provided competitive grant funding, initially as part of the American Recovery and Reinvestment Act of 2009. Race to the Top requires states to develop policies linking student performance to teacher tenure and promotion, to get rid of state caps on the number of charter schools, to use national rather than state tests to assess student performance, and to provide additional financing to schools that need to improve (U.S. Department of Education, 2009).

Although it is difficult to assess the legacy of a presidency that ended so recently, Obama's biggest actions and policy initiatives include the Paris Climate Agreement, a treaty ratified by 173 countries in the United Nations agreeing to take steps to significantly reduce carbon emissions (United Nations, 2017), the passage of the Patient Protection and Affordable Care Act (2010), the development of the Deferred Action for Childhood Arrivals (2012) program for immigrant children, and the continuation and expansion of military involvement in the Middle East.

These policies are all being challenged as this book is being written. Some ways in which the policies are being modified or eliminated during President Donald Trump's administration include withdrawal from the Paris Climate Agreement, efforts to eliminate or substantially change the Affordable Care Act, including a provision in the 2017 tax bill that eliminated the requirement that all people buy health insurance or be fined, and ending executive action for the Deferred Action for Childhood Arrivals.

CURRENT CONTEXT

Beginning with the Reagan administration and continuing through the Trump administration, there has been a great divide between Democrats and Republicans. Presidents Clinton and Obama were centrists and supported policies that had been considered conservative, reducing benefits to the poor (Clinton), developing a health insurance policy that was modelled after Republican Mitt Romney's Massachusetts plan (Obama), tying health care reform to private insurance companies (Obama), supporting charter schools (Obama), free trade with NAFTA (Clinton), and crime policies that were based on "getting tough on crime" (Clinton; many of which were unchallenged by Obama). President Trump's policies have moved the country further to the right. He ran and has acted on a strongly anti-immigrant platform, rescinded Obama's Deferred Action for Childhood Arrivals, and eliminated temporary protected status for immigrants from El Salvador, Haiti, Honduras, Nicaragua, and Sudan (Park, 2017). Congress passed a tax bill that will provide additional financial benefits to those in higher income brackets through increased ability to put money into tax-free college savings accounts, limiting state and local tax deductions to $10,000, reducing individual tax rates, and other methods (Sullivan & Tackett, 2017). According to the Congressional Budget Office, this tax law will increase the deficit $1.4 trillion over the next 10 years (Carney, 2017). Social justice advocates have raised concerns over President Trump's position toward

Epics/Hulton Archive/Getty

PHOTO 1.4 March for Women's Rights, Washington, DC, 2017

reproductive health, LGBTQ+ rights, immigrant rights, and environmental policy. This spurred over 2 million women in all 50 states as well as 657 countries to participate in the 2017 March for Women's Rights (see Photo 1.4).

Despite that fact that the majority of social work students and professionals focus on individual practice, the profession continues to show its presence in the policy arena through organizations such as ISP, mentioned above, as well the Congressional Research Institute for Social Policy (CRISP) and the Association for Community Organizing and Social Action (ACOSA). The profession also continues to explicitly embrace policy through new educational standards for all social work programs that require students to learn about and demonstrate proficiency in policy practice skills.

Final Discussion

Now that you have finished reading this chapter, reread the vignette at the beginning. Based on what you have learned, answer the following questions. Point to specific references in the chapter that help you answer them.

1. How do Shellie and Julian's responses differ?
2. How does each response comply with the NASW Code of Ethics?
3. Where would their respective responses be deficient as per the Code of Ethics?
4. Propose two examples of how Shellie and Julian might work together in an integrated response.
5. What role might race, class, gender, and other aspects of identity play in this vignette?

2

HOW POLICY IS CREATED AND INFLUENCED

LEARNING OBJECTIVES

2.1: Describe the three fundamental founding documents of the U.S. government and their meaning for the U.S. policy process

2.2: Explain how the structure of the U.S. government affects the policy process

2.3: Recall the political parties and their role in U.S. political decision making

2.4: Identify ways that social workers participate in the process and practice of policy

The social work profession encompasses many types of practice and practice arenas and is particularly well situated to different forms of policy advocacy and analysis. This chapter provides needed background for social work students who are learning how to connect social work careers at different levels and in various fields with social policy and advocacy. This chapter builds on a basic knowledge of U.S. state and federal government. It focuses on the interplay between federal and state systems and branches of government while explaining how and where policy is created, implemented, and challenged. Important features of the U.S. political landscape such as the history and current state of the major parties are here, with attention to the ways these have influenced substantive policies and the policy-making process. It discusses political ideologies and their connection to social work. Finally, the chapter examines how these structures and ideologies provide constraints and opportunities to intervene in the policy process and how social workers can draw on their skills and expertise to participate in these interventions.

Vignette: School Budget Advocacy

Based on what you know from the media or your personal, work, or volunteer experiences, think about the following questions as you read the vignette. When you finish the vignette, answer the questions below.

1. What types of social work skills did Alyx and colleagues use throughout this process?
2. What levels of governments are involved in the changes they are trying to make?
3. What knowledge about the political process did Alyx and the others need to be successful?
4. What options do Alyx and their colleagues have at the end of the process?
5. What role might race, class, gender, and other aspects of identity play in this vignette?

Alyx is a school social worker in a middle school. They have been working hard throughout the Past few years to find funding for programs that will help their students, many of whom come from low-income households, to pay for the necessities they need so they can be successful in school. In February, Alyx and the other social workers in the school district developed a proposal for a before-school program that would combine free breakfast and homework help. They believed that this program would have a number of benefits. It would ensure students were fed before they started the school day, which research suggests will make them more successful throughout the day. It would help students understand the concepts in their homework better, which will be good for them as individuals. This program could also be helpful to the school if students improve their standardized test scores, which are important in how outsiders measure the school's success. Based on advice from a current school board member, who is a social worker, Alyx and their colleagues presented this plan to the school board, including the research that backs up the methods chosen and their projected outcomes. They also provided a detailed budget. In addition to Alyx and the other social workers, several teachers, students, and parents came to the school board meeting to testify in support.

Referendum: A general vote by the electorate on a single question, such as a budget or a ballot question

The school board approved the program and agreed to include it in the school board's proposed budget for the following year. The proposed budget then had to go to a **referendum**, meaning every eligible voter in the school district had the opportunity to vote yes or no on the budget. Alyx, the other social workers, teachers, students, and parents worked for a month to share information with the voters in the community to encourage them to support the budget.

On Election Day, only 350 people out of 5,500 eligible voters voted on the referendum. The budget was defeated by a margin of 150 to 200, meaning that if 25 people had changed their votes, or an additional 51 people had come to vote, the outcome could have been different. The town laws say that if the budget fails, the current year's budget will continue to be used, meaning that no additional funding will be available.

THE POLICY PROCESS

As you can see from the above vignette, social workers find that their work is affected by policy in a number of different ways and they need to be prepared to interact with the policy process to make sure their **clients** are being heard and helped. We follow the definition of *client* set out in the National Association of Social Workers (NASW) Code of Ethics: "Clients is used inclusively to refer to individuals, families, groups, organizations, and communities" (2017, Preamble). In this section, we provide an overview of the U.S. policy process. This might be a review for you, or this might be new information. If this is a review, please consider how each piece of information fits into your understanding of the social work profession as you read and what questions this new perspective brings to the information.

Clients: As defined by the NASW Code of Ethics: "Clients is used inclusively to refer to individuals, families, groups, organizations, and communities."

Historical Concepts

The three fundamental founding documents of the U.S. government are the Declaration of Independence, the Constitution, and the Bill of Rights. You can see these original handwritten documents (with transcriptions) in person at the National Archives in Washington, DC, or at https://www.archives.gov/founding-docs. What do these three documents actually mean for the U.S. policy process? Although we are sure you have studied these documents before, think about their context and contents again today, with the present political system in mind.

The Declaration of Independence

The Declaration of Independence was written by Thomas Jefferson, with feedback from Benjamin Franklin and John Adams (National Archives, 2017c). Photo 2.1 shows a dramatization of the signing of this key document. It was amended and passed by the Continental Congress on July 4, 1776. This Declaration outlined the colonists' grievances with Great Britain, their efforts to address these grievances, and, those efforts having failed, their desire to dissolve their political relationship with Great Britain. The Declaration states, "We hold these truths to be self-evident, that all men are created equal, that they are endowed by their Creator with certain unalienable Rights, that among these are Life, Liberty and the pursuit of Happiness." As the character of Angelica Schuyler will note 200 years later in the musical *Hamilton*, women are clearly missing from this declaration (Miranda, 2015). The rights of those who are enslaved are also absent. Importantly, this was a declaration of beliefs that was never intended to have legal authority, so it has never had the force of law (National Archives, 2017c).

Frederick Girsch at the American Bank Note Company, for the Bureau of Engraving and Printing

PHOTO 2.1 Engraving by Frederick Girsch showing John Trumbull's painting of the signing of the Declaration of Independence (c. 1818)

The Constitution

The Constitution replaced the Articles of Confederation, which provided limited powers to the first united government of the colonies but did not create a strong central government. For example, the Articles did not allow the federal government to enforce any rules, tax, regulate commerce, or print money. A Constitutional Convention gathered during the summer of 1787, and rather than tweak the existing Articles of Confederation, the group decided to create a new Constitution (National Archives, 2017b). This was controversial—in fact, after the new Constitution was completed, Congress spent 2 days debating whether the delegates to the Convention had so far exceeded their authority that they should be **censured** or given a formal statement of disapproval (National Archives, 2017d). The document reflected a compromise, with a strong central government but restriction of powers not otherwise specified to states, and three branches of government that checked each other to keep any one branch from gaining too much power (National Archives, 2017b).

Censure: Give a formal statement of disapproval by a governing body

The most significant compromise is that in the Constitution, a document designed to outline and protect independence and rights of the people in our new nation, the rights of some people to enslave others based on race were firmly protected. Although the word *slave* or *slavery* does not appear in the Constitution, its footprint can be seen in three places. Article 1, Section 2, describes how we will count populations for the purposes of representation and taxes. It says,

> Representatives and direct Taxes shall be apportioned among the several States which may be included within this Union, according to their respective Numbers, which shall be determined by adding to the whole Number of free Persons, including those bound to Service for a Term of Years, and excluding Indians not taxed, three fifths of all other Persons.

"All other persons" here refers to enslaved people; Native Americans were completely excluded.

In Article 1, Section 9, in a section that specifically forbids the federal government from a number of acts, the Constitution again refers obliquely to slaves:

> The Migration or Importation of such Persons as any of the States now existing shall think proper to admit, shall not be prohibited by the Congress prior to the Year one thousand eight hundred and eight, but a Tax or duty may be imposed on such Importation, not exceeding ten dollars for each Person.

Based on this section, in 1808, the slave trade was outlawed (Brady, 1972). Slavery, however, remained completely legal until the passage of the 13th Amendment in 1865, which continued to allow slavery or involuntary servitude for those who had been convicted of a crime.

Finally, in Article 4, Section 2, the Constitution states that

> No Person held to Service or Labour in one State, under the Laws thereof, escaping into another, shall, in Consequence of any Law or Regulation therein, be discharged from such Service or Labour, but shall be delivered up on Claim of the Party to whom such Service or Labour may be due.

This clause was designed to prevent enslaved people from fleeing to another state.

The new Constitution was first approved by the members of the Constitutional Convention, and then by the legislatures in the thirteen colonies, shown in Figure 2.1. After a public relations campaign including *The Federalist Papers*, the Constitution was ratified and became law, creating the foundation of the United States as we know it today (National Archives, 2017b).

The Constitution has been amended 17 times, and both the original document and amendments have been interpreted in a variety of ways by the executive, legislative, and judicial branches. The following sections describe the amendments. Next, we look at the three branches of government and see how they have interpreted the Constitution and amendments.

FIGURE 2.1 ■ Map of Original Thirteen Colonies

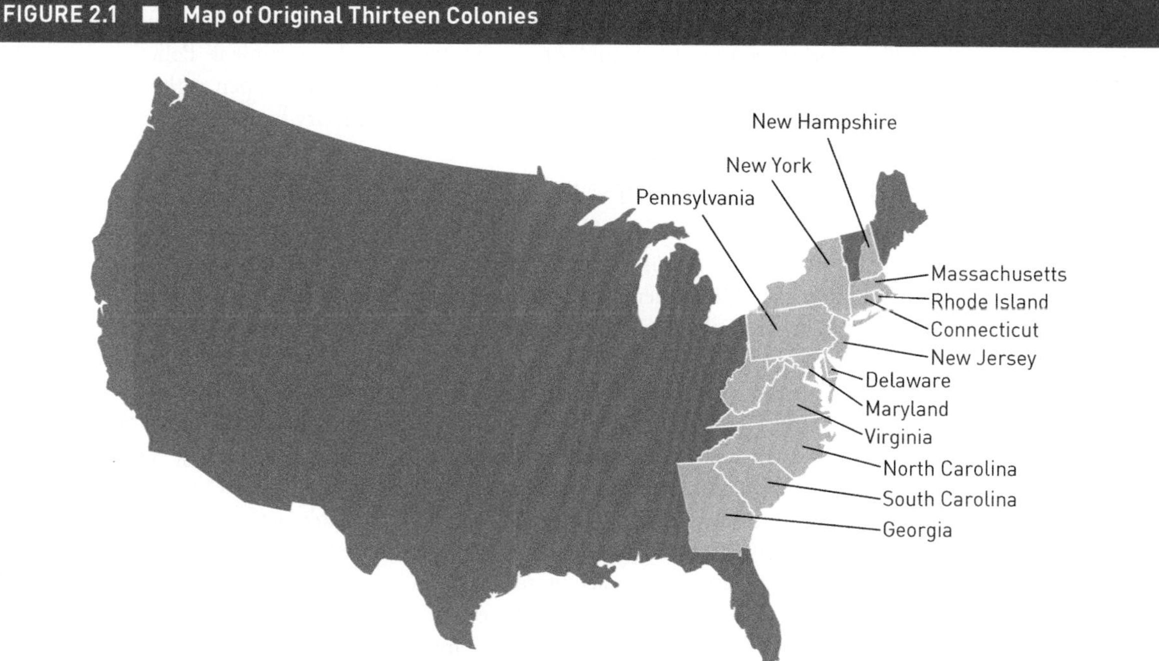

The Bill of Rights

The Constitution was seen by some as vague, providing opportunity for individual rights to be trampled. In the words of Patrick Henry (1788) during the ratifying convention in Virginia, "There will be no checks, no real balances, in this Government: What can avail your specious imaginary balances, your rope-dancing, chain-rattling, ridiculous ideal checks and contrivances?" A Bill of Rights had been hardly discussed at the Convention, because it was assumed that state constitutions would protect the **fundamental rights** of individuals.

Fundamental rights: This is a term that is based on the Constitution and relates to basic rights. Many are included in the Bill of Rights. These rights include freedom of speech, the right not to be incarcerated without a fair hearing, freedom of travel, the right to raise one's children, the right to own property, and the right of privacy.

To address these concerns, the Bill of Rights was developed, shown in Figure 2.2. Primarily written by James Madison, it was ratified by 1791 (National Archives, 2017a). This Bill of Rights, the first ten amendments to the U.S. Constitution, lays out many rights that are still discussed in public debates today. The most significant sources of controversy are Article 1, which protects freedom of speech, the right to assembly, and freedom of religion, among other rights; Article 2, which protects the right to bear arms and is the center of debates about gun laws today; Article 4, which limits unlawful search and seizures; Articles 5 and 7, which provide the right for individuals to be judged by a jury of their peers or equals; Article 6, which allows for a speedy trial; Article 8, which limits excessive bail; and Article 10, which states that all rights not specifically given to the federal government belong to the states.

Constitutional Amendments

In addition to the 10 amendments in the Bill of Rights, the Constitution has been amended an additional 17 times, for a total of 27 amendments. The most recent amendment, the 27th, ratified in 1992, says that members of Congress who vote to increase their pay cannot see that pay raise until after the next election. Many proposed amendments have failed to be ratified by enough states to become law, such as the Equal Rights Amendment and an amendment to give full voting rights to residents of the District of Columbia (Elving, 2018).

Current Structure of U.S. Government

To understand the policy decisions that affect you as a social worker or make an impact on the policy process, you must first understand the structure of government. Policy decisions that affect social workers and the communities and clients we serve happen at the local, state, and federal level and through the legislative, executive, or judiciary branch.

Legislative branch: The division of the government that makes laws. At the federal level, this branch is made up of Congress, which has two houses, the House of Representatives and the Senate.

Executive branch: The division of the government that carries out laws; at the federal level this includes the president, vice president, Cabinet, and most federal agencies

Judicial branch: The division of the government that evaluates laws. It includes many courts, including the Supreme Court that can determine laws unconstitutional.

Branches of U.S. Government

We start with a quick review of the ways the three branches of government are laid out at the federal level and then discuss the division of powers among the different levels of government. While most state governments are structured very similarly, keep in mind that state governments can be structured however the state chooses, so there may be some differences.

You've probably seen similar graphics to Figure 2.3 over the course of your education. It describes the three branches of the federal government and their respective responsibilities to create laws (the **legislative branch**), make those laws reality (the **executive branch**), and evaluate whether those laws are within the limits set by the Constitution (the **judicial branch**). The powers of each branch of government developed and changed over time, and respond to the culture and context of the time period as well as the ideological perspectives of the people who hold power within them (we discuss ideologies in depth later on in this chapter). While some of the processes to allow each branch to check the power of those in other branches were written into the Constitution, others have evolved over time. For example, the Constitution calls for a federal judiciary including a Supreme Court, but the structure of the court with a Chief Justice and associate justices was created in the 1789 Judiciary Act (Supreme Court

FIGURE 2.2 ■ Bill of Rights

The Bill of Rights

Ratified December 15, 1791

Article I

Congress shall make no law respecting an establishment of religion, or prohibiting the free exercise thereof; or abridging the freedom of speech, or of the press; or the right of the people peaceably to assemble, and to petition the Government for a redress of grievances.

Article II

A well regulated Militia, being necessary to the security of a free State, the right of the people to keep and bear Arms, shall not be infringed.

Article III

No Soldier shall, in time of peace be quartered in any house, without the consent of the Owner, nor in time of war, but in a manner to be prescribed by law.

Article IV

The right of the people to be secure in their persons, houses, papers, and effects, against unreasonable searches and seizures, shall not be violated, and no Warrants shall issue, but upon probable cause, supported by Oath or affirmation, and particularly describing the place to be searched, and the persons or things to be seized.

Article V

No person shall be held to answer for a capital, or otherwise infamous crime, unless on a presentment or indictment of a Grand Jury, except in cases arising in the land or naval forces, or in the Militia, when in actual service in time of War or public danger; nor shall any person be subject for the same offence to be twice put in jeopardy of life or limb; nor shall be compelled in any Criminal Case to be a witness against himself, nor be deprived of life, liberty, or property, without due process of law; nor shall private property be taken for public use, without just compensation.

Article VI

In all criminal prosecutions, the accused shall enjoy the right to a speedy and public trial, by an impartial jury of the State and district wherein the crime shall have been committed, which district shall have been previously ascertained by law, and to be informed of the nature and cause of the accusation; to be confronted with the witnesses against him; to have compulsory process for obtaining Witnesses in his favor, and to have the Assistance of Counsel for his defence.

Article VII

In Suits at common law, where the value in controversy shall exceed twenty dollars, the right of trial by jury shall be preserved, and no fact tried by a jury shall be otherwise reexamined in any Court of the United States, than according to the rules of the common law.

Article VIII

Excessive bail shall not be required, nor excessive fines imposed, nor cruel and unusual punishment inflicted.

Article IX

The enumeration in the Constitution, of certain rights, shall not be construed to deny or disparage others retained by the people.

Article X

The powers not delegated to the United States by the Constitution, nor prohibited by it to the States, are reserved to the States respectively, or to the people.

A reminder to be ever vigilant in the protection of these rights
Presented in loving memory of Corliss Lamont 1902 - 1995

National Emergency Civil Liberties Committee
New York, NY 10010

FIGURE 2.3 ■ Three Branches of U.S. Federal Government

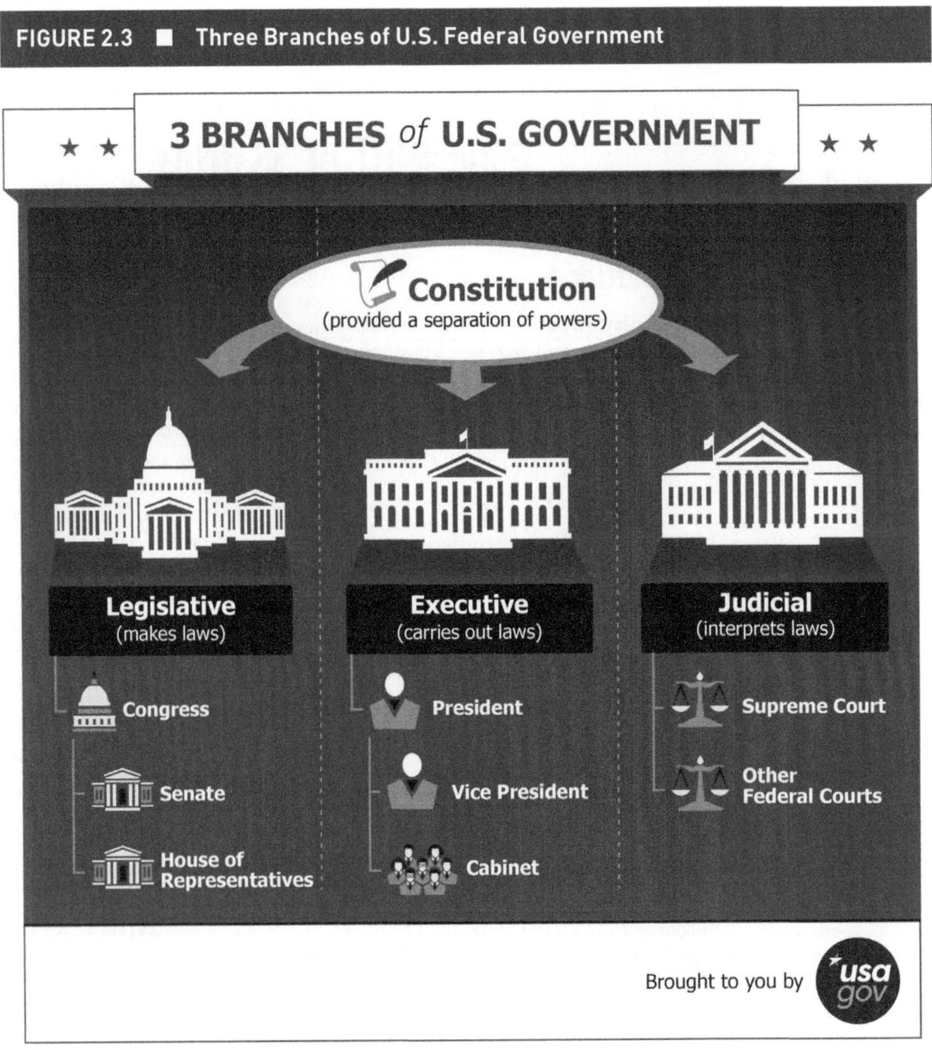

Source: Branches of the U.S. Government. (n.d.). Retrieved from https://www.usa.gov/organization-of-the-us-government#item-211477

Historical Society, n.d.a). The Court gave itself the right to declare a law unconstitutional in 1800 with *Marbury v. Madison* (Supreme Court Historical Society, n.d.b). The two-party structure that today gives leaders of political parties significant influence within the executive and legislative branches did not exist at the writing of the Constitution and was, in fact, actively opposed by many founders of the country.

The general description is that at the federal level, the legislative branch (Congress) makes laws, the executive branch (the president, Cabinet agencies, and other executive branch offices) enforces them, and the judicial branch (Supreme Court and other federal courts) evaluates them is accurate, but not complete. Let's take a specific example and walk it through the three branches.

Licensure: The process by which the government or other authorized body certifies that a person has the qualifications needed to perform a specific job or task

Legislative Process: A Hypothetical Social Work Bill Becomes Law

A common concern for social workers is that social work licensure (like other professional licensure) is regulated at the state level. **Licensure** is the process by which the government certifies that a person has the qualifications needed to perform a specific job or task. Keep in mind that this does not necessarily mean someone is good at that job, but that they meet the minimum qualifications for the license. Although all 50 states use common licensure exams for the LMSW level, other requirements may differ. This can be a challenge if you move from one state to another—you might, for example, have to take additional coursework, training, or an exam to become licensed in a new state, even if you are already licensed in your home state (Association of Social Work Boards, n.d.). One potential solution would be to move social work licensure to the federal level, instead of leaving it to individual states to address.

We are going to take our idea for national social work licensure to a member of Congress who can introduce it, following the process for a bill to become a law as shown in Figure 2.4. Generally you would start with members of Congress who represent your geographic area. That means you have three choices: either your member of the House of Representatives or one of your two U.S. senators. You might also work with a member who doesn't represent you but has a strong interest in your issue. In this case, we start with Representative Barbara Lee, a social worker and member of Congress who chairs the Congressional Social Work Caucus and therefore seems to be a good person to talk to about an issue related to social work (https://socialworkcaucus-lee.house.gov/).

Representative Lee will introduce our bill, which might get the number H.R. 100 (H.R. tells us it's starting in the House of Representatives—if it started in the Senate, the bill number would start with S). Next it is sent to at least one committee, the House Committee on Education and the Workforce (https://edworkforce.house.gov/). Our bill beats the odds—although most bills never get a hearing, Representative Lee works with committee member Representative Carol Shea-Porter (another social worker) to convince the chair to hold a **markup hearing**, which is an opportunity for debate and amendment. Committee members receive many letters and phone calls from social workers in their districts supporting the bill, particularly those who are married to people serving in the military and therefore need to move frequently, who would be really helped by this bill. The committee members are convinced by this argument and the committee votes 30–10 to move the bill forward to the next step. Now all the members of the Social Work Caucus band together with members of the Congressional Military Family Caucus (https://mcmorris.house.gov/congressional-military-family-caucus/) to convince the Speaker of the House to bring the bill to the floor of the House for debate and vote. The **Speaker of the House** is the presiding officer of the House of Representatives. Our bill is one of the 5% of bills that are introduced in the House this session that make it to a vote. The bill passes the full House 235–200 and moves to the Senate to start the process again.

In the Senate, the bill is referred to the U.S. Senate Committee on Health, Education, Labor, and Pensions, also called the HELP committee (seriously, that's what it's called: https://www.help.senate.gov/). None of the 23 members of this committee are social workers, but the committee's Ranking Member is a member of the Senate Military Families Caucus. A **Ranking Member** is the most powerful person on a committee from the **minority party**, the party with less power. If her party had more power in the Senate and became the **majority party**, she would be the committee chair. She advocates on behalf of this bill to her fellow senators, and the bill is unanimously approved 23–0 and moved to the Senate floor for the full Senate to vote. However, the version of the bill that comes out of this committee is **amended** or formally modified. To make it even friendlier to military families, it waives social work licensure fees for the spouses of active duty military members. The bill is successfully introduced and passed in the Senate, but it is not yet ready to go to the president. Because the version that passed the House is different from the version that passed the Senate, it will have to go to a **Conference Committee**,

Markup hearing: The process by which a U.S. congressional committee debates, amends, and rewrites proposed legislation

Speaker of the House: The presiding officer of the U.S. House of Representatives

Ranking Member: The most powerful person on a Congressional committee from the party with less power

Minority party: The political party with less power in a legislative body

Majority party: The political party with more power in a legislative body

Amended: Changed or formally modified

Conference Committee: A committee of the U.S. Congress appointed by the House of Representatives and Senate to resolve disagreements on a particular bill

FIGURE 2.4 ■ How a Bill Becomes a Law

HOW DOES A BILL BECOME A LAW?

1 EVERY LAW STARTS WITH AN IDEA

That idea can come from anyone, even you! Contact your elected officials to share your idea. If they want to try to make it a law, they will write a bill.

2 THE BILL IS INTRODUCED

A bill can start in either house of Congress when it's introduced by its primary sponsor, a Senator or a Representative. In the House of Representatives, bills are placed in a wooden box called "the hopper."

Here, the bill is assigned a legislative number before the Speaker of the House sends it to a committee.

3 THE BILL GOES TO COMMITTEE

Representatives or Senators meet in a small group to research, talk about, and make changes to the bill. They vote to accept or reject the bill and its changes before sending it to:

the House or Senate floor for debate or **to a subcommittee for further research.**

4 CONGRESS DEBATES AND VOTES

Members of the House or Senate can now debate the bill and propose changes or amendments before voting. If the majority vote for and pass the bill, it moves to the other house to go through a similar process of committees, debate, and voting. Both houses have to agree on the same version of the final bill before it goes to the President.

DID YOU KNOW?

The House uses an electronic voting system while the Senate typically votes by voice, saying "yay" or "nay."

5 PRESIDENTIAL ACTION

When the bill reaches the President, he or she can:

√APPROVE and PASS

The President signs and approves the bill. The bill is law.

The President can also:

Veto

The President rejects the bill and returns it to Congress with the reasons for the veto. Congress can override the veto with 2/3 vote of those present in both the House and the Senate and the bill will become law.

Choose no action

The President can decide to do nothing. If Congress is in session, after 10 days of no answer from the President, the bill then automatically becomes law.

Pocket veto

If Congress adjourns (goes out of session) within the 10 day period after giving the President the bill, the President can choose not to sign it and the bill will not become law.

Brought to you by

Source: How Laws Are Made. (n.d.). Retrieved from https://www.usa.gov/how-laws-are-made

a committee appointed by the House of Representatives and Senate to resolve disagreements on a particular bill, for a compromise to be worked out, and then back to both houses for a vote. It cannot move on to the president until both houses of Congress have passed the same bill. Luckily, this issue has become an important one for everyone involved, thanks to continued advocacy by social workers and military families, and it successfully passes the Conference Committee with the Senate change. The House agrees to that version of the bill by a unanimous voice vote.

Executive Process: A Hypothetical Social Work Bill is Implemented

At this point, our proposed policy leaves the legislative branch and moves to the executive branch, represented in this process by the president. The president is not a big supporter of our bill because he wants to reduce rather than add government regulations. On the other hand, he does not want to get on the bad side of military families. Because of these conflicting motivations, the president takes no action on the bill. Since Congress is still in session, our bill becomes law after 10 days, even without the president's signature. As a result, our bill has successfully become a public law. It will get a number that looks something like PL 116-50, for the 50th law that was passed in the 116th session of Congress (each session runs for 2 years, in this case, 2019–2020). We are done! Wait . . . are we done?

For our hypothetical national social work licensure law to be **implemented**, meaning to actually be put into action, the government is going to have to create some rules. Rules, also referred to as *regulations*, are usually much more specific than the laws Congress passes. This process can be even longer and more complicated than the process of getting a bill to become law. An example from the National Archives and Records Administration (NARA) of what that regulatory process might look like is shown in Figure 2.5.

Implementation: The process of enacting a piece of policy that has been approved

In this case, the responsibility within the executive branch for implementation might go to the Department of Health and Human Services (HHS, https://www.hhs.gov/). HHS determines a set of rules they believe are necessary to implement the new social work licensure law, such as clarifying any terms not defined in law and creating a mechanism for implementing the law, which for this law is likely to include an office within the Substance Abuse and Mental Health Services Administration (SAMHSA, https://www.samhsa.gov/) to oversee licensure. HHS proposes those rules, and they are made accessible via https://www.regulations.gov/ for the public and other stakeholders to comment. The time period varies, but this comment period is generally held open for 60 days. The feedback from those comments is incorporated into the final rules, which are then issued publicly at https://www.federalregister.gov/ and sent back to the legislative branch for a final check. If Congress has any changes they want to make, they have 30 days to do so.

Judicial Process: A Hypothetical Social Work Bill is Challenged in the Courts

Now that our hypothetical bill has become law and a mechanism and guidelines for implementation have been established, it is done, right? Not so fast. During the process of creating this law and the related rules, the leaders of state agencies that oversee social work licensure in several different states have become angry. They feel that social work licensure should be regulated at the state level, not the federal level. They think that their state is better equipped to decide practice requirements for social work with their populations. They also do not want to lose the income generated for their state from licensure fees, often called **revenue**. These agencies band together to sue the federal government.

Revenue: Income generated for an organization or government

Their lawsuit is based on Amendment 10 to the Constitution, the last one in the Bill of Rights. It states, "The powers not delegated to the United States by the Constitution, nor

FIGURE 2.5 ■ Regulatory Process

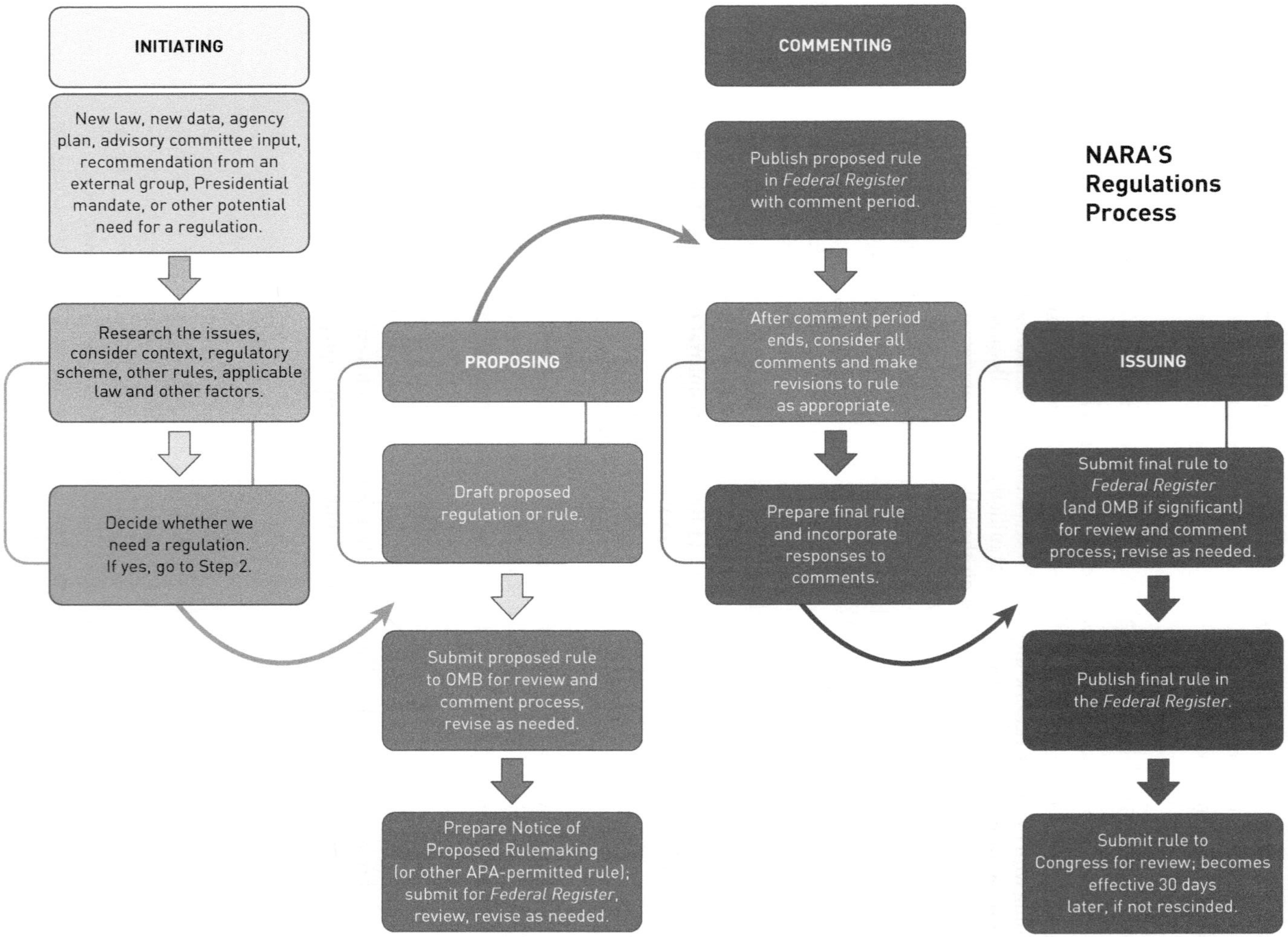

NARA'S Regulations Process

INITIATING

New law, new data, agency plan, advisory committee input, recommendation from an external group, Presidential mandate, or other potential need for a regulation.

Research the issues, consider context, regulatory scheme, other rules, applicable law and other factors.

Decide whether we need a regulation. If yes, go to Step 2.

PROPOSING

Draft proposed regulation or rule.

Submit proposed rule to OMB for review and comment process, revise as needed.

Prepare Notice of Proposed Rulemaking (or other APA-permitted rule); submit for *Federal Register*, review, revise as needed.

COMMENTING

Publish proposed rule in *Federal Register* with comment period.

After comment period ends, consider all comments and make revisions to rule as appropriate.

Prepare final rule and incorporate responses to comments.

ISSUING

Submit final rule to *Federal Register* (and OMB if significant) for review and comment process; revise as needed.

Publish final rule in the *Federal Register*.

Submit rule to Congress for review; becomes effective 30 days later, if not rescinded.

Source: NARA's Regulatory Process. (n.d.). Retrieved from https://www.archives.gov/about/regulations/process.html

prohibited by it to the states, are reserved to the states respectively, or to the people." They argue that this means since licensure is not specifically delegated to the federal government by the Constitution, it is the right and responsibility of the states. Because the state of Massachusetts leads the way, the lawsuit is filed first with the District Court of Massachusetts (see Figure 2.6 for a district court map). Many organizations work on advocacy at this stage by filing briefs called **amicus curiae**, which means *friend of the court* (often just called *amicus briefs*). National organizations representing social workers and military families file amicus briefs on the side of the federal government. National medical associations and other groups that have also been trying to get medical and other professional licenses at the federal level instead of the state level also file briefs on the side of the federal government. Advocacy sometimes brings groups together that you wouldn't expect to be on the same side. Sometimes people who are usually on the same side find themselves disagreeing. In this case, state chapters of social work organizations file amicus briefs siding with the states, because they want to keep control of licensure at the state level, even though the national chapters of their organizations are on the federal government's side.

Amicus curiae: Latin phrase meaning "friend of the court," these are authors of legal documents (called *amicus briefs*) that are filed by those interested in Supreme Court decisions, usually to support the interests of a particular side or outcome

The district courts find in favor of the state agencies and say the new national licensure law is unconstitutional. Most cases will end here. In fact, if the president did not really support the bill, it is likely that the prosecutors he appointed might not wish to pursue the case further (this decision is up to the current leadership of the Justice Department). However, in this case, the federal government decides to **appeal** the decision, which means they ask a higher court to take a look at it to see if the district court made a mistake. It then moves to a federal **appellate court**. The job of this court is to hear appeals of the lower court decisions.

Appeal: In a legal dispute, the procedure to ask a higher court to determine whether a lower court's ruling was correct

Massachusetts is located within the jurisdiction of the U.S. Circuit Court of Appeals, District 1, also called an appellate court. The case moves to this court, which hears both arguments (including more amicus briefs). The appellate court decides that the lower court's

Appellate court: Also called a court of appeals, which hears appeals of lower courts

FIGURE 2.6 ■ U.S. Federal District Court Map

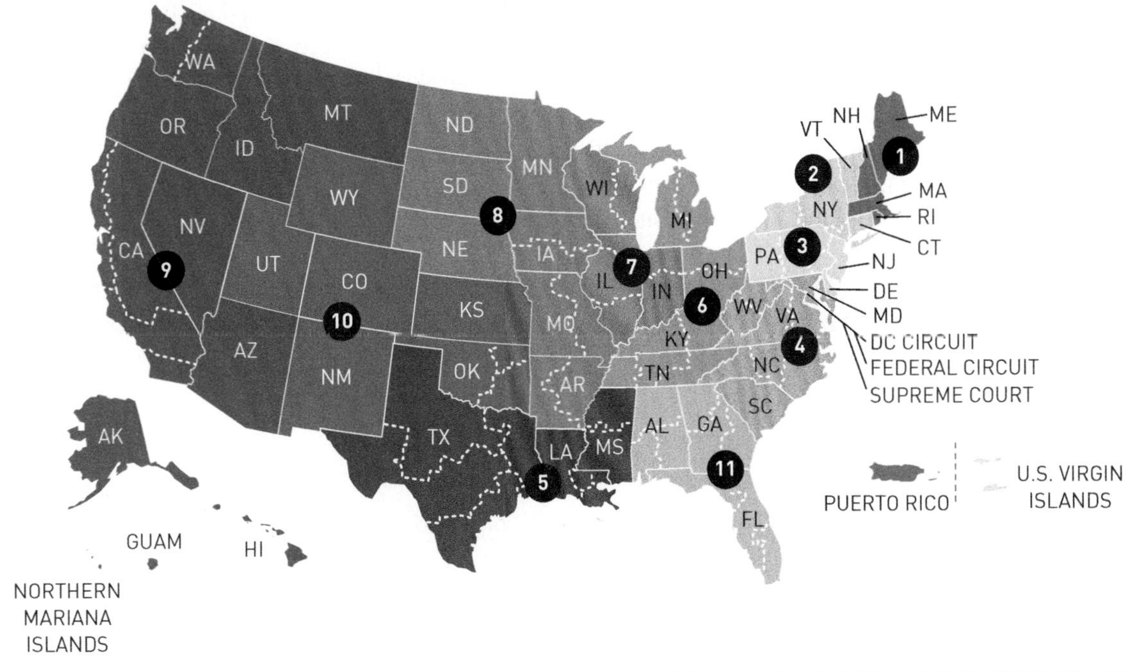

Source: United States Courts. (n.d.). Retrieved from http://www.uscourts.gov/file/document/us-federal-courts-circuit-map

decision was wrong and overturns it, finding in favor of the federal government. The state agencies are unhappy with this decision and appeal to the Supreme Court.

The Supreme Court hears a small fraction of the cases it is asked to consider each year but, against the odds again, it decides to hear this one. The issue of social work licensure on its own might not be enough to convince the Supreme Court, but because the decision seems like it will affect a number of other professions, the Court decides it should be considered. After reviewing the case and hearing oral arguments from both sides, the Court finds in a 5–4 decision that the new law is **unconstitutional** (not in accordance with the U.S. Constitution) because it violates Amendment 10. As a result, social work licensure will remain at the state level and the federal law is no longer in effect. After all this effort, everything goes back to the way it was at the beginning of the process.

Unconstitutional: Not in accordance with the U.S. Constitution

Judicial Process: Are the Courts Political? Though theoretically designed to be nonpolitical, the courts are indeed political and, from time to time, the composition of the courts change, allowing them to be used to support either conservative or liberal agendas. Courts cannot decide which cases they would like to hear; they must wait for someone to bring a case before them. Within the circuits, courts have reputations for liberalism or conservatism. Some circuits, such as the first, second, third, fourth, and ninth are considered to be more liberal, while the fifth and the 11th are seen as more conservative. What does this mean regarding the courts? In general, conservatives are more inclined to focus on limiting government from infringing on individual freedoms, whereas liberals may see the value of laws that limit individual freedoms with the goal of protecting community interests. Using the example of religion, liberal courts tend to support religious freedom defined in terms of keeping religion out of government processes (e.g., separation of church and state) and tend to think that the court's role is to interpret the meaning of laws. More conservative courts tend to consider religious freedom to mean that people should be allowed to practice their religion in any way they see fit even if it may infringe on the rights of others. There are of course disagreements among liberal judges or conservative judges. For example, conservatives can be traditionalists and libertarians. Traditionalists believe that if we have always done something in a certain way, as a result of tradition, it should be allowed to continue whenever possible. Libertarians generally resist government intervention that limits individual liberty for any reason (Feldman, 2012).

Levels of U.S. Government

Often, we think of the U.S. government as a simple triangle, with the power to create policy divided up among local, state, and federal governments (see Figure 2.7).

FIGURE 2.7 ■ Generally Accepted Division of Policy Power

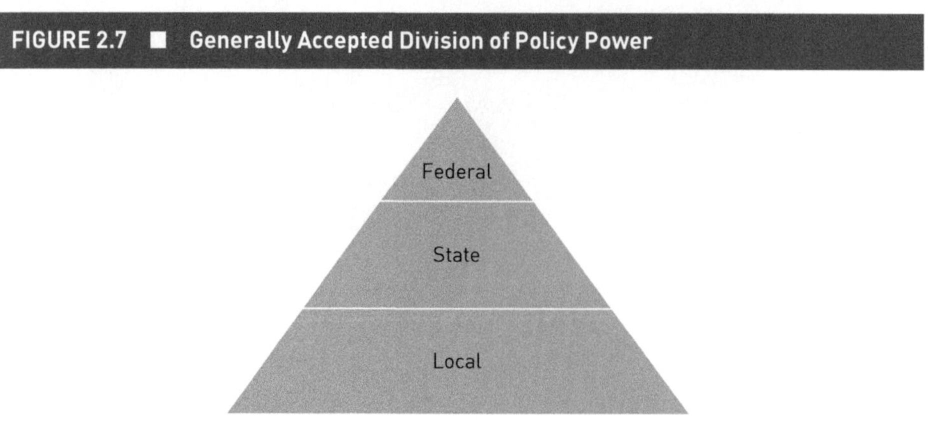

FIGURE 2.8 ■ Actual Division of Policy Power

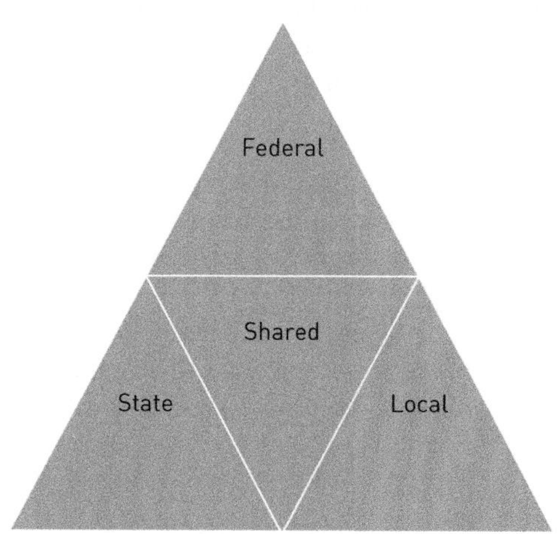

TABLE 2.1 ■ Powers of Government

Appropriate money for programs to promote welfare of residents	Establish local governments	Oversee parks and recreation
Borrow money	Establish military	Oversee post office
Build highways and other major public works	Establish state constitution	Oversee transportation
Charter banks and corporations	Exercise powers not specifically delegated to federal government	Print money
Conduct elections	Issue licenses	Protect against fire
Conduct policing	Make and enforce laws	Provide for public health and safety
Create and collect taxes	Oversee city zoning and planning	Ratify amendments to U.S. Constitution
Declare war	Oversee economic development	Ratify treaties with other governments
Enforce state Constitution	Oversee education	Regulate commerce between states and countries
Enforce U.S. Constitution	Oversee human services	Regulate intrastate commerce (within one state)
Establish courts	Oversee municipal public works	

The truth is probably closer to what is depicted in Figure 2.8, with many powers shared between levels.

Federalism: A system of government in which power is divided between the state and federal government in a defined manner in which each level of government has ultimate authority in some areas

Federalism refers specifically to a system in which power is divided between the state and federal government in a defined manner in which each level of government has ultimate authority in some areas (Galligan, 2007). If every decision made by a state could be overruled by the federal government, we would not have a federalist system. Since there are some areas in which the states have final say no matter what the federal government says, the U.S. system is defined as federalist. We are not alone in this system. While the system in each country looks slightly different, Argentina, Australia, Austria, Belgium, Brazil, Canada, Germany, India, Mexico, Russia, South Africa, Spain, Switzerland, and Venezuela are all federalist (Galligan, 2007).

Discussion: Who is in Charge? Federalism can sometimes feel very abstract, so it might be helpful to look at ways governments in the United States divide up responsibilities in everyday practice. Below you will find a table of activities created by Tanya Rhodes Smith, director of the Nancy A. Humphreys Institute for Political Social Work at the University of Connecticut. Go through the list of activities below and divide them up. Which are exclusive powers of the federal government, exclusive powers of state governments, shared between the federal and state governments, or typically powers of local governments (including towns, cities, and counties)? You may also wish to list other duties of government that we have not included: Which categories do they belong in? When you are finished, discuss with your classmates and/or instructors. Our version of the final table is listed at the end of this chapter for comparison, but some of your conclusions may differ from ours. If so, discuss why and whether you think multiple answers are correct (or that we are wrong!).

In addition to the duties that are divided up among our local, state, and federal governments, many aspects of our social welfare system in the United States are carried out by nongovernmental organizations. For example, nongovernmental organizations may provide services that are paid for by the government (such as hospitals providing services that are billed to Medicare or Medicaid) or are funded through government contracts or grants to provide services. The Urban Institute (Pettijohn, Boris, De Vita, & Fuffe, 2013) lists 52 types of services provided by agencies through state and/or federal government grants and contracts dealing with social welfare areas such as:

- Arts education
- Child abuse prevention
- Civil liberties
- Crisis intervention
- Disaster relief
- Economic development
- Education
- Family counseling
- Food banks
- Homeless shelters
- Job training
- Medical research
- Natural resources conservation
- Rehabilitation services for those who have been involved with the criminal justice system

- Services for survivors of intimate partner violence
- Substance use disorder treatment
- Voter education and registration

Political Parties and Ideologies

While the branches and levels of government discussed above have developed from written documents such as the U.S. Constitution, state constitutions, legislation, and judicial opinions, other aspects of our policy and political systems have developed from common practices. Indeed one aspect of that, the development of political parties, was specifically feared by the founders of our country.

Political Parties

Political parties are groups of people who share similar political goals and opinions who come together to get candidates elected to office. In the *Federalist Papers*, James Madison (1787) refers to parties (using the term *factions* instead of parties) as a "dangerous vice." In George Washington's farewell address (1796), he warned sternly,

> I have already intimated to you the danger of parties in the State, with particular reference to the founding of them on geographical discriminations. Let me now take a more comprehensive view, and warn you in the most solemn manner against the baneful effects of the spirit of party generally.

So how is it that, despite their fervent opposition to parties, every president since Washington has belonged to or represented one of these parties or factions? The credit (or blame) is generally given to Alexander Hamilton (Silbey, 2010). Essentially, Treasury Secretary Hamilton's desire to create a strong central government helped organize Founding Fathers into groups who supported his view of a strong central government, the Federalists, and those who wanted more power to be designated to the states, the Republicans, who became known as the Democratic-Republicans. The latter included such founders as Thomas Jefferson, who in 1789 wrote to his friend Francis Hopkinson, "If I could not go to heaven but with a party, I would not go there at all," and yet by 1800 had been elected president as a Democratic-Republican. The Federalist Party had lost its influence by 1820, to be replaced by the Whigs until the 1850s. Since around 1860, the Democratic and Republican parties have been the two major political parties in the United States; although, as discussed below, the beliefs of those under the umbrellas of those two parties have changed.

While the following discussion includes the two major parties in the United States and the most influential *third parties* or other parties, there are many other smaller parties in U.S. politics. The list from the Federal Election Commission shown in Figure 2.9 includes party labels that appeared next to candidates' names in the 2014 federal elections. You may see other parties' names at the state level, such as New York's "The Rent is Too Damn High" party.

Despite this plethora of options, the Democratic and Republican parties play a major role in U.S. politics, both in the process of choosing and electing candidates and how officials govern once they are elected.

Party labels can also be tricky because parties themselves change over time. The Democrats have gone from the party of slave-owning Southern whites, such as Thomas Jefferson, to parties that have higher turnout by African Americans and Latinos than white Americans. Even within the past 20 years, the two major parties have changed. Within

FIGURE 2.9 ■ List of Party Labels in the United States

A GUIDE TO PARTY LABELS

The following is a list of the abbreviations used in this publication to identify the labels that appeared on the various state ballots for the U.S. Congressional candidates in the 2014 primary and general elections. The party label listed may not necessarily represent a political party organization.

AE	=	Americans Elect	LBU	=	Liberty Union
AFC	=	Allen 4 Congress	LIB	=	Libertarian
AIP	=	American Independent	LMP	=	Legalize Marijuana Party
AKI	=	Alaskan Independence	MSC	=	Send Mr. Smith
ALP	=	American Labor Party	MTP	=	Mountain
AM	=	American Party	N	=	Nonpartisan
AMC	=	American Constitution Party	NAF	=	Nonaffiliated
BBH	=	Bullying Breaks Hearts	NLP	=	Natural Law Party
BP	=	By Petition	NNE	=	None
BQT	=	Bob Quast for Term Limits	NOP	=	No Party Preference
CIT	=	Citizens Party	NPA	=	No Party Affiliation
CN	=	Change is Needed	NUP	=	National Union Party
CON	=	Constitution	OP	=	Of The People
CRV	=	Conservative	PAC	=	Politicians are Crooks
D	=	Democratic	PAF	=	Peace and Freedom
DCG	=	D.C. Statehood Green	PC	=	Petitioning Candidate
DFL	=	Democratic-Farmer-Labor	PET	=	Petition
DNL	=	Democratic-Nonpartisan League	PG	=	Pacific Green
DRP	=	D-R Party	PRO	=	Progressive
EG	=	Economic Growth	R	=	Republican
ENI	=	Energy Independence	REF	=	Reform
FA	=	For Americans	SBP	=	Stop Boss Politics
FEP	=	Flourish Every Person	SC	=	Start the Conversation
FV	=	Future.Vision.	SI	=	Seeking Inclusion
GOP	=	G.O.P. Party	TN	=	911 Truth Needed
GRE	=	Green	TRP	=	Tax Revolt
HRP	=	Human Rights Party	TVH	=	Truth Vision Hope
IAP	=	Independent American Party	UN	=	Unaffiliated
IDP	=	Independence	UPC	=	Unity Party of Colorado
IGR	=	Independent Green	UST	=	U.S. Taxpayers Party
IND	=	Independent	W	=	Write-In
IP	=	Independent Party	WDB	=	We Deserve Better
JP	=	José Peñalosa	WF	=	Working Families
LBF	=	Libertarian Party of Florida	WU	=	Wake Up USA
LBR	=	Labor	WWP	=	Work and Wealth Party

Source: Federal Elections 2014 Election Results by the Federal Election Commission, November 2015. Retrieved from https://transition.fec.gov/pubrec/fe2014/partylabels2014.pdf

the past 100 years, Democrats were more likely to support federal regulation and federally funded social welfare programs. Beginning with the Clinton administration's support for "ending welfare as we know it," the Democrats have become more fiscally conservative and more likely to support arguments that suggested that families living in poverty should "pull themselves up by their bootstraps." This led to reduced social welfare spending. As discussed in Chapter 1, under the Clinton administration, welfare reform changed Aid to Families With Dependent Children, a universal means-tested, federally funded and regulated welfare program, to Temporary Assistance for Needy Families (TANF), a program funded through block grants to states with substantially limited funds, offering many ways in which states and individual workers within the welfare system could remove families from benefits.

Republicans historically focused on providing more control over regulation to states than the federal government. In the recent past, they began to focus more heavily on reduced government spending at both the federal and state levels and maintaining the use of guns without government control, while favoring greater intervention in social areas such as limiting abortion rights and same-sex marriage. Some argue that the political stances of Reagan, considered a standard-bearer of the Republican Party in his time, would not be conservative enough for today's Republican Party (Olsen, 2017).

Political Ideology

Individual political decision making in the United States is influenced by a number of factors (Pew Research Center, 2014, 2015). One of the most significant is **ideology**, that is, beliefs about society and how it should function. When you hear people describe themselves or someone else as the *left* or *right*, they are referring to one measure of ideology that ranks people from a radical or liberal left to a conservative right. However, this distinction erases much of the nuance of political beliefs (Pew Research Center, 2014, 2015). Other political ideologies include socialism, progressivism, and libertarianism. If forced to choose a position described as conservative, moderate, or liberal, most social work students and social workers who have run for office were likely to choose liberal and moderate. Rosenwald's study (2006) found that social work students identified first as liberal (41%), then moderate (34%), and least as conservative (10%). More recent studies using slightly different methods find higher numbers of students identifying with liberal ideologies, above 60%, and a similar number (10%) identifying as conservative (Pritzker & Burwell, 2016; Pritzker & Garza, 2017). Social workers who had run for office (Lane & Humphreys, 2011) identified themselves as more liberal (60%) than the students, with similar numbers identifying as moderate (38%) and conservative (2%).

Ideology: Beliefs about society and how it should function

REFLECTION

CONSIDERING YOUR OWN POSITIONS

1. How would you describe your ideology, using the terms discussed above?
2. After you answer #1, take the quiz: https://www.people-press.org/quiz/political-typology/
3. How does the result of the quiz compare to your answer in #1? What might account for the differences, if any?

Political Parties and Ideology

Political party: Groups of people who share similar political goals and opinions who come together to get candidates elected to office

There tends to be strong overlap between political party and ideology, although not absolute. A **political party** is part of a system in which power is divided between the state and federal government in a defined manner in which each level of government has ultimate authority say in some areas. Socialists support safety nets for the public, redistribution of wealth and resources from the wealthy to the poor and middle class, and single payer health insurance. Socialists are also anti-capitalist, believing that capitalism exploits working people. The party that most closely reflects socialist ideals in the United States is the Democratic Socialist Party. This party supports all the same programs but suggests that rather than getting rid of capitalism, these programs are necessary supports in a capitalist country. In the United States, this tends to be considered radical, but it would not be radical in many European countries. Liberals and progressives tend to be aligned with the Democratic Party, although progressives tend to support broader government involvement in social welfare than liberals. Conservatives tend to be aligned with the Republican Party. Historically, they believe in greater state control over governance than federal control and limited government outside of certain social issues such as abortion. Libertarians believe in limited government, and thus are aligned with many of the same things as Republicans on many issues. Libertarians and conservatives differ on issues that involve government control, such as abortion or the legal distribution of marijuana.

Context is very important in a consideration of political ideology and parties. In more conservative areas of the United States, you will find Democratic candidates who are opposed to gun control laws and in favor of abortion restrictions. In predominately liberal areas of the country, you will find Republican candidates who describe themselves as pro-choice and favor some policies that redistribute wealth. Religion, culture, and local community characteristics can also play a role in deciding what political party people will join, regardless of ideology.

INTERVENTION METHODS: HOW TO ENGAGE WITH THE POLICY PROCESS

In our discussion of the context of policy throughout this chapter, we have touched on many aspects of the policy process. Here, we highlight specific examples of how some social workers participate in this process. You will find activities throughout this book to try some of these opportunities yourself. Before you proceed, answer Questions 1 through 4 for yourself. Engage with your classmates around Question 5 as you move forward.

Social work embraces integration of micro through macro perspectives, using person-in-environment (Karls & Wandrei, 1994; Kondrat, 2002) and the ecological and boundary spanning perspectives (Germain & Gitterman, 1996; Gibelman, 1999; Kerson, 2002). These are useful frameworks to engage all social work students and professionals in policy practice.

Social workers are especially well situated to recognize and create social change. As professionals we are often the face of policy to our clients and communities, or the people who tell clients whether they are eligible for a service or a community how a recently passed policy will affect them. Social workers can see how policies directly impact people. This includes both the intended effects as well as unintended consequences (Gillon, 2000). Understanding the implications of policies on the ground requires social workers to understand how social institutions and structures promote or constrain certain behaviors. Social workers' positioning and training enable them to see these effects clearly.

DISCUSSION

POLICY PRACTICE

1. What are your concerns and fears about engaging in policy practice?
2. What are your hopes and expectations about engaging in policy practice?
3. What skills do you have or hope to gain while you are learning to be a social worker that are valuable to policy practice?
4. What skills or experience to enhance your ability to engage in policy practice might need to come from outside of your social work education? How might you acquire these skills or experience?
5. Interview some of your classmates. Ask how each one of them envisions working to influence policy. What are some of the differences and similarities in the ways that they seek to meet this social work ethical obligation?

Social workers who work with individuals or groups *and* use a policy lens are more likely to connect individuals' experiences to the larger context. They can serve as catalysts when they see a pattern or systemic problem and help galvanize individuals for political action, directly inform agency practices, or influence policy at higher levels (Fischer, 2009). Social workers who work on the micro or mezzo level who recognize broader implications of their work, but who may not know how to address such problems, can link themselves (or their clients) with macro social workers or others in the policy arena. Indeed, social work students and social workers as a group have high levels of interest in, and engagement with, politics and the policy making process than other students (Pritzker & Burwell, 2016), although many report they did not have needed curricular or extracurricular opportunities for engagement in their social work education (Lane, 2011). In a 2008 survey of 270 social workers who had run for or served in political office from 45 states, the majority (63%) felt that their social work education prepared them for their elective career. The social work skills that they most frequently identified as useful for the pursuit of and service in office were communication and active listening, skills that are core components of social work education, regardless of practice area or method (Lane, 2011).

Social workers who dedicate their careers to policy practice take on many different roles. They can be found at all levels of governments across the country serving as elected officials (Congressional Social Work Caucus, n.d.; NASW, n.d.). Others work behind the scenes, running campaigns and serving as political aides, researchers, and in constituent services (Fisher, 2014). Still other policy practice social workers are community organizers, working with groups to identify and advocate around issues that matter before administrative agencies, private actors, and legislative bodies. Other social workers are paid or volunteer lobbyists, building and maintaining relationships with elected officials and their offices in the service of causes or groups to bring about change. Social workers are also citizens who vote and are often well positioned to know the potential benefits and harms of policies on clients, particularly on the vulnerable populations that social workers so often serve.

An example of one method of social work policy engagement is elected public office. Teresa Benitez-Thompson has been representing the 27th District in the Nevada State Assembly since 2010. Like most social workers who are legislators, Assemblywoman Benitez-Thompson is both a woman and a Democrat. She holds a master's degree in social work from the University of Michigan, and she practiced in the areas of hospice care and adoption. In her political career, she is active on issues of importance to women and families that have also had an impact on her own life, including domestic violence that led her mother to bring her and her siblings to Reno, Nevada, to live with her grandparents, and the struggles of growing up in a low-income multigenerational family. These experiences and her social work education inform and influence her practice as an elected official. Assemblywoman Benitez-Thompson describes a family legacy of activism and service. She carried on a tradition of resourcefulness, using a scholarship from the Miss Nevada pageant to fund her undergraduate and graduate education (Elect Teresa, 2017a). Currently, she is the **majority leader** of the Nevada Assembly, which means that she has authority over the day-to-day workings of the legislative chamber, including such tasks as assigning bills to committees and scheduling. In most federal and local legislatures, this position is a sign of respect or seniority and holds power (Ballotpedia, 2017). In 2017, Assemblywoman Benitez-Thompson served on the Nevada Health and Human Services, Ways and Means, and Taxation Committees, reflective of her key interests, which include government spending, jobs, and families (Ballotpedia, 2017; Elect Teresa, 2017b).

Majority leader: Within a legislative body, the head of the party with the most members

ADVOCACY

FIND A SOCIAL WORK LEGISLATOR

Beginning level: Go to Ballotpedia or your state or local government website and identify a lawmaker who is a social worker. If you cannot find a social worker in your state or local government, identify a lawmaker who works on an issue of interest to you or who shares your values. Next, visit their official government and/or campaign website. Based on this research, answer the following questions.

1. What is their party affiliation?
2. What leadership roles do they have?
3. What committees do they sit on?
4. What issues do they seem to care about most?

For the intermediate and advanced level of this activity, go to wwww.edge.sagepub.com/lane

Social Work Contributions Across Policy Arenas

Assemblywoman Benitez-Thompson and others have found that their social work skills are helpful in engaging in the policy and political processes. In this section, we look at the ways in which social work skills benefit social workers in the policy arena and specifically about the ways in which social workers use research to inform their policy work.

In Table 2.2, you will find a list of policy arenas and ways in which social workers may use their social work skills to become involved in action in those areas. After reviewing the list of activities, look through the list of skills. Which skills have you already started to learn in your social work program? Which do you need to develop as you continue your social work education to make you a competent and confident social worker?

TABLE 2.2 ■ Policy Activities and Relevant Social Work Skills

<table>
<tr><th>Policy Arena</th><th>Activities</th><th>Relevant Social Work Skills</th></tr>
<tr><td>Legislative Branch</td><td>Advocacy
• Research
• Sharing insights from practice or stories from clients/communities
• Organizing community members
• Engaging with elected officials and their staff
Electoral politics
• Running for office
• Working on a campaign
• Engaging voters in voter registration, education, or outreach</td><td rowspan="3">Active listening
Administration and management
Advocacy
Assessment on multiple levels
Bargaining/compromising/negotiation
Budget knowledge
Communication
Community engagement
Community organizing
Conflict management/conflict resolution
Critical thinking
Engagement
Facilitating groups and collaboration
Interpersonal skills
Negotiation and conflict resolution
Oral communication
Policy analysis
Research and evaluation
Storytelling
Understanding how programs affect individuals and families
Understanding of human rights, social justice, and diversity
Written communication</td></tr>
<tr><td>Executive Branch</td><td>Participating in regulatory process
• As agency workers
• Weighing in on proposed regulations
• Participating in supervision and oversight
• Budget analysis</td></tr>
<tr><td>Judicial Branch</td><td>Influencing the judiciary
• Writing amicus briefs
• Expert testimony</td></tr>
</table>

Research

To better work within *any* policy arena and understand political reactions to social problems, social workers must first conduct research to understand how particular social problems have been framed, what policies exist to address the problems, and what the existing policies are designed to do. You will discuss research in many places in your social work education; here we focus on the first step in conducting policy research, selecting and evaluating sources. It is often useful to start by looking at an encyclopedia or similar trusted resource such as *Social Work Speaks*, produced by the National Association of Social Workers, or the publications of the Congressional Research Service to get background information on a new topic. Often this type of source includes basic information on the topic and can direct you toward more detailed sources of information.

When finding information from a website or other source you haven't used before, your first step should be to assess the value and trustworthiness of the source. To help us ascertain this, we should ask questions, such as:

- Who made this information available, either by creating it or sharing it? What is the motivation of that person in sharing the information?
- Who created the information? Many resources we use for policy research were created by a government agency, academic institute, individual researcher, or advocacy organization. Does the person or organization who created this information have a specific agenda?
- Were the data collected by a think tank or other organization with connections to a political party or ideology? If so, what is the political leaning of the organization?
- Who funds the organization that created/disseminated the research?
- Who directs the organization—for example, if it is a nonprofit, who are the members of the board of directors?
- What are the goals of the organization?
- Was the information published in a peer-reviewed journal or reviewed by outside sources in some manner for accuracy?
- Are there other perspectives on the same issue? Do these other sources present information from a different political perspective? Who funds those organizations, and so on?

Asking these questions will ensure that you look carefully at the sources of the data that you rely on. It is sometimes tempting to do this only with information that we think is wrong, but not to investigate too strongly information that we think is right. It is important to resist temptation and look as objectively as possible at all the available information before moving forward with policy advocacy.

Newspapers, radio, and television often provide up-to-date information on current policy debates. They may also present skewed data to make a particular point. Figure 2.10 suggests some ways that you might be able to assess how reliable your news source is. It is important to know about the media sources that you seek information from. Who owns them? How are they funded? What are their goals? Often the difference between straight journalism and opinion writing such as op-eds is that the news reporting of an organization aims to be objective, where opinion writing aims to express the political leanings of the author and/or newspaper. Unfortunately, sometimes non-opinion pieces present information in skewed ways as much as opinion pieces do.

In the end, facts alone may not convince other people of your views and they may have trouble identifying which sources of information they should trust, including you. Even if you can, people are often attached to an ideology and try to fit new information into their existing knowledge and belief systems. Well-reasoned, principled people may also simply disagree. As a result, it is important to understand your audience and to frame information so that it can be better received by the person or people that you are trying to teach.

FIGURE 2.10 ■ How to Spot Fake News

HOW TO SPOT FAKE NEWS

CONSIDER THE SOURCE

Click away from the story to investigate the site, its mission and its contact info.

CHECK THE AUTHOR

Do a quick search on the author. Are they credible? Are they real?

CHECK THE DATE

Reposting old news stories doesn't mean they're relevant to current events.

CHECK YOUR BIASES

Consider if your own beliefs could affect your judgement.

READ BEYOND

Headlines can be outrageous in an effort to get clicks. What's the whole story?

SUPPORTING SOURCES?

Click on those links. Determine if the info given actually supports the story.

IS IT A JOKE?

If it is too outlandish, it might be satire. Research the site and author to be sure.

ASK THE EXPERTS

Ask a librarian, or consult a fact-checking site.

IFLA
International Federation of Library Associations and Institutions
With thanks to www.FactCheck.org

Source: The International Federation of Library Associations and Institutions (IFLA)/CC BY 4.0/https://creativecommons.org/licenses/by/4.0/legalcode

Final Discussion

Return to the vignette at the beginning of this chapter and see if your answers to these questions have changed.

1. What types of social work skills did Alyx and colleagues use throughout this process?
2. What levels of governments are involved in the changes they are trying to make?
3. What knowledge about the political process did Alyx and the others need to be successful?
4. What options do Alyx and colleagues have at the end of the process?
5. What role might race, class, gender, and other aspects of identity play in this vignette?

PRACTICAL THEORIES FOR UNDERSTANDING AND ANALYZING POLICY

LEARNING OBJECTIVES

3.1: Identify theories that can inform social work policy practice

3.2: Understand what interest groups are and their role in influencing policy decisions

3.3: Apply policy frameworks to analyze and understand existing policies

3.4: Describe the ways in which theories can be used to analyze policy

In the previous chapter, you learned about our political system. Here we focus on ways of understanding policy. In human behavior class, you are probably learning about systems theory. **Systems theory** (Bronfenbrenner, 1979) suggests that people are influenced by their families, culture, and environment. One's environment includes things like family context, place of work and/or school, neighborhood, religious affiliation, and the larger social and political landscape. Policy is part of what makes up the larger context.

Systems theory: Suggests that people are influenced by a variety of systems that also influence each other, such as families, culture, and environment

What makes something a policy issue rather than a private problem? The transformation of a private trouble into a public problem (Blumer, 1971; Mills, 2000) can be influenced by historical context, key stakeholders, theoretical beliefs, legislators, and interest groups. The frames that describe social problems help define the problems and shape the extent to which they are included or excluded from public policy deliberations and ideally, solutions (Palley & Shdaimah, 2014). Traditional models of policy making are based on the premise that policies are crafted and implemented after a careful review of facts. This assumes that researchers and policy analysts can (1) agree which facts are relevant, (2) prove something works according to an agreed upon definition of success, and (3) use a cost-benefit analysis to assess the least expensive alternative with the best possible outcome. Those of us who live in the real

Economic theory: Theory about how economies, both large (countries) and small (organizations) work. See **micro-** and **macroeconomic** theory for more details.

Social construction: The idea that meaning is created through interaction with our environment and existing values, practices, and norms. According to social construction, much of what we understand as truth is determined by our social and cultural milieu.

Symbolic interaction theory: Suggests that there is no objective "reality" apart from how we describe and think about concepts from our perspective of their reality, which is shaped by the interaction of the individual with others and with society

Feminist theory: Theories based on the assumption that women have been systematically subordinated by patriarchal systems or institutions that privilege men as a group over women as a group

Critical Race Theory (CRT): A race-conscious approach to social policies, practices, and services.

Implementation theory: A form of policy analysis that focuses on the stages after policies have been developed and executed

Interest group: Group of people who unite to further a common political goal

Policy feedback: When the existence of a policy hinders the creation of new policy because of existing constituencies, such as agencies charged with carrying out the initial policy and its beneficiaries, all of whom then have a vested interest in continuing the policy as it is or only making small incremental changes to it

world know that facts alone do not always shape policy and that our understanding of costs, outcomes, and success are not only contested but are also shaped by our beliefs, values, and assumptions. This requires us to understand policy framing.

In this chapter, we provide an overview of different conceptual and practical approaches that social work scholars and activists use to analyze and influence the policy process. In this chapter, we describe how **economic theories, social construction, symbolic interaction theory, feminist theory, critical race theory,** and **implementation theory** shape the debates about policy that most affect our clients and communities. We also look at how **interest groups** and the **policy feedback** process play key roles in shaping policy and policy debates.

It is important to note that many other theories can be used to understand and analyze policy. The theories we focus on here were chosen because of their prominence or relevance to social work's core mission and values. Some examine power and equity and reflect social work's person-in-environment focus. Some, such as neoclassical and Keynesian economic theory, are included because they have been used to shape existing policy. These theories will help you explore how policies are developed and formed, alternative policy ideas that were considered and overlooked, and emerging understandings and societal concerns that challenge existing policy frames. Policy implementation theory can help a practitioner understand the intended and unintended consequences of policies as well as their implications for future policy development and practice. We draw on all these theories throughout the text as tools for both gaining a deeper understanding of policy issues and for developing strategic policy interventions.

Policy theory can sometimes seem dry and disconnected from social work practice. Most social workers like to work with people, whether on a micro, mezzo, or macro level. They want to know, specifically: How do the theories explain how my clients experience the world? How can they guide my work to improve my clients' lives Everything we present in this chapter, and throughout the book, is designed to give you tools to do the best possible social work, whether with individuals, families, groups, organizations, or communities. We hope these theories will challenge you to look at social problems and policies from a variety of perspectives and use those perspectives to serve your clients well.

Vignette: Vaccinations

Based on what you know from the media or your personal, work, or volunteer experiences, think about the following questions as you read the vignette. When you finish the vignette, answer the questions below.

1. Describe different ways in which vaccination policies have been framed
    a. Public good vs. individual rights
    b. Free market capitalism vs. consumer protection through government regulation
2. To what extent are the beliefs described in Question 1 shaped by research?
3. Take the perspective of a particular stakeholder in this debate, such as a parent, medical professional, pharmaceutical executive, or

public health official. How might that person's views be shaped by any of the following:

a. Religious and cultural views
b. Historical experiences
c. Economic interests
d. The mission of their agency or workplace

4. What role might race, class, gender, and other aspects of identity play in this vignette?

BACKGROUND ON VACCINES

Since the advent of vaccines in the late 1800s, there has always been tension between maintaining individual rights and preserving what was then called community safety. Originally vaccines used live cultures that were more likely to make people sick than the ones that are used today. There remains a possibility, albeit relatively remote, that a vaccine can have an adverse effect on the recipient, which is sometimes called "vaccine injury" (Centers for Disease Control and Prevention [CDC], 2017a). Vaccines have been an important tool in reducing and, in some areas of the world, eliminating the incidence and impact of diseases that could be fatal or result in serious and/or chronic illness. Even when some people are not healthy enough to be vaccinated, vaccinating healthy people helps protect the general population.

Current laws in all 50 states require individuals to be vaccinated to participate in state-funded activities such as education and state employment (Colgrove, 2006). Though most people are vaccinated against measles, in 2015, a measles outbreak that started at a California amusement park led to many deaths. People who chose not to be vaccinated or have their children vaccinated were deemed responsible for the outbreak; subsequently, California repealed religious and philosophical exemptions (Aliferis, 2016), as did New York (Rabin, 2019). As of the writing of this book, Michigan, Maine, and West Virginia have laws that only allow vaccine exemptions in public schools for medical reasons and several other states are considering legislation that restricts religious and philosophical exemptions to vaccination (Sandstrom, 2019).

Members of religious groups such as Christian Scientists and Jehovah's Witnesses have been instrumental in getting states to pass religious exemptions to vaccine requirements. "Medical liberty" groups in the late 1800s and early 1900s objected to compulsory vaccination though they were not necessarily against vaccination. In the early 20th century, public health advocates and other medical interest groups such as the U.S. Public Health Service, the American Medical Association, and the American Association for Medical Progress, a group comprised of civic leaders and prominent academics, sought to convince legislators to make vaccinations mandatory. These groups have continued to support vaccine requirements based on a cost-benefit analysis. In other words, considering the population as a whole, the benefit of reducing or eliminating the incidence of deadly or permanently disabling diseases outweighs the potential harm to the few (Colgrove, 2006).

Individual Concerns Versus Public Good: Sarah's Story

Sarah was trained as a nurse but left the profession after a bout of depression. She now works with a nonprofit that supports families with high-needs children. At age 35 she met John and they decided to have a child. Their daughter, Violet, was born prematurely. Sarah was unable to spend her daughter's first few days with her because Violet was hooked up to machines in the pediatric intensive care unit to ensure her survival. After a month, Violet went home with Sarah and her husband but, at that point, Sarah was unable to breastfeed. As a nurse who knows that breastfeeding helps build a child's immune system, Sarah felt guilty about not breastfeeding even though she was aware that it had not been possible. When Violet was healthy enough to get her first dose of the Hepatitis B vaccine, Sarah worried. Though she was aware of the science that suggests that her daughter could not get autism from vaccines, she worked with many parents who firmly believed that their children had been fine until they were vaccinated. The many stories she heard from her patients led Sarah to be skeptical of the research, and her concerns were heightened due to Violet's precarious start and added vulnerabilities. Sarah was not sure what to do. She also wasn't sure what the law in her state allowed. Though not religious, she had been raised as a Christian Scientist. Could she get a religious exemption? Should she try? She talked to John about it. He said that he would acquiesce to her wishes, though he generally thought that vaccines were beneficial and did not share her concerns.

POLICY ANALYSIS THEORIES

In this section, we look at theories that are commonly used to analyze policies. These include economic theories, social construction, feminist theory, critical race theory, and implementation theory. We also look at the ways that interest groups and the policy feedback process affect the ways in which policies are enacted.

Macroeconomics: Government policy regarding monetary policy (how much money a country should print), fiscal policy (how much money a country should spend and how), and tax policy (who should pay for the costs associated with government spending). These three areas together help describe how economies work.

Microeconomics: Financial decision making of individuals and institutions such as companies, firms, and nonprofit organizations

Neoclassical economics: A theory that holds that as long as there is no intervention of outside forces or government, everyone's focus on their own self-interest will allow those who work the hardest to acquire the most wealth

Economic Theories

Though it might seem dry or complex at first read, economic theory is important to understand because it sheds light on people's beliefs about the role of government. Economic theory has been used to guide policy making that impacts every facet of our lives and welfare. Social workers often shy away from economics because it may seem distant from the people we serve. The focus on numbers can feel impersonal and cold. However, to understand policy and policy decision making, it is crucial to develop a basic understanding of economics—a good policy without funding is not helpful to our clients.

The field of economics can be divided into two major categories. **Macroeconomics** focuses on government policy and includes monetary policy (how much money a country should *print*), fiscal policy (how much money a country should *spend* and *how*), and tax policy (who should *pay* for the costs associated with government spending). These three areas together help describe how economies work. **Microeconomics** focuses on financial decision making of individuals and institutions such as companies, firms, and nonprofits.

Neoclassical economics focuses more on microeconomic policy. Analyses using this theoretical framework tend to examine people's ability to think rationally and their ability to work to acquire desired or needed goods and services. This perspective assumes that as long as there is no intervention of outside forces or government, everyone's focus on their own self-interest will allow those who work the hardest to acquire the most wealth. This theory places great faith in the free market[1] to meet the needs of individuals in society (Keynes, 1936; Wolf & Resnick, 2012). The logical outcome of this view is that the inability to achieve desired goals is primarily the failure of the individual, and solutions should focus on changing the behaviors of individual people or organizations.

[1]A free market is the idea that prices for goods and services should be determined by competition between consumers and producers (which will ideally respond to supply and demand) without government intervention.

FIGURE 3.1 ■ Economic Terms

Lawan naklangka/shutterstock.com

Keynesian economic theory, in contrast to neoclassical theory, focuses on how the economy affects individuals. George Maynard Keynes developed his theory in reaction to the depression of the 1930s when unemployment was clearly not the result of individual choices but of systemic problems. In this theory, the key determinants of the economy are the **gross domestic product** (the total amount of goods and services that are produced by a country), the money supply, the cost of goods (consumer price index), national wealth and income, unemployment, and economic growth patterns. According to **Keynesian theory**, individuals make decisions based on broader macroeconomic policy. Keynesians suggest that there may be circumstances when the market does not effectively address social problems such as high unemployment. When that happens, the government should intervene to maintain societal stability (Keynes, 1936; Wolf & Resnick, 2012). Keynesian macroeconomic policy suggests that the government should use **monetary policy**, **fiscal policy**, and **tax policy** to ensure economic stability.

Neoclassical and Keynesian economics both measure economic functioning. Some of the key factors considered important by both are gross domestic product, employment, and poverty (Wolff & Resnick, 2012). Both also compare the costs of a given policy to the monetary benefits or analyze the cost in relation to the policy's effectiveness. Nearly all U.S. policy debates contain a large component of **cost-benefit analysis**, a theory drawn from economics. At its core, cost-benefit analysis suggests that if society can weigh the economic costs and the benefits of a policy, the best possible policy is one in which the benefits outweigh the costs overall. Cost and benefits are often viewed in exclusively or primarily economic terms, particularly in

Gross domestic product: The total amount of goods and services that are produced by a country

Keynesian economic theory: Suggests that the government should use monetary policy, fiscal policy, and tax policy to ensure economic stability

Monetary policy: How much money a country should *print*

Fiscal policy: Policy that designates how much money a country should *spend* and *how*

Tax policy: Who should *pay* for the costs associated with government spending

Cost-benefit analysis: A process in which the cost and benefits of a policy are weighed against each other and the best possible alternative is seen as the one in which the benefits outweigh the costs

neoclassical economics. Analysis that considers noneconomic costs and benefits may be fraught with the difficulties of identifying, agreeing to, and quantifying what the costs and benefits are (Lewis & Widerquist, 2002).

How do you put a dollar value on quality of life? On saving a life? This makes cost-benefit analysis frustrating for social workers who might lean toward value-based arguments that are grounded in our code of ethics. However, to garner support from some constituencies, it may help to present arguments not only in terms of values and social benefits but also economic benefits. In many cases, these may be intertwined. For example, the economic costs of methadone outweigh the economic costs to society of untreated heroin addiction by a ratio of 12 to 1 (National Institute on Drug Abuse, 2012), aligning with the social benefits of addressing addiction. Cost-benefit assessments are further complicated if your analysis looks at overall societal benefits and costs, since in reality the benefits of a policy may go to one segment of the population, while the costs are borne by another. Social workers can add important insights to cost-benefit debates by addressing the specifics of who reaps the benefits and who bears the burdens of a policy.

While both Keynesians and neoclassical economists support privately managed capitalism, Karl Marx thought that capitalism was exploitative by its very nature and should therefore be ended. Marxist theory divides people into three social classes: workers, capitalists, and landowners. His theory focuses on the production of surplus labor, and he considered it exploitation when a capitalist was able to keep the goods or services that were produced by the surplus labor of the worker. Marxist theory is much more value-driven than Keynesian or neoclassical economic theory. Rather than focusing on methods for developing the most efficient economic system, it focuses on the fairest way to distribute resources. Marx's idea, that we consider each according to his (or her) ability and provide for each according to his (or her) need, is inconsistent with basic capitalist values, which suggest that without the ability to acquire wealth or the need to support one's self and one's family, people would have no motivation to work hard and the economy would not thrive (Marx, 1859; Wolff & Resnick, 2012).

As noted earlier, it is important to understand economic policy because it often drives national policy. Historically, Republicans and conservatives were more likely to subscribe to neoclassical economic theory due to a belief in the market and a dislike of government intervention in economic areas. Democrats and liberals, on the other hand, have tended to place more trust in the state and be suspicious of the market and therefore tend more to adopt Keynesian economic policy to help stabilize the economy. Neither perspective historically focused on inequality or inequity. Though Marxist economic theory provides some insight into exploitation, it has historically failed to address inequality associated with gender or racial discrimination. In the sections below, we discuss theories in which the study of inequality and discrimination play a larger role.

Returning to the vaccine debate, there is an economic argument to be made in support of mandatory vaccination. It may be more expensive on the whole for a state or country to provide care for disease treatment and disease conditions, especially those that may cause lifelong disabilities like polio, than to provide vaccinations. Also, an outbreak of a life-threatening disease can be very expensive in terms of loss of work. Another economic consideration asks who will pay for the research and development of vaccines, the costs of vaccination for so many people, the costs of tracking vaccination, and treatment and care provided to victims of diseases. The costs and benefits of vaccinations may accrue to different people and different organizations. Pharmaceutical companies may not consider the development of a vaccine worthwhile unless they expect a profit through incentives such as subsidized research, recommended use for a wide swath of the population, and/or the ability to charge high fees. If doctors or nurses are not reimbursed for administering vaccines, they may not be inspired to administer or require them if they operate only on economic terms. If people have private insurance, the cost of care associated with disease treatment or care may not be public expenses. Insurance companies, therefore, may be motivated to support vaccination because it may lower their costs. Considering how the costs associated with vaccination are construed and who is responsible for them leads us to our next set of perspectives: social construction. As you read, think about how the issue of vaccination is socially constructed.

Social Construction of Social Problems

In 1966, Peter Berger and Thomas Luckman wrote *The Social Construction of Reality.* This book built on symbolic interaction theory and lent credence to the idea that reality is constructed through social interactions. Symbolic interaction theory suggests that there is no objective *reality* apart from how we describe and think about concepts from our perspective of their reality. Culture and language construct belief systems. Social problems or issues take on importance only when individuals believe them to be important. E. E. Schattschneider (1976), a noted political scientist, built on this theory and moved it into the public policy domain by noting that broadening our understanding of the scope of a problem that affects more people is more likely to ensure that an issue becomes part of the public policy discourse. Other factors, such as the values that are invoked or the severity of the problem, will also influence whether and how an issue comes or stays on the public agenda. In other words, the way a policy is socially constructed matters.

Deborah Stone (2012) suggests that social problems are constructed as a result of five different, sometimes overlapping, reasons: symbols, numbers, causes, interests, and decisions. She questions the mainstream belief of policy analysts that it is possible to determine the cause of a problem and suggests that causes of political problems are often framed using symbols and numbers. A symbol "tells a story or, rather, different stories to different audiences" (2012, p. 157). Ambiguity can be used by political leaders or advocates to garner support for causes or to oppose them. Stone also describes how ambiguity can be used in measuring things (numbers). She suggests that while most people consider numbers to be relatively unambiguous, how a phenomenon is measured, including *what* we choose to measure, can affect which policy solutions are developed. Stone notes that our current unemployment measure, for example, excludes people who have been out of the labor force for too long and people who are underemployed or unwillingly part-time employed, which reduces the official count of people who are unemployed. This reduces the perception of the unemployment problem but not the actual amount of unemployment. Another example, pointed out by Victoria Tran (2018) of the Urban Institute is that because Asian Americans, Native Hawaiians, and Pacific Islanders only make up 6.2% of the population, they are often left out official data collection and analysis. Added to the fact that Asians are often assumed to be wealthy even though 12.3% of Asian Americans live below the poverty line, this lack of information means few efforts are made to help Asian Americans access social services (Tran, 2018).

Stone (2012) suggests that policy decisions cannot be understood as the outcome of rational decision making but rather paradoxical ideas related to the interests of influential groups and people:

> Shared meanings motivate people to action and meld individual striving into collective action. Ideas are at the center of all political conflict. Policy making, in turn, is a constant struggle over the criteria for classification, the boundaries of categories, and the definition of ideals that guide the way people behave. (p. 11)

Social construction can be seen by looking at the change in language that has been used to define public assistance, which we described in Chapter 1. Originally called Aid to Families with Dependent Children, the focus of the program was helping dependent children, a category that evokes sympathy and blamelessness. When Congress reduced the availability of assistance to families living in poverty, it did so via legislation called the Personal Responsibility and Work Opportunity Reconciliation Act. The name of the law underscored its function to encourage primarily single-parent families to prioritize work and cast their inability to support their family as a failure of individual responsibility (you should be hearing an echo of neoclassical economic theory here). Tellingly, the program's name was changed to Temporary Assistance for Needy Families, itself emphasizing the temporary nature of assistance to families and away from the support of dependent children.

One example of social construction as a policy analysis can be found in Palley and Shdaimah's 2014 critique of American child care policy. They note that it has been developed and implemented within the frame of an individual family matter with little regard to societal benefits. Due to this framing, child care policy implementation has resulted in several types of programs primarily for those living in poverty, tax benefits for the middle and upper class, and a beginning movement toward universal Pre-kindergarten, which has been framed as education, separate from the child care needs of parents. The existing policies have, they argue, led to diverse interests that have hindered the movement to developing universal early care and education policies in the United States.

DISCUSSION

SOCIAL CONSTRUCTION AND VACCINES

If we apply the social construction of social policy lens, we can see that people's positions and the resulting policy will be driven by how they understand a given problem. Their understanding will be informed by their personal beliefs, values, and experiences and their professional role or obligation. Let's return to our case example of vaccination. Try to imagine what your perspective would be on this issue if you belong to one of the following groups. Then answer the questions below based on that perspective.

- Medical groups such as the American Academy of Pediatrics or the Infectious Disease Society of America
- Representatives of the pharmaceutical industry
- Parents with vulnerable children
- Parents who have religious, philosophical, or medical concerns that conflict with vaccination
- Public health officials

With a classmate or friend who is taking a different perspective, answer the following questions from your person or group's perspective. Consider the similarities and differences in your answers.

1. What is the problem?
2. Who or what do you think might be causing this problem?
3. What intervention or change would fix the problem?
4. Who could make that intervention or change happen?
5. What stories or symbols might you use to illustrate your understanding and to persuade policymakers that it is correct?

Feminist Policy Analysis

Feminist theories are in many ways compatible with social construction. The main foundation of feminist theory is that women have been systematically subordinated by patriarchal systems and institutions that privilege men as a group over women as a group. Many feminists believe that understanding of the world from a woman's perspective is different than that of a man's. People sometimes differ on the extent to which they believe this is informed by biological or inherent characteristics (such as hormones or brain structure) or processes of socialization (such as behavior and role expectations). Many characterize the U.S. feminist movement according to *waves*, with **first wave feminism** taking root in the mid-19th century (Rampton, 2005). First wave feminists fought for many causes, including women's suffrage, and they often challenged what was considered appropriate behavior or clothing for women. The 1848 Seneca Falls Convention drafted the Seneca Falls Declaration, which outlined historical harms to women, affirmed women's worth and equality, and culminated in a resolution that was adopted by the convention:

First wave feminism: Early feminists of the 19th and early 20th century who fought for many causes, including women's suffrage

> That the speedy success of our cause depends upon the zealous and untiring efforts of both men and women, for the overthrow of the monopoly of the pulpit, and for the securing to woman an equal participation with men in the various trades, professions and commerce. (Women's Rights Convention, 1848)

Second wave feminism: The central issues of this movement, which began in the early 1960s, were increased opportunities and choices for women, including equality in the workforce, reproductive and sexual freedom, and combating domestic violence.

The modern feminist movement, referred to as **second wave feminism**, began in the 1960s. In *The Feminist Mystique,* Betty Friedan (1963), one of the founders of second wave feminism, challenged the idea that a woman's place is in the home. Central concerns of this movement were increased opportunities and choices for women, including equality in the workforce, reproductive and sexual freedom, and combating domestic violence.

Third wave feminism viewed second wave feminism as an economically elitist, white women's movement. Iris Marion Young (1990) suggests that democratic theorists often reduce social justice to distribution of material goods and have failed to consider power differentials, institutional discrimination, and the lack of voice given to minority communities. In 1984, bell hooks argued for a broader definition of feminism that would include the concerns of low-income and minority women as well as the need to include men in any movement for women's equality. She suggested that though the needs and interests of women of color and white women may vary, we must hear each other's differences and work together with men to improve the status of all women. Noted sociologist Patricia Hill Collins (2005) further argued that black women's oppression must be seen in a different manner than that of white women as a result of **intersectionality**, a term coined by Kimberle Crenshaw (1989). Intersectionality refers to people's multiple identities, which can result in compounded oppression as well as different experiences among people who may share some (but not all) oppressed identities like woman, racial minority, immigrant, or low-wage worker (see Figure 3.2). Since the early 2000s, a resurgent interest in feminism is sometimes referred to as **fourth wave feminism** (Baumgardner, 2011). This movement, driven by young adult feminists, focuses on sexual harassment and violence, as well as sexuality and gender, and often uses technology and social media (Cochrane, 2013).

Third wave feminism: A branch of feminism that is focused on intersectionality

Intersectionality: Refers to people's multiple identities, which can result in compounded oppression as well as different experiences among people who may share some (but not all) identities like woman, racial minority, immigrant, or low-wage worker

Fourth wave feminism: The resurgent interest in feminism of the early 2000s, driven by diverse groups of young adult feminists, that focuses on sexual harassment and violence, as well as sexuality and gender, and often uses technology and social media

The feminist theories described here have implications for how we understand, make, and implement policy. Although there are a variety of complementary and even conflicting perspectives that inform feminist policy analysis, there are important shared characteristics. One is attention to how policy affects women and women's issues (including what is considered a "women's" issue), such as care work, intimate partner violence, and sexual assault (Hawkesworth, 2006). Another is the importance of attending to relations of power and

FIGURE 3.2 ■ Intersectionality

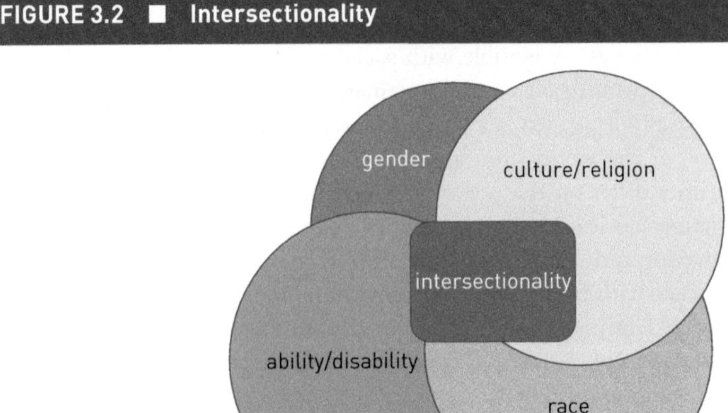

oppression, as drawn from the insights of third wave feminism. A central tenet of feminism, incorporated in the second wave feminist slogan "the personal is political," is the idea that we cannot separate politics from the way they play out in our lives.

Everyday world policy analysis: A method to examine policies by seeking a detailed understanding of how they play out in the lives of ordinary people

Based on these feminist insights, Nancy Naples (2006) developed a type of analysis called **everyday world policy analysis.** This method examines policies by looking at how they unfold in the lives of ordinary people. Shdaimah, Stahl, and Schram (2011) used everyday world policy analysis to examine a Philadelphia home repair assistance program. Naples' theory led the researchers to conduct a step-by-step "walkthrough" of the program with recipients. They found that the requirements of the program as implemented undermined the mission of the home repair policy. For example, homeowners were asked: "Can you see the sky through the roof?" before they could obtain roof repairs. At that point, the cost of repairs usually exceeded program budget limits, leaving homeowners in a situation where they were nearly always too early or too late to qualify. These kinds of revelations that were exposed using everyday world policy analysis may have otherwise been missed.

Just as feminist theories and analysis have built on a variety of insights, including Marxism, democratic principles of equality, and social construction, the insights of feminist policy analysis have informed other types of policy analysis, such as critical race theory, which we discuss in the next section.

Critical Race Theory

Critical race theory comes out of legal and civil rights theory and has been associated with Derrick Bell, Kimberlé Crenshaw, Richard Delgado, Mari Matsuda, and Patricia Williams (among others). Their goal is not only to study but ultimately to change the relationship between race, racism, and power in a broader context than civil rights alone. Critical race theorists tend to believe that most advances in the civil rights movement are due to interest convergence so that any progress made for people of color conveniently coincides with changing economic conditions and the self-interest of whites. Critical race theorists include critical white studies in their research and have found that, as opposed to minority groups, whites do not seem to see themselves as a race, but as individual people. The viewpoints and opinions of whites are considered universally valid as *the truth* while most deny that there is such a thing as white privilege (Cleaver, 1997). Critical race theorists note that this is in stark contrast to minority groups who do not have this advantage (Delgado & Stefancic, 2001; Young, 1990). In fact, often, nonwhite groups are lumped into general categories and their concerns are turned into background noise (Delgado & Stefancic, 2001).

Feeling that theories designed to explore gender discrimination or racial discrimination alone were not adequate to understand the experience of African American women, noted legal theorist and critical race scholar, Kimberle Crenshaw (1989), invented the term *intersectionality* to explain the oppression of African American women, who are oppressed both as a result of their race and gender. Having just read about third wave feminist theory above, you can see how critical race theory and third wave feminist theory overlap. Patricia Hill Collins and Margaret Anderson (1992) built on the language of intersectionality to describe the combined experience of oppression experienced by women of color living in poverty. According to critical race theorists, when an individual is a member of more than one oppressed group, they usually do not fit into one large, unified class and thus, their issues are more specific and less easily generalizable. This makes it much more difficult to locate and target a problem. Critical race theorists use individual narratives to explore experiences based on individual membership in one or more minority groups and to bring to life unique stories with the hope that voices of oppressed people will be better heard (Delgado & Stefancic, 2001).

Analysis using critical race theory and intersectionality can be helpful in examining the impact of policies on different groups. It is useful, for example, when exploring inequality in U.S. education as well as the limitations of civil rights legislation for undocumented workers, home health aides, or nannies who work in their employers' homes and are beholden to them for future employment references. When creating or assessing vaccination policies, we should consider the history of treatment of African Americans by the medical establishment in the United States, especially the Tuskegee experiment. In 1932, African American men were enrolled in a study to track the natural progression of syphilis. In 1945, when penicillin was found to be an effective treatment for syphilis, it was not offered to study participants. The study did not end until 1972, resulting in preventable illness and death of hundreds of African American men, as well as their family members to whom they unwittingly transmitted the disease, so that researchers could study the disease course (CDC, 2017b).[2] It is therefore not surprising that many African Americans may be suspicious of established medical care, including vaccination mandates. This cultural and historical context should be considered when developing public health policies in African American communities to avoid further damage.

Implementation Theory

Implementation is described as a stage after policies have been developed and is the process of fleshing out and executing plans that were outlined in policies. Despite the best intentions of policy creators, policy implementation is often a challenge, as we discuss many times throughout this text. Implementation theory, which comes out of political science, is the study of policies as they are rolled out and tested in real-life settings. Like the everyday world policy analysis discussed in the section on feminist analysis, it looks at how policies unfold. However, implementation theory focuses more on how policies work and their overall impact on institutions, agencies, and individuals rather than solely on the people who are the targets of policy change. Implementation studies were originally conceived as a mechanism to look at what made the achievement of federal policy goals difficult at the local level or what is now referred to as *top-down implementation* (Hill & Hupe, 2011; Pressman & Wildavsky, 1973).

[2]It is important to note that the exposé of the Tuskegee trials and public outcry were key in creating mandatory federal guidelines for the ethical conduct of research. Social worker Dr. Dorothy Height was a part of that movement.

Street level bureaucracy: Frontline social service agencies, like police and child welfare agencies. They are characterized as under-resourced and hierarchical, often charged with internally conflicting mandates and high levels of discretion vis-à-vis the people they serve. Those who work in these agencies are often referred to as street level bureaucrats.

Michael Lipsky's (1980) classic theory of **street level bureaucracy** has been used to describe frontline social service agencies, such as police and child welfare agencies, and those who work in them. According to Lipsky, street level bureaucrats use their limited discretionary power to create policy on the ground within existing resource and program constraints. As Evelyn Brodkin (2012) notes of public service employees, the work of street level bureaucrats is characterized by "the daily struggle . . . to perform their jobs well and, in the process, to do good for their communities and society" (p. 941). While extremely constrained by their circumstances, street level bureaucrats in fact have high levels of discretion and autonomy vis-à-vis the people they serve (Brodkin, 2012; Lipsky, 1980). Many social workers might see themselves in this description of street level bureaucrats.

Others have developed theories designed to integrate top-down and bottom-up implementation (Hill & Hupe, 2011). They note the importance of knowing what is actually happening in the field. Elizabeth Palley's (2004) research on the implementation of special education policy illustrates how policy intentions and implementation may differ. She describes the difference between school policies about inclusion and Functional Behavioral Assessments (FBA) imagined by the drafters of the Individuals with Disabilities Education Act and the reality of the policy as implemented. In this case study, Palley (2004) found that many teachers and school administrators either did not fully understand what an FBA was or were not inclined to use them effectively to alter their strategies of working with students who exhibited behavioral challenges, perhaps as a result of insufficient support. This study found that training and financial resources may be needed to fully implement some policies. It also demonstrated the local nature of implementation. Federal and state policy may be put into practice in different ways in different places, even within the same school district (Palley, 2004). The nature of court interpretation of federal policy suggests that variations in implementation happen at many levels (Palley, 2003).

INTEREST GROUP POLITICS

An interest group is comprised of people who unite to further a common political goal. There are three primary types of interest groups: institutional interest groups whose members belong to the same institution or membership group (such as students who attend the same university or National Association of Social Workers members), economic interest groups whose members join to protect their economic interests (such as members of a union), and public interest groups whose members believe they are furthering a broader public interest (such as members of the National Alliance on Mental Illness or NAMI) (Birkland, 2016).

Concerns about interest groups, or factions as they were previously called, were first identified by the U.S Founding Fathers. As Madison (1787) described them:

> By a faction, I understand a number of citizens, whether amounting to a majority or a minority of the whole, who are united and actuated by some common impulse of passion, or of interest, adversed to the rights of other citizens, or to the permanent and aggregate interests of the community. (para. 2)

The Founding Fathers feared that the passion of interest groups would override reason or the good of the nation—they did not always have a great deal of faith in their fellow citizens. To address this concern, they created several barriers between individual citizens and legislation. For example, until 1914, state legislatures chose U.S. senators, not members of the public (United States Senate, n.d.). They also created the Electoral College, which allows individual voters to vote for *electors* who then actually vote for president. Electors from many states are not required to vote for the presidential candidate for whom their state populations voted. This placed an additional barrier between voters and presidential elections. These and other barriers were designed to keep interest groups and uneducated members of the country from wielding too much power.

Some believe that interest groups have an important and positive role in democracies. In 1951, Truman noted that the competition between interest groups helped create balanced policy. Sociologist Talcott Parsons also believed that social systems tended toward developing systems of what he called *integration*, whereby different groups with different interests developed rules and norms that allowed them to function and persevere through coordination, adjustments, and a sense of shared identity among individual or institutional actors (Wallace & Wolf, 1995). He largely ignored the existence of power differentials among various groups. This idea was challenged by political scientist Theodore Lowi (1979), who suggested that interest groups helped maintain the status quo because bureaucracies relied on outside lobbyists for information and assistance, which led to a structure of privilege that limited the role of citizens in our government. Jurgen Habermas' (1996) more nuanced analysis acknowledges and addresses power imbalances. His theory of communicative action suggests that mechanisms are needed to safeguard fair and robust public debate to ensure access and full participation of people and groups in the democratic process.

Changes in campaign finance laws have led to the growth of membership-oriented interest groups representing business, industry, and those concerned with a specific issue or concern (Cigler & Loomis, 2007). In the 1980s, there was a similar increase in the number of other types of interest groups representing individual corporations, universities, religious groups, foundations, and think tanks (Salisbury, 1984). Two types of interest groups commonly form in relation to government policy: service providers and recipients (Cigler & Loomis, 2007). This can lead to the formation of a phenomenon referred to as *policy feedback*. Policy feedback can limit policy change to only react to existing policies (Pierson, 1993). One reason that policy feedback limits changes is that policies themselves often create constituencies, such as agencies charged with carrying out the policy and beneficiaries, who then have a vested interest in continuing the policy as it is, or adding small changes such as increasing its scope or the population to which it applies.

Concerns have been raised about the limited ways in which nonprofits engage as interest groups in the political process, thus muting the voices of their constituents (e.g., Berry, 2007). Though nonprofits are prohibited from having a substantial part of their work be directed toward lobbying for legislation by the Hatch Act, they are allowed to educate legislators and mobilize constituents (Section 501 of Title 26 [Internal Revenue Code] of the U.S. Code [U.S.C.]). Berry's research suggests that although there are mechanisms to allow nonprofits to engage in significant lobbying without running afoul of tax law, many executives in nonprofits are so fearful of losing their nonprofit status that they simply avoid any connection to the political process. This leads to a socialization process at nonprofits whereby workers become apolitical even though they are affected by policy. Other research suggests that funders may direct their donations to nonprofit organizations to be used for direct services or applied research and are much less likely to fund nonprofit advocacy efforts or movement building (Covington, 2011; Kuttner, 2002).

Conservative think tanks largely backed by wealthy business owners have supported anti-government discourse. Unlike liberal nonprofit organizations, which have shied away from trying to influence political discourse for fear of losing their nonprofit status, conservative groups have actively engaged in political framing. Political scientists Roger Cobb and Charles Elder (1971) note that anti-government discourse can lead to political non-decision making, or keeping new issues off the agenda, which essentially legitimizes the interests of those already in power. For example, groups such as the Heritage Foundation and the American Enterprise Institute have spent their resources developing a conservative agenda to promote tax cuts, privatize government activities, support school choice, and reduce social welfare spending. The Koch brothers, owners of oil refineries and two of the wealthiest Americans, financed

©istock.com/Box5

PHOTO 3.1 Tea Part rally sign

several organizations, including Freedom Works and the Tea Party (see Photo 3.1), also with the goal of opposing government regulation (Palley & Shdaimah, 2014). These conservative interest groups have successfully influenced the U.S.'s political discourse so that at the federal level focus on limiting or reducing government activity exceeds focus on providing services to needy or vulnerable citizens.

Interest group politics can help explain why, despite broad-based support among U.S. citizens for some types of gun control, the National Rifle Association has been able to successfully lobby to ensure limited regulation of guns in the United States. Lobbying efforts by the American Association of Retired Persons and other groups advocating on policies related to older adults also help ensure that a disproportionate amount of social spending in the United States focuses on supporting older adults. The vaccine movement has had several important interest groups: professional medical and related associations (AMA and the AMPHA), government groups such as state and federal public health employees, religious groups, and groups supporting individual rights and opposing government intervention.

USING FRAMEWORKS FOR ANALYSIS

In this chapter, we have presented theories that are central to social work policy analysis. In each subsection, we provided examples of how the theories can be applied to specific policies. In this section, we ask you to apply those theories to the vignette about vaccinations to see how it might inform your policy work in this area.

Choose at least two of the theories that we described in this chapter to analyze vaccination policy. (You may also use this opportunity to analyze another policy that you know about from your field placement, work experience, or have encountered in your life.)

REFLECTION

USING THEORIES TO ASSESS POLICY

1. How does each theory help you understand this policy?
   a. Why the policy was enacted?
   b. How the policy was implemented?
   c. Which different groups were affected by it and how?
   d. What were its unintended or intended consequences?
2. How does each help you understand the policy?
3. How do the theories that you chose complement, contradict, and/or reinforce each other and your understanding of the policy?
4. What does your analysis suggest about assessment of this policy?
   a. To what extent is it compatible with social work values?
   b. How could it be improved?
   c. What kind of alliances could you make to work toward these improvements?

APPLICATION OF THEORIES

In this chapter, we have offered several theories that social workers can use to analyze policies. Each of these theories adds a value to the way you can understand a social problem or policy or the way you can understand the perspectives of others. No single theory can explain all aspects of the complicated social problems that are important to social workers and our communities. Each will add its own perspective and value. Where they differ from one another, you will find opportunities to consider your own assumptions and those of the policymakers or interest groups who were involved in the creation of those policies. Often, you will find that a combination of theories is most useful in understanding a social problem or proposing a solution. As you move forward in this textbook, we highlight how these theories can be applied to specific policy areas such as work, employment, health, behavioral or mental health, child care, education, higher education, criminal justice, housing, homelessness, child welfare, immigration, and the environment. We also look at populations that are particularly affected by social problems of concern and are likely to be important to your social work career, such as families, older adults, and people with disabilities. We encourage you to return to this chapter as a reference and consider how each of these theories describes the social problems that are important to you and the policies that you interact with as a social work student and practicing social worker.

Final Discussion

Now that you have finished reading this chapter, reread the vignette at the beginning. Based on what you have learned, answer the following questions. Point to specific references in the chapter that help you answer these questions. Consider how different theories inform the response to these questions.

1. Describe different ways in which vaccination policies have been framed
    a. Public good vs. individual rights
    b. Free market capitalism vs. consumer protection through government regulation
2. To what extent are the beliefs described in Question 1 shaped by research?
3. Take the perspective of a particular stakeholder in this debate, such as a parent, medical professional, pharmaceutical executive, or public health official. How might that person's views be shaped by any of the following:
    a. Religious and cultural views
    b. Historical experiences
    c. Economic interests
    d. The mission of his (or her) agency or workplace
4. What role might race, class, gender, and other aspects of identity play in this vignette?

FAMILY POLICY

LEARNING OBJECTIVES

4.1: Compare the various perspectives on and meanings of family throughout U.S. history

4.2: Identify U.S. policies that relate to families

4.3: Evaluate alternative approaches to family policy

4.4: Evaluate potential opportunities for advocacy that improves the lives of families

Families are intricately linked with most facets of our lives, and so nearly every policy in this book—employment, housing, and child welfare, to name a few—connects to family policy. This chapter focuses on policies that are significant to the formation and makeup of families in the United States. It begins with a discussion of current family demographic trends, the history of family composition in the United States, and family creation and changes such as marriage, divorce, adoption, and sperm and egg donations that result in different family compositions. It then looks at birth control and abortion, domestic violence, pregnancy, and state and federal policies designed to address and support family needs.

One critical question when discussing family policy is "what is a family?" If you live with a platonic roommate, are you family? If you have a child with someone but choose to live apart, are you family? Are you family with the people you choose, the people with whom you share some genes, the people with whom you share a common upbringing, or some combination? There is a field in sociology dedicated solely to the study of families, and many sociologists have made their careers studying what makes a family. This, of course, has changed over time. The emotional definition of family, the people you choose, may not always parallel the legal definition of family, the people who are defined as your family by law. The legal definition of family has also changed over time, but many policies designed to address the needs of families still reflect an earlier time when a nuclear family was defined as a mother and father who resided together and their children. In addition to tackling the definition of family, in this chapter we discuss the history of family formation in the United States and why it matters who is defined as family.

The second section of this chapter includes a discussion of the many ways in which families are created, including birth, adoption, egg donation, sperm donation, and uterus loaning, and their implications for defining individuals' mutual obligations and relationships in social, educational, legal, and medical settings. The third section explains facets of family policy that have been controlled by the states and by the federal government. We look at the role that lobbying and constituent groups have played in the changing definition of U.S. families and at major federal and state laws regulating family, including marriage laws, child custody and support rules, domestic violence, birth control, abortion and pregnancy, fertility, and the Family and Medical Leave Act. We also discuss policies that affect the development of families and policy responses (or lack of policy responses) to the influx of women of childbearing age into the labor force.

Vignette: Susie and John and a Potential Unplanned Pregnancy

Based on what you know from the media or your personal, work, or volunteer experiences, think about the following questions as you read the vignette. When you finish the vignette, answer the questions below.

1. How does Susie define her family?
    a. If she is pregnant and decides to have the baby, how could this change?
2. What laws would protect Susie if she decided that she did not want to carry her pregnancy to term?
3. What rights might Susie and John have as teenage parents, and how might their rights be limited?
4. If Susie decides to have the baby and give it up for adoption, what support from governmental or private agencies should she expect to receive? Does it matter where she lives?
5. What role might race, class, gender, and other aspects of identity play in this vignette?

At 15, Susie and her boyfriend, John, had sex for the first time. She was not sure if she really wanted to have sex but she also did not want to lose him and he had been pressuring her for a while. She had just had her period so she was pretty sure she would not get pregnant. When she did not get her period the following month, she got scared. What should she do? If she told her mother, her mother would be disappointed in her, or worse. Susie's father did not live with her, and she hardly ever saw him, so she could not imagine seeking his help. She was a good student and did not want to go to the nurse because she did not want to be seen as "one of those girls"—the kind who have sex early and are irresponsible enough to get pregnant. After the first time, she kept having sex with John but made sure he wore a condom. She worried again the next month when her period still had not come. Susie was afraid to tell John, but she finally did. First, he did not believe a baby could be his because he had been wearing condoms. When she convinced him that he was the only one she had ever had sex with, he insisted she get an abortion because he was not ready to be a father. He was planning to go to college and so was she. At church, they had taught her that abortion is murder. Susie was not sure she totally agreed but she did not want to be a murderer.

HISTORY AND SOCIAL CONSTRUCTION OF U.S. FAMILY POLICY

Social construction: The idea that meaning is created through interaction with our environment and existing values, practices, and norms. According to social construction, much of what we understand as truth is determined by our social and cultural milieu.

Structural family: Describes families based on who lives together and often includes some biological relationship

Functional family: Sees families' roles as the socialization of children and adolescents, providing emotional and/or financial support to family members, and connecting with reproduction

Transactional family: Refers to groups that identify as a family and have emotional connections, shared historical experience, and commitment to a shared future

As we have discussed in previous chapters, **social construction** suggests that we, as humans, are products of our interactions with our environment. This perspective leads us to understand that there are many social definitions of family and no one definition is *accurate*. One perspective, informed by many religious traditions, defines a family as a unit that is formed as a result of a marriage between a man and a woman, including their biological children. As noted by the Christian website Focus on the Family (n.d.), "marriage is about more than just love, support, and commitment. It is specifically about love, support, and commitment *between one man and one woman*. In other words, marriage is *heterosexual by definition*." In contrast, the U.S. Census Bureau defines a family household as a "household [that] has at least two members related by blood, marriage, or adoption, one of whom is the householder" (Fields & Casper, 2000). The concept of chosen families originated within LGBTQ+ communities, based on the experience that many individuals who identify as LGBTQ+ have with rejection from their biological families. These individuals often develop a sense of *chosen* family with people who are not related but who offer emotional and/or material support (Miller, 2016).

In general, all these family definitions look at family connections via structure, function, or transactions (Miller, 2016). A **structural family** definition (like the Census Bureau's) describes families based on who lives together and often include some biological relationship. A **functional** definition of families looks at ways in which families socialize children and adolescents, provide support to family members (which could include emotional support, financial support, or both), and reproduce. The Focus on the Family definition above highlights family function. A **transactional** definition of families highlights qualities such as identification as a family, emotional connections, shared historical experience, and commitment to a shared future. The LGBTQ+ chosen family definition is transactional.

REFLECTION
DEFINING FAMILY

How do you define your own family? Is this definition based on structure, function, transactions, or some combination of the three?

What is a family? Of course, one's definition of family is often influenced by one's cultural context. However, in all cultures, families tend to include parents and children. Some include more extended families as well. The formation of families, however, varies from countries in which parents choose their children's spouses (using a heterosexual norm) to those in which adults can choose their own spouses and the gender of said spouse is also a choice. This has also changed over time. In many countries in which parents used to select their children's spouses, children are now finding "love partners" of their own choosing. In some cultural contexts, grandparents as well as aunts and uncles are considered close family, and in other cultures, family usually refers to the **nuclear family** (i.e., parents and children only). In some states, couples who cohabitate for a specific period of time defined by state law, or who register as domestic partners, also defined by state law, may receive many of the same legal protections as spouses.

Nuclear family: Parents and their children

In the United States today, there are many types of families. Nuclear families coexist with families in which children are raised by single parents, by grandparents, or with step- and/or half-siblings. Parents may have children with people to whom they are not and may never be married. Immigration also has a significant effect on families. Immigrants from around the world continue to come to the United States. Not all families immigrate together, so living situations can vary, housing can be temporary, and extended family members may provide parenting supports (Glick, Bean, & Van Hook, 1997). In addition, there may be a variety of immigration statuses within a family, such as a combination of U.S. citizens, green card holders, and undocumented immigrants. Extended families can provide supports with finances, child care, emotional, education, socialization, and keeping cultural traditions. As a social worker, it is important to approach all types of families, even those that are different from the norms in our culture, with curiosity and respect. The National Association of Social Workers (NASW; 2017) Code of Ethics obligates us to respect "the dignity and worth" of individuals and "the importance of human relationships" (para. 3).

Historical View of Families

To understand U.S. family policy, it is useful to have a historical perspective on how families were seen and to understand the changing demographics of family life. In the 1600s, women and men worked on farms and young children also worked to contribute to the family's income. One's family generally superseded one's individual well-being. Many people remarried after the death of a spouse. Prior to the 1800s, colonial women tended to give birth every other year and older siblings had the responsibility of caring for the younger ones. As a result of biblical beliefs about the role of women, married couples were perceived as one person under the law until the mid-1800s in the United States. Women could not inherit money, could not own property, and could not legally keep their own wages. Beginning in the mid-1800s, the rights of married women began to change on the state level (Kahn, 2013). It may be hard to imagine, but this fight continued to modern times. It was not until 1971 that the U.S. Supreme Court overturned statutes that gave preference to men as guardians or trustees and executors of estates (*Reed v. Reed*).

By the end of the 1800s, U.S. birth rates began to decline significantly (Kahn, 2013). In urban settings, children continued to contribute to the family economy by working in factories to add their earnings. As people began to have fewer children, children started to stay with their parents longer and the perception of the length of childhood expanded. From the mid-1800s on, the ideal family division of labor was based on a middle-class white norm, where women took care of the home and children while men earned income outside of the home (Mintz & Kellogg, 1988), although this division did not reflect the realities of life for black, immigrant, or low-income families, as discussed later in this chapter.

While the colonies had provisions for divorce, the process was very difficult and divorce was less common than formal separation. Following the American Revolution, many states made it easier to divorce. American-born women continued to have fewer children throughout this time. *Nativists*, those born in the United States who resented immigration, feared their own lower birth rates would make them outnumbered. As a result, in the late 1800s, they successfully lobbied state legislatures to outlaw abortion in many states (Mintz & Kellogg, 1988). At the beginning of the 20th century, as a result of a reduced birth rate and the highest divorce rate in the world, U.S. states began to develop more restrictive divorce laws. Despite more restrictive laws, by 1927 the divorce rate rose to one in seven.

During the Progressive Era, social workers were involved with developing parenting education programs. They also helped train mothers in "home economics and domestic sciences" so that immigrants and people in poverty could be better parents (Mintz & Kellogg, 1988, p. 119).

From his findings in a cross-national comparative study of families, in 1949 sociologist George Peter Murdock developed a new definition of a family as

> a social group characterized by common residence, economic cooperation and reproduction. It includes adults of both sexes, at least two of whom maintain a socially approved sexual relationship, and one or more children, own or adopted, of the sexually cohabiting adults. (p. 1)

Biological families: Families into which you are born

Families of orientation: Families in which one is raised

Families of procreation: Families with whom one chooses to live and procreate

Talcott Parsons (1943), also a sociologist, divided families into three categories: biological families, families of orientation, and families of procreation. **Biological families** are those to which one is born. His view was that families existed primarily for the social function of raising children as well as to provide emotional support to members and to regulate sexual activity. **Families of orientation** are those in which one is raised, and **families of procreation** are those with whom one chooses to live and procreate. Parson's definitions assumed all partnerships are designed for procreation and, therefore, did not include same-sex couples. During the Industrial Revolution, when families moved from rural farms to urban centers, the nuclear family became more significant. Our definitions and beliefs about families have changed significantly since these definitions were created. However, laws such as the Social Security Act, which was originally passed in 1935 using a similar definition of family, still play a major role in providing support for families. This presents a challenge for social workers who are working to support families who differ from these definitions.

Economic theory of marriage: A theory that suggested that spouses (male/female) gained economically from their mutual dependence in marriage and that men's participation in the labor market supported women's domestic work at home (reproduction and child rearing)

Gary Becker's (1981) **economic theory of marriage** suggests that spouses (male/female) gain economically from their mutual dependence in marriage and that men's participation in the labor market supports women's domestic work at home (reproduction and child rearing). He predicted that as women's labor market participation increased there would be less of an economic need for marriage. This theory predicted the decline of marriage in modern society. Paradoxically, research has shown that men and women who have more education and earn more are more likely to marry (Oppenheimer, 2000), suggesting that marriage exists for reasons other than financial.

U.S. Census Bureau: The agency charged with counting U.S. residents

As noted above, the **U.S. Census Bureau** (2015), the agency charged with counting U.S. residents, currently defines a family as "two or more people residing together, and related by birth, marriage, or adoption." Much of the data that we rely on to understand the current demographics of families is based on U.S. Census data. Households, in contrast to families, can also be defined as all related and unrelated members occupying a housing unit. Multigenerational households include three or more generations living in the home, and shared households consist of a combination of multifamily, including roommates, godparents, and so on (Kim, Spangler, & Gutter, 2016). Last, as a result of court challenges and changes to state and federal law, though gender or sexuality is theoretically no longer a consideration in determining who can be considered part of a family group, the wording of existing laws, systemic oppression, and individual perspectives of people in positions of power often affects the ways in which these policies are implemented. Many social workers struggle with the teachings of their culture or religion regarding the norms of family and the expectations of the code of ethics and professional value statements.

Defining Family Outside of White Middle-Class Norms

During the 1900s, discrimination and limited access to the job market meant that for immigrants, African Americans, and people living in poverty the norm described above of a father working and mother staying home was rarely an option. In these families, women usually worked outside of the home. Women who were enslaved were also required to work, often looking after the children of others, and had limited control over the raising of their own children.

Perceptions of families among those descended from enslaved Africans, Native American tribes, and immigrants often differed from the white middle-class norms, which caused some friction and added to discrimination for these groups. Some of these norms have become part of mainstream America. For example, enslaved families generally prohibited marriage between siblings or cousins, based on beliefs they brought from West Africa that this was incest. European slave-owning families originally allowed siblings or cousins to marry, but gradually came to see such marriages as harmful. Because relatives who were enslaved were often sold to other families, enslaved families developed extended families and what we might think of as *chosen families* today, often including people who were not blood related (Mintz & Kellogg, 1988). Native American tribes often encouraged free selection of spouses by young people, even when the mainstream culture encouraged arranged marriages or selection of spouses by parents. Today, the norm in most U.S. cultural groups is free selection of spouses.

CURRENT FAMILY POLICY

This chapter discusses different ways that biological families are constructed, as well as how they are formed through social configurations, including adoptions. Family policy also includes policy around reproductive technologies, such as that which uses sperm and egg donations, policy related to ending a pregnancy, and policy related to same-sex marriage and adoption. What do all these topics have in common? They all speak to our definitions of who makes up a family and how families are created. In this section, we look at current definitions of families and related policies. The ways in which policies are created, and the people affected by such policies, have social justice implications. For example, child welfare policies are more likely to impact low-income families. In contrast, sperm and egg donation policies may affect both people with resources, often those seeking donors, and people seeking resources, who are often the donors.

What Do Families in the United States Look like Today?

Changes in family structure (see Photo 4.1) over the years have led to much of the debate about family definitions and structures. Within the United States, we have many different ideals of marriage, children and parenting, and household structure. Marrying later in life, divorce, and living together without formal marriage are more common. Americans are having fewer children, giving birth outside of traditional marriage, and giving birth at older ages. These

PHOTO 4.1 There is no typical family; many types of families exist today.

trends, combined with changes in social and cultural attitudes (Daugherty & Copen, 2016), mean that there is no longer a *typical* family. In 2018, while the majority of children under 18 were being raised in homes with two parents (68%), 23% were in homes with single mothers, 4% with single fathers, 3% with other relatives, and 2% with nonrelatives (U.S. Census Bureau, 2018a). Fifteen percent are living in families where one of their birth parents has remarried. Seven percent are living with cohabitating unmarried parents (Pew Research Center, 2015). Compare this to 1950, when 93% of children lived with two parents (U.S. Census Bureau, 2016). In 1960, fewer than 15% of the population lived alone, but that number had nearly doubled to 28% by 2018 (U.S. Census Bureau, 2018c).

The median age when people first marry has changed significantly. In the 1940s, women married on average at age 20.5 and men at age 24. In 2018, the age of women's marriage had increased by nearly 7 years to 27.8, and men are now averaging first marriage at almost 30. The number of people who never marry has also risen from 25% in 1950 to 32% in 2018 (U.S. Census Bureau, 2018c). What are some of the factors that you think might contribute to these changes?

Substantial attention has been paid to the fact that family composition, including marriage and having children, seems connected to race and ethnicity. Marriage rates are lower among African Americans than those who identify as white or Hispanic. Approximately one in two African American children, one in four Hispanic children, and one in five white children under 18 live with only their mothers (U.S. Census Bureau, 2018b). Some factors that impact family composition are the high incarceration of young black men, the higher unemployment rate of black men, educational disparities between black women and black men, and the fact that black men are more likely to marry outside of their race, thus making it more difficult for black women to find partners. Some have argued that given the high rates of unemployment and incarceration (noted above) and lower salaries due to structural oppression and discrimination, it is not economically advantageous for black women to marry men whom they may have to support in addition to supporting children (Raley, Sweeney, & Wondra, 2015). The same may be true for single women living in poverty across race (Edin & Kefalas, 2005). Three out of 10 single mothers live in poverty (Livingston, 2018b).

Childbearing rates have also drastically changed in recent years. Women report having fewer children than they would like, and the U.S. birth rate is rapidly declining to its lowest point ever (Bakalar, 2017; Shdaimah & Palley, 2018). For women ages 15 through 29, birth rates have rapidly fallen. There has been no change for women ages 30 through 34 and a slight increase for women ages 35 through 44 (Stone, 2018). Rates of teen pregnancy, long considered a significant social problem, have declined 67% since 1991 (Bakalar, 2017).

Access to and use of contraception has changed as well. Though only 1.5% of women ages 15 through 44 used Long Acting Reversible Contraception (LARC) like intrauterine devices (IUDs), injections, or implants in 2002, by 2011 to 2013, 7.2% of women were using LARCs. Emergency contraception was used by only 4.2% of women ages 15 through

44 in 2002, rising to 11% by 2006 to 2010. The rate is even higher (23%) for those aged 20 through 23 (CDC, 2017). Alongside the rise in use of various forms of contraception, more women have children later in their final years of fertility. By the time women are ages 40 through 44, 86% are mothers, an increase of 6% since 2006. Today the majority (55%) of women who have never been married have children; while 20 years ago, only 30% of never-married women had children (Livingston, 2018a). In the mid-1970s, 40% of women at the end of their childbearing years had four or more children. Now, 40% have two or more. About 40% of children who were born in 2017 were born to single mothers. The following chart shows the percentage of births to unmarried mothers (Martin, Hamilton, Osterman, Driscoll, & Drake, 2018) (see Table 4.1).

TABLE 4.1 ■ Births to Unmarried Mothers

Highest percentages of births to unmarried mothers	Lowest percentages of births to unmarried mothers
Mississippi (53.5)	Utah (18.5)
Louisiana (52.7)	Colorado (22.5)
New Mexico (51.7)	Idaho (28.1)
Nevada (48.4)	North Dakota (31.5)
Delaware (47.6)	Washington (31.6)
Alabama (47.1)	Minnesota (32)

Source: Table based on data reported in the CDC report *Percentage of Births to Unmarried Mothers by State: 2017.*

Family composition has a significant relationship to access to resources. Single families are at a higher risk of poverty. Single mothers are less likely to accumulate wealth or own assets and often face discrimination in renting and buying homes. Younger households have fewer assets and larger debt (Maroto & Aylsowrth, 2017). However, recent trends indicate that solo parents who are not cohabitating with their partners are more educated and older than those who cohabitate (Livingston, 2018b). There is no longer a significant difference between the number of working mothers and fathers (U.S. Census Bureau, 2017b). In 2015, 62% of mothers and 65% of fathers of children under 18 were working outside the home. Age is significant in decisions about family makeup; members of the millennial generation (born 1981–1996) are more likely to have babies than to marry (Livingston, 2018c). Parenthood status of millennials and members of generation X are compared in Figure 4.1.

In 2019, the Williams Institute reported approximately 642,000 same-sex couples live together in the United States. Sixty-one percent of these couples are married (Jones, 2017). Twenty percent have children. The range of reported same-sex couple households varied significantly by state, ranging from 0.3% in Wyoming to 4% of households in Washington, DC (Lofquist, 2011). Estimates suggest 130,000 children are currently being raised by same-sex couples, including approximately 4% of all adopted children as well as 3% of foster children. Significant discrimination exists for same-sex couples who wish to adopt. Adoption agencies that focus on adoption of babies often prefer to place babies with different-sex couples than with same-sex couples, and some agencies, both private and state-run, have refused to place children with same-sex couples. Birth parents giving up children for

FIGURE 4.1 ■ Marital and Parenthood Status for Millennials and Generation X

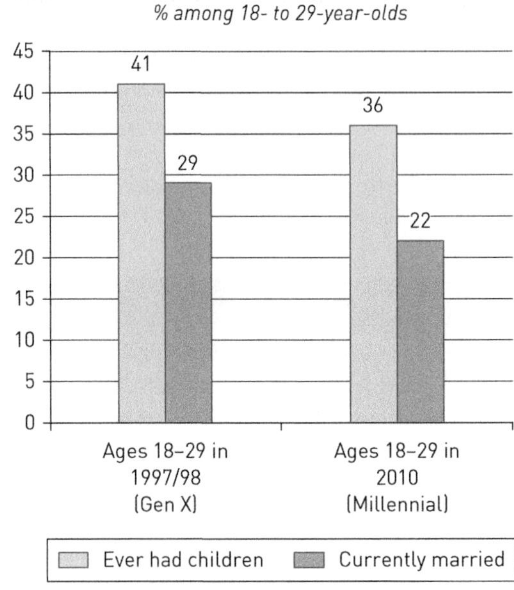

Source: "Marital and Parenthood Status." Pew Research Center, Washington, D.C. (03/09/2011) http://www.pewsocialtrends.org/2011/03/09/for-millennials-parenthood-trumps-marriage/

Note: Percentage of ever had children is based on women.

adoption may also request that their children not be placed in the home of same-sex couples (Brodzinsky & Pertman, 2014).

Child Welfare and Adoption

Domestic adoptions: Adoptions where both the parent/s and child are in the United States

Closed adoptions: Adoptions where birth records are sealed

Hague Convention on Protection of Children and Co-operation in Respect of Intercountry Adoption (HCCH, 1993): An international treaty that was designed to protect the welfare of children who are adopted from other countries and to make sure that they are not the victims of kidnapping

Children can be adopted through foster care or through either domestic (within the United States) or international private adoptions. **Domestic adoptions** include open adoptions when the parent maintains a relationship with the children and the children know their birth parent, as well as **closed adoptions** where birth records are sealed. Policies related to these adoptions vary greatly from one state to another. Some states allow children at age 18 to request that their adoption records be unsealed. The **Hague Convention on Protection of Children and Co-operation in Respect of Intercountry Adoption** (HCCH, 1993) is an international treaty that was designed to protect the welfare of children who are adopted from other countries and to make sure that they are not the victims of kidnapping. The United States signed onto this treaty in 1994, and it has been in full force since 2008. Many countries have their own policies and requirements for international adoptions. The specific laws that govern adoption as a result of child welfare involvement are described in greater detail in Chapter 15.

Sperm and Egg Donations

If you donate sperm, are you legally responsible for the child who is born? Can you have any rights to see the child? What about if you provide an egg donation? What if you carry someone else's fertilized egg for 8 to 9 months? There are no national laws that regulate sperm, egg, or embryo donation. Much is left to the states to regulate and many states have no regulations, leaving the decision to be determined on a case by case basis.

REFLECTION

SPERM AND EGG DONATION

If you donate sperm, are you legally responsible for a child who is produced from that sperm? Can you have any right to see the child? What about if you provide an egg donation? What if you carry someone else's fertilized egg for 8 to 9 months? What do you think the answers should be?

Sperm donation is the most likely area for states to regulate. In 1987, approximately 30,000 children were born as a result of sperm donation (U.S. Congress, Office of Technology Assessment, 1988). Since then, no effort has been made to count the number of children born as a result of sperm donation in the United States, though estimates of anywhere between 30,000 and 60,000 births per year are often used. The Centers for Disease Control and Prevention (CDC) maintains data on Assisted Reproductive Technology (ART), including fertility treatments such as medication, in vitro fertilization, and surrogacy. **In vitro fertilization** is a process by which human eggs are fertilized in labs and then re-implanted into women. **Surrogacy** is a process in which a woman's womb is used to carry a baby for another couple or person. In 2015, approximately 72,000 children were born as a result of ART. Approximately 20,000 ART inseminations involved donor eggs (either previously frozen or fresh). The use of gestational carriers or surrogates, people who are hired to carry the embryo of another couple, rose from 2,251 in 2006 to 4,725 in 2015 (Centers for Disease Control and Prevention, 2017).

In vitro fertilization: A process by which human eggs are fertilized in labs and then, re-implanted into women

Surrogacy: A process in which a woman's womb is used to carry a baby for another couple or person

Because these arrangements operate under state laws, agreements made in one state will not apply to other states with differing laws. This means that social workers working with families who use or consider such options will need to be aware of which state laws apply. For example, the courts in California have had the opportunity to discuss the question of who has parental rights when a surrogate carries a child produced from the sperm and egg of others. Often considered to be a state with liberal courts, California will enforce surrogacy contracts (meaning they will make the parties adhere to them, even if they change their minds). These courts came up with the following test for maternity: "she who intended to procreate the child—that is, . . . to bring about the birth of a child that she intended to raise as her own—is the natural mother under California law" (*Johnson, supra,* 5 Cal. 4th 84, 93, fn. 10, at p. 93, as cited in *KM v. EG,* Court of Appeals 5th Circuit, Div. 5 Cal., 2005). In Pennsylvania, surrogacy contracts are also enforceable (*J.F. v. D.B.*, 897 A.2d1261, 2006). The Appellate Court in Pennsylvania found that a sperm donor who made an oral agreement with a woman to be a donor but not participate in child rearing could not be held liable for support (*Ferguson v. McKiernan*, 940A.2d1236, Pa. 2007). When thinking about surrogacy policy, it should be understood that surrogates are often women with limited financial means whereas those seeking surrogates are more likely to come from higher-income families who can afford this expensive process.

Ohio law explicitly governs artificial insemination. The husband of the woman who is artificially inseminated with someone else's sperm is the father of the child that is created from that sperm; this law also ensures that the donor does not have parental rights to the child. Ohio has a similar law that applies to embryo donations. According to this law, the woman who bears the child is the child's mother, and the egg donor does not have any rights vis-à-vis the child. The husband is the legal father in this instance as well (Ohio Revised Code Title XXXI Chapter 3111, 2001). One of the most interesting surrogacy cases revolves around what surrogates could be paid. In California, in the case *Kamakahi v. American Society for Reproductive Medicine* (ASRM) (2011), the court determined that the ASRM could not limit fees paid for egg donation to between $5,000 and $10,000 because doing so was illegal price fixing and violated federal antitrust law.

As you can tell from the above examples, laws related to the creation of families through donation of eggs or sperm or surrogacy are complicated, which reflects the complicated nature of these arrangements. There are also often very complicated emotional and relationship issues for families to navigate, and so some social workers specialize in working with these families. These social workers must understand the related policies in their states to effectively work with the parents and children involved.

Abortion Rights[1]

Abortion has long been debated in the United States. In 1973, the Supreme Court issued an opinion in the case of *Roe v. Wade* that made it illegal for states to outlaw abortion in all cases. *Roe v. Wade* set up a trimester framework for when states are permitted to interfere with abortion access. According to the court's decision, states cannot outlaw or overly burden a women's right to have an abortion during the first trimester of pregnancy. States can limit women's rights to abortion in the second trimester to protect the mother from harm. The court allowed states to further intervene in the third trimester to protect the unborn fetus because at this point (according to the courts) a fetus was viable, meaning that it could live outside its mother's womb. Although *Roe v. Wade* ensured that some abortion would be legal in the United States, state laws and court cases, such as *Planned Parenthood v. Casey* (1992), have allowed states to regulate and limit abortion rights within the parameters set out by the court. The changing landscape of state laws, court decisions, medical technology, and public opinion have limited access to abortions. Abortion laws largely affect low-income women. As noted by Rob Schenk (2019), an evangelical minister who worked with the pro-life movement, if abortion is outlawed in some states, middle- and upper-income women will always be able to go to another state or country to have the procedure done safely and legally. It is, he notes, the women who are in the weakest position to have children who are often forced by antiabortion policies to have children.

Teens, who are particularly vulnerable to unplanned pregnancies, may be required to obtain parental consent prior to procuring an abortion. In a 2006 case involving a teen required to notify her parents of her intent to have an abortion, the Supreme Court reiterated that state abortion regulations must include provisions to protect women's health (*Ayotte v. Planned Parenthood of Northern New England*). In 2007, in *Gonzales v. Carhart* and *Gonzales v. Planned Parenthood Federation of America, Inc.*, the most recent Supreme Court cases to address abortion, the Supreme Court upheld a federal ban on an abortion technique called *dilation and extraction* that has been referred to in legislation as "partial-birth abortion." Court decisions often contradict one another. The 2007 decisions upheld laws that did not include exceptions to protect the health of the woman, so this decision contradicted and essentially overturned the 2006 decision.

Mifepristone or Miliprex: A drug that is used to pharmaceutically induce an abortion

Federal and state laws also extend to medications that can be used to induce abortion. **Mifepristone** or **Miliprex** is a drug that is used to pharmaceutically induce an abortion. Though legal in France since 1988 and other parts of Europe since the early 1990s, it was not legalized in the United States until 1996. President George H.W. Bush banned the importation of Miliprex. Despite the lower court's approval, the ban was ultimately upheld by the

[1]This section was written and researched in collaboration with Jennifer Dull.

Supreme Court. As a result of antiabortion lobbying, despite research demonstrating that Mifepristone was safe and effective, it was not legally available in the United States until 2000 when it was approved by the FDA (Planned Parenthood, 2016). The availability of the drug has been limited through state government action around prescribing practices or individual actions such as pharmacies' refusal to sell it (Tavernise, 2016).

As a result of the states' authority to regulate abortion within the parameters laid out by the Supreme Court, states have different interpretations of what is legal abortion, who has access to abortions and under what circumstances, when and if minors require parental consent, when fetuses are considered viable, and the amount of public funding that is allocated to enable women to have abortions. Understanding the landscape of abortion law requires understanding your own state laws. The Guttmacher Institute (2018) provides an overview of state laws and their prevalence, although as discussed below, this area is rapidly changing and therefore some of these numbers may have changed by the time you read this, including the following:

- 37 states require parental consent or notification when minors have abortions.
- 41 states mandate that licensed physicians provide abortions.
- 19 states require a second physician for late-term abortion.
- 27 states require waiting periods between the time that a woman attends a counseling session and the time she can legally have an abortion.
- 13 states require a 24-hour waiting period, and 14 require longer waiting periods, which can require at least two visits to a clinic to get an abortion.
- 43 states have regulations limiting abortion with either specification for a timeline in the pregnancy or circumstances around health issues such as life or death of the mother.
- 17 states allow the use of state funding for abortion services.
- 32 states allow the use of federal funds in lieu of state funds when available or in the case of rape, incest, or if a woman's life is in danger.
- South Dakota is the only state that limits the use of federal funds to cases when the woman's life is in danger.
- Individual health care providers can refuse to participate in abortion in 45 states.
- 42 states allow health facilities to refuse abortion services.
- 16 states specifically allow private or religious institutions to refuse to perform abortions.
- Abortion coverage is restricted in private insurance plans in 11 states.
- In contrast to restrictions on teens seeking an abortion, 40 states allow teen parents to place a child up for adoption and only 10 of those require parental consent.
- All states allow teen parents to consent to medical care for their children.
- 18 states have mandated counseling laws that include different disclosure regulations, including the link to breast cancer, the ability of a fetus to feel pain, and the potential mental health consequences of getting an abortion.

Mental health and medical professionals challenge the accuracy of much of the state-mandated disclosure described in this last bullet point. For example, the American Psychological Association (APA) (2008) says,

> [t]he best scientific evidence published indicates that among adult women who have an unplanned pregnancy the relative risk of mental health problems is no greater if they have a single elective first-trimester abortion than if they deliver that pregnancy. The evidence regarding the relative mental health risks associated with multiple abortions is more equivocal. Positive associations observed between multiple abortions and poorer mental health may be linked to co-occurring risks that predispose a woman to both multiple unwanted pregnancies and mental health problems. (p. 4)

In other words, though many antiabortion activists argue that abortions harm women's mental health and have instituted waiting periods to "assist" women, the APA suggests that abortions are not associated with harm to women.

At the beginning of 2019, there was an uptake in antiabortion legislation. Georgia, Kentucky, Louisiana, Mississippi, and Ohio made it illegal to have an abortion after 6 weeks, which is before many women become aware that they are pregnant (Nash, 2019). Alabama completely outlawed aborton, including in cases of rape and incest (Williams & Blinder, 2019). It is likely that these laws will be challenged and that the Supreme Court will revisit *Roe v. Wade* in the near future.

DISCUSSION

HOW DO BELIEFS SHAPE POLICY?

1. How do beliefs about what is family shape abortion policies/politics?
2. How do antiabortion politics affect conservative beliefs about providing government support for families?
3. What is the connection between beliefs about what constitutes a family, what the role of a family is, and who should or should not be able to have an abortion?

You can see where the United States fits in relation to the rest of the world in relation to abortion rights in Figure 4.2.

Social Security Spousal Benefits and Survivor Benefits

The first federal law designed to assist families who had lost a breadwinner was the Social Security Act (1935). Originally, only women were eligible for spousal benefits, but the benefits are now available to a wider group. In the 1970s case of *Califano v. Goldfarb*, 430 U.S. 199 (1977), a widower successfully challenged the gender bias of the law, and the Supreme Court ordered that spousal survivor benefits be available for both men and women. People who are partnered but not legally married cannot access survivor benefits. Before 2015, individuals in same-sex marriages could be eligible for their partner's spousal benefits, but individuals in civil unions were not. This was one reason that advocates continued to push for same-sex marriage. As a result of the *Obergefell v. Hodges* case described below (2015), same-sex spouses

FIGURE 4.2 ■ The World's Abortion Laws

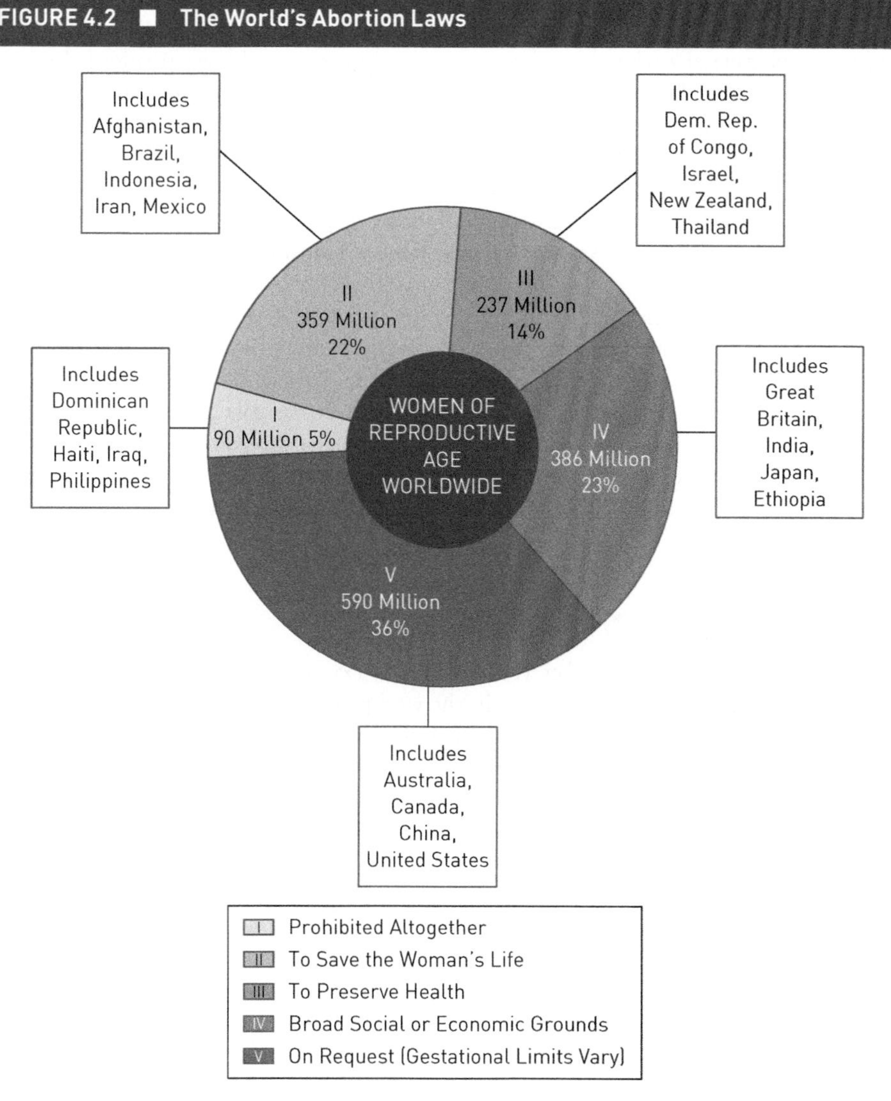

Source: Based on information from the Center for Reproductive Rights, retrieved from https://reproductiverights.org/sites/default/files/documents/World-Abortion-Map.pdf

are now eligible to receive the Social Security benefits of their partners in all states. One criticism of this system is that Social Security privileges the nonworking spouses of high earning partners over low-income working spouses. In some ways, this can be shown as society's preference for women (given that women are typically the lower paid spouses) to obtain financial security through marriage instead of work. Survivors' benefits may also be available to the children of deceased workers and the children of workers who become disabled. Children of deceased adults may be eligible for monthly benefits if they are 18 and under, and remain eligible until age 19 if they are enrolled in school, or age 22 if they have a disability that was identified before they turned 18 (Social Security Administration, 2017). Because these policies are based on an ideal of two parent homes and legal marriage, they are often unavailable to families who might benefit from them.

Temporary Assistance for Needy Families

Aid to Dependent Children (ADC): Part of the Social Security Act. The program was created primarily to support widowed mothers so they could remain at home to care for their children.

Temporary Assistance for Needy Families (TANF): A federal program that provides block grants to states for families in poverty. This program replaced Aid to Families with Dependent Children.

Block grants: Federal grants to states in lieu of direct federal support for programs

Prior to the passage of national legislation, many cities set up widow's pensions. In 1935, as a part of the Social Security Act, **Aid to Dependent Children (ADC)** was created, primarily to support widowed mothers so they could remain at home to care for their children. The name was later changed to Aid to Families with Dependent Children. In 1994, under President Bill Clinton, this assistance changed from a right to temporary support, and it changed from a fully federally funded program to a federal block grant program called **Temporary Assistance for Needy Families (TANF). Block grants** are federal grants to states that allow broad discretion in implementation. TANF limits its support to most families with children for up to 5 years over a lifetime and requires parents to work to receive benefits; states can create shorter time limits and additional requirements as part of their discretionary powers. As a result of a failure to keep pace with inflation, benefits have fallen 20% in real value over the past 20 years, and in every state, as of 2017, benefits were at least 60% below the U.S. poverty line (Floyd, 2017). While this program may offer temporary assistance to families who are struggling (hence the name), it is unlikely to offer them enough money to live on, or the assistance needed to leave poverty.

The Pregnancy Discrimination Act

The Pregnancy Discrimination Act (PDA) (PL 95-555) was passed in 1978 to prevent discrimination against pregnant women in the workplace. At the time, it was legal to fire a woman when she became pregnant. The PDA clarified that Title VII of the Civil Rights Act, which had been passed as a response to civil unrest and race-based discrimination in 1964, should consider pregnancy discrimination as a form of gender discrimination. Title VII of the Civil Rights Act prevents employers who have 15 or more employees from discriminating against employees on the basis of race, religion, or gender. The PDA specifies that if employers provide work accommodations to nonpregnant employees with work limitations, they must provide comparable accommodations to pregnant employees. The most recent challenge to this law was heard in 2015, in the case of *Young v. UPS*. Peggy Young sued United Parcel Service because, though she was able to perform her work duties, the official job description required her to lift 70 pounds and her doctor had told her not to lift more than 20 pounds. Even though her colleagues had offered to help her in such circumstances, UPS felt that she was not capable of working for them while she was pregnant. The U.S. Supreme Court heard the case and decided that since UPS accommodated workers with disabilities and people who had suspended driver's licenses, they should also accommodate pregnant women. They were careful not to say that companies had a duty to accommodate pregnant women generally, but rather *if* they accommodated others, *then* they should also accommodate pregnant women. Following this decision, several states, including Delaware (S.B. 12, 2014) and New York (S. 8, 2015), passed laws that explicitly require reasonable accommodations for pregnant women and nursing mothers in the workplace.

Paid and Unpaid Leave to Care for Family

The most recent federal policy designed to assist families regarding workplace leave is the 1993 Family and Medical Leave Act (FMLA). The FMLA requires employers who have 50 or more employees to provide 12 weeks of unpaid leave to employees who have worked at least 1,250 hours in the past 12 months in the event of a birth, adoption, or fostering a child or if that employee, his or her spouse, parent, or child becomes seriously ill or is active military and is deployed. Employers are not required to return employees to their former position when they return, but are required to return them to an equivalent job. Some states have developed more expansive policies. For example, by 2020, California, the District of Columbia, New Jersey, New York, Rhode Island, and Washington State will all provide paid leave (National Women's Law Center, 2018) and Connecticut will have paid family leave by 2021 (Peck, 2019). In all these states, domestic partners can also receive the leave and, in all but California, the leave is also available for grandparents. Connecticut allows "any other blood relation or person who is the 'equivalent of a family member'" to be covered (Peck, 2019, para. 4). This definition of family was requested by advocates for LGBTQ+ and African American communities for whom chosen families are particularly significant. In most states, funding for family leave comes from employee payroll taxes. New York uses a combination of employer and employee payroll taxes (National Women's Law Center, 2018). State laws provide for up to 16 weeks of leave (Connecticut) and generally cover employers who employ fewer than 50 people, such as Maine, which covers employers of 15 or more people (National Conference of State Legislators, 2016). Despite these innovations, a 2014 report by President Obama's Council of Economic Advisors stated that only 60% of workers had access to unpaid leave for the birth of a child and only 39% reported having some access to paid leave for the birth of a child. Since some of these laws are either newly implemented or have yet to be implemented, the number of families covered may be growing. However, it is still difficult for many employees to take leave to care for new children, sick children, sick spouses, and sick parents because of limited access to paid leave.

Divorce, Child Custody, and Domestic Violence

Family law is traditionally regulated at the state level and therefore subject to wide variation in how families split up as well as how they are formed. Often, there is a minimum residency requirement to file for divorce once you have moved to a state. The residency requirement ranges from nothing in Alaska, Iowa, and Washington, to a year in Connecticut, Nebraska, New Jersey, and New York (Family Law Quarterly, 2012). In many states, partners must be separated for a minimum amount of time to file for divorce. In some states, spouses must provide legal justification to be eligible for a divorce. In others, they can get what is called a *no-fault divorce*, where no legal justification is necessary. If you work with families who are in the midst of divorce or a child custody dispute, it is important to familiarize yourself with your own state's laws. Even though these are regulated at the state level, once the status of a family (marriage, divorce, adoption, parentage) is determined, family law has traditionally been recognized by other states and the federal government under the Constitution's Full Faith and Credit Clause.

Since the 1970s, judges have relied on the *best interests of the child* standard to determine child custody. This gives judges broad discretion to decide what they think is best. In the recent past, there was a maternal preference for child custody. However, the concept of maternal preference has been largely eliminated formally. Though each state has guidelines, to comply with federal law, child custody determinations are generally made based on what is perceived to be in the best interests of the child. At times in US history, courts have been more likely to keep children with their fathers than their mothers in contested custody situations (Dotterweich & McKinney, 2000). The fathers' rights movement has been successful in strongly advocating for joint custody, whereas the mothers' rights movement has sought blanket custody limits for those found to be guilty of domestic violence (Scott & Emery, 2014). There is a federal office to enforce the responsibility of noncustodial parents to pay child support to provide financially for their children. Federal guidelines regulate this process. One federal requirement is that state law may not treat people who are in jail as voluntarily unemployed (Office of Child Support Enforcement, 2016). The federal Office of Child Support Enforcement was created as part of the Department of Health and Human Services to get money for children whose custodial parents were receiving welfare or other benefits as a result of lack of support from the noncustodial parent. As a result of federal law, states are required to create child support guidelines (81 FR 93492, 2016).

Both state and federal laws regulate services for survivors of domestic violence and penalties for perpetrators. Many statutes require that the partners not only be in a romantic relationship but also live together to fall under the purview of domestic violence protections. At the local level in a civil court, victims of domestic violence can file something called a protective order or a no-contact order. These court orders enable victims of domestic violence to seek police protection and have the perpetrator arrested when he or she attempts to contact them or comes within a specific radius (Slater & Fink, 2012). The Violence Against Women Act (VAWA) was passed in 1994 and signed by President Clinton. It is a federal law that has implications at the state level largely because it provides funding for training and support to states to address domestic violence and because it requires state reciprocity with protective orders. A more in-depth discussion of VAWA is provided in the criminal justice chapter.

Caregiving

A traditional role of families is providing care to sick members and children. According to the National Alliance for Caregiving (NAC) and the American Association of Retired Persons (AARP) (2015), about 43.5 million adults provide unpaid care for either a child or an adult with physical health, mental health, or cognitive impairments. The majority (60%) of caregivers are female, and 85% provide care for a relative (49% for a parent, 10% for a spouse). The majority of caregivers also work for pay. Thirty-four percent have a full-time job and 25% work part-time. About 50% of those interviewed stated that they had no choice but to be a caregiver. This work is complicated. While 82% take care of a single person, the rest take care of more than one person. Those being cared for who are over the age of 50 are likely to have long-term physical conditions (59%), memory difficulties (26%), or multiple conditions (37%). However, younger people also need care, and although those aged 18 to 49 are less likely to have a long-term condition (32%), they frequently have a mental health diagnosis (36%) or multiple conditions (37%). Care for this group also includes planning for when a parent or older family member will no longer be able to care for them.

For families with children, child care is a crucial concern. Mothers spend an average of 15 hours a week providing child care, up from 10 in 1965. Fathers spend an average of 7 hours a week providing care for children, up from 2.5 hours in 1965 (Parker & Livingston, 2017). The hours parents spend providing care for children with special needs is greater. In 2009, 16.8 million people provided unpaid care for children up to 18 years old with special needs (medical, cognitive, behavioral disability). As with those caring for older adults, the majority (72%) of caregivers are female (NAC & AARP, 2009).

For public policy purposes, child care is generally supported for low-income families on a less eligibility basis. Federal supports are provided through Head Start, the Child Care Development Block Grant, and the tax code. States and local governments may also provide some child care supports for families either by subsidizing programs, supporting early education teacher training, or directly subsidizing families. A more in-depth discussion of child care policy is found in Chapter 6.

According to a review of 120 nations conducted by the Organisation for Economic Cooperation and Development, the United States and Papua New Guinea are the only countries that do not have any national policy to provide paid maternity leave. Many countries also provide paid paternity leave (Gault, Hartmann, Hegewisch, Milli, & Reichlin, 2014; Taylor, 2019). A review of other countries' paid parental leave provides some comparison for the extent to which families are supported in the United States. In addition to paid parental leave, other countries, specifically European countries, provide support to families by limiting work hours and providing guaranteed paid vacation and sick time (European Union, 2003). FMLA, as noted above, requires that some employers provide 12 weeks of unpaid leave for caregiving associated with birth, adoption, or to care for oneself or for a sick relative.

ADVOCACY

CREATE YOUR OWN CHART OF FAMILY POLICY

1. Create a chart with policies that affect families.
2. Determine which are state, which are federal, and which overlap.

TABLE 4.2 ■ Relevant Federal Family Policy Laws and Their Oversight

Topic	Laws	Oversight Agency	Website
Child Support	Child Support Enforcement Amendments of 1984 Family Support Act of 1988 Child Support Recovery Act of 1992	Office of Child Support Enforcement (OCSE) Department of Justice (DOJ)	https://www.acf.hhs.gov/css/resource/final-rule-implementation-of-child-support-enforcement-amendments-of-1984 https://www.acf.hhs.gov/css/resource/family-support-act-of-1988 https://www.gpo.gov/fdsys/pkg/BILLS-103s922enr/pdf/BILLS-103s922enr.pdf https://www.acf.hhs.gov/css/resource/child-support-recovery-act-of-1992
Income support	Temporary Assistance for Needy Families	U.S. Department of Health and Human Services	https://www.acf.hhs.gov/ofa/programs/tanf
Pregnancy discrimination	Pregnancy Discrimination Act (PL 95-555)	Equal Employment Opportunity Commission	https://www.gpo.gov/fdsys/pkg/STATUTE-92/pdf/STATUTE-92-Pg2076.pdf
Family leave	Family and Medical Leave Act (FMLA) 1993	U.S. Department of Labor	https://www.dol.gov/whd/fmla/
Food assistance	Supplemental Nutrition Assistance Program (SNAP)	U.S. Department of Agriculture Food & Nutrition Service	https://www.fns.usda.gov/snap/short-history-snap

PHOTO 4.2 A pro-marriage equality march

POLICY INFORMED BY ALTERNATIVE LENSES

Social action and legal advocacy have changed the landscape of legal rights available to those who identify as LGBTQ+. This action and the resulting changes in laws would not be possible without the changing definition of family described above. Here we talk more about how this changing perspective on LGBTQ+ families happened and the implications for social work today.

Social Action and Same-Sex Marriage: Past and Present[2]

One of the most momentous occurrences in LGBTQ+ history were the 1969 Stonewall riots at Manhattan's Stonewall Inn, which led to the immediate formation of advocacy groups such as the Gay Liberation Front, the Gay Activists Alliance, and Fight Repression of Erotic Expression (FREE). The first court case over the denial of a same-sex marriage license was in the Minnesota Supreme Court in *Baker v. Nelson* (1971). The court ruled that the ban on same-sex marriage licenses was constitutional. Other cases followed, but upheld that marriage was heterosexual and defined only in terms of family and sexual structure. In 1973, Maryland became the first state to officially ban same-sex marriage. This led the movement advocating for LGBTQ+ rights (commonly called the gay rights movement at that time) to try to create alliances with feminists to dismantle patriarchal understandings of marriage, gender roles, and homophobia (Boucai, 2015) (see Photo 4.2 for a marriage equality demonstration). Efforts to redefine family, marriage, and traditional gender norms were met with strong resistance, and there was a conservative backlash against both gay rights and feminism (Polikoff, 2009).

In the 1980s, gay and lesbian advocates began to push for domestic partnerships in lieu of marriage and worked to redefine traditional family structures (Polikoff, 2009). In 1984, the first domestic partnership law was passed in California, and both California and New York established laws to define same-sex couples as families beginning in 1989. In the early 1990s, more states began to legally recognize same-sex unions. Massachusetts granted domestic partner benefits to same-sex couples in 1992. The next year, in *Baehr v. Lewin* (1993), the Hawaii Supreme Court declared prohibitions against same-sex marriage as a form of gender discrimination: "[W]hen a man cannot marry a man but a woman can, a discrimination based on one's gender has occurred" (Frank, 2014). This did not allow same-sex couples to marry but led to the case being remanded (sent back) to a lower court. In 1998, the state legislature of Hawaii allowed the ban on same-sex marriage to continue, but state law was changed in 2012 to allow same-sex civil unions, which include some of, but not all, the protections of marriage.

In 1996, President Clinton signed the Defense of Marriage Act (DOMA) into federal law, which was unusual, given that marriage had generally been overseen by state government until this point. Under DOMA, states did not have to recognize marriage of a same-sex couple if

[2]This section was researched and written by Jennifer Dull.

their license was issued in a different state. DOMA also declared that all federal legislation regarding marriage applied only to heterosexual couples (Chambers & Polikoff, 1999). Shortly after the passage of DOMA, the Vermont Supreme Court held in 1999 that the state's ban on same-sex marriage was unconstitutional and therefore that same-sex couples should receive the same benefits and protections as heterosexual couples.

The 2000s brought both legislation supporting and banning same-sex marriage, which was accompanied by court challenges, ending in an ultimate victory for same-sex rights at the federal level. States traveled many paths toward legalizing same-sex marriage. In 2003, in the case of *Goodridge v. Department of Health*, the court in Massachusetts held that it was illegal to deny same-sex partners the right to marry, making Massachusetts the first state to legalize same-sex marriage. Vermont passed a law enabling same-sex partners to obtain many of the same rights as heterosexual married couples in civil unions, and in 2009, the state legislature recognized same-sex marriage. California joined Vermont as a civil union state when it passed the Domestic Partner Rights and Responsibilities Act of 2003 giving same-sex couples the same legal rights and responsibilities as their heterosexual counterparts. New York and New Jersey legalized same-sex marriage a few years after Massachusetts. In 2012, ballot measure voters approved same-sex marriage in Maine, Maryland, and Washington (Frank, 2014). In *Obergefell v. Hodges* (2015), a case which consolidated six lower court cases from Kentucky, Michigan, Ohio, and Tennessee, the Supreme Court found that the constitutional rights of same-sex couples were violated as a result of laws prohibiting same-sex marriage. As a result, same-sex marriage became legal in all 50 states and U.S. territories, overturning DOMA. However, in states such as Alabama, some judges refused to marry anyone rather than to facilitate a same-sex union (Elliot, 2018).

Although same-sex marriage is legal across the country, many other challenges exist for LGBTQ+ families and those who work with them. Recent legislation at the state level has included banning conversion therapy (which claims, counter to research evidence, to be able to "convert" people from gay to straight), bills that affect access to adoption and other family planning services for those who are LGBTQ+, and legislation to protect those who are transgender from discrimination. What is happening this year in your state about family issues relating to people who are LGBTQ+?

OPPORTUNITIES FOR ADVOCACY

In this section, we look at advocacy related to abortion and family planning. This is an area that affects multiple areas of social work practice, from school social workers who may interact with teens considering or starting sexual activity, to those working with survivors of sexual assault who have concerns about pregnancy and emergency contraception, to health care social workers interacting with families who are navigating planned pregnancies with risks to the health of the mother. Before you read this section, we recommend that you start by considering your own knowledge and views on pregnancy and abortion. We recommend reviewing the official NASW statement on abortion policy in *Social Work Speaks* to get a sense of the profession's formal statements on this issue.

Advocacy and Family Planning

There is room for advocacy around abortion and family planning on a national and international level. In many places, women have both poor family planning options and limited or no access to abortion even in the case when their own life is at risk. Planned Parenthood and Planned Parenthood International are nonprofits that take leadership positions in such advocacy in favor of abortion access, although not without controversy within the United States. The Center for Reproductive Rights and Amnesty International also provide leadership through research and advocacy around reproductive rights.

Laws regarding abortion vary significantly across the world. As described above, in the United States, women have the right to seek abortions, but many federal and state initiatives. such as parental consent and waiting periods, are designed to limit women's access, as does the lack of available health clinics in states such as Texas and the majority of U.S. counties. Some countries, such as Canada, understand abortion as a component of a woman's right to control her own body and make her own medical decisions. In Canada, as a result of national health insurance combined with understandings of abortion as a matter of women's autonomy, abortion is easily accessible. Other countries have laws that are based on religious beliefs that view abortion as infanticide due to a belief that a fetus is a separate living entity from the moment of conception. In contrast, Chile, Egypt, El Salvador, Iran, Nicaragua, and the Philippines ban abortion in all instances. Other countries with restrictive abortion policies include Nigeria and Senegal, where abortion is illegal except when a mother's life is in danger. Many of these countries are religious states (Center for Reproductive Rights, 2019). See Figure 4.2 to review an overview of abortion laws in countries throughout the world.

Final Discussion

Now that you have finished reading this chapter, reread the vignette at the beginning. Based on what you have learned, answer the following questions. Point to specific references in the chapter that help you answer these questions. Consider how different theories inform the response to these questions.

1. How does Susie define her family? If she is pregnant, and decides to have the baby, how could this change?
2. What laws would protect Susie if she decided that she did not want to carry her pregnancy to term?
3. What rights might Susie and John have as teenage parents, and how might their rights be limited?
4. If Susie decides to have the baby and give it up for adoption, what support from governmental or private agencies should she expect to receive? Does it matter where she lives?
5. What role might race, class, gender, and other aspects of identity play in this vignette?

5

CHILD WELFARE POLICY

LEARNING OBJECTIVES

5.1: Summarize how child welfare has been practiced throughout U.S. history

5.2: Explain how current state and federal child welfare policy laws apply to social work practice

5.3: Describe the benefit of child sensitive protocols for U.S. child welfare

5.4: Determine opportunities for advocacy using research on social problems surrounding the well-being of children

For many, the title *social worker* conjures up an image of people entering others' homes to remove their children. Despite the facts that (1) many social workers work outside this field and (2) many child welfare workers are not trained social workers, the profession of social work has been deeply intertwined with the history of child welfare policy. We use the term *child welfare* to describe the state acting in its role as ***parens patriae***, or the protector of those who are vulnerable and cannot protect themselves. This role is balanced against other important state roles, such as the responsibility for safeguarding the rights of individuals, families, and communities. Striking such a balance can be difficult, particularly when assessments of what constitutes appropriate parenting are influenced by values, beliefs, and political considerations. This chapter begins with the history of child welfare from orphanages and workhouses and continues through the development of current child welfare agencies.

***Parens patriae*:** A Latin term describing the state as protector of those who are vulnerable and cannot protect themselves

In this chapter, we examine how government responses to child welfare were often fed by underlying fears around immigration and urbanization, and by efforts to reform and change individuals and families who struggled to survive and adapt in a capitalist system with few safety nets. As Lindsey (2004) poignantly describes in his in-depth critical history, the U.S. child welfare system has been fundamentally **residual**, meaning it seeks only to meet the needs of individuals in the most dire crises. This is in stark contrast to systems that take a comprehensive approach through the provision of ongoing and regular supports to encourage optimal growth and well-being of children and families, which are often referred

Residual (policy): A policy that seeks only to intervene or meet the needs of individuals in the direct crises (in contrast, see **institutional** policy)

Institutional (policy): Approaches that see intervention or regulation as a regular and appropriate function of government (in contrast, see **residual** policy)

to as **institutional.** Institutional approaches see intervention or regulation as a regular and appropriate function of government. This chapter pays special attention to how child welfare has been understood and practiced. Native American and African American families and communities, who have been and continue to be disproportionately affected by child welfare policies, have often challenged government policy. This chapter examines how and why the state simultaneously strives to protect children and reunify families by focusing on parental behavior, while ignoring the context in which child maltreatment occurs. It also reviews the impact of systemic problems such as poverty, housing inadequacy, and poor mental health services and delivery on child welfare. This chapter addresses recent state and federal supports and programming for children aging out of foster care, including the voluntary extension of foster care through the age of 21. It concludes with some areas for advocacy and a discussion of self-advocacy efforts by current and former foster youth.

Vignette: Social Work Responses to Families in Distress

Based on what you know from the media or your personal, work, or volunteer experiences, think about the following questions as you read the vignette. When you finish the vignette, answer the questions below.

1. What are the roles or responsibilities of the different professionals here (the teacher, Larry, his supervisor)?
2. What skills and training might Larry have from his BSW program that can help guide him in working with this family?
3. Who is Larry's client (the state? the family? the parents? the child/children)? What conflicting concerns might these stakeholders present?
4. What resources might this family benefit from, and who should provide them?
5. What role might race, class, gender, and other aspects of identity play in this vignette?

Larry recently graduated his BSW program and was in his first job with a local child welfare agency. He practiced in rural Oklahoma where he grew up and knew many of the families in his town. Recently, he received a call from a teacher in the local public school who was concerned about a student who was frequently absent, arrived in clothing that was too small and unclean, and seemed listless in the afternoon. Although the teacher had been concerned for the past few weeks, what prompted her call was her observation as a lunch duty monitor that the child did not have lunch for much of the week and relied on friends who shared their meals. Larry took the report, which he discussed with his supervisor. She advised him to visit the family during the day, while the child was in school. Larry arrived at the child's home and was greeted by her parents. When he told them about the reason for his visit, they were distraught. The mother told Larry that they were both unemployed and had been threatened with eviction and water and electrical shutoffs. They were told they were ineligible for cash support through Temporary Assistance for Needy Families (TANF), and their unemployment benefits have come to an end. They had two younger children at home, one of whom required medical care and equipment, which limited their ability to enter the shelter system (such that it was in their rural county) or move in with friends, should they be evicted. Larry knew that legally children should not be separated from their families as a result of poverty. He also knew that the children's health and well-being may be compromised. He was particularly worried about the child with medical needs. With a heavy heart and some confusion about his mandate as a child welfare worker, Larry drove back to the office to consult with his supervisor.

HISTORY AND SOCIAL CONSTRUCTION OF U.S. CHILD WELFARE POLICY

While initially designed to respond to the needs of orphaned children, the U.S. child welfare system has changed, over time, to respond to children who are abandoned, neglected, abused, or victims of poverty. In this section, we look at the changing U.S. child welfare system from the Orphan Trains to modern child welfare. The treatment of children by the state has changed as views of children have developed from that of a liability or property to objects of nurturing and care. Institutions and systems have evolved and changed as children, originally seen as laborers, are now seen as unable to care for themselves both globally and in the United States (Schneider & Macy, 2002).

From the Colonial Era Through Urbanizing America

In early U.S. history, the majority of what we would consider child welfare centered on orphaned children. The state of medical knowledge combined with high rates of infection and disease, including maternal mortality rates in childbirth, led to far more orphans than we see today (Lindsey, 2004). The introduction of smallpox and other European diseases to indigenous American populations also resulted in the death of care providers for children (Schneider & Macey, 2002; but see below section). The population of children labeled "orphans," however, also included many—perhaps even a majority—of children with one or two living parents who were unable to care for them, often due to ill health or poverty. The death of a breadwinning father or a caregiving mother was a common reason for temporary or permanent child dependency on the state.

In the country's early years, indigent children could be employed as indentured servants for their labor, as we describe in Chapter 9. Not only were U.S. children placed out in this manner, poor children dependent on local governments in England were sent as indentured servants to the United States and other colonies. Initially, there were no institutions specifically designed for children and they were therefore placed in almshouses or workhouses with adults. Where asylums for the mentally ill were available, orphaned children were also placed in these institutions. No attention was paid to developmental needs or supervision and protection of children, who were often at the mercy of adult residents and older children. Many suffered terribly. The following description was provided to the 1884 National Conference on Social Welfare:

> A group of boys were found in the wash-house, intermingled with the inmates, and around the cauldrons where the dirty clothes were boiling. Here was an insane woman raving and uttering wild gibberings; a half crazy man was sardonically grinning; and an overgrown idiotic boy was torturing one of the little boys, while securely holding him, by thrusting splinters under his finger-nails. The cries of the little one seemed to delight his tormentor as well as some of the older inmates who were looking on. The upper apartment of this dilapidated building was used for a sleeping-room. An inmate was scrubbing the floor, which was so worn that water came through the cracks in continuous droppings upon the heads of the little ones below, who did not seem to regard it as a serious annoyance. (Letchworth, 1894, p.133)

Early reformers used difficult conditions such as those described above as an impetus to create dedicated institutions and programming for children.

Orphanages and Orphan Trains

While the earliest recorded orphanage on U.S. soil appeared in 1660 in New Amsterdam (now called New York City), they greatly expanded at the turn of the 18th century (Schneider & Macey, 2002). Widespread calls for orphanages began in the middle of the 1800s as part of the larger asylum movement to create stabilizing institutions in an increasingly diverse and growing country (Rothman, 1971). Orphan asylums were specifically designed to separate children from those deemed mentally ill or criminal, as well as from those who were placed in workhouses to receive indoor aid. In this respect they represented a significant improvement. Often started by religious orders, progressive reformers, and philanthropists, the best orphanages sought to provide care as well as some education and, more frequently, to prepare orphans to learn the skills of a trade. However, there was little oversight and conditions in the institutions were often poor. Illness, neglect, and overcrowding were common. Sensationalized reports of abuse over time led to a preference for care within communities and families over care in large institutions. As with earlier periods, likely the majority of children were not in fact orphans but were instead children whose parents were temporarily or permanently unable to care for them (Ramey, 2012).

Beginning in 1854 and continuing to the 1930s, it is estimated over 150,000 children were transported from cities to the rural United States and Canada on what are called "orphan trains" (Cook, 1995). Charles Loring Brace, a Protestant minister who founded the Children's Aid Society (CAS), began this system of *placing out* in response to a combination of social needs, fears, and opportunities. Brace and other reformers painted a bleak picture of children and adolescents in poor urban environments, whom they viewed as highly susceptible to sin and vice. These youth, many of whom were the children of immigrants, were feared as a threat to middle-class respectability. As was the case with orphan asylums, the term *orphan* included children who were considered abandoned, abused, or neglected. The emergence of trains able to travel west made the large scale transfer of urban youth possible; this coincided with a romanticization of farm life as pastoral and healthy, particularly in contrast to crowded cities that were considered a breeding ground for disease and bad habits (Holt, 1992).

> The founders of the Children's Aid Society early saw that the best of all Asylums for the outcast child, is the *farmer's home* . . . . The United States have the enormous advantage over all other countries, in the treatment of difficult questions of pauperism and reform,

> that they possess a practically unlimited area of arable land. The demand for labor on this land is beyond any present supply. Moreover, the cultivators of the soil are in America our most solid and intelligent class. From the nature of their circumstances, their laborers, or "help," must be members of their families, and share in their social tone. It is, accordingly, of the utmost importance to them to train up children who shall aid in their work, and be associates of their own children. A servant who is nothing but a servant, would be, with them, disagreeable and inconvenient. They like to educate their own "help." With their overflowing supply of food also, each new mouth in the household brings no drain on their means. Children are a blessing, and the mere feeding of a young boy or girl is not considered at all. (Brace, 1872)

While reformers appealed to religious notions of charity in recruiting farmers to take in children from the cities, they also clearly appealed to the value of the children's labor. Most children sent on the orphan trains were adolescent boys. Photo 5.1 depicts orphan children age 7 and up picking cotton at a Baptist orphanage farm in Texas.

Farm work had its own dangers and was often difficult. Due to the dispersed nature of rural communities and the great distance from the sending agencies, there was little oversight of children once they arrived at their destinations. Generally, children sent on the orphan trains were not sent to specific, vetted families, but rather groups of children were met at train stations across the country where they would be examined and chosen by whoever arrived to greet them. The literature shows that, as a group, their experiences varied widely. Some were subject to harsh labor and poor conditions; some ran away to seek their fortunes in mines or elsewhere. Others were taken in by families who treated the children as their own and found new and rewarding lives. Regardless, most were severed from their communities and cultures of origin.

Diane Creagh (2012) describes a Catholic variation on the CAS's orphan trains. Concerned by the growing number of abandoned infants, many of whom perished, Sister Mary Irene Fitzgibbon opened the Foundling Asylum in New York City. As the Foundling Asylum grew, and more babies survived with the advent of proper care and better medical attention, the Foundling Asylum began to place older infants and toddlers whose health was stabilized so the asylum could absorb new babies. The orphan trains were not a viable option for those who sought to keep Catholic children within the faith (Cook, 1995). Brace refused to place children with Catholic families due to prejudice; the orphan trains also did not take such young children (Creagh, 2012). Because these children were not yet able and ready to provide farm labor, and due to the desire to raise Catholic children within their faith, the Foundling's "baby trains" appealed to the altruism and faith of fostering families. This also meant that families were vetted before children were placed, and children were prematched with the Catholic families who were to take them in. As with Brace's orphan trains for older children, the treatment of children and the level of oversight varied greatly.

National Child Labor Committee collection, Library of Congress, Prints and Photographs Division [LC-DIG-nclc-0021]

PHOTO 5.1 A group of boys, aged seven and older, work in the cotton field of the Baptist Orphanage, near Waxahachie, Texas.

The demise of the orphan trains was due to a combination of factors (Cook, 1995). There was a growing recognition that environmental conditions such as poverty affected the ability to parent rather than only individual failing. Improvements in working conditions, the beginnings of public education, and the creation of albeit minimal safety nets, together with improved health and medical care (including safer childbirth), allowed more families to care for their own children. The orphan trains, which were, overall, an improvement over prior systems of care and an important response to need, were also plagued by critical press. Stories that highlighted religious and social reformers' prejudices as well as the dangers of placing out came to outweigh stories of success. A changing agricultural landscape also reduced the availability of families to absorb children from the cities. By the 1930s, the use of orphan trains had largely ended with the beginnings of modern child welfare systems. You can find online and library resources to learn more about where children who rode the orphan train traveled, what their hopes were, and how they fared.

THE MODERN CHILD WELFARE SYSTEM

During the Progressive Era, many charitable organizations such as Brace's Children's Aid Society were started in an effort to assist families. The precursors to modern social workers, "friendly visitors," were primarily middle- and upper-class women who found charitable work one of the few acceptable outlets for their intellect and desire for engagement outside of the home. Indeed, it is precisely because the work of nurturing and assistance to families was viewed as consistent with what were seen as maternal duties that it was an accepted vocation.

The Charity Organization Societies (COS), described in Chapter 1, sought to anchor friendly visiting practices in what they called "scientific charity." COS objected to indiscriminate giving and developed methods to evaluate whether families deserved aid. They also encouraged charitable organizations to use assistance to refashion their recipients' character. According to COS, friendly visitors were to provide not only (or even primarily) material assistance, but also advice, encouragement, and training. Those considered deserving were largely white women who had been widowed or deserted by their husbands. While needs derived most often from poverty, the task of the friendly visitor was to build character and imbue their charges with particular religious or moral values. Linda Gordon (1994) describes how destitute families often had little choice but to invite friendly visitors into their homes. These families gave up privacy, becoming subject to intrusive surveillance and instruction on parenting, character, and habits that were rooted in class-based and anti-immigrant sentiment, in exchange for much-needed material relief. This work of the COS movement was further professionalized by the establishment and adoption of Mary Richmond's (1922) method of social casework. **Social casework** focused on interactions with individuals and families. A foundational method of social work practice, social case work provided a systematic way to diagnose a problem to target an appropriate cure. One of its most vocal early critics was Bertha Capen Reynolds (1939), who felt that social case work methods created ethical conflicts for social workers by training them to encourage client compliance rather than working as allies alongside people to change social structures. The vision and influence of the COS was reflected in the beginnings of modern child welfare. First, it combined assistance with support and, when considered necessary, intervention that could include temporary or permanent separation of families (Lindsey, 2004). Second, it viewed itself as a professional endeavor and sought recognition through the establishment of professional training and practice.

Social casework: Developed by Mary Richmond, social casework was a systematic method focused on interactions with individuals and families

The child welfare system originally was conceived broadly to incorporate the well-being of children within families. The Children's Bureau, created and initially led by social work foremothers such as Julia Lathrop, instituted a variety of programs. One curbed infant mortality by more than half over a 40-year period through education and training that led to better hygiene and increasing availability of prenatal and postnatal maternal and infant care (often considered the beginning of the public health movement). Another began to administer financial assistance to mothers with dependent children. In addition, the Children's Bureau created home visiting programs to train mothers how to care for their homes and children (see Photo 5.2).

This combination of services and functions did not last long. If you look at our current systems, functions related to health and well-being are under the auspices of one agency, while functions related to financial support—what we colloquially have come to refer to as *welfare*—are seen as separate and independent functions of *other* agencies. For purposes of this chapter, what is most important is that child welfare came to be seen as synonymous with good parenting and shifted its attention to whether or not parents (largely mothers) were able to provide for their children's basic well-being.

Library of Congress, LC-DIG-npcc-24900

PHOTO 5.2 Children's Bureau (11/28/23)

The first reported case in which the state removed a child from the care of a legal guardian specifically for abuse was Mary Ellen McCormick (Markel & M.D., 2009). Mary Ellen's case was taken up by the Society for the Protection of Cruelty to Animals (SPCA) because there was no existing child welfare agency at the time. The SPCA filed a petition with the court, who responded to Mary Ellen's egregious and documented abuse by removing her from her adoptive mother. This led to the formation of the New York Society for the Prevention of Cruelty to Children (NYSPCC). The NYSPCC, founded in 1875, was the first agency dedicated to the protection of children from abuse and neglect (New York Society for the Prevention of Cruelty to Children [NYSPCC], 2017). This was followed by the creation of other charitable organizations dedicated to helping children who may be neglected or abused by their caregivers. As often happens today, Mary Ellen's initial removal did not fully ameliorate her situation, although she was ultimately adopted by a caring family and herself became the mother of both biological and adopted children (Markel & M.D., 2009).

Eventually, states began to take a role in the protection of children from neglect and abuse. By the 1950s, most states had created child protective service agencies with workers who had the authority to enter families' homes and place children and families under supervision and surveillance when there was a suspicion of abuse or neglect. If deemed necessary, these agencies were also entitled to remove children from their families temporarily or, in some circumstances, permanently. As Duncan Lindsey (2004) describes, due to lack of resources and a strong belief in the authority of the family as protected from state intervention, child welfare has always been a residual function of government. This means that the government can and will step in only when all else has failed.

REFLECTION

SOCIAL WORK PRACTICE TENSIONS

The tensions raised around social casework have continued into social work today. Form groups that have students who are interested in micro, mezzo, and macro practice.

- How are the tensions we describe above reflected in different types of social work practice?
- How might social workers who practice individual therapy or case management tap into broader social change?
- How might social workers who practice in the areas of community organizing or policy change engage with individuals?
- What kinds of alliances might clinical and macro practice social workers form to address issues that relate to child and family well-being?

Current Child Welfare Policies

Parents and other legal guardians are responsible for the basic welfare of their children. Legislation outlines specific responsibilities, such as compulsory school attendance and child support payments. Legislation also outlines liability for criminal abuse and neglect, including sexual abuse. In this chapter, we focus specifically on the role of child protective services for implementing civil child abuse and neglect statutes. This includes investigating and screening reports of child maltreatment and planning for and working with parents, children, foster, kinship, and adoptive parents. Table 5.3 at the end of this section provides a list of key federal child welfare laws by topic, many of which we also describe here in greater detail.

In its 2016 Child Maltreatment report, the U.S Department of Health and Human Services (2017) reported the following statistics:

- The national estimate of children who received a child protective services investigation response or alternative response increased 9.5% from 2012 (3,172,000) to 2016 (3,472,000).
- The number and rate of victims have fluctuated during the past 5 years. Comparison of the national rounded number of victims from 2012 (656,000) to the national estimate of victims in 2016 (676,000) shows an increase of 3.0%.
- Three-quarters (74.8%) of victims were neglected, 18.2% were physically abused, and 8.5% were sexually abused.
- In 2016, a nationally estimated 1,750 children died of abuse and neglect at a rate of 2.36 per 100,000 children in the national population. (Children's Bureau, 2016a, p. ii)

These figures provide a sense of the scope and type of U.S. child welfare concerns and current trends.

The federal government's initial involvement in the area of abuse and neglect was through the Social Security Act, which included Aid to Dependent Children (ADC) and its later incarnation Aid to Families with Dependent Children (AFDC). This legislation provided money

TABLE 5.1 ■ Children in Poverty by Race and Ethnicity

Race	Data Type	2007	2008	2009	2010	2011	2012	2013	2014	2015	2016
American Indian	Percentage	33	31	35	35	37	37	37	36	34	34
Asian and Pacific Islander	Percentage	12	12	13	38	39	15	14	13	13	12
Black or African American	Percentage	35	34	36	38	39	40	39	38	36	34
Hispanic or Latino	Percentage	27	28	31	32	34	34	33	32	31	28
Non-Hispanic White	Percentage	11	11	12	13	14	14	14	13	12	12
Two or more races	Percentage	19	19	20	23	24	24	23	22	21	20
Total	Percentage	18	18	20	22	23	23	22	22	21	19

Data provided by National Kids Count

to states for use in their own child abuse and neglect prevention and intervention efforts. The first federal legislation that regulated (rather than merely provided funding for) child abuse and neglect was the Child Abuse and Prevention Act (CAPTA) of 1974 (PL 93-247). It was most recently reauthorized in 2010. As stated in the introduction:

> It has long been recognized that parents have a fundamental liberty, protected by the Constitution, to raise their children as they choose. The legal framework regarding the parent-child relationship balances the rights and responsibilities among the parents, the child, and the State, as guided by Federal statutes. This parent-child relationship identifies certain rights, duties, and obligations, including the responsibility of the parents to protect the child's safety and well-being. If parents, however, are unable or unwilling to meet this responsibility, the State has the power and authority to take action to protect the child from harm. (U.S. Department of Health and Human Services, Administration for Children and Families, Administration on Children, Youth and Families, Children's Bureau, 2010, p. 2)

CAPTA defines child maltreatment "at a minimum, [as] any recent act or failure to act on the part of a parent or caretaker, which results in death, serious physical or emotional harm, sexual abuse or exploitation, or an act or failure to act which presents an imminent risk of serious harm" (42 U.S.C.A. § 5106g). CAPTA sets minimum standards for child abuse and neglect, requiring all states to have a system designed to intervene on behalf of children, with guidelines designed to balance parents' rights with the duty of the state to intervene in its role as *parens patriae*. It also set up mechanisms to track and aggregate state level data. The U.S. Department of Health and Human Services Agency for Children and Families Child Welfare Information Gateway website is a reliable source of federal and state data as well as research and information on child welfare policies and programs.

States have wide discretion to implement child welfare laws. In general, states investigate when a suspicion of child abuse or neglect is reported. While anyone can file a report of child maltreatment, all U.S. states have laws that designate people in certain professions or roles, including social workers, teachers, and medical professionals, as **mandatory reporters**, meaning that they have a duty to report a suspicion that a child is being abused or neglected (Children's Bureau, 2015). As a social worker, you must familiarize yourself with the law in your state because the content and process for reporting varies. For example, if a mandated professional in Alaska files a report with her supervisor, this does not relieve her of the responsibility; she must report the incident directly to the relevant agency herself. However, a mandated reporter in Georgia may discharge this duty by reporting to the person in charge of the facility or their designee (Children's Bureau, 2015). Not sure what the rules are in your state? The Child Welfare Information Gateway provides a state-by-state list of statutes that it updates periodically.

Mandatory reporter: A person who by virtue of their profession is obligated to report a suspicion that a child is being abused or neglected

Once a report is filed, the local child protective services (CPS) agencies screen the report. Reports can either be screened out or be placed within the supervisory authority of CPS. Some agencies also provide for voluntary family preservation services, which are designed to assist families who might be struggling but do not reach the level of a "founded" report of child abuse or neglect. When CPS places families under mandated supervision, cases may be tracked according to the assessment of risk. Levels of supervision and intervention vary with the perceived type and severity of risk. Some children remain in their homes. Children who are removed from their home may be placed in foster care, with relatives or kin, or in a congregate care facility such as a group home. Once a child is removed from the home, the CPS agency must file a report with the dependency court, which oversees the process and adjudicates in the case where the removal or any facet of the process is disputed (Children's Bureau, 2016b). Parties to child welfare cases are multiple: They include the CPS agency, the child, and at least one parent. Where the parents' interests may differ, they may be viewed as separate stakeholders. Whether or not all parties' interests are recognized as separate may depend on the state. In some jurisdictions there may be both an attorney who represents the child and a person appointed to represent what is considered the best interest of a child, which may be different from what the child wants. **Court-appointed special advocates** (CASAs) or ***guardians ad litem*** (names and exact roles vary by jurisdiction) are volunteers who may be appointed by the courts to safeguard the best interest of the child and may also be involved in child welfare cases (National CASA Association, 2019).

Court-appointed special advocate (CASA) (see also ***guardian ad litem***): A trained volunteer who is appointed by the court to represent the best interest of the child

In 2016, over 437,000 children were in foster care (U.S. Department of Health and Human Services, Administration for Children and Families, Administration on Children, Youth and Families, Children's Bureau, 2017). Similar numbers entered (273,539) and exited (250,248) foster care during that same year. Some groups are overrepresented in foster care; these same groups fare worse in almost all respects, including services that they (and their families) are provided and outcomes. One group is racial and ethnic minorities; we discuss African American and Native American children and families in greater detail below. Another group that is overrepresented in foster care is LGBTQ+ youth (Van Leeuwen et al., 2006; Wilson, Cooper, Kastanis, & Nezhad, 2014). Like other vulnerable youth, LGBTQ+ youth often have a harder time while in foster care with higher rates of victimization and multiple placements. They may also have fewer social supports and more difficulties when they exit care, including homelessness (Robinson, 2018).

Foster care and other forms of placement are designed to be temporary. Children remain under the supervision of CPS while the agency works with the family, under the review of the courts, toward reunification. Courts are required by law to review child welfare cases every 6 months at minimum and to engage with the child on those occasions to the extent possible given the child's age. There are two possible permanent outcomes for child-welfare involved children, broadly speaking. The first is remaining or reunifying with the child's family of origin, which has been the preferred goal under the law since the enactment of the Adoption Assistance and Child Welfare Act of 1980 (Anyon, 2011). This occurs when CPS and/or the court determines that the family of origin can meet minimum standards of care. The second option is **termination of parental rights** (TPR), which severs the *legal* ties between the parent and the child. This means that the child may be legally adopted by another family.

Termination of parental rights (TPR): Severs the *legal* ties between the parent and the child. This means that the child may be legally adopted by another family.

In 2016, 57,208 children were adopted with public agency involvement nationwide (U.S. Department of Health and Human Services, Administration for Children and Families, Administration on Children, Youth and Families, Children's Bureau, 2017). TPR does not guarantee that a child will in fact be adopted or find a stable home. In particular, older children, racial minorities, and children with special needs may not find adoptive parents. Older children may not want to be adopted. Some family members or kin who serve in a foster role may want to continue to do so without legally and officially severing the ties of their relative or friend. In such cases children must avail themselves of other options, such as continued foster or kinship care, independent living arrangements, or group homes.

Among the most recent changes to CAPTA were in the 1997 Adoption and Safe Families Act (ASFA), which was designed to balance between the preferred goal of reunification of families and the perceived detriment of children remaining in the limbo status of foster care for lengthy periods. ASFA described the obligations of CPS agencies:

> Reasonable efforts shall be made to preserve and reunify families
>
> (i) prior to the placement of a child in foster care, to prevent or eliminate the need for removal of the child from the child's home; and
>
> (ii) to make it possible for a child to safely return to the child's home (Adoption and Safe Families Act [ASFA], §101[B], 1997)

Together with the requirement of reasonable efforts, ASFA also put time limits on reaching these goals. According to ASFA, CPS agencies must petition for TPR for children who have been in care for 15 of the prior 22 months. Despite a declared policy preference for children to remain or reunify with their families of origin, ASFA also made it possible for agencies to work with families toward reunification at the same time as it sought permanent adoptive placements, a process that is called *concurrent planning*.

Current statistics indicate that foster care placement is on the rise. Many attribute this growth to the opioid epidemic, likening it to the crack cocaine epidemic in the 1980s, which was also considered to increase child welfare involvement. According to the Children's Bureau (2016c):

> Although there is variation in how States report factors that contribute to foster care cases, it appears that parental substance use may have contributed to the growth in the child welfare population. From 2012 to 2015, the percentage of removals where parental substance use was cited as a contributing factor increased 13 percent (from 28.5 percent in 2012 to 32.2 percent in 2015)—the largest percentage increase compared to any other circumstance around removal.

Another report by the Children's Bureau (Radel, Baldwin, Crouse, Ghertner, & Waters, 2018) describes the complicated ways in which drug use can interact with child welfare involvement. For example, the lack of family-friendly treatment programs may precipitate involvement in the child welfare system if parents who seek treatment cannot do so while remaining with their children. Case workers overwhelmed with burgeoning caseloads may not be able to provide families with the attention they need to preserve or reunite families. There are also some indications that it is harder to address child abuse and neglect when it is accompanied by parental drug abuse.

Poverty and Child Welfare Involvement

While the law explicitly mandates that children should not be separated from their families because of poverty, poverty may in fact be a leading cause of child welfare involvement (Lindsey, 2004). In Eamon and Kopel's (2004) review of state court decisions, three of the four successful individual challenges to child welfare decisions were based on the finding that children were illegally removed from their parents because of poverty. Regardless of parents' intent or desire, they may be unable to meet their children's basic needs, including nutrition, shelter, or medical care, if they do not have sufficient financial resources (Photo 5.3 depicts a family experiencing homelessness).

©iStock/com/PickStock

PHOTO 5.3 Parents may be unable to provide for their children due to unforeseen circumstances. This family in Iowa was forced to evacuate their home due to a flood.

Sometimes poverty manifests itself in a lack of adequate housing, an inability to afford child care, and/or a lack of access to medical and mental health care, including addiction treatment, that may help parents avoid neglect and abuse. Think back to the vignette at the beginning of this chapter. Like many CPS workers, Larry may find himself in a bind, knowing that he has a duty to look out for children for whom parents are unable to provide minimum standards of care.

Housing is a useful example of how poverty can impact child welfare involvement. Rising housing costs, a decrease in affordable and adequate homes, and a dwindling number of public housing spots create challenges for many low-income families. Families living below, at, or even above the poverty line increasingly spend larger portions of their income on housing (Joint Center for Housing Studies, 2018). This leaves fewer financial resources for other expenses such as medical or child care, clothing, and school supplies. Inadequate housing is consistently correlated with substantiated findings of child abuse and child neglect (Freisthler, Merritt, & LaScala, 2006). Housing problems can precipitate admission into temporary care, as well as result in delayed or failed reunification with parents (Cohen-Schlanger, Fitzpatrick, Hulchanski, & Raphael, 1995; Shdaimah, 2009). Once families become child-welfare involved, their housing comes under scrutiny, even if housing deficiencies were not the reason for their initial involvement (Reich, 2005, pp. 130–132). Child welfare involvement itself may also jeopardize existing housing arrangements. For example, parents whose children are removed may lose public housing slots. In a proverbial Catch-22, if and when these same parents are deemed ready to reunify with their children, they may not be reunified due to lack of adequate housing (Shdaimah, 2009). We discuss housing and homelessness more in Chapter 14.

Child welfare agencies and child welfare professionals who want to help families remain together or to reunify families after children have been removed often cannot address housing problems. They have limited resources with which to help families, and policies and structural impediments, such as limiting criteria for federal housing programs, work against them (Harburger & White, 2004; Shdaimah, 2009). The same is true for most other aspects of poverty. The current federal child welfare policy has, until recently, been internally contradictory. It allowed for provision of financial resources to foster parents, while failing to make them available to families of origin to support the stated preference of the law, which was to keep children in their homes and to reunify separated families. The Family First Preservation Act, a bipartisan bill signed into law by President Trump in 2018, should change this. It allows states to use federal foster care dollars on prevention programs for parents, including addiction treatment, parenting and counseling programs, and mental health treatment. The new policy went into effect in October 2018. This bill was a culmination of years of effort on the part of advocates and was the result of a compromise that paired a reduction in the use of congregate care (group settings) (supported by Republican Senator Orrin Hatch) and provision of funding for families of origin (supported by Democratic Senator Ron Wyden) (Kelly, 2018; McCarthy, 2018). It is too early to tell whether and how this will impact rates of reunification.

Race in Child Welfare

African American children were initially excluded from the rescue impulses of early child welfare efforts. However, as policies focusing on child abuse and neglect were established first at the state and then federal level, the numbers of child-welfare involved African American children began to climb. In 1972, as part of the larger civil rights movement, the National Association of Black Social Workers (NABSW) drew attention to the disproportionate number of African American children under the supervision of child protective services. They were particularly concerned not only with the removal of individual children from their families, but also from the cumulative impact on the larger community through the growing number of foster and adoptive placements with white families (Oliver, 2014). Today, it is widely acknowledged that African American children and families comprise a larger proportion of child-welfare involved families than their representation in the general population, and receive **disparate treatment**, meaning they are treated differently than their white counterparts (Duarte & Summers, 2012).

Disparate treatment: Treating different groups differently, often considered a manifestation of discrimination or prejudice

Disproportionate rates of placement are likely driven by the intertwined nature of race-based discrimination and poverty and their impact on child and family well-being. Table 5.1 above shows ongoing and stark differences between rates of non-Hispanic white children, who have the lowest rates poverty at around 12% to 13%, as compared to African American children, who have the highest rates of poverty, hovering around 35%.

Poverty as associated with race cannot fully explain the disproportionate child welfare involvement with children of color. NABSW and other advocates have pointed to racism as a factor in differential levels of surveillance, perception of abuse and neglect by reporters, as well as to responses to child welfare allegations, including allocation of resources to help families remain together or reunify. They also decried the impact of the removal of African American children from cultural communities as damaging to children's racial identity formation in a racialized society, as well as a source of ongoing trauma to the families and communities from which they are separated (Roberts, 2002). Despite widespread attention to racial disparities, a recent review of the literature reveals its persistence at all stages of child welfare case processing.

> Levels of disproportionality tend to increase at every subsequent stage after a maltreatment report is substantiated. African American children (1) are more likely than youth of other racial/ethnic backgrounds to be placed in out-of-home care rather than to receive in-home services; (2) experience more frequent changes in placement; (3) are less likely to reunify with birth parents; and (4) tend to have longer stays in foster care. Disparities for African American children have also been extensively documented. Previous studies indicate that African American children and families receive fewer and lower quality services, fewer foster parent support services, fewer contacts by caseworkers, less access to mental health services and less access to drug treatment services when compared to other racial/ethnic groups. (Boyd, 2014, p. 15, citations omitted)

Yolanda Anyon (2011) explains how tensions around the causes of and solutions to racial disparities are grounded in larger tensions surrounding the function of child protective services, which is illustrated in Table 5.2. Anyon identifies four main policy perspectives (Column 1) with corresponding outcome goals (Column 2). The means to achieve each goal are different, as are the targets of intervention (Columns 3 and 4). In an ideal world with optimal resources, these goals and the means to achieve them would not be in conflict.

For example, it is easy to see that speedy resolution of child welfare cases only conflicts with cultural continuity when there are more African American children coming into the system than there are adoptive African American families. If sufficient resources—including political will—were devoted to tackling these problems, then they might not be in conflict. However, in the United States we have never devoted sufficient resources to any of these foster care goals.

The Multiethnic Placement Act (MEPA) (1994) and the Interethnic Adoption Provisions Act (IEPA) (1996) provide evidence of U.S. policy priorities (Shakeshaft, 2018). These laws were enacted in response to public outcry over children spending extended periods of time in foster care, deemed to be a result of child welfare agencies prioritizing cultural continuity through requirements or preferences for racial matching over permanent placements. Such practices were also subject to discrimination-based court challenges from white families who were denied permission to adopt nonwhite children. MEPA made it illegal to discriminate in foster care or adoption proceedings on the basis of race or ethnicity (or national origin), to delay proceedings to identify racially or ethnically matched families, or to require that caseworkers justify adoptions that are transracial (Anyon, 2011). IEPA made these prohibitions stronger and created a right to sue if race is considered in planning for permanency.

TABLE 5.2 ■ Characteristics of the Four Policy Perspectives

Policy Perspective	Developmental Outcome Prioritized	Framing the Problem of Disproportionalities and Disparities	Preferred Intervention Strategies
Expedient permanency	• Stable attachment	• Exit dynamics—unrealistic efforts to reunify troubled families or find foster youth racially matched adoptive parents • Exit dynamics—insufficient pool of African American adoptive families	• Color-blind placement decisions • Exemptions for providing reasonable efforts toward reunification • Timelines for terminating parental rights • Concurrent permanency planning • Adoption incentives
Social advantage	• Long-term self-sufficiency	• Exit dynamics—undue emphasis on biological and community connections in placement decisions	• Placement decisions that emphasize prospective families' access to material and social capital • Out-of-origin community placements • Adoption incentives
Cultural continuity	• Positive racial identity	• Entry dynamics—history of racism and ongoing discrimination in the child welfare system and society at large • Exit dynamics—barriers faced by African American families wanting to adopt	• Race matching in placement decisions • Targeted recruitment of African American foster and adoptive parents • Cultural competency training for transracial adoptive parents • Subsidized kinship care
Family preservation	• Biological connections	• Entry dynamics—risk factors and related stress disproportionately experienced by African American families who lack the resources necessary for providing stability and safety	• Concrete prevention and reunification services • Subsidized kinship care • Open adoption

Source: Reprinted from Children and Youth Services Review, Vol 33, Yolanda Anyon, Reducing racial disparities and disproportionalities in the child welfare system: Policy perspectives about how to serve the best interests of African American youth, Pages 242-253, Copyright 2011, with permission from Elsevier.

Finally, IEPA required that states develop plans to recruit and train a diverse cadre of foster parents. MEPA/IEPA clearly and explicitly identified the chief concern regarding the plight of African American children as lengthy stays in foster care. These policy changes were designed to create a speedier path to permanency, while failing to address other facets of child welfare placement. This legislation is reinforced by the Adoption and Safe Families Act (ASFA, 1997) provisions described above, which are also designed to expedite permanent placements for children.

The Indian[1] Child Welfare Act (ICWA)

From our beginnings as a nation, the U.S. government tried to dismantle indigenous tribal structures, seize control of lands, and destroy the cultural integrity of indigenous communities. This began in earnest during the American Indian Wars, which started in the 1770s and lasted until the 1920s, while the United States fought with multiple tribes over land and control. As the U.S. government expanded the scope of its power, treaties with Indian tribes turned into executive orders designed to subjugate and control the lives of indigenous peoples. Over time, the federal government created assimilationist policies to incorporate indigenous peoples into U.S. political, economic, and social systems.

One major component of this assimilationist approach by the federal government was a series of efforts to Americanize indigenous children by forcibly removing them from their tribes and families at a young age. Beginning in 1878, the Bureau of Indian Affairs developed a network of boarding schools designed to hold children who were removed from their families and inculcate these children with dominant U.S. cultural values (Garner, 1993). Over several decades, government agents and reservation police seized indigenous children and forcibly removed them to schools over their parents' protests, while noncompliant parents were placed in jail or otherwise penalized. Although these schools provided an education that may not have been available on Indian reservations, they also deliberately deprived indigenous children of their cultural heritage to erode tribal integrity. The children were held at off-reservation boarding schools for periods of 4 years to 8 years and often denied visits by their parents or families (Johnson, 1999). Meanwhile, orphaned indigenous children were denied the opportunity to remain with their tribes and were placed in nonindigenous households. These practices continued late into the 20th century; between 1969 and 1974, 25% to 35% of all those who were defined as *American Indian* children continued to be separated from their families and placed in nonindigenous homes or other institutions (Johnson, 1999; Jones, 1995). In some states, indigenous children were placed outside of their homes at a rate more than 20 times the national average (Garner, 1993). Disproportionate involvement of indigenous children in the child welfare system continues.

The Indian Child Welfare Act (ICWA) represents the federal response to mounting pressure from activists who defined themselves as American Indian, who prior to the 1960s lacked a strong enough voice to attract the attention of a nation "unconcerned with the survival of Indian traditions or culture" (Johnson, 1999). Beginning in 1969, organizations such as Indians of All Tribes, led by graduates of boarding schools, mounted more than 70 protests in which they seized and occupied properties across the country (Johnson, 1999). In July 1970, President Richard Nixon strongly supported a policy of Indian self-determination in a message to Congress (Garner, 1993). In 1973, a 10-week confrontation between Indian activists and the U.S. Army at Wounded Knee highlighted the discrimination and alienation faced by indigenous peoples, as well as their call for greater autonomy (Johnson, 1999). It was in this sociopolitical context that ICWA was passed in 1978. ICWA aims to protect the best interests of indigenous children, families, and tribes by establishing federal requirements in relation to child custody proceedings involving what ICWA describes as Indian children. For example, ICWA affirms the right of Tribal Courts to oversee cases of adoption, abuse, and neglect involving children on reservation land and grants them preference in ruling on these proceedings.

[1]There is much debate within and outside of indigenous communities in the United States about the terms Native American, American Indian, and other terms. In general, we use the term indigenous or Native American throughout this chapter unless referring to the official law, which in the United States often still says "Indian," or to research that has used these or other categorical designations. For more information about this debate, see activist Russell Means' writing on this: http://compusci.com/indian/.

ICWA built on the knowledge and experience of activists, including many Native American lawyers and social workers who had worked with families torn apart through removal. However, not all those involved with child welfare knew about the tragedy of historic child removal policies. As Margaret Jacobs (2014) describes:

> To thousands of non-Indian Americans, the testimony of Indian activists and the passage of ICWA came as a shock. Many social workers, adoptive families, and nonprofit agency directors were accustomed to seeing themselves as caring rescuers. Now some perceived themselves anew through Indian eyes: as child snatchers. For some this was a sobering moment that led to self-question. Others resisted the implications of ICWA and opposed it wholeheartedly. For most Indians, the passage of ICWA brought a new mood of hopefulness as Indian social workers and tribal leaders organized to put the act into full effect. (p. 128)

The efficacy of ICWA in protecting indigenous children and preserving indigenous communities has been repeatedly been called into question by research. A study assessing ICWA compliance in 1988 found that ICWA did not reduce the flow of Indian children into non-Indian care. In fact, figures in 1987 reflect an increase in the percentage of children placed in nonindigenous care from the years prior (Johnson, 1999). Other research indicates that foster care placement rates for Indian children decreased in the 1980s, although they remained higher than those for non-Indian children (MacEachron, Gustavsson, Cross, & Lewis, 1996). Research in 2013 supports this conclusion, finding that although foster care placement of Indian children has continued to decrease, Indian children are still twice as likely to be in the foster care system than children in the general population (Summers & Wood, 2014). Because compliance is partial and may be slow, or because it might take time to identify a child as falling under the jurisdiction of ICWA, to identify relatives, or to solve complex legal issues, a number of cases have arisen where children were placed with non-Native American foster parents and the placements were challenged under ICWA. Such cases are difficult for all involved, whatever the outcome. They raise questions of individual and community belonging, the relative importance of cultural identity, the extent to which cumulative community impact should be considered, and the long-term consequences when cumulative community impact is ignored. For example, in *Adoptive Couple v. Baby Girl* (2013 U.S. LEXIS 4916), the court ruled that a noncustodial parent (in this case a father who was a registered member of the Cherokee Nation) could not invoke ICWA, and the child stayed with her adoptive parents. In another case, the California Supreme Court ordered that a Choctaw child be returned to live with biological relatives after 4 years with her foster family (Branson-Potts, 2016). To promote compliance with ICWA requirements, the Bureau of Indian Affairs proposed new regulations and ICWA guidelines in 2015 and again in 2016 (Bureau of Indian Affairs, 2018).

The case of ICWA demonstrates an ongoing need for the federal government to preserve and protect the welfare of indigenous communities, as well as the need to view and respond to not only individual cases but also broader policies. The treatment of Native American children and communities also show how what are sometimes promoted as beneficial attempts at rescue may (intentionally or inadvertently) serve as a cover for biased and discriminatory policies and policy implementation that oppresses and controls minority populations (Crofoot & Harris, 2012). Social workers are often at the front lines of such policies. The NASW Code of Ethics prioritizes cultural humility, social justice, and human dignity and requires that we engage in critical analysis of any policy and pay particular attention to voices of those who are most affected.

DISCUSSION

REMOVAL OF NATIVE AMERICAN CHILDREN

Think about the responses of different groups of social workers after learning of the systematic removal of Native American children.

1. What do you think are some of the feelings they might have had after learning of these stories, and why?
2. How might a stance of cultural humility have changed well-intentioned social work practice with Native American children?
3. Provide an example of a more recent instance of policy-guided social work practice that might cause unintended harm.
   a. Which groups are impacted by this policy?
   b. Who are the different actors or agencies in charge of carrying it out?
4. What steps do you think social workers and social services agencies at individual, agency, and policy levels of practice can take to prevent harmful consequences of well-intentioned policies?

TABLE 5.3 ■ Relevant Federal Child Welfare Laws

Topic	Laws	Oversight Agency	Website
Child protective services	Child Abuse Prevention and Treatment Act Adoption and Safe Families Act	U.S. Department of Health and Human Services Administration for Children and Families	https://training.cfsrportal.acf.hhs.gov/section-2-understanding-child-welfare-system/2999S
Provisions for particular communities and populations	Indian Child Welfare Act Interethnic Placement Act	No federal agency has oversight responsibility for ICWA (Children's Bureau/ACYF/HHS, 2018)	https://www.childwelfare.gov/pubPDFs/icwa.pdf
Material support	Social Security Act (Survivors Benefits) Temporary Assistance for Needy Families (cash benefits for families living below federal poverty line) McKinney-Vento Homeless Education Assistance Improvements Act of 2001	Social Security Administration (SSA) U.S. Department of Health and Human Services Administration for Children and Families, Office of Family Assistance U.S. Department of Education	https://www.ssa.gov/ https://www.acf.hhs.gov/ofa/programs/tanf https://www2.ed.gov/programs/homeless/legislation.html
Maternal and child health	Special Supplemental Nutrition Program for Women, Infants, and Children (WIC) Supplemental Nutrition Assistance Program (SNAP)	U.S. Department of Agriculture Food and Nutrition Service	https://www.fns.usda.gov/wic/women-infants-and-children-wic https://www.fns.usda.gov/snap/supplemental-nutrition-assistance-program-snap

POLICY INFORMED BY ALTERNATIVE LENSES

In all its iterations, U.S. child welfare has been residual, addressing only the direct situations when children are in need of assistance due to abuse and neglect. A recent report of the United Nations Special Rapporteur on Extreme Poverty and Human Rights on His Mission to the United States of America (Alston, 2018) describes the tremendous and growing inequality and the extreme poverty in the United States. In a footnote (15), the report points to the dubious U.S. distinction as "the only country in the world that has not ratified the Convention on the Rights of the Child, which protects the economic and social rights of children." Further evidence of this is the fact, also noted by the report, that the United States has the highest infant mortality rate in the developed world and the highest youth poverty rate among all countries in the Organisation for Economic Cooperation and Development (OECD).

The United States has some programs that hint at a more holistic approach to child welfare, including the state Children's Health Insurance Program (CHIP) and the Supplemental Nutrition Assistance Program (SNAP), both of which are discussed in Chapter 11. However, these programs are themselves residual in that they are designed to ensure the barest of benefits to the most poverty-stricken children, with many hurdles to proving eligibility and accessing them even for families who qualify. What does it look like in other countries that take a holistic, institutional approach to child welfare? Similar to the ways the Annie E. Casey Foundation uses the Kids Count database (described later in this chapter), the OECD looks at multiple dimensions of child well-being: "material well-being, housing and environment, educational well-being, health, risk behaviours, and quality of school life." In a 2007 report of overall child well-being, the United States ranked 21 of 22 wealthy countries, ahead only of the United Kingdom. The top-ranking countries were the Netherlands and Sweden (Organisation for Economic Cooperation and Development, 2009, p. 27).

The Global Coalition to End Child Poverty is a coalition that includes UNICEF, OECD, and Save the Children. This coalition (2017) recently advocated what they call Child-sensitive Social Protection (CSSP) as the best way to ensure that families can raise their children safely and with the proper attention to developmental and educational needs.

> Child-sensitive Social Protection (CSSP) includes all social protection measures that address children's needs and rights and which improve elements of child well-being. It is an approach under which all social protection measures aim to maximise impacts and minimise any possible harms for girls and boys, across all ages, by systematically incorporating child risk and benefit (impact) analysis into each stage of policy and programme design, implementation and monitoring. It recognises and takes into account the long-term benefits of investing in children that not only help realize the rights and potential of individuals but also strengthen the foundations for economic growth and inclusive development of society as a whole. (p. 4)

What might this look like? While concrete understandings of child well-being will differ according to local resources and cultural beliefs, the report contends that CSSP can be achieved in any country. Looking through a CSSP lens means that all policies would be examined for their impact on children's well-being. Some policies may be explicitly directed at children. Many countries have what is called a *child grant*, which is provided to families after the birth of a child to help support expenses associated with raising a child. This is also a societal expression of valuing children as a societal good rather than the products of individual family decisions. For example, in Israel, families receive a one-time *birth grant*, as well as a monthly payment until the child reaches the age of 18. These grants are universal: They are provided to all families regardless of income. This means that there is no need to prove eligibility (National Insurance Institutes of Israel, n.d.). Another indicator that may not be targeted to children but that impacts their well-being is the extent and coverage of health care. In countries that provide minimum levels of universal and accessible health care for all, children and the families that care for them have greater access. In the absence of health care, not only might children's health be directly compromised, but there may also be an indirect impact on their well-being when parents or other family members are unable to function fully as caregivers due to untreated health problems. This may be exacerbated by lack of sufficient financial assistance for families where a parent may have a disability that prevents them from working and/or caring for a child without additional financial or in-kind supports. As another example, even Nepal, with many fewer resources than the United States, has increased its general disability benefits as part of its effort toward CCSP (Global Coalition to End Child Poverty, 2017).

ADVOCACY

USING CHILD-SENSITIVE SOCIAL PROTECTION AS A TOOL FOR ANALYZING U.S. POLICY

Pick any area of social policy in this textbook. Imagine that you are a social worker who is working with a child or someone who is connected to the child as a caregiver or professional (parent, grandparent, family with children, doctor in a hospital setting, teacher).

1. How would your chosen policy impact the individual with whom you work?
2. What are the direct or indirect positive contributions of this policy to child well-being?
3. What are the direct or indirect negative consequences of this policy to child well-being?
4. What changes might you propose to mitigate any negative impact of the policy on children?

OPPORTUNITIES FOR ADVOCACY

You may have recently taken a required class in research, or you may be taking such a class now or soon. While it may be clear to you how you can use research in clinical social work practice, you might be somewhat confused about its relevance to policy practice. The Annie E. Casey Foundation's Kids Count Data Center is an excellent example of research that is designed to analyze and shape policy around the well-being of children.

On its website, which allows anyone to access Kids Count resources, the Annie E. Casey Foundation (2019) explains:

> The Kids Count Data Book provides a detailed picture of how children are faring in the United States, ranking states on overall child well-being and . . . key indicators covering economic well-being, education, health and family and community. Each year, the release of the Data Book generates significant media attention and a unique opportunity to discuss ways of improving the lives of children and families.

This description highlights several important features for advocacy. The kind of information provided by the Casey Foundation can be extremely helpful to policy advocates, who otherwise might not have the financial resources or personnel expertise to collect or analyze state-level data. The Data Center can be accessed online, allowing advocates to make their own charts or graphs by selecting relevant measures or comparison state(s). In fact, one of the charts in this chapter was made using data from the Data Center. The annual publication of the Kids Count Data Book keeps tabs on how states progress (or regress) from year to year, tracking investments in different areas that impact children's lives. This, in itself, may provide incentives for improvement and allows advocates to keep a watchful eye on local policymakers. It also compares states, allowing advocates to point out how their own state can improve or maintain its role as a leader, depending on how it compares to other states. Such comparisons may also help policy advocates at the state or national level identify other states with similar problems, or states that might provide models to emulate, or be potential collaborators or allies. Finally, media coverage of this annual publication encourages ongoing public discussion about issues of importance to child well-being, which can assist local and national organizations in their attempts to frame child well-being within a broad set of social, economic, and community-related concerns. Evidence-informed media coverage may also enrich public dialogue and sustain interest in child welfare, which can waver or wane over time.

Social workers such as Karina Jimenez Lewis, MSW, help collect and analyze the data in the Kids Count Data Book, as well as disseminate the information found to the media, advocates, and policymakers (Annie E. Casey Foundation, 2016). Social workers have the training and knowledge to participate in and lead data collection efforts as well as the dissemination of information as they gain expertise. Think about how you might use these or other resources in your field placement or your future professional career to learn more about problems that touch communities you work with.

Final Discussion

Now that you have finished reading this chapter, reread the vignette at the beginning. Based on what you have learned, answer the following questions. Point to specific references in the chapter that help you answer these questions. Consider how different theories inform the response to these questions.

1. What are the roles or responsibilities of the different professionals here (the teacher, Larry, his supervisor)?
2. What skills and training might Larry have from his BSW program that can help guide him in working with this family?
3. Who is Larry's client (the state? the family? the parents? the child/children)? What conflicting concerns might these stakeholders present?
4. How might a CSSP or an institutional approach to child welfare be different?
5. What role might race, class, gender, and other aspects of identity play in this vignette?

6

EARLY CHILDHOOD EDUCATION AND CARE POLICY

LEARNING OBJECTIVES

6.1: Describe the history and changing perspectives of child care and early education in the U.S.

6.2: Appraise key policies affecting child care and early education in the United States

6.3: Assess alternative methods of successfully providing child care and early childhood education

6.4: Develop opportunities for advocacy that improves the lives of children and families

This chapter reviews historical and current policies that govern the education and care of children from birth through prekindergarten and consider what they reveal about U.S. understandings of children and the social constructions of childhood. It explores child care policy in light of the high numbers of children with parents in the paid labor market and a growing recognition of the importance of early childhood education. The chapter considers different interest groups and constituents who have been involved in the creation of the current patchwork of U.S. policies including Head Start, the Child Care Development Block Grant, and tax policies. We also discuss the impact that these laws have on state policies. Early education and child care policies have implications for children and families and broader society through their connection to gender equality, employment, and the lifelong impact of early socio-emotional development and educational attainment. Throughout this chapter, we highlight the dynamics of gender, class, and race that have influenced social policy around early child care and education. The chapter will conclude with an analysis examining who benefits and loses from current policies and a consideration of social constructions of child care and early education that can inform new policies.

Vignette: Children and Young Families Struggling on Their Own

Based on what you know from the media or your personal, work, or volunteer experiences, think about the following questions as you read the vignette. When you finish the vignette, answer the questions below.

1. What policies limit or expand Marcie's options to secure appropriate, high-quality education and care for Max and Rose?
2. What challenges does Marcie face in ensuring that the federal policies are implemented in her children's school?
3. What strengths and resources does Marcie have that she can draw on?
4. What roles could a social worker play in helping Marcie and her family (think micro, mezzo, and macro level social work)?
5. How would this situation be different in a two-parent family? If the family was headed by a single father? Would the issues be the same? Would the same policies apply? Why or why not?
6. What role might race, class, gender, and other aspects of identity play in this vignette?

Marcie is a widow raising two children, Rose (age 5) and Max (age 2). She works at a local fast food chain. Although the family lives in a state that offers free and universal pre-kindergarten, it is only provided for a half-day window of either 9 to 12 or 1 to 3, depending on the child's assignment. Marcie has therefore kept Rose enrolled at a regulated private family day care facility, for which she received a subsidy through her state's welfare-to-work program. This arrangement has been a lifesaver for Marcie, because her child care provider, Joan, accommodates Marcie when she runs late due to her job or public transportation holdups. Joan is also flexible when medical or other expenses leave her behind on child care payments. Joan allows Marcie to change her hours to accommodate Marcie's schedule, which changes bi-weekly. This flexibility has limits, though. Lately, Max has had frequent ear infections, and Joan strictly enforces her "no sick children" policy. Marcie's employer is required to provide family leave, but because it is unpaid, Marcie can't afford to take it. Sometimes she can leave Max with her elderly aunt. Other times, she gives him cold medicine, takes him to Joan's, and hopes for the best.

Marcie's employer recently offered her a position as shift manager, which comes with a pay increase and more regular hours. At first Marcie was thrilled. She had been working hard toward this position, which would strengthen her résumé. However, when she reviews the compensation package with her case manager, she learns that the small increase in pay would trigger what researchers have called the **Cliff Effect**, meaning that it would push her out of financial eligibility for a host of programs on which she and her children depend. These include the child care subsidy and food assistance. Marcie learned that there are tax benefits available for child care, but even with the raise, she would not make enough money to take advantage of these. When Marcie calculates the lost benefits, she realizes that she cannot afford to take the new position.

Cliff Effect: The abrupt cutting off of eligibility for public benefits due to small increases in income that generally result in recipients being worse off because income increases do not match the loss of benefits

The brief hope provided by the prospect of her promotion has left her even more frustrated with her current plight. One option that Marcie considered is becoming a day care worker herself. She thinks it will allow her to be with her children. She looked into a number of day care centers that had job openings, but even with reduced tuition for employees, she could not afford to place her own children in such a center. She has decided to open her own family-based child care. However, she does not plan to register it or seek licensure due to the high cost of accreditation. This will mean that she cannot accept children with subsidies, but she can charge less. Many of her neighbors, who struggle to afford care, would be willing to place their children with her. Although ideally Marcie would want training to make sure that Rose, Max, and the children she cares for would be well-prepared for school, at this point, Marcie cannot afford it. She plans to look into free courses offered by her state.

HISTORY AND SOCIAL CONSTRUCTION OF U.S. EARLY CHILDHOOD EDUCATION AND CARE

Early childhood education and care (ECEC) describe the provision of care and nurturing of young people, whether accomplished by a parent, family member, or paid provider, as well as the theory and practice of educating young children (David & Powell, 2015). ECEC in the United States can be carried out in children's own homes or outside the home in child care centers, home-based family child care, or through preschool or prekindergarten programs. While most programs are run by private for-profit or nonprofit organizations, some government programs are available for low-income families or families with specific needs. Programs can be religious, secular, or based on particular educational philosophies. In these settings, including private in-home arrangements, the majority of ECEC is provided by a low-income, female workforce, many of whom earn poverty-level wages (Whitebook, McLean, & Austin, 2016).

The United States has a huge need for paid child care. The majority of U.S. parents with young children, including mothers, are in the paid labor force (Bureau of Labor Statistics, 2019) and their children are cared for by non-parental providers (Mulligan, Brimhall, West, & Chapman, 2005). While this is a matter of choice for some, most two-parent families rely on mothers' incomes. Most single parents have no choice but to work. ECEC is therefore sometimes referred to as **custodial care**, underscoring its purpose as a means to keep children safe and cared for as a substitute for their working parents. Although women have always worked outside the home, their rates of employment have changed substantially over time. In 1900,

Custodial care: Describes child care when used primarily as a means to keep children safe and cared for as a substitute for their working parents

18% of women and 84% of men over the age of 13 participated in the workforce. That number increased for women to 28% by 1940, while remaining relatively unchanged for men. During this time, the average take-home pay for women was substantially lower than for men. For example, Schweitzer (1980) notes that women took home $525 per year on average in 1937 as compared to men, whose annual pay averaged $1,027. In 2018, 71.5% of women with children under 18 were in the workforce, and 65.1% of those had children under age 6 (U.S. Department of Labor, 2019).

In addition to a work support for parents, ECEC is used as a means to socialize children and parents. It is also a source of employment for low-skilled workers, who are primarily women (Palley & Shdaimah, 2014). Early childhood education and care is a place for learning and early intervention. Early childhood is often cited as the most important stage in ensuring healthy biopsychosocial development over the course of the lifespan (Heckman, Grunewald, & Reynolds, 2006; Katner, 2010; Shapiro & Applegate, 2002). As such, child care programs have sometimes been seen as a means to provide a more level playing field across class by providing equal or enhanced educational opportunities for families.

Discussion of ECEC must include the social construction of public and private spheres, and the differences between the experiences of families from different racial, ethnic, and income groups. In industrialized U.S. society, with a growing separation between home and the workplace, women have historically borne the primary responsibility for the private sphere, including child rearing. Men have been seen as the primary agents in the public sphere, including work and public decision making. Early movements around women's suffrage began to shift this idea by suggesting that women also had a place in the public sphere. White and nonwhite groups as well as new immigrants in the United States had very different options and experiences. African American women, both during and after slavery, generally worked outside the home, often taking care of others' homes and children (Arnott & Matthei, 1996; Michel, 1999). Native American/First Nations women shouldered multiple responsibilities. For example, women from tribes in the Great Plains were responsible for much of the work of farming and transforming hides to be sold (Wishart, 2011). Immigrant women frequently worked outside the home, as did poor white women (Arnott & Matthei, 1996). Child care combines the public and private spheres, and policy relating to it often reflects ambiguity or disagreement about appropriate gender roles. Child care policy also reflects the power relationships between men and women (Harris, 2008). In the United States, the social construction of motherhood as the primary responsibility of women has been connected to weak funding for child care and limited support for out-of-home child care (Harris, 2008) by, for example, prioritizing women's pensions rather than support for child care.

Early social reformers often focused on the family domain and relationships. One of the first agenda items of Jane Addams and the Hull House was the provision of child care to low-income immigrant women in the slums of Chicago (Knight, 2005). Their focus was often one of necessity: While low-income families needed child care to ensure the safety of their children, it was considered inferior to the care of children by their own mothers. Many of today's feminists and scholars who are in favor of ECEC policy reform emphasize the need to acknowledge care work to mitigate the burden on care providers. They emphasize the connection between recognizing care work and the ability of women to fully participate in society (Fineman, 1995; Young, 1990). Quality stable child care is not only important for women's equality in the workplace, but it can improve childhood outcomes as well as future economic potential (National Institute of Child Health and Human Development, 2006; Oden, Schweinhart, Weikart, Marcus, & Xie, 2000).

While some scholars have recognized the importance of child care (Kamerman & Kahn, 2001; Waldfogel, 1998), child care has not been viewed as a core U.S. social policy concern (Palley & Shdaimah, 2014). Existing U.S. policy, since the age of industrialization, has been built on the assumption that men are breadwinners and women should remain at home to care for children at least until they are old enough to attend school. As a result, other than a handful of tax policies that reduce a small percentage of taxes for higher-income families with children in care, most existing policies provide financial support for child care only for children living in poverty. These policies treat women's work as an individual decision that, if chosen, should be the sole financial obligation of the family. The implicit message is that families who cannot afford to have a parent stay at home or privately fund other alternatives should not have children.

Early Care as a Necessary Evil

In 1840 Massachusetts, approximately 40% of 3 year olds attended some form of school. However, as a result of "popular and scientific fears that early intellectual development led to later insanity," by 1960 almost no 3 year olds remained in Massachusetts schools (Vinovskis, 2015). Following the move away from the integrated education of young children in public schools, early education (school before age 6) began in several different ways. Early child care for immigrant children living in poverty in the late 1800s was designed to ensure their safety while their mothers worked and socialize them to develop middle-class values. Partial-day private-pay nursery schools served well-to-do children in the 1920s. Kindergarten began in the early 20th century for children in poverty and was quickly adopted by the public schools as a part of universal public education (Rose, 1999).

When U.S. child care centers were first formed in the 19th century, the need for day care was perceived as pathological or aberrant. Many programs were, therefore, connected to other social welfare services and required that families meet with case managers or early social workers as a condition of participation (Michel, 1999; Steinfels, 1973). Child care services, called **day nurseries**, were run as charities and were generally established by philanthropic women for families where mothers had no choice but to work and could not afford care (Harris, 2008). Prior to the Progressive Era, families with no one available to provide child care were faced with the choice of leaving the children alone, perhaps with older siblings, or placing their children in institutions or with other families (Klein, 1992).

Day nurseries: Charity-based child care programs of the 19th century that were established to serve families of women who had no choice but to work

During the Progressive Era (1890–1920), there was a strongly held social belief that women should remain at home while their husbands worked to support them. At this time, there was greater political support for mothers' pensions, which would enable single or deserted mothers to care for their own children, than for child care assistance (Rose, 1999). Paid work by mothers was seen as a social problem caused by family crisis and breakdown, which may have led to the lack of governmental support for child care. Some civic groups, such as women's clubs, supported free kindergarten. These kindergartens were established inside public schools, resulting in the connection that now exists between kindergarten and government-supported education. However, social work icon Jane Addams argued in 1918 that new day nurseries should not be established because low-income women should receive pensions so that they could remain at home with their children (Harris, 2008).

Beginning with the Progressive Era, social workers were involved with the early administration of child care. Those who were part of the Charity Organization Society (COS) screened mothers applying for care. If they deemed mothers worthy of assistance because they needed to work due to widowhood or desertion, they granted them access to care. If they deemed mothers unworthy because they had a husband who drank or was able to work but unemployed, they denied them access to care. The settlement houses, in contrast, "provided day nursery services without investigating the character of the mother and the family" (Klein, 1992, p. xv).

Spain (2001) describes the child care provided by the settlement workers for children of immigrants as "tangible evidence of its support for employed women" (p. 6) and saw them

H. Howard Miller, War Production Co-ordinating Committee

PHOTO 6.1 "We Can Do It!" poster for Westinghouse, closely associated with Rosie the Riveter

as more valuable than the academic discussions of women's rights that were occurring simultaneously within settlements. Day cares and kindergartens in settlements provided child care and taught academic skills, English, and American values through lessons about cleaning and how to buy and sell safe food. In this way, these programs were meant for socialization and assimilation, not only for children but also for the families. Settlements also built many of the first playgrounds in the United States. New York's College Settlement, which opened in 1889, provided a nursery, a kindergarten, music classes for children, and playgrounds. During the same time, educational reformer Pauline Aggassiz Shaw had created 14 kindergartens and multiple nurseries within Boston (Spain, 2001). Her kindergartens were taken over by the Boston School Committee in 1887, creating one of the nation's first public kindergartens (Hurd Smith, n.d.).

Shifting Views on Childhood Education and Women's Work

By the 1920s, the kindergarten movement and shifts in the day nursery movement added more educational components to early childhood care beyond the basic custodial services (Klein, 1992). This change occurred as ideas of childhood shifted. Educational reformer Maria Montessori (who was also an advocate for women's and children's rights and proposed equal pay for equal work by women at the International Congress for Women's Rights in 1896) developed her first nursery school in 1907 in Rome. She wanted to create a learning environment that would "free children to realize their innate human potential" (Giardiello, 2015, p. 29) and valued the empirical study of child development (Giardiello, 2015). These ideas were adopted in the United States in the 1920s.

It was not until the end of the Great Depression and the beginning of World War II that support for child care reemerged. During World War II, women were encouraged to work while their husbands were away. The federal government began to provide funding for child care. This was a shift from societal views that mothers had to be home to care for their children. Child care was no longer perceived as aberrant but rather a necessary support, with positive images, such as Photo 6.1, encouraging women to enter the workforce. The effects of men being overseas during World War II and the resulting need for women to fill their jobs led to a sharp increase in the percentage of women in the workforce. By 1945, 34% of women over 16 were in the workforce (Acemoglu, Autor, & Lyle, 2004).

Women with children were encouraged to be part of this group, but many did not join the paid labor market until 1943 because they lacked child care. As Schwietzer (1980) describes,

> In the absence of sufficient day care, many women simply left their children alone. The Women's Bureau found in 1944 that 16 percent of working mothers in ten war production areas made no arrangements at all for their children's care; most mothers left them with husbands who worked other shifts, with older children, or with other relatives. Only 5 percent had children in day care centers. Historian William Chafe writes that "a social worker in the San Fernando Valley counted forty-five infants locked in cars in a single war plant parking lot." Magazines ran features on "door key

> children" who roamed city streets during the day with a housekey tied around their necks. A reporter who visited a Southern California trailer camp during working hours found nine children (and four dogs) chained to their trailers while the children's parents were at work. (p. 93)

Legislation popularly known as the Lanham Act was passed to support the war industry (Stolfutz, n.d.). As part of this legislation, $52 million was provided from 1943–1946 to subsidize high-quality, full-day, year-round child care for up to 6 days a week. As a part of the Works Project Administration, day care centers were developed not only as a work support for women in the war and home industries, but also to provide employment for women as child care providers. The care provided in these centers was limited to 18 months and was provided by women who had not received any special training (Michel, 1999). The child care supported by these funds enabled women to work when their country needed them. At the end of the war, women stayed in the workforce in relatively similar numbers, although most moved back into traditional female occupations (Schweitzer, 1980). Lanham Act funding was short-lived, ending in 1946, when women were sent home to give up their jobs for returning veterans and resume care for their children (Michel, 1999).

A significant mechanism for private child care in the United States has been the use of nannies. In the American South, prior to the Civil War, many of these were enslaved black women who were forced to care for others' children, breed more slaves, and endure the sale of their children and other family members (Spaights & Whitaker, 1995). When slavery ended, however, care for the children of middle- and upper-middle-class women often continued to be supplied by black women. While providing this care for white women, many left their own children in the care of older relatives or neighbors (Amott & Matthei, 1996). In the North, single immigrant women historically took positions as nannies in the households of wealthy families. Today, many nannies continue to be immigrant women, with some sending money to family in other countries so they can care for U.S. children whose parents need or desire to work (Michel & Peng, 2017).

Child Care and Early Education as a Matter of Fairness and Equity

As a part of John F. Kennedy and Lyndon Johnson's War on Poverty, Head Start, an educational program for 3 and 4 year olds, was created in 1965. The goal of Head Start was to provide compensatory early education experiences for children at risk of school failure due to poverty. The idea was to give them a *head start* when they began school with a similar foundation to that which middle-class families were able to provide their children. Local control of programs led to great variation in quality. In addition, from the time Head Start was created, it has always been underfunded (Zigler & Muenchow, 1992). As a result, many potentially eligible children are unable to access programs. In the late 1960s, the Social Security Act was amended to provide additional funding to subsidize child care for the children of women who currently or recently received public benefits. Children whose care was subsidized under this program were often eligible for longer day programs than Head Start. Unlike Head Start, those programs were not necessarily designed to be educationally based (Steinfels, 1973).

Women again began entering the workforce in large numbers in the 1970s (Bureau of Labor Statistics, 2011). In 1971, Senator Walter Mondale introduced the Comprehensive Child Development Act (CCDA), a bipartisan bill to provide care for all U.S. children. Feminists, unions, and employers came together to support the legislation (Self, 2012). Proponents used arguments that noted the unfairness of forcing parents to choose between work and family obligations (Palley & Shdaimah, 2014). Many of those who opposed the bill expressed fear that the federal government would create unreasonable mandates for religious child care centers and would have required women to place children in uniform child care arrangements (Michel, 1999). In his veto of the bill that passed Congress with bipartisan support, Richard Nixon played on Cold War fears that public child care would "Sovietize" American families (Cohen, 2013). He said he was concerned that it would "commit the vast moral authority of the National Government to the side of communal approaches to child rearing over against the family-centered approach" (Nixon, 1971).

For more than 30 years following Nixon's veto, little effort was made to create broad national policies to address the universal child care needs of U.S. families (Michel, 1999). For example, in 1988, the less comprehensive Act for Better Childcare Services (ABC) (H.R. 3660 [100th]) was introduced by Democratic Senator Christopher Dodd and Republican Senator John Chafee to address the child care needs of low-income families. During the legislative hearings for ABC, advocates, including parents, state legislators and administrators, and representatives of both liberal and conservative interest groups, pointed to the growing body of research that showed the importance of quality education on childhood development (National Scientific Council on the Developing Child, 2009; Yoshikawa et al., 2013). They also argued that workers who had stable child care would be more productive and less likely to leave their jobs (Palley & Shdaimah, 2014). Initially, this bill passed both chambers of Congress. Due to technical difficulties, however, it needed to pass the House again. Instead of returning the bill to the House, a series of compromises led to the creation of the Child Care Development Block Care Grant (CCDBG) (Cohen, 2001; Lynch, 2014). CCDBG provides funds to states for child care for income eligible families. More recently, funds have also been provided to improve child care safety and quality. However, the focus of government support for child care and early education remains on families and children living in poverty (Office of Child Care, 2017).

Social Movements

Social movements have affected the availability of ECEC in the United States. Although many groups have had an impact, including businesses and unions, we focus here on the work of women reformers from the late 19th century forward. These include the Progressive movement, the primarily white women's movement, and African American social reformers.

As noted earlier, during the Progressive Era (1890–1920), social workers actively helped develop child care centers in settlement house communities to support working immigrant women and to help socialize their children. Progressives advocated for the creation of state and local widow's benefits to support single mothers rather than the expansion of child care. Harris (2008) argues that the women's movement during this time influenced the government to provide social services through both legislation and grants from the government to female-run charitable organizations providing the services. At the time, women were not protected by contract law (because they could not legally form contracts), and therefore they looked to government protection. The women's movement sought legislation that would protect women from participation in the workforce rather than ensure their right to participate. It was not until World War II when the stigma surrounding women's paid participation in the workplace was temporarily lifted that the National Federation of Day Nurseries requested aid from the government (Harris, 2008).

Maternalist: Perspective which elevates women's roles as primary nurturers and keepers of the home and family

While many early reformers sought to help women, they did so within what has been called a **maternalist** framework, which elevated women's roles as primary nurturers and keepers of the home and family. These reformers focused on protective labor legislation for women, eliminating child labor, and advocating for pensions for women who lost a male breadwinner through death or desertion. These adjustments were designed to accomplish several goals. They helped some women support themselves and their children without a man's income.

However, the pensions were meager, involved often impossible eligibility criteria, and were almost always given only to white women. As a whole, these efforts did not eliminate the need for women to work, but rather they stigmatized women's labor outside the home and reinforced gendered spheres. Further, they largely steered clear of government intervention, preferring to keep child care efforts within the realm of charitable endeavor rather than an entitlement (Michel, 1999).

Feminists in the latter 20th century elevated the virtue of women's labor as part of a movement for equality. According to Burrell (cited in Goertz & Mazur, 2008), the agenda of the National Women's Political Caucus included "equal representation in the National Commission for Neighborhoods tax reduction for childcare facilities, flexible hours for federal civil servants, family planning, federal abortion subsidies, rise of minimum salaries, and gay rights" (p. 89). In the 1960s, there was general agreement amongst feminist groups that child care should be a right. The National Organization for Women deemed child care necessary to achieve women's equality in the workforce (Dinner, 2010). Despite this initial inclusion of childcare in the early 1970s platform for women's equality, women's roles as mothers and caregivers were largely ignored as third wave feminism shifted to downplay maternal responsibilities to advance an agenda of workplace equality (Palley & Shdaimah, 2014). This led to what many considered to be **double shifts** where women carried out their unacknowledged maternal labor while working for wages outside the home. The early 2000s saw what has been called the **opt-out movement** and the **mommy wars**, where primarily higher-income women were seen to be choosing between a satisfying maternal role and a career. The continuing historical thread is the failure to recognize that paid work and parenting have always been a necessity for many families who struggle to balance work and family obligations (Williams, Manvell, & Bornstein, 2007).

Double shift: Refers to unacknowledged labor, typically but not always by women, when they are primarily responsible for work at home while also working for wages outside the home

Opt-out movement: Trend of the 2000s where women who had or could have pursued high-earning successful careers chose to "opt-out" of the paid labor market to perform uncompensated maternal labor

Mommy wars: Debates in which value judgments pit the virtue of women who work in the paid labor force against the virtue of women who perform uncompensated labor as primary caretakers for their children and home

Cisgender: Describing those whose gender identity matches their assigned gender at birth

Iris Marion Young (1990) suggests that women's interests can also be seen as the perspectives that women bring to situations. The priorities of the women's movement have reflected the identities of those who were most visible within it. In the United States, the dominant women's movement has been historically associated with the perspective of white middle-class women, often heavily represented by those who were straight and **cisgender** (i.e., those whose gender identity matches their assigned gender at birth). Parallel and powerful women's movements have existed within other groups as well. The stigma and ambivalence of maternal employment was never a feature of black reformers' efforts. This may be due to the harsh economic realities that so many black families faced as a result of racism, or due to the fact that many of the early black reformers, unlike their white counterparts, were more familiar with the need to work. Another factor might also be that child care for black children was financially supported by the communities they served, and so there was less of a social difference between those providing and receiving assistance (Michel, 1999). The difference between the white reformers' motivation of paternalistic noblesse oblige that grew out of class differences may have made them less empathic than the more communal attitude that often lay at the base of black reformers' efforts. A racial divide has continued to the present day in attitudes toward child care and women's work (Clemetson, 2006; Parker, 2005).

CURRENT CHILD CARE AND EARLY EDUCATION POLICIES

Several mechanisms currently support public financing of early education and care. In this chapter, we focus on policies that impact financing, quality, and access to early education and care.

These comprise the patchwork of U.S. child care policy. At the end of this section, Table 6.2 provides an overview of many relevant laws.

Tax Code Provisions, Head Start, and the Child Care and Development Fund

The tax code provides some financial assistance to help families pay for ECEC. The Child and Dependent Tax Credit allows families who earn sufficient income with dependent children under age 13 to receive up to $3,000 in tax credits for one child and up to $6,000 for two or more children. The credit is calculated based on earned income to defray some costs of child care that enabled the parents to work or seek work (Internal Revenue Service, 2019). Other than tax credits and deductions that are available to all tax-paying parents, most federal and state spending on early childhood education is designed to meet the needs of families living at low-income thresholds and occasionally families who have children with disabilities. With the exception of tax credits that were created in the 1950s and have not kept pace with inflation, existing federal child care policies such as the Family Medical Leave Act or Head Start only help parents in temporary and extreme circumstances: birth, ill health, and poverty (Dinner, 2010; Internal Revenue Service, 2019). They do not meet the regular and ongoing needs of working families.

The major federal funding for ECEC is through Head Start and the Child Care and Development Fund (CCDF). The CCDF provides funding for care with the primary goal of moving women who receive Temporary Assistance for Needy Families (TANF) into the workforce. Little of this money focuses on quality of care—approximately 4% of the funding from CCDF in 2000 was earmarked for quality assurance. However, states have discretion in how they wish to ensure quality improvements and, in the past, little has been done to monitor the quality of programs receiving federal funding (Government Accountability Office, 2002; Vucic, 2013). Other laws that provide funding and services to children younger than five include the Child Find provision and Part C of the Individuals with Disabilities Education Act. States are required to develop programs within the community and work with doctors to identify children with developmental disabilities and to provide early intervention services to children from birth to 2 years old. Each state must develop its own plan, and as a result, services vary from state to state. Though originally a program for children who met income-eligibility criteria, spots are now set aside in Head Start programs for children with disabilities regardless of income (Sheradin, 2015). As with Head Start, these programs as well as the funding for families receiving TANF are chronically underfunded and unable to meet the needs of all eligible families (Harris, 2008).

In addition to the financial obstacles facing parents who seek to access quality ECEC, many struggle to find care during the hours they need it. Child Care Aware reported 68,000 parents from 28 states seek child care for nonstandard hours (Ho, 2017). In addition, one survey found only 6% of child care centers reported offering overnight care, 2% reported offering evening care, and only 3% reported providing weekend hours (National Survey of Early Care and Education Project Team, 2015).

Setting Standards for Child Care

Oversight of child care (see photo 6.2) is generally provided at the state level. ECEC regulations are developed by state and territory governments to establish the rules that child care providers must comply with to operate legally. These rules vary significantly from state to state. In addition to meeting the regulations of their state, early childhood programs may be required to meet local or federal requirements, depending on their population, funding, and location. For example, programs receiving payments from the federal Child Care and

Development Fund must meet a set of state health and safety requirements. In addition, to be eligible for diverse sources of funding, programs may choose to meet other standards, such as Quality Rating and Improvement System (QRIS) standards or prekindergarten program requirements (Office of Child Care, n.d.). Managed through the U.S. Department of Health and Human Services, QRIS is a set of child care standards created by the National Child Care Information and Technical Assistance Center in 1998. QRIS is designed to raise standards of quality and to provide parents with information to help them choose satisfactory care. QRIS has tiers, with graduated requirements for achieving each level. The requirements include factors such as carer-child ratios, staff training and credentials, learning environment, family involvement, and leadership and management skills of the provider or agency. Assessment is based on a combination of self-report and independent evaluation. Many states provide incentives to participate in QRIS, such as grants or bonuses.

PHOTO 6.2 Nursery teacher playing with children in a classroom

School Readiness for All Children and Head Start

In 1964, the Office of Economic Opportunity, directed by Sargent Shriver, was developing programs to help fight the **War on Poverty**. At the time, 30 million Americans lived in poverty; half of those were children, most of whom were younger than 12. The agency developed a Head Start Planning Committee to create a program that would include preschool and health care. One of the planning committee members, Urie Bronfenbrenner, used an ecological approach to child development that emphasized the environment within which children spend their time rather than just the few hours they are in school. (You will likely learn more about Bronfenbrenner and the ecological approach in other places in your social work education.) He advocated the involvement of parents of children from low-income households in the planning and delivery of services—a radical view at the time (Zigler & Muenchow, 1992).

War on Poverty: A set of programs and policy initiatives created by President Lyndon B. Johnson to combat poverty in the United States

Because one of Head Start's goals was to support the employment of mothers and communities were concerned about outsiders determining the best method of educating their children, Head Start did not originally employ teacher training standards nor did it specify curricular requirements. Though some standards have since been developed, there is still great variation in program quality (Vinovskis, 2005). Head Start (for children age 4–5) and Early Head Start (birth to age 3) programs are also required to ensure that at least 10% of the children whom they serve are children with disabilities (Sheridan, 2015).

Early Education for Children with Disabilities

All states currently receive federal funding to support the education of children with disabilities and are, therefore, required to develop Child Find programs to identify children who may have disabilities, beginning at birth. As we discuss more in Chapter 12, the Individuals with Disabilities Education Act (IDEA), originally called the Education for All Handicapped Children's Act and passed in 1975, was most recently updated in 2004. It provides federal guidance and funding not only for school-age children but also for children ages birth to age 5. Part C provides specific guidance to assist states to provide early intervention services to children birth to age 2 who are born with developmental delays. States have wide latitude to determine the developmental delays on which to focus and which services they provide. Children identified with developmental delays under Part C of the IDEA are eligible for Individual Family Service Plans, which unlike plans for children in higher grades focus not just on the individual student with the delay but may include services for parents to enable them to better support their infant or toddler.

When children are 3 years old, Part B of the IDEA (covering school-age children) begins to apply to them. If a disability is identified, the local school district is required to provide an Individual Education Plan (IEP), detailing the tailored early intervention services for that child. According to the IDEA (2006), a

> (1) Child with a disability means a child evaluated in accordance with §§300.304 through 300.311 as having mental retardation, a hearing impairment (including deafness), a speech or language impairment, a visual impairment (including blindness), a serious emotional disturbance (referred to in this part as emotional disturbance), an orthopedic impairment, autism, traumatic brain injury, another health impairment, a specific learning disability, deaf-blindness, or multiple disabilities, and who, by reason thereof, needs special education and related services. (34 CFR 300.8(a))

Whereas Part C of the IDEA is designed to help children who are "at risk of having substantial developmental delays" (IDEA 34 CFR 303.1(e), 2006), Part B, as you will learn in the next chapter, is not designed to help children reach their optimal development but rather to make "meaningful educational progress" (*Board of Education of the Hendrick Hudson Central School District v. Amy Rowley*, 458 U.S. 176, 1982). How do you think these two goals might be different?

State-Funded Prekindergarten (PreK) Programs

One exception to a trend of defunding in the wake of a struggling economy is the recent funding of programs to supply care and education for young children through state-based universal PreK programs for children ages 3 and 4. Funding for these initiatives, overall, expanded annually from 2005 to 2011 (Pew Center on the States, 2011). Where states have experimented with universal PreK programs, findings show an increase in the supply and quality of programs for children of this age. However, vagaries of funding, changes in eligibility and other requirements, or changing regulations can adversely impact programs and the families that rely on them (Schilder, Kimura, Elliott, & Currenton, 2011).

In many places, PreK programs do not address the family care needs of working parents and are designed more to meet educational and school-preparedness goals (Pew Center on the States, 2011). They typically provide only a few hours of daily education, although in some locations, mixed-delivery systems with options for center-based care allow them to be combined with full-day care (Schilder et al., 2011). As a result of this and, possibly, parental preference for private or full-day care, a small percentage of children are actually enrolled in state PreK programs: In 2016, 32% of 4 year olds and 5% of 3 year olds participated in state-funded prekindergarten programs (Barnett, Friedman-Krauss, Weisenfeld, Horowitz, Kasmin, & Squires, 2017).

One concern raised by child care advocates is related to PreK program implementation. For example, in states where PreK programs are designed to build on the existence of elementary schools, they may financially jeopardize the operation of private child care centers. Because of insufficient funding for child care, many ECEC providers rely on cost shifting, using money received from the care for older children to help subsidize the care for younger children, enabling them to meet the higher ratio of carers per children for infants and young toddlers required by law. In focus groups conducted with child care providers by the authors (Shdaimah, Palley, & Miller, 2018), providers expressed concern that school-based PreK implementation would pose a threat to their economic sustainability by creaming off the most profitable programs. Such a loss would harm not only providers but also families with younger children who are dependent on their care. In some states, such as Pennsylvania, discussions around implementation have included child care providers, making it less likely that such unintended harm may occur. In Table 6.1 we highlight some of the many variations in child care and early education policy in different states throughout the United States.

ADVOCACY

REVIEW OF SOURCES

Choose one of the federal laws listed in Table 6.2. Visit the federal government agency's website that discusses that law.

1. What information did you find there?
2. Who do you believe is the audience for that webpage?
3. Was the information clear?
4. What information was not available that you would like included?

TABLE 6.1 ■ Variation in Child Care and Early Education Policies and Programs at the State Level

Topic	Overview
Child care quality	Quality Rating and Improvement System (QRIS) at the federal level includes graduated child care standards designed to raise standards of quality and provide parents with information to help them choose satisfactory care. It is not mandatory for states. State variation in adoption and implementation: • Participation is voluntary in most states that adopted QRIS. • Some (e.g., Oklahoma) mandate that all child care facilities meet minimum standards, and others (e.g., Wisconsin) require this of child care facilities that receive subsidies for children of low-income families. • Most adopting states provide financial incentives to participate.
Tax policy	• Twenty-six states (including Washington, DC) offer tax credits. • Twelve states offer refundable credits that provide income-eligible parents benefits even if these exceed taxes due (National Women's Law Center, 2015).

(Continued)

TABLE 6.1 ■ Continued

Topic	Overview
Licensing of child care facilities	State licensed and regulated • Some states subject home- and center-based care to registration. • Some states subject only center-based care to registration; states rely on QRIS (see above) for licensing. Local licensing requirements can include: • Safety and health criteria • Minimum child-to-caregiver ratios • Inspection and oversight requirements • Educational or training qualifications for providers
State-funded prekindergarten	• A few states provide PreK for all (universal, e.g., Vermont) • Most are for income-eligible children only • Six states provide no prekindergarten program (Idaho, Montana, New Hampshire, North Dakota, South Dakota, and Wyoming) (Diffey, Parker, & Atchison, 2017) • Programming generally lasts a few hours a day • Teacher qualifications and curricula vary

TABLE 6.2 ■ Relevant Federal Child Care and Early Education Laws and Their Oversight

Topic	Laws	Oversight Agency	Website
Financial support for child care	Child and Dependent Care Tax Credit (1976)	Department of the Treasury/ Internal Revenue Service	https://www.irs.gov/individuals/child-and-dependent-care-information
Quality, accessibility, and provision of information for parents and guardians	Child Care and Development Block Grant (2014)	Department of Health and Human Services	https://www.acf.hhs.gov/sites/default/files/occ/child_care_and_development_block_grant_markup.pdf
Support for income-eligible children and their parents	Head Start (passed as Economic Opportunity Amendments, 1966)	Department of Health and Human Services	https://www.gpo.gov/fdsys/pkg/STATUTE-80/pdf/STATUTE-80-Pg1451.pdf
Education for children with disabilities	Individuals with Disabilities Education Act (IDEA, 2004)	Department of Education	https://sites.ed.gov/idea/about-idea/
Child care for military dependents	Military Child Care Act (1989)	Department of Defense	https://elibrary.cnic-n9portal.net/document-library/?documentlibraryaction=view&id=47
Grant resources for states to fund preschool programming	Every Student Succeeds Act (2015)	Department of Education	https://www.ed.gov/essa
Parental leave	Family Medical Leave Act	Department of Labor	https://www.dol.gov/whd/fmla/

POLICY INFORMED BY ALTERNATIVE LENSES

ECEC policies vary according to their purpose. Different models of care are often a reflection of society's values or efforts at social engineering. In this section, we examine alternative perspectives and the policies they might suggest. We also examine policies in particular settings to see how alternatives might work in practice. For example, as a result of declining birthrates, some countries have used child care policy as a tool to encourage women to have children (Grant et al., 2004). Such policies support mothers' work by increasing options for the provision of paid child care. On the other hand, a number of socially conservative countries have sought to encourage women to leave the workforce and remain home to care for their children, which both reinforces traditional gender roles and "frees up" employment opportunities for men; such countries have policies that allow for extended paid leave for parents rather than support for public child care (Morgan & Zippel, 2003). Norway, which sought to equalize gender roles at home and in the workplace, mandates that a portion of the generous 46-week of fully paid leave[1] can only be used by fathers (Clapp, 2016). What would ECEC look like in the United States if we examined it through different lenses? The following sections examine ECEC from perspectives that differ from dominant U.S. approaches and paradigms.

Feminist Perspectives

Marxist feminist thought offers an alternative lens to frame the work of caring for and educating children (as well as for others) by demanding that such efforts be valued in the same way that we value paid work done in offices or factories. Political philosopher Karl Marx distinguished between **productive labor**, which results in goods that have a market value in that they can be bought and sold, and nonproductive (also referred to as **reproductive labor**), work that is necessary but has no commercial value. Feminist scholars have challenged the juxtaposition of productive and reproductive labor, criticizing Marx for his "inability to conceive of value-producing work other than in the form of commodity production and his consequent blindness to the significance of women's unpaid reproductive work in the process of capitalist accumulation" (Federici, 2012, p. 92). They note that Marx's failure to acknowledge the importance of such work in sustaining production overlooked the capitalist exploitation of women's labor within the private sphere of the family. Even when these tasks are carried out by individuals outside the family and therefore become **commodified** (i.e., given a monetary value), they are considered caring labor and are low-pay and low-status jobs. Commodified care work is disproportionately carried out by women. This is true not only of child care, but also of teaching—especially the teaching of younger children.

Productive labor: Labor that results in goods that have a market value in that they can be bought and sold (in contrast, see **reproductive labor**)

Reproductive labor: Work that is necessary but has no commercial value (in contrast, see **productive labor**)

Commodification: Giving something a monetary or exchange value. This can refer to labor or products.

Martha Albertson Fineman (1995) argues that the designation of caretaking[2] as part of the private rather than the public sphere has perpetuated the dependency of both those who receive care and those who care for others. Because caretaking is either completely unremunerated or poorly paid, those who carry it out must depend on the earnings or support of others for their own survival (upon which the care of their charges also hinges). In the idealized nuclear heterosexual family, providing support through productive (i.e., wage earning) labor is the role of men. Families who do not have a successful male breadwinner to support those needing and giving care are seen as incomplete or failing. Feminist theorists like Iris Marion Young (1990), who propose a reframing of caretaking as a valued activity, note that it requires that we challenge the

REFLECTION

THINKING THROUGH A FEMINIST LENS

Imagine that we lived in a society that valued child care as an important social and fiscal activity as feminist theorists like Fineman and Young suggest:

1. How might our policies be different?
2. How might policies informed by increasing the value of care work impact Marcie, Max, and Rose's situation?
3. What other policy areas might be fruitfully analyzed using feminist perspectives?

> deeply held assumption that moral agency and full citizenship require that a person be autonomous and independent . . . . Female experience of social relations, arising both from women's typical domestic responsibilities and from the kinds of paid work that many women do, tends to recognize dependence as a basic human condition (cf. Hartsock, 1983, chap. 1). (p. 55, citation in the original)

In other words, Young and other feminist thinkers ask us to recognize that we are all dependent on someone else at points in our lives. Therefore, dependency should not diminish or stigmatize either the person receiving or providing care. Recognizing the value and worth of caring and being cared for means acknowledging and supporting care work as part of human interdependence rather than relegating it to the invisible realm of the private sphere where families must fend for themselves as best they can.

Child Care Alternative: U.S. Military Child Care

For those people who suggest that high-quality, universal child care that is available in other countries could never be provided in the United States, the U.S. military serves as a local model. As a result of poor quality child care, excess cost, and the long wait lists faced by military personnel, in 1989, the U.S. Congress passed the Military Child Care Act. Like the examples we provide above, there was a purpose for this legislation that goes beyond caring and education of young children. It was designed to retain talented workers in the military as they began to have families and to allow active military personnel focus on their very important jobs without the distraction caused by concern over their children's well-being. This system of care for the children of military personnel is a home-grown model that could be used for the rest of the country. Military personnel go to a centralized place to find family child care, child development centers, and care for school-aged children. Military child care must meet Department of Defense (DOD) certification standards, and child development centers must be in compliance with standards set out by the National Association for the Education of Young Children (NAEYC), a nonprofit accrediting body and advocacy group (Pomper, Blank, Campbell, & Schullman, 2004).

In 2005, 91% of military child care centers were accredited by NAEYC as compared to 8% of civilian child care centers. Military child care workers are paid salaries commensurate

[1]Norwegian parents are entitled to 56 paid weeks at 80% of their salary.

[2]Fineman (1995) chooses the term *caretaking* because she believes it denotes the value and importance of the activity, whereas she sees the term *caregiving* as reinforcing the devaluation of caring for others (p. 9).

with the pay of other military personnel with similar levels of education and training. This means full-time workers receive health benefits, sick leave, retirement benefits, and life insurance; some supervisors earned up to $76,000 a year in 2004 (Pomper et al., 2004). Child care workers in these programs receive extensive initial and ongoing training, which contributes to the stability of the child care workforce and maintains their knowledge base and credentials. Parents pay fees based on a sliding scale and providers are given subsidies to enable them to provide care for children from lower-earning families, making care affordable to all parents. In 2004 and 2005, costs ranged from a low of $43 to $59 dollars a week to a high of $107 to $126 a week, depending on parental income, approximately 8% to 13% of income for lower-earning parents and 9% for higher-earning parents. The armed forces subsidize home-based family care and center-based care, both of which are licensed and regulated (Pomper et al., 2004).

OPPORTUNITIES FOR ADVOCACY

Social workers can and should familiarize themselves with existing and proposed ECEC policies at the state and federal level. These can impact clients including local communities, child care providers, families receiving benefits, labor unions, or families whose children have educational or developmental needs. The National Conference of State Legislatures provides links to local ECEC enacted and proposed legislation in all the U.S. states and territories (National Conference of State Legislatures, 2019). On a federal level, the Early Education and Care Consortium (2017) has a website that provides updates for all federal policies relating to child care and early education. Some longtime advocacy organizations, such as the National Women's Law Center, Child Care Aware, and the Economic Policy Institute, provide data that include the type of care, child care providers' earnings, quality of care, number of children in subsidized care, as well as analyses of who would be helped by proposed legislation. This information is helpful to anyone interested in learning more about and advocating in the area of ECEC.

Many national and local organizations continue to advocate for the expansion of ECEC, quality improvement, and strategies to reduce the cost and/or subsidize the cost of care. One challenge is that advocacy groups sometimes work at cross purposes. Head Start, for example, seeks greater funding and support for Head Start whereas PreK advocates are focused on getting federal and state money to support the development and expansion of PreK programs. These programs address the needs of 4-year-old and sometimes 3-year-old children. With a limited supply of resources, these groups as well as those who are advocating for tax reform may find themselves fighting for the same dollars. However, there seems to be a growing recognition that all aspects of child care are connected, and advocates are exploring collaborative work, including cooperation between child care advocates and child care providers (Palley & Shdaimah, 2014). That many in the field now use the term early childhood education and care illustrates the recognition that quality care must involve developmentally appropriate educational programming in addition to basic safety. Social workers can play a role in organizing across priorities, strengthening the ties among groups that have shared goals and agendas, and framing the issue in ways that speak to potential allies and the broader public.

There has been recent federal momentum to address the cost of care and provide greater financial support for middle-and upper-income families. For example, in January 2017, Republican Senator Richard Burr and Independent Senator Angus King introduced a bill designed to increase the amount of money that families can place in flexible spending accounts and to make the Child Care and Dependent Tax Credit refundable (Child Care Aware of America, 2017). There are also several state level bills that address ECEC. For example, Colorado outlawed suspension in publicly-funded preschools (Open States, 2019). A 2019 Massachusetts proposal would require preschools to develop policies that confine the use of suspensions and expulsions to instances of grave danger.

Some groups, including the First Five Years Fund, have aligned themselves with tax policy advocacy. These groups have suggested that the Child and Dependent Tax Credit become fully refundable and that it be increased from $3,000 per child to $12,000 for a 4 year old or $17,000 for an infant to reflect the real cost of care. They also advocate for the expansion of the Lifetime Learning Credit, which currently applies only to college tuition and allows for a credit up to $2,000 per tax return, to include early childhood education (First Five Years Fund, 2017).

Another area for advocacy is to fight for better compensation for child care providers as a crucial workforce that contributes to children's well-being and employment support. More than 50% of this low-wage workforce, disproportionately comprised of women, immigrants, and people of color, is eligible for means-tested benefits (Whitebook et al., 2016). These workers are simultaneously undervalued and the subject of a growing number of regulations and credentialing requirements (Shdaimah et al., 2018). England and Folbre (1999) have claimed that the reason we have publicly supported education is because it is viewed as a public good and that society as a whole is considered to benefit from a well-educated workforce and citizenry. However, research on early childhood development over the past 20 years has consistently demonstrated the importance of early childhood experience on the development of the human brain (Center on the Developing Child at Harvard University, 2016) and on a child's future outcomes (Heckman et al., 2006). Advocacy can draw attention to systemic factors that affect providers, children, and families and build alliances between these groups as well as with families with children and child care and early education providers. Coalition building for advocacy has been a hallmark of social work policy interventions as you have seen throughout this book. The area of child care and early education can similarly benefit from coalition building. Can you think about some of the ways that the interests of different groups may diverge or align? What kind of social work expertise and skills might help different groups come together to identify common cause and work together for policies that can support families while providing meaningful employment at living wages? No doubt there are other stakeholders, like employers, who may also need to be involved in such a coalition.

DISCUSSION

CHILD CARE AS PART OF AN EDUCATION CONTINUUM

Some proposals, such as a recent discussion in Minnesota, suggest treating funding for early childhood education much as we fund K–12 education.

- Consider the ramifications of child care policies that would treat child care the way that we treat K–12 education.
- How might this change the price and availability of child care (for individuals, families, or government)?
- How might this affect the qualifications of child care workers? How might this affect the salaries of child care workers?
- How might this affect standards for child care facilities?

Final Discussion

Now that you have finished reading this chapter, reread the vignette at the beginning. Based on what you have learned, answer the following questions. Point to specific references in the chapter that help you answer these questions. Consider how different theories inform the response to these questions.

1. Can you identify the specific policies that impact Marcie and her children?
2. How do existing policies limit or expand Marcie's options to secure appropriate, high-quality education and care for Max and Rose?
3. How might policies affect current and future opportunities for Max and Rose?
4. What roles could a social worker play in helping Marcie and her family (think micro, mezzo, and macro level social work)?
5. What role might race, class, gender, and other aspects of identity play in this vignette?

EDUCATION POLICY, KINDERGARTEN THROUGH HIGH SCHOOL

Co-authored by Jennifer Dull

LEARNING OBJECTIVES

7.1: Describe the history and meaning of schools

7.2: Critique how educational policies affect the education of various groups of students

7.3: Analyze the role of education using social construction theory

7.4: Develop advocacy opportunities that improve education for marginalized groups

The field of education is a common social work practice area. Access to education also affects social work clients on many levels. This chapter reviews federal education policies for children from kindergarten through high school and their implications for state and local districts. It begins by providing background on the history and social construction of relevant policies and identifies different constituents who have been involved in their creation. We discuss how childhood has been understood, has affected the development of education policy in the United States, and how such policies shaped and were shaped by class, race, and gender inequality. We also examine the implications of specific national and state-based education policy, and the impact of segregation and funding formulas on the quality of education. This chapter further explores debates over the role of federal and state government in determining curricula, overseeing educational quality accountability, and balancing the demands of public education with calls for parental control over their children's education.

Vignette: Arvin's Educational Challenges

Based on what you know from the media or your personal, work, or volunteer experiences, think about the following questions as you read the vignette. When you finish the vignette, answer the questions below.

1. Can you identify the specific policies that impact Arvin?
2. How do existing policies limit or expand Judie and Sandra's options to secure appropriate, high-quality education for Arvin?
3. What are the challenges Ms. Reyes, Arvin, and his parents face in ensuring that the federal policies are implemented in this school?
4. What role might race, class, gender and other aspects of identity play in this vignette?

Lately Arvin has been having trouble in school and his teacher, Ms. Reyes, suspects that he may have a learning disability. Arvin, a usually cheerful 7 year old, complains that he doesn't understand his homework, and he often asks to stay home from school. Ms. Reyes suggested that Arvin's parents, Judie and Sandra, request to have him evaluated. They submitted a formal request for an evaluation that the school must complete within 60 days to comply with state law. However, school budget cuts now mean that there are only two district psychologists for the three elementary schools serving 1,500 children. Sandra and Judie have also heard rumors that the school might be shut down for failing to make **adequate yearly progress** for several consecutive years. This means that a high percentage of students are performing under grade level, as measured by statewide annual standardized tests. They have looked into a number of charter schools in their city, but they don't believe that any of these have the resources or the teachers with special education training that Arvin might need.

Adequate yearly progress: Grade-level performance on statewide annual tests based on federal or state standards related to No Child Left Behind and its newer version, Every Student Succeeds

Sandra reached out to her cousin Celina, who lives just over the city line in a wealthy suburban school district. Celina has offered to have the family stay with her so that they can send Arvin to a better school. It would be crowded if Judie, Sandra, and Arvin moved in, but if they can manage, then they might be able to have Arvin assessed and begin to receive services. At some point, they could try to find an affordable rental home in the district with Celina's help, but Judie and Sandra are unlikely to be able to find a place before school starts and there are few affordable places to live in the district. Even if Arvin's assessment does not reveal a learning disability that would entitle him to services, the classroom sizes in Celina's district are capped at 23 students, whereas Arvin now has 35 classmates. Sandra and Judie believe that the greater opportunity for individual attention would be helpful. The elementary school in Celina's neighborhood also offers free homework help and sports programming twice a week, which would provide Arvin with some after-school supervision and enrichment, as well as a highly-subsidized summer enrichment camp. However, Sandra and Judie are a little concerned. They know they would have to have a rental contract with Celina or something that seems official because they heard about a case in another state where parents faced criminal charges for registering their children at a school when they did not live in the district. Even if the arrangement is temporary and risky, Sandra and Judie want to provide Arvin with the best education that they can, and they worry that he is already falling behind.

HISTORY AND SOCIAL CONSTRUCTION OF U.S. EDUCATION

The history of U.S. education includes many different ideas about what education is and which students should be eligible to participate. In this section, we look at the changing meanings of education in the United States and how those affect our view of education today. We also look at some key groups that have been involved in shaping education policies.

Public Schools for Whom?

Public education efforts predate the founding of the United States. In 1647, the Massachusetts Bay Colony required that any town with 50 or more families establish an elementary school as part of the Old Deluder Satan Law (Massachusetts Court System, n.d.).

Although schooling was beginning to be offered as a public good prior to and during the Revolutionary War period, it was far from a general public right. Often, education was divided into separate systems for children from families of limited means and their well-off counterparts. In 1814, Thomas Jefferson proposed that "the laboring" and "the learned" receive different types of education. "[T]he laboring will need the first grade of education to qualify them for their pursuits and duties: [T]he learned will need it as a foundation for further acquirements" (p. 2). In 1790, Pennsylvania suggested the state should be responsible for educating children from families with limited financial resources, but families of means should pay for their own children's schooling. The type of schooling believed appropriate for state-educated children was exemplified by the New York Public School Society, formed in 1805, to teach in the Lancasterian model. One master would give a rote lesson to older students, who shared it with younger students, who shared it with those even younger. In this method, one teacher could teach hundreds of students, and students would learn "discipline and obedience qualities" desired by factory owners (Brown-Martin & Tavakolian, 2015). These students were educated to be workers who would serve elites rather than educated to be leaders. Separate systems also existed for male and female children and white and nonwhite children. Compulsory public education in 17th century Massachusetts Bay Colony was primarily comprised of programs for white male children (Osgood, 2008). As a result, in 1780, the literacy rate for women was half that of the rate for men (National Women's History Museum, n.d.).

In 1817, the Boston Town Meeting considered a system of free primary schools, although wage earners were concerned about the expense to taxpayers. In 1820, the country's first public high school, Boston English, opened, and by 1827, Massachusetts had made public school free for all. Though Massachusetts' free education system began as voluntary, the state made education mandatory in 1851. Their efforts focused specifically on children of immigrants, who were considered by the government to need socialization and "Americanization" (Osgood, 2008). With a similar goal of socializing the Native American population, federal law was enacted to force thousands of Native American children to attend public boarding schools to "solve the Indian problem." The attitude of these schools was captured by Captain Richard H. Pratt, who founded the first boarding school and said these schools needed to "kill the Indian in him and save the man" (Bear, 2008, n.p.). In 1880, the Under Secretary of the Interior issued regulations requiring that all instruction of Native American children be in English (Prucha, 1973). The Indian Bureau provided guidance to enforce these regulations under threat of removal of children and of support for education:

> You will please inform the authorities of this school that the English language only must be taught the Indian youth placed there for educational and industrial training at the expense of the Government. If Dakota or any other language is taught such children, they will be taken away and their support by the Government will be withdrawn from the school. (Atkins, 1887)

Outside of a few states, in the 1800s, most children received no formal education. Most lived in rural communities and were either apprenticed or worked on their family's farms. In areas where schooling was available, while both boys and girls were allowed to attend, girls were generally steered toward home economics or other vocational classes (Madigan, 2009). In the late 1800s, as a result of urbanization and increased immigration, there was an expansion of government regulation, some of which was designed to support children (Osgood, 2008). However, for the majority of our country's history, education was voluntary, tuition-based, and, as was the case in Massachusetts, locally funded and supervised. Eventually, the federal government provided money from the sale of unsettled lands to fund public education and required that all states admitted to the Union after the Civil War create nonsectarian public schools, for which it provided minimal funding (Rhodes, 2012).

Library of Congress, LC-USZ62-120428

PHOTO 7.1 Early U.S. school; date and location unknown

While educational opportunities were expanding for white students from the laboring and immigrant communities in the North, by the 1930s, Southern states were passing laws making it illegal to teach reading to those who were enslaved (see Photo 7.1 of an early 20th century rural school). Despite such laws, about 5% of enslaved people were able to become literate. Free public education came to the South after the Civil War and, once instituted, benefited white children more than African American children (Center for Racial Justice Innovation, 2006). Not only were schools that served African Americans severely under-resourced in relation to schools that served their white counterparts, but the Supreme Court ruled that separation itself was not inherently unequal. In 1896, the Supreme Court decision in *Plessy v. Ferguson*, while technically about rail cars, allowed for "separate but equal" segregated public schools across the country. It was not until the *Brown v. Board of Education* decision in 1954 that school **segregation**, or separating groups of people by race, religion, ethnicity, or gender, was ruled unconstitutional. While this ruling technically meant that educational segregation became illegal, *de facto* segregation persists through residential patterns that often group people by race and class (Felton, 2017).

Segregation: Separating groups of people by race, religion, ethnicity, or gender

Public education through high school developed to "inform the citizenry so they could govern and to assimilate the immigrants" (Graham, 1995, p. 11). Students were routinely required to repeat grades if they had not been able to master the material and were extremely likely to leave school before they could graduate. For example, for every 1,000 students who entered elementary school in New York City in 1908, 263 would graduate from eighth grade and only 56 would graduate from high school (Graham, 1995).

The history of U.S. education is marked with racial, socioeconomic, and gender inequities. Once black children were allowed to attend school, educational segregation based on race and religion maintained racial and cultural hierarchies. Girls were also often excluded from educational opportunities afforded to their brothers, a phenomenon that Title IX sought to address. Education in the United States has always provided fewer opportunities and resources for children from lower-income families compared to their higher-income counterparts. This has been caused by or exacerbated by the ways in which our education is paid for. The localized nature of school funding means that wealthier districts are better able to support education and enrichment, and poor districts have fewer resources to deal with higher needs. Diane Ravitch, Assistant Secretary of Education under George H.W. Bush, summed up many of these ideas: "In America, we have often been satisfied with the democratic principle that all children could attend school. We have not been insistent that all children would not only attend but also learn" (Graham, 1995, p. 5).

Education as a Tool for Social Change

Although educational policies have often reflected and deepened inequalities in our society, education has also been used positively as a mechanism to create social change. Some view the education of new immigrants following industrialization as a positive example, even as others criticize its patronizing and assimilationist stance. **Assimilation** refers to losing one's original cultural identity and practice, which may include losing native languages. Education was seen initially as a means to socialize children and influence their families and, as such, as much for the benefit of broader society as the children who were being educated. In the 1960s, education was seen as a mechanism to address racism. As the ideals of the country and the needs of the workforce have changed, education has been seen as a tool to produce educated democratic citizens, train factory workers for the industrial age, create strong scientists to compete in the Space Race and in the international STEM economy, as well as a place to help integrate children with disabilities into mainstream society. Beginning with *Brown v. Board of Education* (1954) and the Elementary and Secondary Education Act (ESEA, 1965), the federal government began taking a role in using public education as a mechanism to reduce inequality, an area of policy previously left to states and localities, with mixed results.

Assimilation: Adjusting to the surrounding cultural context. This is often associated with losing one's original cultural identity and practices and may include losing native languages.

Oversight and Accountability

The Elementary and Secondary Education Act (1965) was designed to equalize the playing field and help children from disadvantaged backgrounds improve their educational opportunities and make them more commensurate with that of well-to-do students. According to Patricia Albjerg Graham (1995), ESEA was politically palatable precisely because no one knew exactly what "equal educational opportunity" was or how to implement it. In fact, this law was viewed suspiciously by educators because of their concerns about its implementation. As a result of questions raised by Robert F. Kennedy and Wayne Morse about how to judge the success of the law, as well as pushback from educators and others about federal over-involvement in education, then–Secretary of Education Frances Keppel turned to the Carnegie Foundation to develop a measure. The **National Assessment for Educational Progress** was the first significant measure used to assess student performance. Use of this measure began a tradition of federal push for oversight and accountability (Graham, 1995).

National Assessment for Educational Progress: A national testing tool used to assess student performance

In 2001, the Elementary and Secondary Education Act was replaced by the No Child Left Behind Act of 2001 (NCLB, 2002), which expanded federal oversight of schools and established more specific accountability standards. This highly popular legislation, which was supported by Republicans, Democrats, civil rights advocates, and business groups, was signed into law by George W. Bush (Klein, 2015). While many believed it would equalize educational opportunities, the law was problematic for many schools, teachers, students, and families. It was designed to maintain protections for students with high needs and continue to enforce the importance of annual statewide assessments measuring progress toward standards. It was also designed to provide more opportunity for local innovation by allowing states to develop their own assessment measures and emphasized the needs of students in the lowest-performing schools (U.S. Department of Education, n.d.a). Among other requirements, NCLB mandated that all students in Grades 3 through 8, regardless of race, income, disability, language, or background, achieve state-defined proficiency standards in reading and math by 2014. Under NCLB, schools were assessed based on the achievements of their students. States were given the discretion to set their own educational goals and measures, but were required to show "adequate yearly progress" (AYP) through "continuous and substantial improvement," with particular emphasis on the achievements of students who were economically disadvantaged or with limited English language proficiency (U.S. Department of Education, 2009). Schools that did not achieve AYP could be closed and their students transferred to other schools. A central critique of NCLB was that schools with the highest need populations did not receive the resources to make the improvements. Adding insult to injury, these schools and the communities they served were punished for their failure to improve. These consequences created incentives for schools to suspend or remove students who had learning and other difficulties, so those students' test results would not impact the school's overall scores. Finally, many teachers complained that state measures and the need to perform on tests led to the phenomenon of *teaching to the test*, encouraging teachers and students to practice a narrow set of skills and provide limited educational content to score well. In many schools, parents and educators felt the policy left little to no space for creative learning or development of critical thinking skills (Kozol, 2005).

Efforts to reform the law to address critiques continued as it was renewed and amended, but critics raised concerns with each incarnation. In 2015, NCLB was replaced with the Every Student Succeeds Act (ESSA), which was implemented beginning in 2017. ESSA allows states more local control than No Child Left Behind to set achievement goals for students and to develop strategies to address the needs of schools that are struggling with low student performance and high drop-out rates. States must set challenging academic standards for students in math, reading, and science. They can use the federal Common Core Standards for this purpose, but do not have to. States are also now required to consider more than student test scores when evaluating school performance and can determine what those additional factors should be.

Role of the Federal Government

Since the federal government began to take a role in education, there have been tensions between states' desire for federal support for education and local resistance to federal oversight and direction. Federal involvement in education has developed over the years amid uncertainty of the role the federal government should play in education and a general desire to have decisions about schools made at the state and local level. The U.S. Department of Education's website (n.d.b) starts with this disclaimer for visitors: "Please note that in the U.S., the federal role in education is limited. Because of the Tenth Amendment, most education policy is decided at the state and local levels."

Education is not mentioned in the federal Constitution despite its guarantee in all 50 state Constitutions. The Department of Education was created in 1867 with a budget of $15,000 and four employees, marking the federal government's first foray into education, but it was demoted back down to an Office of Education the following year, amid fears that the federal government would exert too much control over schools (U.S. Department of Education, 2010). It remained small, moving from the Department of the Interior to the Department of Health, Education, and Welfare.

With the exception of the small operations within the then–Office of Education, the federal government was largely not engaged in education policy until the landmark decision in *Brown v. Board of Education* (1954), which was designed to desegregate schools. The federal government did not provide direct financing for public education until 1965 when the Elementary and Secondary Education Act (now Every Student Succeeds), (2015) was passed, which provided funding to support compensatory services for low-income and minority students who had been historically disadvantaged (Rhodes, 2012). Following the 1960s, some states began to provide funding to local districts to create some minimum standards designed to provide equity for historically disadvantaged children. However, curricular decisions were largely relegated to localities. The Department of Education was reinstituted as a Cabinet-level office under the 1979 Department of Education Organization Act and became active in 1980. To date, there is a debate about whether the Department should be abolished and all control of schools returned to states and communities or whether there should be more intensive federal standards. The timeline below provides a lens to indicate how quiet the federal government has been about education in some time periods and how active they have been in others.

Profile of Social Worker and Education Secretary Wilbur Cohen. Wilbur J. Cohen was born in Wisconsin in 1913 (DeWitt, 2011). He studied economics at the University of Wisconsin-Madison, and despite the fact that he never completed any graduate education, he went on to become, among other things, one of the founding voices behind the Social Security program, a Secretary of Education, and a social work professor. In 1935, at age 22, Cohen moved to Washington, DC, to work with social workers, such as Eveline Burns and Frances Perkins, on the creation of Social Security. He was offered a tenured position teaching Public Welfare Administration at the University of Michigan in 1956 (remember that he had only an undergraduate degree), where he developed expertise in education policy and became a strong policy advocate. He returned to government in 1961 at the request of President Kennedy, and he served as Assistant Secretary of Health, Education, and Welfare before becoming President Johnson's Secretary of Health, Education, and Welfare in 1968.

In his position as secretary, Cohen fought for 65 major pieces of legislation, including the Elementary and Secondary Education Act and Medicare. He played a part in American social welfare policy from 1935 until his death in 1987 (DeWitt, 2011). One obituary read,

> It is rare for someone to come to Washington at the age of 21, spend decades in the bureaucracy and rise to a position in the Cabinet. It is even rarer for a high political appointee to be widely admired for his expertise and renowned for his amiable nature. This was Wilbur Cohen . . . Like his friend Hubert Humphrey, Wilbur Cohen cared not only about "the people," but about individual people. Through a lifetime of working to improve the lot of others, he never lost his enthusiasm or his largeness of spirit.
>
> (Wilbur Joseph Cohen, 1987, p. A19)

History of Education in the U.S.: Timeline of Federal Education Actions

- 1867: First federal Department of Education created by Andrew Johnson, demoted to an Office of Education in 1868
- 1953: Department of Health, Education, and Welfare (HEW) established by Reorganization Plan No. 1 of 1953
- 1958: National Defense Education Act provided $900 million for federal aid to guidance, counseling, and testing; support for teaching science, mathematics, foreign languages, vocational training, training teachers and language specialists, research in use of media, and college loans, spurred by the Soviet Union's success with Sputnik
- 1964: Civil Rights Act of 1964 required the Commissioner of Education to report on the extent to which public educational opportunities were limited by discrimination in race, color, religion, or national origin and provided funding to overcome problems of desegregation
- 1965: Elementary and Secondary Education Act of 1965 authorized $1.33 billion to public schools, including $1 billion for those deprived of education; amended in 1966 and 1968, part of President Johnson's War on Poverty
- 1965: Head Start authorized
- 1966: Office for Civil Rights created
- 1967: Advisory Committee on Mexican-American Education and Office of Indian Affairs created within the Office of Education
- 1968: Under Secretary and social worker Wilbur Cohen became HEW Secretary
- 1969: Office of Child Development established within HEW and Head Start was transferred here
- 1970–1971: Office of Education grants $7 million to the Children's Television Workshop to develop *Sesame Street* (for early childhood) and The Electric Company (to help 7 to 10 year olds learn to read)
- 1972: Title IX passes
- 1974: Family Educational Rights and Privacy Act
- 1975: Education for All Handicapped Children Act (EAHCA)
- 1979: Department of Education Organization Act passed, paving the way for a standalone Cabinet-level Department of Education in 1980 (U.S. Department of Education, 2010)
- 1990: Individuals with Disabilities Education Act (IDEA)
- 1994: Public School Redefinition Act
- 2002: No Child Left Behind Act
- 2015: Every Student Succeeds Act

Source: U.S. Department of Health and Human Services. (1972). A common thread of service: A history of the Department of Health, Education, and Welfare. Retrieved from https://aspe.hhs.gov/report/common-thread-service/history-department-health-education-and-welfare

PHOTO 7.2 Demonstrators in Arizona protest funding cuts.

Labor Unions and Education

In 1916, the American Federation of Teachers (AFT) formed a national union incorporating local unions from most of the major cities across the United States. However, these groups were not authorized to collectively bargain on behalf of teachers. It wasn't until 1962, as a result of a strike, that New York City teachers won the first collective bargaining agreement in public education (Moe, 2011). **Collective bargaining** is a technique where the union bargains for an entire group of members rather than individuals to make a group contract with an employer. The percentage of teachers covered by collective bargaining rose to 65% in 1978, and has remained relatively stable. Teachers currently enjoy collective bargaining rights in 34 states (Moe, 2011).

Collective bargaining: A technique used, generally by unions, where the union bargains for an entire group of members rather than individuals to make a group contract with an employer

Unions: Organized membership groups of workers that advocate for fair wages and better working conditions for employees as a group

Unions are organized membership groups of workers that help advocate for fair wages and better working conditions for employees as a group. Unions have been a source of strength for teachers enabling them to negotiate for better pay, better benefits, and even breaks and planning time during the day. However, teachers' unions have also been criticized for supporting and protecting incompetent teachers as well as for advocating for pensions that are no longer available to many workers in the private sector. Unionized teachers are also paid based on salary schedules so that the amount of seniority and formal education determines one's salary rather than one's merit as a teacher. Some mayors and both school and district level administrators have argued that the benefits and tenure that teachers' unions have been able to achieve as a result of negotiations challenge their ability to improve the quality of education for children in public schools (Moe, 2011) (see Photo 7.2 for a protest sign for a demonstration to support funding public education).

CURRENT EDUCATION POLICY

In this section, we highlight key education policies, primarily federally directed policies that are implemented at the state and local level. This section reviews policies that address student record keeping, discrimination, and school discipline. At the end of this section in Table 7.1, you will see a review of federal policies, and in Table 7.2, you can review a summary of state level variation in selected educational policies.

School Segregation

Though the Supreme Court ruled that districts could not segregate schools in *Brown v. Board of Education* in 1954, many schools and districts remain de facto segregated. Following that court decision, legislation created explicit rules about discrimination in public programming. Title VI of the Civil Rights Act of 1964 stated, "No person in the United States shall, on the ground of race, color, or national origin, be excluded from participation in, be denied the benefits of, or be subjected to discrimination under any program or activity receiving Federal financial assistance." The Department of Health, Education, and Welfare toured schools in the South within a week of the law's passage and met with superintendents of schools to discuss voluntary compliance with the new law (U.S. Department of Health and Human Services, 1972). However, schools in many states, Northern and Southern, waited decades to integrate. In many cases they did not do so unless forced through parents' lawsuits.

Even though legal segregation is no longer allowed, integration of students from different racial and ethnic backgrounds is far from finished. Since 1970, when the results of this law might have been expected to start, the number of schools that are severely segregated, with enrollment of white students between 0% and 10%, has more than tripled. According to the Civil Rights Project at the University of California-Los Angeles, 18.6% of schools in the United States had white enrollment between 0% and 10% and 18.4% had nonwhite enrollment between 0% and 10%. This means that 37% of students in the United States—more than one in three—attend schools comprised almost entirely of white students or students of color, with particularly isolating effects for African American and Latino students (Orfield, Ee, Frankenberg, & Siegel-Hawley, 2016). Often described as a process of **resegregation**, the short-lived and arguably marginally successful efforts to desegregate have been reversed. Many attribute this to a combination of seemingly private choices to live in highly segregated residential patterns. However, such patterns are a product of a legacy of institutional racism and economic inequality that lead to and reinforce wealth and income divides. Federal housing policies that have caused segregation contribute to this resegregation (see Chapter 14 for more details on these policies). As a result of resegregation, low-income, often black and other minority, students do not have access to the same quality of education that students in wealthier school districts, often white, receive.

Resegregation: Reintroducing segregation where it may have been reduced or previously ended. This is often done through policies that do not explicitly support segregation but their impact results in segregation.

Desegregation occurs when people in schools are no longer separated by race. The newest front in the fight for desegregation is rezoning districts. Across the United States, communities have been rezoning or separating existing school districts in ways that reduce communities economic and racial integration. According to Felton (2017), "[W]hite parents are leading a secession movement with dire consequences for black students." Though *Brown v. Board of Education* (1954) made it illegal to segregate schools solely on race, it was not until the early 1970s that many districts were forced to bus students between school districts in an effort to break up segregated schools (*Stout v. Board of Education of Jefferson County*, 1971). Since that time, the Justice Department has exercised little authority to stop school redistricting or the end to forced busing. As a result, Southern public schools are now more racially segregated today than they were 40 years ago (Felton, 2017).

Desegregation: An end to separating people by race in schools or other public accommodation

Student Privacy

The Federal Education Reporting and Privacy Act (FERPA, 1974) provides parents of minors and students age 18 and over with the right to access, inspect, and challenge their own educational records. It also allows adult children and parents the right to grant written authorization to share educational records with other parties. FERPA applies to all agencies that receive either direct or indirect federal funding for education and as a result, applies to public schools, charter schools, colleges, and universities. FERPA allows records to be shared within schools if they are being shared as a result of legitimate educational reasons, when a student is transferring schools, and with other state agencies including the juvenile justice system when required by state law. These laws also apply in all educational settings where the federal government provides funding, including college, but once students turns 18, they can determine who should have access to their records, including whether to allow parent access.

Gender Discrimination, Sexual Assault, and Sexual Harassment

Title IX: Ensures all students have the right to be free of discrimination based on gender

While gender discrimination, sexual harassment, and sexual assault are often discussed at the college level or in the working world, they are also significant problems in the secondary school setting. **Title IX** of the Educational Amendments Act of 1972 ensures all students the right to be free of discrimination based on gender. Though originally used in secondary education as a mechanism to increase girls' access to school athletics, this law has also led to the end of publicly financed single-gender education. It has further been used to limit the sexual harassment and unequal treatment of students as well as employees of educational institutions. Title IX requires schools to protect all students against sexual assault and harassment, regardless of sex, sexual orientation, race or national origin, age, disability, or documentation status, and to provide resources on these topics to students.

Often social workers are charged with helping implement the rules set out by Title IX. Social workers are often assigned to work both with victims and perpetrators of sexual assault. Gender identity was not a priority of Congress when this legislation was passed in 1972, but legal decisions since then have expanded the law's protections to gender, not only biological sex, affecting students who identify as transgender. Much of the policy on gender identity from the federal government since 1972 has come through regulations or guidance from federal agencies rather than specific legislation. Individual states may also have stronger protections for transgender individuals than the federal government offers (Buzuvis, 2013).

School Discipline

School discipline policy, which includes discipline, searching students' possessions, drug testing, and suspension, is a key area for social workers working with school-aged children. Nineteen states still allow corporal punishment in public schools, and 48 allow private schools to use it (Gershoff & Font, 2016). Further, school personnel need only have *reasonable suspicion* that a student is violating a school policy to search their belongings when they are in school (*New Jersey v. T.L.O.*, 1985). Though schools and districts cannot randomly subject students to drug tests, they can develop policies requiring drug testing for students who wish to participate in student athletics or other extracurricular activities (*Board of Education of Independent School District 92 of Pottawatomie County v. Lindsay Earls*, 2002; *Veronia School District v. Acton*, 1995). Based on the Supreme Court decision in *Goss v. Lopez* (1975), most school systems have policies requiring that if a student is suspended for 10 days or less that the student be given notice of the charges and an opportunity to present his or her version of the story generally prior to the disciplinary action. If the child is suspended for 10 or more days or expelled, most districts require hearings with school district personnel. Some schools use restorative justice policies, policies designed to be nonpunitive and to repair the social fabric by reintegrating victims and offenders into the school environment. A randomized study in Pittsburgh Public Schools found that these practices were effective in reducing school suspensions, including reducing the disparate treatment of black students, although New Haven Public Schools have not yet found the same effect (Peak, 2019). This practice is covered more thoroughly in Chapter 13 on criminal justice.

Special Education and Disabilities

Before the 1970s, education for children with disabilities, when it happened, occurred in a different realm, separated from all other students. Much of it was privately funded. In

1838, Boston established separate schools for children needing special instruction, such as schools for older immigrants and students who struggled academically. In addition, by the late 1800s, many school districts had created segregated schools for both deaf and blind students (Osgood, 2008).

Today, federal law affords certain rights for students with disabilities. Section 504 of the Rehabilitation Act of 1973 was the first law to provide an affirmative right for students with disabilities not to experience discrimination in public schools. Section 504 applies to all organizations that are federally funded and, therefore, also applies to colleges and universities. The Americans with Disabilities Act (ADA) expanded this provision in 1990 to apply to all schools other than parochial schools (which are excluded from the ADA) so private schools are now prohibited from discriminating against children with disabilities.

The Individuals with Disabilities Education Act (IDEA, 2004), originally the Education for All Handicapped Children Act (1975) provides federal funding to support the education of children with disabilities beginning with newborns who demonstrate developmental delays and continuing through high school (up to a maximum of age 21). The original law proposed that the federal government would cover 40% of the cost of special education, because it was assumed this amount would cover the difference in spending between children with and without disabilities. In practice, the federal government has never paid more than 17% to 20% of the cost of educating students with disabilities (Tiede, 2016).

According to the IDEA, all children with disabilities are entitled to receive a "free appropriate public education" in the "least restrictive environment." The Supreme Court has noted that a **free appropriate public education** need not be the best possible education but rather one that is "reasonably calculated to enable a child to receive meaningful educational benefit," or an adequate education as opposed to one that is designed to help a child reach his or her potential (*Board of Education of Hendrick Hudson School District v. Rowley*, 1982, pp. 206–207). Though the IDEA excludes medical services, the Supreme Court has found public school systems are obligated to pay for nursing services, such as catheterization that are necessary for a student to attend school (*Irving v. Tatro*, 1984; *Cedar Rapids School District v. Garret F.*, 1999).

Free appropriate public education: the legal standard for educating children with disabilities in publicly funded schools. The education must be "reasonably calculated to enable a child to receive meaningful educational benefit" (Board of Education of Hendrick Hudson School District v. Rowley, 1982)

Under the IDEA, each state must develop a plan to actively locate and identify children with disabilities. Parents may also request that their child be evaluated to determine if the student is eligible for special education services. Once a parent has signed a written consent to have their child evaluated, the IDEA requires that the evaluations must be completed within 60 days. Parents can also request an independent evaluation at public expense if they disagree with the school's initial evaluation.

Once a school district determines that a child is eligible for special education services under the IDEA, they must develop a plan, called an **Individual Education Plan** (IEP). This plan identifies the student's disability, his or her needs, and describes how these needs will be addressed, including what services will be provided, by whom, how often, and the extent to which the student will be educated with nondisabled peers. It also includes a section on student accommodations and specialized services. Once a student is 16, his or her IEP must include a section on transitioning the student to independence.

Individual Education Plan (IEP): A plan, mandated by the Individuals with Disabilities Education Act for special education students, which identifies the student's disability and needs. It also includes an explanation of how these needs will be addressed, including what services will be provided, by whom, how often, and the extent to which the student will be educated with nondisabled peers.

School Finance

School finance refers to the systems that are put into place by each state to fund their public education. Because schools in the United States are primarily funded through local government, the state-level funding mechanisms mean that children who live in wealthier areas can generally attend better-resourced public schools. The Elementary and Secondary Education Act (1965) was established to provide some supplemental funding for children in lower-income districts. It remains the primary source of federal funding for public education in the United States. Baker, Farrie, Johnson, Luhm, and Sciarra (2017) found that many states, including California and Texas, provide low percentages of their economic capacity to education. Only four states in the United States (Delaware, Massachusetts, Minnesota, and New Jersey) use progressive school finance systems in which they provide high funding for education generally and increased funding for high-poverty districts. Fourteen states, including Illinois, New York, North Dakota, and Pennsylvania, had policies that actually provide less state funding to students in high needs areas.

In the early 1970s, in an effort to address the inequity of school funding mechanisms, a group of parents sued the San Antonio School District on behalf of children from low-income and minority households in Texas. Their claim was that the unequal funding that existed between schools in richer and poorer neighborhoods violated the Equal Protection Clause of the U.S. Constitution (*San Antonio Indep. Sch. Dist. v. Rodriguez*, 1973). The Supreme Court ultimately rejected the idea that the Equal Protection Clause of the U.S. Constitution applied. The court claimed that education was not a fundamental Constitutional right or liberty interest and found that no suspect class of citizens was particularly disadvantaged by the Texas school finance policies. A **suspect class** is a group who has experienced historical discrimination and/or one who is powerless to protect themselves in the political process. The court found that the Texas school finance policies were rationally related to a legitimate government purpose and, as such, could remain.

Suspect class: The Supreme Court has held that laws that affect one of these groups should be held to a higher standard of review. Suspect classes include race, religion, alienage, and national origin.

REFLECTION

IS EDUCATION A RIGHT OR A PRIVILEGE?

Choose one of the following positions to argue in a debate. Research your position and be prepared to make at least three arguments to back up the position. Consider the role that the values of the social work profession have in supporting your position. Be prepared to carefully consider the opposing position and respond thoughtfully.

Position 1: Education is a fundamental right and should be free for all.

Position 2: Education is a privilege that can be earned but should not be automatically available to all.

Because of the 1973 *Rodriguez* decision by the Supreme Court, lawsuits arguing against the current system of state finance have relied on challenges based on state constitutions alone. Though parents and advocacy groups have sometimes won cases at the state level, most cases have been won by states that have not had to address the inequality of school financing (Koski, 2003). Koski (2003) suggests that when judges have found fault with state financing mechanisms for education, they have provided little guidance for state departments of education or legislatures to fix them. Between 1973 and 1989, plaintiffs filing suit on behalf of students or parents won only 7 of 23 school finance cases. Between 1989 and 2001, they won in about half of the cases.

The California Supreme Court found that education was a fundamental right as early as 1874 (*Ward v. Flood*, 1874). In 1971, the California courts found that education should be subject to a high standard of judicial review and that how money was being allocated for

ADVOCACY
EDUCATION LAW

1. Choose one of the education laws listed in Table 7.1.
2. Visit the federal government agency's website that discusses that law.
   a. What information did you find there?
   b. Was the information clear?
   c. What information was not available there that you would like included?
   d. Assess the extent to which you think this law is aligned with social work values.

education violated the Equal Protection Clause of California's state constitution. They found that children from poorer families were getting a lower-quality education and that the state had no compelling reason for this disparity. Since then, different states have taken different stances on the importance of education. For example, the Florida Supreme Court held that the Florida constitution did not denote education as a fundamental right (*Fla. Dep't of Educ. v. Glasser*, 1993). In 2016, the Connecticut State Superior Court ruled that "Connecticut is defaulting on its constitutional duty" through not only the system the state uses to allocate aid to school districts, but also graduation standards, teacher evaluation, and teacher pay (Harris, 2016, para. 2).

Because many education policies are controlled at the state level, it would be impossible to describe all state level education policies in this book. Table 7.2 describes some examples of educational policy variation from state to state.

TABLE 7.1 ■ Relevant Education Laws and Their Oversight

Topic	Law	Oversight Agency	Website
K–12 education	Elementary and Secondary Education Act of 1965	Department of Education	https://www2.ed.gov/about/offices/list/oii/nonpublic/eseareauth.pdf
	Every Student Succeeds Act	Department of Education	https://www.ed.gov/essa?src=ft
Privacy	Federal Education Reporting and Privacy Act (FERPA, 1974)	Department of Education	https://www2.ed.gov/policy/gen/guid/fpco/ferpa/index.html
Education for children with disabilities	Individuals with Disabilities Education Act (IDEA, 2004)	Department of Education	https://sites.ed.gov/idea/about-idea/
	Section 504 of the Rehabilitation Act of 1973	Department of Labor	https://www.dol.gov/oasam/regs/statutes/sec504.htm
Discrimination	Title IX of the Educational Amendments of the Civil Rights Act of 1964	Department of Justice	https://www.justice.gov/crt/overview-title-ix-education-amendments-1972-20-usc-1681-et-seq
	Title VI of the Civil Rights Act of 1964	Department of Health and Human Services	https://www.hhs.gov/civil-rights/for-individuals/special-topics/needy-families/civil-rights-requirements/index.html

TABLE 7.2 ■ Selected State Educational Policy Variation

Topic	Overview
Civics education	Arkansas, Florida, Missouri, New Mexico, and South Dakota do not include civics or citizenship education in their curricula, whereas New Jersey, New York, and North Carolina do. Accountability models: while many states have developed content standards in civics or government, only two states have attached consequences for students and schools based on required civics assessments, Florida and Tennessee have this taken into account in their school's rating (Education Commission of the States, 2016).
Common core	Common Core State Standards have been adopted by 42 states, the District of Columbia, four territories, and the Department of Defense Education Activity (DoDEA). South Carolina, Texas, and Virginia, among other states, have not adopted Common Core Standards (Common Core State Standards Initiative, n.d.).
English language learning	State funding for English language learning (ELL) varies significantly. Thirty-three states and the District of Columbia include it in their primary funding formula. Twelve states provide categorical funding through separate line items. In five states, school districts are reimbursed after ELL costs are accrued. Delaware, Mississippi, Montana, and Rhode Island do not provide any state funding for ELL (Millard, 2015).
Fine arts education	Twenty-nine states define the arts in statute or code as a core or academic subject. States that do not define the arts as a core or academic subject include Alaska, Colorado, and Connecticut. Most states require districts or schools to offer arts instruction at the elementary, middle, and high school level. Alaska and Hawaii do not require districts to offer arts instruction at any educational level. Twenty states provide funding for an arts education grant program or a state-funded school for the arts including Oklahoma, South Carolina, and Utah (National Center for Education Statistics, 2017).
Social studies	States like California, Illinois, and Iowa do not require students to illustrate their knowledge of social studies through summative assessments, whereas states like Arizona, Minnesota, and North Dakota utilize the U.S. citizenship test as a summative assessment. Other states use different frameworks for summative assessments. For example, New York employs a global history and geography as well as a U.S. history and government summative assessment (Education Commission of the States, 2017).
Students with disabilities	As discussed in the chapter, in 2016, the federal government only covered approximately 16% of the cost of the average per pupil expenditure for each child with a disability (U.S. Department of Education, 2015). As the local district level, this funding may come through the state's primary funding formula (33 states and the District of Columbia), separate line items (12 states), or reimbursement to districts after costs are accrued (5 states, including Vermont, Wisconsin, and Wyoming) (Millard & Aragon, 2015). Because of the IDEA's (2004) guidelines, categories of disabilities are the same throughout the United States. However, there is significant variation among the services that are available from district to district, because local districts generally bear the burden of the costs of the services that are provided.
Teacher evaluation	As of 2015, 27 states require all teachers to have annual evaluations, up from 15 states in 2009. New probationary teachers must be evaluated annually in 45 states. In 2015, there were just 5 states in the nation—California, Iowa, Montana, Nebraska, and Vermont—that had no formal state policy requiring teacher evaluations (National Council on Teacher Quality, 2015).
Teacher Licensing	Twenty-two states require elementary teachers to demonstrate content knowledge through testing in each core subject they will teach. In 2015, 22 states required elementary teachers to demonstrate content knowledge by obtaining passing scores on academic content tests in each core subject (rather than obtaining a general or composite score that may mask weaknesses in certain subjects, or requiring no tests at all). This policy change comes as numerous states require teachers to pass the Praxis II Elementary Education: Multiple Subjects test. Five states—Alaska, Hawaii, Iowa, Montana, and Ohio—do not require all elementary teachers to pass any content tests as a requisite for licensure (National Council on Teacher Quality, 2015).

Topic	Overview
Teacher preparation	Core subject area content tests are required for middle school students in a majority of states (26). Just five states require secondary teachers to demonstrate content knowledge for all subjects they will teach—Indiana, Minnesota, Missouri, South Dakota, and Tennessee. Ten states require that secondary teacher candidates have the ability to build content knowledge and vocabulary through careful reading of informational and literary texts, to incorporate literacy skills as an integral part of every subject, and to intervene and support students who are struggling (National Council on Teacher Quality, 2015).
Teacher tenure	In 2009, teacher effectiveness was not formally connected with tenure decisions anywhere in the United States. By 2015, 23 states required that tenure decisions be informed by teacher performance. In 9 states—Colorado, Connecticut, Delaware, Florida, Hawaii, Louisiana, New York, Oklahoma, and Tennessee—evidence of teacher performance is required as the most significant criterion for granting teachers tenure or contract renewal (National Council on Teacher Quality, 2015).

POLICY INFORMED BY ALTERNATIVE LENSES

Social construction theory provides a mechanism to look at the role and type of education. Western views of childhood and the learning process draw much from rational constructivist views, such as Piaget's theories that conceptualize children as "independent egocentric self[s]" (Gupta, 2015, p. 148) who learn as they interact with their physical environment. According to this theory, children learn in a linear manner and pass through a series of stages as logic develops and allows cognition and skill to advance, ending with adulthood. This view places the individual in the center of the learning process and makes the environment of secondary importance—basically the child is an active learner who will not benefit from a rich environment until they are cognitively ready. Such views are based on a normative Western middle- to upper-class view of childhood. There is little allowance for diversity of social, cultural, or political context and a diminished importance of the people in the environment, their language, traditions, customs, rituals, and so on. Reasoning, logic, and independence are prized.

An alternative view comes from Vygotsky, who believes that the learning context is priority, with individual cognitive development secondary (Gupta, 2015). This view suggests that children who participate in activities with adults or older children will develop tools to accomplish their own learning by making meaning of what they see, and learning how their community or culture interprets the world through language and social interaction. In addition to supporting a nonlinear view of development, this perspective focuses less on an individual child's intellectual aptitude and more on the social environment. Cultures, such as India, that reflect the second worldview tend to be collectivist and see child-rearing as a societal responsibility that reflects history and culture as a public activity (Gupta, 2015).

Education policies vary according to the purposes that they serve and are often a reflection of broader societal values. In this section, we consider what U.S. education policies might look like through different ideological perspectives, in contrast with dominant approaches and paradigms.

School Choice

Charter school: Independent schools that are publicly financed but may not be held to legal and union requirements of local public schools. Many are not regulated by a central school board.

The charter school movement in the U.S. is the result of a number of different ideas about education and the perception of an educational system in crisis. **Charter schools** are independent schools that are publicly financed but not held to public school legal and union requirements. During the 1970s, Ray Budde, who was a professor at the University of Massachusetts in education administration and who had been an educator and assistant principal in East Lansing, Michigan, proposed the *charter* concept. He asserted that charter schools would foster greater accountability by empowering teachers to innovate in the classroom (Budde, 1996). Though many called for public school reform to counter declining test scores and improve public education, there was little support for restructuring (Kolderie, 2005). In 1983, the Department of Education under the Reagan administration published their seminal report, "A Nation at Risk." The report opened with a declaration of obligation to children and society:

> All, regardless of race or class or economic status, are entitled to a fair chance and to the tools for developing their individual powers of mind and spirit to the utmost. This promise means that all children by virtue of their own efforts, competently guided, can hope to attain the mature and informed judgement needed to secure gainful employment, and to manage their own lives, thereby serving not only their own interests but also the progress of society itself. (National Commission on Excellence in Education, 1983)

The highly publicized report garnered national attention that fed and was fed by widespread criticism of the U.S. educational system that highlighted, among other failings, the country's global standing.

Criticism of the U.S. public education system coincided with more widespread calls for devolution of public services and attacks on centralized government that gained traction during the Reagan era (Nathan & Gais, 2001) and continue to be a central feature of U.S. governance. Budde reintroduced an expanded proposal for charter schools (1988), which had gained important political allies. In a 2017 NPR interview, one of the founders of the charter school movement, Ted Kolderie, explained core elements of charter schools that cut across state and local variation:

> The term "charter" really refers to the decision by states to turn public education into a two-sector system. One is a traditional school district, centrally managed. The other, charter schools, are independent, not owned by a central school board. Both are public, but they're organized in radically different ways . . . The charter sector was supposed to encourage innovation—pedagogical laboratories that would push new ways to teach, even if it was disruptive. The charter sector [operates on] limited contracts. Their renewal is subject to performance. Charters are authorized by [groups] defined in state law. In New Jersey and Massachusetts, for example, the state is the only authorizer. Some states have created separate boards that authorize charters. Authorizers are usually non-profits and include universities, but in most cases, local school boards authorize charter schools. (Sanchez, 2017)

Albert Shanker and the American Federation of Teachers (AFT) embraced Budde's concept of *restructuring* through charter schools. Minnesota was the first state to adopt charter school legislation in 1991 (Kolderie, 2005). To date, 44 states and the District of Columbia have legislation that enabled the creation of charter schools (Education Commission of the States, 2018).[1] The federal government became an early partner in the charter school movement. In 1994, Congress adopted legislation originally introduced by Republican Senator Dave Durenberger and Democratic Senator Joseph Lieberman as the Public School Redefinition Act. This bill eventually evolved to become the Federal Charter School Grant Program (FSCP) authorized through the Elementary and Secondary Education Act (ESEA). The FSCP provides assistance with starting new charter schools and funding charter school facilities (Smole, 2005).

While the political origins of the charter movement were moderately left-leaning, today many of its major proponents identify as politically conservative. Liberal charter school supporters initially viewed them as an opportunity to counter private school voucher[2] efforts by offering an option that would safeguard union-won job protections for teachers and combat disparities among racial and socioeconomic groups. Conservatives supported charter schools, on the other hand, to discontinue collective bargaining protections for teachers and advocated that charters not be bound by union protections, which has become the case nationwide (Kahlenberg, 2008). Charter schools are also more racially and religiously segregated than traditional public schools because of their systematized recruitment of specific groups based on targeted curricula and patterns of self-segregation (Frankenberg, Kotok, Schafft, & Mann, 2017). Many charter schools have come under fire from civil rights groups because of their targeting of low-income and minority populations for suspensions, expulsions, and other disciplinary actions against students as well as fiscal and management concerns (Prothero, 2016). They have often been accused of taking the highest performing students out of the public schools while leaving those with more intensive needs, particularly students with learning disabilities and those who face discipline problems, in a more poorly funded public education system (Strauss, 2017). Increasing efforts by religious groups to obtain charters have pushed against the boundaries of separation of church and state (Hillman, 2008; Vieux, 2014; Weinberg, 2009). The effectiveness of charter schools has been difficult to determine because charter schools vary widely from state to state, with varying oversight, regulation, and evaluation mechanisms. It is clear, however, that given the continued expansion and creation of new charter schools across the nation they remain an integral part of the education reform policy landscape for the foreseeable future.

DISCUSSION

CASE STUDY OF NEW ORLEANS RECOVERY SCHOOL DISTRICT

Perhaps the most comprehensive example of charter school implementation in the United States is the post-Katrina New Orleans' Recovery School District. Following the devastation of the storm in 2005, New Orleans faced the opportunity and challenge of completely rebuilding its school system. When the State of Louisiana assumed control of schools in New Orleans, they largely dismantled the existing public school system and replaced it with a labyrinthine conglomerate of charter schools. While results are mixed and new problems have arisen, New Orleans is surely the city to watch regarding the charter school movement. By most accounts, test scores have improved across the school district, which has no remaining traditional public schools. In addition to learning what works, the charter network in New Orleans has been a laboratory of trial and error, with some arguing that the errors have created more racial and socioeconomic inequity (Brinson, Boast, Hassel, & Kingsland, 2012). One of the major differences between the New Orleans model and other cities with large charter networks, like Detroit, is its insistence on closing low-performing schools. Autonomy comes with an accountability mandate that school leaders have not shied away from enforcing.

Discuss the following:

1. If you were a social worker working with a family in a poorly funded school system, would you recommend that they look to place their children in a charter school?
2. How might this intersect with your obligation as a social worker to the larger community?
3. What advocacy opportunities for the family and community do you see?

---

[2]Vouchers are coupons or "scholarships" offered by states that parents can use to send their children to schools of their choosing, including private and religious schools, thus diverting public funds from public to private education (Turner, 2016).

[3]As of 2018, Montana, Nebraska, North Dakota, Vermont, and West Virginia were the only states without laws that enable the creation of charter schools (Education Commission of the States, 2018). South Dakota allows charter schools only for schools serving primarily Native students from recognized tribes under a federal grant.

School Financing in Finland

The education system in Finland consistently scores among the top of most global education ratings. Finnish schools and the system that governs them are heralded for academic excellence, equity, and organizational efficacy. Many Finnish system constructs run counter to standards and practices in the U.S. education system. For example, the compulsory school age is 7 (as opposed to a typical age of 6 in the United States), class sizes are small, there is recess every hour in 15-minute intervals, the school day ends between 1 p.m. and 2 p.m., and there are no national standardized tests (Gross-Loh, 2014). Perhaps what is most striking about the Finnish education system is the way it is funded. Education is free, accessible, and equal for all children (National Center on Education and the Economy, 2017).

Equity has not always been the bedrock of the Finnish education system. During a period of economic downturn in the 1960s, the Finnish government decided to stake economic recovery on providing a quality public education for all its citizens. This was a bold declaration of Finland's newfound independence from Soviet control. Finland saw unification and equality as a way forward in stark contrast to previous educational opportunities, when luck and privilege reigned (Hancock, 2011). This major shift in values in the education system also resulted in an unprecedented redistribution of resources as Finland has prohibited market-based, fee-for-service private schooling. All schools in Finland, including the few remaining private schools, receive the same public funding and are free. Schools also adhere to centralized national education standards and a curriculum that is combined with local control at the municipal levels (Organisation of Cooperation and Economic Development [OECD], 2013). They admit students based on a single set of criteria and all have access to identical programming and resources (Antikainen & Luukkainen, n.d.). Teachers in Finland are also well paid and respected, following educational reform that increased professional gatekeeping and educational requirements (OECD, 2015). The results of Finland's steadfast investment in educational equity continue to pay dividends. Finnish students remain at the top of the global academic charts, with little impact of student background on educational performance (OECD, 2013; Paratanen, 2011).

OPPORTUNITIES FOR ADVOCACY

The areas we have discussed throughout this chapter offer many opportunities to improve on current policies and create change. For example, you can become involved with existing advocacy groups to challenge school financing, discrimination against LGBTQ+ children in schools, school testing policies, and school segregation. You can learn about your state's financing system at http://www.schoolfundingfairness.org/. The National Education Law Center does research, engages in litigation and works with state community organizations to help challenge existing school financing systems.

In 2017, the Equality Act was proposed at the federal level to amend the Civil Rights Act of 1964 "to include sex, sexual orientation, and gender identity among the prohibited categories of discrimination or segregation in places of public accommodation" (S.B. 1006). The amendment of this law would protect gay, bisexual, and transgender students from discrimination in schools. You could become involved with the Human Rights Campaign and other civil rights organizations supporting this bill in its recent incarnations.

Final Discussion

Now that you have finished reading this chapter, reread the vignette at the beginning. Based on what you have learned, answer the following questions. Point to specific references in the chapter that help you answer these questions. Consider how different theories inform the response to these questions.

1. Can you Identify the specific policies that impact Arvin?
2. How do existing policies limit or expand Judie and Sandra's options to secure appropriate, high-quality education for Arvin?
3. What are the challenges Ms. Reyes, Arvin, and his parents face in ensuring that the federal policies are implemented in this school?
4. What role might race, class, gender, and other aspects of identity play in this vignette?

8

HIGHER EDUCATION POLICY

LEARNING OBJECTIVES

8.1: Identify groups that have historically access to higher education

8.2: Evaluate the current needs of students in higher education

8.3: Appraise how alternative lenses can affect U.S. higher education policy

8.4: Develop opportunities for advocacy in the areas of affordability and the admission process

Higher education: Or postsecondary education; the range of options for schooling beyond high school

Higher education or postsecondary education refers to the range of options for schooling beyond high school. What might be an ideal description of access to higher education? Frawley, Larkin, and Smith (2017) write in their discussion of Indigenous peoples and college:

> University is not for everyone, but a university should be for everyone. To a certain extent, the choice not to participate in higher education should be respected given that there are other avenues and reasons to participate in education and employment that are culturally, socially and/or economically important for society. Those who choose to pursue higher education should do so knowing that there are multiple pathways into higher education and, once there, appropriate support is provided for a successful transition. (p. 3)

In this chapter, we discuss the current system of higher education, the policies that affect who can access the system, and policies that affect students, employees, taxpayers, and graduates such as Title IX, the GI bills, and DACA. Particular attention is paid to marginalized groups who have often been denied access, such as women, people of color, and immigrants. Social movements of those who have demanded access for those shut out, such as the DREAMers, are discussed. The chapter highlights opportunities for advocacy, such as college affordability and equal access to higher education.

---

[1]Thank you to Francis Furmanek, MSW, and Adilene Garcia, MSW, for their help in drafting this chapter.

Vignette: Struggling to Pay for College

Based on what you know from the media or your personal, work, or volunteer experiences, think about the following questions as you read the vignette. When you finish the vignette, answer the questions below.

1. Can you identify the specific policies that impact Kai?
2. How might policies affect current and future opportunities for Kai?
3. What strengths and resources does Kai have that she can draw on?
4. What roles could a social worker play in helping Kai (think micro, mezzo, and macro level social work)?
5. What role might race, class, gender, and other aspects of identity play in this vignette?

Kai is the first person in her family to go to college. Her family did not have the resources to help her. They encouraged her and supported her desire to go to college. She was accepted out of high school into a private college in a neighboring state. Because she figured out her college applications and financial aid on her own, she applied late and was not able to access a Pell Grant or other similar aid. During her first semester, she excelled in the classroom, especially in math and science classes, but she could not stay in school because her student loans did not cover the cost of tuition, room and board, fees, and books. She was upset to leave school and visited the college counseling center for help. The social worker with whom she met was very understanding and helpful, but was only allowed to see her for two sessions. After she left school, Kai moved into her own apartment and took a few classes online from a for-profit university. That university has just gone bankrupt, and she is not sure she will receive any credit for those classes. She is now taking two community college classes per semester and working full time as a nursing assistant at a nursing home. She likes helping people, but the work is hard. Without a college degree, Kai has little chance for advancement. Since she is taking classes less than half time, her student loan payments will start soon. She is worried that the cost of the student loans will mean she has to choose between paying rent and continuing to take classes. She has heard that there might be programs that are specifically for women who are interested in math and science, but she has no idea if she qualifies, how to learn more, or whom to ask. She is considering giving up on college to focus on full-time work.

HISTORY AND SOCIAL CONSTRUCTION OF U.S. HIGHER EDUCATION

The history of higher education in the United States is very different for disparate groups of students. Higher education for white men in the United States became possible in 1636, with the establishment of Harvard College (n.d.). The next U.S. college was not founded until 1693, the College of William and Mary in Virginia (William & Mary, n.d.). The first college for women, Salem College, was established in 1772 in North Carolina (Salem College, n.d.). In 1837, the African Institute, now called Cheyney University of Pennsylvania, was founded to serve African Americans (Cheyney University of Pennsylvania, n.d.) and, in 1854, Ashmun Institute was founded as the first **Historically Black College and University** (HBCU), and later renamed Lincoln University after President Abraham Lincoln (Lincoln University, n.d.). These HBCUs primarily focused on providing the primary and secondary education that most black students were not able to get through the public school system and were not able to focus on postsecondary education until after 1900 (U.S. Department of Education, Office of Civil Rights, 1991). The Columbia Institution for the Instruction of the Deaf and Dumb and Blind, now called Gallaudet University, which began to confer college degrees in 1864, was the first higher education institution for people with disabilities (Gallaudet University, n.d.). As you can see, the question of who should have access to higher education was one that was unsettled for much of our country's history. The history of higher education for able-bodied white men is 100 years longer than the history of college education for able-bodied white women and 200 years longer than the history of college education for people with disabilities or members of other racial groups.

Historically Black College and University: A college or university that was originally founded to educate students of African American descent

Education for the Elites

Early colleges were, according to their records, designed to serve the greater good as much as advance the careers of the individuals who attended them. Many of the early institutions of higher education in the United States, including Harvard, had religious backing and content. While there was no religious test to enter Harvard College (as there was in the English institutions it took inspiration from), in the early days, students participated in twice-daily Scripture readings and daily prayer. Half of 17th century Harvard graduates became ministers (Kohlbrenner, 1961). Early college and university charters declared their purpose "the harmony of the whole community," "the common good," and the promotion of the "grand interests of society." This focus on the greater good continued for the first 200 years of American higher education, but was supplanted by individualism, personal gain, and practicality after the Civil War. The tensions between the greater good and individual advancement remain in higher education today (Dorn, 2017).

Higher education expanded to include agricultural schools, institutions for women, teachers' colleges (called *normal schools*), HBCUs, junior or community colleges, and research-focused institutions. Dorn (2017) argues that the system of what we call *higher education* today is really made up of different types of institutions that developed throughout this time. He also argues that although individualism came to the fore, higher educational institutions continued to prioritize the greater good. In the period following World War II, the rising consumer society, along with the growing numbers of people attending college thanks to government supports such as the GI Bill, Pell Grants, and subsidized student loans, made education a requirement for many higher paying jobs. At the same time, greater numbers of people were able to access it. The period between 1945 and 1970 is sometimes called the golden age of higher education. At the same time, all white men were not given equal access to education. In the early 20th century while excluding blacks entirely, quota systems also limited access to higher education, particularly elite institutions, for minorities such as Jews and Catholics. It was not until the 1960s that Yale University stopped using quotas to limit access for Jewish applicants (Johnson, 1986; Steinberg, 1971). The financial tightening required by the recessions of the 1970s widened the gap between students who were studying the liberal arts or other *lofty* subjects and those studying more *vocational* subjects, particularly at community colleges.

REFLECTION

ASSESS YOUR UNIVERSITY

Dorn (2017) describes several ways in which universities can be classified:

- Public or private
- Parochial or secular
- Single-gender/single-sex or coeducational
- Racially segregated or racially integrated (or a combination)
- Two-year, 4-year, and/or graduate universities

What university are you attending now? How would it be classified in all these categories? How do those classifications affect your education?

Education for Non-elites

Public higher education in the United States got a major boost in 1862, when President Lincoln signed the First Morrill Act. Also called the Land Grant Act (or by its long title: the Act Donating Public Lands to the Several States and Territories, which may provide Colleges for the Benefit of Agriculture and the Mechanic Arts), it provided states with land that they could sell. Under the act, proceeds had to be used to create and maintain colleges that would teach agriculture and the mechanical arts in addition to any other subjects they chose (Library of Congress, n.d.). Many of today's universities, such as Cornell University, Massachusetts Institute of Technology, and University of Wisconsin-Madison, trace their roots to this act. Any institution of higher education funded under this act or the Second Morrill Act is called a **land-grant institution**.

Land-grant institution: A college or university designated by a state to receive the benefits of the Land Grant Acts

The Supreme Court decided in *Plessy v. Ferguson* in 1896 that public accommodations such as universities could be segregated by race as long as the accommodations for African Americans were "separate but equal" (U.S. Department of Education, Office of Civil Rights, 1991). Following this decision, the Second Morrill Act was passed in 1890, requiring states that segregate their public higher education systems by race to provide land-grant institutions for black students whenever land-grant institutions for white students were created. This resulted in several public land-grant institutions for black (primarily African American) students in southern and border states, reaching 16 institutions in total. Generally, these offered education in agriculture, mechanical sciences, industry, and teacher training, to the exclusion of other college-level courses and degrees.

In the 1890s, William Harper was serving as the president of the University of Chicago. He wondered whether the first 2 years of college were really a continuation of secondary education rather than being "university-level" based in part on the German model of education, which includes those 2 years in high school. University of Chicago created a *junior college* and *senior college* and began awarding the first associate's degrees for those who finished the 2 years of junior college. In 1901, his friend J. Stanley Brown, a high school principal, introduced college-level courses in Joliet High School and created the first junior college in America, Joliet Junior College. While today community colleges often make postsecondary education available to more students, they were created from a desire to separate students considered elite from everyone else (Drury, 2003).

In 1965, the Special Subcommittee on Indian Education, formed out of the U.S. Senate Committee on Labor and Public Welfare and chaired by Senator Robert Kennedy, commissioned a report on education for Native American children. That report, poignantly called *Indian Education: A National Tragedy, A National Challenge* detailed the crisis in education for Native children when it was released in 1969. The findings related to higher education included the startling statistic that 18% of students in Federal Indian schools attended college (well below the national average at that time of 50%), and only 3% of those graduated (compared to the national average of 32%). Only 1 of every 100 Indian college graduates went on to graduate study. The report also included a series of recommendations to improve education for Native Americans and provide more ownership of the education to the tribes and their peoples. The dedication of this report is a poem called Brave Heart by John Belindo, which begins with:

> This Brave Heart Light surrounded by Brown Faces,
>
> so sad to be themselves.
>
> We have seen him staring
>
> at primitive landscape,
>
> broken treaties and broken hearts.
>
> The Brown Children have sung:
>
> garbled chords of muted war-like
>
> music from tiny buffalo robes,
>
> "We are no longer little hopes from the hogans and pueblos,
>
> we are no longer little pinion
>
> hulls in a bowl." (p. vii)

Tribal college: Educational institutions controlled and operated by Native American tribes

Following the Kennedy report, Navajo Community College (now Diné College) was established as the first **tribal college**, controlled and operated by a tribe, in 1968. The call for more ownership of higher education by tribes contributed to an environment in which tribal colleges founded their own American Indian Higher Education Consortium in 1973 (American Indian Higher Education Consortium, n.d.). Federal funding came from the Tribally Controlled Community Colleges Assistance Act, or the Tribal College Act, in 1978. With a budget of approximately $2,831 per student as of 1981, the Carnegie Foundation, in a 1989 report, called these schools "underfunded miracles" that were "shaping the future of Native America." As of this writing, the U.S. has 38 recognized tribal colleges.

Opening of higher education for a new group of non-elites does not always mean equitable access. For example, when women began to seek higher education, they were often able to access only a small number of options. This was especially true for women of color. In a speech to social work students in 2009, the great civil rights and women's rights leader Dorothy Height explained that when she graduated from high school in 1929, she had two options: to be a teacher or a social worker (personal communication, Dorothy Height, October 29, 2009). She chose social work. Today we still see significant racial and gender disparities in many of the degrees chosen by incoming college students. For example, women are still overrepresented in social work, nursing, and teaching and underrepresented in computer science and engineering.

This expansion of availability of higher education has also raised questions of whether everyone should pursue college, which has informed current debates on free college (see this chapter's advocacy section). Economic research shows that while in 1964, the financial benefits of college outweighed the costs of college for nearly everyone who attended, by 2010, as many as 1 in 10 people who attend college would be financially better off had they not attended college (Strohush & Wanner, 2015). However, the financial rewards of college do not reflect other potential benefits, such as social interaction with peers, access to consumer credit markets, access to unique experiences or specific careers, positive effects on local communities, increased health outcomes, and increased family stability, or costs, such as effects on fertility rates (Strohush & Wanner, 2015). Any policy changes that address the availability of higher education should also consider larger issues: Is higher education a right or a commodity? Should everyone have access to higher education? Should everyone be encouraged to attend college?

Education and the Military

One of the biggest landmarks in higher education history and policy came in 1944. The Servicemen's Readjustment Act of 1944, commonly called the GI Bill of Rights, unanimously passed both houses of Congress and was signed into law by President Franklin Roosevelt. This law provided resources for homeownership, business development, and unemployment compensation to returning World War II veterans and provided significant funding for higher education. By 1951, 8 million veterans took advantage of these opportunities for higher education or training, and the 2 million who attended college or university changed the perception of higher education as only appropriate for the wealthy.

This bill was modified in 1952 to include Korean War veterans (CQ Almanac, 1952) and in 1966 to include Vietnam-era veterans (Mattila, 1978). In 2008, the Post-9/11 GI Bill included veterans who have served more than 90 days active duty since September 10, 2001, and in 2017 was modified to make funding available longer for post-9/11 veterans (Dortch, 2018). Other connections between the military and higher education include the 1958 National Defense Education Act, which provided $900 million for a variety of areas, including loans, college teacher training, and training of language specialists. It focused on areas that were considered important to the national defense (U.S. Department of Health and Human Services, 1972). By 1962, $225 million in National Defense Student Loans had been received by 350,000 students. If your social work practice provides you the opportunity to work with veterans, remember that many veterans of the armed forces may be eligible for help for college through one of these GI bills. The supplemental materials for this book online provide some helpful places to start researching those benefits.

Military students on campus today are shown in Photo 8.1. Because of these policies and others, veterans' services and Reserve Officer Training Corps (ROTC) chapters are a common feature of many campuses. The relationship between universities and the military is not always an easy one—universities were also the site of significant anti-war protests by both student and faculty during the Vietnam era (Schreiber, 1973) and have gone on to be the homes of many social movements and protests on issues, such as war, racism, income inequality, and sexual assault.

PHOTO 8.1 Military students

Higher Education Act

President Lyndon Johnson signed the Higher Education Act (HEA) (PL 89-329) into law in 1965 as part of a group of policies called the *Great Society*, ranging from Medicaid to the Elementary and Secondary Education Act to voting rights (Hannah, 1996). One purpose of this act was to combine existing programs, that affected higher education, including work-study, the GI bill, and very limited student loan programs, to allow colleges to grow to address expanding enrollments. The bill's authors used two strategies to increase access to college. First, by including these bills in a large package of policies (called an **omnibus bill**, which puts separate proposals together in one large bill), the authors made it more likely that redistributive policies would not be noticed. In addition, by framing access to college as a problem that affected those in poverty rather than students of color, they avoided triggering the racist attitudes that were prevalent in legislators of both parties and prevented other such legislation from being passed. As a result, this bill (while still incremental) included programs such as the Upward Bound from Poverty Program for minority students, made federal work-study programming permanent, created subsidized federal student loans, and modified the National Defense Education Act loan program. This bill also included resources for universities to update libraries and facilities, conduct research, and encouraged them to provide services to their communities. Funding for a National Teacher Corps and grants for institutions to provide teacher training and for individuals enrolled in that training were also included. In only 4 years, loans that were part of the HEA's Guaranteed Loan Program were approaching $3 billion and affecting 2.5 million students.

Omnibus bill: A piece of legislation that combines several proposals together

In 1970, the Ford Foundation funded a report to the Secretary of Education about the status of higher education after this period of rapid expansion (U.S. Department of Health and Human Services, 1972). The Newman Report called into question inequality within higher education that was affecting women, students of color, and low-income students (U.S. Department of Health and Human Services, 1972). It found that the 2,500 institutions of higher education in the United States were essentially all the same, providing students with no real choice. This report recommended that colleges focus on education rather than other activities, consider specialized education that was based more on experiential learning and less on classroom learning, and address the significant numbers of students who started college without finishing. Following this, a significant overhaul of the HEA's in 1972 established equal opportunity for higher education as a federal policy priority. Toward that end, the amendments established federally funded grants (today called Pell Grants), to be matched by the state, created the Student Loan Marketing Association (now called Sallie Mae), expanded resources for nonuniversity post–high school programs (such as vocational training), and added more accountability for higher educational institutions, particularly around the way they spent money. By 1978, Pell Grants were available to financially eligible full- and part-time undergraduates, the amount of money available for loans was increased, and loans were available to parents and to all students regardless of income (Hannah, 1996).

As a result of a change in public support for higher education, the election of Ronald Reagan, and an increase in student loan default rates, when this bill was reauthorized in the 1980s, there were restrictions on students who received aid, especially student loans, as well as student loan lenders and universities themselves. The 1992 updates to this law included a single form to fill out for federal financial aid (you might be familiar with the FAFSA form, which stands for Free Application for Federal Student Aid), made aid more available to those with higher incomes, and increased state oversight of universities.

Public, Private, and For-profit Higher Education

Today, fourteen million students (73% of all students in degree-granting programs) pursue degrees at public universities. This is followed by four million students at private nonprofit colleges (20%), and one million students in private for-profit programs (6%) (National Center for Education Statistics [NCES], 2016). Since Harvard was founded in 1636, higher education in the United States has been comprised almost exclusively of public universities (primarily funded through government dollars) and private not-for-profit universities. Prior to 1976, for-profit higher education in the United States consisted primarily of what were considered career colleges or technical schools that educated fewer than 25,000 students per year, received little or no federal or state aid, and were a small part of the overall higher education conversation. This changed in 1976 when the University of Phoenix started offering classes, marketing primarily to adults working full time and first-generation college students (Tierney, 2011).

Concerns have been raised about for-profit institutions, particularly regarding admissions policies and rates of completion, as well as the tuition costs and the resulting debt of graduates. Policy in this area has generally put the responsibility for assessing the quality of a university on accrediting bodies. These are not government agencies, but are recognized and overseen by the U.S. Department of Education (n.d.). Table 8.1 provides comparisons of the student population and outcomes of community colleges, public 4-year colleges, for-profit colleges, and private 4-year colleges (Center for Analysis of Postsecondary Education and Employment, 2018). Unless otherwise noted, the provided numbers are from the 2016–2017 school year; some numbers are not available for all four types of schools.

TABLE 8.1 ■ Comparison of Community Colleges, Public, Private, and For-Profit Colleges

	Community Colleges	Public 4-Year Colleges	For-Profit Colleges	Private 4-Year Colleges
Number of students	8.7 million	14 million	1 million	4 million
Percentage of all students	31	51	4	14
Percentage of enrolled students who are older than 24	19	4	40	68
Percentage of enrolled students who are African American	13	13	21	13
Percentage of enrolled students who are female	53	55	63	58
Percentage of enrolled students who are single parents	9	3	27	
Percentage of enrolled students with a high school diploma	86	96	76	
Annual tuition and fees for a full-time student	$4,100	$8,200	$16,000	$27,300
Associate degree recipients with $20,000+ debt (2012)	9%	n/a	55%	n/a
Bachelor's degree recipients with $20,000+ debt (2012)	n/a	39%	78%	53%
Median earnings 10 years after first enrolling	$32,700	$42,400	$28,700 (2-year colleges) $38,700 (4-year colleges)	

(Continued)

TABLE 8.1 ■ (Continued)

	Community Colleges	Public 4-Year Colleges	For-Profit Colleges	Private 4-Year Colleges
Students who first enrolled in 2003 who were no longer enrolled and employed in 2009	78%	84% (average for public and nonprofit schools)	71%	84% (average for public and nonprofit schools)
Three-year default rate for those in repayment as of 2014		11%	16%	7%
Twelve-year default rates for all first-time students who started college in 2003–2004	13%	12%	47%	13%
Twelve-year default rates for borrowers who started college in 2003–2004	26%		52%	

CURRENT HIGHER EDUCATION POLICIES

In this section, we discuss a range of policies that currently apply to higher education in the United States, including the Higher Education Opportunity Act, policies that affect retention and completion, student privacy, violence, sexual assault and harassment, and behavioral health. In addition, we address policies that affect specific populations such as people who work for universities, students who are immigrants, online students, and independent students. At the end of this section, Table 8.3 outlines significant federal policies that are addressed in this chapter.

The Scope of Higher Education Today, Including Social Work Education

In fall 2018, 19.9 million students were enrolled in U.S. colleges and universities. Overall public funding for higher education comes primarily from the federal government ($75.6 billion in 2013), state government ($72.7 billion), and municipal government ($9.2 billion). Additional funding comes from student loans ($103 billion) and education-related tax credits, deductions, exemptions, and exclusions ($31 billion) (Pew Charitable Trusts, 2015). You might wonder how social work fits into this picture. As of 2017, the Council on Social Work Education (CSWE) reported more than 60,000 BSW students, 63,000 MSW students, and 3,000 doctoral students in accredited programs. From 1898 when the Charity Organization Society of New York started the first Summer School in Philanthropic Work, then the New York School of Philanthropy, now Columbia University School of Social Work, social workers have been intimately involved in higher education (Columbia School of Social Work, n.d.).

Although you might have an image of a typical college student, would it surprise you to find out 39% of all college students attend part time and 38% of college students are older than 25? Each year, one million students will earn an associate's degree, 1.9 million will earn bachelor's degrees, and 786,000 will earn master's degrees. As of 2016, 54% of college students identified as white, 13% each as black or Hispanic, 6% as Asian, and less than 1% as Pacific Islander or American Indian/Alaska Native. Just over 3% identified with more than one race

(NCES, 2016). The demographics of social work education have also shifted. Although the earliest social workers and social work students were primarily elite white women, today 40% of BSW students, 45% of MSW, and 45% to 50% of doctoral students come from historically underrepresented groups (CSWE, 2017). More than 80% are female.

Higher Education Opportunity Act

The Higher Education Opportunity Act (HEOA, Public Law 110-315) was enacted on August 14, 2008, reauthorizing the Higher Education Act. As of this writing, it has been overdue for another reauthorization since 2013. The American Council on Education (2018), a membership organization of U.S. colleges and universities, calls it "the single most important piece of legislation overseeing the relationship between the federal government, colleges and universities, and students" (para. 2). This Act regulates most aspects of U.S. higher education, including federal financial aid, work-study, and support for students to attend college, international education, and graduate studies. Specific programs covered in this policy include teacher education, support for institutions serving historically disenfranchised students, student loans, as well as grant and scholarship programs such as Pell Grants, TRIO, GEAR UP, Byrd scholarships, TEACH grants, and scholarships for dependent members of veterans' families. The HEOA also describes the role of states and accrediting agencies in the oversight of higher education and services for students with disabilities. These policies affect access to higher education for all students, including social work education, as well as many of the communities with which we work.

DISCUSSION

VOTER REGISTRATION ON YOUR CAMPUS

HEOA requires colleges and universities to make voter registration available to students. There is a lot of variety in how this is implemented on campuses, from a single email to all students to an entire office that focuses on helping students to vote. Here is what the law requires: https://www.aacrao.org/resources/compliance/voter-registration

Here are samples of what some campuses do:

https://www.wcu.edu/learn/academic-enrichment/center-for-service-learning/student-democracy-coalition/

https://vote.adelphi.edu/

Discussion questions:

1. Why does the HEOA require colleges to engage students in voting?
2. What does your university *currently* do to engage students in voting?
3. What do you think your university *should* do to engage students in voting?

Retention and Completion

The typical way to measure graduation rates is to look at the number of students who complete a degree within 6 years from the college where they started. In 2016, 60% of students had finished a bachelor's degree from the college they started attending in 2010. Public and private 4-year colleges have similar rates (59% and 60%, respectively), with for-profit schools lagging significantly (26%). **Completion rates** are measured by the number of students who finish

Completion rates: The measure of students who finish the degree they start within a set time period and are highest for most selective institutions that accept fewer than 1 in 4 applicants (88% completion) and lowest at those with open admissions policies (32%) (NCES, 2018b).

Retention rate: The measure of students who stay at the same college from their first year to their second year

One of the most challenging times for students is in the beginning of their education. In 2016, 62% of students who started their first year of college returned to the same college for their second year (referred to as **retention rates**), while an additional 12% continued college at another location (referred to as persistence), meaning 26% of students did not continue past their first year. This means that out of every nine students who start college, one will transfer to a different school, two will stop attending after their first year, and six will continue to their sophomore year at the same school. These rates vary by students' race and ethnicity, whether they attend full time or part time, whether they are older than 24 when they start, and whether they are at a community college, public, private, or for-profit school (National Student Clearinghouse Research Center, 2018).

One policy effort to help students make more informed choices and perhaps affect graduation, retention, and persistence has been the College Scorecard, a website hosted by the U.S. Department of Education at https://collegescorecard.ed.gov/, which includes data collected since 1996 regarding colleges' graduation rate and cost, as well as the average salary of graduates.

Student Privacy

Social workers who work in K–12 education or higher education or who communicate with school staff should be aware of the Federal Education Reporting and Privacy Act (FERPA) (Protecting Student Privacy, n.d.). FERPA regulates which student information can be shared by school personnel, with whom they can share it, and under which circumstances. This is particularly important because this applies to information often controlled or requested by social workers in their various practice capacities. FERPA provides parents of minors and students age 18 and over with the right to access, inspect, and challenge their own educational records. Students over 18 and parents of minors also have the right to grant written authorization to share educational records with other parties. FERPA applies to all agencies that receive either direct or indirect federal funding for education and, as a result, applies to public schools, charter schools, colleges, and universities. FERPA allows records to be shared within schools if they are being shared for legitimate educational reasons, when a student is transferring schools, and with other state agencies including the juvenile justice system, when required by state law. Once a student turns 18, the student can determine who should have access to records, including whether to allow parent access.

Data privacy is also a concern, given the amount of information about students that is collected by schools at all levels. Advocates look at policies related to data to find out whether it is collected in a systematic fashion and whether it is securely maintained. Since 2013, more than 70 laws regarding the privacy of student data have been passed around the country (Data Quality Campaign, 2016). This is still an emerging area for policy.

Violence on College Campuses

Violence in colleges and universities can take many forms, including sexual assault, domestic violence, and suicide. According to the Department of Education, in 2015, 27,500 criminal incidents against people or property were reported on campuses, at a rate of about 18.5 per incidents per 10,000 full-time-equivalent students (NCES, 2018a). The most common crime reported was burglary (12,300), which made up 45% of reports;

followed by forcible sex (8,000), 29% of crimes; auto theft (3,300), 12% of crimes; aggravated assault (2,300), 9%; and robberies (1,000), 4% (NCES, 2018a). Reporting of crime on campuses is governed by the Crime Awareness and Campus Security Act as well as the Clery Act (discussed below) (U.S. Department of Education, 2017). These figures may be underestimates of actual crime rates because understanding crime on campus can be complicated. Not only are some crimes, such as sexual assault, extremely underreported, but crime may not be counted as related to a college campus if it occurs in an off-campus location.

Violence on campus in the form of gun-related crime has received a significant amount of attention since the 2007 mass shooting at Virginia Tech University killed 33 and wounded 15. Since 2007, 122 people have been killed and 198 wounded in gun-related violence on college campuses (Jones, 2018), ranging from a shooting on campus at Northern Illinois University in 2008, where six died and 17 were wounded (Saulny & Davey, 2008), to the death of one University of Utah student in 2017 in an incident that started as a domestic violence call (Phillips, 2017). The American Association of State Colleges and Universities (2018) has ranked this as one of the top 10 concerns facing colleges for the 6th year in a row. Policy solutions to this problem are controversial and often related to larger policy debates about gun violence and gun rights, with some arguing that more weapons on campus are the solution and others arguing the opposite. For example, Table 8.2 shows a breakdown of state laws about carrying concealed weapons on college campuses as of 2018 (National Conference of State Legislatures, 2018). You can find the laws in your area on the National Conference of State Legislatures website.

TABLE 8.2 ■ Concealed Carry Laws and College Campuses

Policy Solution	Number of States	States
Allow citizens to carry concealed weapons if they meet certain state requirements	50	All
Ban carrying concealed weapons on college campuses	16	California, Florida, Illinois, Louisiana, Massachusetts, Michigan, Missouri, Nebraska, Nevada, New Jersey, New Mexico, New York, North Carolina, North Dakota, South Carolina, Wyoming
Each college or university makes the decision about concealed carry rules on campus	23	Alabama, Alaska, Arizona, Connecticut, Delaware, Hawaii, Indiana, Iowa, Kentucky, Maine, Maryland, Minnesota, Montana, New Hampshire, Ohio, Oklahoma, Pennsylvania, Rhode Island, South Dakota, Vermont, Virginia, Washington, West Virginia.
Concealed weapons allowed on public postsecondary campuses	10	Arkansas, Colorado, Georgia, Idaho, Kansas, Mississippi, Oregon, Texas, Utah, Wisconsin
Faculty members with licenses can carry concealed weapons, but not students or the general public	1	Tennessee

ADVOCACY

CAMPUS GUN POLICIES

Do your own research to find policies related to guns on your campus or on a campus near to you if you are studying online. The National Conference of State Legislatures website at http://www.ncsl.org/research/education/guns-on-campus-overview.aspx may be a good place to start, along with your college's website or public safety office. Next, visit the National Conference of State Legislatures database to find out what legislation has been proposed http://www.ncsl.org/research/education/education-bill-tracking-database.aspx, search under "Postsecondary-Campus Safety." Discuss the following:

1. What are the current policies related to guns on your campus?
2. What do you think the policies related to guns should be?
3. If the policy needs to change, what would be the first step?

Sexual Assault and Harassment on Campus

As discussed in Chapter 7, Title IX of the Education Amendments Act of 1972 was designed to address gender discrimination in education. The presence of Title IX on a college campus is more structured than in K–12 education, especially in coordination with other applicable policies. Reporting of related data is covered by the Jeanne Clery Act, which requires that universities track sexual assault and rape, and the Violence Against Women Act (VAWA), which amended the Clery Act to require that crimes related to domestic violence, dating violence, and stalking be included as well (Federal Register, 2014). These data are collected by the Title IX Coordinator and the public safety department on the college campus and must be reported annually to the campus community, including prospective students, faculty, and staff, generally via the internet (U.S. Department of Education, n.d.). The Clery Act does not mandate any specific intervention to address any of these crimes, only the reporting of statistics. Do you know what these statistics are for your school or where to find them?

Between Title IX and VAWA, higher education institutions are required to provide primary prevention and awareness programming to new students and employees regarding dating violence, domestic violence, sexual assault, stalking, and sexual harassment. These requirements are tied into federal financial assistance received by most colleges. Despite these requirements, we know that the crimes described here are still very underreported on campuses, with researchers estimating that only one in four crimes is reported to any authority (Sloan, Fisher, & Cullen, 1997). Confidentiality and student privacy make reporting complicated, as discussed below regarding behavioral health. One of the most challenging aspects of work related to sexual assault on college campuses is that states have a variety of definitions for sexual assault and rape, which differ from the definitions in the Title IX statutes. Colleges also handle reports of sexual assault and work together with law enforcement in very different ways. As a result, strong disagreements exist about whether sexual assault offenses should be handled by college administrations or processed by the criminal justice system (DeMatteo, Galloway, Arnold, & Patel, 2015). The "Times Up" and "It's On Us" initiatives have been pushing in recent years to update campus, local, state, and federal policies about sexual assault and sexual harassment, as demonstrated in Photo 8.2. For a vivid description of the way these problems play out for college students who are assaulted or accused of assault, as well as the administrators and law enforcement officials who adjudicate these cases, we recommend the book *Missoula: Rape and the Justice System in a College Town* by Jon Krakauer.

Tim Clayton-Corbis/Corbis Sport/Getty

PHOTO 8.2 Army personnel wave T-shirts supporting the "It's On Us" initiative, an awareness campaign to help put an end to sexual assault on college campuses, during the Army Black Knights vs. Air Force Falcons, college football match at Michie Stadium, West Point, New York

Behavioral Health on Campus

Identifying and addressing mental health and substance use–related needs in the United States is hindered by stigma and shame—a fact that social work students are generally aware of well before they begin their studies. College campuses are no exception. For example, alcohol use disorders are an extremely common challenge for today's college students, but research shows that only a minority of students utilize college-based services for substance use disorders (Bourdon, Moore, Long, Kendler, & Dick, 2018). Students report many barriers, including stigma, access to insurance, and especially privacy, that discourage them from acknowledging and addressing problematic substance use and other behavioral health concerns. Given that many major mental illnesses have their first onset by age 24 (Kessler, Berglund, Demler, Jin, Merikangas, & Walters, 2005), significant occurrences of behavioral health concerns are likely to occur in college, perhaps for the first time, in an environment that does not encourage addressing those needs. Unaddressed needs have serious consequences: One study found the two top causes of student death among college students were accidental injury and suicide and that accidental injuries included a significant number of deaths related to alcohol use (Turner, Leno, & Keller, 2013). Binge drinking and hazing related to Greek life, sports teams, and other group activities contribute to this latter group of injuries (Bendlin, 2015).

One significant concern for students is the question of disclosure of mental illness or other related concerns. Some members of a college community are mandated reporters, meaning they are required by Title IX to report suspicion of abuse, neglect, sexual assault, and imminent danger to a higher authority, and reports of mental health or substance use concerns may trigger this reporting. Mandated reporters are typically college professors, administrators, and residential staff. Staff members in campus health, campus psychological services, or campus ministry may be able to serve as confidential resources for students. However, even staff allowed to keep most topics confidential have a duty to warn of imminent danger and, under emergency circumstances, are mandated to break confidentiality. Requirements of federal law, state law, and professional licensure and ethics, are balanced in some situations with legal protections such as the Privacy Rule of the Health Insurance Portability and Accountability Act (HIPAA), preventing unauthorized release of health records.

University Employees

Higher education employment, including all who work for public, private, and for-profit colleges and universities, community colleges, and other technical, trade, and training schools, accounts for about four million jobs, approximately 2.6% of all jobs in the United States at any given time. The majority (77%) are at 4-year institutions, with community colleges (18%) the next biggest group (Higher Ed Jobs, 2018).

Individuals who work for colleges and universities are affected by many of the policies we discuss in this chapter, including Title IX, as well as the policies discussed in Chapter 9 regarding labor. However, not all university employees benefit from the protections of labor laws. Two groups who have been advocating for policy change in recent years include adjunct faculty members and graduate students.

The most commonly known model for faculty in higher education are tenure-track positions, meaning that faculty are hired with essentially a 5- or 6-year probationary period. If they meet requirements for teaching, research, and service to the university by the end of that time, they receive **tenure**, which entitles them to significant job security and a relatively permanent post. Specific requirements vary significantly from one university to another and may be different in different departments within a university; some universities prioritize teaching, others prioritize writing books, articles, or getting grants to fund research, and others prioritize service to the university. Generally, some combination of the three is required. Faculty who are not in these positions are called **contingent faculty**. This group includes full-time faculty who are on fixed-term contracts but are not eligible for tenure and those who are part-time faculty, often called **adjunct faculty**. Today, 70% of faculty positions in higher education are contingent, including full-time contingent faculty members, adjunct faculty members, and graduate students with teaching responsibilities (American Association of University Professors, 2017).

Tenure: A relatively permanent post, often as a teacher or professor

Contingent faculty: Faculty without significant job security, including those who are full time without the protections of tenure and those who teach part time on a semester-by-semester basis

Adjunct faculty: Part-time faculty without the job-security protections of tenure, often given contracts one semester at a time

Adjunct faculty are assigned to teach on a per course basis and are considered part time. At many institutions, they are limited to three or fewer classes per semester. Because they are parttime, at most universities they are not eligible for benefits such as health insurance and they may not be included in collective bargaining agreements or union membership. While many adjunct faculty members work part or full time in other jobs, some teach at multiple institutions to create full-time employment. Recent public attention highlighting the poverty of individuals in this situation has led to advocacy for benefits and higher salaries for adjunct faculty members.

Graduate students who are teaching or conducting research on college campuses on a part-time or adjunct basis often struggle to make ends meet. Recent advocacy for graduate students has included efforts to unionize and efforts to raise the stipends received by graduate students to be the equivalent of $15 per hour, or a "living wage" (Flaherty, 2018).

Students Studying Online

Students who take all their classes in a traditional in-person college classroom still comprise the majority of college students at 69%, but online education is increasing quickly. In 2016, 31% of students took at least one distance education course, and 15% of students took classes exclusively through distance education or online (Lederman, 2018). Online programs range from University of Phoenix, which started offering online courses in 1989 and in 2018 was thought to have 100,000 students (down from 470,000 in 2010), Western Governors University with 97,000 students, and Southern New Hampshire University, which has 100,000 students primarily online, to traditional on ground or brick-and-mortar campuses that offer a few courses online (McKensie, 2018). Online education is also part of social work education. There are 21 BSW programs (4.5% of overall programs), 44 MSW programs (19%), six DSW programs (60%), and two PhD programs (3%), which are fully online (CSWE, 2017).

Although online education has the potential to expand access to education, at least three million Americans live in places beyond the physical reach of public universities and without access to adequate high-speed internet to allow for online education. American Indian and Alaska Native students and families with low incomes are the most likely to live in areas out of reach of both types of education. In addition, students who are not as well prepared for higher education tend to be less successful in completely online classes than in face-to-face classes (Rosenboom & Blagg, 2018).

Students who study completely online find several advantages, as illustrated by Photo 8.3, including an increase in choices of schools and majors, and flexibility that allows for full-time work or care of family members. One disadvantage is access to health and wellness services, particularly behavioral health services. While it is not required by current policy, best practices suggest that behavioral health services should be available to any enrolled student, regardless of their status as a face-to-face or online student, both in the interest of the student's health and because access to support services, such as counseling, increase the likelihood of students' successful degree completion (Barr, 2014). Future policies might require resources for online students such as pre-enrollment services that accurately describe the expectations and requirements of the program, mental health education, crisis services, such as suicide hotlines that are publicly available to all students, access to services about self-evaluation and strategies to address issues, clear referral to disability services when needed, and access to counseling services for all students.

PHOTO 8.3 Many students today study online, which allows them flexibility in location.

Students Who Are Immigrants

As of 2012, an estimated 1.8 million people in the United States were unauthorized youth who came to the country as children (American Immigration Council, 2012). In 2001, Lucille Roybal-Allard, then a California state legislator, heard the story of a young woman who had come to the United States as a child, lived in the United States through college, but was not documented and faced obstacles in working and building her life. Roybal-Allard worked with a Democratic member of the U.S. Congress from California and a Republican member of Congress from Utah to introduce the Student Adjustment Act to allow in-state tuition rates to be available to undocumented youth. Soon, the bill was renamed the Development, Relief, and Education for Alien Minors Act (the DREAM Act) and affected students called **DREAMers**. Newer versions are discussed further in Chapter 15. Versions of this legislation have been reintroduced in every Congress until 2017, with the most recent being a bipartisan bill introduced by Senators Lindsey Graham and Jeff Flake (Republicans) and Dick Durbin (Democrat) in July 2017 that includes a road to citizenship for DREAMers, individuals who are part of the temporary protected status program (TPS), and others (National Immigration Law Center, 2017).

DREAMer: A person who has lived in the U.S. without official authorization since coming to the country as a minor who may be eligible for a special immigration status under federal legislation

Because legislative action had not been successful, on June 15, 2012, President Barack Obama announced the Deferred Action for Childhood Arrivals (DACA) program, giving these DREAMers temporary permission to stay in the United States and authorization for employment for an initial 2 years with potential to renew. Proponents argue that DACA allowed young immigrants the opportunity to unlock their full potential. Critics of this move include those who felt that it did not provide enough opportunities for enough immigrants, those who felt it was too lenient and should not reward coming to the United States illegally, and those who felt executive action was an inappropriate way to address this problem. Concerns have also been raised about the information collected through DACA and how it will be used by the federal government. On September 5, 2017, the Trump administration announced plans to end DACA, originally stating that October 5 would be the last day that U.S. Citizenship and Immigration Services would accept applications for DACA.

This decision was immediately challenged in court by immigrant rights groups, and in 2018, several states, including Texas, filed their own lawsuits challenging the DACA program as a whole. While the current status of DACA is confusing and likely to change, as of this writing the program is still available to those who were already enrolled but not for new applicants (National Immigration Law Center, 2018). See Chapter 15 for more information about how both of these policies affect other members of the immigrant community.

Students Who Are Independent

Fifty-one percent of students in 2012 met at least one of the following criteria used by FAFSA to determine if a student is "independent":

- Age 24 or older
- Married and/or has legal dependents other than a spouse
- Attending graduate school
- A veteran or active member of the armed services
- An orphan, foster care resident, or ward of the court
- An emancipated minor
- Homeless or at risk of becoming homeless (Institute for Women's Policy Research, 2018)

Students who fall into these categories, compared to other students, are more likely to be female, students of color, earn low wages, work at least 20 hours per week, have substantial unmet financial need (based on the calculations in their FAFSA, at least $5,000 in unmet need), spend more than 20 hours per week caring for dependents, and be part-time students. They are also half as likely as their peers to graduate. On average, only 33% of this group will graduate within 6 years (Institute for Women's Policy Research, 2018).

Government and university policies have been slow to adjust to this new "typical" student. Current policies for assessing the cost of attending college do not include many of the costs experienced by this group of students, particularly child care and transportation. The process of determining eligibility for financial aid through the FAFSA (laid out in the Higher Education Act) also penalizes students who worked in the prior year by assuming that income will continue. This group of students might benefit from a policy that would allow them to indicate whether they will reduce their work hours in the upcoming year, so their student aid could reflect projected decreases in income. Because many of these students have no choice but to work and attend college part time, they are often ineligible for many types of student financial aid (Institute for Women's Policy Research, 2018).

Many of the students in this group, as well as growing numbers of traditional students choose 2-year colleges, either as their complete education, or as a place to start before transferring to a 4-year institution. Nationally, approximately one-third of undergraduates in 2016–2017 were in 2-year colleges, and nearly half of all students who completed a 4-year degree in 2016 had enrolled at a 2-year college in the previous 10 years. This group is affected by policies related to access to remedial classes and financial aid. While community colleges enroll a higher proportion of low-income students than 4-year colleges, the proportion applying for and receiving federal financial aid is lower than 4-year colleges (Community College Research Center, n.d.). Proposals for free college (discussed later in the chapter) often center around 2-year colleges and would significantly affect this population.

TABLE 8.3 ■ List of Relevant Federal Laws

Topic	Laws	Oversight Agency	Website
Access to college, paying for college	Higher Education Act/Higher Education Opportunity Act	Department of Education	https://www2.ed.gov/policy/highered/leg/hea08/index.html
	GI Bills	Veterans Administration	https://benefits.va.gov/gibill/
	College Scorecard		https://collegescorecard.ed.gov/
Higher education and disabilities	Workforce Innovation and Opportunities Act	Department of Education	https://www2.ed.gov/about/offices/list/osers/rsa/wioa-reauthorization.html
	Rehabilitation Act of 1973		https://legcounsel.house.gov/Comps/Rehabilitation%20Act%20Of%201973.pdf
	Americans with Disabilities Act		https://www2.ed.gov/policy/rights/guid/ocr/disability.html
Gender discrimination, sex discrimination, sexual harassment, sexual assault	Title IX	Department of Education, Office for Civil Rights	https://www2.ed.gov/policy/rights/guid/ocr/sexoverview.html
	Clery Act	Department of Education	https://ifap.ed.gov/.../attachments/HandbookforCampusSafetyandSecurityReporting.pdf
	Violence Against Women Act	Department of Justice, Office of Violence Against Women	https://www.justice.gov/ovw
Student privacy	FERPA	Department of Education	https://www2.ed.gov/policy/gen/guid/fpco/ferpa/index.html
	HIPAA	Department of Health and Human Services	https://www.hhs.gov/hipaa/for-professionals/compliance-enforcement/index.html
Immigration	DACA	Citizenship and Immigration Services	https://www.uscis.gov/humanitarian/deferred-action-childhood-arrivals-response-january-2018-preliminary-injunction
Racial discrimination	Civil Rights Act	Department of Education, Office for Civil Rights	https://www2.ed.gov/policy/rights/guid/ocr/raceoverview.html
Safety on campus	Clery Act	Department of Education	https://ifap.ed.gov/.../attachments/HandbookforCampusSafetyandSecurityReporting.pdf
	Crime Awareness and Campus Security Act		https://www2.ed.gov/admins/lead/safety/campus.html

POLICY INFORMED BY ALTERNATIVE LENSES

In this section, we look at how other countries organize their higher education systems. In addition, we examine the potential for free college and the way that critical race theory might inform a discussion of race in college admissions.

International Alternatives

Disparities within postsecondary education are not unique to the United States. An annual survey of the 36 members of the Organisation for Economic Cooperation and Development (OECD) find that background, socioeconomic status, and immigration status have a strong impact on the likelihood that a child will attend college. Students who come from families where parents have not attended college are underrepresented in college and earn 65% as much as their college-educated peers. Across these countries, women are more likely than men to graduate high school and attend college—50% of women aged 25 to 34 were college educated in 2017, compared to 38% of men. This hasn't affected the gender gap in employment or wages. Only 81% of young college-educated women are employed in these countries, compared to 89% of comparable men, and only 78% of the same group who are foreign born are employed. Women who are college educated also earn on average 26% less than their male counterparts (OECD, 2018).

Tuition cost is one way in which U.S. colleges differ from their peers in other countries. The average cost of a year's tuition for an undergraduate degree across the OECD countries surveyed was $2,364, and, across the OECD, countries spent an average of 1.5% of their gross domestic product on higher education. Total spending by government on education in the United States is slightly lower than average, while spending by individuals and nongovernmental agencies on college education is more than three times the average—the highest in the world (OECD, 2018).

In approximately one-third of OECD countries, residents of the country are charged nothing for tuition for undergraduate, graduate, or doctoral degrees. This includes Denmark, Estonia, Finland, Norway, Poland, the Slovak Republic, Sweden, and Turkey. Austria, Belgium, Hungary, Italy, Luxembourg, and Switzerland offer all three types of degrees at the equivalent of $2,000 or less per year. Only Chile, the United Kingdom, and the United States have an average cost of $7,000 or more per student per year (OECD, 2018). Countries that strive to make postsecondary education available to low-income students are split between those that make the cost of education as low as possible and those that offer means-tested support to students in need. One final note: In Australia, Canada, New Zealand, Sweden, and the United States, foreign students are charged significantly more than national students. This is not the case in other OECD countries, where foreign and resident students are charged the same rate, including Finland, Norway, the Slovak Republic, and Slovenia, where tuition is free for all (OECD, 2018).

Free College

In June 2014, the governor of Tennessee signed legislation creating Tennessee Promise, a scholarship and mentoring program that provides 2 years of tuition-free community college or technical school for high school graduates who meet high school requirements, commit to ongoing community service and mentoring meetings, and maintain at least a 2.0 GPA in college. This is one of 238 *promise* programs available at the state or local level in 44 states, which offer aid above and beyond traditional federal and state aid to those who either come from a specific geographic area or agree to go to a specific school (Tennessee Promise, n.d.). They can take the form of place-based programs like Kalamazoo Promise, or free tuition programs like New York State's Excelsior Program (PennAHEAD, n.d.). Although most of these programs are in their early days, outcomes so far are mixed. Like many others, Tennessee's program is funded through the lottery, which raises a challenges for replicability (Fain, 2014). Free college has yet to be enacted on the federal level, although it was proposed in 2015 during the Obama administration (America's College Promise) (Gross, 2015) and has been suggested by some political candidates.

Critical Race Theory and Affirmative Action

Should race be a factor in admissions policies for higher education? This is an ongoing area of debate, policy making, and legal action. While racial quotas (requiring a specific number of a college's students to come from certain racial or ethnic backrounds) are not allowed under federal law, a number of Supreme Court decisions have allowed race to be considered as a factor in the admissions process to balance out systemic bias against college applicants of color, resulting in policies that fall under the general category of **affirmative action**. This term refers to policies that favor individuals because of their membership in groups that have previously experienced discrimination. The term comes from Title VI of the 1968 Civil Rights Act, which authorizes colleges to "take affirmative action in setting goals and timetables to remedy the racial discrimination found in U.S. society" (p. 9). Since this provision was challenged in 1978, disagreements about affirmative action have continued to be addressed in the court system, and resulting decisions have considerably narrowed the ways in which affirmative action can be used by colleges and universities. In 2018, a group of students sued Harvard, arguing that the university's admissions policies disadvantage Asian-American applicants, and had their case heard by a federal court. It is expected at the time of this writing that the case will eventually be heard by the Supreme Court (Anderson, 2018) and this case might change the legality of affirmative action across the country.

Affirmative action: Favoring individuals who belong to groups that have faced historical discrimination

As discussed in Chapter 3, critical race theory (CRT) can help our analysis of public policy by ensuring the voices of people who have been marginalized are present in policy discussions and that policy outcomes for these groups are included in the debate. Common arguments for and against affirmative action generally highlight (1) the need to create **color-blind** admission systems that do not take race into account, (2) the benefit of systems that increase the diversity of students at predominantly white institutions to make a better learning environment, or (3) the need for systems that compensate current students of color for past discrimination. A CRT perspective might ask whether integration that forces change on predominantly white institutions is the best way to assure equity in education for students of color. CRT challenges us to consider whether we are considering white students as the norm who benefit from diversity, and whether we accept color-blind policies only when they benefit white individuals or communities over communities of color. A CRT analysis suggests that students of color who are affected by affirmative action policies generally highlight their past experiences of discrimination and the need for an affirmative action policy to address that past discrimination, while institutions that are developing and even defending affirmative action policies are reluctant to acknowledge systemic racism within their own institutions. For example, in a case at the University of Michigan regarding affirmative action, students "asserted that racism continues to exist in both its overt and covert forms and that, as long as it remains, policies and practices need to be in place to compensate for the barriers that racism erects in higher education settings" (Yosso, Parker, Solórzano, & Lynn, 2004, p. 15), and that the campus climate sends a message that "[w]hites enjoy a sense of entitlement and members of racial minority groups are viewed as unqualified, unworthy, and unwelcome" (p. 15).

Color-blind: Systems that make decisions without regard to race

OPPORTUNITIES FOR ADVOCACY

There are many opportunities for advocacy related to higher education, both on your campus and at the state and federal levels. In this section, we highlight college affordability and student debt as well as inequality in access to higher education.

College Affordability/Student Debt

The College Scorecard discussed above (https://collegescorecard.ed.gov/) was developed as one way to emphasize the rising cost of college and therefore affect students' decisions about colleges and related student loan debt. A coalition working in this area is the Student Aid Alliance (n.d.), a group of 85 higher education groups and universities that advocate for policies related to college affordability and student debt. They use the hashtag #savestudentaid and encourage members to advocate on student aid–related policies. Most recently, they worked to stop the PROSPER Act (Promoting Real Opportunity, Success, and Prosperity through Education Reform Act) that they argued would make college more expensive for students using financial aid. They also seek increases in funding for programs like federal work-study, Pell Grants, and GEAR UP. This organization and others like it work to balance the cost of higher education with the available funding for students and look at ways to help students understand the cost of higher education and make acceptance and financial aid decisions that will serve them well in the long run.

Inequality in Access to Higher Education

We began this chapter with a quote from Frawley, Larkin, and Smith (2017) arguing that "[u]niversity is not for everyone, but a university should be for everyone" (p. 3). These authors argue that the choice whether to participate in higher education should be available to all. In Chapter 7, we discussed the ways that school funding and segregation result in unequal access to K–12 education. This chapter includes many examples of policies that attempt to address inequitable access to higher education, such as affirmative action policies designed in an attempt to address inequality in higher education access. We have also raised the question of whether some individuals should be supported in options other than higher education. Review this chapter and look for other examples of policies that address unequal access to higher education. Choose one policy that affects a population of interest to you and find an interest group active in advocating for or against that policy. Subscribe to updates from that organization and look for ways you can act on that policy.

Final Discussion

Now that you have finished reading this chapter, reread the vignette at the beginning. Based on what you have learned, answer the following questions. Point to specific references in the chapter that help you answer these questions. Consider how different theories inform the response to these questions.

1. Can you identify the specific policies that impact Kai?
2. How might policies affect current and future opportunities for Kai?
3. What strengths and resources does Kai have that she can draw on?
4. What roles could a social worker play in helping Kai (think micro, mezzo, and macro level social work)?
5. What role might race, class, gender, and other aspects of identity play in this vignette?

9

WORK AND EMPLOYMENT POLICY

LEARNING OBJECTIVES

9.1: Identify the historical conceptions of work in the United States and their effect on policy

9.2: Critique the strengths and gaps in current policies related to work

9.3: Compare and contrast U.S work and employment policy with those of the U.S. military and the European Union

9.4: Assess wage policy approaches for improving the quality of life for the working poor

This chapter begins with a history of paid labor including efforts to regulate the employer-employee relationship and collective bargaining. This is followed by a discussion of the creation of **social safety net** programs as they relate to work. These programs grew from a recognition of the governmental role in mitigating the risks of economic trends that impact large segments of the labor market. This section closes with a discussion of changes brought about by globalization and other economic shifts. Much of U.S. social policy hinges on people's status as employees. In contrast, unpaid labor, such as family care, is often devalued or not acknowledged as work. This belief has persisted as a theme through U.S. history and has implications for different populations, such as family caregivers and women who perform the bulk of domestic labor. Building on the social construction of work, we discuss the central U.S. employment and worker-based federal, state, and employer policies and describe mechanisms for the inclusion and exclusion of coverage. The chapter then explores the broader cultural values that these policies demonstrate. It concludes with a discussion of alternative labor policies and active advocacy campaigns to address unmet needs of employees.

Social safety net: The basic set of government programs that mitigate of economic risks

Like many other areas of U.S. social policy, work and employment policies are characterized by a focus on individual choice over the well-being and safety of workers. As we have seen throughout the book, many safeguards are **residual**, meaning that they only intervene when other systems fail. This is in contrast to **institutional** approaches, which see intervention or regulation as a regular and appropriate function of government. This approach treats work concerns, such as unemployment or underemployment, as individualized and fleeting rather than structural. Fewer economic interventions target the economy or workforce as a whole. Additionally, approaches to work and employment largely ignore power imbalances, seeking instead to treat most actors (whether they are individuals or large corporations; small farmers or agribusinesses) similarly in terms of their ability to establish, maintain, and terminate their work relations. One final, overarching thread throughout the history and implementation of U.S. work and employment policy is the sole recognition of paid labor as a form of work and the failure to consider unpaid work, upon which the economy and most paid labor depends, as work. As we trace key points in the history of U.S. work and employment policy, keep these ideas in mind and consider how, under each era or category, they have influenced policy.

Vignette: Protections for Workers and Their Families

Based on what you know from the media or your personal, work, or volunteer experiences, think about the following questions as you read the vignette. When you finish the vignette, answer the questions below.

1. What kind of resources would you like to be able to offer Elijah, Noreen, and their family regarding
    a. Elijah's concussion
    b. His possible PTSD
    c. Assistance to the family if Elijah is laid off or has a reduced income
2. Make a list of the possible concerns that are raised for you when you read Elijah's story. Who might be responsible for making things better regarding each concern?
3. What are the different policies that may be relevant here?
4. To which other professionals might you turn for assistance?
5. What role might race, class, gender, and other aspects of identity play in this vignette?

Elijah is 48 years old. A father of three children (ranging in age from 9 to 15 years old) and a husband, he is the main breadwinner and earns a living as a forklift operator. He lives in the town where he grew up, and he had hoped to support his family with the same blue collar, union employment that his father held when raising Elijah and his siblings. Things have changed, though. At first, changes were slow. Perhaps the most notable change is that while his father earned sufficient wages to meet the family's needs, buy a car, and take annual vacations, his own family needs the salaries of two people to maintain their lifestyle. His wife Noreen has worked since their youngest entered first grade. To be able to greet the school bus each day, drive the children to their extracurricular activities, and be on call for any illnesses or teacher conferences, Noreen works only part time as a switchboard operator at a call center. Because she is a part-time employee, they rely on Elijah's job for health benefits. Another change is that Elijah's father was a proud union member at a time when most of the factories were union shops. Elijah's company is not a union shop. Frankly, Elijah never wanted money to be taken out of his paycheck for union dues and didn't see much benefit from unions.

Recently, Elijah suffered a concussion while on the job when a package became dislodged from the load he carried on the forklift. He was home on paid part-time disability, but that ran out a week ago. He returned to work, although he is unable to operate the forklift due to continuing symptoms. His wife suspects that this might be more than just a concussion. She thinks it might be a form of posttraumatic stress disorder, a condition she has heard about from friends, because his symptoms include irritability and disproportionate reactions to loud noises or movement from above. Elijah thinks she is overreacting but has agreed to discuss it with his primary care physician during his next checkup. His employer has offered him a desk job for lower pay. Elijah has concerns that the desk job will not pay sufficiently and that he will lose his position if he is out for much longer. He also has some concerns about the responsibility of his employer for the accident, because he had lodged a number of safety concerns informally with his supervisor in the few months prior to the accident. However, he is afraid that any confrontation or complaint may lead to his being laid off completely, which he and his family cannot afford.

HISTORY AND SOCIAL CONSTRUCTION OF U.S. WORK AND EMPLOYMENT

Work and employment policies have evolved over the course of U.S. history from being relatively unregulated to the complex array of policies that govern different aspects of employment. Work and employment policies currently address job training, work supports, employer-employee relations, workplace safety, and retirement. A host of local and federal laws, overseen by different regulatory agencies, respond to changing social and economic conditions as well as changing notions of the appropriate role and scope of government.

The Early Years

In the early years of the republic, the United States was made up of small, family-run farms that provided sustenance for individual families together with small towns and growing cities that were home to small businesses. These small businesses, many also family run, generally had a small number of workers. Such workers included apprentices, who labored in exchange for learning a trade; servants, often young people who moved frequently and exchanged labor for room, board, and small wages; or indentured servants. Still others, many of whom were children, were involuntarily sent to the United States from England as a result of their poverty by local parishes under the English Poor Laws. They were poorly treated and suffered under harsh conditions (Dahlberg, 2012). Indentured servants, who first came to the colonies in the early 17th century, contracted to work for periods of time generally ranging from 4 to 7 years in exchange for passage to the United States, room, and board. At the end of their indenture, they were declared free of their obligations and given a *freedom package* that could include land, livestock, clothes, and food for a period of time. The work was difficult, and the conditions were meager. Indentured servants could be punished for various breaches of contract; one punishment was to extend their period of indenture. One example of such a breach was for women indentured servants who became pregnant, which in Virginia could result in an additional 2 years of service (Library of Congress, n.d.). Some colonies offered protection to indentured servants. For example, Massachusetts required contract holders to support indentured servants who became ill and were unable to work. Though conditions were harsh, indentured servitude enabled many people who were escaping war and other hardships in Europe to come to the colonies when they lacked their own resources (Tomlins, 2010).

As the country grew, so did demand for labor, thus increasing the leverage of laborers and their cost. This fed a growing trans-Atlantic slave trade of Africans abducted and sold into slavery (Graden, 2016). Larger farming operations that existed primarily in the South relied heavily on the uncompensated labor of enslaved people until slavery was finally outlawed in the United States in 1865 by the Thirteenth Amendment. Labor relationships were only minimally regulated by the government, and no specific worker protections existed. As Diane DiNitto (2011) describes, throughout the 19th century the government solved problems of employment through making land available for people to settle and farm. This met the multiple goals of quelling unrest, providing a way for citizens to become self-sufficient, and establishing a U.S. presence in expanding geographic areas.

Industrialization and the Beginnings of Workplace Protections

As the U.S. economy grew and changed from primarily agrarian to industrial, the ways people earned their livelihoods changed. Manufacturing relied on low-wage labor in factories and in the building of infrastructure, such as railroads. Capital was concentrated in the hands of a relatively small group of individuals and companies who employed large numbers of laborers drawn from U.S. farms and immigrant communities (Boyer, 1978). As we described in Chapter 1, workers labored long hours for little pay; machinery, equipment, and environmental conditions were often hazardous. Women worked for even lower pay than men, and child labor, as yet unrestricted, yielded even lower wages. Photo 9.1 depicts children working at a glass factory in Indiana at midnight.

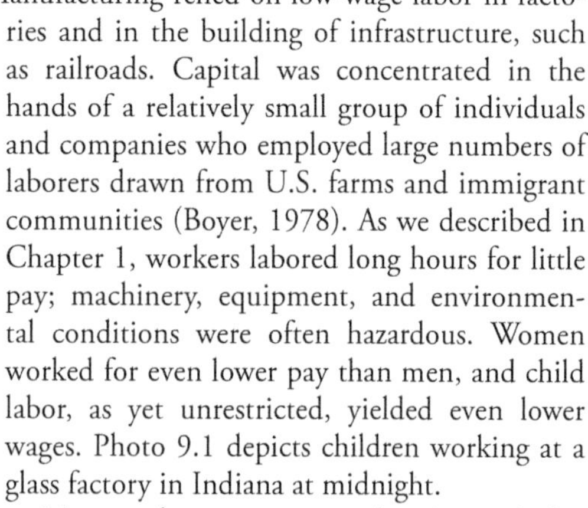

Lewis Wickes Hine, Library of Congress, LC-DIG-nclc-01151

PHOTO 9.1 Glassworks, midnight

Most workers were extremely poor, with few options for employment or the means to otherwise sustain themselves. They also had virtually no assets, so they had nothing to fall back on if they became injured, ill, or unemployed. This meant that individual workers wielded virtually no leverage against employers, who set the terms of their employment, including wages, salaries, hours, and working conditions. In extreme cases, such as company towns, employers

Department of Labor

PHOTO 9.2 Demonstration of protest and mourning for the Triangle Shirtwaist Factory fire of March 25, 1911

might also be landlords and run the company store, which was the only place that people could buy what they needed (Green, 2012). Long-term oppression and hardship led to the formation and growth of unions, which allowed workers to join forces. United, they compensated for their lack of power as individuals through grassroots campaigns that took advantage of their strength in numbers. Social workers were deeply involved in the steady work to build labor unions and supported their long-term campaigns (Scanlon & Harding, 2005). Unions met with strong, often violent resistance. In many cases, unions and union members fought back. Unions used collective tactics, including picketing and strikes, such as the famous nationwide Pullman railroad workers strike of 1894 (Basset, 1997), to seek concessions from employers. Workplace disasters resulting from hazardous conditions also played a role in the creation of workplace protections. One horrifying example is the 1911 Triangle Shirtwaist Factory fire. One hundred forty-six employees, most of whom were Italian and Jewish immigrant women and girls lost their lives, and 71 were injured when they were trapped in a locked building with piles of flammable cloth (McEvoy, 1995). Such tragedies fed a growing social consciousness, and strengthened support for unions such as the Ladies Waist and Dressmakers Union, depicted in Photo 9.2.

Workplace protections enacted in the early 20th century were modest and focused on populations that were perceived as both worthy and especially vulnerable. These included the first laws prohibiting child labor, as well as protections for women, such as setting maximum working hours. Other laws protected certain trades, such as bakers. Many of these laws were enacted at the state level; federal legislation took longer. More than half of states had laws regulating child labor by the turn of the century. However, it was only in 1916 in the Owen Keating Act that the U.S. Congress first attempted to regulate child labor by banning products of child labor through its power to regulate interstate commerce. In 1918, a conservative Supreme Court declared this law unconstitutional (Whittaker, 2004). The Pomerene Child Labor Tax Act (1919), which placed a 10% tax on goods produced with child labor, was similarly struck down by the court in 1922 (Whittaker, 2004).

Filling Gaps in the Worker Safety Net

The period following the stock market crash and the **Great Depression of 1929** is often considered a turning point in the history of social welfare. In response to widespread unemployment and unrest, the **New Deal** programs—often referred to as Alphabet Soup for the plethora of acronyms to which they referred—created jobs for the huge number of unemployed. The first of these was the Federal Emergency Relief Act (FERA). Like many other New Deal programs, this was temporary and ran from 1933–1935. The federal government invested $500 million to reduce unemployment by creating unskilled jobs in local and state governments. Similarly, the Civil Works Administration (CWA), which operated from 1933–1934, employed four million workers in low skill level work projects such as building roads and grading airport runways (Schwartz, 1984). Not only did these programs provide relief by creating jobs, but they also stimulated the economy and provided long-term benefits for the country through work done at the local level and building national infrastructure. Projects such as the Hoover Dam, the nation's highway system, and the National Parks were born of New Deal programs, such as the Works Progress Administration (WPA) and the Civilian Conservation Corps (CCC) (Lurie, 1934; Reading, 1973). The WPA, CCC, and other programs created by the National Industrial Recovery Act (NIRA) of 1933 were considered emergency relief. At their height in 1934, these programs collectively employed nearly 2.5 million workers. Economist Scott McConnell (2014) suggests that similar work relief programs that benefit workers and the economy should be considered in times of deep unemployment despite their costs.

> These workers [in NIRA created programs] performed various jobs, but most of the labor was geared toward conservation, infrastructure development, and other forms of public service. The Civil Works Administration alone was responsible for laying twelve million feet of sewer pipe, building or improving 255 thousand miles of roadway, and repairing 40,000 schools, 3,700 playgrounds, and nearly one thousand airports. As of February 1939, the Public Works Administration had engaged in 17,780 projects, totaling $1.8 billion of direct investment (Public Works Administration 1939). (p. 544, citation in the original)

REFLECTION

ALPHABET SOUP PROGRAMS

Pick an acronym from one of the New Deal Alphabet Soup programs listed below.

- What was the full name of the program, and what did it do?
- Who were the people who were employed, trained, or received support under it?
- What was the public benefit that it sought to provide?
- Do you think that such a program still exists at the federal, state, or local level?
- How might a proposal for such a program be received today?

Programs by acronym: FERA, CWA, PWA, CCC, UI, WPA, SSA

A number of safety net programs that help people in relation to their status as workers were also created during the New Deal. Unlike the programs we just reviewed, these were not temporary and many of them have expanded since their enactment. The Social Security Act is considered the centerpiece of the New Deal. It set up programs that provide assistance to individuals who had paid into the program as workers (or their spouses and dependents) and is the foundation for the current Social Security system that provides benefits in the event of disability, death, and after reaching retirement age.

Federal unemployment insurance (UI) was also established in the wake of the Great Depression. While voluntary unemployment programs were instituted by individual employers, unions, and joint employer-employee ventures in the early 20th century, these were insufficient to mitigate unemployment, which reached as many as 18 million U.S. workers at the height of the Great Depression. Individual state responses that began in the early 1920s were also insufficient to mitigate the havoc of the Great Depression. Where local government capacity was often outstripped by need, the federal government had deeper resources. It was also able to redistribute resources to ensure that needs were met across the country (Skocpol, 2003). The Social Security Act set up a system to require employers to pay into unemployment compensation funds that are paid through state agencies. Though the federal government regulates unemployment insurance, each state has its own system with different levels of taxation, different benefits, and different eligibility criteria.

One of the critiques of these and other New Deal programs (not just those related to work) is that they were discriminatory. For example, one official from the National Association for the Advancement of Colored People (NAACP) who testified against the Social Security Act described it as "a sieve with holes just big enough for the majority of Negroes to fall through" (Katzenelson, 2005, p. 48). Farm laborers, seasonal or migrant workers, and domestic workers were excluded from the Social Security Act. These exclusions were specifically targeted at women and African Americans. Similarly, while the National Labor Relations Act gave unions the right to organize, they were not prohibited from discrimination and many, in fact, discriminated against women and minorities. Many employment and training programs, such as the WPA, discriminated by race and gender in hiring practices as well as wages. While worker protections that grew out of the Great Depression were an important part of the developing U.S. safety net, they were far from comprehensive or fair.

This is also the case in relation to work and labor relations. Many legislative changes that had been struck down for decades by the Supreme Court finally succeeded following activism by groups who were concerned about working conditions. For example, in 1938, the federal Fair Labor Standards Act (FLSA) was enacted, finally setting minimum working-age limits at 16 years old for employment during school hours, 14 for certain after-school jobs, and 18 for work considered dangerous (Grossman, 1978; Mayer, Collins, & Bradley, 2013). The FLSA also set a federal **minimum wage** and rules around record-keeping and overtime (Wage and Hour Division, 2016).

Minimum wage: The minimum hourly wage that workers must be paid by law

Much of the policy that emerged from this period reflected a shifting belief in the role of government, which now used its power not only to regulate and intervene in individual employee-employer relationships, but also at the broader level of political economy. For example, the **National Labor Relations Board (NLRB)** established in the National Labor Relations Act of 1935 (National Labor Relations Board [NLRB], 2015), which officially recognized the role of organized labor, provided certain protections to workers, and established a process for employees to file complaints in response to unfair practice (NLRB, n.d.a). The NLRB describes its work, "Starting in the Great Depression and continuing through World War II and the economic growth and challenges that followed, the NLRB has worked to guarantee the rights of employees to bargain collectively, if they choose to do so (NLRB, n.d.b). As was the case during the prior era of union activism, social workers such as Forrester

National Labor Relations Board (NLRB): The federal agency housed in the Department of Labor that is charged with protecting workers' individual and collective rights

DISCUSSION

"A SWITCH IN TIME SAVES NINE"

A turning point in the ongoing tensions between the Supreme Court and Congress came in the 1937 decision in *West Coast Hotel Co. v. Parrish.* Elsie Parrish, a chambermaid at the West Coast Hotel, sued her employer for the difference between the state of Washington's minimum wage and what the hotel actually paid. The Washington state Supreme Court declared the minimum wage unconstitutional, and the state of Washington appealed to the Supreme Court. When it seemed that the Supreme Court would uphold the state-level decision, President Roosevelt started efforts to "pack the court" by expanding the number of justices. Had this succeeded, the appointment of justices who were less hostile to government intervention would dilute the votes of the justices known as the *Four Horsemen* who had consistently voted against such interventions. It is largely thought that fear of such intervention was what motivated the two swing voters to side with those who upheld the constitutionality of the law. Thus "the switch in time" saved the Supreme Court composition of nine justices (Carson & Kleinerman, 2002).

1. What were the different powers held by the Supreme Court and Congress in this case (hint: you can look at the Constitution, which is discussed in Chapter 2)?
2. What does this incident tell you about the relative strength of each of these institutions?
3. What might be some of the reasons behind the differences in the position of Congress and the position of the Supreme Court?
4. What does this incident tell us about the balance of these powers?
5. What does this incident make you think about the ability to make social change?

Blanchard Washington, Harry Hopkins, and Frances Perkins played key roles in the New Deal. What can you find out about these social workers and how they shaped U.S. policy during this period?

A Larger Mission: Equality in the Workplace

The next wave of employment-related policy changes came as a result of activism during the Civil Rights era of the 1960s. In 1963, President John F. Kennedy introduced a proposal for the Civil Rights Act (CRA) to the American public in a famous televised address that still resonates with many:

> We are confronted primarily with a moral issue. It is as old as the scriptures and it is as clear as the American Constitution. The heart of the question is whether all Americans are afforded equal rights and equal opportunities, whether we are going to treat our fellow Americans as we want to be treated . . . Now the time has come for this nation to fulfill its promise. The events of Birmingham and elsewhere have so increased the cries for equality that no city or state or legislative body can prudently ignore them. We face, therefore, a moral crisis as a country and as a people. It cannot be met with repressive police action. It cannot be left to increased demonstrations on the streets. It cannot be quieted by token moves or talk. It is a time to act in Congress, in your state and local legislative body and, above all, in all of our daily lives. Next week I will ask the Congress of the United States to act, to make a commitment it has not fully made in this century to the proposition that race has no place in American life or law.

These concerns were reflected in the organizing and social movements that shaped public opinions and discussions of civil rights, including the Freedom Riders, the Alabama Christian Movement for Human Rights, and the Student Nonviolent Coordinating Committee (SNCC) (PBS Learning Media, n.d.). These groups were predominantly led by African American leaders such as Dr. Martin Luther King, Jr. Many women, such as social worker Dr. Dorothy Height, were integral members of the movement but were rarely given credit in public (Keyes, 2010).

The Civil Rights Act was signed into law in 1964 by President Lyndon Johnson, after President Kennedy's assassination. Although this federal legislation was enacted primarily in response to race-based discrimination, Title VII of the CRA prohibited discrimination based on race, color, national origin, sex, religion, and retaliation (Equal Employment Opportunity Commission [EEOC], n.d.b). Title VII set up the **Equal Employment Opportunity Commission** (EEOC), which can investigate and help resolve complaints when the agency determines that discrimination has occurred. Individuals who want to file discrimination lawsuits against an employer or labor union must first file a complaint with the EEOC unless they are suing under the Equal Pay Act (EEOC, n.d.a). When such complaints are not resolved, individuals can file private lawsuits. If the EEOC determines that systematic discrimination occurred, they can refer the complaint to the Department of Justice which can sue the employer or union (Civil Rights Act [CRA], 1964). The CRA has been expanded over time. In 1978, the Pregnancy Discrimination Act (PDA) was passed to include discrimination against pregnant women (for more on the PDA, see Chapter 4).

Equal Employment Opportunity Commission (EEOC): The federal agency that can investigate and help resolve complaints when the agency determines that discrimination has occurred

Workplace protections have not expanded equally for all. While there are no legislative protections for workplace discrimination on the basis of sexual orientation or gender identity (SOGI), an EEOC interpretation of the Civil Rights Act that has been upheld by the courts includes sexual orientation and gender identity under federal sexual discrimination provisions (*Baldwin v. Foxx*, 2015; EEOC, n.d.a). However, the Department of Justice **Civil Rights Division**, also a federal agency, takes a different stance. The Civil Rights Division has informed the Supreme Court that it does not consider Civil Rights Act provisions to protect against discrimination on the basis of sex to include gender identity (Opfer, 2018). This question is being taken up by the Supreme Court in three cases as of this writing (Minter, 2019). Notwithstanding official policy, and perhaps because of its lack of consistency, LGBTQ+ individuals continue to be overrepresented in unemployment and firing. They also fare worse in terms of hiring and promotion. LGBTQ+, in particular transgender individuals, report high levels of workplace unwelcoming and sometimes hostile work environments (Out & Equal, 2019). Due to such concerns, many LGBTQ+ employees hide their gender identity or sexual orientation, which can be detrimental to their advancement and workplace relationships and deprives employers of the full benefit of their talents and potential contributions (Hewlett, 2011).

Civil Rights Division: The U.S. Department of Justice arm charged with oversight of the Civil Rights Act that has the authority to investigate and bring forward cases of discrimination

Additional federal protections were enacted during the Civil Rights era. These include the Age Discrimination in Employment Act (1967), which prohibits employers from discriminating against people who are 40 years old or older in "hiring, promotion, discharge, compensation, or terms, conditions, or privileges of employment" (U.S. Department of Labor, n.d.b, para. 2). Additional protections against discrimination on the basis of age have been added through subsequent federal legislation, such as the Age Discrimination Act (1975). Disability rights were not recognized in employment until the Rehabilitation Act of 1973. This law, which is covered in more detail in Chapter 12 on disability policy, only applies to organizations that receive federal funding. In 1990, civil rights for people with disabilities were expanded under the Americans with Disabilities Act (ADA). Title 1 of the ADA requires equality of opportunity in employment for employees who work (or seek to work) and applies to companies that employ over 15 workers (U.S. Department of Justice Civil Rights Division, n.d.).

Occupational Safety and Health Administration (OSHA): The federal agency housed in the Department of Labor that sets, provides education about, and enforces regulations regarding workplace safety in government and private employment

Whistleblower: An employee who alerts OSHA to safety and health violations under OSHA or other statutes. These individuals are entitled to certain protections against retaliation.

Alongside new forms of employment protections, workplace safety was also enhanced during this era. The Occupational Safety and Health Act (1970) created the **Occupational Safety and Health Administration (OSHA)** to set regulations regarding workplace safety in government and private employment. OSHA also conducts outreach and training (U.S. Department of Labor, n.d.a). The agency has authority to investigate compliance and impose sanctions, which may include fines, and the publication of safety and health violations intended to punish, inform, and deter future noncompliance. OSHA also provides guidelines and outlines protections from retaliation for **whistleblowers**—employees who alert the agency to safety and health violations under OSHA or other statutes.

CURRENT WORK AND EMPLOYMENT POLICIES

There are many policies that regulate employment, some of which we have described in our historical overview. Table 9.1 at the end of this section lists key topics in work and employment policy and the agencies that oversee them. In this section, we describe in greater detail areas that are often of interest to social workers and subject to policy debates. These include a changing employment settings and the labor market; retirement benefits; unemployment; and job creation, education, and training.

The Changing Employment Context

From the 1960s to the 1990s, labor rights were expanded through programs designed to enhance equality and protect workers. As new laws were implemented, the courts, government agencies, workplaces, and employees struggled to interpret the meaning and scope of these protections. For example, a Supreme Court decision in 2007 limited equal pay litigation by saying that cases needed to be brought within 180 days of the discrimination occurring, even if the person who was being paid less did not know about the discrimination until after that deadline (*Ledbetter v. Goodyear Tire & Rubber Company*). These limitations were addressed by Congress in the Lilly Ledbetter Fair Pay Act (2009), the first bill signed into law by President Obama. This law defines every new unequal paycheck as a new discriminatory act, and therefore increases the likelihood that those who are discriminated against are able to sue (National Women's Law Center, 2013). However, debates about such protections continue to evolve, as exemplified by our discussion of the inclusion of gender identity and sexual orientation sex-based discrimination in the prior section. These debates are also informed by increased attention to more insidious forms of discrimination such as structural oppression and microaggressions. Contentious debates over interpretation of workplace protections have been further complicated by beliefs about the proper role of government and the extent to which it should intervene in business as well as employer-employee relationships. Many employment-related trends have either eluded the policy agenda or are still in emerging stages. For example, as we document in Chapter 6, U.S. child care policy has not addressed the growing numbers of women with children who make up an increasing proportion of the paid labor force, creating more need for paid care for children during their parents' work hours (Palley & Shdaimah, 2014).

Gig economy: Newer employment areas that are characterized by temporary employment and decreasing employer commitment to their employees

Newer employment areas that are characterized by a policy void include decreasing employer commitment to their employees. This is caused by a number of trends, including employees' more frequent job changes, the increase in part-time employment, contingent work (sometimes called the **gig economy**), and outsourcing. In a political economy where so much of social welfare, such as health benefits and retirement income, is tied to one's status as an employee, these trends are concerning and have made many individuals and families vulnerable to market changes and personal circumstances such as health crises. **Shift work**, often at atypical and changing hours, is an increasing feature of low wage employment, which can make it hard to sustain employment in the face of care responsibilities (Lefrançois, Messing, & Saint-Charles, 2017). Recently, the popular media exposed the practice in which workers are assigned changing schedules, often by a computer algorithm designed to save the employer money with no regard to work patterns for the employee (Kantor, 2014). For some, this results in "clopening," where a worker might close the store in a final night shift, only to return early the next morning to open. Employers also spread shifts to avoid paying overtime or enhancing benefits. While there has been no legislative response to these practices at the federal level, a number of cities and states have enacted laws that prohibit or regulate these practices. One example is New York City's Fair Work Week Act (New York City Government, n.d.), and other laws that require practices such as restrictive or secure scheduling to give employees a more humane and predictable schedule.

Shift work: Work that is often carried out during atypical and changing hours, often a feature of low-wage employment

Another trend is the increase of part-time work, often against the wishes of workers who would prefer full-time positions. Part-time work is associated with a precarious work status and higher rates of poverty (Golden, 2016; Henly & Lambert, 2014). This trend is fed by decreasing demand for low-skilled workers in living wage jobs. **Living wage** is defined as the hourly wage that is considered sufficient to meet a worker's needs. Poverty wages are associated with poor health and well-being and limit family ability to pay for quality child care. People with non-living wages are also unlikely to be able to save for future hardship, such as a health crisis, loss of existing employment, or home or car repair (Lambert, Fugiel, & Henly, 2010). Part-time workers are unlikely to be able to save for retirement and are likely to earn less Social Security benefits than full-time workers (see discussion below). One report finds mixed predictions for how growing automation and technology might impact workers, with different impacts by gender as well as race and ethnicity. For example, women and people of color are disproportionately represented among low-wage direct care workers such as child care providers and health aides, jobs that are unlikely to be replaced by technology (Hegewisch, Childers, & Hartmann, 2019).

Living wage: The hourly wage that is considered sufficient to meet a worker's needs

Retirement Benefits

Current work and employment policies exist at both the state and the federal level. The Social Security Act is one of the primary federal policies that provide benefits to individuals and family members through their current or past connection to the labor market, as described above. Contributions paid into Social Security are required from both workers and employers. Retirement benefits represent approximately two thirds of Social Security benefit claims (the remainder includes approximately 20% that are disability-related and 10% for survivor benefits) (Veghte, 2013). Although described as a social insurance program, workers' contributions pay for current recipients rather than being placed in savings accounts for their own future use. The **Social Security Administration (SSA)** (2017), the federal agency charged with administering the policy, explains:

Social Security Administration (SSA): The federal agency charged with administering policies and programs under the Social Security Act

> The money you pay in taxes isn't held in a personal account for you to use when you get benefits. We use your taxes to pay people who are getting benefits right now. Any unused money goes to the Social Security trust funds, not a personal account with your name on it. (p. 2)

Social Security is what we call an **entitlement program**, which means that the government is *obligated* to pay benefits. (You may hear this term used incorrectly in policy discussions.) The current generation of workers funds the payments to current beneficiaries. This means that

Entitlement program: A benefit that government is *obligated* to provide benefits for disability, retirement, and loss of a breadwinner are always dependent on a current pool of workers. We might ask, then, why these benefits have been framed as insurance? Many believe that this framing underscores the universal nature of the benefits that fosters broad-scale investment and support, making this one of the most stable and popular U.S. social welfare policies. Social Security has a dedicated funding stream through these contributions, which means that it does not rely on money from other sources. In fact, the government has often borrowed *from* these funds for other purposes.

When the Social Security Act was signed into law in 1935, its retirement benefits were considered one leg of a three-legged stool upon which workers could depend when they retired (DeWitt, 1996). The other two "legs" were employment-related retirement plans, such as pensions, and personal savings. From the discussion above and your own experience, you may see why many individuals, particularly those who rely on low-wage or part-time employment, rely exclusively on Social Security benefits when they are no longer able to work. Social Security is credited with lifting many American workers and their families out of poverty (Romig, 2018). This is particularly true of older Americans (see Chapter 10). It is important to underscore that individuals are only entitled to retirement benefits under the Social Security Act if they or their spouse have paid into the system while employed for a minimum number of 40 quarters (10 years), which do not have to be consecutive (Social Security Administration, 2018).

The solvency of Social Security, or its ability to pay future benefits, has long been a concern. The Social Security Administration's Office of the Chief Actuary (OCA) provides an Annual Report on the state of Social Security funds. The most recent report, which is based on current and projected fiscal information including revenue streams and interest rates, shows that the Social Security benefits to be paid out will begin to exceed funds available in 2023 (Social Security Administration, Office of the Chief Actuary, 2019b). The Social Security Administration, Office of the Chief actuary also summarizes a variety of proposed changes designed to address or mitigate projected shortfalls. The most recent report (2019a) outlined eight different types of proposals, which would make changes to any or all of the following: cost-of-living adjustment, level of monthly benefits, retirement age, type of family members who are entitled to benefits, payroll taxes (including maximum taxable income levels), trust fund investment in equities, taxation of benefits, and coverage of employment. The United States has already enacted changes in the age at which retirees are entitled to full benefits, which was gradually raised from age 65 to 67 by legislation enacted in 1983 (Li, 2019).

While Social Security provides retirement benefits to the largest group of Americans, workplace retirement plans are another common type of retirement benefit. According to one estimate, over one third of U.S. employees do not have access to any employer-sponsored retirement plans; fewer part-time workers have access than full-time workers (Pew Charitable Trusts, 2016). Even when companies provide pensions, many workers are ineligible or do not access their employer-sponsored plans because they cannot afford to. This set of benefits is more likely to be accessed by management and professional workers than service workers. As might be expected, if employers create incentives for retirement savings through matching contributions, employees are more likely to save for retirement.

The two main types of employment-sponsored retirement benefits are defined benefit plans and defined contribution plans. Defined benefit plans are those in which the employer guarantees payment of a specified monthly amount upon retirement. These plans are protected by a special federal insurance provided by the Pension Benefit Guaranty Corporation (U.S. Department of Labor, n.d.d). This type of plan is increasingly rare in the private employment sector though it is still common for federal, state, and local public sector employees. As the name suggests, defined contribution plans only set the amount that the employee (and the employer, if it has a matching plan) will contribute—it does not guarantee what the employee will receive. These kinds of plans include 401(k)s and 403(b)s, Simplified Employee Pension Plans (SEP), or employee stock ownership plans. The value of plan savings fluctuates depending on how the plans are invested, which means that it may be hard to predict what one's retirement income will be from such a plan. Many such plans provide tax benefits that encourage investments in employee retirement savings. Each program has its own rules and guidelines that can include eligibility criteria, contribution caps, or insurance and disclosure requirements.

The most common private sector plans are 401(k) plans, which allow employees to put a portion of their salary into a tax-deferred savings account. This means that that they do not pay income taxes on this money at the time they earn it. Employees pay taxes on these funds when they take them out, which usually saves money in taxes (Internal Revenue Service [IRS], 2018b). Under the Employee Retirement Income Security Act of 1974 (ERISA), 401(k) plans are subject to Labor Department oversight and are covered by minimum standards designed to protect employees who invest in them. Among these is the requirement that those who oversee the plans act in the best interest of employees who own them. Employers can contribute to these accounts as well, and such contributions are designed both as a work benefit and to incentivize retirement saving. Another plan available for those who work in nonprofit organizations are 403(b) accounts (IRS, 2018a). Primarily offered to public school teachers, they are also available to tax-exempt organizations that include many religious organizations and nonprofits (IRS, 2019). These accounts are exempt from ERISA requirements, and are therefore not as secure or as transparent in their operation and oversight as 401(k) plans. Like 401(k) plans, employers may also contribute to employee savings.

Unemployment

The Bureau of Labor Statistics, which is the government agency charged with keeping track of characteristics of the U.S. workforce, considers people unemployed when they are not working but are interested in working and have actively looked for a job during the past 4 weeks (Bureau of Labor Statistics, 2015). Actively looking for work includes a wide variety of activities, such as sending out a resume or contacting a prospective employer (Bureau of Labor Statistics, 2015). Those who have graduated from school and have never worked are not counted in the unemployment statistics. The United States has been measuring unemployment every month since 1940 based on a sample from the **Current Population Survey (CPS)**. Figure 9.1 graphs a 50-year trend in U.S. unemployment, which at the time of this writing is in a historically low range.

Current Population Survey: A survey carried out by the U.S. Census Bureau

Some consider current unemployment rates to be deceptively low because they believe that the CPS-based measure is underinclusive. For example, it does not include individuals who are underemployed (i.e., working fewer hours than they would like). It also does not include what are called *discouraged workers*, people who want to work but have not sought employment in the 4 weeks prior to the survey (Bureau of Labor Statistics, 2018b). Research suggests that the longer one is unemployed, the more difficult it is for one to find work, suggesting that unemployment is a compounded phenomenon that may become persistent. Including these groups of people could double the U.S. unemployment rate according to some estimates (Ginsburg, Ayers, & Zaccone, 2018).

The Federal Unemployment Tax Act (FUTA) regulates a federal-state partnership for temporary (usually up to a maximum of 26 weeks) support for workers when they become unemployed. This law requires that employers pay a federal tax that funds assistance to states to pay unemployed workers in the form of cash benefits and support for job service programs. FUTA will also pay half of unemployment benefits when unemployment benefits are extended during periods of high unemployment. For example, during the **Great Recession**, Congress extended unemployment benefits to allow beneficiaries to access benefits for up to 99 weeks between 2009 and 2013. States can also borrow money from this fund to pay their portion of extended benefits. States have wide discretion in calculating state contributions,

Great Recession: An economic downturn in the U.S. and global markets, lasting from 2007 through 2009, that especially impacted the real estate and the banking industry, which originated with a crisis in the mortgage industry (loans secured by property, often someone's home)

as well as setting rules regarding eligibility and duration of benefits. State unemployment contribution rates are generally calculated either in the aggregate for the state or using calculations that factor in employers' individual records regarding workers layoffs (Vroman, Maag, O'Leary, & Woodbury, 2017). To qualify for benefits, workers need to demonstrate that they are actively seeking employment and are willing to accept suitable employment. Workers must also register with the U.S. Employment Service. Understanding unemployment insurance will likely come in handy during your social work career—many Americans will be eligible to access these benefits at some point in their working career. You or your family members may have used them, and whatever fields of social work you pursue, you are likely to work with those who are eligible for unemployment insurance at some point. It is important to understand eligibility criteria, applications processes, and rules for specific benefits and programs for your state and for federal benefits. You can access your state-specific unemployment benefits and programs through the federal Department of Labor website, which maintains links to all state programs.

Workers' compensation insurance programs for workers who are hurt or killed in work-related incidents exist at the state level. Federal workers' compensation is available for some employment sectors or incidences (e.g., for miners suffering from black lung disease, longshore and harbor workers, and federal employees) (U.S. Department of Labor, n.d.e). Workers' compensation also provides benefits to the dependents of workers killed on the job. All states have workers' compensation programs, which vary in types, levels, eligibility, financing, and administration of benefits (Sangupta, Reno, & Burton, 2007). The compensation is intended to substitute for wages that have been lost due to accident, illness, or death. They often include medical coverage. These programs are largely seen as beneficial to both employers and employees. Employees, for their part, are guaranteed to receive benefits without having to prove any fault on the part of the employer through relatively quick and standardized process. Employers, for their part, reduce the risk of costly lawsuits (DiNitto, 2011).

FIGURE 9.1 ■ Labor Force Statistics from the Current Population Survey

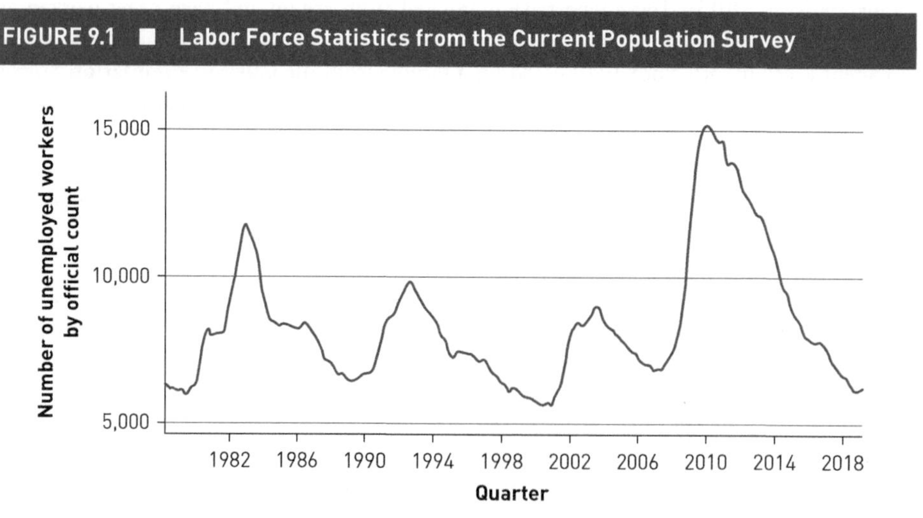

Source: This chart was created 6/12/19 using the Bureau of Labor Statistics calculator for years 1978–2018; https://data.bls.gov/pdq/SurveyOutputServlet

Creating Jobs, Education, and Training Workers

According to the Bureau of Labor Statistics (2018a), there are 22.7 million government employees in the United States, including municipal, county, state, and federal workers. Government employees tend to have relatively good work hours, job stability, and benefits. However, these jobs are not the product of programs specifically designed to create employment or mitigate unemployment but rather workers who fill regular functions of government, such as law enforcement or municipal services.

The only time in U.S. history that the U.S. federal government and some local governments saw themselves as creators of jobs to raise employment rates was during the New Deal. The federal government has continued to support programs designed to train youth and adults to enter the workforce and to retrain workers to create a better match between their skills and the existing job market. The Employment and Training Administration (ETA), housed at the Department of Labor, has a mission "to contribute to the more efficient functioning of the U.S. labor market by providing high-quality job training, employment, labor market information, and income maintenance services primarily through state and local workforce development systems" (U.S. Department of Labor Employment and Training Administration [ETA], n.d.). Under the Workforce Investment Act (WIA) (1998), reauthorized in 2014 as the Workforce Innovation and Opportunity Act (WIOA), money is provided to states to fund workforce development programs. States have wide discretion regarding programming and eligibility criteria (U.S. Department of Labor ETA, 2016b). Under this umbrella, a mechanism was designed to quickly provide grants to what are referred to as *dislocated workers*, those who lose their jobs through systemic unemployment such as mass layoffs, disasters, or emergencies. WIOA provides grants to states to develop "one-stop" centers in local communities that provide training, retraining, job skills, education, and employment referrals. In some states, *core services*, such as job searching, may be available to all workers. More intensive training and services are generally offered only to unemployed or dislocated workers. WIOA also provides grants to states for youth programs, including vocational training and transitions to postsecondary education, with a special emphasis on "out-of-school and at-risk youth" (U.S. Department of Labor ETA, 2016a, p. 3).

Another group that may receive job training and supportive services to enable employment, such as child care or transportation subsidies, are those receiving public welfare benefits (e.g., TANF). Sometimes referred to as *workfare*, the United States makes receipt of TANF benefits contingent on employment or work-related activities. These programs have received mixed reviews, and many scholars find that workfare programs do not reduce poverty (Pavetti, 2016). Many workplace supports, such as child care subsidies, are insufficient to cover all those who are eligible (Palley & Shdaimah, 2014). In some locations, such as New York City's Work Experience Program under Mayor Rudolph Giuliani, workfare workers have been tasked with jobs otherwise performed by salaried (and sometimes, unionized) workers, such as sanitation and parks employment (Devinitz, 2013). This was harmful to non-workfare workers whose wages were undercut, as well as to the workfare workers who performed labor for below minimum wage and often without important protections such as safety equipment (Devinitz, 2013). Another factor influencing the success of welfare-to-work programs is the extent to which these programs prepare workers for jobs that are available and the extent to which current employers would hire workers coming from workfare programs. The programs with the best outcomes are those that support participants' efforts to acquire skills and education rather than just find work (Pavetti, 2016).

TABLE 9.1 ■ List of Relevant Federal and State Labor and Employment Laws

Topic	Laws	Oversight Agency	Website
Wage and hour standards	Fair Labor Standards Act	Department of Labor, Wage and Hour Division	https://www.dol.gov/whd/
Workplace safety	Occupational Safety and Health Act of 1970	Occupational Safety and Health Administration (OSHA)	https://www.osha.gov/about.html
Pension benefits	Social Security Act	Social Security Administration (SSA)	https://www.ssa.gov/benefits/disability/
Disability	Social Security Act	Social Security Administration (SSA)	https://www.ssa.gov/benefits/disability/
Unemployment insurance	Social Security Act	Department of Labor (federal and state levels)	https://www.dol.gov/general/topic/unemployment-insurance
Family and sick leave	Family Medical Leave Act	Department of Labor	https://www.dol.gov/general/topic/benefits-leave/fmla
Workers' compensation	Federal Employees Compensation Act Longshore and Harbor Workers' Compensation Act Black Lung Benefits Reform Act Energy Employees Occupational Illness Compensation Program Act Radiation Exposure Compensation Act	Department of Labor (federal and state levels)	Federal: https://www.dol.gov/general/topic/workcomp State: https://www.nasi.org/research/2007/report-workers-compensation-benefits-coverage-costs-2005

POLICY INFORMED BY ALTERNATIVE LENSES

Workplace policies take many different models, both inside the United States and in other countries. Here we discuss two. The first is the U.S. military's approach to child care as an important work support to a crucial workforce. The second is the European Union's Working Time Directive to regulate labor conditions.

Family Leave for the U.S. Armed Forces

As we discussed in Chapter 6, child care policies in the military are an alternative model to the rest of the country. The military also provides extended workplace leave for service members and their families to care for family members or themselves in the event of birth, adoption, or sickness. This is a result of the 2009 Congressional expansion of the Family Medical Leave Act (FMLA) for service members as part of the National Defense Authorization Act, which received bipartisan support, passing quickly and without contention (Karin, 2009). It expanded coverage for individuals on active duty or pending active duty for up to 26 weeks, longer than the 12 weeks to which other FMLA-covered employees are entitled (Martin, 2009). The primary impetus for the bill sheds further light on the important connection between work and family. One of the reasons for passage of the law was growing recognition of the caregiving role that service members play, particularly with the increasing number of women in the military. Other countries provide even more comprehensive systems of child care that both support parents in the workforce and ensure dignified employment and living wages for providers, but the U.S. military model is an example close to home that may be more readily accepted as a policy strategy.

The European Union's Working Time Directive

The European Union's Working Time Directive (2003/88/EC) sets minimum standards for member countries' regulation of labor conditions. These standards limit work hours and set standards for leave and breaks on the job (European Commission, n.d.) including requirements such as:

- Work weeks not to exceed 48 hours, including any overtime
- Eleven consecutive hours of daily rest in every 24-hour period
- Rest breaks for employees on duty more than 6 hours
- Uninterrupted rest periods of 24 hours for every 7-day period
- Four weeks of paid annual leave

This directive also includes special protections for specific types of workers, including night workers, doctors in training, and transportation workers. In some cases, individuals can choose to opt-out of the 48-hour limit; more flexibility regarding leave is granted if it is the result of collective agreements, which generally can mitigate power imbalances between individual workers and employers or government (European Commission, 2017). A European Commission (2017) report on the implementation of the directive shows that member states are largely in compliance. Some forms of noncompliance are when countries exclude certain categories of workers by law (rather than collective agreement, which is permitted). For example, Ireland excludes "firefighters, prison staff, and marine emergency personnel" (p. 4); Belgium, Luxembourg, Sweden, and the UK exclude domestic workers. Trade unions have also criticized the directive's opt-out provisions, which they see as counter to the goal of the directive to protect workers' health (European Commission, 2017). In many cases, member states provide more protection than the European Union minimum directive requires.

OPPORTUNITIES FOR ADVOCACY[1]

> No business that depends for existence on paying less than living wages has any right to continue in this country . . . and by living wages I mean more than a bare subsistence level. I mean the wages of decent living. (President Franklin Roosevelt, Presidential Papers, 1933)

In the wake of rapid industrialization during the 19th century, a confluence of moral and economic forces led to passage of new labor laws mitigating low wages, long working hours, child labor, health risks, and poor conditions in the workplace as described above. As we note earlier in this chapter, after decades of unrest around labor laws, the Great Depression in the 1920s and '30s drove issues around employment to the forefront of U.S. politics (Samuel, 2000). It was in this sociopolitical context that federal minimum wage first became law in 1938. Despite meeting significant resistance, minimum wage was signed into law by President Franklin Roosevelt as part of the Fair Labor Standards Act (Grossman, 2015).

[1]This section was researched and written by Jonas Rosen, MSW.

FIGURE 9.2 ■ Federal Minimum Wage, 1938–2016

Bureau of Labor Statistics, retrieved from http://www.pewresearch.org/fact-tank/2017/01/04/5-facts-about-the-minimum-wage/

Note: Wage rates adjusted for inflation using implicit price deflator for personal consumption expenditures.

Minimum wage was initially established at $0.25 per hour. Since enacted, the federal minimum wage has been raised 22 times, most recently in 2009, when it was increased to its present level of $7.25 per hour (Wage and Hour Division, 2015). The current federal minimum wage actually represents a decrease from the "peak" minimum wage, (see Figure 9.2).

As of 2018, 29 states and the District of Columbia established their own rates, ranging from $0.25 to $6.00 above the federal rate (Bradley, 2018).

Who are Minimum Wage Workers?

The minimum wage directly affects a small portion of the workforce. Approximately 2.7% of all hourly paid workers, around 2.2 million people, work at wages equal to, or below, the federal minimum wage of $7.25 per hour (Bradley, 2017). This marks a significant decrease from the 13.4% of people paid minimum wage in 1979, when data were first collected (Bureau of Labor Statistics, 2017). However, it is estimated that around 20 million people in the United States work at "near-minimum-wage" (DeSilver, 2017). The majority of minimum- and near-minimum wage earners work in the restaurant and food service industry, which continues to be the biggest occupational field for these hourly paid workers, following the decline in manufacturing jobs from the 1970s (DeSilver, 2017). Employers may be permitted to pay workers below minimum wage for a variety of reasons. For example, employees who work for tips may be paid below minimum wage if their hourly wage plus their average hourly tips are at or above minimum wage. Employers may also be allowed to pay some categories of workers, such as youth or people with disabilities, subminimum wage to encourage their employment (U. S. Department of Labor, n.d.c).

Workers younger than 25 comprise 20% of hourly paid workers, however they make up about 50% of all individuals paid the federal minimum wage or less (Bureau of Labor Statistics, 2017). About 10% of employed teenagers aged 16 to 19 earned minimum wage or less (Bureau of Labor Statistics, 2017). The percentage of minimum wage workers varies by race or ethnicity and gender. About 3% of white and black workers earned minimum wage, compared to about 2% of Asian and Hispanic workers (Bureau of Labor Statistics, 2017). Though women make up less than half of the workforce, approximately 60% of all minimum wage workers are women (Mejia, 2015).

Living Wage and the "Fight for 15"

Even though all U.S. laborers are guaranteed a minimum wage, in many cases full-time minimum wage employment provides an income that is simply insufficient for hourly paid workers to meet their basic needs. Minimum wage is often far lower than the **living wage:** the minimum income necessary to satisfy basic expenses for food, housing, and other essential needs. Living wage advocates also note that the cost of living varies by location and family size. The Living Wage Calculator created by Amy Glasmeier (2018) indicates that the living wage for a single adult living in San Francisco is $19.63, as compared to the city's minimum wage of $11.00. If the same individual has two children to support, his or her living wage calculation rises to $44.19, while the minimum wage remains unchanged at $11.00. While elimination of poverty was a major objective of the U.S. minimum wage policy, research indicates that the creation of a minimum wage has had little or no effect on poverty (Vedder & Gallaway, 2002).

Over the past few decades, poverty-level conditions in minimum wage service occupations have sparked a wide array of campaigns and protests pressuring local government to pass living wage ordinances (Freeman, 2005). In 1994, Baltimore, Maryland, was the first U.S. city to pass a living wage ordinance for city contract workers (Bernstein, 2004). Living wage advocates have accumulated many victories; by 2003, over 100 cities and jurisdictions instituted living wage ordinances (Freeman, 2005). While the living wage movements began at the local level, the campaign for living wage burst onto the national scene in 2001, when students at Harvard seized the main administrative building, demanding living wages for dining hall staff, janitors, and guards at the university (Freeman, 2005) (see Photo 9.3). Following a 3-week sit-in and national press coverage, 26 student protesters finally emerged from the administrative building after Harvard administrators agreed to reexamine and negotiate university wage policies (Goldberg, 2001). Soon afterward, students at numerous other universities, including Johns Hopkins, Stanford, Swarthmore, University of Virginia, and Wesleyan followed suit, effectively protesting to raise worker pay (Freeman, 2005). The fact that these small-scale, student-initiated wage campaigns proved effective demonstrates the power and potential in grassroots activism. These campaigns were well-organized and persistent, and they used traditional and social media effectively.

Darren McCollester/Getty Images News

PHOTO 9.3 Sit-in at Harvard University

A more recent campaign, "Fight for 15," mobilized thousands of service workers across the nation, particularly in the fast food industry, and has resulted in significant victories. The cities of Los Angeles, New York, San Francisco, and Seattle will progressively raise their minimum wage to $15 over the course of several years (Mcgeehan, 2015). Connecticut, Maryland, and New Jersey authorized statewide gradual increases in the minimum wage up to $15 (National Conference of State Legislatures, 2019; Reiss, 2019). Living wage advocates continue their campaigns in the hopes that local efforts will build a national movement to raise the federal minimum wage (last raised in 2009) for all U.S. workers. Although raising minimum wage may intuitively seem like a positive step toward reducing poverty and wealth inequality, some opponents warn of negative economic consequences. For example, efforts to impose a living wage lead to higher labor costs, which may compel some employers to decrease their workforce, and potentially lead to higher rates of unemployment amongst unskilled workers. A 2015 survey found that the majority of economists believed that raising the minimum wage to $15 per hour would have negative effects on employment levels in both youths and adults (Fowler & Smith, 2015). The same survey found that 67% of economists surveyed believed that a $15 minimum wage would make it harder for small businesses to stay in business. Meanwhile, other economists have urged Congress to raise minimum wage to at least $10.10. Opponents to local living wage campaigns are also concerned about losing businesses that can easily migrate to other cities or states. They also raise concerns that if wages are too high, it may lead to human workers being replaced by automation (Khatib, 2017).

ADVOCACY

MINIMUM WAGE

Debate around the federal minimum wage provokes thoughts about how we, as social workers, might fight for a more equitable and just world. It also raises questions about how to consider the efficacy and costs of various mechanisms to achieve these goals, and how these might be framed. Think about the following questions:

1. What does framing the issue of income around the idea of "minimum wage" suggest?
2. Why did more recent advocates invent the concept of "living wage"?
3. Review the benefits and risks of raising wages as discussed in the chapter. Can social work ethics and values inform your assessment? Should they? If so, how?
4. The campaign for living wages illustrates interplay between local, state, and federal government. What are the advantages and disadvantages of advocacy at each level?

Final Discussion

Now that you have finished reading this chapter, reread the vignette at the beginning. Based on what you have learned, answer the following questions. Point to specific references in the chapter that help you answer these questions. Consider how different theories inform the response to these questions.

1. Can you identify the specific policies that impact Elijah, Noreen, and their children?
2. What health and financial resources might be available to them?
3. What do you think should be the responsibilities borne by Elijah and his family? His private employer? The government?
4. How do existing policies limit or expand the Elijah and his family's options to provide for them? What additional programs or policies do you imagine would be helpful?
5. What role might race, class, gender, and other aspects of identity play in this vignette?

POLICY FOR OLDER ADULTS

LEARNING OBJECTIVES

10.1: Identify how the changing social construction of aging has affected policies related to older adults over the course of U.S. history

10.2: Critique existing U.S. policies that affect older adults

10.3: Assess the ways in which a relational perspective would improve U.S. policies toward older adults

10.4: Plan advocacy opportunities that address the needs of LGBTQ+ older adults

What do we mean when we use the term *older adults*? While we often think of the age of 65 as a demarcation point, different definitions result in a variety of entry or cut-off points for age-related programs or benefits. In addition, the American Geriatrics Society (AGS) raises a number of important questions that provide insight into some of the factors we might consider when reviewing or designing programs for older adults: "Are we trying to optimize vitality over the life cycle? Promote longevity? Minimize health care use and costs? Enable individuals to work as long as possible? Plan services to match needs? Increase the "**longevity dividend**"?" (Friedman et al., 2019, p. 18). Based on their assessment of a complex and differentiated calculus, the authors of the AGS report "support a multifaceted definition of healthy aging that acknowledges the importance of broad-ranging concepts central to geriatrics, such as culture, function, engagement, resilience, meaning, dignity, and autonomy, in addition to minimizing disease" (p. 18). This goal is compatible with social work values and reflects a comprehensive understanding of aging in the context of relationships, environment, and society.

Longevity dividend: the social and economic benefits of healthy aging essentially by using preventative medicine

This chapter examines policies that impact the growing population of older adults. In addition to examining challenges related to aging in areas such as health, it looks at aging through the life course. This includes decisions that older adults make as they approach the age when they can take advantage of public or private retirement benefits instead of (or in addition to) work in the paid labor force. Many older adults remain in their own homes; some reside with or are cared for by family. Caring for older adults greatly affects the lives of caregivers, the overwhelming majority of whom are women (be they spouses, children, or other family members). As with many U.S. policies, caring for adult family members is viewed as a private concern. This has resulted in a policy vacuum. Many older adults themselves also act as care providers for other older adults or for younger family members. In this chapter, we explore struggles faced by families around caregiving and the implications of existing policies for older adults, their families, and their communities.

This chapter analyzes the framing of older adults as a demographic group and social movement. How did older adults come to be seen as a group that is considered to be deserving of protections and benefits? Which older adults can avail themselves of public policy benefits, such as retirement or medical benefits, and why? Which cannot? How do recent conceptions of aging and longer life expectancies change the way we view older adulthood? What is the relationship or intersection between older adulthood and other demographic categories, such as race, gender, and class? We hope you will think about these questions as you read through this chapter to learn more about policies that affect this population.

Vignette: Parenting for a Second Time

Based on what you know from the media or your personal, work, or volunteer experiences, think about the following questions as you read the vignette. When you finish the vignette, answer the questions below.

1. What kind of services or information might be helpful for Darla and John? For Larissa? For Kendra? The family unit?
2. What roles might social workers working with this family have?
3. What steps might you take to try to resolve ethical conflicts that may arise for you as a social worker in this role?
4. What broader systemic factors influence the choices available to Darla, John, Larissa, and her daughter, Kendra? What advocacy efforts might social workers take to address them?
5. What role might race, class, gender, and other aspects of identity play in this vignette?

Darla is a retired child care provider in her early 70s. She worked until she was 65, but did not receive a pension or benefits from her employer. She still babysits for extra cash. Her husband John, who ran a small business, is also retired. They support themselves with modest savings and Social Security benefits. Their daughter Larissa has struggled with addiction that has led to arrests for drug and prostitution offenses. Larissa's addiction and incarceration have resulted in their taking on a kinship caregiving role for their 4-year-old granddaughter Kendra. Kendra's child welfare caseworker has suggested that they consider moving toward formal adoption. Darla and John are reluctant to take this step because they know it will be hurtful to their daughter. They also are hopeful at Larissa's renewed prospect of reuniting with Kendra following Larissa's participation in a court-affiliated diversion program that has connected her with resources. The program has helped her maintain sobriety for the past year, and they want the possibility of reunification to remain open because it is an important incentive for Larissa. Darla has continued to work whenever she can to pay additional bills, although she does not always have the energy to supervise active young children. John is Kendra's primary caregiver, which he enjoys but finds tiring.

Kendra is experiencing behavioral problems. Although John and Darla receive some support from the child welfare agency in the form of clothing stipends and guidance from Kendra's helpful case manager, they are unable to receive funding to support the recommended therapies, which include individual and family interventions. Kendra's behavioral problems have also made grandparenting harder, making John and Darla question whether they are equipped to see Kendra through this difficult period, which they hope will end with Larissa and Kendra's reunification. Their budget is tight, and the additional expenses are beginning to feel burdensome. They have also found themselves emotionally conflicted in their role parenting Kendra, because some of their decisions on her behalf have been painful to their daughter Larissa. They are grateful that they have been able to help Kendra and Larissa, whom they love dearly, but these are not the golden years that they envisioned.

HISTORY AND SOCIAL CONSTRUCTION OF U.S. POLICY FOR OLDER ADULTS

Attitudes toward older adults have undergone many cultural shifts (Fischer, 1977). In the 1600s through 1800s, those who were older were treated with respect and deference, possibly because Puritans saw longevity as a sign of God's favor. In the 1800s, a rise in slurs reflected increased disdain for older adults. There is some evidence that suggests that older adults may have been treated with disdain and viewed as a burden in agricultural societies that were heavily dependent on hard physical labor. Hillier and Barrow (2011), drawing on other historians, caution that attitudes toward groups, including older adults, were often based on multiple facets of identity. The way that older adults were viewed and treated in the United States was grounded not only in their age, but also their social status, which was affected by their perceived race and/or ethnicity, immigration status, land ownership, and wealth. Think about how this illustrates the concept of intersectionality, which we discuss in Chapter 3.

As in many countries at the time, no U.S. social policy specifically addressed older adults. This may have been, in part, because illness and death were much more evenly spread throughout the life course than they are today. Health vulnerabilities that are currently more heavily concentrated among aging populations occurred from the moment of birth and were a constant concern (Demos, 1986). Life expectancies were much lower, so a much smaller percentage of the population lived into older adulthood. As you may recall from Chapter 1 in which we discussed the Elizabethan Poor Laws, local governments who ran relief programs were very much concerned with sorting those whom they considered worthy or deserving of assistance from those who were not. Under the principle of less eligibility, assistance was never supposed to leave recipients better off than even the least paying jobs, so it was not too attractive. According to Deborah Stone (1984), people who were unable to work due to older age or disability presented a complicated problem for those providing relief. Older adults were first seen as a target for government intervention in this context of their financial vulnerability. Older adults were categorized with others who were considered deserving, such as people who were incapacitated due to illness or infirmity. While those considered deserving were more likely to be afforded outdoor relief and spared the workhouse, authorities still wanted to ensure that people not see assistance as an attractive option. Assistance was therefore still meager, recipients were still subject to investigation, and assistance to the elderly people living in poverty waxed and waned subject to changing local sympathies and political winds.

Retirement and Health as Worthy of Public Investment

The Great Depression is often seen as the pivotal moment in which age was first viewed as a separate area of public policy. John Myles (1988) describes a path of gradual development that he calls a "ratchet approach" (p. 273). By the Great Depression, many found themselves in need. As a result, poor law distinctions between the deserving and undeserving poor lost their foothold. As we describe more fully in Chapter 9 on employment, the Social Security Act was a centerpiece of the New Deal that provided different kinds of benefits to many. These benefits were provided most fully to some retired workers and their families. The original provisions were limited by political concessions resulting in blatantly racist policies such as the exclusion of farm and domestic workers from Social Security retirement benefits (Quadagno, 1988). Retirement benefits for older adults with histories of work under the Social Security Act were both universal and substitutive, living up to Myles' (1988) definition of a modern welfare state. A **substitutive benefit** is a replacement for something to which it is of similar or equal value. In this case, the retirement benefit was intended to replace a portion[1] of income from work. Such an approach is very different from the principle of less eligibility. The universality of Social Security's retirement and other benefits has often been credited as the chief source of its popularity. Since 1975, Social Security benefits have automatically risen by **Cost-of-Living Adjustments** or COLAs, which are linked to the Consumer Price Index. This automatic linking was designed to retain the value of the benefits over time (Social Security Administration, n.d.a).

Substitutive benefit: Benefits that are designed to replace something of equal or similar value

Cost-of-living adjustment: Adjustments that are made to benefits to ensure that they retain their value

Changing Political Power Among Older Adults

The idea of older adults as a constituent group coalesced in the 1960s. Inspired by the other movements, including the civil rights movement, the women's rights movement, and the disability rights movement, older adults began to conceive of themselves as a category entitled to certain basic rights and dignity. At a time when older people were viewed through dismissive and patronizing stereotypes as weak, irrelevant, or cute, anti-ageism activists fought for recognition, rights, and inclusion. Not only did they achieve many of their goals, but their activism itself disrupted these stereotypes (Sanjek, 2010).

The American Association for Retired Persons (AARP) was founded by Ethel Percy Andrus in 1958 as a response to elderly poverty and the experience of caring for her own ailing parents

[1]These benefits were meant to be substitutive when viewed together with the expectation that retirees would also have work-based pensions and some savings. For more on this, see the discussion in Chapter 9 about Social Security benefits as part of a "three-legged stool."

(Day, 2017). Percy credited Hull House in Chicago, where she spent her formative years, as an important influence (American Association for Retired Persons [AARP], n.d.b). The organization, for which membership is available to people over the age of 50, was founded to assist people in making choices about how they live in older adulthood. AARP engages in political advocacy and securing marketplace advantages using its formidable consumer constituency buying power. AARP describes itself and its mission as member-driven and evolving over time.

> Input from AARP's diverse membership shapes everything we do as an organization. Feedback comes from surveys, public opinion polls, phone calls, emails, social media, face-to-face conversations with volunteer leaders and staff, letters to the editors of our publications and more. Members' views shape our decisions about everything from advocacy positions to volunteer opportunities to new online health tools. (AARP, n.d.a)

Another advocacy group for older adults is the Gray Panthers. This more activist group was founded by Maggie Kuhn in 1970. It consisted of local chapters across the country (Sanjek, 2009). Although this group was founded by older adults, the organization was multigenerational and had a vision of aging along a continuum with dignity. It viewed **interdependence**, or the dependence of two or more people or things on each other, as a natural part of the human condition, and fought for policies that would support a sustainable vision of people and communities. The Gray Panthers also saw aging as a universal process that could unify diverse groups of people. They have advocated against mandatory retirement ages and for expanding Social Security and health care for all (not just older adults). They have also advocated for environmental protections and antinuclear causes, accessibility, and LGBTQ+ rights.

Interdependence: A concept expressing the mutual and reciprocal reliance of people and communities

The Gray Panthers was founded on principles of equality, democracy, and anti-racism. According to Sanjek (2010), a member and chronicler of the Gray Panthers, the organization thrived through charismatic leadership and an inclusive and dynamic ideological vision. It gained media attention and political traction by countering stereotypes. These included "being where older people were not expected to be" (e.g., testifying in Congress and on popular media); "doing what older people were not expected to do" (e.g., picketing and performative protests); and connecting with allies across generational lines by "including young Gray Panthers in causes affecting the elderly" and "taking actions on issues that affect the young" (Sanjek, 2010, pp. 139–140).

Some scholars point to another shift in how older adults, as a group, are viewed by the public. This is in large part due to the success and growth of movements of older adults. We can see examples of many adults who meet the policy-related definition of 65 or older with active and prominent political careers and in the nonprofit and business worlds.

> [T]he political standing of the aged has shifted twice over the course of roughly the last 75 years, moving first from a longstanding marginalized existence to one manifesting a robust and established political presence, and second from that widely accepted standing to one now seen as more imposing and threatening to others. (Hudson & Gonyea, 2012, p. 273)

The growth of AARP and its increased political power is a clear example of this shift. AARP, which in 2018 had nearly 38 million members, is the largest member organization in the United States. It topped the *Washington Business Journal*'s 2018 list of the largest Washington, DC, area associations ranked by revenue (Proctor, 2018), with $1.6 billion (Beard & Williamson, 2011). AARP was a powerful and controversial force in lobbying for the 2003 changes that created Medicare Part D, which covers prescription drugs (see below) (Day, 2017, p. 54), largely seen to benefit the organization as a major player in the private health insurance market. These changes, supported by Republicans and opposed by Democrats, resulted in the resignation of between 45,000 and 120,000 AARP members who opposed this position. The perceived power of organizations advocating for older adults has been used to discredit their positions. For example, in their attempts to make significant changes to Social Security, some conservative advocates juxtaposed the relative security and wealth of older adults against the needs of younger people (Beard & Williamson, 2011). Such groups condemned older adults for using their disproportionate political power in their own self-interest at the expense of other worthy groups. Ironically, one reason for the relative financial security of older adults may be precisely because of policies such as Social Security retirement benefits in contrast to much more meager and limited support to families, young children, and younger adults, as discussed in the following box.

ADVOCACY

COMPARING DIFFERENT ADVOCACY APPROACHES

In this chapter, we describe two organizations that advocate against ageism and for improvements for older adults. It is common for different advocacy organizations to work with or on the same or overlapping populations or issue areas. These organizations may work together and/or be in competition for resources or to frame the issues. Think about differences and similarities between AARP and the Gray Panthers as you answer the following questions. You can also find more information about these groups in the sources we cited or online.

- How are the missions, tactics, and constituencies of the organizations similar or different?
- How might the organizations' respective structures influence the specific problems they choose to address? The manner in which the organization addresses them?
- What do you think might be the relationship between the two organizations, and why?
- Try to apply these questions to two advocacy organizations in an area of interest to you. How does the different topic or organizations that you chose impact your answer to these questions?

Current Overall Trends and Policies

In general, people in the United States are living longer due to improvements in health, nutrition, and medicine that have both reduced mortality and improved how we manage disease. According to the U.S. Census Bureau (2018), sometime during the 2030s the number of older people in the United States is projected to surpass the number of U.S. children for the first time. These demographic shifts are illustrated in Figure 10.1, which show distributions of the U.S. population by age in 1960 as compared to the projections for 2060.

Dependency ratio: The ratio of those who provide support to those who receive support

In many industrial nations, such as Japan and across Europe, this shift has already occurred and is a cause for concern (Vespa, 2018). This change is a result of declines in fertility coupled with gains in life expectancy. One reason for concern is the shift in what is called the dependency ratio. The **dependency ratio** is an expression of the balance between those who *provide* support through caregiving, financial support, and taxes, and those who *receive* support regardless of age. Many programs that are designed to benefit older adults, such as Social Security and Medicare (discussed below), are financed by younger,

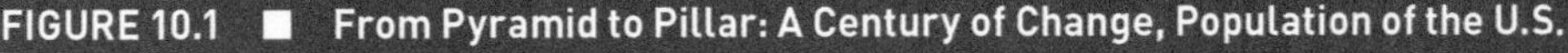

FIGURE 10.1 ■ From Pyramid to Pillar: A Century of Change, Population of the U.S.

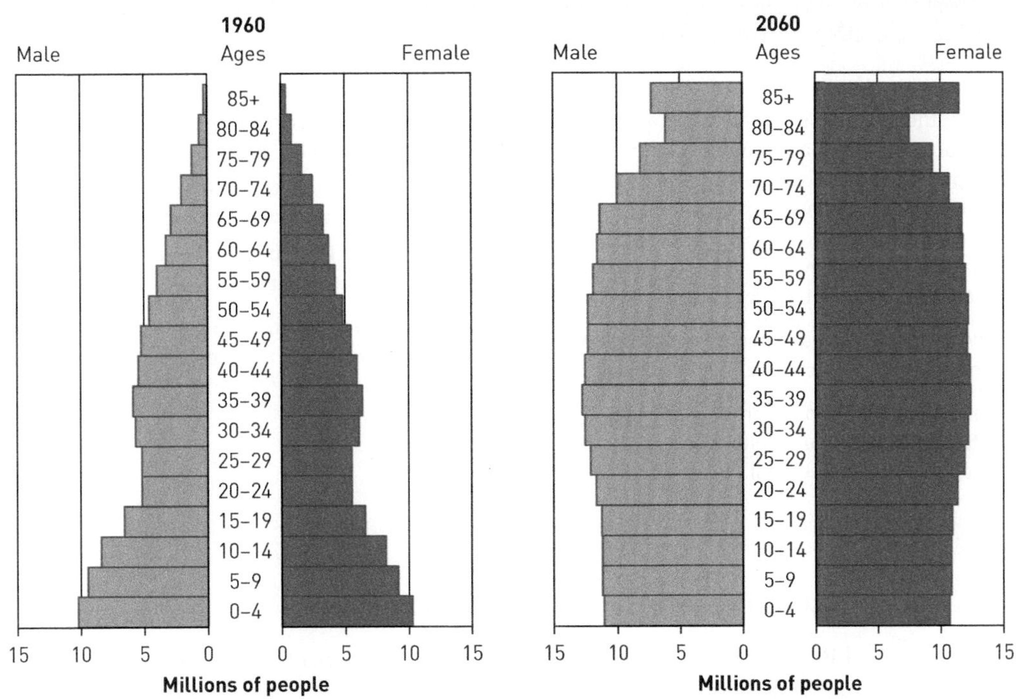

Source: U.S. Census Bureau. (2018, October 1). From pyramid to pillar: A century of change, population of the U.S. Retrieved from https://www.census.gov/library/visualizations/2018/comm/century-of-change.html

working-age populations. When those in the workforce are outnumbered by nonworking populations, the social and financial costs of caring and supporting older adults may be become burdensome.

At the individual and family level, people who find themselves in situations where they are simultaneously providing care for older and younger family members are often referred to as the **sandwich generation** (Miller, 1981). The majority of those providing such dual care are women, who often balance their roles as caregivers with paid labor (Evans et al., 2016; Halinski, Duxbury, & Higgins, 2018). The extent to which children take on caregiving responsibilities for their parents as they age is influenced by gender, financial situation, and cultural norms and expectations, which vary significantly by race and ethnicity (Cravey & Mitra, 2011). This means that social workers in the area of aging—whether they are working with potential caregivers and recipients or community planners—must consider a range of factors in their practice and strive to be culturally responsive.

Sandwich generation: A term describing the cohort of people who simultaneously provide care and support to both older and younger family members, such as parents of young children who also provide care for their own aging relatives

The World Health Organization (WHO) and the U.S. Centers for Disease Control and Prevention (CDC) view aging through a holistic lens, which looks to the absence of disease or pathology as well as well-being more generally. This can include social connections and living environments that contribute to health and well-being, such as transportation, access to healthy food, and safe, stable housing. Many agree that although increased longevity is a benefit, our societal solutions to address problems associated with aging have not caught up with the needs of many (Davitt, Madigan, Rants, & Skemp, 2016).

DISCUSSION

PERSPECTIVES ON OPTIMAL AGING

Think about the questions posed by the American Geriatrics Society at the chapter outset and the closing paragraph prior to this box that juxtaposes holistic and pathology-based perspectives.

1. What are the most important factors to focus on when we think about optimal aging?
2. How do these factors impact the families and communities in which older adults reside?
3. Think of a policy or program that provides services to older adults (either specifically or among other constituents).
   a. Given your responses to Questions 1 and 2, create a list of program strengths.
   b. How might these strengths be enhanced or replicated in other programs?
   c. What kind of improvements would make the program better?
4. What perspectives on aging do you think fit best with social work values and why?

Disparities and Cumulative Disadvantage

Life expectancy: The median age of death for a particular group

Disparity: Inequality; differences in outcomes between different populations or groups

Cumulative disadvantage: a term that refers to the compounding nature of disadvantage that accrues across the life course.

Life expectancy (the median age of death for a particular group) in the United States is not uniform. Within an overall trend of growing life expectancy there have been sporadic reductions in life expectancy attributable to public health crises, such as the AIDS epidemic. There are also educational, socioeconomic, and racial and ethnic **disparities** in life expectancy (U.S. Census Bureau, 2018). Older women outnumber older men. Accai, and Firebough (2017) attribute recent declines in U.S. men's and women's life expectancy to different causes. Black men have consistently shown lower life expectancy than black women, white men, and white women, which many be attributed to much greater exposure to a variety of risks, including social, economic, and health-related hardships, over their life course (Jermane Bond & Herman, 2016). **Cumulative disadvantage** is a term that refers to the compounding nature of disadvantage that accrues across the life course and therefore intensifies with age. As Hudson (2016) explains, in looking at inequality

> [w]here age and generation are concerned, a longitudinal lens is required, one that acknowledges the cumulative accretion of opportunities and constraints over time and throughout the life course. In the absence of midlife course corrections, there is no reason to believe that early life inequalities will somehow be lessened by the time individuals attain old age. Indeed, in the United States, where public policies on behalf of those aged 18–64 are stunningly absent, there is every reason to think that matters will get worse rather than better with the passage of life and time. (p. 39)

For example, unsafe housing and poor access to preventative medical care as a child may lead to chronic health conditions and lower academic achievements, which in turn impact employment. This, in turn, may influence how an individual is situated at retirement age regarding housing, retirement income and benefits, health, wealth accumulation, social support networks, and the ability to support younger generations.

Economic inequalities are often compounded by both racial and gender based inequality. (Davitt & Baik, in press). Race- and gender-based disparities are, of course, maintained across the age span. Women, who earn less than men for the same work, will accrue smaller savings, be less likely to build equity, and earn fewer pension and Social Security benefits. Women also do the bulk of unpaid care work, and therefore are more likely to have lower lifetime earnings due to dropping out of the paid labor force for periods or working part time. All these factors result in lower incomes, wealth, and financial benefits in older age for women throughout the world (Paz, Doron, & Tur-Sinai, 2018). Critical race theory also suggests the importance of considering cumulative disadvantages that accrue due to racial discrimination. Intersectionality reminds us that race intersects with other facets of identity that can result in cumulative disadvantage, such as gender, social class, and sexual orientation. As noted above, there is a need to understand aging through a wide variety of lenses. Throughout the rest of this chapter, we describe some of the ways that various facets of people's identity may be considered in aging policy.

CURRENT POLICIES FOR OLDER ADULTS

Older adults are a heterogeneous group; while older adults may share some similarities, there are also different subpopulations within this group that deserve attention. For example, some researchers look at loosely defined age cohorts, such as early, middle, and late older age. People in these groups share many health and social characteristics, including family roles. In this section, we provide greater detail on three areas of policy that have significant effects on many groups of older adults: the Older Americans Act, Social Security retirement benefits, and Medicare. We also highlight two subgroups of older adults that have made important contributions to society and their families: veterans and older adults providing care for younger family members. These groups have been identified as facing special challenges that would benefit from specialized policies and programs. Below, Table 10.1 lists federal laws and programs with particular relevance for older adults.

The Older Americans Act and Aging in Place

The United States has a dearth of resources to address the many different facets of aging in a coordinated manner. This may be due to a focus on illness and out-of-home care, even though the overwhelming majority of older adults in the United States age in their own homes and communities. The Older Americans Act (OAA) was passed in 1965 and has been reauthorized most recently in 2016 (U.S. Dept. of Health and Human Services, Administration for Community Living [ACL], n.d.). It provides funding to local governments for services to people aged 60 and older, with the primary goal of supporting older adults who live in their own communities. Services provided through the OAA are universal (not dependent on income eligibility) and are not reliant on prior work history. The OAA is designed to support services that allow adults to age with optimal health and well-being:

> Although older individuals may receive services under many other federal programs, today the OAA is considered to be a major vehicle for the organization and delivery of social and nutrition services to this group and their caregivers. It authorizes a wide array of service programs through a national network of 56 state agencies on aging, 629 area agencies on aging, nearly 20,000 service providers, 244 Tribal organizations, and 2 Native Hawaiian organizations representing 400 Tribes. The OAA also includes community service employment for low-income older Americans; training, research, and demonstration activities in the field of aging; and vulnerable elder rights protection activities. (ACL, n.d.)

As its description suggests, many different programs are provided under the OAA. One example is the Older Americans Act Nutrition Program (OAANP). The OAANP is available to all, but it targets population groups with the greatest social and financial needs (Lee, Frongillo, & Olson, 2005). Food is provided in congregate (group) settings as well as in people's homes by programs such as Meals on Wheels. The program is designed to meet nutritional needs that are key to good health and to meet social needs of older adults. Whether delivered into a person's home or provided in a congregate context, the OAANP is an opportunity for regular social interaction. This may be particularly important to older adults, who report higher levels of loneliness and isolation (Lyons, 2018). In one study of Georgia's OAANP, Lee, Sinnett, Bengle, Johnson, and Brown (2011) found that people waitlisted for the program fared much more poorly on social, financial, and nutritional indicators than program participants. This suggests that the program is successful in meeting its goals, but insufficiently available to all those who are eligible for and in need of services.

Within the rich array of services and supports provided for older adults, there are many unmet needs. In addition to insufficient access and coverage of the OAANP, researchers have identified other areas for improvements in research, interventions, and portrayal of the lives of older adults. For example, there is insufficient attention to mental health (Kim, Lehning & Sacco, 2018), substance use (Kuerbis, Sacco, Blazer, & Moore, 2014), sexuality (Solway, Clark, Singer, Kirch, & Malani, 2018), and sexual health (Ports, Barnack-Tavlaris, Syme, Perera, & Lafata, 2014). Reasons for these oversights may include stigma, prioritizing other concerns that are perceived as more pressing, a dearth of competent geriatric providers, a lack of coordination among providers, a lack of access to services, and misconceptions about older adults. As Levinson (1986) noted in his formative article on understanding the life course, research

> must include all aspects of living: inner wishes and fantasies; love relationships; participation in family, work, and other social systems; bodily changes; good times and bad—everything that has significance in a life. To study the life course, it is necessary first to look at a life in all its complexity at a given time, to include all its components and their interweaving into a partially integrated pattern. (p. 4)

Similarly, policy and programming that focuses only on particular aspects of the life course and ignores others is bound to be incomplete. Priorities must also be derived from what older adults believe to be most important to them, and therefore they (like all people and communities that are targets of policies and programs) must be included in policy making at all stages.

Across the world, countries struggle to adapt to challenges brought about by changing demographics and living patterns (Fitzgerald & Caro, 2014). These including longer lifespans, smaller and geographically dispersed families, and insufficient public infrastructure. The Village Model is an example of one U.S. community-based response to fill public policy gaps for adults who are aging within their own homes and communities. First formed by a group of older adults in a relatively wealthy area of Massachusetts, villages vary in their structure, whom they serve, and the services they provide. Most villages are independent, collaborative membership organizations run primarily with the help of volunteers and members and drawing on existing community resources (Greenfield, Scharlach, Lehning, Davitt, & Graham, 2013). They provide services as diverse as home repair and maintenance, transportation, shopping, telephone help lines, visitors, and fitness classes. Villages are designed not only to fill a gap in services, but also to provide opportunities for altruism and social networking through volunteering and organizational engagement.

Though these partial, private solutions fill an important policy vacuum, they are limited and have the potential to be exclusionary (Davitt, Lehning, Scharlach, & Greenfield, 2015). Villages tend to exist in already well-resourced communities, like middle- and upper-income neighborhoods, although there are a few in lower-income communities, and some villages provide discounted or sliding-scale fees. There is some evidence to suggest that villages reinforce **homophily** (the tendency for people to live and associate with people like themselves), which contributes to de facto segregation (see Chapter 14 regarding housing).

Homophily: The tendency for people to live and associate with people like themselves

Social Security Retirement Benefits

Social Security is designed to provide U.S. workers and their dependents with financial resources should they become unable to work due to disability or death and when they age. As discussed in Chapter 9, retirement benefits were supposed to be only one leg of a three-legged stool upon which retired workers could depend (DeWitt, 1996). Photo 10.1 is a poster distributed throughout post offices and by labor unions beginning in 1936 when Social Security numbers were first issued. You can see that its focus is on the retirement component of the program.

The other two parts of the design were employment-related benefit plans and personal savings. However, many people, particularly those who rely on low-wage or part-time employment, lack pension benefits. Many also may not be able to accumulate retirement savings. Such individuals may be solely reliant on Social Security benefits after retirement, with significant impacts on poverty for older adults. According to analysis by the Center for Budget and Policy Priorities:

> For 65 percent of elderly beneficiaries, Social Security provides the majority of their cash income. For 36 percent of them, it provides 90 percent or more of their income. For 24 percent of them, it is the sole source of retirement income.
>
> Reliance on Social Security increases with age, as older people are less likely to work and more likely to have depleted their savings. Among those aged 80 or older, Social Security provides the majority of income for 76 percent of beneficiaries and nearly all of the income for 47 percent of beneficiaries. (DaSilva, 2015)

While social security benefits by design ensure a minimum income, as noted above they are protected from erosion by COLAs.

Social Security is credited with lifting a large number of U.S. workers and their families out of poverty (Remig & Sherman, 2016). This is particularly true of older adults: Figure 10.2 below compares the incomes of older U.S. adults *with* and *without* Social Security benefits. We can see that a significant percentage of older adults would be in poverty if not for these benefits.

Social Security Administration

PHOTO 10.1 Historical Social Security poster

Despite the importance of Social Security benefits in reducing poverty, today's benefits are still insufficient to meet most older adults' basic needs. As compared to other Organisation for Economic Cooperation and Development countries, U.S. Social Security pensions replace a much smaller percentage of the preretirement income of older adults (Organisation for Economic Cooperation and Development, 2019). This means that older adults who are least likely to have savings or work-based pensions are living on just over half of their income before they retire with no supplemental sources. There are also incentives to delay receipt of benefits through the age of 70. The United States has a much higher percentage of individuals who continue to work at higher ages than other countries.

Medicare

Medicare, created by an amendment to the Social Security Act, is a federal program that has covered people over age 65 since 1965. In the early 1960s, the cost of medical care, particularly hospital based care, was rapidly increasing. Though people who were hospitalized made up only 8% of the population receiving medical care, their care was responsible for 50% of all U.S. health care spending. (Marmor, 2017). While all Western European and many other countries were decades into universal health insurance, these efforts had failed in the United States, as we discuss in Chapter 11. When signing the bill, President Lyndon Johnson said

> No longer will older Americans be denied the healing miracle of modern medicine. No longer will illness crush and destroy the savings that they have so carefully put away over a lifetime so that they might enjoy dignity in their later years. No longer will young families see their own incomes, and their own hopes, eaten away simply because they are carrying out their deep moral obligations to their parents, and to their uncles, and their aunts. (Social Security Administration, n.d.b)

Since 1972, people with permanent disabilities have also been able to get health care through Medicare. An individual who is 65 or over, eligible for Social Security, and has paid payroll taxes for 10 or more years, or who is married to someone who is eligible for Social Security and

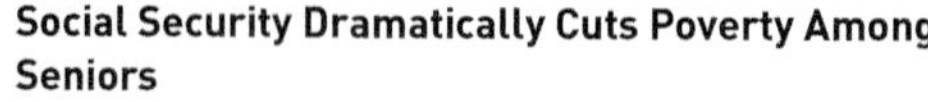

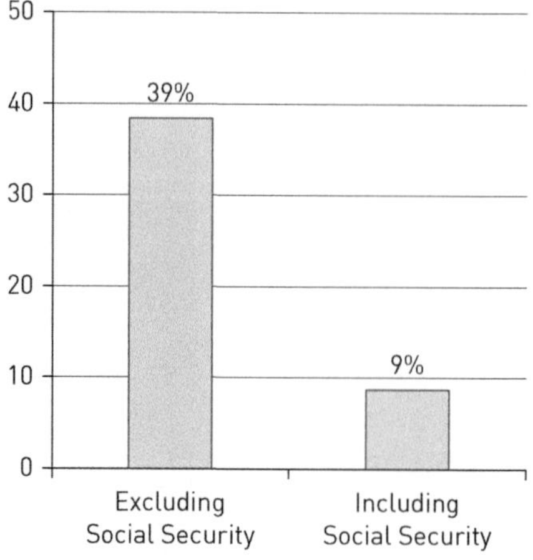

Source: "Social Security Dramatically Cuts Poverty Among Seniors," Retrieved from https://www.cbpp.org/social-security-dramatically-cuts-poverty-among-seniors-5

has paid payroll taxes for that time, can receive Medicare Part A (Kaiser Family Foundation, 2017). Currently, Medicare covers approximately 59 million Americans (Centers for Medicare and Medicaid Services, 2018). See Figure 10.3 for more information about Medicare recipients. Many Medicare recipients are also recipients of Medicaid. In Chapter 11, we discuss Medicaid in greater detail. While Medicare is the primary federal health insurance program for older adults regardless of income, Medicaid is the primary public health insurance for people, including older adults, with low incomes. Medicaid also helps low-income older adults pay for out-of-pocket expenses through the Medicare Savings Program.

Medicare is run by a federal agency called the Centers for Medicare and Medicaid Services (CMS), which is under the authority of the Department of Health and Human Services. Medicare services are covered in four "parts" (Kaiser Family Foundation, 2017). Part A covers hospital and nursing facility care, some home health care, and hospice. After they meet their deductible ($1,364 per year in 2019), recipients may still be charged coinsurance payments for hospital or skilled nursing facility care. **Coinsurance** means that Medicare covers most of the cost, but the participant must pay for the rest. This can be very expensive. Part B includes visits to doctors, outpatient services, preventive care, and some home health. It also has a deductible ($185 in 2019) and a 20% coinsurance payment for services (meaning Medicare covers 80% and the recipient covers the rest), although annual wellness visits and much preventive care are not counted against the deductible or coinsurance. Parts A and B cover the largest number of participants—59 million in 2017, including 50 million over the age of 65 and the rest with disabilities. Enrollment in Medicare Part A is automatic if one meets the work credit requirements. Enrollment in Part B is optional and requires that beneficiaries enroll proactively. Despite this additional step, most choose to enroll in Part B due to lower premiums relative to what can be obtained in the private market.

Coinsurance: The portion of payment for a service such as a doctor's visit that the beneficiary must pay

FIGURE 10.3 ■ Characteristics of the Medicare Population

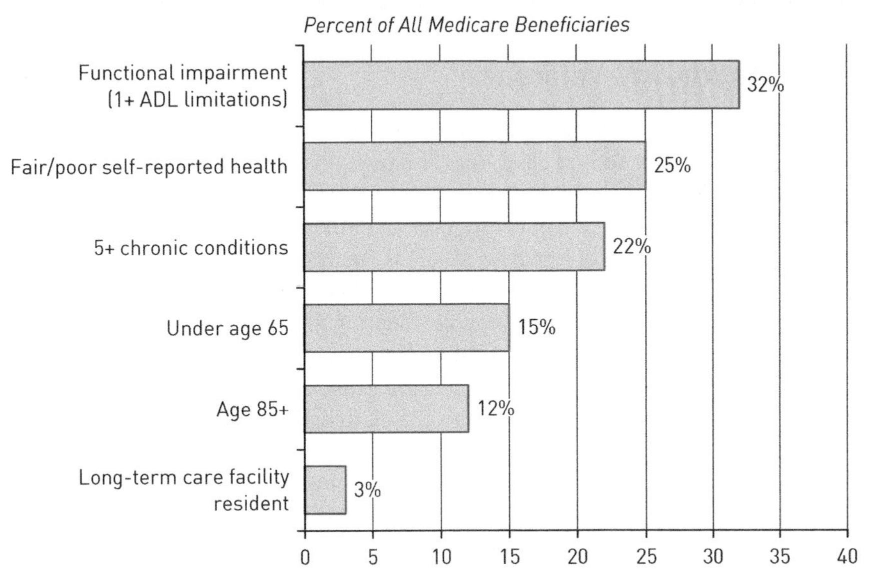

Source: KFF analysis of the Centers for Medicare & Medicaid Services 2016 Medicare Current Beneficiary Survey

Note: ADL is activity of daily living.

Part C is also called Medicare Advantage. Beneficiaries who enroll in Part C are essentially enrolling in a private health plan like a health maintenance organization (HMO) or preferred provider organization (PPO) that must provide all the benefits that a traditional Medicare plan provides. Not all Medicare Advantage programs include prescription drug coverage, in which case this must be purchased separately. The plans that do offer this are called MA-PD plans. Approximately 19 million people (around one third of all Medicare recipients) enrolled in Part C in 2017.

Part D, the most recent addition to Medicare, was created by the Medicare Prescription Drug, Improvement, and Modernization Act of 2003. It provides coverage for outpatient prescription drugs for Medicare recipients, either through Medicare Advantage or stand-alone prescription drug plans. Enrollment in Part D is optional, but 42 million people (about 73% of all Medicare recipients) chose to enroll in it in 2017. Costs for recipients vary depending on which plan they choose and their income. They include monthly premiums and cost sharing for prescriptions.

As you might imagine given the size of this program and the complexities of the health conditions faced by those who use it, spending on Medicare is considerable. In 2016, Medicare made up 15% of all federal spending. From another perspective, one in four dollars spent on prescription drugs, hospital care, or doctors' services in the United States comes from Medicare (Cubanski & Neuman, 2017). Medicare is funded from two different sources, both of which are under the U.S. Treasury: the Hospital Insurance Trust Fund and the Supplemental Insurance Trust Fund. The first draws funds from payroll taxes (paid by employers and employees); the second is from funds that Congress authorizes (Centers for Medicare and Medicaid Services, n.d.). Both also draw from interest and from premiums that are required in certain instances. Each trust fund pays for different services.

As a practicing social worker, you may find yourself trying to help a client determine their eligibility or helping your agency seek funding to provide or be reimbursed for services. You may also identify systemic concerns such as gaps in services or seek to advocate regarding proposed changes to complex policies like Medicare. Government websites, many of which we have cited here, contain helpful information including links to state-specific websites.

Older Adults Who Are Veterans

Veterans are a social group who share a unique set of life experiences and challenges as they age. In many ways they are seen as deserving (although this was not true for veterans of conflicts such as Vietnam), and they were among the first groups in the United States to receive pension benefits (Skocpol, 1992). As of 2014, over 13 million, or almost 70%, of U.S. veterans were age 55 or older (National Center for Veterans Analysis and Statistics, 2016). Over the next 20 years, the proportion of veterans aged 85 and older, a group often in need of more health and long-term care, is expected to double (Housing Assistance Council, 2016). Veterans with combat experience often carry physical and psychological burdens from their military service, which must be addressed in comprehensive gerontological care. Approximately 25% of all veterans have some sort of service-connected disability, and this rating is higher among older veterans (Bureau of Labor Statistics, 2019).

Older veterans with disabilities tend to experience anxiety and depression at increased rates as well as higher rates of poverty (Gould, Huh, Brunskill, McConnell, & Tenover, 2015). Among behavioral health concerns are histories of trauma following veterans' participation in combat. According to Clark and Rouse (2018), approximately 30% of older veterans meet the criteria for a formal PTSD diagnosis. The aging process may exacerbate psychological suffering. Real and perceived losses such as retirement, debilitating illnesses in self or relatives, and death of loved ones can aggravate the symptoms of PTSD (Sherwood, Shimel, Stolz, & Sherwood, 2003). It is therefore crucial to develop programs and policies that raise awareness of and provide services for psychological distress in aging veterans. Mental health conditions are underdiagnosed in older veterans because many trauma survivors cope by avoiding discussing their experiences (Clark & Rouse, 2018).

Demographic characteristics have important implications for where and how gerontological services should be provided. Research suggests that within the Veterans Affairs health system, as in other health care settings, racial disparities persist for important clinical health outcomes (Trivedi, Grebla, Wright, & Washington, 2011). A disproportionate number of veterans, particularly older veterans, live in rural areas and small towns and therefore may have limited access to services (Housing Assistance Council, 2016). In some ways, veterans have greater resources than their nonveteran counterparts. They are also less likely to be uninsured or live in poverty and they tend to have higher personal incomes (National Center for Veterans Analysis and Statistics, 2016). However, veterans older than 55 tend to be worse off financially than their younger counterparts, with a substantial number living on annual incomes of less than $20,000, even with Social Security and additional retirement income (Housing Assistance Council, 2016). These factors can affect a veteran's access to care and the blend of financial or health services that should be considered in policies and programs for veterans.

The Veterans Affairs (VA) system provides tailored benefits for older veterans, which "include disability compensation, pension, education and training, health care, home loans, insurance, vocational rehabilitation and employment, and burial" (U.S. Department of Veterans Affairs, 2017b, para. 2). Veterans' benefits vary. The type and scope of benefits for eligible veterans may depend on whether a veteran served during a war, saw active duty, or was injured, and the veteran's length of service.

The VA provides a range of long-term care geriatric programs for veterans with complex needs, including home-based and community services. Financial assistance is available to VA beneficiaries who are homebound, bedridden, in need of help performing daily functions, or in a nursing home. The Geriatrics and Extended Care Services targets veterans with chronic illness and older veterans (U.S. Department of Veterans Affairs, n.d.). It also runs national model programs such as the GeriPACT, or Geriatric Patient-Centered Care Teams, which uses interdisciplinary teams to facilitate patient decision making and access to care (Sullivan, Eisenstein, Price, Solimeo, & Shay, 2018). Because the VA is a federally funded system that serves a large and diverse population and has a research infrastructure, it can be an important testing ground for model programs. Another resource for veterans and families is the wide range of local and national nonprofit organizations that provide services specifically to veterans. For a sense of the type and scope of such organizations, you can see the *Veterans and Military Service Organizations Directory* published by the U.S. Department of Veterans Affairs (2017a). In addition, many issue-specific organizations such as legal services or mental health organizations provide specific programming for older veterans. Many programs for veterans have peer-to-peer components grounded in the idea that veterans may share similar experiences that differ from their civilian counterparts.

Grandparents and Kinship Caregivers

Older adults fill many different roles in the lives of their relatives. While much of the research cited here focuses specifically on grandparents, older adults provide primary care or assistance for a range of younger relatives in their capacity as aunts, uncles, or cousins.

One study found that type and intensity of caring can be influenced by the age of the grandchildren and grandparents, their geographic proximity to each other, the relationship between the grandparents and parents of the child, as well as resources including finances and time (Silverstein & Marenco, 2001). Often these relationships are a source of mutual satisfaction and joy, as it appears in Photo 10.2.

Like Darla and John in our opening vignette, grandparents and other kinship caregivers have filled the role of primary or sole caregivers for their grandchildren in an increasing number of U.S. families. Figure 10.4 shows these trends. In 2015, approximately 2.9 million U.S. children were living in households with their grandparents who were responsible for their care, an increase of 400,000 over 2005 statistics (Wiltz, 2016). Raising grandchildren is more common among racial minorities and families of lower socioeconomic status. Research indicates that African American grandparents raise grandchildren at a higher rate than grandparents from other racial and ethnic groups (Peterson, 2018).

Many factors contribute to the phenomenon of grandparent and kinship care, including parental substance abuse, incarceration, death, and mental illness (Jendrek, 1994). Similar to past spikes in drug addiction, the recent U.S. opioid crisis caused a significant increase in the number of children whose parents cannot care for them (Radel, Baldwin, Crouse, Ghertner, & Waters, 2018). Many of these children have come into the care of relatives (Intergenerational Family Services, 2018). The circumstances by which children come into primary care of grandparents and other kin can create a complex array of challenges and rewards for caregivers and children. Research on these consequences is mixed. Though a number of studies have indicated a link between grandparent caregiving and poor physical health (Kelley, Whitley, Sipe, & Yorker, 2000), low financial resources (Fuller-Thomson, Minkler, & Driver, 1997), and conflict with children's parents (Sands & Goldberg-Glen, 2000), a recent study found no evidence to suggest that caring for grandchildren has dramatic and/or widespread negative effects on grandparents' health (Hughes, Waite, LaPierre, & Luo, 2007). Hughes, Waite, LaPierre, and Luo (2007) attribute health disadvantages found among grandparent caregivers to previously existing conditions rather than to providing care.

Rewards for caregivers include gratification, feelings of usefulness, and pride in their own abilities to meet new challenges. Research suggests that grandparents who derive more psychological rewards from raising grandchildren are better able to cope with the variety of challenges and stressors they encounter than those who derive fewer psychological rewards from caregiving (Giarrusso, Silverstein, & Feng, 2000). The contribution that older adults make to younger family members when they provide care is also a benefit to society at large, and therefore should be recognized and supported. Many programs and interventions have been developed to provide such support, particularly to grandparents living in poverty who are most likely to serve as primary caregivers despite their own financial strain. One study emphasized the importance of professional assistance and community services in minimizing the negative impact of child-related challenges on grandparents' well-being (Gerard, Landry-Meyer, & Roe, 2006). Another suggested that a model of education combined with social support holds potential for addressing unmet needs of this population (Dunn & Wamsley, 2018).

PHOTO 10.2 Some grandparents are the sole caregivers for their grandchildren.

FIGURE 10.4 ■ Children in Foster Care Raised in Grandfamilies or Kinship Care

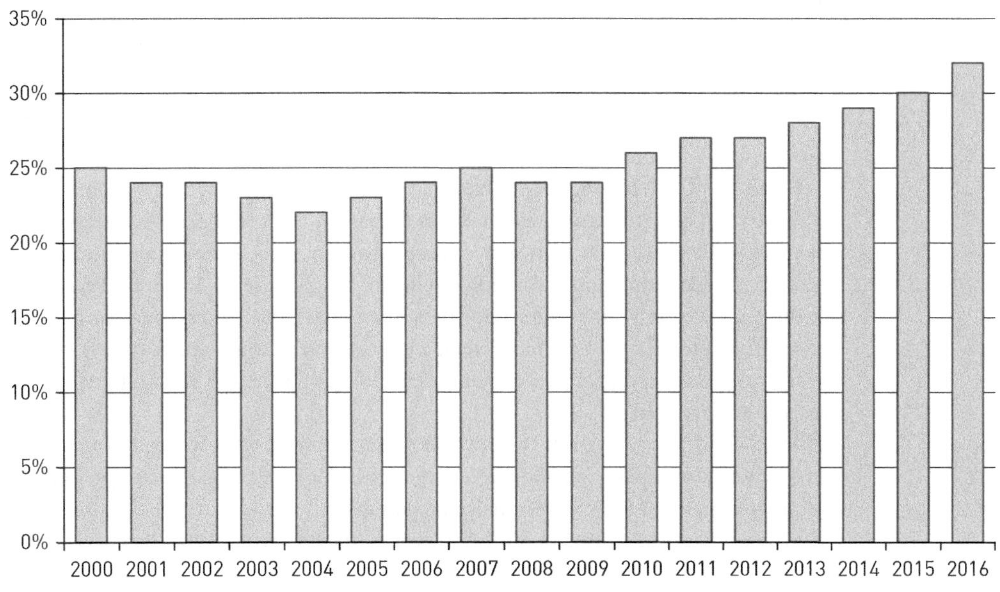

Source: Data from Annie E. Casey Foundation Kids Count Data Center.

TABLE 10.1 ■ Federal Laws Relevant to Older Adults

Type	Laws	Oversight Agency	Website
Services and programs	The Older Americans Act	Administration on Aging	https://acl.gov/about-acl/administration-aging
Retirement	Social Security Act Employment Retirement Security Income Act (ERISA)	Social Security Administration Department of Labor, Department of Treasury, and Pension Benefit Guaranty Corporation	https://www.ssa.gov/ https://www.dol.gov/general/topic/retirement/erisa
Health	Social Security Act Title XVIII (Medicare) Social Security Act Title XIX (Medicaid)	Centers for Medicare and Medicaid Services	https://www.medicare.gov/
Elder abuse	Elder Justice Act, Older Americans Act	National Center on Elder Abuse	https://ncea.acl.gov/
Discrimination	Age Discrimination in Employment Act	U.S. Equal Employment Opportunity Commission	https://www.eeoc.gov/laws/types/age.cfm
Older adults as a resource	National and Community Service Act of 1990 (Senior Corps, federal and local)	Corporation for National and Community Service	https://www.nationalservice.gov/programs/senior-corps

POLICY INFORMED BY ALTERNATIVE LENSES

The United States has often been characterized as a society that values individual achievement and responsibility. While such beliefs are thought to foster initiative, innovation, and drive, they can also devalue the importance of relationships and mutual support. Relational lenses, in contrast, focus on interdependence not as a hindrance or problem, but as part of what it means to be human. This framing recognizes that every person is dependent on others at points in their lives, not only for assistance, but also as part of the collaborative endeavor of creating a just society. According to the idea of "relational autonomy," dependence should not be viewed as antithetical to individual autonomy or choice (MacKenzie, 2013). Interdependence, including the ability to rely on social safety nets, may foster individual opportunities and choices because they provide a secure base. Such a conception of interdependence is compatible with social work values and practice, which sees individuals as nested within families, the community, and society (NASW, 2017).

One of the drawbacks of our current policy environment is that we tend to analyze and address social concerns as separate or siloed problems. Not only are people interdependent, but policies and programs also are interconnected. For example, the child care policies that we reviewed in Chapter 5 have a direct impact on the resources that John and Darla have available to care for Kendra (keep this in mind when you return to the final discussion questions). Separating policy spheres by issue or by singling out certain populations as particularly vulnerable can have risks and benefits. While this strategy may be helpful in identifying resources or drawing attention to problems, it can also feed into stereotypes that portray different groups as particularly needy or problematic. Separate policies for older adults may feed into ageism by supporting assumptions that older adults are frail and incapacitated. One example is mandatory reporting laws for elder abuse, like the ones that exist for children. These laws can be beneficial in protecting vulnerable older adults, but they can also be used to challenge the decision-making capacity of older adults in ways that may reduce their autonomy.

Interdependence, for example, would consider the important role of older adults raising or providing child care for younger family members. Some U.S. policies have more of an interdependent framing. Policies that support veterans and Social Security are built in part to support older people who have contributed to our well-being as service members and workers, respectively. These policies help people who contributed while they were physically and developmentally able, and we reward their contributions by providing for them when they may no longer be able to support themselves or others. The policies that we described look to older adults as people who are both in potential need of services and also people who make important societal contributions. Older adults have long been viewed as a resource, as in the case of grandparents caring for grandchildren. The Corporation for National and Community Service (CNCS) is a federal agency that acts like a clearinghouse for older adult volunteers and helps older adults connect to organizations and programs to volunteer in their communities. It is one example of how policies, in combination, can treat older adults simultaneously as a group with special vulnerabilities and as an important resource. If you research U.S. National Service Programs Senior Corps, you will see that the CNCS believes that older adults can also benefit through giving to others—recognizing that helping relationships can be mutual.

OPPORTUNITIES FOR ADVOCACY

Attention to LGBTQ+ adults as they age provides many opportunities for advocacy. Older LGBTQ+ adults face challenges, including discrimination and disparate treatment, in many areas of life. These include heteronormative assumptions about family formation and caregiving and the need for culturally responsive health care and appropriate housing. Relationships among LGBTQ+ partners and family members may also be complicated by a lack of legal recognition. Even after some laws have changed to provide recognition for these relationships through marriage or second-parent adoption (see Chapter 4), older LGBTQ+ adults may have hidden their sexual orientation and intimate relationships because of stigma. Lack of legally recognized relationships may create hurdles for older LGBTQ+ adults particularly around retirement benefits, caregiving, inheritance, and medical decision making (Knochel, 2010). Because social change and advocacy takes place at all levels of social work practice, Vanessa Fabbre (2016) calls for social workers to "incorporat[e] queer perspectives into practice with older adults" not only for service provision but also as a means of "resisting norms around gender and sexuality to promote individual and social change" (p. 74).

Advocacy efforts have included the identification, development, and implementation of guidelines for practice and provide resources for social workers in an effort to ensure effective practice designed to treat people equitably (see, e.g., Fredriksen-Goldsen, Hoy-Ellis, Goldsen, Emlet, & Hooyman, 2014). A number of organizations have developed and disseminated knowledge and resources to agencies, advocacy groups, and to LGBTQ+ individuals and families. One example is the National Resource Center on Aging (NRCA, n.d.), which is also partially supported by the U.S. Department of Health and Human Services. SAGE is another group that provides services and advocacy on behalf of LGBTQ+ older adults. Founded in 1978, it has local affiliates and a website with a rich array of service information, blogs, research, and advocacy materials that is an excellent resource for older LGBTQ+ adults and anyone who works with them (SAGE, 2018).

The importance of advocacy was recently underscored in the controversial decision to remove questions about sexual orientation and gender identity (**SOGI**) from the National Survey of Older Americans Act Participants, administered by the federal Administration of Community Living (ACL) (Morabia, 2017). In 2014, the ACL added a question to the survey asking respondents whether they self-identified as lesbian, gay, bisexual, or straight, and a question designed to elicit whether a person identifies as transgender (Cahill, 2017). Documentation as a form of recognition has symbolic meaning. This survey is also an important tool for the ACL to shape the services that it provides to older adults living in the community (as described above). LGBTQ+ older adults may have additional or different needs than their straight counterparts, and they face different obstacles to access (Zodikoff, 2006). If needs are not identified or populations are not included in the survey, then services provided under these federal programs many not serve everyone equally nor meet existing needs. Activists challenged the removal of the SOGI questions as a politically motivated action under the guise of scientific rationale. Public health scholar and activist Sean Cahill (2017) explained:

SOGI: An acronym often used as shorthand for sexual orientation and gender identity

> The collection of data on LGBT program recipients is critical to ensuring that programs meet the needs of LGBT seniors and LGBT people with disabilities, who experience high rates of economic insecurity, social isolation, and discrimination. The government is rolling back essential tools that it requires to determine whether it reaches all elders and disabled individuals effectively and equitably. Collecting SOGI data to better understand barriers to accessing services and reduce health disparities should not be a political or partisan issue. (n.p.)

Responses drew on the expertise of researchers, scholars, and activists. For example, the American Journal of Public Health published a "Dossier on the Erasure of Sexual Orientation Question from the National Survey of Older Americans Act Participants" (Morabia, 2017). The dossier included opinions from scholars as well as former Assistant Secretary for Aging Kathy Greenlee (2017), who presided over the development and initial implementation of this survey question. These advocacy efforts halted the removal of the sexual orientation question from the survey, but the gender identity question has not been restored (Cahill, 2017).

REFLECTION

SOCIAL WORKERS ADVOCATE ON BEHALF OF OLDER LGBTQ+ ADULTS AND OTHERS

Removal of the sexual orientation and gender identity (SOGI) questions from the ACL survey is one of many battles around who is recognized and counted. For example, SOGI questions were also intended to be added to a survey around demographic information and services needs of people with disabilities. There have been recent controversies on whether questions about immigration status should be included on U.S. Census counts and the accuracy of counting people experiencing homelessness (see Chapter 14). These controversies have taken place at both the local and federal level. Drawing on what we have described in this section and from your own personal or professional experiences, reflect on the following questions:

1. What is the importance of collecting information about specific populations?
2. Can you think of any risks in collecting information about those populations?
3. What roles might social workers have in the creation, implementation, and use of such surveys?
4. How might actions of government agencies such as the ACL shape implementation of the law?

Final Discussion

Now that you have finished reading this chapter, reread the vignette at the beginning. Darla and John are helping Larissa raise her daughter. In doing so they are providing for their own family. They often feel as though they are doing so in the vacuum of their individual family without any outside social support. Based on what you have learned, answer the following. Point to specific references in the chapter that help you answer these questions. Consider how different theories inform the response to these questions.

1. What kind of social supports are available for them as a family? (Hint: You might have found these in answering the questions at the beginning of the chapter or generated ideas as you read.)
2. Do these supports come from a premise of interdependence, or quid pro quo (getting something in exchange for giving something)?
3. How might their lives look different if we were living in a society that prioritizes interdependence rather than individual self-reliance?
4. What role might race, class, gender, and other aspects of identity play in this vignette?

11

HEALTH POLICY

LEARNING OBJECTIVES

11.1: Assess perspectives on whether health care is a right or privilege throughout U.S. history

11.2: Outline the effects of various current health care policies in the U.S. on significant groups served by social work

11.3: Assess solutions to U.S. health care problems today using a variety of perspectives

11.4: Develop opportunities for advocacy related to health policy

As former senator and health advocate Tom Daschle says, health "affects all of us in an intensely personal, emotional way" (Daschle & Nather, 2010, p. 2). This chapter explores policies addressing physical and **behavioral health**[1] in the United States, affecting everything from availability of health insurance to addiction services. We look at perspectives about whether access to health care is a right or a privilege and ways in which groups such as professional medical associations, patient advocates, and pharmaceutical companies affect the policies that result from public debate. This chapter examines how race, class, and gender inequality affect access to care and, ultimately, health care outcomes. Policies including Medicaid, the Affordable Care Act (ACA), and the Mental Health Parity and Addiction Equity Act are reviewed. This chapter also discusses policies that affect specific communities with which social workers often partner, such as veterans or members of Native American/indigenous groups. This chapter ends with an examination of gaps in policy and services and opportunities for advocacy ranging from universal health care to access to nutrition for those in poverty.

Behavioral health: The field related to the promotion of well-being through assessment, diagnosis, treatment, and prevention of mental illness, substance use, and other addictions

[1]A note about terminology: behavioral health is defined by the National Association of Social Workers (n.d.) as a subset of social work practice which "promotes well-being through . . . assessment, diagnosis, treatment, and prevention of mental illness, substance use, and other addictions" (para. 1). Many still prefer the terms mental health and substance use, but behavioral health is used here and in other places to refer to the broader range of issues including mental health and substance use. There are arguments against using this term, with some suggesting that it conflates individual decision making about behaviors with underlying mental health issues.

Vignette: Hepatitis C and Medicaid

Based on what you know from the media or your personal, work, or volunteer experiences, think about the following questions as you read the vignette. When you finish the vignette, answer the questions below.

1. What policies are relevant to this vignette?
2. Would the outcome of Jamie's case be any different if he lived in a country with universal health care?
3. What factors should a state take into consideration when deciding whether to cover this medication?
4. What social work values are relevant to this vignette?
5. What role might race, class, gender, and other aspects of identity play in this vignette?

When Jamie was 8 years old, he had a relatively minor medical procedure. During the procedure, he lost a lot of blood and needed a transfusion. Unfortunately, because prior to 1992 donated blood was not tested for Hepatitis C, the blood he received was contaminated and he contracted Hepatitis C. He is one of three million to four million Americans who have this illness, although as many as 75% do not have symptoms, so they are unaware they are infected. Jamie discovered that he had Hepatitis C during a routine physical. He had health insurance through his employer, a cell phone company where he served as a call center employee. Shortly after the diagnosis, he lost his job and has not found a new position. He currently has health insurance through Medicaid.

In 2014, Jamie was 60 and living in Indiana and looking for work. He went to the doctor because he was feeling tired and nauseated and had noticed that his skin looked a little yellow. The doctor told him that he had developed chronic Hepatitis C, meaning the virus that had been quietly present all those years was now attacking his liver. If not treated soon, he would need a liver transplant.

A new treatment that has recently become available for Hepatitis C allows it to be fully cured for the first time. While the treatment is amazing, it is very expensive—generally it costs somewhere between $55,000 and $90,000. When Jamie's doctor submitted his information to Medicaid, he found out that Indiana's Medicaid program refused to pay the cost of this treatment. Even though all state Medicaid programs get a discount of 23% off the cost of the medication, Indiana argued that it was still too expensive for them to provide this treatment to everyone who might need it. Indiana Medicaid said that they would only pay if Jamie had significant liver damage. Basically, Jamie must get sicker to be eligible for the treatment, even though he is already so sick that he is unable to look for work.

HISTORY AND SOCIAL CONSTRUCTION OF U.S. HEALTH CARE

Health: A state of complete physical, mental, and social well-being and not merely the absence of disease or infirmity

What is health? The World Health Organization (WHO) defines **health** as "a state of complete physical, mental and social well-being and not merely the absence of disease or infirmity" (1948, n.p.). Healthy People 2020 is a research-based 10-year initiative of the Department of Health and Human Services that is designed to improve the health of every American. Their vision is "[a] society in which all people live long, healthy lives" (Healthy People 2020, n.d., para. 3). As you already know, health, health care, and health policy are complex issues that touch every part of people's lives. Here is a snapshot of the news stories discussing health on one morning in 2018:

- Syphilis cases hit a 70-year high in England
- The World Health Organization recommends everyone attending the World Cup be vaccinated against measles before they leave home
- Sixteen people are reported dead from the Nipah virus in India
- Twelve people are reported dead from the adverse effects of weight loss balloons in the United States
- Researchers argue (in separate studies) that feeling disgust is good for your health, that lack of sleep is bad for your health, and that a new blood test might be able to detect cancer early
- San Francisco bans the sale of flavored tobacco products because they might encourage teens to smoke
- A 113-year-old woman in Ohio becomes the oldest known living person in the United States
- Singer Ariana Grande discusses her posttraumatic stress disorder, caused by a suicide bombing at her concert in Manchester, England, in 2017
- The Food and Drug Administration recalls an opioid overdose antidote because the syringes might be contaminated with loose particulates and warns people to be on the lookout for Medicare fraud related to a dementia medication
- Mussels in Puget Sound test positive for opioids and other chemicals that are likely flushed down toilets and therefore into public waterways

Health Care: Right or Privilege?

Because health is such a complicated and significant issue, we hope this chapter gives you as many questions about health policy and resources in your area as it does answers. There is a lot of overlap between health policy and disability policy, so Chapter 12 includes information relative to these questions as well. We start with a big one: Is health care a right? Or is health care a privilege?

Health insurance: A type of insurance coverage that pays for certain health-related expenses incurred by the insured

As hard as it is now to imagine, **health insurance**, a type of insurance coverage that pays for certain health-related expenses incurred by the insured, is a relatively modern invention. Health insurance was pioneered by Otto Bismarck in Germany in the 1880s and was not discussed in the United States until the presidency of Theodore Roosevelt in the Progressive Era. Since that time, reformers have argued that health care should be a right, not a privilege, and should be available to all through systems such as compulsory health insurance (Hoffman, 2009). Others, such as U.S. Senator Ron Johnson, have argued that health care is a commodity to be purchased by those who have access to the resources (Benen, 2017). The idea of health insurance gained momentum during the 1930s, when rising costs for health care and related technologies made it inaccessible for low-income and many middle-class Americans. During this time, hospitals also changed from institutions designed to care for those with chronic illnesses or people in poverty to places where Americans accessed surgery and other services on a temporary basis. This expansion and change of services was expensive and meant that hospitals needed to be funded by more than just philanthropy and private donations. As a result, those using hospitals were expected to pay for their costs (Ross, 2002).

Health insurance was not the only health policy discussed during the Progressive Era. This era also saw the Sheppard-Towner bill, the first federal law funding maternal and infant health care. This bill was possible because of the work of the U.S. Children's Bureau, created in 1912 and headed by Julia Lathrop. After 6 years of careful study, the Children's Bureau reported that one in every 10 babies born in the United States died, and for families making less than $450 per year, one in every 6 babies died. This put the United States well behind other wealthy countries, such as New Zealand, where only one in every 20 new babies died. Jeannette Rankin, the first woman to be elected to Congress and a social worker, found that the mortality rates were even worse for rural women. She and Senator Joseph Robinson introduced a bill in 1918 to decrease maternal and infant mortality across the country. Rankin did not win reelection, due in part to her advocacy for the safety of coal miners in her native Montana, her public work on behalf of women's suffrage, and her anti-war efforts. After she left Congress, others picked up the fight and the bill was reintroduced. In 1921, those fighting against the bill included the American Medical Association (AMA), which argued that public health should be managed at the state level rather than the federal level and that despite the Children's Bureau's statistics, there was no existing emergency around maternal and infant health. Others who opposed the bill included "medical liberty organizations" that believed there should be no regulation of health care, medical education, or licensure of doctors, and groups such as the "Women Patriots" who had been opposed to women's suffrage and believed the bill was a socialist conspiracy. Those who supported the bill included the Women's Joint Congressional Committee. This coalition of 20 national women's organizations used community organizing around the "Save the Babies" campaign slogan and advocacy to overcome the opposition most members of Congress had to this bill with the threat of angering 20 million women who had recently acquired the right to vote. Cooper (1987) argues:

> Its passage was a turning point in American history in two ways. First, the act represented the beginning of federal support in an American health program. Second, and more importantly, the law represented the emergence of women as a dynamic voting group capable of securing reforms for themselves and their children. (pp. 36–37)

This bill and the process of its passage and implementation also led to the creation of child welfare departments in more than 30 state governments.

In the 1940s, Franklin Roosevelt outlined his "Economic Bill of Rights" or "Second Bill of Rights" in his State of the Union Address to Congress, including "[t]he right to adequate medical care and the opportunity to achieve and enjoy good health" as a right that all Americans should possess. The Universal Declaration of Human Rights, passed by the United Nations' General Assembly in 1948, includes as one of its 50 fundamental human rights that

> [e]veryone has the right to a standard of living adequate for the health and well-being of himself and of his family, including food, clothing, housing and medical care and necessary social services, and the right to security in the event of unemployment, sickness, disability, widowhood, old age or other lack of livelihood in circumstances beyond his control. (Article 25)

National health insurance was suggested in early versions of the Social Security Act, but was not included in the final bill due to economic concerns and strong opposition from the AMA, Republicans who opposed government expansion, and Southern Democrats. However, the Social Security Act did include some funds for public health and maternal and child health services (Hoffman, 2009).

Significant national health reform has been proposed five times since Roosevelt's speech. In the 1940s, President Truman proposed a national health insurance plan in the model of Roosevelt's economic bill of rights proposal, part of his Fair Deal proposals. Again the AMA was opposed. They called his plan *socialized medicine*, which played into the national anti-communist mood. However, aid for hospitals was passed separately, and labor unions worked with business to begin building employer-based health insurance (Hoffman, 2009).

Employer-provided health insurance became more common, but because health insurance companies could choose not to cover those who were older or in poorer health, or charge them more money, affordable coverage became less accessible for all. Because of this, in the 1960s, it became a policy priority to develop a strategy to provide health coverage for older Americans and, to a certain extent, those in poverty. Elements of several different proposals were signed into law by President Johnson in an update to the Social Security Act in 1965, as shown in Photo 11.1. This formed the basis of Medicare Part A, which was designed to cover hospital, skilled nursing, and home health care for older adults and individuals with long-term disabilities; Medicare Part B, which was designed to pay for physician care for older adults and people with long-term disabilities with some costs borne by individuals through premiums; and Medicaid, which was designed to cover health care costs for people who were poor or had disabilities. These initiatives passed despite opposition from (you guessed it) the AMA, but with the support of the American Hospital Association, labor unions, and the health insurance industry. Long-term care, prescriptions, and vision care were not covered for the elderly. None of these plans included any mechanism for government to control costs (Hoffman, 2009). Catherine Hoffman notes,

> [t]he confluence of presidential leadership and urgency, Johnson's political skills in working with a large Congressional Democratic majority, growing civil rights awareness, public support, and the support of hospitals and the insurance industry contributed to the achievement of the most significant health reform of the century. (2009, p. 5)

Hoffman also notes that the United States did not have federal agencies that estimated the costs of new proposals during that time. In just 8 years, health spending (primarily Medicare

LBJ Presidential Library

PHOTO 11.1 President Lyndon Johnson signs the Medicare bill at the Harry S. Truman Library and Museum in Independence, Missouri.

and Medicaid) grew from 4% of the federal budget to 11%. In the 1970s, President Nixon and Senator Ted Kennedy offered competing proposals for a national health insurance program. Although the idea had overwhelming bipartisan support, the politics of navigating the competing proposals and the effect of the Watergate hearings and President Nixon's resignation doomed it. During the Carter administration, economic woes and rising health costs led to more focus on cost containment than expanding access to health insurance.

In the 1990s, President Clinton proposed a massive reform to the health care system (Blendon & Benson, 2001). This plan, called the Health Security Act, developed out of a process chaired by First Lady Hillary Clinton into a complex 1,400-page plan that failed to gain traction. However, as a result of this work, the Children's Health Insurance Program (CHIP) was created to shore up Medicaid by providing health insurance for low-income children (Hoffman, 2009). Do you know what the Children's Health Insurance Program in your state is called? How would you find out?

ADVOCACY

ARE LINDSAY AND HER FAMILY ELIGIBLE FOR HEALTH INSURANCE?

You are a case manager working with Lindsay, a single mother in Connecticut. Lindsay has a 6-year-old daughter (Ashley) and a 2-year-old son (Henry). She also takes care of her mother, Marie, who lives with them. Lindsay makes $2,000 per month and struggles to make ends meet. She is starting to max out her credit cards. Her job does not offer health insurance, and she is scared that if one of the children gets sick, she won't be able to take care of them. The social worker at her daughter's school referred Lindsay to you to see if she is eligible for any assistance, particularly for health care. Go to https://www.connect.ct.gov/ and click on "Am I Eligible?" Make a list of all the questions that you will have to answer to find out if Lindsay is eligible then answer them. For the information not given here, do your best to estimate what you think reasonable answers might be for her. Based on this process, answer the following questions:

1. How difficult is this process for the average person?
2. Based on the information you entered, what assistance is Lindsay eligible to receive?
3. Do the answers you found help with her concerns about health care?

The social construction of health in the United States reflects the fields that have primarily shaped it: medicine and public health (Mann et al., 1994). While these two disciplines share many concerns and ideas, they reflect our core disagreements about health: Are we concerned with health of individuals, as in medicine, or the health of populations, as in public health? Medicine looks at whether an individual is healthy or not healthy, or capable or incapable of performing functions of daily life. Public health looks at the conditions that promote or inhibit health in the environment, family, health care systems, or other institutions. If we return to the WHO definition of health above, "a state of complete physical, mental and social well-being and not merely the absence of disease or infirmity" (1948, n.p.), some might argue that *complete well-being* reflects the public health perspective while *absence of disease and infirmity* reflects the medical perspective. In general, the public health approach is associated with seeing health care as a right, and the medical approach is associated with seeing health care as a privilege, although many in the medical community see health care as a right, and some public health practitioners argue the limits of rights to health care.

The World Health Organization Constitution (1948) includes the following:

- Health is a state of complete physical, mental and social well-being and not merely the absence of disease or infirmity.
- The enjoyment of the highest attainable standard of health is one of the fundamental rights of every human being without distinction of race, religion, political belief, economic or social condition.
- The health of all peoples is fundamental to the attainment of peace and security and is dependent on the fullest co-operation of individuals and States.
- The achievement of any State in the promotion and protection of health is of value to all.
- Unequal development in different countries in the promotion of health and control of diseases, especially communicable disease, is a common danger.
- Healthy development of the child is of basic importance; the ability to live harmoniously in a changing total environment is essential to such development.
- The extension to all peoples of the benefits of medical, psychological and related knowledge is essential to the fullest attainment of health.
- Informed opinion and active co-operation on the part of the public are of the utmost importance in the improvement of the health of the people.
- Governments have a responsibility for the health of their peoples which can be fulfilled only by the provision of adequate health and social measures.

The debate about whether health care is a right or a privilege has been heavily shaped by professional groups, insurance companies, pharmaceutical companies, lawmakers, and individuals. When surveyed, members of the American public generally agree health care is a right and should be accessible to all, but when asked about specific portions of policies that make that possible, such as policies that include significant individual costs or mandates, they are not supportive (Hoffman, 2009). In general, the public views on these issues are complicated. The public is likely to support the idea of health reform, but not favor specific reforms, and to support more government involvement in health care even as they lack trust in the government to handle this responsibility (Blendon & Benson, 2001).

Health care providers may have a different perspective perhaps because they rely on payment for their livelihoods and are fearful that government involvement may reduce their incomes. They often have a lot of influence on the process. For example, a recent article in *The Washington Post* quotes national and state legislators describing the lobbying efforts of the American Dental Association as powerful, unified, and relentless, comparable to the National Rifle Association in their political strength (Jordan, 2017). The power of these professional organizations, particularly the 200,000 strong AMA, has influenced not just policy but also the ways in which the American public and lawmakers talk about health. Through most of this history, the AMA was adamantly opposed to any type of government-regulated insurance and has been able to slow the progress and substantially shape the end results of related legislation (Ross, 2002).

In recent debates about health care reform and health policy, insurance companies and pharmaceutical companies have also heavily influenced debate and outcomes. Questions have been raised about the collaboration between professional associations, federal regulators, such as the Food and Drug Administration (FDA), and organizations in the private market that provide and make a profit from health care, such as pharmaceutical companies and insurance companies. For example, the FDA allowed the following statement to be placed on the drug label for OxyContin, which turned out to be not borne out by clinical research: "[D]elayed absorption as provided by OxyContin tablets is believed to reduce the abuse liability of a drug" (McFadden, Breslauer, & Connor, 2018, n.p.). In 2002, when the FDA convened a panel of experts to address opioid addiction, eight out of the 10 experts had ties to the pharmaceutical industry (McFadden et al., 2018). The AMA and other groups have struggled to develop clear conflict of interest policies about funding for medical research, conferences, and training and the connections between their lobbying efforts and the best interests of doctors, pharmaceutical companies, and health insurers (Nissen, 2017). These conflicts of interest, or at least the appearance of conflicts of interest, have affected public trust in doctors and the health system (Nissen, 2017). Are these relationships inevitable? Generally, doctors believe that "physician interaction with pharmaceutical and medical device companies is vital to scientific progress" (Nissen, 2017, p. 1737).

Mental Health

Mental health: A person's condition with regard to their psychological and emotional well-being

Throughout history, people with **mental health** concerns related to psychological and emotional well-being were likely to end up in institutions, prison, or on the streets, particularly if they lacked family or resources for support. Mental institutions often appeared much like prisons. When Benjamin Franklin and Thomas Bond founded a hospital in Philadelphia in 1752, it included care for "lunaticks," complete with shackles attached to the walls. By 1890, a public hospital for people needing mental health care was present in every state in the country (U.S. National Library of Medicine, n.d.). The first textbook that addressed mental health was written by Benjamin Rush, sometimes called the father of American psychiatry, in 1812. Dr. Rush, one of the signers of the Declaration of Independence, believed that mental illness resulted from irritated blood vessels in the brain. Suggested treatments in his writings and lectures included "bleeding, purging, hot and cold baths . . . mercury . . . a tranquilizer chair . . . and a gyrator" (U.S. National Library of Medicine, n.d., n.p.). Others at the time believed that mental illness had "'moral' causes such as worries and anxieties" (n.p.).

Mental health care became more standardized within health care in the mid-1800s, with the establishment of the Association of Medical Superintendents of American Institutions for the Insane (now the American Psychiatric Association) in 1844 and a Committee on Insanity within the AMA in 1854. However, the "care" given to people with mental health needs was often still inhumane and cruel. Thanks to advocates like Dorothea Dix and journalists like Nellie Bly, resources began to be allocated to provide better care, although the challenges of providing adequate services within institutions continue today (U.S. National Library of Medicine, n.d.).

Mental illness has been criminalized or used as a tool of power throughout history, as in the case of Elizabeth Packard of Illinois, who was forcibly placed in an asylum by her husband in 1860 because she disagreed with his religious beliefs. Patients were forcibly restrained as a matter of common practice, and today, medication used as chemical restraints are often used to pacify mental patients. The size of mental hospitals made any care other than restraints difficult—by 1954, Long Island, New York's Pilgrim State Hospital had 13,875 patients, and included "its own water works, electric light plant, heating plant, sewage system, fire department, police department, courts, church, post office, cemetery, laundry, store, amusement hall, athletic fields, greenhouses, and farm" (New York State Office of Mental Health, n.d., para. 4). Mental health problems were also used as grounds for treatments such as lobotomies, imprisonment, restriction from getting married, and sterilization. As an example, in 1907, when Indiana enacted a eugenics law, 2,500 people in state custody were sterilized. **Eugenics** refers to procedures that are designed to "improve" the human population by increasing desirable characteristics and decreasing undesirable characteristics. The law stayed on the books until it was declared unconstitutional in 1921; laws that prevented "imbeciles, epileptics, and those of unsound minds" from marrying were not repealed in Indiana until 1977 (Indiana Historical Bureau, n.d.).

Eugenics: Procedures that are designed to "improve" the human population by increasing desirable characteristics and decreasing undesirable characteristics, primarily through manipulation of reproduction (e.g., sterilization)

The roots of modern-day U.S. mental health care come from the time following World War II when the care for people with mental illness in asylums was increasingly seen as problematic and efforts were made to medicalize and standardize treatment. The National Mental Health Act of 1946 created the National Institute of Mental Health. Since 1952, the ***Diagnostic and Statistical Manual of Mental Disorders (DSM)*** has been the model of psychiatric classification used by social workers and other behavioral health practitioners and is often the basis for determining whether treatment will be covered by insurance companies. This has been true despite the significant critiques of the DSM and its use in treatment of women, members of the LGBTQ+ community, and nonwhite communities.

Diagnostic and Statistical Manual of Mental Disorders: The handbook used as the authoritative guide to the diagnosis of mental disorders

The use of community services became preferable in the United States and Western Europe through the 1950s. These were designed to move individuals from care in institutions and asylums to care within community-based agencies. While the move away from asylums was successful in the United States, with 120 hospitals closing and the population of mental hospital residents decreasing from a peak of 553,979 in 1964 (the first year that antipsychotic drugs were available) to 61,722 in 1996, the replacement for that care has been less successful. Inpatient mental health care in the United States is offered through psychiatric beds in traditional hospitals. Care offered in outpatient settings

> has been somewhat less successful, often leading to considerable care gaps or to a complex network of poorly coordinated institutions including ambulatory clinics, psychiatrists or psychotherapists in private practice, community mental health centers, case management teams, day clinics, workshops, sheltered accommodations and nursing homes. (Novella, 2010, p. 228)

Under President Kennedy, the Community Mental Health Act of 1963 was designed to create community-based preventative care and treatment, but the act was never funded.

REFLECTION

COMMUNITY MENTAL HEALTH ACT

Read President Kennedy's statement on the Community Mental Health Act of 1963. How would mental health services today look different if this act had been funded as he imagined? http://www.presidency.ucsb.edu/ws/?pid=9546

Substance Use

The history of attitudes toward substance use and addiction follow similar trends. Alcohol has been a constant part of our history, despite efforts like temperance and prohibition to restrict drinking. In 1830, the average person in the United States drank five to seven gallons of alcohol every year (Henninger & Sung, 2014). The presence of a person in the house with a drinking problem was enough to remove families from eligibility for services from Charity Organization Societies (Henninger & Sung, 2014). Dr. Rush and other medical professionals proposed sober homes that would include moral and religious instruction as well as more exotic treatments such as "cold baths, vomiting, and aversion therapy to the practices of bleeding, blistering, and sweating the patient" (Henninger & Sung, 2014, p. 2258). The term *alcoholism* entered the medical language in the 1800s, reflecting the treatment of alcoholism as a disease rather than a criminal offense, including detoxification and inpatient treatment as well as continued care supervised by a physician in the community. Some of these treatments included the use of other drugs, such as opioids, as part of the recovery process. Societal responses to alcoholism have swung back and forth between the need for everyone to abstain from alcohol (significant segments of the Temperance Movement), to the development of programs focused on abstinence only for those who were diagnosed with alcoholism (the Washington Societies and Alcoholics Anonymous and other 12-step programs), to an acceptance of alcohol and a focus on moderation.

Prohibition: Efforts and movements to criminalize the use of substances such as alcohol or other drugs; often refers to the movement in the United States between 1929 and 1933 to prevent the making and sale of alcohol

Prohibition and other efforts to criminalize all use of alcohol and other drugs decreased the availability of treatment and, through legislation such as the Harrison Act of 1914, moved dealing with substance use from the public health arena to the criminal justice system (Henninger & Sung, 2014). These policies criminalized substance use and were particularly used to target African American men. This is discussed more in Chapter 13, which focuses on criminal justice.

The next wave of substance use treatment, including efforts such as the Minnesota Model designed to build recovery based on mutual respect, have often been led by those who have struggled with substance abuse (Henninger & Sung, 2014). Substance use policies passed in recent years have often focused on evidence-based treatments such as Screening, Brief Intervention, and Referral to Treatment (SBIRT), medication-assisted treatment (MAT), and harm reduction.

Medication-assisted treatment (MAT): Treatment for substance use that combines behavioral therapy and medications

Both the Substance Abuse and Mental Health Services Administration (SAMHSA) and the Drug Enforcement Administration (DEA) at the federal level oversee **medication-assisted treatment**, which combines behavioral therapy and medication to treat substance use disorders, because many of the medications used in MAT are themselves controlled substances. States also hold responsibility to license and regulate providers in their states who address substance use. For example, in Florida, agencies are regulated by the State Substance Abuse and Mental Health Program Office if they do any of the following: addiction receiving facilities, detoxification, intensive inpatient treatment, residential treatment, day or night treatment, outpatient treatment, continuing care, intervention, prevention, and medication-assisted treatment (Florida Department of Children and Families, n.d.).

Harm reduction: Strategies and policies that aim to minimize negative health, social, and legal impacts associated with drug use in a nonjudgmental manner

Harm reduction strategies and policies focus on "reducing [drug use's] harmful consequences, including death, HIV, hepatitis C, criminal activity, and incarceration," rather than decreasing drug use (Hawk, Vaca, & D'Onofrio, 2015, p. 239). Harm reduction methods include the distribution of nalaxone (also known as Narcan). Nalaxone can reverse the effects of an opioid overdose and can be used with minimal training. Relevant policies include Good Samaritan laws and those that allow nalaxone to be distributed without a prescription or prescribed to a family member of someone dealing with opioid addiction.

Opioid Epidemic: Case study

In 1994, Fred Coulter was working in a printing plant in Ontario, Canada (Webster, 2012). A heavy roller fell and ruptured Fred's spine. His doctor prescribed a number of painkillers to help him manage the severe pain, and Fred was soon given a prescription for OxyContin. He was not alone—in 1996, over eight million Americans had a prescription for opioid painkillers, and today 29% of Canadians over 18, nearly one in three, report that they have used some sort of opioid in the last 5 years. Like many users, Fred was soon buying OxyContin on the street, spending roughly $100 per day on his addiction.

By 2012, Fred had stopped using OxyContin and was in methadone treatment (Webster, 2012). He had joined one of several class action lawsuits against Purdue Pharma, the makers of OxyContin, and other pharmaceutical companies. These lawsuits accused pharmaceutical companies of failure to disclose risks of addiction, and deception in advertising. For example, Purdue Pharma distributed the video *"I got my life back"* to doctors' waiting rooms across the country. This video featured a doctor who said about opioids:

> They don't wear out; they go on working; they do not have serious medical side effects . . . . So, these drugs, which I repeat, are our best, strongest pain medications, should be used much more than they are for patients in pain. (Moghe, 2016, n.p.)

As of 2017, class action lawsuits like Fred's had resulted in courts requiring approximately $971 million in payments from pharmaceutical companies, although relatively small amounts have gone to individual members of the suits. In most of the lawsuits, the companies were not required to admit any wrongdoing (Haffajee & Mello, 2017). While this number sounds large, keep in mind that Purdue made $2.8 billion (with a B) from OxyContin in 2012 alone. In 2018, Purdue agreed to stop marketing opioids to doctors (McCausland & Connor, 2018).

What is the total cost of the opioid epidemic? In 2015 alone, more than 33,000 people died from drug overdoses, including prescription drugs like OxyContin and street opioids like heroin and fentanyl, and during that one year, the economic cost was $504 billion (Council of Economic Advisers, 2017). Other estimates put the total cost of the opioid epidemic at more than $1 trillion (Allen, 2018).

Policies that respond to the opioid epidemic include making it more difficult to get prescription opioids, encouraging those who are struggling with addiction to get treatment, funding, training, and awareness of Narcan and other medications for first responders and members of the public to block the effects of an overdose, and access to methadone and other medications for those who are addicted. They can also include Narcotics Anonymous and other 12-step programs, help for communities who have been hard hit by the epidemic, funding of programs that use text messages to alert local communities when dangerous substances are mixed with drugs, and more. These policies vary in their capacity to address the systemic causes of the epidemic, the challenges of individuals who are affected, and the damage done to communities with high rates of opioid use.

CURRENT HEALTH POLICY

In this section, we discuss the significant issue of inequality of access to health care, and the resulting disparity in outcomes for whites and nonwhites. We also review a range of health policies, including the Affordable Care Act and the policies and programs that provide health care to older adults, people with low incomes, Native Americans, and veterans. At the end of this section, Table 11.4 outlines significant federal policies that are addressed in this chapter.

Compared to other countries in the world, the United States spends an extraordinary amount on health insurance. Health care spending per capita (meaning total spending divided by the number of people in the country) in the United States was $9,892 in 2016, 20% more than the next highest country (Switzerland at $7,919), and more than twice what is spent by Canada ($4,752) or the United Kingdom ($4,192) (OECD, 2018). Spending has also grown over time—as recently as 1998, the United States spent $4,270 per capita (Kim & Lane, 2013). The cost of health care was significant in the debate around the Affordable Care Act. Spending on health care includes spending by individuals, governments, and health insurance companies on health care goods and services, including prevention and public health. This disparity in spending between the United States and other countries has been true for a long time (Kim & Lane, 2013), but does not lead to better health outcomes. Health outcomes for Americans are below average in life expectancy, infant mortality, birth weight, cancer, diabetes, and suicide, although at the top in perceived health status (OECD, 2017).

Many argue the U.S. health system is able to be dynamic and innovative because of the significant spending and that new procedures and treatments that are developed in the United States benefit other countries with lower spending and less investment in health innovation (Carroll & Frakt, 2017). To get a sense of how much the United States spends on health care in comparison to other countries, and how that translates into health outcomes, review the chart in Figure 11.1 that shows average life expectancy in comparison to health expenditures in 24 countries.

Underinsured: Individuals or families who have access to some health care that does not fully meet their needs

Health care in the United States is provided by a fragmented set of providers and insurers. Some Americans have access to excellent health care, generally provided through employer-sponsored health insurance or Medicare. The cost of care for individuals and families for employer-sponsored health care are growing rapidly. Other Americans are **underinsured**, meaning they have access to some health care but it does not fully meet their needs. Finally, a significant group of Americans are uninsured and have no access to care. Those who are in poverty and are nonwhite are more likely to fall into the uninsured and underinsured groups (Butterfield, Rocha, & Butterfield, 2010). Approximately 91% of the United States is covered by insurance—in comparison to other OECD countries, only Greece has fewer people covered by health insurance (OECD, 2017). In 2018, 55% of those under 18 were covered by private insurance, while 42% were covered by public insurance and 5% were uninsured. The 42% covered by public insurance includes children across the country who get health coverage from Medicaid or CHIP—without those programs, the number of uninsured in the United States would be substantially higher. Of adults between 18 and 64, 70% are covered by private health insurance, 19% by public insurance, and 13% were uninsured (Cohen, Martinez, & Zammitti, 2018).

Health Care and Inequality

Health outcomes for people in the United States who are not white are significantly worse than for those who are white, including higher rates of diabetes, heart disease, infant mortality, cancer, and HIV/AIDS. This inequality is caused by limited access to preventive care, racialized health care practices, unequal access to health providers, and limited empirical research that examines health considerations of nonwhite populations (National Association of Social Workers [NASW], 2018). Public health professionals internationally, including those associated with the WHO, describe the social factors that contribute to these inequities as **social determinants of health**, which they define as

Social determinants of health: The conditions in which people are born, grow, live, work, and age

> [t]he conditions in which people are born, grow, live, work and age. These circumstances are shaped by the distribution of money, power and resources at global, national and local levels. The social determinants of health are mostly responsible for health inequities—the unfair and avoidable differences in health status seen within and between countries. (WHO, n.d., para. 1)

FIGURE 11.1 ■ Life Expectancy vs. Health Expenditure Over Time (1970–2014)

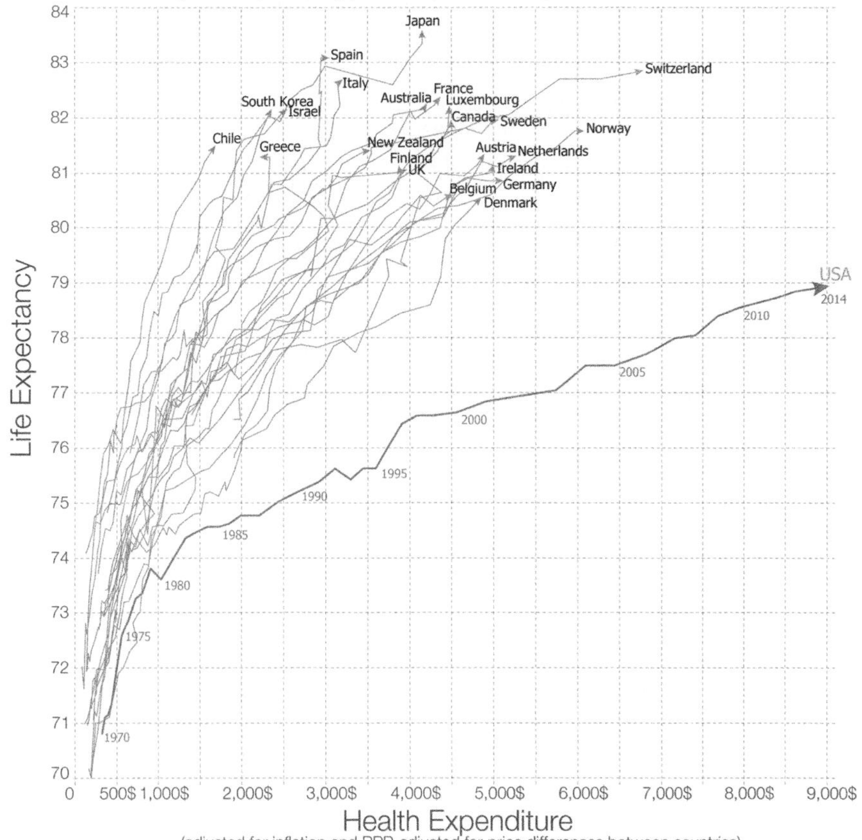

Source: Licensed under CC-BY-SA by the author Max Roser

Social determinants of health include employment and working conditions; social exclusion; income, gender, racial, and sexual inequality; early childhood development; globalization; urbanization; income; housing and living conditions; education; food security; and exposure to violence (NASW, 2018; WHO, n.d.). Racism in particular is a key social determinant of health that results in significant health disparities (Vanidestine, 2018).

The Affordable Care Act

The most recent large-scale changes to U.S. health care policy have occurred since 2010 as a result of Public Law (PL) 111-148, the Patient Protection and Affordable Care Act (often called the Affordable Care Act, ACA, or Obamacare). After his election, President Obama told Senator Tom Daschle, "Tom, health care is the most important thing we will ever do. It will be my legacy. And it is more important to me now than ever before. Don't ever

Tom Williams/CQ-Roll Call Group/Getty

PHOTO 11.2 Demonstrators gather in the atrium of the Hart Office Building to protest the Senate's health care bill on July 25, 2017

doubt that" (Daschle & Nather, 2010, p. 117). The political fight over this law has already taken years, as demonstrated by Photo 11.2, and its implementation is changing as you read this book.

In 2010, prior to the Affordable Care Act, the United States government spent an estimated $2.6 trillion on health expenditures, including spending on Medicare, Medicaid, and so on. This averaged approximately $8,402 per American and totaled 17.9% of the gross domestic product for that year (Kaiser Family Foundation, 2012). Various cost estimates on the bill projected that spending would be $938 billion over 10 years and that the bill would reduce the deficit by $124 billion over those ten years, with savings from reductions in spending and fraud through Medicare and Medicaid, and through the installation of new taxes and fees in the legislation. This analysis is the subject of much debate (factcheck.org, 2012). One significant area that was expected to lead to increased expenses by insurers was the inclusion of **essential health benefits** that all health plans must cover. These benefits include those listed in Table 11.1 (healthcare.gov, n.d.).

Essential health benefits: Those procedures and services that must be covered by insurance according to the Affordable Care Act

Birth control and breastfeeding support services must also be covered. Health plans may choose to cover other services not listed here, such as dental care, vision care, and medical management for things like weight management, back pain, and diabetes (healthcare.gov, n.d.).

The Affordable Care Act was designed with a lofty goal, that an estimated 95% of U.S. citizens and legal residents would have health insurance coverage within 6 years (*Washington Post*, 2010). Mechanisms to achieve that goal are shown in Figure 11.2 (*National Federation of Independent Business et al. v. Sebelius, Secretary of Health and Human Services, et al. [NFIB]*, 2012; *The Washington Post*, 2010).

The Affordable Care Act was also designed to expand Medicaid to cover a larger pool of individuals. The original legislation required that all states expand Medicaid to cover those under 65 with incomes less than 133% of the poverty line. A 2012 Supreme

TABLE 11.1 ■ Essential Health Benefits
Ambulatory patient services (outpatient care you get without being admitted to a hospital)
Emergency services
Hospitalization (such as surgery and overnight stays)
Pregnancy, maternity, and newborn care (both before and after birth)
Mental health and substance use disorder services, including behavioral health treatment (this includes counseling and psychotherapy)
Prescription drugs
Rehabilitative and habilitative services and devices (services and devices to help people with injuries, disabilities, or chronic conditions gain or recover mental and physical skills)
Laboratory services
Preventive and wellness services and chronic disease management
Pediatric services, including oral and vision care (this does not include adult dental and vision coverage, which are not essential health benefits)

Court ruling held Congress could not require states to do so, but states can still offer Medicaid to these people if the states choose to (*NFIB*, 2012). As a result, 31 states and the District of Columbia have expanded Medicaid, while the remaining 19 states have not (Witters, 2018).

Implementation of the ACA is complex and is the subject of 31,000 scholarly articles and books written on the topic since 2010. It relies on legislation, which has been changed by Congress several times, including in the tax bill passed at the end of 2017, which repeals the individual mandate and is likely to increase the number of people who choose not to buy into health insurance (PBS Newshour, 2017). Governors and state legislatures also have power over how they implement the law in their states, ranging from state governments that expanded Medicaid, fully funded the legal mandates required by the law, and enshrined protection of the essential health benefits into law to those who refused Medicaid expansion, are deliberately underfunding the law, and are actively working for its repeal. Changes to this legislation are likely to be under active debate for the foreseeable future, as is advocacy related to these changes.

Medicare

Medicare is the most universal health insurance program in the United States. It was designed to cover adults over the age of 65 when it was enacted as an expansion to the Social Security Act in 1965. It includes four major parts. Part A covers hospital and nursing facility care. Part B covers doctor visits and outpatient services. Part C covers HMOs. Part D covers prescription drugs (Kaiser Family Foundation, 2017). If you have not yet read the previous chapter on older adults (Chapter 10), we recommend that you review the section of that chapter on Medicare before you continue.

FIGURE 11.2 ■ Timeline of Affordable Care Act Implementation

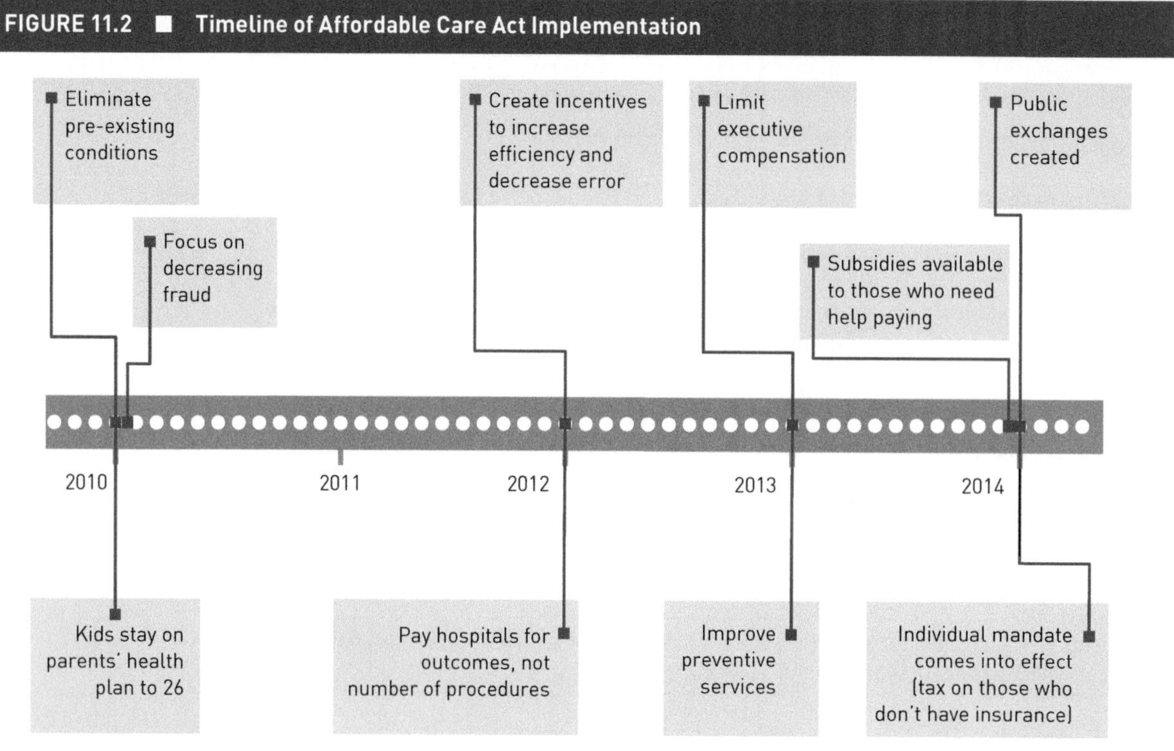

Source: National Federation of Independent Business et al. v. Sebelius, Secretary of Health and Human Services, et al. [NFIB], 2012; *Washington Post,* 2010

Medicaid

According NASW (2018), "Medicaid is the nation's single largest social safety net program" (p. 147). Medicaid is involved in health care services for 72 million Americans living in poverty (Centers for Medicare and Medicaid Services, 2018), about one in every five Americans, and was also created as part of the Social Security Amendments of 1965. Recipients of Medicaid are diverse, and include pregnant women, children, people with disabilities, and older adults (NASW, 2018). Medicaid is structured by a set of federal requirements, which allow states discretion to provide services within those guidelines. Funding for Medicaid comes from both federal and state governments. Essentially, the federal government agrees to pay each state a percentage of its total Medicaid expenses (this percentage is called the Federal Medical Assistance Percentage or FMAP). In recent years, the federal government has issued guidance to allow states to create work requirements for Medicaid recipients. These requirements are being challenged in the court system but have the potential to result in a significant number of Medicaid recipients losing access to health services (Aron-Dine, Chaudhry, & Broaddus, 2018).

Medicaid affects individuals and families who receive services, hospitals and health centers located in low-income areas who serve a significant number of Medicaid beneficiaries, nursing homes, and community-based long-term health care providers and recipients (see Table 11.2 for some examples of the role Medicaid plays in the U.S. health care system). The Kaiser Family Foundation estimated in 2016 that Medicaid paid for approximately 16% of overall personal health spending in the United States, including more than 50% of spending on long-term care and approximately 10% of spending on prescriptions. This program totaled $553 billion in spending in 2016. The majority (63%) of that funding was federal and the remainder (37%) was state based (Rudowitz & Valentine, 2017).

TABLE 11.2 ■ Medicaid's Role in Our Health System

Function	Groups Assisted
Health insurance coverage	Low-income families—33 million children and 19 million adults
	Elderly and persons with disabilities—16 million
Assistance to Medicare beneficiaries	Elderly and persons with disabilities—10 million (21% of Medicare beneficiaries)
Long-term care assistance	Institutional residents—1.5 million
	Community-based residents—2.9 million
Support for health care system and safety-net	National health spending—16%
	Long-term care spending—50%
State capacity for health coverage	In FY 2015, FMAPs range from 50% to 73.6%

"Medicaid's Role in Our Health Care System," KFF, https://www.kff.org/health-reform/issue-brief/medicaid-moving-forward/.

In the 32 states (and Washington, DC) that have chosen to expand Medicaid in the wake of the Affordable Care Act, individuals who earn 138% of the federal poverty level are eligible for services. This includes people who earn approximately $16,753 for an individual or $34,600 for a family of four in 2018. As of 2014, Medicaid and CHIP together covered just more than 29 million American children (Paradise, 2015).

Medicaid requires that states cover of a variety of services for all Medicaid recipients, from hospital and physician care to family planning and birth services. Non-emergency transportation to medical care must also be covered, which is a challenge in rural areas and for those without reliable transportation options. States can decide to cover other services as well, such as prescription drugs, home based services, and medical equipment; Table 11.3 describes these mandatory and optional services.

Medicaid **reimbursement rates**, payments that providers receive in return for services, are lower than those for other government-sponsored programs. For example, Medicaid pays only 75% of the rate that Medicare pays for the same services. As a result, it can be difficult to find physical and mental health care providers who will take Medicaid and treat Medicaid patients (NASW, 2018). Many states have gaps in services, in particular services provided by psychiatrists, professionals who treat substance use, and dentists (Paradise, 2015). In many states, clinical social workers cannot be reimbursed for services through Medicaid, which adds to both cost and availability challenges (NASW, 2018). Research also suggests that stigma, access to transportation, lack of care outside of usual business hours, and lack of enforcement by state Medicaid oversight agencies are hurdles to care (Paradise, 2015). Find out whether your state allows clinical social workers to be reimbursed through Medicaid. Where would you find that information? How could you affect this policy?

Reimbursement rates: Payments that health care providers receive in exchange for services rendered to patients

Indian Health Services

The federal government signed many treaties with Native American and Alaska Native populations that promise "all proper care and protection" in exchange for the lands and resources that the federal government has taken from tribes. Included in this care and protection is health care. This legal obligation, specifically through court cases such as *Cherokee Nation v. Georgia* in 1831, the Snyder Act of 1921, the Indian Health Care Improvement Act (IHCIA) of 1976, and IHCIA reauthorization in 2010 as part of the Affordable Care Act, has resulted in the provision of services through Indian Health Services (IHS).

TABLE 11.3 ■ Medicaid Benefits

Medicaid Benefits: Mandatory and Selected Optional Services	
Mandatory services	**Selected optional services**
• Inpatient and outpatient hospital services • Physician, midwife, and nurse practitioner services • Early and periodic screening, diagnosis, and treatment (EPSDT) for children up to age 21 • Laboratory and x-ray services • Family planning services and supplies • Federally qualified health center (FQHC) and rural health clinic (RHC) services • Freestanding birth center services (added by ACA) • Nursing facility (NF) services for individuals age 21+ • Home health services for individuals entitled to NF care • Tobacco cessation counseling and pharmacotherapy for pregnant women (added by ACA) • Nonemergency transportation to medical care	• Prescription drugs • Dental care • Durable medical equipment • Personal care services • Home and community-based services (HCBS)

Note. The services shown here apply to Medicaid beneficiaries who qualify under pre-ACA eligibility rules. Newly eligible adults under the ACA Medicaid expansion receive Alternative Benefit Plans (ABPs), which must include the 10 categories of "essential health benefits" specified in the ACA as well as family planning services and supplies, FQHC and RHC services, and nonemergency medical transportation, and provide parity between physical and mental health/substance use disorder benefits.

"Medicaid Benefits," **KFF,** https://www.kff.org/health-reform/issue-brief/medicaid-moving-forward/.

Indian Health Services care is significantly underfunded compared to all other federal government health expenditures. Figure 11.3 illustrates funding for health benefits per capita, showing that funding for each person who uses IHS is substantially lower than Medicare, veterans' services, Medicaid, and Federal Employees Health Benefits (FEHB) (the health insurance program for most federal employees). This is a particular concern given the lack of resources available for Native Americans and their chronic complex health and economic issues, including significant poverty and systematic oppression.

Today, more than half of the IHS budget is managed by individual tribes (Warne & Frizzell, 2014). These programs can also bill to Medicaid, Medicare, and Children's Health Insurance Programs, which can bring resources to this population and increase their access to services. Services are offered through three entities: directly from IHS, through programs managed by tribes, and through 34 Urban Indian Health Programs (UIHPs) that are run as nonprofits and funded primarily through federal grants, contracts, and Medicaid. Funding for these services has not kept up with the increase in health care costs. A 1998 estimate suggests that IHS had less than half of the resources needed to achieve its goals. IHS is not health insurance, so it is not covered by all the aspects of the Affordable Care Act (Warne & Frizzell, 2014), meaning that the disparities in access to treatment for this population could be exacerbated.[2]

[2]More information about the potential effects of the Affordable Care Act on health care for Native Americans and Alaska Natives can be found through the National Conference of State Legislatures (http://www.ncsl.org/documents/health/IndHlthCare.pdf) and through Indian Health Services (https://www.ihs.gov/aca/). These effects depend heavily on the levels at which programs are funded through Congress.

FIGURE 11.3 ■ Graph of Per-Capita Spending in 2010 on U.S. Government Health Programs

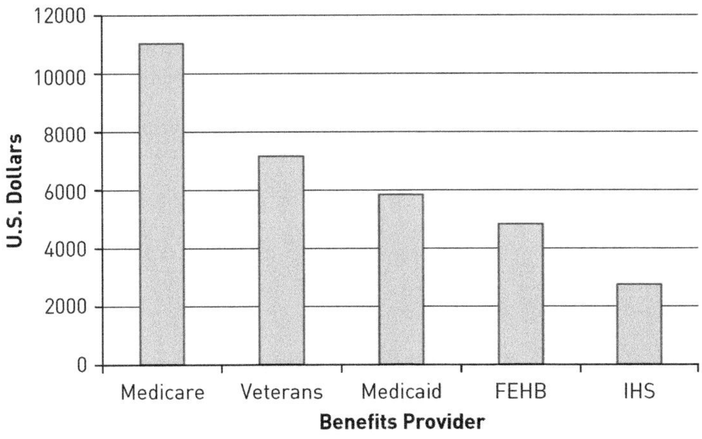

"National Tribal Budget Formulation Workgroup. National tribal budget recommendation for the Indian Health Service: fiscal year 2013 budget. US Department of Health and Human Services: Washington, DC; 2011.

Source: https://www.ncbi.nlm.nih.gov/pmc/articles/PMC4035886/

Veterans' Health

Veterans' health care in the United States covers a large range of veterans and health needs. The Veterans Administration (VA) was established in 1930. It expanded in 1944 after the passage of the Servicemen's Readjustment Act (also called the GI Bill of Rights) and became a cabinet-level Department of Veterans Affairs in 1989. In 1996, the Veterans Health Care Eligibility Reform Act transformed health care within the VA from primarily a series of hospitals to a health care system. This change resulted in the current system of 21 Veterans Integrated Service Networks (VISNs), which are designed to coordinate care and resources among veterans medical centers and other facilities, including more than 850 community-based outpatient clinics and more than 300 long-term care facilities, residential facilities, veterans' counseling centers, and home-care programs (Perlin, Kolodner, & Roswell, 2004). Veterans facilities offer care to veterans who need physical health care, mental health care, substance use services, and long-term care, and care to those who are homeless or at risk of homelessness.

REFLECTION

GETTING TO THE VHA

Find the closest VHA facility to you by using the VA website or another source. How long would it take a veteran in your town to be able to access services from this facility? Would the veteran be able to access that facility if they do not have access to a car? How do the answers to these questions affect the likelihood of veterans in your local area accessing services regularly?

Today, the Veterans Health Administration (VHA) has 1,240 health care facilities around the country that provide services to more than nine million veterans with a budget of approximately $68 billion. The VHA employs more than 300,000 full-time staff and trains more than 127,000 trainees in health professions, including social work, every year (U.S. Department of Veterans Affairs, n.d.).

TABLE 11.4 ■ List of Relevant Federal Laws

Topic	Laws	Oversight Agency	Website
Health system	Patient Protection and Affordable Care Act (often called the Affordable Care Act, ACA, or Obamacare)	Department of Health and Human Services (HHS)	https://www.hhs.gov/healthcare/about-the-aca/index.html
Senior Health	Social Security Act Amendments of 1965, which created Medicaid and Medicare Medicare Prescription Drug, Improvement, and Modernization Act of 2003, which created Medicare Part D	Department of Health and Human Services, Centers for Medicare and Medicaid Services (CMS)	https://www.cms.gov/
Mental health and substance use	Mental Health Parity and Addiction Equity Act	Department of Health and Human Services	https://www.hhs.gov/about/agencies/advisory-committees/mental-health-parity/task-force/resources/index.html
	Drug Addiction Treatment Act (DATA) of 2000	Substance Abuse and Mental Health Services Administration (SAMHSA) and Drug Enforcement Administration (DEA)	https://www.deadiversion.usdoj.gov/pubs/docs/dwp_buprenorphine.htm
Children's health	Balanced Budget Act of 1997/ Title XXI of Social Security, which created the Children's Health Insurance Program (CHIP)	Department of Health and Human Services, Centers for Medicare and Medicaid Services	https://www.insurekidsnow.gov/
Maternal and child health	Child Nutrition Act of 1966 Amendment, which created the Special Supplemental Nutrition Program for Women, Infants, and Children (WIC)	United States Department of Agriculture Food and Nutrition Service	https://www.fns.usda.gov/wic/women-infants-and-children-wic
	Food Stamps Act of 1964, which created what is now called the Supplemental Nutrition Assistance Program (SNAP)	United States Department of Agriculture Food and Nutrition Service	https://www.fns.usda.gov/snap/supplemental-nutrition-assistance-program-snap
Native American/ Alaska Native health care	Indian Health Care Improvement Act of 1976	Department of Health and Human Services, Indian Health Services (IHS)	https://www.ihs.gov/
Veterans' health	Veterans Health Care Eligibility Reform Act of 1996	Department of Veterans Affairs (VA), Veterans Health Administration	https://www.va.gov/health/

POLICY INFORMED BY ALTERNATIVE LENSES

Many controversies in U.S. health care policy today concern how services are delivered. If you return to the debate from the beginning of the chapter about health care as a right or a privilege, you can see that people and organizations see the problem and potential solutions from fundamentally different perspectives. Here, we look at some alternatives from perspectives emphasizing capitalism as opposed to perspectives emphasizing human rights. We also use the German health insurance system and Portuguese response to substance use problems as two examples of different approaches to health care and health insurance.

Capitalism

A **capitalist** approach to health care argues that using the private market to deliver services creates a system that is more innovative, less bureaucratic, and less prone to fraud than systems that rely on government-provided health care. Those who support capitalist health care policies emphasize individual choices, competition, and substantial limits to government programs. Examples of capitalist health approaches include managed care, high-deductible plans, and health savings accounts (Gratzer, 2006). For example, Robinson and Casalino (1996) suggest that **managed care**, which moves health decision making to a competitive system of private actors, can create a better and more efficient coordination of services if implemented correctly with "economies of scale, efficient risk bearing, reductions in transaction costs, and the development of capabilities for innovation" (p. 18). Managed care has been added to government health programs such as Medicare Part C and Medicaid and informs employer-sponsored health coverage (NASW, 2018). In a general sense, managed care is the mechanism that organizes health care providers (including social workers) into systems. Within those systems, providers agree to set fees for services or payments per client (Vandiver, 2013). Proponents highlight its cost-effectiveness, and opponents point out that it struggles to manage complex care, including care for those who have mental health and substance use needs (NASW, 2018).

Capitalism: A belief system that privileges private ownership of goods and property for profit, rather than by the state. Capitalism also sees individualism and competition as drivers of economic growth and overall prosperity.

Managed care: A system of health decision making by a competitive system of private actors

Human Rights

A human rights approach to health looks at the positive and negative effects of health policies, programs, and practices on **human rights** (Mann et al., 1994), rights inherent to all human beings, regardless of race, sex, nationality, ethnicity, language, religion, or any other status. Take the question of collecting data about a person's HIV status. That information can be crucial in developing programs and policies to address HIV, but is that information collected in ways that protect the privacy and safety of those who are vulnerable because of their HIV status? We could also look at ways in which health policies prioritize different problems and whether those decisions about priorities and funding are discriminatory in their intent or impact. Are we equitably funding breast cancer prevention in communities of color and predominantly white communities? Are we providing health services in the languages spoken by those who are affected by the problem? Do we teach our doctors that members of one group feel pain differently than those of another group, and therefore provide some people with less adequate pain management than others?

Human rights: Rights inherent to all human beings, regardless of race, sex, nationality, ethnicity, language, religion, or any other status

Another aspect of the human rights approach to health is to examine ways in which human rights violations affect health. Mann et al. (1994) note that "[t]orture, imprisonment under inhumane conditions, or trauma associated with witnessing summary executions, torture, rape or mistreatment of others have been shown to lead to severe, probably life-long effects on physical, mental and social well-being" (p. 17) and suggest that other less severe human rights violations also have significant health implications.

A challenge of human rights approaches is that they are nuanced and complex, which creates many opportunities for misunderstandings or misapplication through the process of passing and implementing policy. These approaches also have the potential to add cost and time to the process of providing health care. This approach is aligned with social work values, but may require significant shifts in the ways that health systems and the public think about health care.

International Alternatives: Germany and Portugal

Under the German system of health insurance, all citizens and permanent residents are required to obtain health insurance through a combination of public and private services and pay a mandatory contribution of 14.6% of their gross wages. This "universal" system does not cover temporary residents or undocumented immigrants, although the latter are eligible for coverage for pregnancy, childbirth, and acute conditions. An analysis by Bozorgmehr and Razum (2015) suggests that the cost to the system of excluding asylum-seekers and refugees from care is higher than the cost of granting this group regular access to care. Regardless of cost, including asylum-seekers and refugees in health insurance is not currently a politically popular policy option.

Financial responsibility and decision making in Germany are shared between government, for-profit, and nonprofit entities. In 2015, the act to Strengthen SHI Health Care Provision and Act to Strengthen Health Promotion and Prevention were passed to increase services in rural areas, shorten the time that Germans wait for specialist appointments to a maximum of 4 weeks, encourage innovative care, and improve preventative care and health promotion (Blumel & Busse, 2016).

Another alternative approach, this one for substance use disorders, can be found in Portugal. In the 1990s, 1% of Portugal's population was addicted to heroin, one of the worst rates in the world. While other countries, such as the United States, have turned to the criminal justice system to address addiction, Portugal took a different path. Since 2001, possession and use of all drugs are considered a health issue rather than a crime, unless the person has more than a 10-day supply. As Dr. João Goulão, head of Portugal's General-Directorate for Intervention on Addictive Behaviours and Dependencies (SICAD), says, "We are dealing with a chronic relapsing disease, and this is a disease like any other. I do not put a diabetic in jail, for instance" (Frayer, 2017, n.p.). Since the passage of this law, drug cases are down 75%, death from drug-related causes are five times lower than the average in other European countries, and drug-related HIV infections have decreased by 95%.

Decriminalization: The process redefining a behavior or activity that has been designated as illegal so that it is no longer a criminal offense, even if it is not legal

The Portuguese government emphasizes that they have decriminalized drug use, not legalized it. The term **decriminalize** describes the process of changing a system so that something that has been illegal is no longer considered a criminal offense, even if it is not deemed legal. This means that drug use is still illegal, but it is considered an administrative violation rather than a criminal violation; drug trafficking is still a prosecutable criminal offense (Greenwald, 2009). The policy remains popular with both Portuguese politicians and the general public (Frayer, 2017; Greenwald, 2009).

OPPORTUNITIES FOR ADVOCACY

Health care policy includes both written policy and implementation. Any discussion of health advocacy should include the ways in which people of color have been harmed by organized health care in the United States, and the resulting, understandable, suspicion that members of these communities have toward the health care system and health care providers. This suspicion often extends to social workers. This section provides a few examples of these previous harms, as well as a discussion of current issues and areas for advocacy.

Discriminatory Treatment of People of Color in Health Care

There is a long history of discrimination and abuse against people of color by the health care system (Chen, Vargas-Bustamante, Mortensen, & Ortega, 2016). For example, students of medical history are often introduced to J. Marion Sims as the father of modern gynecology, but critics have pointed out that the medical procedures he pioneered were tested on enslaved women without the use of anesthesia (Wasserman, Flannery, & Clair, 2007). The women who were the subjects of these experiments would not have been able to consent to the research. Those who study research ethics also document how the Tuskegee and Guatemala syphilis experiments keep communities of color from believing that public health officials have their best interests at heart (Rodriguez & García, 2013). In the Tuskegee syphilis study, the U.S. Public Health Service withheld treatment from African American men who had syphilis without their knowledge or consent. In Guatemala, the U.S. Public Health Service infected with syphilis many people with mental illness, prisoners, and people in the military, in order to study them. Those who study genetic research can attest that Henrietta Lacks and her family were unaware that her genetic code was still alive and actively used in medical research after her death (Skloot, 2010).

In the United States, racial and ethnic minority groups are affected by discrimination in many ways:

- Inadequate medical care given because of stigmatizing assumptions about the ways people of different races feel pain (Hoffman et al., 2016)
- Less medical research about health conditions, treatment, and outcomes
- Lack of access to preventative care
- Higher rates of death from diabetes, health disease, infant mortality, cancer, HIV/AIDS, childbirth, and more (NASW, 2018)

For example, black women are 243% more likely to die of causes related to pregnancy or childbirth than white women (Martin & Montagne, 2017).

Imagine that you are a social worker in a hospital. What are some of the ways you might see discrimination play out in your workplace? What are some tactics you can use in that setting to address discrimination as you see it occur?

Nutrition Programs

Access to nutritious and adequate food is an important aspect of health. U.S. policy often deals with nutrition separately from health, through agencies such as the U.S. Department of Agriculture. One example of this is the Special Supplemental Nutrition Program for Women, Infants, and Children (WIC), which became law in 1975 (PL 94-105). WIC is a program for pregnant and postpartum women and young children who are at risk of nutritional problems and is "designed to influence lifetime nutrition and health behaviors in a targeted, high-risk population" (National WIC Association, n.d., para. 1). WIC provides supplemental food packages to pregnant women who are low-income until 6 months **postpartum** (after giving birth) and to their children until age 5. As a part of President Johnson's Great Society Programs in 1964, the Food Stamps program was created by the Food Stamps Act of 1964 to give agricultural surplus to poor families (Social Security Administration, n.d.). In the late 1980s, the federal government began to mandate that states develop **electronic benefit transfer systems** (EBT), which allow beneficiaries to pay for their benefits with a card that looks like a credit card, making it easier and less stigmatizing for participants to use their benefits. In 2008, the name Food Stamps was changed to Supplemental Nutrition Assistance Program or SNAP, although many people still use the original name. Since its creation in the 1960s, Food Stamps/SNAP has been expanded and contracted many times depending on funding and the state of the overall economy. As of August 2019, SNAP provided benefits to approximately 33.4 million Americans in just under 17 million households, many of whom are working, people with disabilities, older adults, and young children, on a monthly basis.

Postpartum: The time following childbirth

Electronic benefit transfer system (EBT): Technology that allows money to be automatically placed on an encoded payment card that can be used to pay for goods or services

This program cost $36 billion in Fiscal Year 2019 and provided an average of $135 per person per month or $1.40 per meal (Center on Budget and Policy Priorities, 2018). Eligible families must have a gross income at or below 130% of the poverty line (today that would be $20,784 per year for a family of three) and have limited or no assets. Adults without families may be eligible, but, generally, they must work at least 20 hours a week to be able to receive benefits ("Snap Data Tables," 2019). The delivery of SNAP benefits varies from state to state; for more information about the SNAP program in your state, visit https://www.cbpp.org/research/food-assistance/snap-online-a-review-of-state-government-snap-websites.

Universal Health Care

Universal health care: Health system that provides quality medical services to all regardless of their ability to pay

Single-payer health care: Access to the full continuum of physical and mental health services for all people regardless of age, race, ethnicity, religion, gender or gender expression, sexual orientation, cognitive or physical functioning, socioeconomic or immigration status, or geographic location

Universal health care refers to systems that provide quality medical services to all, regardless of their ability to pay. The NASW (2018) supports a version of this, including proposals for a single-payer health insurance system, to achieve the goals of Healthy People 2020, improve patient outcomes, advance the health of the overall population, and reduce health care costs. **Single-payer health care** proposals include "access to the full continuum of physical and mental health services for all people regardless of age, race, ethnicity, religion, gender or gender expression, sexual orientation, cognitive or physical functioning, socioeconomic or immigration status, or geographic location" (NASW, 2018, p. 149). Such policies are common in other countries but are still hotly debated in the United States. For example, Australia, France, Germany, Great Britain, and Switzerland all have higher levels of coverage than the United States with good health outcomes (Carroll & Frakt, 2017). The debate on this issue tends to emphasize two main concerns. First, those who support universal health care see health care as a right, while those who oppose it generally view health care as a privilege or commodity. Second, the cost of universal health care is seen as a negative by those who believe that universal health care would be too costly for the government to provide.

DISCUSSION

RECOMMENDATION ON UNIVERSAL HEALTH CARE

You are the staff member for a social worker who is a state legislator. She has asked you to research the most recent proposal for universal health care in your state (it might be called "Medicare for All" or "single-payer health care"). Write a memo with the pros and cons of this legislation. Compare your list with a classmate, and together make a recommendation. How would you recommend she vote?

Final Discussion

Now that you have finished reading this chapter, reread the vignette at the beginning. Based on what you have learned, answer the following questions. Point to specific references in the chapter that help you answer these questions. Consider how different theories inform the response to these questions.

1. What policies are relevant to this vignette?
2. Would the outcome of Jamie's case be any different if he lived in a country with universal health care?
3. What factors should a state take into consideration when deciding whether to cover this medication?
4. What social work values are relevant to this vignette?
5. What role might race, class, gender, and other aspects of identity play in this vignette?

12

DISABILITY POLICY

LEARNING OBJECTIVES

12.1: Illustrate the history of disability policy and social views of people with disabilities in the U.S.

12.2: Analyze the effect of the current federal laws and policies on the lives of people with disabilities

12.3: Compare and contrast alternative approaches to disability-related policy

12.4: Determine opportunities for advocacy regarding language, awareness, and self-advocacy

This chapter begins with a discussion of disability. What is a disability? How has disability been constructed over time? Using a historical lens, this chapter examines intersectionality in relation to disability policy, by recognizing that discrimination as a result of disability status often overlaps with discrimination as a result of gender and race. It explores the history of disability policy in the United States, including the influence of the disability rights movement in lobbying for civil rights, inclusion, and visibility. This chapter also describes the social work profession's connection to disabilities and the historical role that social workers have played in processes that influence the availability and scope of benefits for different groups (i.e., veterans, those with physical disabilities, and people with mental disabilities and substance use disorders). It examines existing policies that have been designed to address problems associated with disabilities, including Social Security Disability Insurance, the Americans with Disabilities Act, the Individuals with Disabilities Education Act, the Rehabilitation Act, and provisions in federal housing policies that make people with disabilities eligible for subsidized housing. This chapter then looks at the challenges associated with implementing current disability related policies. Last, it provides avenues for advocacy in the field of disability policy.

According to the United States' Census Bureau, in 2014, 27% of U.S. residents had disabilities and 18% had severe disabilities (Taylor, 2018). As people age, they are more likely to become disabled. According to the Institute on Disability at the University of New Hampshire, approximately 6% of children ages 5 to 17, 11% of 18 to 64 year olds, and 35% of people over 65 had a disability. People with disabilities are approximately twice as likely to be unemployed than people without disabilities. In 2016, only around 36% of people with disabilities were in the workforce as compared to approximately 77% of nondisabled people (Institute on Disability, 2017). If you do not have a disability right now, you are likely to at some point, or to be living with or caring for someone who has a disability. As a social worker, even if the field in which you work is not explicitly designed to serve people with disabilities, it is likely that a large number of your clients will be people with disabilities or need to know about services for people with disabilities to care for their loved ones. Policies that have been designed to address the needs of people with disabilities will be crucial to your work as an ethical effective social worker.

Some, particularly parents of children with disabilities, have questioned the use of the term *disability* and have suggested it be replaced with the term *special needs* (Gernsbacher, Raimond, Balinghasav, & Boston, 2016). We chose to use the word disability in this chapter because all major statutes and laws require people to meet the definition of the term disability to qualify for benefits and all of the major databases that collect data on people with disabilities also use that language. The term special needs has been falling out of favor with disability rights advocates. For example, disability rights activist and blogger Emily Ladau (n.d.) challenges disability euphemisms, including the term special needs. She writes, "Everyone has needs. What makes mine so 'special' just because I have a disability? Nothing." She questions why people are trying to find a word to replace disability rather than allowing people with disabilities to embrace their disabilities and live with them. Research on a sample of over 500 adults comparing the terms special needs and disabilities found people were more likely to associate developmental disabilities and cognitive slowness with the term special needs rather than the word disability, and they found that the term disability led to greater inclusion (Gernsbacher et al., 2016). As with any language, when there is discrimination toward a population, words that are meant to be inclusive can become associated with stigma over time. Throughout this chapter, we generally use the term disability. As discussed in the advocacy section, we recommend that when working with people with disabilities, you talk with them about the language they prefer, just like you might do for members of other groups.

Vignette: Navigating School and Benefit Systems

Based on what you know from the media or your personal, work, or volunteer experiences, think about the following questions as you read the vignette. When you finish the vignette, answer the questions below.

1. What other services that are not discussed below might the family be eligible for, both in school and outside of school?
2. Are there any child welfare concerns, and if so, what are they?
3. What do you think the role of a school social worker would be in this case? How do you think he or she could advocate for Bob to get support in school?
4. Is there another agency outside the school system that might be able to help Bob and his family?
5. What role might race, class, and gender, or other aspects of identity play in this vignette?

Jane is 35. She has two children, ages 14 and 16. She married her high school boyfriend and had children right after graduation, so she has never worked full-time outside of the home. After five years of marriage, her husband's domestic violence became so brutal that she suffered a traumatic brain injury. She left and divorced her husband. For two years, her parents took care of her and her children while she recovered from her injury. Her parents were sent back to Haiti because immigration authorities discovered they had overstayed their visas. Jane and her children now live alone. Though she is generally able to function and parent her children, she gets frequent migraines. As a result of her headaches and other related injuries, she is unable to work and receives Supplemental Security Income (SSI).

Jane's son, Bob, has always struggled in school and was diagnosed with a severe learning disability as a result of his low IQ and difficulty learning new tasks when he was in elementary school. He is now 16. In his most recent school evaluation, his IQ rose to the low normal range and, as a result, his special education services were suspended and he stopped receiving SSI benefits. Jane relied on both her and her son's benefits to pay the rent for their small two-bedroom apartment and for food. She has been on a waitlist for a Section 8 housing voucher for the past 8 years and is nowhere near the top of the list. She also worries that even if she could get subsidized housing she would not be able to find someone to accept the voucher.

When Bob's benefits were denied, she started pressuring him to try to get a job. He applied for work as a clerk in the local grocery store and the local dollar store but was not hired. He developed anxiety, and his mother encouraged him to stop attending school. Without extra support, school had been even more difficult, so he was happy to stop going to school. You are the school social worker and must figure out how to address this situation. In your state, at 16 Bob is not mandated to attend school, but you are worried about his future and would like him to get a high school diploma. You realize that without the diploma, his prospects are much bleaker than they would be if he was able to graduate from high school.

HISTORY AND SOCIAL CONSTRUCTION OF U.S. DISABILITY POLICY

Disability has had many different definitions over the years. In this section, we look at different constructions and definitions of disability, as well as the evolution of U.S. disability policy.

Models of Disability

An understanding of disability can be broken into four models: the medical model, the social model, the functional limitations model (the Nagi model), and the World Health Organization's (WHO) international classification of functioning model (Mitra, 2006).

The medical model assumes that disability is experienced only by the person with the disability and that it is caused by a medical problem or condition that requires some treatment or rehabilitation. It assumes that the goal is for the person with the disability to eventually be able to function "as a normal person does" (Mitra, 2006, p. 237). The Nagi (1976) model refers to a disability as "inability or limitations in performing social roles and activities such as in relation to work, family, or to independent living" (p. 411). This suggests a **relativist** view in which a person's disability is defined in part by societal expectations of what people should be doing (e.g., relative to others). For example, if you are born in a culture where women are not taught to read and write, it is not a disability if a woman cannot hold a pencil or has a reading disability, but if a woman is born someplace where everyone is expected to be able to read and write, these limitations would be considered disabling. In contrast, the **social model** suggests that disability "is created by the social environment and requires social change" (Mitra, 2006, p. 237) rather than focusing on the individual as the source of the problem. In other words, it is not the individual with the disability who is limited, but rather the environment that limits the individual. For example, in the case of a person who uses a wheelchair, this model would suggest that the problem is that a particular building is inaccessible rather than that the person using the wheelchair is operating outside the norm. The most comprehensive definition of disability is that of the World Health Organization. Their Classification of Functioning, Disability, and Health (WHO, 2002) uses a biopsychosocial model that suggests that disability is a result of

Relativist: An approach in which societal expectations of what one should be doing are defined in part in relation to what others are doing

Social model: approach that views the environment rather than any particular individual attribute or functioning as a limiting factor

> three levels of human functioning . . . functioning at the level of body or body part, the whole person, and the whole person in a social context. Disability therefore involves dysfunction at one or more of these same levels: impairments, activity limitations and participation restrictions. (p. 10)

Under this definition, disability is a result of the interaction between the individual and the environment. This model incorporates aspects of the medical, functional, and social models of disability. With this model, **activity** refers to the execution of a task or action by an individual. **Activity limitations** refers to difficulties an individual may have executing activities, generally focused on activities of daily living. **Impairments** are defined by WHO as problems in body function or structure resulting in an inability to do something that a *typical* person is expected to be able to do. **Participation restrictions** refer to problems individuals may experience in involvement in life situations.

Activity: Execution of a task or action by an individual

Activity limitations: Difficulties an individual may have executing activities, generally focused on activities of daily living

Impairments: Problems in body function or structure resulting in an inability to do something that people are generally expected to be able to do

Participation restrictions: Problems individuals may experience in involvement in life situations

Many U.S. disability-related policies are based on the medical model and the Nagi or functional limitations model. None rely on the WHO's international classification of functioning or the social model. Federal laws use various categories of disabilities for different purposes. The U.S. Census has categories of disability related to hearing, vision, ambulatory function, cognitive function, independent living, and self-care. One category of disabilities that has been the subject of advocacy includes invisible or *non-apparent* disabilities. Invisible or **non-apparent disabilities** are those that cannot necessarily be seen by others and encompass a wide range of diagnoses, including dyslexia, Crohn's Disease, chronic pain, mental illness, and attention-deficit/hyperactivity disorder (ADHD). Many invisible/non-apparent disabilities do not fit into clear cut legal categories. In addition, to be protected against discrimination and to receive accommodations, people with these disabilities must disclose them in the workplace. As you can imagine, people with mental illness may avoid disclosure because of the cultural stigma associated with the disability (Prince, 2017). In addition, it may be stressful for people with invisible disabilities to have to convince others that they have a disability (Davis, 2005).

Non-apparent disabilities: Disabilities that cannot necessarily be seen by others and encompass a wide range of diagnoses, including dyslexia, Crohn's Disease, chronic pain, mental illness, and attention-deficit/hyperactivity disorder

The Early U.S. History of Disability

During Colonial times, people with disabilities were treated with a mixture of fear, disgust, pity, and fascination. People with disabilities had no basic human rights and were seen as a burden because of their dependence on their families and their towns. During the 1700s and 1800s, people with disabilities were seen in such a negative light that there was a belief that having a child with a disability was a bad omen. Sometimes parents were even accused of witchcraft and were punished (Neuhaus & Smith, 2014).

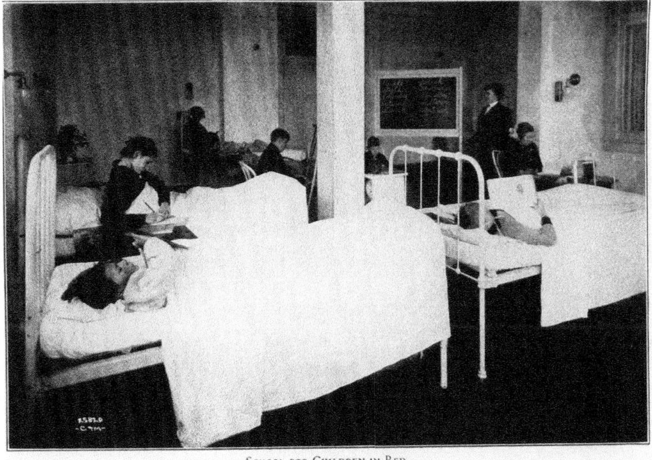

Edith Gertrude Solenberger

PHOTO 12.1 Children's Orthopedic Hospital, Seattle, Washington, 1914

From the 1880s until about the 1970s, ugly laws prohibited beggars and those who were "unsightly" from being in public. The laws stated that those who are

> diseased, maimed, mutilated or in any way deformed so as to be an unsightly or disgusting object, or an improper person to be allowed in or on the streets, highways, thoroughfares or public places in this city shall not therein or thereon expose himself or herself to public view. (Coco, 2010, p. 23)

The history of disability and mental illness are intertwined during this time. In the early 1800s, the first classifications for mental illness were recognized: dementia, melancholy, and mania with and without delirium. In the 1800s, states began to form large asylums for people with mental illness and physical, developmental, and intellectual disabilities. The mid-1800s saw the rise of almshouses with terrible living conditions. Dorothea Dix was one of the first advocates for people with cognitive disabilities and mental illness. Dix fought for better living conditions and challenged the stigma that people with disabilities and mental illness were helpless and a burden (Switzer, 2003). Schools for children with orthopedic disabilities were also founded during this time (see Photo 12.1).

Eugenics sterilization laws emerged in the early 1900s, and the eugenics movement forced sterilization onto people with disabilities (Baynton, 2011). The eugenics movement was based on the theories of Sir Francis Galton in England. This movement held that the human species could be improved by selective breeding practices such as forced sterilization of those with undesired traits such as "the feeble minded" or "insane" (O'Brien, 2011). The eugenics movement was supported by the 1927 Supreme Court ruling in *Buck v. Bell.* It allowed states to impose forced sterilization on people with disabilities, the poor, and minority women. This case has not been explicitly overturned, which suggests that if states chose they can still engage in forced sterilization of people deemed to have limited cognitive ability.

Eugenics sterilization: Sterilization carried out against people with disabilities in an effort to rid humans of "bad genes"

Social Security Act and Disability Rights Movements Begin

During the early 1900s, public health emergencies such as large polio outbreaks left many people dead or with permanent disabilities. As a result of World War I, there was also an increase in the number of people with disabilities. The first government policies designed to support people with disabilities were for veterans who had become disabled

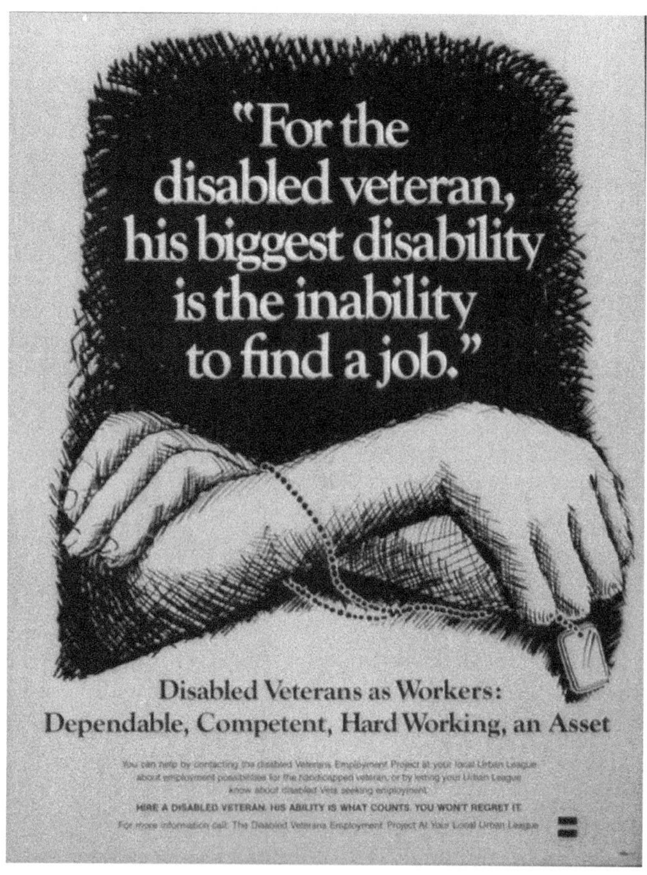

PHOTO 12.2 Poster supporting access to employment for veterans with disabilities

as a result of service to their country (see Photo 12.2). Franklin D. Roosevelt, who used a wheelchair after he was diagnosed with polio, was the first president to have a known disability, but even this was hidden somewhat from the public. In 1935, he signed the Social Security Act that provided support for those who couldn't work as a result of age. During the Great Depression, a group called the League for the Physically Handicapped, comprised primarily of people with polio and cerebral palsy, staged a sit-in in New York to protest their exclusion from New Deal jobs provided through the Works Progress Administration (WPA). During World War II, veterans began to advocate for support and disability rights grew (Shapiro, 1994).

It was not until 1956 that Social Security benefits were added for those aged 50 to 64 who could no longer work due to disability and their adult children. In 1960, Social Security was expanded to cover all workers with disabilities and their adult children (Social Security Administration, n.d.a). In 1972, Geraldo Rivera's documentary, *Willowbrook: The Last Great Disgrace*, brought light to the horrendous conditions of institutions for people with intellectual, cognitive, developmental, and mental disabilities. This sparked an advocacy movement that led to the creation of the Protection and Advocacy (P & A) System in the Developmental Disabilities Assistance and Bill of Rights Act (1975); the Education for All Handicapped Children Act, (1975), which was later renamed the Individuals with Disabilities Education Act (IDEA); and the Civil Rights of Institutionalized Persons Act (CRIPA) (1980). The P & A systems are federally funded state agencies designed to advocate on behalf of people with disabilities. Much of the work that they do is provide legal support and representation to underserved populations to help them navigate the legal system (U.S. Department of Health and Human Services, 2018). These agencies can often be a useful support for social workers who are working with people with disabilities who believe that the civil rights of their clients are not being protected. They may also be useful if you are not sure whether your client's treatment is simply a difficult challenge or may be discriminatory.

Modern Disability Rights Movement

It was not until the 1960s that the modern disability rights movement began in earnest. Many people with disabilities had watched the African American and women's civil rights movements and wondered why they too could not be fully included as citizens. In the early 1960s, Ed Roberts, a young California man with paraplegia and an iron lung as a result of polio in his early teens, finished junior college and wanted to pursue a 4-year degree. Initially, the Department of Rehabilitation Services refused to pay for his college tuition at the University of California-Berkeley because they felt that he would never be able to work. When he was denied the funding, the president of the college as well as his advisor and the dean of students advocated for the Department of Rehabilitation to support his education. When their initial efforts were unsuccessful, they published an op-ed in the local paper, and the resulting negative attention changed the decision. Once the Department of Rehabilitation agreed to pay for Roberts to go to college, he had to get Berkeley to admit him. To do that, he also had to figure out where he could live. He spoke to many people, and finally, the Director of Student Health Services agreed to allow him to live on a floor of the hospital. As a result of California law, he was able to hire state-funded attendants to help him dress and eat. Others who learned of his success began to apply to Berkeley, and the university accepted more students with severe physical disabilities. In the fall of 1970, Roberts founded the Physically Disabled Students Program (PDSP) as a mechanism for people with disabilities to support and mentor students with disabilities and prevent them from dropping out of college. The mission of this organization, providing people with disabilities with control of their own lives, became the foundation of the independent living movement. Employees of the PDSP then founded the Center for Independent Living. This center, which was run by people with disabilities, identified the lack of integration of people with disabilities as a social problem rather than an individual medical issue, and had a primary goal of community integration (Shapiro, 1994).

The first federal law to protect the civil rights of people with disabilities was Section 504 of the Rehabilitation Act of 1973 (known as Section 504), based on a bill drafted by Senator Hubert Humphrey from Minnesota and Representative Charles Vanic from Ohio to expand the Civil Rights Act that had failed as a stand-alone bill. The proposal called for the expansion of the Civil Rights Act to include people with both physical and behavioral disabilities (at the time called physical and mental handicaps) and became the basis for Section 504 of the Rehabilitation Act. This law replaced and expanded the Vocational Rehabilitation Act and because it required no additional federal funding was not controversial. According to the well-known disability rights author David Shapiro (1994), "the first civil rights bill for disabled people . . . [was not the] result of a hard fought battle. Disabled people did not even ask for it." (pp. 64–65). At the time of its introduction, members of the disability rights movement had been more focused on litigation as a strategy to gain civil rights, but when they learned what was in the bill, they immediately began to support it (Shapiro, 1994). Once the law was passed, the Berkley disability rights community was frustrated by the failure of the federal government to implement regulations and had a sit-in at the San Francisco office of Health and Human Services (Scotch, 1984).

Though passed by both houses of Congress, Nixon originally vetoed the revision of the entire Rehabilitation Act suggesting that the costs would be too high. Interestingly, there was no testimony about Section 504, the portion that includes the statement:

> No otherwise qualified handicapped individual in the United States, as defined in Section 7(6), shall, solely by reason of his handicap, be excluded from the participation in, be denied the benefits of, or be subjected to discrimination under any program or activity receiving Federal financial assistance. (n. p.)

In 1973, the Rehabilitation Act was revised and the overall funding was reduced. Nixon signed it into law. Section 504 was left unchanged (Scotch, 2001).

In the late 1970s, the same people who started the independent living movement at Berkeley founded the Disability Rights Education and Defense Fund. In 1980, this group sent their first lobbyist, Patrisha Wright, to Washington, DC. In 1986, the National Council on the Handicapped, whose members had been appointed by President Ronald Reagan, issued a report recommending a law be passed to promote equal opportunity for people with

National Archives

PHOTO 12.3 President Bush signing the Americans with Disabilities Act in 1990

disabilities. Their report led to the introduction of the Americans with Disabilities Act, written by Senators Harkin and Kerry, working with Wright, which passed and was signed into law by President George HW Bush in 1990 (see Photo 12.3). A broad, nearly universal, coalition of disability rights organizations supported the bill's passage (Scotch, 2001). As Shapiro (1994) notes, the fight for civil rights for people with disabilities was fought by "a largely invisible, almost underground, movement" (p. 117). This movement challenged the medical model of disability that assumed people needed to be treated or cared for and focused more on integration and changing society to accept people with differences as equals.

CURRENT DISABILITY POLICIES

The following section reviews existing benefits and protections that are available to people with disabilities. It starts with a discussion of benefits that include veterans' benefits, Supplemental Security Income, and Social Security Disability Insurance. It then describes the civil rights benefits that are provided by the Rehabilitation Act of 1973 and the Americans with Disabilities Act. It explains the educational services that are available as a result of the Individuals with Disabilities Act and concludes with a discussion of **self-directed** medical services. Table 12.1 highlights significant federal policies that affect people with disabilities and their families.

Self-directed services: Services that provide the option for people to select staff, services, organizations and scheduling of services that they believe works best for them

Veterans' Benefits

The first federally established disability benefits were designed for veterans. There was a belief that because many veterans were disabled as a result of their service to the nation, the nation should help them, in other words, they were worthy of assistance (Skocpol, 1992). The first veterans' benefits were provided by the Pilgrims who provided aid for veterans injured defending the colonies. They passed a law that demanded the colonies assist soldiers who were maimed during the war with the Pequot Indians (U.S. Department of Veteran Affairs, 2018). During the Revolutionary War, the Pension Act of 1776 was passed to provide money for injured veterans. As a result of the Civil War, in 1862, pensions were provided for disabled veterans (Skocpol, 1992). Following World War I, the Veterans Bureau was established to address the needs of veterans, and veterans' benefits were expanded to include vocational rehabilitation and mental health services for "**shell shock**" (which we now call posttraumatic stress disorder) in addition to previously existing pensions. An expansion of military hospitals accommodated the needs of injured veterans (Day, 2006). As a result of World War II, there were many more visibly disabled adults in the United States. A group called the Paralyzed Veterans of America was formed to advocate to improve their access to medical care and rehabilitation services. Their advocacy led to the creation of a Presidential Committee on Employment of the Handicapped, which was designed to encourage businesses to hire disabled veterans. This was the start of the independent living movement discussed in the previous section (Shapiro, 1994). In 1944, the GI Bill was passed, which provided money for veterans' education.

Shell shock: A clinical and colloquial term used to describe what is now generally diagnosed as posttraumatic stress

This benefit was provided for both disabled and nondisabled veterans and led to an increase in the number of students with disabilities attending college.

Social Security Disability Insurance and SSI

Prior to the creation of Social Security Disability Insurance, many states provided pensions for people with specific disabilities. For example, in the 1920s and '30s, 23 states provided relief assistance for people who were blind. Some advocates, such as Robert Irwin who led the American Foundation for the Blind at that time, were opposed to automatic pensions and specialized schooling because he believed it disempowered people (Shapiro, 1994). The 1935 Social Security Act included Aid to the Blind. It was not until 1956 that it began to include aid for people with other disabilities (Day, 2006).

Currently, Social Security disability programs provide cash assistance to people who are deemed to have long-term disabilities and are unable to work. Those who cannot work can apply for benefits through two programs. Social Security Disability Insurance (SSDI) is a program for people who have sufficient work history, their widows or widowers if they are at least 50, and dependent children, as well as people who were designated as disabled before they turned 22 years old. Supplemental Security Income (SSI) is a program for people who are in poverty, regardless of work history. SSI provides financial assistance to people with severe disabilities, no matter their age or work history as long as they are sufficiently disabled and income eligible (Social Security Office of Policy, 2005/2006). When applying for SSI or SSDI, eligibility criteria include: the disability must be long term, meaning it has lasted at least 12 months; the disability must be sufficiently limiting, which is determined by a review of medical and school records; and for SSI, the family income and resources must be sufficiently low (SSA, 2018). If the person with a disability has been able to work, there is a cap on the income that he or she can earn and retain eligibility. As of 2019, the cap was $1,220/month for those without visual impairment and $2,040/month for those who are visually impaired.

Every 3 years, applications must be reviewed for those aged 17 and under, and supporting evidence must be provided, or the family will be at risk of losing the benefits. Plan to Achieve Self-Support (PASS) is a program that enables those receiving SSI to save money for resources that will help them work, such as education, training, or other items or services that will help with a work goal (Social Security Administration, n.d.b). As noted in Chapters 9 and 10, respectively, Social Security also provides survivor's benefits and retirement income.

Some problems associated with SSDI and SSI are that the definition of disability is strict, and the rules for determining whether someone qualifies as having a disability according to Social Security are complicated. Many must hire lawyers and appeal initial disability determinations, often waiting years before they become eligible for SSDI or SSI (Social Security Administration, Office of Policy, 2005/2006). As a result of the Deficit Reduction Act of 2005 (PL 109-171), retroactive payments of more than three times the monthly benefit must be made in installments. These installments can be equivalent to no more than three times the monthly benefit at 6-month intervals unless the individual receiving the benefit can prove that he or she has incurred debt and will experience undue hardship (Social Security Administration, 2018). For example, if someone is owed $20,000 in back payments but should only have been getting $800 a month, the person will not be able to get more than $2,400 paid every six months rather than a lump sum back payment. As a result, it could take up to 10 years for the person to receive all their back payments. If someone has been unable to pay their mortgage and needs the money more quickly, they can get it, but it requires the completion of more forms and another administrative process, again delaying the actual payment. As a result, delays in retroactive payments can produce further hardship.

Another limitation is that neither program adequately addresses chronic illnesses that may flare up for less than a year, making people temporarily unable to work but not long enough to be eligible for SSI or SSDI. In addition, because you must receive SSDI for a year before you become eligible for Medicare, people with disabilities who begin to receive SSDI or SSI have perverse motivation to remain or continue to claim disabled status even if they could technically return to the labor market. Many are ineligible for Medicaid or Medicare as a result of assets or earnings that are too high, thus disqualifying them from public coverage until they deplete their assets or reduce their employment earnings. If a person chooses to return to the labor market and he or she has a flare up of their disability, the person has no recourse and must await a redetermination of disability, often foregoing income and access to health care in the interim.

Section 504 of the Rehabilitation Act of 1973 and the Americans with Disabilities Act (ADA)

As described above, Section 504 made it a civil rights violation for federal agencies and any agency receiving federal funding, including colleges, to discriminate against people with disabilities based on their disabling condition. This law provided many of the founding principles and guidelines on which the Americans with Disabilities Act was based. It also ensures that children who do not qualify for special education services as a result of the Individuals with Disabilities Education Act do not experience discrimination in public schools.

The Americans with Disabilities Act (ADA) was designed to expand on the rights that were created in Section 504 of the Rehabilitation Act so that these rights would apply to agencies beyond those receiving federal dollars. To be covered by a law as a person with a disability, one needs to have "a physical or mental impairment that substantially limits one or more major life activities . . . ; a record of such an impairment; or [be] regarded as having such an impairment" (42 U.S. Code § 12102, 1990). Major life activities include "caring for oneself, performing manual tasks, seeing, hearing, eating, sleeping, walking, standing, lifting, bending, speaking, breathing, learning, reading, concentrating, thinking, communicating, and working" (42 U.S. Code § 12102, 2009). Title I of the ADA requires that all employers other than religious organizations, who employ 15 or more people, make reasonable accommodations in employment. Title II of the ADA applies to public services and transportation, and Title III applies to public accommodations (public and private facilities used by the public, including stores, schools, etc.).

In accordance with the ADA, the U.S. Equal Employment Opportunity Commission (2002) has defined reasonable accommodations as:

> (i) modifications or adjustments to a job application process that enable a qualified applicant with a disability to be considered for the position such qualified applicant desires; or
>
> (ii) modifications or adjustments to the work environment, or to the manner or circumstances under which the position held or desired is customarily performed, that enable a qualified individual with a disability to perform the essential functions of that position; or
>
> (iii) modifications or adjustments that enable a covered entity's employee with a disability to enjoy equal benefits and privileges of employment as are enjoyed by its other similarly situated employees without disabilities.

Requests for reasonable accommodations can include: physical accessibility (use of elevator, ramp, modifying workspace layout); modified work schedules (part-time, various hours); modifying equipment (lighting, assistive technologies, computer software); modification of tests, policies, and/or training materials (longer time for exams, oral instead of written);

communication (readers, interpreters, large print); policy enhancement (service animals); or a reassignment to a vacant position. The law specifically notes that reasonable accommodations must not cause undue hardship for the employer, which may include changing the job description or functions of the job, lowering production standards, or providing a service that is needed both on and off the job (e.g., a wheelchair) (U.S. Equal Employment Opportunity Commission, 2002). To qualify for a reasonable accommodation, the person must tell their employer what accommodation they need (verbally or in writing), and the accommodation must be related to a medical condition. While employers cannot ignore a request, they can ask for supporting documentation, and if the accommodation is unreasonable, they can deny the request even if the person has a medical reason.

One of the first significant cases to be litigated as a result of the ADA was *Olmstead v. L.C.* in 1999. The Supreme Court decision in this case suggested that people should not be institutionalized if they could receive treatment in the community by making "reasonable modifications" to existing state resources as opposed to "fundamental alterations." The Supreme Court decided that the ADA applied to individuals living in state-supported housing. This suggested that the ideal was to provide people with disabilities long-term care in community settings rather than in institutions. However, states were exempted from this requirement if they could demonstrate that to do so they would have to fundamentally alter their existing system of service provision and that doing so would be unduly burdensome.

As a result of the *Olmstead* decision, there has been an effort to rebalance Medicaid funds from supporting institutional, skilled nursing care, to providing more supportive community-based care. Self-directed services are services in which people with long-term health needs are given a pot of money and can select staff, services, organizations, and scheduling of services that they believe work best for them (National Council on Disability, n.d.). Both the Medicaid Innovation Accelerator Program and the Affordable Care Act have provided several incentive programs to promote community inclusion and self-directed services. Medicaid has several other programs for states that specifically promote self-directed care for individuals who are otherwise eligible for Medicaid services and need acute or long-term care (Medicaid, n.d.).

The Supreme Court ruling in *Board of Trustees of the University of Alabama v. Garrett* (2001) determined that individuals have no right to sue states for money damages under the ADA in federal court. However, the Court held that they can sue for injunctive relief (to stop the government's behavior). In addition, the federal government can sue the states for both monetary damages and **injunctive relief**. The right to sue for injunctive relief was further upheld by the Supreme Court in 2004 (*Tennessee v. Lane*). In *Barnes v. Gorman*, (2002), the Supreme Court further weakened the ADA by determining that there are no individual rights to punitive damages available for ADA or Section 504 cases. **Punitive damages** are designed to punish the accused (so that they have greater motivation to follow the law) rather than just make up for the harm that was caused. In this case, Jeffrey Gorman, who has paraplegia, was arrested for fighting with a bouncer at a nightclub. The arresting officer did not let him empty his urine bag before transporting him to the station. Then he was improperly transported to the station. As a result of his experience in transportation, he "suffered serious medical problems—including a bladder infection, serious lower back pain, and uncontrollable spasms in his paralyzed areas—that left him unable to work full time" (*Barnes v. Gorman*, 2002). The Supreme Court held that he was unable to sue for punitive damages because they felt that punitive damages were beyond the scope of what Congress intended when passing the ADA.

Injunctive relief: A court order that requires someone to stop engaging in a particular behavior

Punitive damages: Court order designed to punish the accused (so that they have greater motivation to follow the law) rather than just make up for the harm that was caused

Many lawsuits have been filed that have helped further define and clarify individual rights under the ADA. There were four major cases in the late 1990s and early 2000s in which the Supreme Court limited the rights of people with disabilities under the ADA. In *Sutton et al. v. United Airlines, Inc.* (1999), the Court held that employers could choose not to hire employees because of a vision condition that could be corrected when they determined that the condition was not significant enough to warrant their being protected as disabled. In other words, they could choose not to hire employees as a result of a condition and then claim that the condition was not significant enough to warrant them being protected as disabled. In *Toyota Motor Manufacturing, Kentucky, Inc. v. Williams* (2002), the Supreme Court held that a woman who could not perform the manual tasks associated with her job, but was able to perform other manual tasks associated with daily living, did not satisfy the definition of disabled. In *U.S. Airways, Inc. v. Barnett* (2002), the Court held that requiring a company to alter a seniority system to accommodate a disability could be considered an undue hardship for an employer. Last, in *Chevron U.S.A., Inc. v. Echazabal* (2002), a man who worked in an oil refinery as a contractor applied to Chevron for a job. Chevron chose not to hire him because during his physical they learned of a liver condition that they thought would make it dangerous for him to work at the refinery. They asked his employer to reassign him. Ultimately, he was fired by that employer. Chevron defended their position based on Equal Employment Opportunity Commission (EEOC) regulations, which stated that an employer need not employ someone whose employment poses a risk to their health. The Supreme Court supported this position and determined that Echazabal had not experienced disability discrimination.

In 2008, the Americans with Disabilities Amendment Act (ADAA) was passed essentially to overturn the decisions in *Toyota* and *Sutton*. This law clarified that the intention of the legislators when they passed the ADA was that disability be construed broadly. The ADAA specifically states that in *Sutton* and *Toyota*, the Supreme Court narrowed the definition of disability beyond what Congress had intended when the ADA was passed. It further states that uncorrected vision cannot be used as a standard for employment unless it is "job related and consistent with business necessity" (42 U.S. Code § 12102 [5][c]) and "whether an impairment substantially limits a major life activity shall be made without regard to the ameliorative effects of mitigating measures" (42 U.S. Code § 12102 4[E][1]). Like most other employment discrimination claims based on federal law, except the Equal Pay Act, you must first file a complaint with the EEOC before you can file a lawsuit charging discrimination based on disability in the workplace (Equal Employment Opportunity Commission, 2018).

The ADA (1990) requires that people with disabilities be given equal access to transportation and that public buildings, sidewalks, and transportation be made accessible. Its implementation has challenged cities, counties, and states. Disability rights advocates have needed to remain vigilant and continue to fight for these legally established rights. For example, on May 19, 2019, a class action case was filed against the New York Metropolitan Transportation Authority for renovating subway stations and not making them accessible (Disability Rights Advocates, 2019). Organizations, such as the Disability Rights Advocates, file class actions and other cases and produce reports to support disability rights advocacy.

Individuals with Disabilities Education Act (IDEA)

During the 2016–2017 school year 14%, or 6.7 million, students who were enrolled in public schools received special services under the IDEA as a result of a diagnosed disability (National Center for Education Statistics, 2018). As noted in Chapter 7, the Individuals with Disabilities Education Act has four major parts; Part A sets out the overarching guidelines, Part B addresses the educational needs of infants and toddlers until age 3, Part C addresses the educational needs of children from age 3 through 12th grade, and Part D includes provisions for discretionary grants to improve education for children with disabilities. The IDEA requires schools and school districts to provide special educational services to children with the following diagnoses: deaf-blindness, deafness, intellectual disability, specific learning disability, other health impairments, speech/language disability, traumatic brain injury, autism spectrum disorder, emotional disturbance, hearing impairment, orthopedic impairment, multiple disabilities, and developmental delay. To be eligible for special education services under the IDEA, the disabling

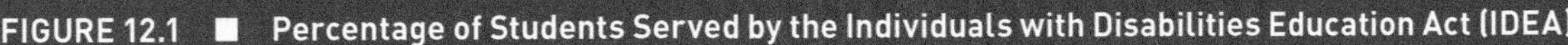

FIGURE 12.1 ■ Percentage of Students Served by the Individuals with Disabilities Education Act (IDEA)

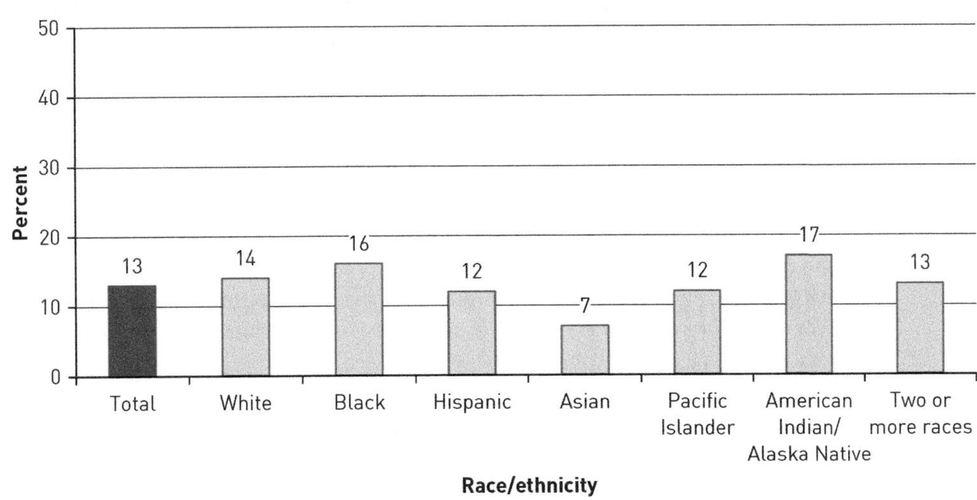

Source: U.S. Department of Education, Office of Special Education Programs, Individuals with Disabilities Education Act (IDEA) database, https://www2.ed.gov/programs/osepidea/618-data/state-level-data-files/index.html#bcc; and National Center for Education Statistics, Common Core of Data (CCD), "State Nonfiscal Survey of Public Elementary/Secondary Education," 2015 -16. *See Digest of Education Statistics 2017*, table 204.50.

condition must adversely affect a student's educational performance. In other words, if you use a wheelchair but it does not affect how you perform in school, you would not be eligible for special education services under the IDEA. You would, however, be eligible for protection under Section 504 of the Rehabilitation Act of 1973, which prohibits discrimination on the basis of disability. The first Supreme Court case to address the IDEA was the case of Amy Rowley, who was able to understand only about 80% of what was going on in the classroom as a result of her hearing impairment. Despite her hearing limitation, she was getting passing grades. Her parents wanted her to be eligible for a sign interpreter to help her better understand what was going on in the classroom. They argued that she needed these services to receive a free, appropriate public education (FAPE), a requirement of the IDEA. Holding that no student had the right to receive services necessary to enable them to reach their full potential in public schools, the Supreme Court said that the services that a student with a disability should receive must only be sufficient to ensure that a student with a disability makes "meaningful educational progress" (*Board of Education of Hendrick Hudson Central School District v. Rowley*, 1982).

Fourteen percent of all children who attend public schools are diagnosed with a disability and, as a result, are eligible for special education services. Thirty-four percent of students eligible for special education services are labeled as having a specific learning disability. Historically, these children were separated from their peers without disabilities. Now, more than 60% of students with disabilities spend over 80% of their time in regular education classes (National Center for Educational Statistics, 2018). As noted in the education chapter, a disproportionate number of students with discipline-related disabilities are students living in poverty and students of color, particularly African American or Latino.

The Patient Protection and Affordable Care Act (ACA)

The Patient Protection and Affordable Care Act (2010) provides many benefits to people with disabilities. First, Section 1557 of the ACA prohibits discrimination by insurance companies and health care programs based on race, color, religion, sex, national origin, age, or disability.

The ACA also prohibits excluding people from receiving insurance because of preexisting health conditions, which allows people with disabilities to get employment-based insurance that covers conditions associated with their disability. This means that insurance companies cannot refuse treatment or charge more for that treatment if a person has a disability. Prior to the passage of the ACA, exclusion clauses restricted coverage and treatment for people with disabilities (Yee, 2015). The provision that allows children to stay on their parents' insurance until they are 26 years old can also benefit people with disabilities; it can allow parents to help transition their children to adulthood and give them time to navigate the sometimes complex systems of services or agencies for adults with disabilities.

Due to the limited availability of health insurance coverage for people with disabilities prior to the ACA, many had to forgo work opportunities to stay eligible for Medicaid. This relegated many people with disabilities who may have otherwise opted for employment to remain in poverty just so that they could receive necessary medical care. In states that chose to take advantage of the Affordable Care Act's Medicaid expansion, people with long-term disabilities have access to broader coverage, which has put less pressure on them to choose not to work so they can be eligible for health care benefits. Since procedures differ across states, some people with disabilities have more limited service options than others (National Council on Disability, 2016). Overall, Medicaid expansion has led to an increased number of people with chronic conditions who have access to health care by establishing Essential Health Benefits (EHB) categories, which apply to both private individuals and small group health insurance plans. This allows people with disabilities more access to certain services such as prescriptions, services for substance use, clinical mental health treatment, and rehabilitation and habilitation services and devices (Yee, 2015). There are still barriers to effective treatment for people with disabilities because appropriate health care is not always accessible (lack of sign language interpreters, accommodations, equipment, training, etc.) or affordable as a result of potentially high deductibles. Advocates are trying to show the importance of defining quality health care for people with disabilities, which may include different services than those for people who are not disabled. In addition, as a result of anti-ACA activism, the future of the ACA is uncertain.

In 2018, Congress voted to get rid of the individual mandate that required everyone to have insurance or pay a penalty (Mangan, 2018). As of July 2019, a lawsuit filed in the Fifth Circuit Court of Appeals in Texas challenged the constitutionality of the ACA on the grounds that without the individual mandate, the law is unconstitutional (Zhou, 2019). According to the Commonwealth Institute, if the law is overturned, 17 million people who are currently insured will become uninsured (Commonwealth Fund, 2019). If the law is overturned, this may pose a significant problem for people with disabilities who, as a result of the ACA, were able to get insurance to cover preexisting conditions. Without the ACA, some may cease to have insurance for major health conditions. This may ultimately cause people with disabilities who can work to leave work and become impoverished in order to qualify for Medicaid. Social workers who work with clients with disabilities are well situated to understand the impact that reducing the coverage afforded by the ACA can have for people with disabilities and to help advocate for them.

In addition to the federal laws described above, many state programs and policies affect individuals with disabilities. As noted above, the implementation of the ACA varies by state. Programs for people with disabilities are often assessed by quality of care, including how well they support independent living, productivity (jobs, social roles), inclusion/access (access to supports, staying with families/communities), and quality of life (health, safe environments). Some states, such as California, have long histories of support for independent living whereas other states, such as Arkansas, Illinois, Mississippi, and Texas, have minimal services to support people with disabilities. In 2014, 15 states had no state institutions that segregated people with intellectual and developmental disabilities (IDD) and 9 states had only one state institution, meaning that state institutions like Willowbrook (discussed above) were closed and generally not replaced with less restrictive humane alternatives. Twenty-seven states reported that 80% of people with IDD were supported in family and other home-like settings (United Cerebral Palsy Association, 2016). In 2016, 15 states reported at least 10% use of self-directed services for people with disabilities and 5 states (Florida, Illinois, New Hampshire, Utah, and Vermont) reported 20% of people with disabilities used self-directed services. Ten states (Connecticut, Maryland, New Hampshire, New Mexico, Oklahoma, Oregon, Rhode Island, Vermont, Washington, and West Virginia) reported that 33% of people with IDD in the state were employed, and 15 states reported that 60% of people with disabilities were in vocational programs. **Vocational programs** are designed to help people either enter or return to the workforce. They are sometimes referred to as *vocational rehabilitation* programs. According to the United Cerebral Palsy Foundation (2016), Arizona is the top-ranked state for the inclusion of people with disabilities, and Texas and Mississippi are the lowest ranked. Advocates for people with disabilities, including social workers, can be influential in the development and implementation of these programs.

Vocational programs: Programs designed to help people either enter or return to the workforce, sometimes referred to as *Vocational Rehabilitation* programs

Disability and the Workplace and Higher Education

Integrating people with disabilities into society requires the integration of people with disabilities into all facets of life, including education and the workforce. Education, job training, and employment opportunities have been increasing for people with disabilities. On August 14, 2008, PL 110–315, the Higher Education Opportunity Act (HEOA), was signed into law. In addition to the other aspects of this law discussed in Chapter 8, this law made postsecondary education more accessible and affordable for people with disabilities. There are currently 238 college-level programs specifically designed for students with intellectual disabilities. These programs include universal design for learning, financial aid, training for teaching staff, and access to specialized instructional materials. **Universal design** is the idea that education or workplace structures can be designed in a way that is optimal for everyone, so that there is less need for adaptation to account for individual needs; this also encompasses the idea that accommodations for some can be helpful for everyone. One of the most prominent features of the act was providing access for students with intellectual disabilities (ID) with transition services that could enable them to participate in postsecondary programs. Previously, it was rare for these students to go to college. These programs have different supports and focuses including job training, credit bearing college classes, mentorship, allowing students to audit college classes, support with English language instruction and math, independent living skills, self-advocacy skills training, as well as communication and social skills training.

Universal design: The idea that education or workplace structures can be designed in a way that is optimal for everyone so that there is less need for adaptation to account for individual needs; this also encompasses the idea that accommodations for some can be helpful for everyone

In addition, through grants from the U.S. Department of Education, 25 Transition and Postsecondary Programs for Students with Intellectual Disabilities (TPSIDs) were funded from 2015 to 2020. These programs are specifically designed to expand inclusion for people with intellectual disabilities into college as a result of transition and postsecondary support programs.

REFLECTION

DISABILITIES AND THE WORKPLACE

Think of some strategies to include people with disabilities in the workplace.

1. What policy strategies do you think could help further this goal?
2. How might you work toward putting these strategies in place?

FIGURE 12.2 ■ Employment for Those With and without Disabilities

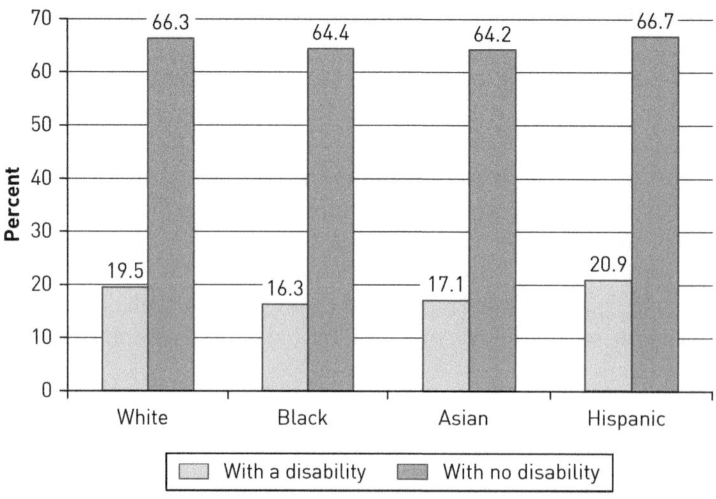

Source: U.S. Department of Commerce

U.S. Bureau of Labor Statistics, Division of Labor Force Statistics (2019). Persons with a disability, 2018 current population survey (CPS). Retrieved from: https://www.dol.gov/odep/pdf/DOL_ODEP_2018_Briefing_with_notes_ODEP.pdf

In 2014, the Workforce Innovation and Opportunity Act (WIOA) updated and replaced the 1998 Workforce Investment Act (WIA), a program designed to provide job training for disadvantaged youth and adults so that they could successfully enter the workforce. The WIOA added individualized assessments, specific training, access to jobs, transition services for youth, and programs and incentives for employers to hire more people with disabilities. In addition, it required increased monitoring and mandated performance measurements. This may have created disincentives to provide services to people with disabilities because they have greater barriers to employment and therefore, their success is more expensive (Spaulding, 2015). In addition, funding has not matched the increased mandates of WIOA (Bird et al., 2014). This is important because there is a wide gap between people with disabilities and those without in the workforce. In fact, in over 34 states, the gap between the employment rate of people with disabilities and those without disabilities in the workforce is at least 40%. The type of disability further influences one's likelihood of employment (Institute on Disability/UCED, 2017) (see Figure 12.2).

TABLE 12.1 ■ List of Relevant Federal Laws

Topic	Laws	Oversight Agency	Website
Accessibility	Air Carrier Access Act Architectural Barriers Act (ABA) ADA Title II: Public Transportation	Department of Transportation Aviation Consumer Protection Division, C-75 Architectural and Transportation Barriers Compliance Board Office of Civil Rights	https://www.transportation.gov/airconsumer/disability www.access-board.gov www.fta.dot.gov/ada www.ada.gov

Topic	Laws	Oversight Agency	Website
	ADA Title III: Public Accommodations ADA Title IV: Telecommunications Relay Services Telecommunications Act of 1996 Section 508 of the Rehabilitation Act of 1973	Federal Transit Administration Department of Justice Civil Rights Division Federal Communications Commission General Services Administration Office of Government-wide Policy IT Accessibility & Workflow Division (ITAW)	https://www.fcc.gov/general/disability-rights-office www.fcc.gov/cgb/dro www.gsa.gov/portal/content/105254
Civil rights	ADA Title II: State and Local Government Activities Civil Rights of Institutionalized Persons Act (CRIPA)	Department of Justice Civil Rights Division	www.ada.gov https://www.justice.gov/crt/civil-rights-institutionalized-persons
Education	Individuals with Disabilities Education Act (IDEA) Section 504 of the Rehabilitation Act of 1973	Office of Special Education and Rehabilitative Services Department of Justice Civil Rights Division	www.ed.gov/about/offices/list/osers/osep www.ada.gov
Employment	ADA Title I: Employment	Equal Employment Opportunity Commission (EEOC)	www.eeoc.gov
Housing	Fair Housing Act, amended in 1988	Department of Housing and Urban Development	www.hud.gov/offices/fheo www.fairhousingfirst.org
Voting	Voting Accessibility for the Elderly and Handicapped Act of 1984	Department of Justice Civil Rights Division	https://www.ada.gov/ada_voting/ada_voting_ta.htm

Source: U.S. Bureau of Labor Statistics

POLICY INFORMED BY ALTERNATIVE LENSES

Disability is treated very differently in different countries. In 2006, the United Nations adopted the Convention on the Rights of Persons with Disabilities. This document was ratified by 177 countries. The United States has signed, but not ratified, this treaty.[1] Through Article 4, the United Nations established general obligations that ensure the rights and freedoms for people with disabilities; it also provides protection against discrimination and includes provisions

[1]The UN Glossary website provides the following definitions of terms that relate to international treaties (Dag Hammarskjold Library, 2018).

Signature Subject to Ratification, Acceptance or Approval

Where the signature is subject to ratification, acceptance or approval, the signature does not establish the consent to be bound. However, it is a means of authentication and expresses the willingness of the signatory state to continue the treaty-making process. The signature qualifies the signatory state to proceed to ratification, acceptance or approval. It also creates an obligation to refrain, in good faith, from acts that would defeat the object and the purpose of the treaty.

[Arts. 10 and 18, Vienna Convention on the Law of Treaties 1969]

Ratification: The action of a state that binds it to a treaty that people with disabilities be part of the legislative planning process. Article 4 mandates that countries agree to pass appropriate laws that protect and promote the rights of people with disabilities; abolish laws or programs that discriminate; conduct research on technology, goods, services, and equipment that support access for people with disabilities; provide information to people with disabilities regarding affordable assistive technologies; provide appropriate training for those who provide supports and services for people with disabilities; and have an overall agreement to follow the guidelines established in the Convention (Convention on the Rights of Persons with Disabilities: Article 4, 2006). Ten years after the Convention was signed, some progress has been made but much more is needed. The World Policy Analysis Center at UCLA analyzed the implementation of the Convention's goals. According to the Center, only 10% of the signatory countries have followed up on their promise to guarantee the rights of people with disabilities. Only 28% of countries ensure the right to education for students with disabilities with the lowest enrollment in low- to medium-income countries. Five percent of countries have no provisions, and 12% have separate schools for students with disabilities. Only 24% of countries had constitutional protections enabling people with disabilities to work as of 2016. Only 26% of countries explicitly guarantee health care access (World Policy Analysis Center, 2016). The United States provides neither constitutional protection for people with disabilities to work nor guarantees health care access.

Norway

An example of a country with an excellent system for providing support for people with disabilities is Norway. Not only does Norway provide guaranteed health care for all as well as a constitutional protection for people with disabilities, it also provides a social security income for those with a loss of income up to 50% as a result of a disability or illness. People with disabilities are eligible for 3 years of benefits from the date of a claim once a commission has determined that their claim is legitimate. Unlike other countries, this right is universal and does not require a previous work history. Those who are entitled to benefits receive 66% of their prior wages or 50% of the average wage if they were not working. To be eligible, someone must be undergoing treatment or have undergone treatment, or be getting vocational training and seeking employment (NAV, 2018; Social Security Administration, 2016).

DISCUSSION

DISABILITY AND LABELS

All the laws that protect people with disabilities in the United States require people to have diagnosed disabilities. This is particularly problematic under the Individuals with Disabilities Education Act because some parents may not want their child to be labelled as a child with a disability or to have a specific disability label, such as an intellectual disability or an emotional disturbance, because of the stigma associated with those labels. This can get in the way of children receiving needed services.

1. Discuss ways in which this challenge could be addressed.
2. How might cost be an issue?
3. At what age should a child have a say in determining whether he or she wants to be diagnosed with a condition that might enable him or her to receive needed services but also carries a stigma?

OPPORTUNITIES FOR ADVOCACY

Beginning with Dix, and gaining momentum following the Civil Rights movement, many agencies and organizations have advocated for the rights of people with disabilities. There are many opportunities for policy advocacy around disability issues. The fight for access to jobs and services, independent living, and inclusion in schools and communities is ongoing. The fight to maintain health insurance for preexisting conditions continues as long as the existence of the ACA remains tenuous. Senator Chuck Schumer of New York introduced the Disability Integration Act that is designed to provide more services for those who need long-term services and supports (Sensenbrenner, 2017). Mental health advocates strive to decrease the stigma and improve services for those with mental health issues. Here, we start with discussions about language and disability awareness, and highlight opportunities for self-advocacy.

Use of Language

Best Buddies is an international not-for-profit agency that aims at inclusion for people with disabilities through friendships. They created the Spread the Word to End the Word Campaign, which tackles stigmatizing language used for people with disabilities. This campaign is built on the idea that changing the language we use to describe people with disabilities will help people see people with disabilities as full human beings and encourage treatment of all people with respect.

Another example of the importance of language is the push for what is often referred to as *person-first language*. This means that we refer to people first rather than a particular attribute. In the context of disability, this means that we say *people with disabilities* rather than *disabled people* or describe a *person with Autism Spectrum Disorder* as opposed to an *autistic person*. However, as we have noted before in this text, language can be contested. For example, some adults with autism prefer *identity first* language and like to be called autistic people (Brown, 2019). Many self-advocates argue that it is better to ask the person their preference because some people feel that hiding the disability may play into a stigma that they wish to combat or because their disability defines who they are (Collier, 2012). This is consistent with social work values that we should both respect and empower the populations with whom we work. The importance of language also comes through in people's struggles to be defined the way they wish to be. For example, the advocacy organization The Arc (n.d.) of the United States describes how it changed its name from the "Association of Retarded Citizens" to "The Arc":

> We, as an organization have been sensitive to the impact of terminology on our constituency and have adapted accordingly. As the words "retardation" and "retarded" became pejorative, derogatory and demeaning in usage, the organization changed its name to "The Arc." (n.p.)

We believe that explicit discussion of language and identity are important. They acknowledge the power of words and the ability of individuals and groups to evolve how they think and to articulate how they wish to be perceived and referred to. Such explicit discussions can also bring fundamental tensions to the surface where they can be publicly debated.

Disability Awareness

In television shows and movies, there are few characters with disabilities, and individuals with disabilities are often portrayed by actors without disabilities. Many disabilities are hidden, so although the statistics suggest there are many people around us with disabilities, we may not know how these disabilities affect people's everyday lives. As a result, many advocacy activities around disability include increasing awareness of different types of disabilities and their effects, and the capabilities of people with disabilities to equally participate in work and social environments.

Advocacy groups are pushing to train law enforcement officers on disability awareness, in light of recent altercations. The Arc's Center on Criminal Justice and Disability is currently running is a campaign called "Found a Pathway to Justice" to train law enforcement officers to recognize and appropriately respond to people with disabilities or mental illness. Some have suggested that training police how to deal with mental health issues is the wrong strategy and instead, we should have trained mental health professionals responding to mental health crises (Vitale, 2018). This too is an area of potential advocacy for social workers. Similar concerns exist for people on the autism spectrum who may be understood by police officers to be unresponsive or dangerous. The National Autism Association has created a safety initiative for people with autism, their families and police officers.

Self-Advocacy

A lot of advocacy around disability rights has been initiated and sustained by people with disabilities. This, of course, is consistent with social work values. Many self-advocacy organizations are active today, such as the National Disability Rights Network, the Autistic Self Advocacy Network, the Center for Disability Rights, and the Learning Disability Association of America. These groups and others help keep the voices of people with disabilities and their family members at the forefront of their leadership and decision-making processes. In addition, many state and local areas have self-advocacy groups that are led by people with disabilities. The self-advocacy movement has even begun reaching into the schools in the form of student-led IEP meetings, where students not only participate in their IEP meetings, but staff collaborate with and prepare students to learn about their disability and how it affects them so they can better advocate for themselves (Diegelmann & Test, 2018). **Person-centered planning** is another tool that involves putting the person in the center of their support planning by looking at his or her goals, barriers, and the services that are needed to overcome those barriers (Stanhope, Ingoglia, Schmelter, & Marcus, 2013).

Person-centered planning: An approach that involves putting people in the center of their support planning by looking at their goals, barriers to achieving them, and the services that are needed to overcome those barriers

ADVOCACY

THE AMERICAN ASSOCIATION OF PEOPLE WITH DISABILITIES

The American Association of People with Disabilities promotes advocacy through policy letters, call-in campaigns, rallies, and research. They are currently advocating for increased IDEA funding and an end to the requirement that people with disabilities must deplete their assets and have a low income to qualify for long-term services and supports through Medicaid. Find their website and contact them to learn about steps you can take to help advocate for people with disabilities in your community and nationally.

Final Discussion

Now that you have finished reading this chapter, reread the vignette at the beginning. Based on what you have learned, answer the following questions. What have you learned from this chapter that might help you if you were Bob's social worker? How might you help advocate for Bob, and how might you try to advocate for policy changes to better help Bob at both the local district level and state and federal levels? Point to specific references in the chapter that help you answer these questions. Consider how different theories inform the response to these questions.

1. What other services that are not discussed below might the family be eligible for both in school and outside of school?
2. Are there any child welfare concerns, and if so, what are they?
3. What do you think the role of a school social worker would be in this case? How do you think he or she could advocate for Bob to get support in school?
4. Is there another agency outside the school system that might be able to help Bob and his family?
5. What role might race, class, gender, and other aspects of identity play in this vignette?

13

CRIMINAL JUSTICE

LEARNING OBJECTIVES

13.1: Describe the history and impact of U.S. criminal justice policy on marginalized groups

13.2: Describe the current state of the criminal justice system and its effects on specific populations

13.3: Assess whether diversion programs and restorative justice policies could address the injustices of the current criminal justice system

13.4: Plan advocacy activities to address solitary confinement and negative actions of criminal justice system actions toward people with mental illness

Understanding the criminal justice system and its impact on individuals, families, communities, and society is critically important to the social work profession. This commitment is embraced in social work's commitment to "promote smart decarceration":

> Guided by our profession's social justice orientation and commitment to working with vulnerable populations, social work scholars and practitioners should be leaders in efforts to reform the criminal justice system in the era of decarceration. Decarceration entails more than simply not incarcerating – it involves developing an array of more effective and socially just alternatives to replace incarceration. This work provides an opportunity to engage and mobilize social work scholars and practitioners in developing and executing an actionable agenda for smart decarceration. (Grand Challenges for Social Work, n.d.)

The way that a nation defines criminal behaviors reflects its underlying social values. It also reflects beliefs about the purposes of state action toward sanctioned behaviors, which can include revenge or retribution, deterrence, control, rehabilitation, and/or symbolic action. How societies define and respond to criminal behavior changes over time with shifts in cultural norms and values. For example, less than 50 years ago, most U.S. states considered homosexuality illegal. At that time, spousal rape was not a crime. Physical violence within a marriage was considered a private matter. Many of you may also be paying attention to battles over the legal status of marijuana at the state and federal levels. Similarly, the reasons for and length of incarceration have changed over time.

The United States has the dubious distinction of having the highest rate of incarceration in the world (Organization for Economic Co-operation and Development [OECD], 2016). Indeed, many argue that our country uses criminal justice primarily as a means of societal control and surveillance, particularly of racial and ethnic minorities (Simon, 2007) and immigrants (Hernández, 2017). This chapter examines historical shifts in the framing of criminal justice such as the war on drugs as well as the implications of this framing for communities and families. The impacts of criminal justice policies on social work practice include significant family and community financial instability, mental health consequences, and the disenfranchisement of individuals and communities. In this chapter, we explore interest groups engaged in criminal justice advocacy. In addition, we look at the implications of criminal justice policy on family formation and changing roles and responsibilities within families.

Vignette: Responses to Offending

Based on what you know from the media or your personal, work, or volunteer experiences, think about the following questions as you read the vignette. When you finish the vignette, answer the questions below.

1. How do you think the criminal justice system should respond to Larissa's offending behavior, and why? In considering your answer to these responses, think of who you are considering (Larissa, her neighborhood, the broader community) and your goals for the response.
    a. What do you think would be the most effective response?
    b. What do you think would the fairest (most just) response?
    c. Is the fairest response necessarily the most effective one?
2. What are some of the hopes and concerns that you might have if you were the social worker visiting Larissa with the public defender?
3. What steps might you take to try to resolve any ethical conflicts that might arise for you as a social worker in this role?
4. What role might race, class, gender, and other aspects of identity play in this vignette?

Larissa grew up in a low-income neighborhood where her family was just able to make ends meet. When she entered high school, her father was unemployed and her family could not afford to buy her new clothes or school supplies. They were unable to pay for any extra activities, which included field trips and, later, her junior prom. Larissa complained to a friend, who told her that one of the teachers "likes younger women" and suggested that she offer to date him in exchange for prom tickets. Larissa figured that older men (and her teenage peers) often "hit" on her anyway, so why not get something out of it? Ten years later, Larissa struggles with substance abuse and health problems including Hepatitis C. She sometimes sells sex to purchase drugs and to keep a roof over her head. She has trouble getting or keeping a legal job due to her bouts of ill health, criminal record, and housing instability. Her daughter Kendra lives with Larissa's parents. They only allow Larissa to see Kendra if she is not actively using drugs and only in their home where they can supervise. Larissa has sought addiction treatment several times, but Medicaid covers only inpatient stays. She is successful during treatment, but when she returns to her friends and the neighborhood where she has support, she is also surrounded by opportunities to buy and use drugs. The drugs help her cope with some of the trauma that she experienced while selling sex on the streets.

Larissa was recently arrested for prostitution. She told her public defender that although she has sold sex in the past, this time she was out on the streets because she had nowhere else to go. While some police officers have helped her by trying to connect her to outreach services or warning her when they learn about violent customers, in this case she told her public defender that the officer arrested her when she refused to provide him with free sexual services. A lawyer and social worker from the public defender's office meet with Larissa, who is incarcerated because she cannot post bail. Based on her experience with similar cases, the public defender is skeptical that Larissa will be believed and offers her entry into a diversion program. To access the diversion program, Larissa will have to plead guilty to the charges, but she will not be punished with fines or jail time if she successfully completes the 1-year program. Larissa is exhausted and wants help. Regardless of her innocence, she knows that participating in the program will get her longer-term services than she can access outside of the criminal justice system. The public defender also explains that if she "takes the program" she will get out of jail faster. Not only is Larissa eager to get out of jail soon for her own sake, but she knows that her parents will not bring Kendra to visit her in jail and she is eager to get out quickly to see Kendra. After Larissa hears this, she tunes out the rest of the explanation offered by the public defender. This includes what can happen to her if she fails to complete the program, in which case her guilty plea is officially entered, and she will be sentenced with no opportunity to go to trial to share her version of events.

HISTORY AND SOCIAL CONSTRUCTION OF U.S. CRIMINAL JUSTICE POLICY

Definitions of crime and ideas of the appropriate social response to crime have changed substantially since the founding of the United States. In this section, we look at the transition in the United States from colonial times, when one might be transported across an ocean as a punishment, to the current era of mass incarceration.

The U.S. in Its Founding Years

Colonial American history was heavily influenced by British criminal justice policy. The British sent people convicted of crimes (called *convict transport*) and destitute people (as we discuss in Chapter 9) to the North American colonies, often over the objections of the receiving colonists (Butler, 1896; Vaver, 2013).

> Rebellious subjects from England and Wales, Ireland and Scotland as well as Catholics and the wrong sort of Protestants such as Quakers and Covenanters were despatched to the West Indies and North America. In the later seventeenth century, serious offenders, initially sentenced to death and pardoned on condition of 14 years transportation, emerged as a dominant feature in the transatlantic trade. (Morgan, n.d., para. 2)

As may be imagined, conditions of the transatlantic crossing were difficult. Once in the United States, those who survived served their sentences in hard labor (Morgan & Rushton, 2004). The majority were sent to Virginia and Maryland, which relied heavily on labor of enslaved people for agricultural production. Most were men, although some women were also sent to the United States. This practice, and the involuntary nature of convict labor, reflected a disregard for the rights or welfare of prisoners.

Similar to its European counterparts, criminal justice in the early U.S. colonial era was marked by physical punishment for transgressions or fines, many of them religiously or morally based. For example, early settlers could be punished for violating a 1662 Virginia law that required regular Sunday church attendance (Cox, 2003). Punishments were meted out by local governments, often through the church or parish. Localities were required to have stocks such as those depicted in Photo 13.1, in which those convicted could be punished on public display.

> Most self-respecting settlements also had a ducking stool, a seat set at the end of two beams twelve or fifteen feet long that could be swung out from the bank of a pond or river. This engine of punishment was especially assigned to scolds—usually women but sometimes men—and sometimes to quarrelsome married couples tied back to back. Other candidates were slanderers, "makebayts," brawlers, "chyderers," railers, and "women of light carriage," as well as brewers of bad beer, bakers of bad bread, and unruly paupers. In the absence of a proper ducking stool, authorities in some climes, as in Northampton County, Virginia, ordered the offender "dragged at a boat's Starn in ye River from ye shoare and thence unto the shoare again." (Cox, 2003)

Carol M. Highsmith, Library of Congress, C-DIG-highsm-44994

PHOTO 13.1 The stocks at historic Cold Spring Village, Cape May, New Jersey

Such punishments were motivated not only by vengeance, but also as a means of deterrence. Public punishments were shameful, and convicted criminals provided both entertainment and a cautionary tale to spectators. Some punishments left permanent marks, such as the branding of a thief with the letter T, lopped off ears, or slit nostrils (Friedman, 2005). The bodies of those who were punished in such manner carried living reminders for themselves and others.

The Rise of the Criminal Institution

As early as the 18th century, there was a move to change punishment in ways that were less gruesome, but arguably more effective. Philosopher Jeremy Bentham (1798) designed what he called the "panopticon" intended to maximize control and reform. He described it as a circular building:

> By blinds and other contrivances, the keeper concealed from the observation of the prisoners, unless where he thinks fit to show himself: hence, on their part, the sentiment of an invisible omnipresence.—The whole circuit reviewable with little, or, if necessary, without any, change of place . . . affording the most perfect view of every cell. (Bentham, 1798, p. 96)

Key to Bentham's design is that prisoners would know that they could always be watched, no matter where they were or what they were doing. They also would never be sure when they were being surveilled. Bentham believed that this would be an efficient and effective motivation to change criminal behavior through the internalization of constant self-vigilance.

According to philosopher Michel Foucault (1995), mechanisms that are designed to foster self-discipline became a pervasive tool of governing that exists in many facets of our lives, including schools and workplaces. In some cases, this may be a positive development for society. Others are concerned about forms of surveillance that make people less likely to challenge the power of those in authority. When rules are internalized, they may begin to feel natural, thus making it harder for people to recognize rules as something that can be changed. Prison proponents like Bentham, who attempted to influence behavior, were considered progressive in their time. Their reforms were often improvements on crueler responses to societal transgression.

While prisons initially were designed as temporary holding places for those awaiting trial, sentencing, or punishment, over time they became places where people could be held for punishment after conviction. The move toward prisons rather than the infliction of harsh physical punishment was in part spurred by a desire for reform. The work of Bentham, and people like Italian philosopher Cesare Beccarria who advocated for rational, just, and proportionate punishment designed to preserve social bonds, influenced early prison reformers (Bessler, 2009). Quakers who built the first prison in Philadelphia, like their European reformer counterparts, saw prisons as a place of rehabilitation where inmates would receive adequate food and have opportunities for self-reflection (in some cases through solitary confinement) and work. The Quakers also sought to abolish capital punishment. Although these new prisons were intended to be an improvement over earlier forms of punishment, they quickly became a target for reform. As the U.S. population grew, so did the numbers of those who were incarcerated (Rothman, 1980). Prisons were overcrowded and understaffed, and treatment of prisoners—whether due to lack of care or under the guise of rehabilitation—could be cruel. Prisons were also ripe for exploitation, with reports of prison wardens hiring out prison labor for their own financial benefit. The fact that so many prisoners were immigrants or indigent contributed to societal indifference to their plight.

David Rothman (1980) documents the Progressive prison reform movement of the post–Civil War period, which sought to ameliorate those conditions through building more and newer prisons, enhanced oversight and supervision, and individualized opportunities for rehabilitation through parole and probation. While these led to some improvements, poor conditions were often replicated. Many of these same concerns are raised by today's prison reform movements. Rothman documents that the use of other means of supervision outside of prison—rather than *replace* incarceration—largely set up *additional* systems of surveillance that widened the reach of the criminal system. Many of these practices came to be seen as routine and necessary, just like surveillance or oversight practices that you may have experienced, such as random drug testing, traffic cameras, searches of school lockers, and pop quizzes. Critics of surveillance practices ask us to reflect on what such practices are designed to accomplish, and who is targeted and controlled by them.

Policing

The Bureau of Justice Statistics reported that as of 2016 there were about 18,000 law enforcement agencies in the United States across all levels (local, state, federal). While the first federal law enforcement officer, the federal marshal, was created by Congress in 1879, early U.S. policing was largely informal and the province of the private sector. Local volunteers, or people who were required to serve as punishment, would work as night patrols whose duty it was to watch out for danger. Night watch patrols were overseen by publicly paid constables, for whom this was one of several public duties. In other cases, merchants paid people to keep watch over goods. Boston was the first city to establish a regular police force in 1838, at the urging of merchants who were largely concerned with theft and the suppression of working class strikes and riots. According to Potter (2013, citation included in original), by the 1880s most of the major U.S. cities had

> "modern police" organizations [that] shared similar characteristics: (1) they were publicly supported and bureaucratic in form; (2) police officers were full-time employees, not community volunteers or case-by-case fee retainers; (3) departments had permanent and fixed rules and procedures, and employment as a police officers was continuous; (4) police departments were accountable to a central governmental authority. (Lundman, 1980)

In the south, police forces had their origins in early slave patrols, who were tasked with deterring revolts and hunting, capturing, and return enslaved people who had run away (Hadden 2003). In major cities, like Charleston and Savannah, police grew out of efforts to manage mobile slave populations working away from the homes of their owners in workshops, wharves, and warehouses (Vitale, 2017). After the Civil War, when slavery was outlawed, these patrols morphed into police departments that controlled formerly enslaved people. They enforced laws that were designed to deny economic and political rights to formly enslaved persons as part of Jim Crow laws. Vagrancy statutes, convict leasing, and prison plantations were used to force those who had been enslaved into menial work such as sharecropping or forced labor through the criminal justice system (Oshinsky, 1997).

Although the police forces were established ostensibly to protect people from crime or harm, they were seen as corrupt and cruel, often working with equally corrupt politicians (who appointed them) and with organized crime (Walker, 1997). The Wickersham Commission report, issued in 1931, acknowledged these problems and led to some changes in policing (Strecher, 1998). The Wickersham Commission was appointed by President Hoover in 1929, about 8 years into Prohibition. Prohibition was largely considered a policy disaster that led to increased crime and violence while doing very little to achieve its goal of curtailing alcohol consumption. The report documented widespread corruption among the police forces across the country. It portrayed a disorganized system that allowed for discretion that was used in often exploitative ways. While the timing of the report during the Great Depression meant that it had little immediate effect, it was an important milestone in (re)conceptualizing policing as a professional regulated activity (Walker, 1992). This meant creation of rules and guidelines, professional screening and training, and policies and programs for supervision.

The report also called for separation of policing from official politics by shifting from appointment by favoritism among politicians to government service processes that are designed to be apolitical.

What do these historical roots of policing have to do with social work? From its earliest days, social workers collaborated with police departments. The Buffalo Charity Organization Society relied on police investigations as part of their comprehensive information gathering to decide which families to serve and how (Hansan, n.d.). The intentions of these proto-social workers were arguably to provide assistance. However, historically and today, this often leads to complicity in implementing policies to surveil and control, a problem that was recently noted in a social work and law enforcement collaboration in Arizona's Project ROSE. This project was designed to assist women engaging in prostitution by arresting them through street sweeps, but the program arguably caused more harm than good through negative police-community relations, collateral consequences, and net-widening (Strangio, 2017; Wahab & Panichelli, 2013). Policing, particularly of vulnerable populations, has social justice implications. Though the targets of policing may have changed over time, as we describe in the sections below, it remains important to think critically about who is policed and what the consequences of policing are. Some of the more high-profile cases of recent years which we discuss are portrayed in the U.S. Department of Justice Civil Rights Division reports on cities, such as Ferguson, Missouri (2015), and Baltimore, Maryland (2016), in which young African Americans were killed by police. These reports expose systems that are plagued by endemic racial and gender bias as well as failures of proper supervision and discipline. Social workers have been among the many calling for investigation of the police departments in these cases and may also play a role in addressing them (Giwa, 2018).

Getting Tough on Crime: The 1980s

In the 1960s and 1970s, concerns about social upheaval were brought on by demonstrations across the country. Riots in largely African American urban centers such as Baltimore inspired fear among many white Americans (Csicsek, 2011). The proliferation of drugs and related crime added to the sense of social dislocation and lack of control. In the 1980s, harsh political rhetoric was used to draw on fears of chaos and crime, which led to the passage of laws that expanded policing and legal control as well as harsher punishments (Simon, 2007). It is not coincidental that this trajectory also took place during a backlash against the welfare state that had sought to curb social ills of poverty and disenfranchisement through provision of opportunities and resources rather than blaming and punishing individuals for their personal failure (Schram, 2000). In both cases, the U.S. political environment was moving toward punishment over assistance and targeting individuals rather than systems as the locus of blame and intervention for societal problems.

Several different policies were part of this shift. Congress and state legislatures passed mandatory minimum sentencing laws that restricted judges' authority to be lenient in their sentencing (McCoy, 2003) but gave them leeway to provide harsher sentences than the minimum. New York's Rockefeller Drug Laws started a trend of very harsh punishments for most drug offenses. Local district attorneys also played a major role by demanding tougher plea deals and calling for longer sentences (Pfaff, 2017).

Broken Windows Theory: A theory that claims visible signs of social disorder (such as vandalism or littering) encourage more widespread criminal activity in that same area

One theory that is emblematic of this shift was the **Broken Windows Theory**, first proposed in 1982 by James Wilson and George Kelling in an article by the same name, which uses the symbol of broken windows as a metaphor for social disorder or criminality (Greene, 2016). Wilson and Kelling asserted that visible signs of social disorder in an area—such as vandalism, littering, or public intoxication—encourage more widespread criminal activity in that same area. According to Wilson and Kelling, social disorder and criminality are inextricably linked, and one broken window, if left unrepaired, may soon lead to another broken window. In other words, neighborhoods decline into high-crime zones through disorderly conditions.

This theory became popular and influential in social science and criminal justice, leading to the emergence of "order maintenance policing," which aimed to limit disorder and thus limit criminality (Harcourt, 1998). This led to policing strategies that targeted minor offenses such as vandalism or public drunkenness to reduce more serious offenses. In the 1990s, New York City Mayor Rudy Giuliani famously implemented this policing strategy and claimed credit for significant reductions of crime that far exceeded the national average (McKee, 2017; Vitale, 2008). However, critics pushed back against these findings, claiming that many factors were involved in crime reduction, such as the significant decrease in unemployment and the growing size of the New York City police force (Greene, 2016). Additionally, critics of this theory state that it neglects the complex array of factors that contribute to crime, such as race, wealth, class, and education (Vitale, 2008). Other critics assert that broken windows policing strategies (and their recent outgrowths such as "Stop and Frisk" policies) are unjust because they target impoverished minority communities (Bernard, 1998; Vitale, 2008).

Research into the efficacy of order maintenance policing remains mixed. Some research suggests that broken windows and other cues of social disorder have smaller effects in stimulating crime than previously thought (Beate, 2017). And while some studies in the 1990s and early 2000s indicated significant reductions of crime from broken window policing, other studies found no significant effects (Welsh, Braga, & Bruinsma, 2015). Meta analyses of these criminological studies suggest that, overall, disorder policing strategies are associated with modest reductions in crime (Welsh et al., 2015).

CURRENT CRIMINAL JUSTICE POLICIES

Criminal justice is influenced by laws and policies at the local, state, and federal levels. Elected officials pass laws that establish which behaviors constitute crimes and classify them according to levels of seriousness (e.g., felony, misdemeanor, and infraction). These levels also correspond with types and levels of punishments, which typically include citations, fines, and/or incarceration. The U.S. Code is the official compilation of permanent federal statutes, updated every 6 years by the House of Representatives. Title 18 of the U.S. Code of Laws is the main federal criminal code.

The U.S. Constitution contains protections pertinent to criminal prosecution. These include the 4th Amendment (prohibition of unreasonable searches and seizures), the 5th Amendment (the right to trial by jury for serious crimes), the 6th Amendment (the right to counsel by defense), and the 8th Amendment (prohibition of cruel and unusual punishment). What these mean in practice has been subject to debate and has changed over time. For example, you may have heard of a Miranda Warning, which comes from the famous 1966 Supreme Court case *Miranda v. Arizona*. Relying on the 6th Amendment, the Supreme Court ruled that

> the person in custody must, prior to interrogation, be clearly informed that he has the right to remain silent, and that anything he says will be used against him in court; he must be clearly informed that he has the right to consult with a lawyer and to have the lawyer with him during interrogation, and that, if he is indigent, a lawyer will be appointed to represent him. (p. 437)

Since this is a Supreme Court decision, it is binding on all the court levels below, which means it applies to all interactions with state and federal law enforcement agencies (see Chapter 2).

Many different law enforcement agencies operate at federal, state, and local levels to implement laws. Table 13.2 at the end of this section lists select criminal laws that may be particularly relevant to social work practice. Most criminal laws exist at the state level, since the Constitution stipulates that the federal government can only make laws where it has explicit powers and all other powers are left to the states (often called **residual powers**). Some examples of federal crimes are mail fraud, drug trafficking, identity theft, electoral fraud, kidnapping, and tax evasion. The federal and state systems are separate. Federal crimes are activities that the U.S. Congress has determined are illegal. Someone who is charged with a federal crime will be prosecuted in the federal system, sentenced according to federal guidelines. If found guilty, they will be punished within the federal system. Those who allegedly violate laws created at the state level will go through this process in the state system. In some areas there is exclusive jurisdiction (authority) of either the state or federal system; in other areas there may be overlap. When there is overlap, there may be cooperation and assistance, bringing greater investigative or prosecutorial resources to bear. There may also be instances of conflict due to competition over decision making or if laws themselves are in conflict. For example, some state laws that permit marijuana use may contradict federal laws that criminalize such use. This can lead to confusion among targets of law enforcement, those who provide advice, and those who implement the laws (Chilkoti, 2017).

Residual powers: Powers that are not explicitly granted to the federal government in the U.S. Constitution and are therefore considered to be within authority of state governments

Juvenile Delinquency

Juvenile delinquency: Criminal offenses that are committed by minors and status offenses

Status offense: A behavior that is prohibited for minors but otherwise legal, such as violations of curfews, running away, truancy, possessing alcohol, or ungovernability

Juvenile delinquency describes two different kinds of minors' involvement with the legal penal system. The first are criminal offenses that are committed by minors. The second are what are referred to as **status offenses**, which are behaviors that are prohibited for minors but otherwise legal (Office of Juvenile Justice and Delinquency Prevention, 2015). These are not considered crimes but acts of delinquency that can include violations of curfews for minors, running away, truancy, possessing alcohol, or ungovernability. A separate system for managing minors who have committed crimes or status offenses was conceived in the early 20th century by reformers. It grew from a combination of growing beliefs that children are inherently different from adults in their capacity for development and change through rehabilitation and the desire to control (initially) immigrant and (later) racial minority youth through punishment and supervision (Tanenhaus, 2004). Social work foremothers from Hull House were intricately involved in the creation of the first juvenile court, located in Cook County, Chicago. Then, as now, the crimes that brought girls before the courts often had to do with sexuality; boys were often brought before the courts for theft (Schlossman & Wallach, 1978). Picture 13.2 depicts a boy charged with theft in a Missouri juvenile court.

Tensions between helping and controlling continue. The purported benevolence of the delinquency system has sometimes resulted in according juveniles fewer rights and protections. For example, juveniles do not have the right to bail or trial by jury. In other areas, juveniles are afforded the same rights that adult criminal defendants have, such as constitutional due process rights, as affirmed in the landmark Supreme Court decision *In re Gault* (1967). There are also certain rights that juveniles enjoy that adults do not, such as a right to an attorney in criminal proceedings, sealing of their records, and the right to educational programming while incarcerated (Juvenile Law Center, n.d.). It is important to note that the definition of *juvenile* can differ; some states set the definition of juvenile at a maximum age of 16, while in others it is 18. Some jurisdictions allow older juveniles who commit certain crimes (often violent ones) to be tried as adults. This is determined by the relevant state laws and judicial discretion.

Increasingly harsh school disciplinary practices and protocols have been found to increase the likelihood that students will end up in juvenile justice systems (McCarter, 2017). For example, since the 1990s, students in the United States have been increasingly affected by the "criminalization of education," with growing numbers of police in schools (sometimes called *safety resource officers*), security guards, and security cameras (Mallett, 2017). Combined with stringent disciplinary practices and the implementation of **zero tolerance** measures for infractions, the number of suspensions, expulsions, and arrests in schools has risen exponentially since the 1990s (McCarter 2017). A single suspension increases the likelihood that a student will drop out and/or come in contact with the juvenile justice system (Losen, Hewitt, & Toldson, 2014). Once a child drops out of the school system, they are eight times more likely to be incarcerated than youth who graduate from high school (Schept, Wall, & Brisman, 2014).

Library of Congress, LC-DIG-nclc-04645

PHOTO 13.2 Juvenile Court. An 8-year-old boy charged with stealing a bicycle. Thursday May 5, 1910. Location: St. Louis, Missouri

Many people have used the term **school-to-prison pipeline** to refer to the collection of policies and practices in schools that increase the probability that some students are more likely to face criminal involvement than they are to obtain a quality education (Mallett, 2016). The school-to-prison pipeline involves millions of children and adolescents in school and juvenile justice systems. It disproportionately affects students from vulnerable or socially disadvantaged groups, including those who are impoverished, racial and ethnic minorities, LGBTQ+ adolescents, and/or have disabilities. In the United States, students of color are disproportionately represented in school discipline statistics, and there are large gaps in rates of suspensions and expulsions (McCarter, 2017).[1]

School-to-prison pipeline: The collection of policies and practices in schools that lead to greater likelihood of criminal justice involvement

Zero tolerance: A term referring to policies that prohibit waiver or reduction of consequences for offenses

Mass incarceration: Describes the extremely high rates of incarceration in the United States, both historically and in comparison to other countries

Incarceration, Reentry, and Collateral Consequences

As we noted, the United States has the highest incarceration rate of any nation. The term **mass incarceration** is often used to describe the volume of those directly and indirectly affected by incarceration in the United States. Figure 13.1 shows a huge increase in incarceration rates in the United States between 1992 and 2010, and a slight decline in incarceration trends between 2010 and 2016. The U.S. imprisonment rate still remains not only well above the average worldwide (as indicated by the red bar) but also higher than that of any other country.

One study (Wildeman, 2016) comparing 21 wealthy democracies found that the negative consequences of incarceration are far worse in the United States than in other countries. This research suggests that the way we *do incarceration* in the United States is significantly more negative than it is elsewhere. We therefore need to pay attention not only to rates of incarceration but also to how incarceration and reentry may be improved for better outcomes. In the sections below we discuss two areas of current criminal justice trends that are subject of debate.

The 1980s saw a rise in the privatization of U.S. prisons at the federal and local levels, with approximately 8% of all incarcerated persons as of 2015 in facilities owned by private

[1]Jonas Rosen researched and drafted the section on the school-to-prison population here and the discussion of Social Workers Against Solitary Confinement below.

FIGURE 13.1 ■ Prison Population per 100,000 Population, in 1992, 2010, and 2013 (or nearest year)

Downward trends in crimes in most OECD countries between 2008 and 2013, particularly among youths

Rate of persons brought into formal contact with the police and/or criminal justice system per 100000 population, in 2013 (or nearest year), all crimes taken together, index 100 in 2008

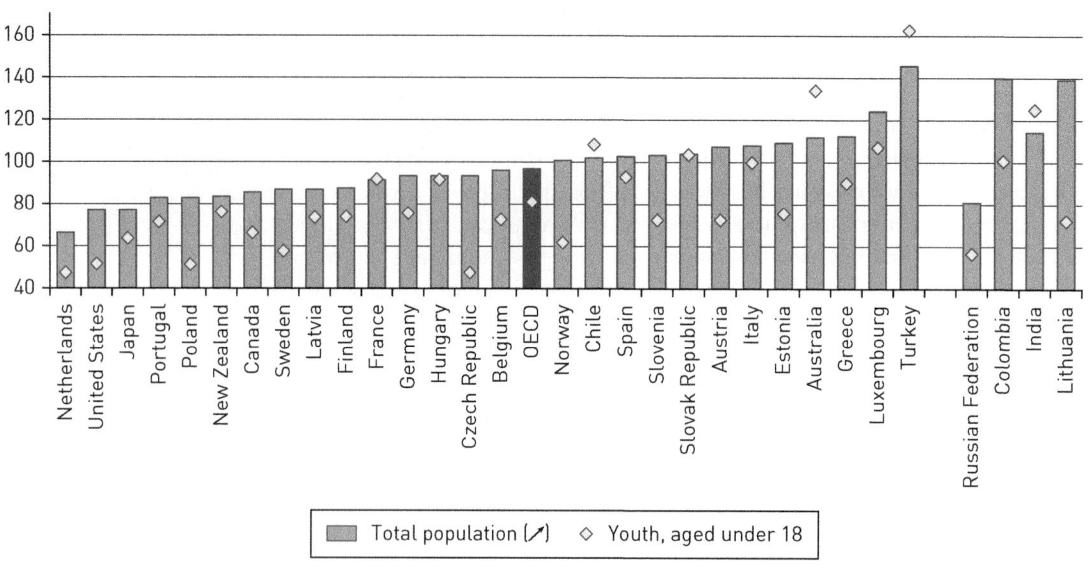

Source: OECD (2016). Society at a Glance 2016: OECD Social Indicators. OECD Publishing, Paris, http://dx.doi.org/10.1787/9789264261488-en

Privatization: The outsourcing of government functions to the private for-profit or nonprofit sector, often with financial incentives and reduced oversight

Neoliberalism: An orientation toward government characterized by the belief that market or business-oriented approaches are more effective and less costly than government-run programs and therefore, includes a preference for minimizing government involvement. It focuses on individual behavior rather than system factors as causes of success or failure programs based on this theory tend to create interventions that focus on individual behavioral changes.

companies rather than by the government (Bureau of Justice Statistics, 2015). **Privatization** is the outsourcing of government functions to the private for-profit or nonprofit sector, often with financial incentives and reduced oversight. This was part of a larger trend of privatizing social services that some see as a hallmark of **neoliberalism**. One central characteristic of neoliberalism is the belief that market or business-oriented approaches are more effective and less costly than government-run programs. However, this has not proven to be the case. Private prisons are not less expensive than publicly run facilities, and they are no more effective at reducing recidivism or enhancing the health and well-being of those who are incarcerated, their families, or communities impacted by crime. Studies are mixed regarding how those imprisoned in private systems fare as compared to their counterparts in public institutions (see, e.g., Lukemeyer & McCorkle, 2006). Regardless of efficacy, privatization of prisons has introduced perverse incentives to expand the criminal justice system due to its function as a place of potential profit, and their moral legitimacy has been contested (Burkhardt, 2014). Some have asked whether it is appropriate or ethical to make prisons into profit-bearing ventures. Put another way, why should any *excess* money go into the hands of prison owners or stockholders rather than into programming or services that assist communities grappling with crime or rehabilitation? If there is money to spare in the running of prisons, might such excess taxpayer dollars be used to fund education, food safety, or reducing taxes? Some of the same companies that own for-profit prisons are now entering the field of for-profit immigrant detention facilities.

Incarceration in the United States has an impact not only on those who are incarcerated, but also on their families and communities. For example, at the individual level incarceration has been linked to chronic health problems (Schnittker & John, 2007) and debt. Families with incarcerated members are at increased risk of divorce (Massoglia, Remster, & King, 2011), and children of incarcerated parents have lower educational performance than their peers (Turney & Haskins, 2014). At a community level, higher rates of incarceration can result in a form of **gerrymandering**, skewing legislative representation (Nonprofit Voter Engagement Network, n.d.). This is because the U.S. Census counts include prison populations in the locations where they are incarcerated even though prisoners are unlikely to be from the communities in which they are incarcerated, regardless of the fact that most do not have the right to vote. This can give *host* communities disproportionately higher representation and deprive *sending* communities of their fair share of legislative representation. Because the distribution of government resources is often based on population, it also means that the communities with the highest rate of incarcerated community members are provided fewer resources than they deserve.

Gerrymandering: Manipulation of voting districts by a more powerful political party seeking to secure or strengthen a majority by drawing voting maps around different population groups

Another major issue related to criminal justice is predatory ticketing. When low-income people receive fines, many for auto-related infringements, that they are unable to pay, they may ultimately end up being incarcerated. In Ferguson, Missouri, in 2015, prior to Michael Brown's death, fees and fines collected by law enforcement, predominantly from community members of color, made up 10% of the city's budget. Some who cannot pay all the fees up front end up making payments over time and face both interest fees and additional costs. For many of those who initially can pay the fees, this is still a huge burden. A Justice Department report found extreme racial bias in policing in Ferguson (2015), using collection of fees and fines as one example of the disparity within the police force's activity.

Collateral consequences are the harmful individual, family, and community effects of criminal system involvement.

Collateral consequences: Legal and regulatory sanctions and restrictions that limit or prohibit people with criminal records from accessing employment, occupational licensing, housing, voting, education, and other opportunities

> Collateral consequences are legal and regulatory sanctions and restrictions that limit or prohibit people with criminal records from accessing employment, occupational licensing, housing, voting, education, and other opportunities. Collateral consequences most frequently affect people who have been convicted of a crime, though in some states an arrest alone—even an arrest that doesn't result in a conviction—may trigger a collateral consequence. (National Inventory of Collateral Consequences of Conviction, 2019)

When individuals are engaged with the criminal justice system, collateral consequences can compound the difficulties to successful reentry to society. Such consequences extend to and exacerbate exclusion from important social-economic supports (e.g., public benefits and housing), employment and educational opportunities, and citizenship (voting or running for office) at a time when people seeking to reenter society may most need them. In her widely cited book, *The New Jim Crow*, Michelle Alexander (2012) argues the disproportionate impact of our criminal policies on racial minorities is not coincidental. She argues that they are a new, ostensibly colorblind, way to disenfranchise African Americans as individuals and communities in the way that the Jim Crow laws did.

Many of these measures have been criticized and, in some cases, people have successfully fought to reverse them. In the 2018 midterm elections, Florida citizens passed a ballot referendum that restored voting rights to people convicted of felonies. According to The Sentencing Project estimates, this would restore voting rights to about 1.5 million people, increasing the eligible voting population in the state by 10% (Uggen, Larson, & Shannon, 2016). Subsequent to the passage of this referendum, the legislature in the state of Florida passed a law requiring people convicted of felony crimes to pay all outstanding court fees prior to being able to vote (Mower & Mahoney, 2019). One study that examined restoration of voting rights in Virginia suggests that those citizens who have become re-enfranchised show more positive attitudes about the government generally and the criminal justice system, both factors that are associated with lower rates of crime (Shineman, 2018).

Social workers play crucial roles at all junctures of the criminal justice system, including in prisons and in assisting formerly incarcerated individuals to reenter society. In the latest figures available from the Bureau of Justice Statistics (2018) in 2002, 592,000 offenders were released from state prisons, the majority of whom continued to be under some form of supervision in the community. Some social workers provide mental health or rehabilitation services, often within the constraints of underfunded and stressful environments that are not conducive to optimal human functioning such as prisons. Social workers may also provide services to the families of incarcerated individuals, who may, as noted above, experience heightened difficulties. Social workers may also facilitate visits or communication with incarcerated family members. Many social workers are involved in the process of reentry. For example, the University of Maryland School of Social Work clinic housed at the School of Law helps geriatric prisoners reenter their communities by developing services that enable their earlier release and reacclimation to civilian life (Siegel & Ozug, 2016). Such services include housing, employment, medical, and reconnecting with families. In addition to this kind of case management, social workers advocate for policy changes that can ease reentry and mitigate or eliminate collateral consequences (Patterson, 2013). One such example is "ban the box" campaigns that have been conducted at the state and local level (Avery & Hernandez, 2018). Ban the box campaigns seek legislative action to remove barriers to employment by prohibiting check-off boxes on job applications related to criminal convictions where such convictions have no relevance to the particular job.

In thinking about the deleterious effects of incarceration and collateral consequences, it is worth asking ourselves as a society what are our goals for the criminal justice system? If we wish for incarceration to serve as a means to rehabilitation, it is clear that different systems must be put in place. The disproportionate impact of incarceration on marginalized communities highlights ways in which the current system is not only ineffective, but also unjust.

ADVOCACY

COLLATERAL CONSEQUENCES

Research the collateral consequences of criminal charges and/or conviction in your state.

1. What charges or convictions give rise to collateral consequences?
2. In what areas of life (employment, housing, benefits, etc.)?
3. What do you think is the underlying rationale for these policies are (this may be explicitly stated)?
4. What is the duration of these consequences?
5. How might this impact your advice as a social work case manager to someone who is reentering society after a criminal conviction?
6. Which (if any) of these sanctions do you believe
    a. Impact a client's ability to desist from criminalized activities
    b. Reasonably protect citizens
    c. Impact a client's citizenship rights

(note: particular sanctions or consequences might fall in more than one of these categories)

The Impact of Criminal Policies on Specific Populations

The well-documented disproportionate impact of criminal justice policies is one reason they should be of interest to social workers who are professionally obligated to combat oppression and work for justice (NASW, 2017). These include people who identify (or are identified as)

LGBTQ+, racial and ethnic minorities, women, immigrants, and people who live in poverty. Policing practices, and the resultant criminal processing that these groups are subject to, is sometimes referred to as the **over-policing under-policing paradox**. Over-policing refers to the fact that certain groups or communities are more often targeted for heightened surveillance and enforcement. The under-policing part of the paradox refers to the fact that these same groups also experience a dearth of protection and safety services, particularly for serious crimes (Levoy, 2015; Vitale, 2017). These experiences are an understandable source of distrust and can erode people's perceptions of the system's legitimacy (National Institutes of Justice, 2016). The following subsections provide information on three groups that experience disproportionate impact and disparate treatment in the criminal justice system: women, African Americans, and low-income communities.

Over-policing under-policing paradox: The paradox that marginalized communities or groups are both the targets of more surveillance and enforcement and experience a dearth of protection and safety services

Women and Girls

Increasing numbers of U.S. women are involved in the criminal justice system (Kajstura & Immarigeon, n.d.). Some have attributed the growing rates of female arrests and incarceration to a rise in female violence. Chesney-Lind and Pasko (2013) challenge this assumption, pointing out that not only do women and girls continue to commit far fewer crimes than their male counterparts, but also the majority of these are nonviolent property crimes or prostitution. According to The Sentencing Project (2018), the change in women's criminal justice involvement "is the result of more expansive law enforcement efforts, stiffer drug sentencing laws, and post-conviction barriers to reentry that uniquely affect women." Figure 13.2 shows the rise in women's incarceration during the last century.

Feminist criminologists highlight the ways experiences of women and girls in the criminal justice system differ from that of men and boys. Their rates of, reasons for, and types of offending are different; they are also surveilled and punished for different behaviors and actions. Historically and in current times, women's and girls' (and even more so African American women and girls) sexual behaviors and perceived promiscuity are regulated and

FIGURE 13.2 ■ Women's Incarceration Rate, United States, 1910–2014

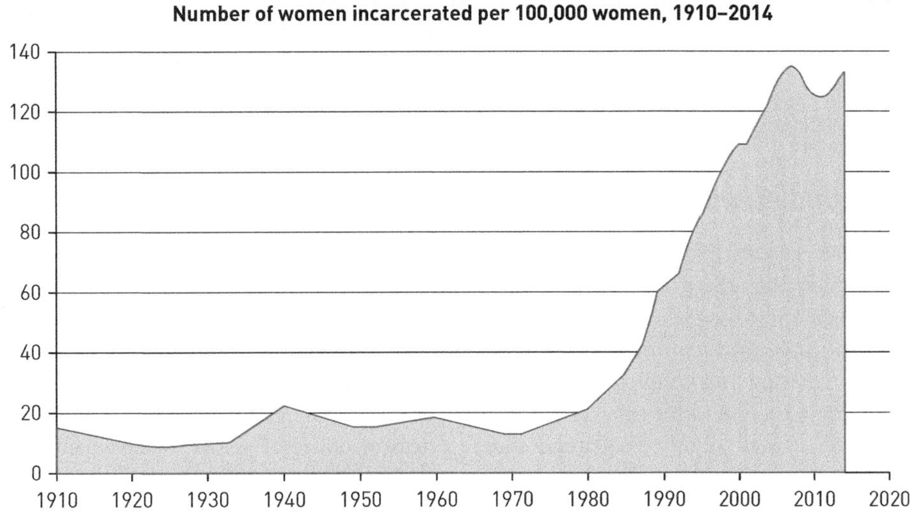

Source: Graph complied by Prison Policy Institute from the following: Bureau of Justice Statistics' Historical Corrections Statistics in the United States, 1850-1984; Bureau of Justice Statistics' State and Federal Prisoners, 1925-85; Bureau of Justice Statistics' National Prisoner Statistics Program punished (see e.g., Bowler, Lilley, & Leon, 2016; Pasko, 2017; Richie & Jones-Brown, 2017). Examination of other crimes, which are often drug related, show that women are disproportionately involved as accessories to their male counterparts. Women also face special hurdles that relate to sexual assault, reproduction, childbearing, and their role as parents. More than 60% of women in state prisons have a child under the age of 18 (The Sentencing Project, 2018).

Incarceration as well as the attendant criminal justice contact leading up to (i.e., arrest) and following (i.e., probation) incarceration may also negatively disrupt caregiving. Although a report for the National Conference of State Legislatures (Christian, 2009) found that the majority of children of those who are incarcerated are in the care of another parent, relative, or kinship caregiver, 11% of incarcerated women (the majority of whom are single parents) had children in foster care. Some studies have found that most children of incarcerated parents in foster care were placed before their parents' incarceration (Moses, 2006). Regardless of whether incarceration precipitates placement, children in foster care experience more hurdles visiting and staying in touch with their incarcerated parent (Christian, 2009), even though strong relational bonds serve as a protective factor for some of the negative consequences of having an incarcerated parent (Martin, 2017).

Many women and girls in jail and prison have long histories of abuse. Some are forced into illegal activities such as drug transport and sales and sex work by abusive male partners. Others are there for violence against abusive partners. For girls, prior sexual assault and other trauma are major predictors of incarceration. The Human Rights Project for Girls found that over half of all incarcerated girls had experienced sexual assault and many more had endured multiple adverse childhood experiences such as physical abuse, psychological abuse, and profound neglect (Saar, Epstein, Rosenthal, & Vafa, 2015).

One recent controversy includes the practice of shackling pregnant women while they are giving birth (Clark & Simon, 2013). This has been challenged in many states, but is still occurring across the country. Access to menstrual supplies has also been discussed in the news and state legislatures. Even where correctional facilities are required to provide these free of charge, leaving their distribution in the hands of individual facilities and correctional officers means that menstrual supplies can be managed in ways that humiliate and punish individual prisoners or women as a group (Greenberg, 2017). You can research the laws and practices in your state around such issues or others as well as actual or potential advocacy efforts that have been mounted to address them. Social workers are often well positioned by virtue of their different roles working within the criminal justice system or with people and communities affected by it to better understand the intended and unintended consequences of criminal justice policies.

Communities with High Rates of Poverty

Individuals who are living in poverty are much more likely to be involved with the criminal justice system than those with greater wealth. As Table 13.1 shows, annual incomes of all men and women and for racial and ethnic subgroups who are incarcerated are much lower than their non-incarcerated counterparts.

Those arrested and convicted of crimes are also more likely to have been unemployed or working part time prior to arrest than other people (Looney & Turner, 2018). A criminal record, as well as other collateral consequences of criminal justice involvement such as restrictions on licensure, types of employment, and public benefits, make it harder for people with criminal records to find and maintain employment. As a result, people with criminal records are less likely to be employed, even several years after incarceration (Looney & Turner, 2018).

TABLE 13.1 ■ Median Annual Incomes for Incarcerated People Prior to Incarceration and Non-Incarcerated People Ages 27 to 42, in 2014 Dollars, by Race and Ethnicity and Gender

	Incarcerated People (prior to incarceration)		Non-Incarcerated People	
	Men	Women	Men	Women
All	$19,650	$13,890	$41,250	$23,745
Black	$17,625	$12,735	$31,245	$24,255
Hispanic	$19,740	$11,820	$30,000	$15,000
White	$21,975	$15,480	$47,505	$26,130

Source: Prison Policy Imitative, using data from the Bureau of Justice, retrieved from https://www.prisonpolicy.org/reports/income.html

Researchers and the popular press have chronicled how criminal fines and fees burden low-income defendants, often turning minor infractions into financial punishments or deprivations of liberty that exceed what the legislature intended to be the punishment for specific crimes. What are referred to as **LFOs (legal financial obligations)** can include court costs, criminal fines, and fees assessed for procedures (like DNA testing) and supervision or monitoring. LFOs can be levied as a form of restitution when crimes involve harms to victims (Washington State Superior Court, 2018). LFOs are also used as part of a criminal penalty to heighten the *cost* of offending. Some LFOs are a mechanism of shifting costs from the state to those who are tried and convicted, a practice that has become more prevalent as criminal justice systems have been crushed by the costs of charging and incarcerating people in growing numbers. As a result of research on the LFOs and advocacy efforts, in 2018, San Francisco passed an ordinance to abolish all court fees (San Francisco Ordinance No. 131-18, 2018).

LFOs (legal financial obligations): Fines and fees beyond what is set out as punishment for a crime and can include restitution, court costs, criminal fines, and fees assessed for supervision or monitoring

Defendants who cannot pay LFOs when they are assessed also pay interest; in Washington State, for example, LFOs bear a mandatory rate of 12% interest annually (ACLU Washington, n.d.). This is just one of the ways that LFOs are far more onerous on low-income individuals than their wealthier counterparts. Whereas middle- and upper-income individuals can generally pay costs and fines immediately, those who struggle financially can find themselves saddled with debt that follows them for their whole lives, increasing over time. These reinforce and deepen already existing inequalities by making it harder for people living in poverty convicted of crimes to start afresh after having served their sentences (Martin, Sykes, Shannon, Edwards, & Harris, 2018). Failure to pay can lead to more fines, more supervision, and incarceration. They also lead to loss of credit, often barring those with criminal convictions from financial transactions that are a basis for stability, such as renting or buying a house or car. Alec Schierenbeck's (2018) *The New York Times* op-ed opens with an illustrative comparison of how fines that are the same for everyone are often **regressive** (meaning that they have a harsher impact on people with less money):

Regressive fines: Fines that have a disparate impact on people with fewer economic resources

> If Mark Zuckerberg and a janitor who works at Facebook's headquarters each received a speeding ticket while driving home from work, they'd each owe the government the same amount of money. Mr. Zuckerberg wouldn't bat an eye. The janitor is another story.

While many LFOs are required, judges often have discretion at the upper end. Research shows that judges tend to assess fees in excess of minimums and often do not have or do not use mechanisms to consider income as a factor (Harris, 2016). In contrast, the differential impact of LFOs is mitigated in other legal systems such as Finland's, which adjusts fines by income (Shierenbeck, 2018). Measures that employ **progressive fine** systems, which may be tied to a person's earnings or the value of the car that was driven during a speeding incident, may be fairer and serve as better deterrents to high-income offenders than our current system.

Progressive fines: Fines that are calculated to have a relatively equitable impact by, for example, considering a person's income bracket

Race and Ethnicity

Racial and ethnic minority communities consistently suffer from both high levels of crime and intensive and sometimes abusive policing. Despite high levels of arrests and proactive interventions, most major crimes go unreported to police and only about half of those reported are ever solved (Vera Institute 2019a). At the same time, people in these communities are surveilled, policed, charged, and punished more harshly and at disproportionate rates. Inequities exist at all points in the system, from policing through charging, convicting, and sentencing. As Cassia Spohn (2017) sums up in her historic and current review of racial disparities in the U.S. criminal justice system:

> Racial minorities—and especially young black and Hispanic men—are substantially more likely than whites to be serving time in prison; they also face significantly higher odds than whites of receiving life sentences, life sentences without the possibility of parole, and the death penalty. (p. 171)

Conviction of innocent people is thought to be a result of unacknowledged and unchecked psychological biases, misidentification, media, and political and prosecutorial incentives (Godsey, 2017; Gould & Leo, 2010). Nearly all U.S. states have what are called **innocence projects**, which have helped overturn **wrongful convictions** that have resulted in innocent people serving sometimes decades of their life in prison. As with other inequities in our criminal justice system, wrongful convictions disproportionately impact racial minorities. Of the 1,900 people on the National Registry of Exonerations, which tracks people who are convicted and later found innocent, 47% were African American (Gross, Posley, & Stevens, 2017). African Americans are also much more likely to be found innocent among people who are discovered to have been framed in policy scandals. Given the greater harm and lower benefit that racial minorities experience vis à vis the criminal justice system, it is unsurprising that they show higher levels of distrust of the criminal justice system (Morin & Stepler, 2016).

Innocence projects: Organizations or programs devoted to overturning wrongful convictions

Wrongful conviction: When an innocent person is convicted of a crime

These concerns have been highlights in the wave of protests in response to high profile, but unfortunately not unusual, killing of black men and women. The #BlackLivesMatter movement, the most prominent voice, was started in 2013 by black organizers Alicia Garza, Patrisse Cullors, and Opal Tometti after the acquittal of George Zimmerman for Trayvon Martin's murder. In this case, Zimmerman was acquitted of criminal charges, on the basis of a defense that rested on what the jury determined was a legitimate fear, for murdering the unarmed black teenager who was out to purchase a candy bar. In the years following, the killing of young black men at the hands of police, including Freddie Gray in Baltimore, Michael Brown in Ferguson, and Eric Garner in Staten Island, sparked protests across the country. Police brutality was also implicated in the death of Sandra Bland, a young black woman who died in custody following a Texas traffic stop.

The protests in the streets (see Photo 13.3) were aimed not only at the deaths, but also in frustration over a lack of accountability within the criminal justice system. These included—depending on the case—complaints regarding insufficient disciplinary actions, prosecution, conviction, and policy reform and education. Such concerns were shored up by evidence produced in federal investigations of local police in Ferguson and Baltimore, which we have cited above. Despite the 2018 directive of former Attorney General Jeff Sessions to decrease federal investigation of local police, according to a bipartisan federal U.S. Commission on Civil Rights (2018) report:

Joe Raedle/Getty Image News

PHOTO 13.3
Demonstrators in Miami, Florida, stood with tape reading reading, " I Can't Breathe", on December 7, 2014. The protest was one of many that took place nationwide after grand juries investigating the deaths of Michal Brown in Ferguson, Missouri and Eric Garner in New York failed to indict the police officers involved in both incidents.

> The best available evidence reflects high rates of use of force nationally, and increased likelihood of police use of force against people of color, people with disabilities, LGBT people, people with mental health concerns, people with low incomes, and those at the intersections of these groups.
>
> Lack of training and lack of funding for training leave officers and the public at risk. Critical training areas include tactical training, de-escalation techniques, understanding cultural differences and anti-bias mechanisms, as well as strategies for encounters with individuals with physical and mental disabilities.
>
> Repeated and highly publicized incidents of police use of force against persons of color and people with disabilities, combined with a lack of accurate data, lack of transparency about policies and practices in place governing use of force, and lack of accountability for noncompliance foster a perception that police use of force in communities of color and the disability community is unchecked, unlawful, and unsafe. (p. 5)

This report is careful to note that better information, training, and accountability are important not only for the communities adversely impacted by problematic policing, but also by police and broader society.

The police are a gateway into the criminal justice system, and racial disparities and disproportionate punishment continue at all points. One example at the punishment end is in death penalty cases. African Americans are disproportionately among those who are executed or awaiting execution; 42% of the 2,553 prisoners awaiting death in 2016 identified as black (Davis & Snell, 2018). A qualitative study of death penalty juries document racial bias (Fleury-Steiner, 2004). How the government responds at all levels, including the point of investigation, shapes the criminal justice system and how it is perceived. Will it be considered a trustworthy protector of individuals and communities and their rights? Or will it be considered a liability and threat to the safety and security of individuals and communities? We can see from the information presented in this chapter that the answer to these questions may vary depending on one's perspective and identity. Social workers' responsibility to protect vulnerable populations directs our actions to challenge the detrimental impact of the criminal justice system on racial minorities, women, and low-income communities, among others.

TABLE 13.2 ■ List of Relevant Laws

Topic	Laws	Oversight Agency	Website
Criminal offenses	Title 18 of the U.S. Code Federal and state penal codes	Department of Justice U.S. Sentencing Commission Local and state law enforcement, prosecution, and judiciary	https://www.justice.gov/ https://www.law.cornell.edu/uscode/text/18
Parole and probation	Prisoner Rehabilitation Act of 1965 Pretrial Services Act of 1982 Sentencing Reform Act 1984	Probation and Pretrial Services System Parole Commission Local and state agencies	http://www.uscourts.gov/services-forms/probation-and-pretrial-services https://www.justice.gov/uspc
Law enforcement	The Civil Rights Act of 1964 and 1968 Comprehensive Drug Abuse Prevention and Control Act of 1970 Anti-Drug Abuse Act of 1986 Violent Crime Control and Law Enforcement Act of 1994 Violence Against Women Act of 1994 Office of Community Oriented Policing Services (established by the Violent Crime Control and Law Enforcement Act of 1994) Patriot Act (2001)	Department of Justice (oversees Federal Bureau of Investigation [FBI], Drug Enforcement Agency [DEA], other federal agencies) Department of Homeland Security (oversees Immigration and Customs Enforcement [ICE], Customs and Border Protection, Coast Guard) State departments of public safety Office of Juvenile Justice and Delinquency Prevention	https://www.justice.gov/ https://www.dhs.gov/ https://cops.usdoj.gov/
Hate crimes	The Civil Rights Act of 1964 Violent Crime Control and Law Enforcement Act 1994 Church Arson Prevention Act of 1996 Hate Crime Statistics Act of 1990 Matthew Shepard and James Byrd, Jr. Hate Crimes Prevention Act of 2009	Department of Justice	https://www.justice.gov/ https://www.adl.org/adl-hate-crime-map https://www.aclu.org/
Prisons and jails	Eighth Amendment of the U.S. Constitution Anti-Drug Abuse Act of 1986	Federal Bureau of Prisons Department of Corrections Bureau of Justice Statistics State and local departments of corrections	https://www.usa.gov/corrections
Juvenile justice	Juvenile Justice and Delinquency Prevention Act of 1974	Office of Juvenile Justice and Delinquency Prevention	https://www.ojjdp.gov/
Data collection and research	Justice Systems Improvement Act of 1979	Bureau of Justice Statistics	https://www.bjs.gov/

POLICY INFORMED BY ALTERNATIVE LENSES

Just as many of the reforms outlined in our historical description were a (sometimes) well-intended outgrowth of moral outrage and/or a desire to more effectively address what are perceived as problematic behavior (Rothman, 1980), there are also well intentioned recent reform efforts. As advocates of, or participants in, such reforms, social workers would do well to heed the cautionary tales of history that tell us that while reforms may bring important improvements, they likely have their own socially problematic intended and unintended consequences.

Alternative Criminal Justice Programs

Diversion programs are a common alternative criminal justice response that grows out of the perception that existing responses to criminalized activities are ineffective or unfairly punish people for behaviors they would avoid if they had the choice (see, e.g., Leon & Shdaimah, forthcoming). Grounded in **therapeutic jurisprudence** (Winnick & Wexler, 2003), diversion programs seek to enhance the therapeutic implications of legal system encounter and minimize those that may exacerbate underlying problems. They involve multidisciplinary teams that can include social workers, public defenders, prosecutors, judges, police, probation officers, mental health providers, and community partners, including social service agencies and nonprofit organizations (many of which are run or staffed by social workers).

Therapeutic Jurisprudence: A term that describes the therapeutic and anti-therapeutic consequences of encounters with the criminal justice system. Therapeutic jurisprudence proponents seek to minimize the anti-therapeutic aspects of criminal justice involvement and maximize its therapeutic potential.

Diversion programs do not fundamentally change the legal status of offenses, but as the name suggests, they divert individuals from consequences at different stages of the criminal process. At the earliest stage of criminal justice involvement are programs such as the Law Enforcement-Assisted Diversion Program (LEAD), started in Seattle, that divert individuals at point-of-arrest by police officers. In programs that require a guilty plea, defendants waive their legal rights to challenge the charges in court and are diverted from punishment while they remain in the program. If successful, they have charges dismissed and expunged. Progress in diversion programs is met by rewards, and breaches result in sanctions. Most programs subscribe to a philosophy by which sanctions are graduated and customized to provide an opportunity for reflection and learning (National Drug Court Resource Center, 2016). These can include essays that are read in open court, community service, and incarceration. In phased programs, sanctions can be accompanied by a program phase restart, lengthening defendants' required supervision. Continued breaches or expulsion may lead to termination of the defendant's participation, thus triggering consequences from which defendants were originally diverted.

Concerns about diversion programs include defendants' rights, unequal distribution of opportunities, and **net-widening** effects when they capture individuals who might not otherwise be arrested (Strangio, 2017; Wahab & Panichelli 2013). Many programs require a guilty plea as a condition of participation, raising concerns about coercion if programs serve as a gateway to much-needed resources. Others criticize the diversion of scarce community resources, such as treatment beds or housing slots, into the criminal justice system. Concerns have also been raised about the appropriateness and quality of treatment and the tension that arises from the provision of rehabilitative services, particularly therapy, within the criminal justice system requiring public disclosure and the threat of punishment. Equally important, diversion programs rarely address systemic conditions that contribute to people's motivation for engaging in illegal activities, such as affordable housing, discrimination, the availability of adequate and appropriate treatment, and living wage employment (Shdaimah & Bailey-Kloch, 2014). One overview of drug court evaluations found mixed results, with some drug courts effective

Net-widening: A term used to reflect the expansion of the criminal justice system to include more people or behaviors due to programmatic, policy, or implementation changes for some participants (Boldt, 2010). Problem-solving courts may have worse outcomes than traditional criminal justice responses for participants who do not succeed (Orr et al., 2009). Diversion programs' incorporation of rehabilitative services within the criminal justice system present both opportunities and challenges.

REFLECTION

SOCIAL WORK PRACTICE AND ETHICS

Think back to Larissa from the opening vignette who is being offered entrance into a prostitution diversion program. Imagine again you are the social worker who coordinates this program. You have noticed that, while many women benefit from the program, the prosecutor often pushes for things that go against your Code of Ethics. For example, she asks you to reveal the content of therapy sessions, even though it was initially agreed informally that she would only ask about whether and how often you meet with participants. You push back on these requests, but the judge only reluctantly supports you, saying, "Please remember that we are all on the same team."

1. To what extent does this program change the underlying characterization of prostitution?
2. To what extent might this program change Larissa's immediate, short-term, and long-term circumstances?
3. Consider your potential responses to the prosecutor and the judge; some options might be to
   a. leave the program,
   b. educate them on your Code of Ethics,
   c. push back on a case-by-case basis, and/or
   d. ask the stakeholder group to revisit the policies to clarify the different obligations and agreements of each professional involved in the program.

Restorative Justice

Restorative justice: A theory of justice, drawing inspiration from indigenous practices, that emphasizes repairing the community when a harm is committed through a collaborative process that includes recognition of the harm. Solutions based on restorative justice often include reparations, reconciliations, and reintegration.

While diversion programs are firmly nested within the existing criminal justice system, **restorative justice** (Zehr, 1990) is an alternative response that can take place within or outside of this system. An umbrella term used to include a range of programs, restorative justice approaches are said to have originated in indigenous practices that focus on harm that is caused to individuals and to communities when a person offends. The community seeks to hold the offender accountable and to create an opportunity for the offender to acknowledge responsibility and repair the harm. Restorative justice is largely viewed as compatible with social work values in that it is a holistic perspective that incorporates a variety of perspectives and views harm within the context of the individual and their environment (Gumz & Grant, 2009). According to Van Wormer and Bednar (2001), it is also compatible with social work's strength-based approaches. There is some debate about whether restorative justice approaches are appropriate in all situations, and in all cases the parties must agree to participate. While we introduce them here in the context of criminal justice, restorative justice is also practiced in other settings with the potential to repair harms such as in child welfare team decision making (Drywater-Whitekiller, 2014) and education (see Chapter 7). Harms that may be perceived as appropriate for criminal justice processing or resolution are also addressed, with the agreement of the parties. This sometimes occurs within communities either prior to engagement with the criminal justice system or in cases where restorative justice is presented as an alternative (diversion) from a part of the process, such as when a judge refers to community mediation with the agreement of the parties. Some restorative justice programs are also in addition to rather than instead of the regular criminal justice process as in the case where convicted offenders who have served or are serving their sentences and victims or their families choose to engage in a restorative practice.

Rethinking Our Goals for Criminal Justice

In our introduction to this chapter, we describe several criminal justice goals, including retribution, deterrence, and rehabilitation. After reading the chapter, it should now be clear that dominant themes of U.S. criminal justice are deterrance, largely through incapacitation and punishment. The designated legal consequences for offenses are amplified through collateral consequences which are compounded for low-income and otherwise marginalized populations. For example, when people go to jail, they often lose their jobs. While some programs exist for rehabilitation or to address the root causes of offending, as with the case example, they are located in court programs that may involve coercion and punishment. This often makes for internally contradictory messages and programming. For example, after successfully completing a diversion program, graduates may still find it impossible to secure sustainable legal employment due to collateral consequences including LFOs and restrictions on housing and work. The pervasive and ongoing surveillance that disparately impacts low-income communities, people of color, women, and LGBTQ+ individuals has also led many to the conclusion that the criminal justice system is used to control and keep down minority populations.

Many researchers have attributed the punitive nature of the U.S. system to its use as a tool for social control. A number of theorists argue the criminal justice system is the political system's response to an overly fearful, irrational, and vengeful public. Responses are often disproportionate, with fear of crime seemingly decoupled from actual crime rates. Many believe that our system is very punitive especially due to *racialized othering*, in which predominantly white policymakers enact often overly punitive policies due to fear of African American communities which has led to the high rates of disproportionate criminal justice involvement and disparate treatment for blacks.

In her cross-national comparative study, Lisa Miller (2016) provides a different theory for the punitive nature of U.S. criminal justice policy. She analyzed policy proposals and political rhetoric in regard to violent crime, with a specific focus on homicide. Miller found that fear-based, punitive policies that target marginalized groups in the United States are more often a result of political framing by policymakers than a response to public fear. She therefore argues that public fear is *created and exploited* by policymakers rather than being a motivating factor for policy change. Miller theorizes that policymakers are not responding to public demand so much as serving existing powerful interests. The influence of money plays a role in this case through growing power of the prison industry, which works against responses that differ from our current forms of punishment (Brickner, & Diaz, 2011). Policymakers shape options through framing the debate and constructing particular policy options. When policymakers offer *only* punitive policies as solutions, these policies find public support in the face of alternatives to do nothing. In contrast, Miller (2016) finds that when rising crime rates gave rise to similar fears in England, policymakers offered punitive policy options that were accompanied by social welfare policies designed to addresses social causes to crime, such as investment in early childhood education. These were supported by the public as a package, indicating that if more comprehensive approaches to crime were offered, they may have public support (Miller, 2016). Data indicate that the U.S. public might similarly support more comprehensive programming in relation to low-level offenses such as drug- or mental health–related offending or prostitution, such as the diversion programs discussed above. They may also be supported by communities (see e.g., Shdaimah, Kaufman, Bright, & Flower, 2014) and professional associations such as the American Psychological Association (see e.g., Benson, 2003). Such a shift would be compatible with a person-in-environment stance that attends to the complex interaction of structural opportunities and constraints with community, neighborhood, and family influences, as well as individual agency.

ADVOCACY

FRAMING

This section returns to frames that guide U.S. criminal justice policy. The chapter has many examples where social workers and others point out injustices and work to effect change, such as the #BlackLivesMatter movement, SWASC, and diversion programs. Some of these target large systems; others seek to make smaller but meaningful changes at the local or program level. Social workers have the skills and the obligation to work at all these levels.

1. What goals do you think should guide our criminal justice policy?
2. What activities can you do to foster discussions of your vision and engage with others who may have similar and different views?
3. What specific policy or program might you target as an area to implement small but meaningful changes?
4. What specific policy might you target as an area for broader change?

OPPORTUNITIES FOR ADVOCACY

Many opportunities for social work advocacy exist within and around the criminal justice system. In this section, we highlight efforts to address solitary confinement and advocacy that specifically focuses on people with mental illness and developmental disabilities when they interact with police.

Solitary Confinement

Social Workers Against Solitary Confinement (SWASC) was formed in October of 2014 to engage with criminal justice reform. More specifically, its mission is to abolish solitary confinement and offer support to those who have been affected by this practice. SWASC (n.d.) views solitary confinement as "a torturous, cruel, and inhumane practice that violates United Nations Conventions and Covenants." SWASC calls on social workers and mental health professionals to recognize that solitary confinement is a violation of basic human dignity, rights, and welfare, and therefore in opposition to the social work Code of Ethics. Solitary confinement is a practice that also disproportionately affects low-income, minority populations. SWASC is not the only group of professionals to make a statement against the use of solitary (APHA) confinement, which has also been challenged by the American Public Health Association (APHA) (2013) and the National Commission on Correctional Health Care (2016).

SWASC operates a range of initiatives. On a micro level, SWASC offers social work support and rehabilitation to those who have been held in solitary confinement, as well as to professionals who work with them. On a macro level, SWASC raises awareness, mobilizes resources, and influences policy toward the abolition of solitary confinement. SWASC runs advocacy campaigns urging lawmakers to limit the use of solitary confinement and calling for mental health workers and correctional personnel to halt participation in solitary confinement practices (SWASC, 2018). SWASC also partners with national and international organizations to develop alternative measures for disciplining and protecting inmates.

DISCUSSION

SOLITARY CONFINEMENT ADVOCACY

Efforts to curb the use of solitary confinement have been spearheaded by social workers and other professionals in different practice areas (e.g., mental health, criminal justice) using different strategies (e.g., clinical, administrative, organizing, policy). Think about a criminal justice issue of interest to you:

1. What are the different ways in which social work practice intersects with that issue?
2. How would you find more information on this topic? What can you find out about whether this topic is handled differently in other states or countries?
3. Given what you know, what changes might you like to see?
4. Sketch out some strategies for making these changes. When crafting your strategy, consider
   a. Who might be your allies and how you can work together?
   b. What tactics would you use to achieve your goal?
   c. What outcomes would you consider a success?

People Experiencing Mental Illness

People who are killed by police, incarcerated, placed in solitary confinement, and who commit suicide disproportionately experience mental illness. Some reports have found that people with mental illness are 15 times more likely to be killed by police than others (Fuller, Lamb, Biasotti, & Snook, 2015). The American Public Health Association (APHA) (2018) has identified police violence as a major public health issue creating trauma and stress for citizens in communities being policed. A recent Vera Institute report (2019b) noted that approximately 15% of men and 31% of women in prison suffer from serious mental illness, including bipolar disorder, schizophrenia, and major depressive disorder and 68% suffer from substance abuse disorders. These individuals are also more likely to be placed in solitary confinement than others (Metzner & Fellner, 2010). Solitary confinement has been shown to worsen psychiatric symptoms (Weir, 2012). Nonetheless, fewer than 15% of those with mental illness receive appropriate treatment while incarcerated (Vera Institute, 2019b). Perhaps this is why those with mental illness are more likely to commit suicide in jail than others (Daniel, 2006). A number of organizations such as the National Alliance on Mental Illness (NAMI) conduct outreach and trainings with police departments to raise awareness and train law enforcement in responding appropriately. This can include de-escalation tactics, providing resource and referral information, and understanding how people with mental illness may behave or respond in a police encounter (National Alliance on Mental Illness (NAMI), 2019). Some have criticized existing police training, suggesting that interventions should be provided not by police officers but rather by social workers or other professionals with expertise in mental illness. Social workers should also think critically about the larger context of policing and advocate at the macro level rather than trying to train the police to behave better, noting that the research on the effectiveness of police trainings suggests that they are often ineffective (Vitale, 2017).

Final Discussion

Now that you have finished reading this chapter, reread the vignette at the beginning. Based on what you have learned, answer the following questions. Point to specific references in the chapter that help you answer these questions. Consider how different theories inform the response to these questions.

1. How do you think the criminal justice system should respond to Larissa's offending behavior, and why? In considering your answer to these responses, think of who you are considering (Larissa, her neighborhood, the broader community) and your goals for the response.
2. What different policies may be relevant here?
3. How might you explain to Larissa the pros and cons of her options when you visit with the public defender?
4. What steps might you take to try to resolve any ethical conflicts that might arise for you as a social worker in this role?
5. What role might race, class, gender, and other aspects of identity play in this vignette?

14

HOUSING AND HOMELESSNESS POLICY

LEARNING OBJECTIVES

14.1: Describe the history and social construction of homelessness in the United States

14.2: Describe the history and social construction of housing in the United States

14.3: Critique how various policies address challenges for people who are homeless or struggle with housing discrimination

14.4: Apply a Housing First framework to supporting homelessness

14.5: Plan advocacy actions to address homelessness using criminal justice reform and the racial disparity tool

Social workers who work in homeless shelters, transitional housing, or public social services work directly with individuals experiencing homelessness and are affected by housing policy every day. Social workers who work with families and children in schools, survivors of intimate partner violence, children in child protective services, those in substance use treatment, and in health care need to navigate housing systems on behalf of communities and individuals experiencing homelessness, at risk of homelessness, and those who have been harmed by housing systems, landlords, or housing policies. This is true of social workers who work in urban, suburban, and rural communities in economically well-off areas and in economically struggling communities.

In the United States, an individual or family's experience of housing or homelessness is heavily influenced by characteristics such as race, gender, family composition, and sexual orientation. In this chapter, we describe perspectives on shelter in the United States, beginning with the history of housing and homelessness policy, and how it affects today's housing segregation, homelessness, and related social problems such as health and educational inequities. We define homelessness and look specifically at the role of structural racism in access to assets, adequate housing, and homeownership. We also examine how housing and homelessness policy affect the larger social context in many important facets of life.

Vignette: Larissa and Housing First

Based on what you know from the media or your personal, work, or volunteer experiences, think about the following questions as you read the vignette. When you finish the vignette, answer the questions below.

1. What systems could be involved in Larissa's life?
2. What steps might you take to try to resolve any ethical conflicts that might arise for you as a social worker if you were working with Larissa?
3. What are the broader systemic factors that influence the choices available to Larissa?
4. Are there government policy changes that could help Larissa and, if so, what are they? What advocacy efforts might social workers make to bring these about?
5. What role might race, class, and gender, or other aspects of identity play in this vignette?

Larissa, whom you met in Chapter 13, has trouble getting or keeping a steady job due to her bouts of ill health, criminal record related to prostitution and drugs, and housing instability. She has attempted to stop using drugs several times, but struggles to stay sober when back on the streets or in neighborhoods where she has previously used drugs. Larissa recently completed a 1-year diversion program as part of a plea agreement for her prostitution charge. Since she graduated, she has not been able to find stable long-term housing. Most of the housing programs available to Larissa require that she stay sober, follow stringent rules, and take frequent urine checks (often daily) to remain housed. If she fails to follow all the program rules, she will be without a place to live and back on the streets. A friend she met in a treatment program thinks Larissa might be eligible for a program that follows the Housing First model, but this is the first she has heard of this program and is not sure what she should do or whom to ask. A top priority for Larissa is to regain custody of her daughter, Kendra. She knows that she cannot get custody unless she has a place to live, but is not sure what else she needs to do to demonstrate that she has a safe place where Kendra can live with her. Larissa is also unsure whether she would be allowed to live with Kendra while she is in a Housing First program, even if she does regain custody.

HISTORY AND SOCIAL CONSTRUCTION OF U.S. HOMELESSNESS

As Elaine Abelson noted in 2003, "Historical memory is short and we have forgotten (if we ever knew) that homelessness has been a recurrent problem in the United States" (p. 105). In this section, we look at the historic roots of homelessness. While homelessness became more visible to the American public after the 1980s, when federal budget cuts and deinstitutionalization of people with mental illness made the problem impossible to ignore, it has existed in some form throughout our nation's history (Hopper, 1991). Today, **homelessness** is defined as a state of housing for individuals and families who lack a fixed, regular, and adequate nighttime residence; will imminently lose their primary nighttime residence; unaccompanied youth and families with children and youth; and individuals and families who are fleeing, or are attempting to flee, domestic violence, dating violence, sexual assault, stalking, or other dangerous or life-threatening conditions.

Homelessness: A state of housing for individuals and families who lack a fixed, regular, and adequate nighttime residence; will imminently lose their primary nighttime residence; unaccompanied youth and families with children and youth; and individuals and families who are fleeing, or are attempting to flee, domestic violence, dating violence, sexual assault, stalking, or other dangerous or life-threatening conditions

An early example of inadequate housing existed in the late 19th century in the New York City **tenements**, a room or rooms within a house or block of apartments in which people often lived in crowded and unsanitary conditions. These residences held 290,000 people per square mile and still could not contain all who needed housing (Reynolds, 1893). Lubove (1963) describes the New York tenements:

Tenements: A room or rooms within a house or block of apartments in which people often lived in overcrowded and unsanitary conditions

> By the 1850's, one might notice squat three- and four-story boxes of wood or brick in the downtown area, filled with workingmen and their families. These flimsily constructed railroad flats contained as many as twelve or sixteen families. No ray of sunlight penetrated the tiny interior bedrooms, not much larger than closets. Those who could not afford the luxury of an apartment in a reconverted one-family home or in a tenement frequently landed in dark, damp cellars or renovated stables and warehouses. (p. 3)

The Progressive Era: Homelessness and the "Married Vagabond"

In 1895, Mary Richmond, generally viewed as one of the founders of modern social work, spoke at the 22nd Annual Conference of Charities and Corrections in New Haven, Connecticut—the closest thing to a national conference for the profession at that time. During this professional conference, the many people addressed the systemic problem of tenements and poor housing (Barrows, 1895). For example, Marion I. Moore of Buffalo, NY, called out tenement house landlords and the local Board of Health for their roles in contributing to the unsanitary and unsafe conditions of tenements. Dr. E.R.L. Gould of the University of Chicago suggested that giving women more responsibility in the administration of tenements would lead to better outcomes. In contrast to these views, Mary Richmond focused on the moral deficits of individuals whom she called "married vagabonds." **Vagabond** was a derogatory term used to conjure an image of people experiencing homelessness as people who wandered from place to place irresponsibly.

Vagabond: Derogatory term used to describe a person who is experiencing homelessness

Here is an excerpt:

> I have ventured to give this title [Married Vagabonds] to my paper, because I am anxious to bring the *man* of the neglected family out of that retirement—behind wife and children—into which he has so discreetly withdrawn. A great deal has been written about the single vagabond. His nomadic habits have been described

> by specialists and some have even ventured to turn tramp and take the road, in order to secure data at first hand for their studies. No specialist, however, has been able to study the married vagabond in the same way. He is well protected from scientific scrutiny—too well protected. It has been my fortune to know individually a considerable number of both the single and the married fraternity, and I confess to a preference for the former. It is true that the tramp is a barbarian, openly at war with society; but then, he is not so prompt to claim from society the privileges and protection which she so willingly extends to the head of a family. In short, he is not such a cowardly, unenterprising creature. (p. 514)

This writing by Richmond and others like it highlight the moral judgment that was common to the work of Charity Organization Societies and other charity workers during that time, as discussed in Chapter 1. They assumed those who experienced homelessness or were in danger of becoming homeless had done something to cause that situation and sought policies to force these "barbarian[s], openly at war with society" (p. 514) to own up to their responsibilities. These writings ignore the larger societal issues of industrialization, family separation, unemployment, and inadequate housing. The attempts by charities and governments to address these concerns were generally inadequate to remedy systemic problems and focused primarily on individuals. For example, the first Salvation Army mission offered "soup, soap, and salvation" in New York's Bowery district (U.S. Department of Housing and Urban Development [HUD], 2011). Generally, social service programs run by the Charity Organization Societies or government, including workhouses, almshouses, or poorhouses, focused first on determining who was worthy of help (Riis, 1890/1967). Those with no place to stay were also given the opportunity to sleep on the floor of police stations, with nearly 450,000 doing so in the 1874–1875 winter (Johnson, 2010).

Great Depression: Homelessness and Societal Factors

The economic upheaval of the Great Depression made it harder (but not impossible) to view homelessness as an individual failing, given that the 1933 census counted 1.5 million persons experiencing homelessness (Crouse, 1986). This number was almost entirely comprised of people experiencing what we would today call "unsheltered homelessness" and very likely vastly undercounted those who were doubled-up with families, living in their cars, or otherwise invisible to the system, bringing the total number of people actually experiencing homelessness to at least two million. **Unsheltered homelessness** refers to people experiencing homelessness who are sleeping outside, in places not meant for human habitation, such as parks, public transportation stations, the street, and wooded areas. Even given the clear systemic failures that caused homelessness and housing instability during this time, the responses of many charities and governments were inadequate to the task. A homeless family during this time is illustrated in Photo 14.1.

Unsheltered homelessness: People experiencing homelessness who are sleeping outside, in places not meant for human habitation, such as parks, public transportation systems, the streets or wooded areas.

Women and people of color were affected first by the Great Depression and had the least ability to recover, given that they had fewer employment opportunities, were ineligible for many New Deal programs, and had fewer financial resources available to them (Abelson, 2003; Johnson, 2010). As the New Deal and World War II manufacturing helped bring the Great Depression to a close, homelessness persisted but became less visible, and "allowed most Americans to think of homelessness as someone else's problem throughout the next 20 years" (McClendon & Lane, 2014, p. 349). Housing problems borne of the economic downturn compounded the discrimination African Americans had historically faced in housing. Since the end of the Civil War, African Americans from the south who migrated north in search of jobs often faced limited housing options due to segregation and discrimination

(Johnson, 2010). For more about how women and African Americans in particular were disadvantaged in finding housing throughout American history, we highly recommend two articles: Johnson's "African Americans and Homelessness: Moving Through History" and Abelson's "'Women Who Have No Men to Work for Them': Gender and Homelessness in the Great Depression, 1930–1934", both listed in the references for this chapter.

Farm Security Administration - Office of War Information Photograph Collection (Library of Congress)

PHOTO 14.1 Homeless family photographed by Dorothea Lange in 1939

Deinstitutionalization: The Modern Era of Homelessness Begins

The next time homelessness became too visible to be ignored by the public at large and policymakers was when the Community Mental Health Act of 1963 attempted to **deinstitutionalize** or move people with chronic mental health conditions from a lifetime in state-run institutions to community-based mental health clinics. In principle, this was an idea that had the opportunity to provide a much higher quality of life for people with mental illness and their families, many of whom advocated for these changes (Gollaher, 1993). This deinstitutionalization movement failed not necessarily because the idea was wrong, but because of its poor implementation and insufficient funding (Lamb, 1994). Signed by President Kennedy right before his death, this act was designed to provide a network of services to support individuals with psychiatric disorders in community settings. Instead, these individuals were discharged into communities without access to care, treatment, or the ability to maintain housing (Feldman, 1983). This ushered in the modern-day era of services for people experiencing homelessness, including soup kitchens and emergency shelters for men and women. Increased urban homelessness combined with decreased federal assistance for cities in the 1980s resulted in an increase in need and a decrease in capacity. Between 1980 and 2003, federal support for low-income housing, including public housing and Section 8, was cut in half (Wardrip, Pelletiere, & Crowley, 2005). Federal funding for housing has continued to decline. From 2011 to 2016, the combination of federal funding on all housing programs decreased between 4% and 13% annually (Rice, 2017). This combined with increasing need and increased cost of living in cities have moved some of the burden of housing and homelessness services into suburbs and rural areas (HUD, 2011).

Deinstitutionalize: Discharge individuals from institutions; deinstitutionalization refers to a policy strategy designed to release individuals with mental illness from institutional care

HISTORY AND SOCIAL CONSTRUCTION OF U.S. HOUSING

Today's U.S. residents are very likely to live in a neighborhood where other people share their racial or ethnic background, particularly if they are white or African American. Today, if you are white, you are likely to live in a neighborhood that is 75% white and 8% African American. If you are African American, you are likely to live in a neighborhood that is 45% African American and 35% white (Greene, Turner, & Gourevitch, 2017).

Housing Segregation and Federal Policy

***de facto* segregation:** Segregation in fact, meaning the existence of segregation even where policy does not explicitly segregate

***de jure* segregation:** Segregation caused by laws

Structural racism: A system in which institutions and policies within our nation disadvantage nonwhites in ways that are often compounding and cumulative

Integration: A situation in which people live together or near others who are racially and ethnically different from them

Why does housing segregation, where people are likely to live near people of their own racial or ethnic background, happen? Is it because Americans choose to live in neighborhoods with other people who come from our same racial background because of our own racist beliefs and/or have a desire to live near others who we identify with (a concept known as homophily)? Or is it because racist real estate agents or landlords steer us into segregated neighborhoods? Is it a direct result of slavery and the attitudes that created slavery? All these factors play a role in housing segregation, but they are not the whole story. In *The Color of Law*, Richard Rothstein (2017) argues that government at all levels used explicitly racist policies to define where different racial and ethnic groups, particularly those who are identified as white and African American, should and can live. These policies have deliberately segregated communities across the country, creating *de jure* segregation. Both ***de facto* segregation** (segregation in fact, meaning that legislation does not overtly segregate people by race, but nevertheless segregation exists) and ***de jure* segregation** (segregation created by laws) are intimately linked with structural racism, both existing as a consequence of it and perpetuating it. **Structural racism** is the system within which institutions and policies in our nation disadvantage nonwhites. In this instance, African Americans are particularly affected. Rothstein also suggests that the reasons for housing segregation are important. If, as he contends, segregation was caused by government policies, it is not just the government's option but the government's *responsibility* to address it. "African Americans were unconstitutionally denied the means and the right to integration in middle-class neighborhoods, and because this denial was state-sponsored, the nation is obligated to remedy it" (Rothstein, 2017, p. xiv). **Integration** is defined as a situation in which people live together with those who are different from them.

REFLECTION
YOUR NEIGHBORHOOD

In the supplemental materials for this book, you can find maps of your area that show you how integrated or segregated your area is. Think about the neighborhood where you live or grew up. How racially and ethnically diverse is that area? Are there any other kinds of obvious diversity?

Racist policies coexist with policies that specifically prohibit racism in public policy. The Fifth Amendment prohibits unfair treatment of citizens, the Thirteenth Amendment prohibits slavery and its byproducts, and the Fourteenth Amendment states that,

> [n]o state shall make or enforce any law which shall abridge the privileges or immunities of citizens of the United States; nor shall any state deprive any person of life, liberty, or property, without due process of law; nor deny to any person within its jurisdiction the equal protection of the laws.

In 1866, following the end of the Civil War, Congress passed a Civil Rights Act (over the veto of President Andrew Johnson), which made it illegal to act in ways that replicated the characteristics of slavery. Racial discrimination in housing was included in this ban. In 1875, Congress passed another Civil Rights Act, influenced by the testimony of seven African American members of Congress, which prohibited discrimination by private business owners. During debate on this bill, African American Representative James Rapier of Alabama characterized the question to be answered as simply "either I am a man or I am not a man"

(United States House of Representatives, n.d., para. 1). However, the effects of these laws were short lived. For the next 100 years, the federal government actively worked to promote racial segregation and discrimination. In 1883, the Supreme Court ruled that Congress had overreached its authority in trying to keep private business owners from discriminating (The Civil Rights Cases, n.d.). This 1883 decision laid the groundwork for a century of legal discrimination against African Americans, including in housing. It took the 1968 *Jones v. Mayer* decision and the Fair Housing Act to give the government the authority to address discrimination in private markets and to provide the government with a way to enforce that law.

The Legacy of Redlining—Segregation and the Fair Housing Act

Deliberate segregation in government housing policy is most commonly associated with "redlining" (Rothstein, 2017). The term **redlining** comes from the Federal Housing Administration (FHA) and is defined as the process of refusing a loan or insurance to someone because they live in an area deemed to be a poor financial risk, which results in significant segregation. Created in 1934, the FHA's Underwriting Manual helped determine whether mortgages in any given area were eligible for federal insurance, which essentially determined the availability and cost of mortgages in any given area. The manual claimed to focus on the "examination of mortgage risk" (Federal Housing Administration [FHA], 1936, para. 2). Regarding race, the manual states,

Redlining: The practice of refusing a loan or insurance to someone because they live in an area deemed to be a poor financial risk that results in significant segregation

> The Valuator should consider carefully the immunity or lack of immunity offered to the location because of its geographical position within the city. Natural or artificially established barriers will prove effective in protecting a neighborhood and the locations within it from adverse influences. Usually the protection against adverse influences afforded by these means include prevention of the infiltration of business and industrial uses, lower-class occupancy, and inharmonious racial groups. (FHA, 1936, para. 229)

The manual specifically speaks to the need to keep schools segregated, saying,

> The social class of the parents of children at the school will in many instances have a vital bearing. Thus, although physical surroundings of a neighborhood area may be favorable and conducive to enjoyable, pleasant living in its locations, if the children of people living in such an area are compelled to attend school where the majority or a goodly number of the pupils represent a far lower level of society or an incompatible racial element, the neighborhood under consideration will prove far less stable and desirable than if this condition did not exist. (FHA, 1936, para. 266)

By 1950, the FHA and the Department of Veterans Affairs (VA), using these same rules, were insuring half of all mortgages in the country. This made it virtually impossible for African Americans to obtain mortgages or forced them to pay substantially higher down payments and higher interest if they sought to purchase homes. By 1973, the U.S. Commission on Civil Rights declared "[t]he housing industry, aided and abetted by Government, must bear the primary responsibility for the legacy of segregated housing" (p. 3). The supplemental materials of this book include the redlining maps for many areas of the country, like the one demonstrated in Figure 14.1—can you find one close to where you live?

As we discuss through the rest of this chapter, the legacy of racist policies like redlining continue today. One potential policy solution to this historic injustice that has been proposed is a set of **reparations**, or compensatory payments, to the communities most affected by redlining, slavery, and other racist policies. One bill to start the reparations process, H.R. 40, has been introduced in Congress continually since 1989 (Owens, 2017).

Reparations: Payments of money to those who have experienced past wrongs

FIGURE 14.1 ■ Home Owners' Loan Corporation (HOLC) "Residential Security" Map of Atlanta

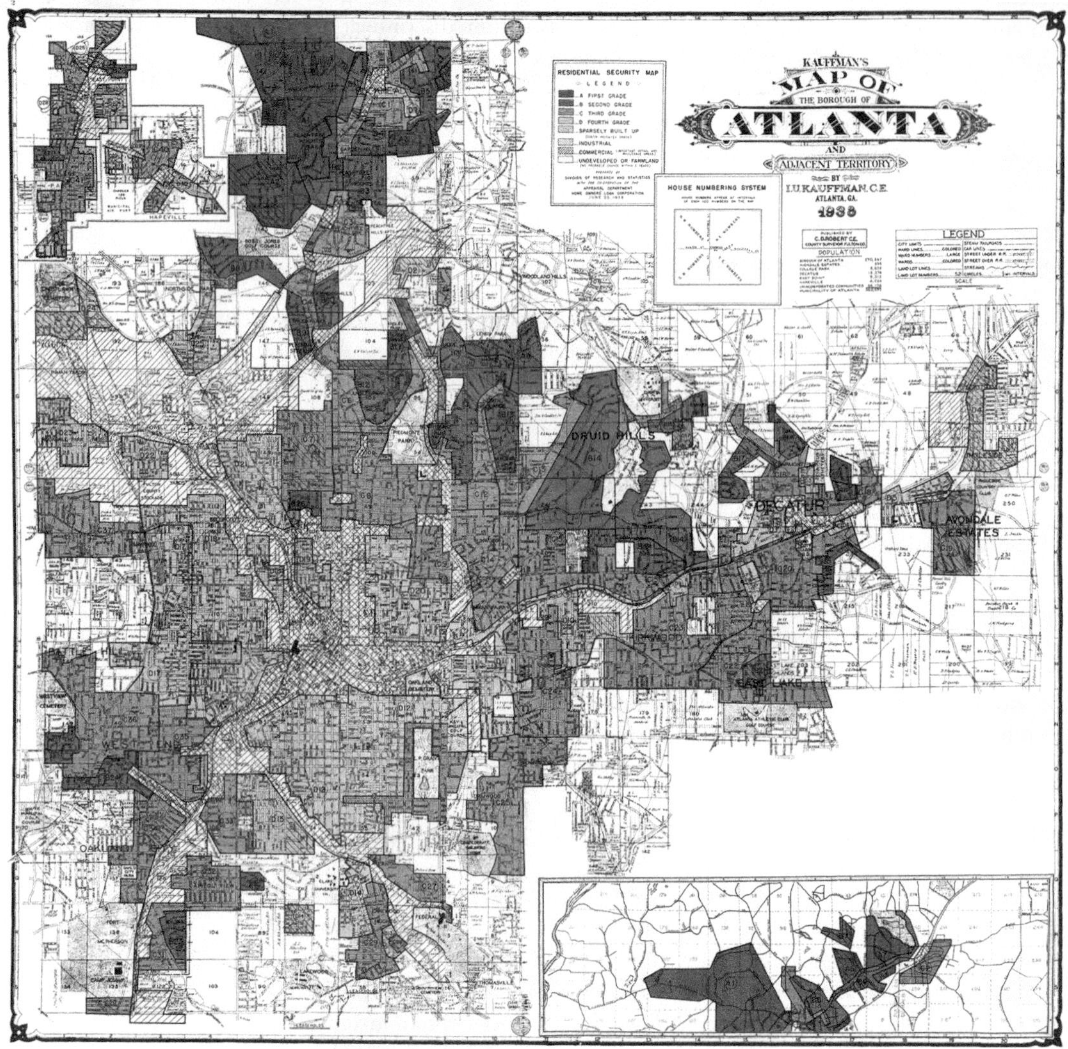

Source: Robert K. Nelson, LaDale Winling, Richard Marciano, Nathan Connolly, et al., "Mapping Inequality," American Panorama, ed. Robert K. Nelson and Edward L. Ayers, accessed March 14, 2019, https://dsl.richmond.edu/panorama/redlining/#loc=11/33.7535/-84.3565&opacity=0.8&city=atlanta-ga&text=bibliograph.

Congress passed the Fair Housing Act as part of the Civil Rights Act of 1968 to address housing segregation. It was signed into law by President Johnson a week after the assassination of Dr. Martin Luther King, Jr. An appellate judge, ruling on the law, noted that Congress' intentions were clear: "Congress was aware that the measure would have a very broad reach, and indeed the legislation was seen as an attempt to alter the whole character of the housing market" (Wilkey as cited in Calmore, 1997, p. 1070). Enforcement of this law has been either weak or troubled (Calmore, 1997), despite some forward movement. One positive development was the Fair Housing Amendments Act passed in 1988, which expanded the protections of the Fair Housing Act to include people with disabilities and families with children and increased the ability of the U.S. Department of Housing and Urban Development (HUD) to enforce the law (Squires, 2017).

Home Ownership: Is It the American Dream?

According to the U.S. Department of Housing and Urban Development (2018a),

> For many Americans, owning a home is an essential part of the American dream that conveys a number of economic benefits, such as the ability to accumulate wealth and access credit by building home equity, reduce housing costs through the mortgage interest deduction, and gain long-term savings over the cost of renting. (para. 1)

However, as described above, government policy has not made home ownership equally available to all. Because home ownership has historically been seen as a way to grow wealth, many people invest their life savings into their homes and go into significant debt to purchase homes. As a result, when events like the Great Recession of 2007–2009 moved many families into foreclosure and bankruptcy, this also led to increased homelessness and loss of accumulated wealth. We might think of **wealth** as a term that only applies to those who are very well-off, but economists use this term to refer to any assets held by individuals and families, including homes and equity in a home, in comparison to any debt they carry. While the overall net worth of American families has not returned to prerecession levels, by 2013, the disparity in wealth between white families and black and Hispanic families had grown significantly when compared to 2007 prerecession levels. As shown in Figure 14.2, Pew Research Center (2014) found that white families had a median wealth of 13 times

Wealth: Assets held by individuals and families, including homes and equity in a home, minus any debt they carry

FIGURE 14.2 ■ Wealth Gap Between White, Black, and Hispanic Households

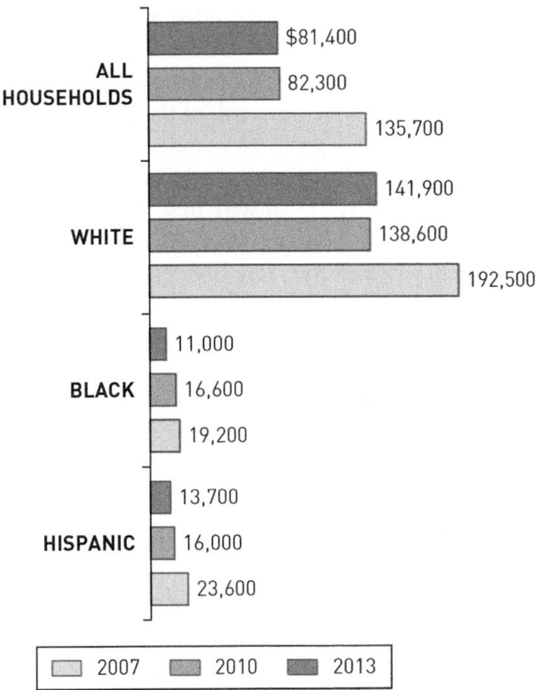

Source: Pew Research Center tabulations of Survey of Consumer Finances public-use data

Note: Blacks and whites include only non-Hispanics. Hispanics are of any race.

that of black families and 10 times that of Hispanic families. Cost and inequities related to health care are also connected with risks in home ownership—think back to the discussion in Chapter 11 about the expenses of health care and the disparities in the quality of care available to different groups in the United States. In 2008, as the Recession was at its peak, half of all households reported that medical expenses had led to their foreclosures (Robertson, Egelhof, & Hoke, 2008).

CURRENT HOUSING AND HOMELESSNESS POLICY

Homelessness is a complex problem that has drawn media and research attention throughout the United States for decades. How big is the problem of homelessness in the United States? In 2018, according to the annual Point-in-Time (PIT) count, approximately 553,000 persons were experiencing homelessness on a single night in January (HUD, 2018b). Two thirds were staying in shelters or transitional housing programs, while one third were living on the street or in other places not intended for sleeping (HUD, 2018b).

Approximately half of those counted as homeless on this night were in the 50 largest U.S. cities, while about 20% were in rural areas. While the public image of homelessness is often of adults who are on their own, this number included 180,000 people who were part of families with children, 91% of whom were in sheltered locations (HUD, 2018b). African Americans, who make up 13% of the U.S. population, make up 40% of those experiencing homelessness and 51% of members of families with children experiencing homelessness. Rates of homelessness are trending downward nationally among many groups including veterans and families (HUD, 2018b), but homelessness, particularly unsheltered homelessness, continues to be a crisis in cities like San Francisco and New York (HUD, 2018b; Wu, 2018).

Today, homelessness exists everywhere in the United States, though it is concentrated in particular areas. In January 2018, 3,900 people were living in shelters following emergencies or natural disasters such as Hurricanes Harvey, Irma, Maria, and Nate and wildfires in the western United States (HUD, 2018b). At the same time, half of the people experiencing homelessness in the United States were in California, Florida, New York, and Texas (the four largest states in the country). Hawaii, Oregon, and Washington also had high rates of homelessness. Nearly half of all unsheltered people in the country (47%) were in California. In Maine, Massachusetts, New York, and Rhode Island, at least 95% of people experiencing homelessness were in shelters (HUD, 2018b). Both Massachusetts and New York have a state constitutional "right to shelter" for individuals and families. This, combined with the harsh winter weather, may explain the high rates of sheltered homelessness as opposed to unsheltered homelessness.

Differences in homeless rates are caused by geography, access to services, and many other factors. The supplemental materials of this book include information collected by HUD about homelessness across the country so you can look at the homeless population in your area. Homelessness is a problem for people who might not be your first vision of homeless individuals, such as college students. The vignette in Chapter 8 was inspired by the story of Daisia Kai Walker, a student at Central Connecticut State University who is one of the 17% of students in her college system who are dealing with homelessness (Megan, 2018). Because she was profiled in a newspaper series on college homelessness, a local hospital reached out and offered Walker a job, but the problem of homelessness remains for tens of thousands of college students across the country.

Most individuals and families who use homelessness services cycle in and out of them. Kuhn and Culhane (1998) classify homelessness as chronic, episodic, or transitional. People experiencing **transitional homelessness** or short-term homelessness make up approximately 80% of shelter users, and associated challenges include unemployment, relationship status, housing availability, or substance use. One third of those in emergency shelters stay for a week or less, and those in this category generally experience one or two shelter stays over a 3-year period. Those experiencing **episodic homelessness**, approximately 10% of shelter users, cycle in and out of homelessness and may stay in shelters five times in 3 years. **Chronic homelessness** or long-term homelessness accounts for a small portion of the overall homeless population, but this population has especially high needs. They account for 24% of all people who are homeless, and two thirds are likely to stay in unsheltered locations. This number has declined by 26% since 2007 (HUD, 2018b).

Transitional homelessness: Short-term homelessness

Episodic homelessness: Homelessness that is experienced in recurring cycles that are relatively short

Chronic homelessness: Long-term homelessness

Housing concerns addressed in today's housing policy range from lack of affordable housing to housing segregation and discrimination. Housing policy covers a wide swathe of U.S. policy at the federal, state, and local levels. Much policy that relates to housing, such as mortgage policies or other financial regulations, has a significant effect on social work practice and the populations with which social workers engage. Table 14.1 at the end of this section outlines significant federal policies relating to both housing and homelessness in the United States.

Defining Homelessness

In order to evaluate policies that affect homelessness, it is useful to have a shared definition of the problem. Definitions vary, which means that those eligible for assistance through one program might not be eligible through another. For example, if you are sleeping in your own apartment, but expect eviction any day, are you homeless? Some might call that "precariously housed" or "housing unstable" instead of homeless; some might not consider it a housing problem until you are officially without a place to stay.

The federal government offers several definitions of homelessness through different programs. The definition used by the HUD as directed by Congress through the McKinney-Vento Homeless Assistance Act as amended by the Homeless Emergency Assistance and Rapid Transition to Housing (HEARTH) Act of 2009 is widely used. This definition provides four possible categories under which individuals and families may qualify as homeless:

1. Individuals and families who lack a fixed, regular, and adequate nighttime residence, including a subset for an individual who resided in an emergency shelter or a place not meant for human habitation and who is exiting an institution where he or she temporarily resided;
2. individuals and families who will imminently lose their primary nighttime residence;
3. unaccompanied youth and families with children and youth who are defined as homeless under other federal statutes who do not otherwise qualify as homeless under this definition; and
4. individuals and families who are fleeing, or are attempting to flee, domestic violence, dating violence, sexual assault, stalking, or other dangerous or life-threatening conditions that relate to violence against the individual or a family member. (Federal Register, 2011, p. 75995)

What is the thread that ties these categories together? It is "that the person has no home of his or her own, any available shelter is tenuous or unsafe, sleeping arrangements are precarious, and they have little to no safety or privacy" (McClendon & Lane, 2014, p. 347).

The landscape of work with youth and children experiencing homelessness is even more complicated. There are at least three different definitions of homeless youth used by the federal government, including by the Department of Housing and Urban Development, the Department of Education, and programs authorized by the Runaway and Homeless Youth Act (youth.gov, n.d.a). HUD's definition specifically includes

> children and youth who are sharing the housing of other persons due to loss of housing, economic hardship, or a similar reason; are living in motels, hotels, trailer parks, or camping grounds due to lack of alternative adequate accommodations; are living in emergency or transitional shelters; are abandoned in hospitals; or are awaiting foster care placement. (McKinney-Vento Act sec. 725[2]; 42 U.S.C. 11435[2])

McKinney-Vento and HEARTH

In 1987, the McKinney-Vento Homeless Assistance Act began to address the challenges of modern homelessness and create opportunities for government and nonprofit responses at the local, state, and federal levels. One of the most significant programs created by McKinney-Vento was the Continuum of Care (CoC) program. The CoC

> is designed to promote community wide commitment to the goal of ending homelessness; provide funding for efforts by nonprofit providers, and allow State and local governments to quickly rehouse homeless individuals and families while minimizing the trauma and dislocation caused to homeless individuals, families, and communities by homelessness; promote access to and effect utilization of mainstream programs by homeless individuals and families; and optimize self-sufficiency among individuals and families experiencing homelessness. Programs operated under CoCs include emergency shelter, transitional living programs, and permanent supportive housing for disabled and highly vulnerable populations. There are more than 400 CoCs across the country. (HUD, n.d-a)

In 2009, the HEARTH Act reauthorized and redesigned McKinney-Vento. It funds both prevention activities and efforts to find permanent housing solutions for recently homeless individuals and families as quickly as possible (HUD, n.c). Among other provisions, this law consolidated all of HUD's competitive grants in one place, created a program for rural housing, updated the definitions of homelessness used by HUD, and increased emphasis on both prevention and program performance (i.e., measuring outcomes). In 2017, appropriations for activities under HEARTH/McKinney-Vento included $2.383 billion in funding for street outreach, homelessness prevention and diversion, emergency shelter, rapid rehousing, permanent supportive housing, transitional housing, and coordinated entry (National Alliance to End Homelessness, 2017).

Point-in-Time (PIT) Count: Annual count of sheltered and nonsheltered people experiencing homelessness

Sheltered (homelessness): Individuals or families residing in homeless programs such as emergency shelters, transitional living programs, and rapid rehousing

Unsheltered or street (homelessness): individuals or families sleeping outside, in places not meant for human habitation, such as parks, public transportation stations, the street, and wooded areas

Counting People Experiencing Homelessness

The CoCs described above are heavily involved in a challenging activity: counting the number of people experiencing homelessness within geographic areas to help policymakers understand the needs of each community. One of the challenges in this count is that many people who are experiencing homelessness are difficult to find or do not wish to be found. Two primary methods are used. Each year during the last week in January, every CoC across the nation is required by HUD to conduct a **Point-in-Time (PIT) Count** as a condition of their federal funding. This count includes an annual **sheltered** count of people currently residing in homeless programs such as emergency shelters, transitional living programs, and rapid rehousing, as well as the total number of available beds in their community. At least every other year, programs conduct an **unsheltered** or **street** count of people experiencing homelessness who are sleeping outside, in places not meant for human habitation, such as parks, public transportation stations, the street, and wooded areas. Many communities complete the PIT Count between the hours of 8 p.m. and 5 a.m. to try to find everyone who is experiencing unsheltered homelessness on that night. This count is completed primarily by volunteers, some of whom are social workers or social work students.

The second method used to collect data is a Homeless Management Information System (HMIS), a locally administered database that each CoC must implement as a requirement of HUD funding for homeless assistance projects. Since 2014, other federal funders such as the Department of Veterans Affairs (VA) and the Department of Health and Human Services (HHS) have also required that projects funded through their agencies also participate in HMIS (HUD, n.d).

These data are collected and presented in HUD's Annual Homeless Assessment Report (AHAR), which focuses on identifying and understanding the scale of homelessness. The AHAR, presented to the U.S. Congress, "provides nationwide estimates of homelessness, including information about the demographic characteristics of homeless persons, service use patterns, and the capacity to house homeless persons" (HUD, 2018b). This information helps inform the allotment of resources granted by Congress and HUD to each geographic area to address their local needs to prevent and try to eliminate homelessness (HUD, 2018b). Counting people experiencing homelessness may seem unrelated to the everyday social work practice of working with people who are homeless, but it is an important process that can benefit from social work skills and is crucial to providing our agencies and communities with the resources needed to work with people experiencing homelessness. Knowing how many people are affected by homelessness can help influence policymakers to allocate resources to help them.

Predatory Lending

During the Great Recession, many families were victimized by predatory lending. **Predatory loans** are a type of **subprime loans** that are designed for borrowers with risky credit who may be unable to obtain loans from mainstream lenders. Because of the increased risk, lenders charge higher interest rates than those that are available in the *prime* mortgage market, the term used for mortgages to people considered to have a lower risk of not paying their loans. Predatory loans meet at least one of the following criteria:

1. higher interest and fees than is required to cover the added risk of lending to borrowers with credit imperfections,
2. abusive terms and conditions that trap borrowers and lead to increased indebtedness,
3. fails to take into account the borrower's ability to repay the loan, and
4. violates fair lending laws by targeting women, minorities and communities of color. (National Community Reinvestment Coalition, 2002, p. 4)

Predatory loans: A type of subprime loans with higher interest and fees than is required, abusive terms and conditions that fail to take into account the borrower's ability to repay. These loans violate fair lending laws by targeting women, minorities, and communities of color.

Subprime loans: Loans that are designed for borrowers with risky credit who may be unable to obtain loans from mainstream lenders

Because predatory loans disproportionately *target* vulnerable populations, the financial difficulties, including foreclosure and bankruptcy, that follow from these loans disproportionately affect marginalized groups. Advocates have long fought predatory lending and have had legislative successes at the local and national level. Despite legislation such as the Dodd-Frank Wall Street Reform and Consumer Protection Act of 2010, the Equal Credit Opportunity Act of 1974, and the Fair Housing Act, all of which were designed to stop these discriminatory practices, they persist (National Community Reinvestment Coalition, 2002).

Public Housing

Public housing in the United States has roots in the military, including housing for white military families, which was expanded to civilians working near naval shipyards and munitions plants during World War I (Rothstein, 2017). Housing was a struggle for both African American and nonaffluent white families during the Great Depression, a systemic problem that continued through World War II. As part of the New Deal, public housing for families without a connection to the military was created. As with many New Deal programs, housing projects were segregated by race or designated entirely for white families. Housing available for African Americans was substandard compared to housing offered to white families. The Public Works Administration (PWA) used the "neighborhood composition rule," which said that federal housing projects should reflect the previous racial composition of neighborhoods. Even integrated urban neighborhoods were the recipients of segregated housing in violation of this "rule." Some segregated public housing was built by demolishing existing integrated housing and rebuilding whites-only or blacks-only projects in their place, causing segregation where there was none before (Rothstein, 2017). By 1937, when the federal government ended the building of housing by the PWA and turned this responsibility over to the U.S. Housing Authority (USHA) as part of the Wagner-Steagall Act, segregation was the program's official policy.

In the 1940s, as white access to home ownership increased, public housing became increasingly identified as an African American problem. In 1949, newly elected Senator Hubert Humphrey, who would be a champion of civil rights legislation and one of the first senators to employ an African American staff member, argued for the passage of the 1949 Housing Act. He stated: "I should like to point out to my Negro friends what a large amount of housing they will get under this act" (Humphreys, 1949 as quoted in Rothstein, 2017, p. 31). He and other advocates felt that the need for housing justified supporting the act, even though almost all the housing created would be built as segregated, unequal housing. The housing constructed as a result of this law included Techwood Homes in Atlanta, shown in Photo 14.2, the first public housing project in the country, as well as the Cabrini Green Homes in Chicago, which held 15,000 people at its height and was mostly demolished in the 1990s and early 2000s, and the Van Dyke Houses in New York City, which are in a neighborhood of Brownsville in Brooklyn considered one of the poorest areas in New York City.

Historic American Buildings Survey, Library of Congress, HABS GA,61-ATLA,60C

PHOTO 14.2 Techwood Homes: The first federally funded public housing project in this country, Atlanta, Georgia

Today, African Americans make up 12% of the overall population of the United States and 45% of public housing tenants. Significantly, "African American and Hispanic public housing residents are four times more likely than white public housing residents to live in high poverty neighborhoods" (National Low Income Housing Coalition, 2012, p. 3). Contrary to many public beliefs, the segregation of public housing in the United States is a direct result of deliberate segregationist government policies and actions.

Subsidized Housing, Including Section 8

In addition to public housing, another significant area of federal housing policy is privately owned subsidized housing. Generally, this type of housing involves long-term subsidy contracts between a private owner and a government agency such as the HUD. Section 8 is the most well-known subsidized housing. Another program is the Housing Choice Voucher that allows families to rent from landlords who do not have a long-term contract with the government and, in theory, provides individuals and families with some ability to choose where they want to live (Kingsley, 2017). These programs also depend on the willingness of landlords to participate, which often comes with some form of oversight. This can limit the use of such vouchers, and a number of local government initiatives have sought to curtail discrimination against people using housing vouchers to pay for their rent by outlawing what has become known as "source of income discrimination" in housing (National Housing Law Project, 2017). There are a number of other ways in which the federal government enters into the housing market to address housing needs that are outside the scope of this chapter; the Urban Institute's excellent policy brief on federal housing assistance (Kingsley, 2017) is a useful resource in this area.

Current Policy Areas: Supportive Housing

Supportive housing policies offer opportunities to people who are at risk of homelessness or otherwise have difficulty living independently (U.S. Interagency Council on Homelessness, 2018). These policies generally result in housing options that combine stable housing with support services such as help with household work, therapy, addiction services, or medication management. Supportive housing is often designed for a specific population. For example, the Section 202 Supportive Housing Act of 2010 (which modifies Section 202 of the Housing Act of 1959, hence the name) offers housing to families in which at least one person is over age 62, and the family meets criteria for very low income. It allows independent living with support services that could include cooking, cleaning, transportation assistance, and more (HUD, n.d). This program is often just referred to as Section 202. This program is similar to the Section 811 Project Rental Assistance Program, called simply Section 811 or PRA, authorized by Section 811 of the National Affordable Housing Act of 1990 and updated by the Frank Melville Supportive Housing Act of 2010, which provides similar services for very low- and extremely low-income people with disabilities, generally those who have an income of 30% or below their area's median income. To find out what incomes would qualify someone for these programs in your area, you can visit the HUD website and search "income limits."

Violence Against People Experiencing Homelessness

Between 1999 and 2017, the National Coalition for the Homeless (2018) documented 1,758 violent crimes against people experiencing homelessness resulting in 476 deaths. According to the Coalition,

> [t]hese crimes are believed to have been motivated by the perpetrators' biases against people experiencing homelessness or by their ability to target homeless people with relative ease. The crimes include an array of atrocities such as murder, beatings, rapes, and even mutilations. (p. 4)

The true number of attacks is undoubtedly higher than reports indicate because many individuals experiencing homelessness will not report victimization out of fear of engaging with law enforcement. Violent crime adds to the trend that those who experience homelessness have a life expectancy 20 to 30 years less than the general population. Victims of bias crime are among the 13,000 people experiencing homelessness who die each year (National Coalition for the Homeless, 2018). Laws that cover hate crimes such as civil rights laws do not generally include crimes against individuals experiencing homelessness in the definition of hate crimes, but homeless advocates such as the National Coalition for the Homeless are pushing for the laws to be changed to include this category.

Youth Homelessness

Youth experiencing homelessness include those who are members of families, those who have aged out of foster care programs, those who have been released from juvenile justice programs, and those who have left or been forced to leave family homes or abusive relationships (Miller, Unick & Harburger, 2017). A disproportionate number of homeless youth, somewhere between 20% and 40%, identify as lesbian, gay, bisexual, transgender, and queer/questioning or other sexual or gender identities (LGBTQ+). Some studies found as many as 20% of youth shelter residents came to the shelter directly from foster or group homes (Bass, 1992). Systemic hurdles such as lack of access to affordable housing, systemic racism, and poverty are also significant for this population (Miller et al., 2017). Homeless youth have multiple vulnerabilities. Those who are with families may be afraid that their homeless status will cause them to be removed from their families. Those who are alone may be ineligible for services or financial support or fearful they will be returned to unsafe family or institutional settings. Youth on the streets are likely to engage in high-risk survival behaviors such as **survival sex** (prostitution, or trading sex for shelter). Runaway and homeless youth are likely to experience problems such as school failure, substance abuse, delinquency, malnutrition, sexually transmitted infections, serious mental disorders, and premature death from suicide, murder, or drug overdose (Greene, Ringwalt, & Iachan, 1997; Haber & Toro, 2004; Robertson & Toro, 1999). Miller, Unick, and Harburger (2017) also emphasize the resiliency of this group—homeless youth are often resourceful in finding ways to make ends meet, stay in school, and work, despite the challenges they face. Although the resources available do not match the need, federal policy includes programs for runaway and homeless youth such as the Basic Center Program that encourages reunification or alternative placements. Services available also include the Transitional Living Program, which includes long-term housing; programs for youth aging out of foster care; and programs for those who are pregnant or parenting (youth.gov, n.d.b).

Survival sex: Sex that is exchanged for shelter or other basic necessities

Local Policy: Rent Control

Rent control: A system where the government uses price controls to keep the cost of rent down for some rental units

Rent control is a system where the government uses price controls to keep the cost of rent low for some rental units. Though originally a European idea, rent control was introduced in the United States during World War II to ensure affordable housing, particularly for soldiers and their families. The first rent control policies were rent freezes. Though in most places rent control laws expired in the late 1940s, they continued in New York. As a result of high inflation and tenants' rights organizing, additional U.S. cities such as Baltimore, Chicago, and Seattle as well as parts of California adopted rent control policies in the 1960s and 1970s. These rent control policies allowed for slight increases in rent (Jenkins, 2009). As of 2019, the only states that currently have municipalities with rent control laws are California, Maryland, New Jersey, New York, and the District of Columbia. Most other states have state laws preempting rent control thereby prohibiting localities from passing or enforcing rent control laws (National Multifamily Housing Council, 2018). On February 28, 2019, Oregon enacted the first statewide rent control policy in the United States that will limit rent increases to 7% a year in addition to inflation. Some opposed to this law argued that rent control has historically advantaged higher income families and created housing shortages while reducing the quality and quantity of rental housing (Ingber, 2019; Lazo, 2019).

TABLE 14.1 ■ List of Relevant Federal Laws

Topic	Laws	Oversight Agency	Website
Homelessness services	McKinney-Vento Homeless Assistance Act/Homeless Emergency Assistance and Rapid Transition to Housing Act (HEARTH)	National Center for Homeless Education/Department of Education Department of Housing and Urban Development	https://nche.ed.gov/mckinney-vento/ https://www.hudexchange.info/homelessness-assistance/
Homeless youth	Runaway and Homeless Youth Act	National Center for Homeless Education/Department of Education Family and Youth Services Bureau/Department of Health and Human Services	https://nche.ed.gov/runaway-youth/ https://www.acf.hhs.gov/fysb/programs/runaway-homeless-youth
Homelessness, mental health and substance use	Community Mental Health Act Community Mental Health Services Block Grant	Substance Abuse and Mental Health Services Administration/US Department of Health and Human Services	https://www.samhsa.gov/grants/block-grants/mhbg
Public housing and subsidized housing	Section 8 Housing Choice Vouchers	Department of Housing and Urban Development	https://www.hudexchange.info/programs/public-housing/
Housing discrimination	Fair Housing Act/Civil Rights Act of 1968	Office of Fair Housing and Equal Opportunity/Department of Housing and Urban Development	https://www.hud.gov/program_offices/fair_housing_equal_opp
Financial protections for mortgages	Dodd-Frank Wall Street Reform and Consumer Protection Act of 2010 Equal Credit Opportunity Act of 1974	Bureau of Consumer Financial Protection/Federal Reserve Board Department of Justice	https://www.consumerfinance.gov/ https://www.justice.gov/crt/equal-credit-opportunity-act-3
Hate/bias crimes		Civil Rights Program/Department of Justice	https://www.fbi.gov/investigate/civil-rights/hate-crimes
Supportive housing	McKinney-Vento Homeless Assistance Act/Homeless Emergency Assistance and Rapid Transition to Housing Act (HEARTH) Section 811 Section 202		https://www.hudexchange.info/programs/shp/ https://www.hudexchange.info/programs/811-pra/ https://www.hudexchange.info/programs/section-202/

POLICY INFORMED BY ALTERNATIVE LENSES

Housing, homeless policies and housing rights have changed many times because of our understanding of homelessness and its causes. In this section, we will focus specifically on current programs and services for people experiencing homelessness. We ask you to think about the following question: Is housing a basic human right that should be provided to people even if they are actively using substances or have not yet successfully managed a mental health issue or should it be a reward for people who meet certain program criteria?

Treatment First or Housing First?

Approximately one quarter (20% to 25%) of people experiencing homelessness have severe mental illnesses—significantly higher than the 6% of the general population with similar health status. Mental illness is a significant factor in homelessness for both single adults and families. One mechanism that has proven successful in serving people experiencing homelessness and mental illness is coordination between homeless service providers and mental health providers. Another effective strategy is supported housing, which as discussed above combines housing services with treatment for mental and physical health problems, education and employment, and significant peer and professional support (National Coalition for the Homeless, 2009).

The traditional approach to working with people with mental illness or substance use disorders who are experiencing homelessness is to focus on treating any underlying addiction or illness first (treatment first). For example, for those with substance use disorder, this approach requires individuals to go through detoxification, attend treatment, and/or achieve sobriety as a condition of independent living. In this model, the dominant choice of policymakers and programs from the 1960s to the 1990s, individuals needed to comply with treatment rules, prove abstinence, and give up a significant amount of privacy. In return, they gained access to housing and supporting services; breaking the rules was likely to get them expelled from such programs and returned to the streets. The paradigm in common use since then, called Housing First, considers housing "a fundamental need and human right" (Padgett, Gulcur, & Tsemberis, 2006, p. 75). Housing is maintained even if a person has a relapse or is incarcerated, and individuals have as much choice as possible in the treatment of their or mental health and substance use disorders (Padgett et al., 2006).

In the supplemental materials for this chapter, we offer examples of communities that have used both models. We encourage you to review those materials and find out which models are currently being used in your area.

DISCUSSION

HOUSING FIRST

Research the difference between Housing First and other approaches to chronic homelessness. Discuss with a friend or classmate what approaches you feel are most effective.

OPPORTUNITIES FOR ADVOCACY

Housing and homelessness provide countless areas for social work advocacy intervention. Here we focus on two areas with direct connections to social injustice: the interaction of the criminal justice system with homelessness and racial disparities among people experiencing homelessness.

Criminal Justice Reform

The connection between homelessness and incarceration is significant. Those who are released from jail or prison have significant rates of homelessness due to challenges with employment, access to housing, and interruptions of pre-incarceration living situations; many of these reentry issues are discussed in Chapter 13. In addition, homelessness is a risk factor for incarceration, as many communities have criminalized the daily activities of homelessness, including panhandling (asking for money), loitering (sitting in a public place), sleeping outdoors, and even possessing a grocery cart (National Coalition for the Homeless, 2006). While some cities have decriminalized behaviors associated with homelessness and worked toward providing services instead, other cities have passed regulations on **urban camping**, or sleeping outside in an undesignated area, that reinforce this criminalization. Because the criminal justice system disproportionately affects members of marginalized populations such as racial and ethnic minority groups, this means that the relationship between incarceration and homelessness significantly affects particularly vulnerable groups (Commission on Equity and Opportunity, 2019). Criminal justice involvement, particularly with drug-related offenses or sexual offenses, may also keep people from accessing public or subsidized housing through many programs.

Urban camping: Sleeping outside in an undesignated area

ADVOCACY
CRIMINAL JUSTICE AND HOMELESSNESS

Choose one of the criminal justice issues tracked by the National Conference of State Legislatures.

http://www.ncsl.org/research/civil-and-criminal-justice.aspx

1. What is happening in your state related to this issue? How will that affect individuals who are experiencing homelessness or are at risk of homelessness? What is one advocacy activity you could participate in to make change to improve this problem?

Racial Disparity Tool

The U.S. Department of Housing and Urban Development recently published a tool that facilitates analysis at the local community level of racial disparities among people experiencing homelessness. They note that "such an analysis is a critical first step in identifying and changing racial and ethnic bias in our systems and services" (HUD, 2018). To access the tool, visit https://www.hudexchange.info/resource/5787/coc-analysis-tool-race-and-ethnicity/ and follow the instructions. If you're not sure what Continuum of Care (CoC) is closest to you, visit this list: https://www.hudexchange.info/resource/5693/fy-2018-continuums-of-care-names-and-numbers/

The information provided here can be shared with policymakers in your state to develop plans to address the issues regarding race and poverty that cause vulnerability to homelessness and develop policies to address those vulnerabilities. What action could you take to address racial disparities and homelessness in your home state?

Final Discussion

Now that you have read this chapter, please return to the vignette and see if your answers to the following questions have changed.

1. What systems might be involved in Larissa's life right now?
2. What steps might you take to try to resolve any ethical conflicts that might arise for you as a social worker in this role?
3. What are the broader systemic factors that influence the choices available to Larissa?
4. Are there government policy changes that could help Larissa and if so, what are they? What advocacy efforts might social workers take to address them?
5. What role might race, class, and gender, or other aspects of identity play in this vignette?

15

IMMIGRATION POLICY

LEARNING OBJECTIVES

15.1: Review the various waves of immigration and views of immigrants throughout U.S. history

15.2: Assess current immigration policies and their impact on children and families

15.3: Critique current policies using intersectionality and economic theories

15.4: Devise opportunities for immigration advocacy with federal, state, and local governments

As with other areas of policy, social workers often find themselves on the front lines when dealing with issues related to immigration. Immigration policy is a particularly hot topic as this book goes to press. There have always been tensions about immigration in the United States, and arguably new concerns arose as a result of the 9/11 terror attacks. Since the beginning of the Trump administration, these tensions have increased. In January 2019, a government shutdown resulted from Democratic leaders' refusal to agree to Republican leaders' demands for funding to expand the U.S. border wall with Mexico. Shortly before that, several children died in U.S. immigration holding facilities. Social workers, including those who work in schools, hospitals, and other community-based settings, increasingly find themselves struggling with immigration-related ethical conflicts. How do we follow the law and ensure that basic human rights are upheld? To what extent do social workers know what rights and protections are available, and how these can be mobilized to help individuals and communities? Are existing laws fair to all? If not, how can we change them? How can we work with other professionals, such as doctors and lawyers, to ensure the safety and well-being of vulnerable immigrants?

Beginning with the settlement house movement, social workers have helped new immigrants adjust to life in the United States and provide them with necessary supports. We have also lobbied for immigrant rights and for immigrant needs to be addressed through the political system. Both these roles continue today. When the Trump administration announced a "zero tolerance" immigration policy that would prosecute families who attempt to cross the border and forcibly separate children from parents, the NASW called such a policy "malicious and unconscionable" and declared "the National Association of Social Workers (NASW) will press lawmakers to rescind this egregious action" (NASW, 2018, para. 1). As a result of political efforts and lobbying from many groups, this policy was ultimately rescinded (Lyons, Levin, Glenza, & Hopulch, 2018), although the border policy is constantly changing at the time of this writing.

In this chapter, we look at the history and roles that immigration, as well as immigration limits and quotas, have played in the United States. We explore some of the economic impacts of both inclusive and exclusive immigration policy. Who benefits and how? We explore different ideological perspectives on immigration and look at the recent development of immigration policy and the ways our system of checks and balances has attempted to limit it. We examine the social construction of different immigrant populations and the way it has shaped views on their contributions to our social and economic systems. As you read this chapter, carefully consider the different words that can be used to describe members of the immigrant community and their underlying meaning. For example, what is the difference between a documented and an undocumented resident? What do people mean when they refer to illegal aliens, and why is that term so offensive to some? What is the difference between a migrant and a refugee? Last, we look at the rhetoric and policies that have been developing during the administration of President Trump that address immigration.

Vignette: Jose's Path from Guatemala to New York to ICE

Based on what you know from the media or your personal, work, or volunteer experiences, think about the following questions as you read the vignette. When you finish the vignette, answer the questions below.

1. As a school social worker, if Jose was one of your students, what steps could you take to support him on an individual (micro) level?
2. Before he was arrested by ICE, what supports would be appropriate for his parents, who may have feared advocating for themselves or their child due to their undocumented immigration status?
3. Are there organizational changes (mezzo level changes) that could help ensure that future students like Jose would not be arrested and sent back to their birth countries with minimal support?
4. What government policy changes might help Jose?
5. What role might race, class, gender, and other aspects of identity play in this vignette?

Jose is a 15-year-old boy from Guatemala. His father came to the United States as an undocumented immigrant when Jose was five. Like many other immigrants, Jose's father has sent money to Jose, his mother, and younger brother in Guatemala since then.[1] Jose was raised in an economically stable home with lots of family nearby. When Jose began high school, gangs began to take an interest in him. He mostly kept to himself and tried to avoid them but was often beaten up and threatened. Because his family was better off economically than many of their neighbors, Jose's home was periodically burglarized. When Jose refused to join the gang, his family was threatened: They could pay for his safety, or the gang would kill him.

Given the threats, his father wanted the family to join him in the United States. With the help of a **coyote** (a person who smuggles people across borders), whom they paid $8,000, the family made it to the United States and settled on Long Island, New York, where Jose's father had been working. Jose's mother found work cleaning houses, and the family was able to afford a two-bedroom basement apartment. Though it was not nearly as nice as their home in Guatemala, they felt safe and, initially, they were. Jose began school and enjoyed making friends. He lived in the town of Huntington, which was known for its high-quality schools and low crime rate. He was admitted to a bilingual program and was flourishing. Jose, his mother, and his brother filed for refugee status and awaited the determination.

Coyote: A person who smuggles people across the U.S. borders

One day, however, Jose was bored in math class and began doodling on the side of his worksheet. He drew the school mascot (which unbeknownst to him was also a gang symbol) and the area code to his hometown in Guatemala. When the teacher saw it, he reported it to the school principal. The principal brought Jose into his office and included the school safety official (who was not a school employee) in the meeting. Jose was told not to draw such characters or the phone extensions in Guatemala because this might indicate gang involvement. Jose swore that he had no gang involvement, and in fact, there was no known gang in the school. He was released and sent home for the rest of the day. His parents were invited to the school to discuss the offense but could not attend because it would have meant taking unpaid time off of work. They all assumed the incident was over.

Two months later, when watching TV, Jose was arrested by Immigration and Customs Enforcement (ICE). Apparently, the school safety officer was required by the county police to report the accusation against Jose to ICE. Jose was kept in solitary confinement, ostensibly for his own protection, for 6 months. After that time, he agreed to plead guilty and return to Guatemala with a 20-year ban from returning to the United States. Although his parents hired a lawyer and wanted him to fight the accusation, he felt that his sanity was slipping away during his solitary confinement. Jose was returned to Guatemala and lives with a distant relative in a town far from where he grew up. However, there are gangs in the town where he lives, and he continues to fear for his life.[2]

---

[1]Monies that immigrants send to people in their countries of origin are referred to as **remittances**. They are often important financial supports **not** only for family members but also for communities and local economies.

[2]This vignette is a slight adaptation of a story that was reported in *The New York Times* by Hannah Dreier on December 28, 2018.

Remittances: Monies that immigrants send to people in their countries of origin

HISTORY AND SOCIAL CONSTRUCTION OF U.S. IMMIGRATION POLICY

Many people think of the United States as a diverse country that has allowed people to immigrate from all over the world. However, U.S. history has also always included hostility toward outgroups, including immigrants.

Following the initial colonization of North America by the British, the first major wave of immigration into the United States occurred from 1840 to 1860 and included many unskilled laborers escaping the Irish Potato Famine and German Jews fleeing religious persecution. During this time period, the U.S. labor market needed people with low skills to work in factories and build railroads. Most remained in cities. As a backlash, the No Nothing Party emerged with an anti-immigrant platform. This party largely died out during the Civil War (DeSipio & de la Garcia, 2015).

The second major wave of U.S. immigration that included people from Asia and Europe occurred from 1870 to 1920. This led to the first major immigration policy in the United States: the Chinese Exclusion Act of 1882. This law banned Chinese people from immigrating to the United States as a result of their race and ethnicity. Prior to this time, the United States had no laws restricting immigration (Vitale, 2017). The Chinese Exclusion Act was gradually expanded to include other Asians (Foner, 2006). Chinese immigrants were unable to become citizens until 1943, and in 1952, the McCarran-Walter Act extended this right to others of Asian descent. In 1895, when a California court required the State to provide public education for Chinese children, many districts created special segregated schools for them (Foner, 2006). Though most of these immigrants remained in cities, Scandinavians, Mexicans, and Germans often moved to rural areas (DeSipio & de la Garcia, 2015).

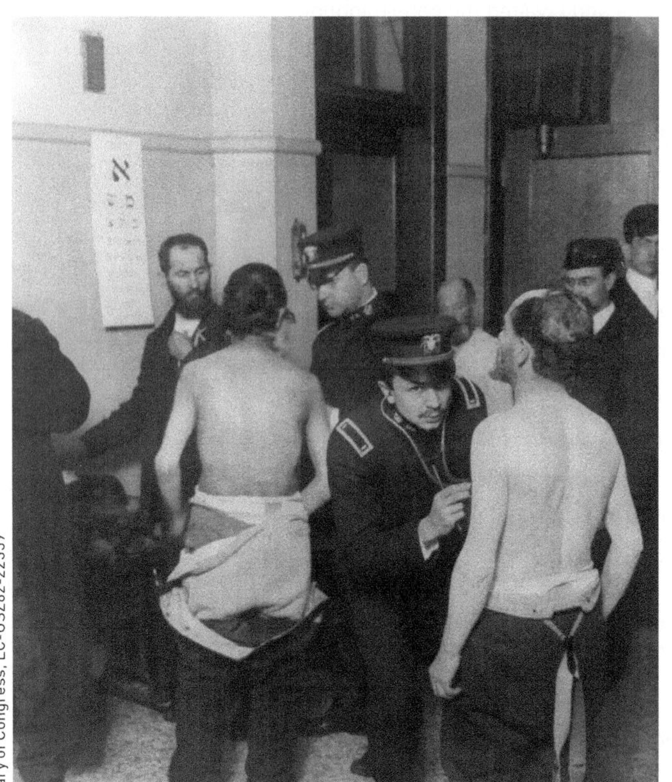

Library of Congress, LC-USZ62-22339

PHOTO 15.1 Jewish immigrants being examined by doctors at Ellis Island around 1907

State commissioners enforced federal immigration law with direction from the U.S. Department of the Treasury (U.S. Citizenship and Immigration Services [USCIS], 2012). In 1892, the United States opened its first immigration center on Ellis Island where federal inspectors determined who could enter the country. One hundred nineteen of the agency's 180 employees worked at Ellis Island (USCIS, 2012), shown in Photo 15.1. With the rise of immigration from the Austro-Hungarian Empire, Italy, and Russia during the end of the 19th and beginning of the 20th centuries, more effort was made to restrict immigration. Several laws in the 1920s created quota systems. The Immigration Act of 1924, referred to as the *Johnson Reed Act*, lasted the longest. It created a system of national quotas on immigration based on numbers that were equivalent to 2% of the U.S. population in 1890, and the immigrants who were allowed to come were based on the percentage of that population already in the United States (U. S. Department of State, n.d.b). It capped the total number of immigrants at 164,667. In

1929, this number was reduced to 153,879 (U.S. Holocaust Memorial Museum, n.d.). This system was designed to discriminate against people from Eastern and Southern Europe, many of whom had begun to immigrate to the United States in the early 20th century. Because this law was based on the 1890 census rather than the 1920 census, fewer Eastern and Southern Europeans were eligible to immigrate to the United States (DeSipio & de la Garcia, 2015). As a result, preference was given to immigrants from Germany, Ireland, and the United Kingdom, and there were long waitlists for immigrants from Eastern and Southern Europe (Luden, 2006). This Act completely excluded Asian immigrants (U.S. Department of State, n.d.b). The system was based heavily on racist ideas about the superiority of people from certain Northern European countries (Luden, 2006). At this time, there were no numerical restrictions on immigrants from Latin America as long as they could meet literacy requirements and were not perceived as likely to become dependent on public welfare (De Sipio & de la Garcia, 2015).

The U.S. Border Patrol was established to enforce the Immigration Act of 1924 and focused largely on limiting Mexican immigration to the United States (Vitale, 2017). During periods of heightened labor needs, the U.S. Border Patrol largely overlooked the literacy requirements for Mexicans (De Sipio & de la Garcia, 2015). The opposite was also true: during the Great Depression of the 1930s Many states and localities deported not only Mexicans but also naturalized citizens of Mexican descent (Balderrama & Rodriguez, 1995).

During World War II, there was little support to amend the Immigration Act of 1924 despite the large number of refugees. A **refugee** is defined as someone who flees their country to avoid war, persecution, or as a result of a national disaster. In the 1940s, native-born Americans feared that new immigrants would compete for jobs following the Great Depression, which had economic impacts that continued into the beginning of the War. According to the U.S. Holocaust Memorial Museum (n.d.), "only 23% of Americans were in favor of the immigration of German refugees—and these congressmen believed that legislation reducing immigration would prevail if the subject came up for debate" (para. 9). Though legislation was introduced in 1939 in both the House and Senate to allow 20,000 Jewish children to immigrate outside of the Immigration Act caps, the legislation was never brought to a vote. On December 1945, though a Gallup poll found that only 5% of Americans wanted to allow Holocaust survivors to immigrate to the United States, President Truman granted displaced people priority visas under the existing caps (U.S. Holocaust Memorial Museum, n.d.). In 1948, Congress passed the Displaced Persons Act allowing 200,000 Holocaust survivors to enter the United States. However, because the act was limited to people who had entered Austria, Germany, or Italy before 1945, it discriminated against Jews who were in Soviet Bloc countries. The Refugee Relief Act of 1953 dropped the cap on immigration and allowed more refugees from World War II to resettle in the United States (U.S. Citizenship and Immigration Services, 2012).

Refugee: As defined by the U.S. Code, is someone who leaves their native country and "has a well-founded fear of persecution on account of race, religion, nationality, membership in a particular social group, or political opinion"

In 1951, the United States and Mexico entered into an agreement called the **Bracero Program** that allowed seasonal workers to come to the United States temporarily as agricultural workers for registered American employers. Between 1951 and 1968, hundreds of thousands of Mexicans participated in this program. At the same time, the Immigration and Naturalization Service (INS) deported many Mexicans, some of whom were American citizens, through **Operation Wetback** (U.S. Citizenship and Immigration Services, 2012) a program whose racist name reflected its harsh portrayals of Mexican immigrants as dirty and irresponsible and the use of military tactics to forcibly remove Mexican immigrants, often to unfamiliar parts of Mexico.

Bracero Program: A program from the 1940s that enabled Mexican immigrants to legally enter the United States to work on farms

Operation Wetback: A U.S. immigration program in 1954 where military tactics were used to forcibly remove Mexican immigrants, some of whom were naturalized citizens, often to unfamiliar parts of in Mexico

Immigration policy continued to be heavily restricted based on racial quotas until the 1960s. In 1965, shortly after President Kennedy was assassinated, President Lyndon B. Johnson signed the Hart-Cellar Immigration Bill, which ended quotas based on national origin. The law created our current system where immigration is primarily based on family reunification and needed work skills. It never occurred to policy makers at the time that skilled workers from Asian and African countries would wish to immigrate to the United States and bring their families (Luden, 2006).

In 1986, the Immigration Reform and Control Act granted legal status to many undocumented immigrants. It also created sanctions for employers who hired undocumented immigrants (Cohn, 2015). In 1990, the United States again changed immigration eligibility so that new immigrants had to fall into one of three categories: family sponsored, employee sponsored, or diversity candidates who were chosen by lottery. The reason for diversity candidates is to allow people to immigrate to the United States from underrepresented countries. Anyone with a high school degree and 2 years of work experience from all except 19 nations is eligible to apply to the lottery. This law also granted the INS authority to grant or deny naturalization petitions, an authority that had previously been judicial (U.S. Citizenship and Immigration Services, 2012).

The United States did not have a formal refugee policy until the Refugee Act of 1980 (U.S. Citizenship and Immigration Services, 2012). The United States has a history of providing refugee status to people from countries with which it has poor relations rather than those with which we have good diplomatic ties, regardless of the danger particular citizens face (Kerwin, 2014). The number of refugees who are admitted to the United States has fluctuated. In 1980, President Jimmy Carter increased the number of refugees who were admitted to about 200,000. More typically, approximately 110,000 refugees are admitted annually (Krogstadt & Radford, 2017). In 2017, President Trump issued an Executive Order limiting the number of refugees to 50,000, less than half of a typical year.

In 2002, the Homeland Security Act was passed and transferred the responsibilities that had been under the Immigration and Naturalization Services into three different agencies: Customs and Border Patrol, Immigration and Customs Enforcement, more commonly referred to as ICE, and U.S. Citizenship and Immigration Services (USCIS) (U.S. Citizenship and Immigration Services, 2012). In 2016, the Obama administration suggested 110,000 refugees be admitted in 2017. However, the Trump administration reduced the number to 50,000. In 2018, although the cap on refugees was 45,000, only 16,230 refugees were admitted to the United States. This was equivalent to 102 refugees per one million residents. This can be seen in contrast to Canada, which resettled 725 refugees per million residents; Australia, which resettled 618 per million residents; and Norway, which resettled 528 per million residents (American Immigration Council, 2018).

Ingroups: Those in the majority or accepted by the majority

Outgroups: Minorities or unfavored populations

One cannot really understand immigration to the United States without discussing race. Historically, immigration and construction of national identity can be understood by the construction of what Sociologists refer to as **ingroups**, comprised of people who were considered acceptable, and **outgroups**, minorities or unfavored populations. In the context of immigration, outgroups were often comprised of those who were considered nonwhite. As Noel Ignatiev (1995) argues, the Irish who came to the United States to escape the potato famine were not originally considered white. A result of their improving social class and power gained through unionization, they "became white" in the eyes of the public and policy makers. Similarly, it was only after World War II that restrictive immigration policies for Jews, specifically Jewish refugees, were made more expansive. In one 1939 example of the anti-Jewish immigration policies, the United States rejected entry to a ship of 935 German Jews and sent it back to Germany. Karen Brodkin (1998) notes that Jewish immigrants became white, like their Irish counterparts, as a result of racist policies that helped white people, including Jews, achieve economic success while disadvantaging black people. These policies included redlining (discussed in Chapter 14) and local control of the Servicemen's Readjustment Act of 1944, known as the GI Bill, that allowed states and private actors (such as universities) to discriminate in its implementation. Race, class, and power played a role in helping both Irish and Jewish immigrants become white. Once perceived as white, both these immigrant groups experienced less discrimination.

TABLE 15.1 ■ History of Federal Immigration Laws Until the 1980s

Topic and Date	Website
Naturalization Act of 1790, 1795	https://legisworks.org/sal/1/stats/STATUTE-1-Pg103.pdf
Alien Friends Act/Alien Enemies Act 1798	http://library.uwb.edu/Static/USimmigration/1798_alien_laws.html
Naturalization Act of 1870	https://www.loc.gov/law/help/statutes-at-large/41st-congress/session-2/c41s2ch254.pdf
1862 Anti-coolie law	http://library.uwb.edu/Static/USimmigration/12%20stat%20340.pdf
Page Act of 1875	http://library.uwb.edu/Static/USimmigration/18%20stat%20477.pdf
Immigration Act of 1882/ Chinese Exclusion Act	https://www.loc.gov/law/help/statutes-at-large/47th-congress/session-1/c47s1ch376.pdf
Immigration Act of 1903/ Anarchist Exclusion Act	https://www.loc.gov/law/help/statutes-at-large/57th-congress/session-2/c57s2ch1012.pdf
Immigration Act of 1917	http://library.uwb.edu/Static/USimmigration/39%20stat%20874.pdf
Emergency Quota Act 1921	http://library.uwb.edu/Static/USimmigration/1921_emergency_quota_law.html
The Nationality Act 1940	http://library.uwb.edu/Static/USimmigration/1940_naturalization_act.html
Displaced Persons Act 1948	http://library.uwb.edu/Static/USimmigration/62%20stat%201009.pdf
Amerasian Immigration Act 1982	http://library.uwb.edu/Static/USimmigration/96%20stat%201716.pdf

Source: https://www.usa.gov/become-us-citizen

As presented above, U.S. immigration history has, with rare exception, been based on xenophobia and racism. Immigrants from Asia, Ireland, Italy, and Latin America and Jewish immigrants from Eastern and Western Europe all have histories of mistreatment by U.S. immigration policies. Although many of these have, over time, come to be seen as ingroups, newer waves of immigrants face similar hurdles. As you continue to read this chapter, think about how these patterns have changed or remained the same. A review of the major historical federal immigration laws is provided in Table 15.1.

CURRENT IMMIGRATION POLICIES

Approximately 13.5% of the U.S. population, or 40 million people, were born outside of the United States. At our peak immigration in 1890, 14.8% of the population was foreign born. Approximately 25% of current immigrants are of Mexican descent, and 20 million Americans trace their roots to Asian countries. Since 1965, one fourth of the immigrants to the United States have come from one of 20 Asian countries (López, Luis, & Patten, 2017). Seventy-six percent of the immigrant population have legal U.S. resident status, either as naturalized citizens (45%) or as lawful permanent residents (green card holders, 27%); the rest are undocumented. From 1990 to 2007, the number of unauthorized immigrants coming to the United States tripled; however, the number of these immigrants declined from 2015 to 2017. There is some indication that this trend is changing. Despite crackdowns and policies separating families, in early 2019, border patrol reported 76,000 undocumented migrants crossing the U.S. Mexican border monthly, indicating a precipitous rise in immigration (Dickerson, 2019). Nonetheless, the number of Mexican immigrants leaving the United States has surpassed the number of those coming to the United States. At the end of this section, Table 15.3 outlines significant federal immigration policies.

In 1948, following World War II, the United Nations (UN) adopted the Universal Declaration of Human Rights. This document expressly defined 30 basic human rights. In relation to immigration, the main relevant right is Article 13, which declares that "(1) Everyone has the right to freedom of movement and residence within the borders of each State. (2) Everyone has the right to leave any country, including his own, and to return to his country." In addition, other articles speak to the right "to recognition everywhere as a person before the law" (Article 6) and not to be "arbitrarily deprived of his nationality nor denied the right to change his nationality" (Article 15). The Declaration also includes the right to equal protection of the law for all, including those of different races and genders. Unfortunately, the Universal Declaration of Human Rights is not a binding law in itself (although some of its principles have been elaborated in treaties) but an aspirational statement. It nonetheless provides an important perspective for how some people feel that immigrants should be viewed and treated and is consistent with the NASW Code of Ethics.

There are four paths to U.S. citizenship (see Figure 15.1). Citizenship provides a number of rights, including voting for elected officials, serving on juries, traveling with a U.S. passport, bringing family members to the United States, holding some elected offices and government jobs, and obtaining many government benefits. One can be born in the United States, marry an American citizen, serve in the military, or reside or work in the United States long enough with a green card (also known as a permanent work visa) to establish permanent residency and apply for citizenship. A green card or lawful permanent resident card will be reissued assuming the U.S. resident does not violate any laws. A permanent resident must reside in the United States for 5 years to be eligible for citizenship or 3 years if the person is married to an American. A felony conviction renders people permanently ineligible for citizenship (U.S. Department of Homeland Security, n.d.a). In general, the term **documented resident** refers to someone who has been issued legal papers by the U.S. federal immigration authorities allowing them to both reside and work in the United States. These documents can grant temporary or permanent rights.

Documented resident: Someone who has been issued papers by the U.S. federal immigration authorities allowing them to reside and sometimes work in the United States

There are three ways to become a documented resident or to legally immigrate to the United States. People who are not U.S. citizens must apply for a visa to enter the country if they wish to work here. People can get visas if they are sponsored by a family member. Preference is given to spouses and minor children (U.S. Department of State, n.d-a). Temporary work visas restrict employment to the reason indicated on the visa as well as the length of stay that has been approved. A permanent work visa/Green Card allows an immigrant to remain in the country and work in whatever capacity he or she chooses as long as the person complies with the Green for Card requirements. Green Cards are awarded according to priorities; the first priority group is for those with some extraordinary ability; the second is for those holding an advanced degree; the third is for conducting professional work for which there are no comparably skilled U.S. citizens; and the fourth is for people who have worked for the U.S. military, children who have been abused, neglected, or abandoned by their parents, U.S. broadcasters who have worked in Europe or Asia, religious leaders, and certain types of physicians. The last priority is given to people who make a large investment in the United States that is designed to create or maintain 10 full-time permanent jobs in the United States (U.S. Department of Homeland Security, n.d-b).

U.S. federal immigration policy is currently based on a preference system. Despite the long list above of professional categories, the system we currently have prioritizes family over skilled workers. Though President Kennedy's original bill gave preference to skilled workers, churches and unions who feared competition lobbied for family preference, which was incorporated into the law (Luden, 2006). This has led to something that has often been referred to in the media as *chain migration*. **Chain migration** describes the potential of one family member who comes to the United States who brings their relatives who, in turn, bring other

Chain migration: Describes what occurs when one person a comes to the United States and brings family members who, in turn, bring other relatives

FIGURE 15.1 ■ Pathway to U.S. Citizenship

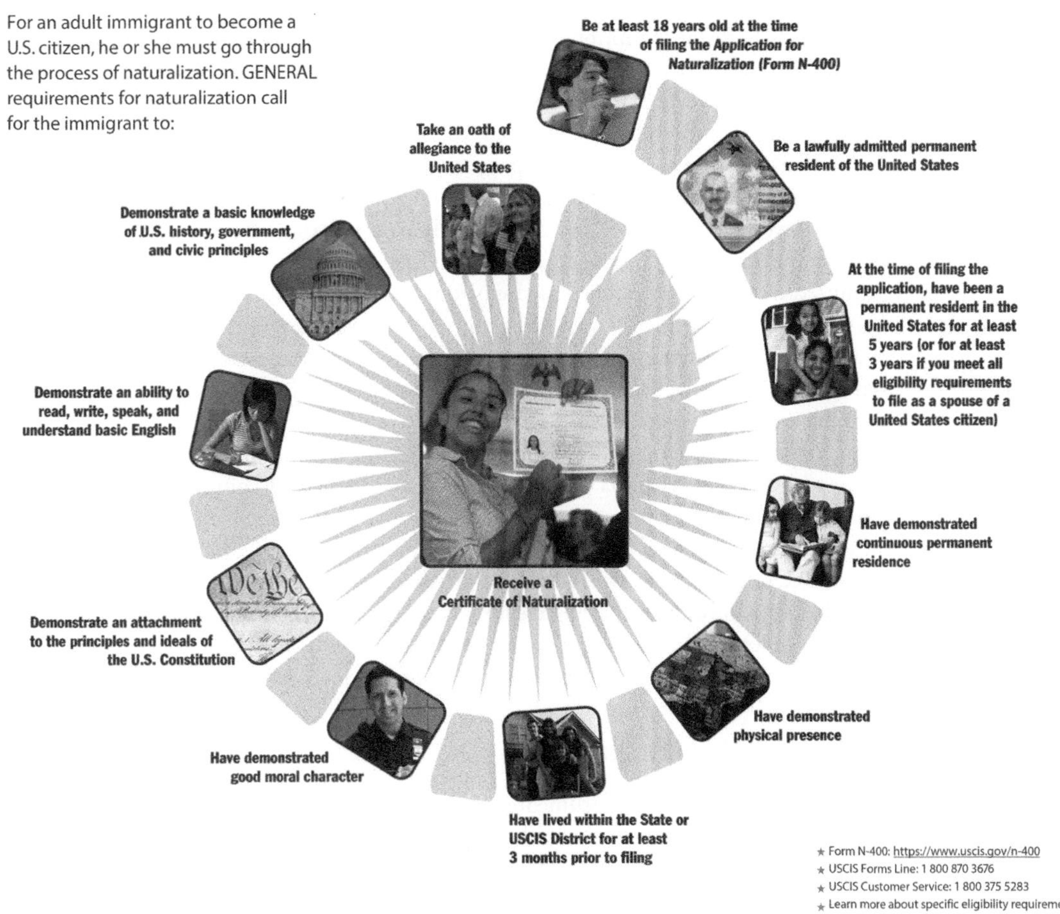

Source: https://www.usa.gov/become-us-citizen

relatives. Because allowing one person to come may ultimately allow for a larger family group of immigrants, this is called chain migration. An **anchor baby** is another colloquial term, used to describe a child who is born in the United States to non-American parents. This is predicated on the idea that the baby somehow serves as an anchor, attaching a non-American family to the United States. This term persists even though children in this situation are generally not a source of any rights or legal status for their parents or siblings.

Anchor baby: A political term used for a child who is born in the United States to parents who are not U.S. citizens

Immigrants who come to the United States without visas are called *undocumented* immigrants. In the past, they were often referred to as *illegal* immigrants. However, it has been noted by many that their existence is not illegal and that calling people illegal immigrants is dehumanizing. It is more respectful to refer to someone who does not have proper documentation as unauthorized or undocumented. Some **undocumented residents**, or those who come

Undocumented resident: Immigrants who reside in the United States without legal documentation or status to the United States without visas, seek legal status as refugees once they enter the country. Others simply try to hide from authorities for fear of being caught and sent back to their countries of origin.

A refugee, as defined by the U.S. Code, is someone who leaves their native country and "has a well-founded fear of persecution on account of race, religion, nationality, membership in a particular social group, or political opinion" (Immigration and Nationality Act, USC 101[a][42][A], 2013). As described above, the president and Congress determine a ceiling on the annual number of refugees allowed into the United States, although the actual number admitted may be substantially lower than this cap.

Guest workers: Immigrants who are given short visas to work in seasonal labor

H-2B visa: A work visa for nonagricultural workers

Another way in which one can legally work in the United States is to be a guest worker. **Guest workers** are given short visas to work in seasonal labor. The **H-2B visa** is for nonagricultural workers. These workers are typically paid less than the average wages for workers who do the same work and are citizens or legal residents. The number of these workers permitted in the United States has risen from 82,000 in 2013 to approximately 148,000 in 2018 (Huennekens, 2018). The H-2A program is for seasonal agricultural workers. Both the H-2A and H-2B programs have been associated with brutal treatment, squalid conditions, and enslavement as well as employers cheating their employees out of their wages (Garrison, Bensinger, & Singer-Vine, 2015).

Temporary Protected Status (TPS): A U.S. immigration status that enables people from countries that had experienced a major natural disaster or war-torn countries to temporarily live and work in the United States

In 1990, the United States created a mechanism for temporary immigration called **Temporary Protected Status** (TPS), which enables people from countries that had experienced a major natural disaster or war to temporarily live and work in the United States. Prior to 1990, the executive branch designated residents from some countries eligible for Extended Voluntary Departure, a status, much like TPS, which enabled people to temporarily live and work in the United States. The only people eligible for TPS status are those who are currently in the United States. In other words, people cannot apply for TPS from abroad, but if they come on a travel visa, they can apply for TPS to remain in the United States (Messick & Bergeron, 2014).

Undocumented Workers

In 2014, two thirds of undocumented arrivals to the United States were individuals who had come to the United States with a valid visa and then stayed past their allotted time (Warren & Kerwin, 2017). It is unclear how many undocumented immigrants walk across the border but, according to U.S. Customs and Border Protection (2017) data, there was a decrease in apprehensions of such people from 1.6 million in 2000 to 303,000 in 2017. This number spiked in early 2019. For undocumented immigrants who come to the United States on foot, migration itself is dangerous. According to the UN's International Organization for Migration (2018), in 2017, 412 people died attempting to migrate to the United States. Getting to the border itself is dangerous. Traveling through Mexico at the southern border, many immigrants face kidnappings, extortion, and rape, and some are murdered (Shetty, 2019).

The challenges that immigrants experience often begin as soon as they enter the United States. The international organization Human Rights Watch (2018) documented abusive conditions in U.S. Border Patrol holding cells, where undocumented migrants, including women and children, are often forced to sleep on the floor with only Mylar (thin tin foil) blankets for 3 to 4 days. Security officials often require them to remove or discard their sweaters for "security reasons," so that they are cold, and migrants reported not being allowed to shower, not being provided with soap, and not being given toothbrushes. In addition, teenagers, as well as fathers, are kept in different holding cells than women so families are forced to separate during a particularly traumatic experience, causing additional trauma.

Once in the United States, undocumented workers and guest workers are especially vulnerable to labor exploitation because they fear that if they report an employer for breaking the law or file for workers' compensation as a result of on-the-job injuries, they may face deportation. In 2008, 37% of undocumented workers reported experiencing wage theft from employers (Bernhardt et al., 2009). In a report for the National Employment Law Project, Berkowitz, Huizer, and Smith (2017) documented cases in Florida and Massachusetts where employers have retaliated against undocumented workers who have filed for workers' compensation by reporting them to ICE, and the workers have been threatened with deportation. In other words, this fear is not irrational. As a result of these practices and anti-immigrant sentiment espoused by federal leadership, fear of deportation has caused many undocumented immigrants not to comply with federal investigations into unfair labor practices and, in some cases, even to avoid officials who are trying to provide them with back pay (Levin, 2017).

The Impact of Current Policies on Children

Widespread reports have shown difficult and inhumane conditions for children and families at the southern U.S. border in recent years. At one point in 2018, amid multiple news reports about maltreatment of children separated from their parents, a U.S. Customs and Border Protection spokesperson denied that families or children were being mistreated and stated that the detention facilities had acceptable conditions (Taxin, 2018). Children interviewed by advocates described being separated from their families and put into crowded rooms. They reported being cold, hungry, tired, and scared and having very little communication with their parents (Taxin, 2018). Many children became sick. In December 2018, two children died of treatable illnesses in the custody of American immigration centers. Since then, more have died. The harsh conditions serve a purpose according to a Department of Homeland Security official, who said, "It's the complete, 100 percent focus on harsher options that will deter the influx, with a disregard for managing what's happening" (cited in Fernandez, Dickerson, & Villegas, 2019). In other words, the deaths may be partially accidental, but the situation that gave rise to them is not.

There have also been abuse allegations in these detention centers, as well. In *E.D. v Sharkey* (2019), a 19-year-old mother of a 3-year-old sought asylum for domestic violence. In a detention center in Pennsylvania, she was sexually assaulted, made the brunt of jokes, and threatened with deportation. This case is one of 1,448 sexual assault allegations against workers in ICE facilities between 2012 and March 2018. This number is likely under-representative; a Government Accountability Office report cited by the ACLU showed that 40% of 2013 sexual abuse allegations were not reported (Lopez & Park, 2018), meaning those numbers could be higher. Some children in detention centers who were separated from their families were either lost or placed in foster care. The *AP News* (Raff, 2018) reported that in the summer of 2018, more than 300 parents were deported to Central America, leaving 66 children in the custody of the U.S. government. These children are not eligible for reunification, meaning they were placed in foster care with the fear of involuntary adoption.

In another change to immigration policy, the Trump administration tried to end Temporary Protected Status for citizens of El Salvador, Haiti, Honduras, Nepal, Nicaragua, and Sudan effective in 2018 (Abramsky, 2019). In the beginning of 2018, the ACLU and some California law firms filed suit to stop this administrative action. Plaintiffs argued that the Trump administration did not follow the proper administrative procedures to end the program and that the president's motivation to do so was largely based on racism. In October 2018, a California district court issued a temporary injunction stopping the Trump administration from being able to roll back the program until the case could be argued in courts. The Trump administration appealed to the 9th Circuit (Abramsky, 2019). As of the drafting of this book, this case is still making its way through the courts.

DISCUSSION

SHOULD IMMIGRATION POLICY BE FEDERAL OR STATE?

Should immigration policy be regulated at the state or federal level?

1. Identify some reasons that federal regulations make sense.
2. Identify some reasons that state-and local-level regulations make sense.
3. Identify challenges of both state and federal regulations.

State Immigration Laws

Despite the establishment of federal control over immigration, states and localities have often exercised a considerable amount of discretion, including the power to deport Mexicans and U.S. citizens of Mexican origin during the Great Depression. As discussed above, during World War II, the federal government established the Bracero Program to enable Mexican immigrants to legally come to the United States to work on farms. However, enforcement was lax and farmers, particularly in Texas, saw the law as unnecessary government intrusion. Enforcement only came when "[w]orkers who complained or organized against low wages and abysmal conditions were simply handed over to Border Patrol for deportation" (Vitale, 2017, p. 177).

Arizona has been on the front lines of state immigration policy. Between 1980 and 2008, the population of Arizona rose from 2.7 million to 6.5 million; two fifths of the growth was Latino (Blau & Frezzo, 2012). By 2017, the population was 7.1 million, 31% of whom identified as Latino (U.S. Census Bureau, 2018). The Arizona legislature passed many anti-immigrant laws including the Legal Arizona Workers Act (2007), which requires employers to use the federal E-Verify system to ensure that all their workers are documented residents or citizens. If employers are found to have hired an undocumented resident, they can be heavily fined or have their business licenses suspended. This law was challenged in the court system and upheld by the U.S. Supreme Court (*Chamber of Commerce v. Whiting*, 2011). Arizona also passed Support Our Law Enforcement and Safe Neighborhoods Act (Senate Bill 1070), which made it legal to demand proof of citizenship from any Arizona residents if law enforcement officers believe that they might be undocumented. It also made it illegal for documented residents to fail to carry their registration papers. In response to the passage of this law, many cities, localities, businesses, and immigrant rights groups boycotted the state of Arizona, and the National Immigration Rights Law Center filed suit against the state. In 2016, they reached a settlement and law enforcement were told not to investigate citizenship based merely on "reasonable suspicion," a relatively low standard, that someone was undocumented, thus raising the standard for stopping people (Duara, 2016).

Other states that have passed anti-immigration legislation include South Carolina, which established a 24-hour hotline for reporting immigration violations. Alabama passed an expansive anti-immigration law in 2011, HB56, making it, among other things, legal for officers to inquire about immigration status during traffic stops and illegal for undocumented immigrants to attend a public university. The law required verification of immigration papers for enrollment in K–12 programs, but that provision was overturned by the 11th Circuit Court of Appeals. The court also blocked the state from arresting people for failure to produce documentation of legal status when pulled over for routine traffic stops (Sarlin, 2013). When Alabama's restrictive immigration policy was originally passed, the legislature feared that police officers might fail to enforce it. They found, however, that the police did enforce the policy and, as a consequence, both documented and undocumented Latino residents were less likely to report crimes or help the police when they were investigating crimes (Sarlin, 2013).

By 2019, 25 states had considered sanctuary bills. **Sanctuary** is a loose term with important symbolic meaning, referring to proposed laws to limit cooperation with federal immigration authorities in various ways. The goal of such legislation is to protect undocumented residents, particularly those undocumented residents who are arrested or detained. By April 2019, California, Colorado, Illinois, Iowa, Massachusetts, New Jersey, New Mexico, Oregon, and Vermont had all passed sanctuary bills (Griffith & Vaughan, 2019). Over 150 cities and counties, primarily on the east and west coasts, have passed similar ordinances on the local level. Most limit the communication that local law enforcement can have with ICE as well as ICE's access to courthouses and jails. In November 2017, the U.S. Justice Department announced that they might block the access of sanctuary cities to federal law enforcement money. On October 8, 2018, a federal district court judge blocked the Justice Department from restricting sanctuary cities access to federal law enforcement money (Slobe, 2018).

Sanctuary: A loose term with important symbolic value referring to proposed city and state laws to limit cooperation with federal immigration authorities in various ways

It is important for social workers working in immigrant communities and those who may come in contact with immigrants, which includes most social workers, to be aware of their own state's laws that relate to immigration. This can help you support your clients as well as advocate to change policies that you think are unfair. For a chart of state immigration laws, see Table 15.2.

TABLE 15.2 ■ State Immigration Laws

Topic	Selected States
Prohibits state officials from to collect information and giving it to federal government	California, Colorado, Connecticut, Illinois, Massachusetts, New Jersey, New Mexico, Oregon, and Vermont
Immigration enforcement laws	Arizona, California, Colorado, Illinois, Iowa, Minnesota, Rhode Island, Tennessee, Vermont, and West Virginia
Bans sanctuary cities	Alabama, Arizona, Arkansas, Florida, Georgia, Iowa, Mississippi, Missouri, North Carolina, South Carolina, Tennessee, and Texas
Provides funds for refugees, naturalization services, health, etc.	Arkansas, Arizona, California, Colorado, Georgia, Iowa, Idaho, Illinois, Kansas, Louisiana, Maryland, Massachusetts, Michigan, Missouri, Mississippi, New Jersey, New Mexico, New York, Pennsylvania, South Carolina, Utah, Vermont, Virginia, Washington, and Wyoming
Education: tuition benefits	California, Colorado, Connecticut, Florida, Illinois, Kansas, Maryland, Minnesota, Nebraska, New Jersey, New Mexico, New York, Oregon, Texas, Utah, and Washington, and the District of Columbia
Education: financial assistance to unauthorized students	California, Colorado, Connecticut, New Mexico, Maryland, Minnesota, New Jersey, Oregon, Texas, and Washington
Education: banned financial assistance to unauthorized students	Alabama, Arizona, Georgia, Missouri, and South Carolina
Employment: workers' compensation, unemployment, licensing, authorization	California, Colorado, Florida, Georgia, Idaho, Illinois, Indiana, Michigan, Minnesota, Mississippi, Missouri, Nebraska, New York, North Carolina, South Dakota, Vermont, West Virginia, and Wyoming

(Continued)

TABLE15.2 ■ (Continued)

Topic	Selected States
Health care	Arizona, California, Iowa, Idaho, Indiana, Maryland, Mississippi, New York, Vermont and Washington
Human trafficking	Louisiana, Maine, Nebraska, and Washington
Identification: driver's licenses	California, Illinois, Kansas, Louisiana, Maine, Michigan, Oregon, Rhode Island, Tennessee, Utah
Public benefits programs	Arizona, California, Connecticut, Georgia, Hawaii, Illinois, Maryland, New York, Oklahoma, and Washington
Voting	California, New Hampshire, and Massachusetts

Source: Based on information obtained from the National Conference of State Legislatures Report on State Immigration Laws, 2019, the Center for Immigration Studies (Griffith, & Vaughan, 2019).

Federal Policy: The Role of Executive Orders

In January 2019, the federal budget process was at an impasse over President Trump's demand for funding for a border wall (see Photo 15.2). The Democrats, who had agreed to increase funding for border security from the current $44 billion (U.S. Department of Homeland Security, 2018) resisted paying for a border wall. Affected by the resulting government shutdown were 800,000 government employees, including employees of the Transportation Security Administration (TSA), the Federal Bureau of Prisons, and active duty members of the U.S. Coast Guard, as well as services like Food Stamps/SNAP, food safety inspections, and financial assistance through the U.S. Department of Housing and Urban Development. After 35 days, the longest government shutdown in history, a bipartisan committee negotiated a budget with much more limited funding than Trump had demanded. Nevertheless, he signed it. After signing the new budget bill and staving off further government shutdowns, President Trump declared a state of emergency to allow him to require the military to build the wall and divert funds from the Department of Defense and other sources to do so. This is a controversial move because, if allowed, it will set a precedent that the president can circumvent the declared will of Congress by using his discretion to call a state of emergency. This use of emergency powers in this manner has been challenged in the courts as unconstitutional by 16 states (Savage & Pear, 2019). Presidents have also used other kinds of executive branch powers to circumvent or challenge the legislative branch. When Obama was unable to get legislation passed to protect DREAMers, he issued an executive order allowing them to receive papers enabling them to go to college and be able to work legally in the United States under Deferred Action for Childhood Arrivals (DACA), which we describe later in this chapter. His executive order required that they continue to register on a bi-annual basis to keep their temporary protected status (U.S. Citizen and Immigration Services, 2018).

PHOTO 15.2 Picture of U.S.–Mexico border near Tijuana from Imperial Beach, California

TABLE 15.3 ■ Selected Federal Immigration Laws

Topic	Laws	Oversight Agency	Website
Changed caps on temporary worker visas	Immigration and Nationality Act 1990	U.S. Citizenship and Immigration Services (USCIS)	http://library.uwb.edu/Static/USimmigration/104%20stat%204978.pdf
Special immigration status for people who have served in the military	Armed Forces Immigration Adjustment Act of 1991	U.S. Citizenship and Immigration Services (USCIS)	http://library.uwb.edu/Static/USimmigration/105%20stat%20555.pdf
Changed category of offenses for which people could be deported	Illegal Immigration Reform & Immigrant Responsibility Act 1996	Immigration and Customs Enforcement (ICE)	http://library.uwb.edu/Static/USimmigration/1996_illegal_immigration_reform_and_immigrant_responsibility_act.html
Consolidated immigration reform and border control, More money for immigration security and border patrol	Intelligence Reform and Terrorism Prevention Act a.k.a. National Security Intelligence Reform Act 2004	U.S. Customs and Border Patrol and Immigration and Customs Enforcement (ICE)	http://library.uwb.edu/Static/USimmigration/2004_intelligence_reform_and_terrorism_prevention_act.html
Money for fencing for the southern U.S. border	Secure Fence Act 2006	U.S. Customs and Border Patrol	http://library.uwb.edu/Static/USimmigration/2006_secure_fence_act.html
Temporary work visas for people who arrived to the United States as minors	Deferred Action for Childhood Arrivals (DACA) 2012	U.S. Citizenship and Immigration Services (USCIS)	https://www.uscis.gov/archive/consideration-deferred-action-childhood-arrivals-daca

POLICY INFORMED BY ALTERNATIVE LENSES

Discrimination against immigrants has been a persistent theme through United States' history. As noted above, people who were identified as Jewish, Irish, and Italians were allowed to become naturalized citizens and had the legal and political rights of "whites," but they continued to be excluded from purchasing property in certain neighborhoods as a result of restrictive covenants and were excluded from some businesses. New immigrants were often paid less than other white residents for the same work. In addition, popular media perpetuated demeaning stereotypes (Foner, 2006). Views on immigrants as "the other" persist in communities and in schools. For example, immigrant children who may have higher needs as a result of needing to learn a language other than the one their parents speak at home and those who may have experienced trauma in their country of origin or during their migration process are still often placed in poorly resourced schools and many are pigeonholed into less academic programs (Olson, 2008).

Critical Race Theory and Immigration

As you may recall from Chapter 3, critical race theory requires consideration of race when evaluating both the construction and implementation of policies. With U.S. immigration policy (and the immigration policy of many other nations), this is not a challenge. One reason for

Xenophobia: Fear of and prejudice against people from other countries

anti-immigration sentiment is **xenophobia**, which means fear of and prejudice against people from other countries. Nationalism and racism have long played a role in xenophobia and anti-immigrant sentiments throughout the world. The popular press has widely cited xenophobia as a chief factor in much of the recent political rhetoric around immigration policy. One example is President Trump's unfounded pronouncements that "criminals and Middle Easterners"—itself meant to invoke xenophobic stereotypes of Middle Eastern immigrants as terrorists—were mixed in a caravan of Central American families walking toward the Mexican border (Bump, 2018).

Intersectionality: Gender and Immigrant Status

Immigrant status often coincides not only with a country of origin, which may be tied to racial or ethnic categories, but other facets of people's identity. Gender, in particular when combined with race, can lead to increased vulnerability and discrimination. Statistics about violent crime committed against immigrant women bear this out. Other factors that intersect to increase vulnerability include limited language skills, different cultural norms between immigrants' country of origin and the United States, and, for those who lack legal status, fear of deportation. As a result of these factors, immigrant women are more vulnerable to domestic violence than native-born women. Nonetheless, twice as many immigrant women as native-born American women lack health insurance. Moreover, federal policy blocks legal immigrants from eligibility for Medicaid for the first 5 years of their residency in the United States, limiting access to prenatal care for many women.

U visas: Visas that provide temporary immigration benefits

There are some protections for particularly vulnerable immigrant women. For example, immigrant survivors of domestic violence and other crimes may be eligible for **U visas** that provide temporary immigration benefits. Immigrant women who are forced into sex work as a result of fraud or coercion are also eligible for special visas. However, these programs do not appear to be well implemented. For example, though there were 5,000 visas available for those who were forced into sex work in 2012, only 674 were distributed (Garcia & Franchim, 2013).

Economic Analysis and Immigration

The economics of immigration are complicated. Though it is true that the overall economy does better when there is an influx of immigrants, all Americans do not benefit equally. An increase in low-skilled workers means that employers can pay low-skilled workers less. This increases the profits of employers. However, a 2016 report from the National Academies of Science, Engineering, and Medicine (2017), which looked at 20 years of immigration data, found that the impact of immigration on the wages of native-born workers is small, and they found little evidence that immigration affected overall employment rates for native-born Americans. The study also found that although first-generation immigrants are more costly than other residents to local and state governments, their children tend to be high earners and contribute more in taxes than native-born Americans.

Immigrants also make more money in the United States than they would have made in their home countries. Based on 30 years of economics research, George Borjas (2016) notes that the increase in low-skilled workers has led to a decline in wages for unskilled work in the United States. He argues that this could be counteracted by government policies designed to redistribute wealth by taxing the companies who make more money as a result of immigrant labor and using that money to support public goods including health, education, and infrastructure.

Were it not for immigrants, the United States would be experiencing population declines. There is a problem if the number of nonworking people becomes too big for the working-age population to support (see Chapter 11). Have you ever heard someone say that Social Security is not going to exist when you retire? The reason for this is that today's workers pay for the Medicare and Social Security benefits of today's retirees. If the number of retirees gets too high, then the tax burden on the workers may also be too high. Potential solutions to this problem could include reducing benefits, increasing the burden on current workers, or finding additional workers to contribute to these systems (Cassidy, 2018). Immigrants could be one solution to this problem. A 2016 World Bank Group report on this topic suggested that the rising age of the U.S. population with the current birth rate statistics was problematic without immigration (World Bank Group, 2016). To keep the population from declining, we would need to have a birth rate of 2.1%. Instead, we have a birth rate of 1.7%. Immigrants could help make up the difference. In 2010, there were 21 Americans age 65 and older for every 100 working Americans. If birth rates continue at their present speed, by 2030, there will be 35 adults aged 65 and older per 100 working-age adults (18–64) and by 2060, there will be 42 (Adamy & Overberg, 2018), numbers that are not sustainable with our current retirement structure.

OPPORTUNITIES FOR ADVOCACY

Though immigrants, particularly undocumented immigrants, are not legally entitled to the same protections afforded to citizens regarding their right to live and work in the United States, many have U.S.-born children. According to the U.S. Constitution, everyone who is born in the United States is a citizen. As a result, many of the policies designed to deport undocumented residents harm U.S.-born children who are citizens. When their parents are faced with deportation, child citizens are often faced with the option of being raised in foster care or being deported to a country where they may not even speak the language (Zayas & Bradlee, 2014). The arrest of parents or other relatives prior to deportation causes sudden separation of parents and children and can be very traumatic (Zayas & Bradlee, 2014). Recent immigration policies such as those that require parents to be separated from their children at the border can cause children to develop mental health problems including anxiety, depression, eating problems, and sleeping problems (Chaudry et al., 2010).

REFLECTION
WORKING WITH IMMIGRANTS

1. What are some of the micro issues that you expect to face as a social worker if you are working with immigrants?
2. How can mezzo level organizational policy help or hurt immigrants?
3. On a macro level, what are the ways that our current immigration policy is consistent or inconsistent with the NASW Code of Ethics? The United Nations Declaration on Human Rights?
4. How do social construction theory, economic analysis, and critical race theory help you understand the current issues of immigration in different ways?

The DREAM Act

One emerging social movement is in support of young adults and children brought to the United States when they were children rather than as adults by choice. Many remember living no other place than the United States. Beginning in early 2000, the National Immigration Law Center and other advocates who helped create the DREAM Act began lobbying for

PHOTO 15.3 Immigration rally, New York City, June 5, 2010

its passage (see Photo 15.3 for a banner used at a rally in New York City). The DREAM Act, an acronym for the Development, Relief, and Education for Alien Minors, was designed to protect such individuals. In the mid-2000, students began to organize themselves. In early 2010, though large national pro-immigration organizations were pushing for full-scale immigration reform policies, young people broke with larger, more traditional pro-immigrant organizations and openly supported and lobbied for the DREAM Act.

Students also conducted acts of civil disobedience such as hunger strikes and sit-ins. One group entered then-Senator John McCain's office and refused to leave. As a result of this action, several students were given deportation orders. In part in response to these actions, the entire pro-immigrant movement began to support the DREAM Act. This movement was also publicly supported by President Obama (Altschuler, 2011). Though introduced every year beginning in 2001, the closest the bill came to passage was in 2010 when the House of Representatives passed it, and the Senate was five votes short of passing it. The inability of Congress to pass the DREAM Act led President Obama to issue an Executive Order allowing DREAMers to work legally by deferring any action on deportation for renewable 2-year periods. This order, which became effective in 2012, is referred to as DACA, Deferred Action for Childhood Arrivals.

DACA created temporary relief for children who were under 18 when they arrived in the United States and had been in the United States for at least 4 years. This order enabled children who were brought to the United States before age 16, who had been in the United States since 2007, and who were younger than 31 to receive temporary, renewable work permits. Amuedo-Dorantes and Francisca Antman (2016) compared DACA eligible and non-DACA-eligible undocumented immigrants, and found DACA reduced poverty by about 38%, demonstrating that even temporary legal status improves the economic well-being of families. Other research (Venkataramani, Shah, O'Brien, Kawachi, & Tsai, 2017) demonstrates that DACA also correlated with improvements in mental health status for participants. Approximately 800,000 people took advantage of DACA. Close to 100,000 of these had their status changed after initial enrollment, meaning they either became eligible for a different type of visa or a green card or lost their DACA status as a result of committing a crime (U.S. Citizenship and Immigration Services, 2017). Shortly after President Trump took office in 2018, he suspended the DACA program and tried to stop DACA renewals. As a result of several federal district court challenges, as of the writing of this book, DACA recipients are currently still able to renew their work permits (U.S. Citizenship and Immigration Services, 2019).

There are many federal, state, and local opportunities for advocacy regarding immigration. You can track your own state's actions on the National Conference of State Legislators website. You can find out about federal legislative action on many established organizations websites, which are listed on the National Immigration Law Center's websites. Other organizations, such as America's Voice and United We Dream, are newer and tend to be more action oriented. These groups create petitions and have organized marches to help garner support for undocumented immigrants.

ADVOCACY

FIND IMMIGRATION-RELATED ADVOCACY GROUPS

Using the internet, research immigration advocacy organizations in your community.

1. Which organizations provide direct services?
2. Which organizations are involved with legislative advocacy?
3. Which do both?

The National Association of Social Workers (NASW) encourages advocacy. As we described above, in 2018 they took a policy position that separating children from their parents at the border is "unconscionable" (NASW, 2018). Though one voice alone may not create a change in policy, organizational statements, petitions, and demonstrations together can create a force powerful enough to create policy change. Membership in organizations like NASW can help you stay informed on issues that are important to you and find actions that might be helpful.

Final Discussion

Now that you have finished reading this chapter, reread the vignette at the beginning. Based on what you have learned, answer the following questions. Point to specific references in the chapter that help you answer these questions. Consider how different theories inform the response to these questions.

1. As a school social worker, if Jose was one of your students, what steps could you take to support him on an individual (micro) level?
2. Before he was arrested by ICE, what supports could you have given his parents who may have feared advocating for themselves or their child due to their undocumented immigration status?
3. Are there organizational changes (mezzo level changes) that could help ensure that future students like Jose would not be arrested and sent back to their birth countries with minimal support?
4. What government policy changes might help Jose?
5. What role might race, class, gender, and other aspects of identity play in this vignette?GI Bill:

16

ENVIRONMENTAL POLICY

LEARNING OBJECTIVES

16.1: Describe the history of U.S. environmental policy

16.2: Assess environmental policies and the framing of these environmental concerns

16.3: Describe the ways that the state of California and international governments address environmental concerns

16.4: Construct opportunities for environmental advocacy

The person-in-environment is a crucial theoretical foundation of social work. From early work in Massachusetts hospitals that required immigrants with tuberculosis be given the opportunity to access fresh air (Praglin, 2007) to current clinical work with individuals and families, social workers are taught to focus on the person in their environment. However, the environment is not always defined broadly to include the actual environment of the planet or even local climate patterns. Though initially recognized in social work as a concern in the late 1980s and early 1990s (Berger & Kelly, 1993; Hoff & McNutt, 1994; Soine, 1987), and identified by the American Academy of Social Work and Social Welfare as one of the Grand Challenges of the Social Work profession in 2015 (Kemp & Palinkas, 2015), relatively few have written about the environment in social work literature. Most of those who have written on the connection between social work and the environment have suggested the need to focus on the social consequences of environmental concerns (Alston, 2015; McKinnon, 2008). Susan Kemp and Lawrence Palinkas (2015) note that social workers are uniquely positioned to develop and implement "strategies to anticipate, mitigate and respond to the social and human dimensions of environmental challenges" (p. 4). In other words, our role is more significant than just responding to hazards; we are also in a position to try to limit them.

Social justice and social welfare are often interwoven with environmental hazards. Clean air and water, exposure to toxic chemicals, and the overall health of the planet affect the health and well-being of all individuals, families, and communities. Global warming results in rising water levels that make many coastal areas uninhabitable, causing people to lose their homes and creating environmental refugees. This contributes to societal instability. Environmental disasters disproportionately affect communities where people do not have the financial resources or insurance to bounce back after major catastrophes. Over 40% of small businesses do not recover from environmental disasters (Morris, 2017). Disadvantaged groups are also more likely to live in areas where man-made environmental hazards are present. For example, children living in low-income neighborhoods disproportionately suffer from asthma (Corburn, Osleeb, & Porter, 2006) and the people living in Flint, Michigan, who were poisoned by water with high lead content, were disproportionately people of color living in poverty (Clark, 2018).

Environmental policy covers many different areas. Major environmental laws in the United States protect the air and water. More recent international environmental treaties have sought to reduce global warming. Despite rising environmental concerns, environmental and conservation policies have been seen by many as a threat to their ability to engage in meaningful labor or make profits. For example, people in towns reliant on coal mines as their sole industry do not want to close mines because of the expectation (based on experience) that this will result in the loss of jobs and threaten the sustainability of whole towns. This chapter reviews the history of environmental hazards and environmental regulation in the United States. Using a critical race lens, we look at the populations who are most vulnerable to environmental hazards. We also discuss the challenges of balancing the interests of citizens with those of profit-making corporations. We examine the barriers to designing policies that balance these interests, their implementation, and policy feedback regarding what is defined as an environmental hazard. Finally, we look at alternative methods of framing environmental concerns by reviewing policies that have been used elsewhere in the world, as well as in California, which has stricter environmental regulations than the rest of the United States. Last, we suggest areas for potential advocacy.

Vignette: Mary Sue and Fracking

Based on what you know from the media or your personal, work, or volunteer experiences, think about the following questions as you read the vignette. When you finish the vignette, answer the questions below.

1. What are some of the social work concerns that were raised in relation to fracking and its impact on Mary Sue and her community?
2. What do you as a social worker need to know about fracking laws in your own state?
3. What actions might social workers take to help improve the situation at the micro, mezzo, and macro levels?
4. What role might race, class, gender, or other aspects of identity play in this vignette?

Background on Fracking

Fracking: The process of extracting fossil fuels, primarily oil and natural gas, from shale or rocks buried deep in the ground

Several groups have been engaged in debates over **fracking**, the process of extracting fossil fuels, primarily oil and natural gas, from shale or rocks buried deep in the ground.

Environmentalists have expressed concerns over the long-term damage to the environment as a result of fracking as well as concerns about clean water and air in areas abutting fracking sites. Energy companies and executives, as well as citizens who owned land, much of which had little value prior to the ability of energy companies to harvest the gas and oil available deep underneath it in the shale, have all profited greatly from fracking. As you read this, many of you are wondering: What does this have to do with social work and social welfare? For those of you who have some familiarity with fracking, you are probably aware of the environmental concerns that accompany it. However, you may still be wondering why are you learning about this in a social work policy class? We hope this vignette will help answer these questions.

Though the fracking process has been around since the 1970s, in 2010, scientific advances made it cheaper for the oil industry to extract oil and natural gas from rocks deep within the ground. Once fracking became an economically viable process, oil companies began to lease land from farmers to drill for oil and natural gas (Warner & Shapiro, 2013).

A 2014 report conducted by the Center for Public Integrity, Inside Climate News, and The Weather Channel (Morris, Song, & Hasemyer, 2014) found that the state of Texas had an insufficient number of air monitors intending to cover a 20,000 square mile area including the area of Eagle Ford, Texas. As a result of this, the majority of oil and gas production sites near Eagle Ford are allowed to monitor themselves. The Texas Commission on Environmental Quality has had its budget cut in half since 2008, and few companies that are found to have broken the law concerning emissions are actually fined. Fracking has been viewed as a problem in many states. In 2014, New York and Maryland banned fracking. Massachusetts and Vermont have also banned fracking, but this ban is mostly symbolic because neither state has the underground resources to frack (Hirji & Song, 2016).

Mary Sue's Story

Mary Sue (a fictional character based loosely on a real story reported by Morris, et al., 2014) is 66 and lives in Eagle Ford, Texas, with her husband, Joe. Though she had suffered from asthma for most of her adult life, when oil companies entered her community and started fracking on her neighbor's property, her breathing deteriorated. Prior to the advent of fracking, she had been able to manage her asthma with a nebulizer and had never been hospitalized. Now, she visits the hospital several times a month. The closest hospital is 150 miles from her home, and both she and her husband worry that one day she will not make it. The neighbor who owns the land is also a friend who tried to stop his relationship with the oil company as a result of his concerns about changes in the air quality and his worry for Mary Sue. However, he could not afford to buy out the 20-year lease he had signed. Several other people in the county also allowed fracking on their property, so he was not sure if the air or water quality concerns would have ended if he had stopped the lease. When his wife got cancer and died, which he thought might also have been associated with the changes to the air quality or the water as a result of fracking, he moved to Dallas to be away from the pollutants and to be closer to his children. Now Mary Sue has fewer local supports.

THE HISTORY AND SOCIAL CONSTRUCTION OF U.S. ENVIRONMENTAL POLICY

The first effort to address air quality in the United States was the Air Pollution Control Act of 1955, which provided federal money to research air quality. Fifteen years of legislation followed. The 1963 Clean Air Act provided federal dollars to monitor and control air pollution within the public health service. In 1967, the Air Quality Act was passed but contained almost no enforcement mechanisms. The Clean Air Act of 1970 established requirements for states to achieve national air quality standards to limit the pollution from industrial and mobile sources. It also authorized the establishment of national emission standards for hazardous pollutants (Environmental Protection Agency, 2017). Rachel Carson's 1962 publication of *Silent Spring*, the first major public exposé on chemical contaminants in our environment specifically **DDT** a (widely used pesticide with significant health side effects), is often considered a turning point. The publication of this book and subsequent public attention helped fuel popular support for the founding of the Environmental Protection Agency, now a cabinet-level department within the U.S. federal government (Lewis, 1985).

DDT: A once widely used pesticide with significant harmful health side effects that has been outlawed in the United States since the early 1970s

In 1969, one of the worst oil spills in U.S. history occurred, second only to the Exxon Valdez spill in 1989. Union Oil had received a waiver from the U.S. Geological Foundation to drill without following the existing guidelines. This spill resulted in a major environmental catastrophe leaving a 35mile oil slick along the California coast. The pictures that were broadcast of dead sea mammals and birds covered in oil led to one of the biggest conservation efforts in U.S. history. California called for a moratorium on offshore drilling off its coast, President Nixon signed the National Environmental Policy Act, and California passed the California Environmental Quality Act (Mai-Duc, 2015). This event also led to the first Earth Day celebration in the United States in April 1970. This time period is often cited as the beginning of U.S. environmentalism. This movement is credited with developing the political will for both Republicans and Democrats to support environmental regulation (Rosenbaum, 2017).

It was during the 1970s that most current U.S. environmental policy was passed including the Clean Air Act of 1970 discussed above, the Clean Water Act (1972), the Coastal Zone Management Act (1972), the Safe Drinking Water Act (1974), and the Resource Conservation and Recovery Act of 1976. This time period also saw the Toxic Substances Control Act (TSCA) in 1976, amendments to the Clean Water Act in 1977 and 1987, and amendments to the Clean Air Act in 1977. Despite a changing scientific understanding of environmental concerns, few federal efforts have been made to update these policies. In the sections below, we provide detail on specific areas of U.S. environmental policy, many of which are also referenced in Table 16.1, which lists major federal environmental laws.

USDA Forest Service, Pacific Northwest Region, State and Private Forestry, Forest Health Protection. Collection: Portland Station Collection; La Grande, Oregon. Imege: PS-1429

PHOTO 16.1 Picture of DDT being sprayed in Oregon in 1955

Air Quality

In 1970, in the wake of the big Earth Day celebrations, Congress amended the Clean Air Act to address some of the earlier versions' failures. The resulting legislation was more national and less regionally focused. As Representative Paul Rodgers (1990), Chair of the House Committee on Health and the Environment during the deliberations pointed out, "air contamination does not stop at neatly defined regional boundaries" (p. 2). The amendments created the first national air quality standards as well as deadlines for compliance with those standards. Representative Rodgers (1990) noted that in addition to changing the law, the 1970 amendments also "raised the consciousness of the american public and American businesses regarding the importance of pollution control" so that pollution was no longer considered something unpleasant but necessary, but seen as a controllable issue (p. 3). The Clean Air Act was again revised in 1977 and 1990.

The original Clean Air Act that established national air quality and auto emissions standards allowed California to set its own standards about what pollution cars can expel into the atmosphere so it could act as a demonstration project for the rest of the country. California's current emissions waiver is set to expire in 2026. During the second Bush administration, the Environmental Protection Agency (EPA) filed a lawsuit against California for setting its own auto emissions standards. Before the federal district court could rule on the standards, Obama became president and the claim was not pursued. However, in 2007, two lower court judges had held that California could have its own emission standards and an appellate court held that the burden of proof is on the EPA not to grant the waiver as opposed to on California to demonstrate the need for a waiver. As of this writing, the Trump administration is again challenging the current California emissions standards (Egelko, 2018; see Photo 16.2).

©iStock.com/Tramino

PHOTO 16.2 Factory chimneys emitting air pollutions. View through the field on clouds of smoke and factory

In 2005, Massachusetts, eleven other states, and some cities brought a claim against the EPA suggesting that the EPA was required by the Clean Air Act to regulate carbon emissions from new cars to lower greenhouse gases. These gases trap radiation within the atmosphere, raising temperatures. Those filing suit claimed that failure to regulate carbon dioxide, a form of greenhouse gas, could result in a loss of coastal lands. The EPA responded to the initial complaint that they did not have to regulate carbon emissions and, even if they did, they needed to complete more research before doing so. The district court upheld the EPA's position. When the case came to the Supreme Court, the Court overturned the district court's decision, finding that the EPA was authorized by the Clean Air Act to regulate any air pollutant from motor vehicles. This law was intentionally written broadly to include new sources of air pollution, including carbon emissions, which were not conceived of when the law was written. They also held that Massachusetts had standing to bring the case because it could be harmed by rising sea levels (*Massachusetts v. Environmental Protection Agency*, 2007).

Drinking Water Quality

The federal regulation of U.S. drinking water began in 1914 with the development of public health standards for bacterial levels. In the late 1960s, public health researchers identified problems with excessive levels of pathogens in 40% of the U.S. drinking water supply. One 1972 study of treated water in Louisiana found 36 hazardous chemicals. This finding and other similar research were largely responsible for the pressure that led Congress to pass the Safe Drinking Water Act in 1974 (EPA, 1999). These only apply to public drinking water and do not affect private well water on which 13 million households rely (EPA, 2019c). Moreover, its failed implementation has recently been widely publicized in the ongoing water safety crisis in Flint, Michigan, and debate over water rights for Native Americans affected by the Dakota pipeline, discussed below in relation to current policy. It is notable, in both of these cases, that the people most affected by lack of access to clean drinking water were and will be primarily black Americans and Native Americans.

Because many people living in rural poverty have private wells, they are not covered by this law. Mining activities such as ash disposal and fracking have polluted private wells. Toxic chemicals used in farming have also affected well water quality (Healy, 2018). Some states have addressed these problems. In Pennsylvania, if well water becomes contaminated after there is mining activity, the activity is presumed to have caused the pollution and the company must provide clean water to the residents (Pennsylvania General Assembly, Title 58 Sec 3218, 2012).

California is home to many laws that are more stringent than federal law; we discuss more in the section about alternative views. In California, the Safe Drinking Water and Toxic Enforcement Act (Proposition 65) was passed in 1986. This is a state law and does not apply nationally. This law protects drinking water and requires the state to post a list of chemicals that are known cancer-causing agents, and it requires businesses to provide warnings on products containing such chemicals (Office of Environmental Health Hazard Assessment, 2018).

Waste Disposal

In 1976, Congress passed the Resource Recovery and Disposal Act. This law remains the primary federal legislation covering the disposal of solid and hazardous waste. It was passed in response to an increased awareness of the harmful effects of this waste on humans. It regulates active municipal and industrial sites that emit waste (EPA, 2019b). Historic or abandoned sites are regulated by the Comprehensive Environmental Response, Compensation, and Liability Act (CERCLA), which was not passed until 1980. This law was designed to collect tax money from both chemical and petroleum industries to pay for cleanup efforts to address hazardous substances that they had released. The money was used to develop a trust fund to pay for the cleanup of abandoned and uncontrolled hazardous waste sites (EPA, 2018b). In 1986, it was amended and renamed the Superfund Amendments and Reauthorization Act. The amendments created new enforcement mechanisms, allowed greater citizen participation in decisions about strategies for clean-up, and increased the amount of money in the trust fund (EPA, 2018b).

Coastal Zone Management

The federal government has also passed laws to address coastal zone management, protect national forests, and consider the environmental impact of chemical exposure on workers. The 1972 Coastal Zone Management Act was designed to facilitate federal-state partnerships to protect and restore the coastal property and to make sure that coastlines are developed responsibly. The law is administered by the National Oceanic and Atmospheric Administration (NOAA) and has three main goals: (1) to align federally funded action with state coastal management programs; (2) to provide money to states to enhance state programs that address, "wetlands, coastal hazards, public access, marine debris, cumulative and secondary impacts, special area management planning, ocean and Great Lakes resources, energy and government facility siting, and aquaculture;" and (3) to financially support state programs to prevent and control pollution from running into coastal waters (National Oceanic and Atmospheric Administration, 2018). The 1976 National Forest Management Act (NFMA) was designed to better manage U.S. forests by making them more sustainable and limiting excess logging. It was also designed to protect streams from logging and to support and encourage reforestation. In addition, the Office of Health and Safety Administration (OSHA, 2018) issues directives designed to protect workers from exposure to chemicals that can be harmful.

CURRENT ENVIRONMENTAL POLICIES

Although environmental policies cover more than we can summarize in this book, we highlight key areas. It is also important to remember that the policies discussed in the previous section—like all policies—can be changed at any time. For example, on May 20, 2019, *The New York Times* reported Trump administration plans to eliminate an Obama-era ruling called the Clean Power Plan. In so doing, the EPA will change the analytic model that they use to calculate air quality harms and will reduce the estimated number of premature deaths thereby affecting the analysis of the costs and benefits of regulation. While decreasing the number of deaths may sound good, the problem is that this method only changes the counted number of deaths, not the number of actual deaths. Advocates have raised concerns that the actual number of deaths may go up if regulations are weakened and air pollution is allowed to increase (Friedman, 2019). This is an example of how politics can shape not only debate but also the facts that are available to the public and policymakers in making policy decisions.

In this section, we highlight current policies related to surface water, Native American water rights, and drinking water safety in Flint, Michigan, and elsewhere. We also discuss regulation of toxic chemicals, climate control, and nongovernmental efforts to address hazards. See Table 16.1 later in this chapter for more information about current environmental laws.

Surface Water

In one landmark case from the 1980s, John Rapanos filled 22 acres of wetland with sand to begin a construction project, without filing for a permit. The EPA interpreted the Clean Water Act's requirement that "navigable waters" not be polluted to include a requirement that wetlands abutting such waters also be protected. Rapanos appealed. Ultimately the case was heard by the Supreme Court. The majority of Supreme Court justices agreed Rapanos was not guilty of violating the Clean Water Act. However, there was no majority opinion. The conservative justices noted that they did not think the wetlands were navigable waters. Justice Kennedy, in his own opinion, noted that though wetlands could be navigable, in this case, the connection to navigable waters was not clear. The case was remanded to a lower court to gather more information (*Rapanos v. United States*, 547 U.S. 715, 2006). To try to clarify the intent of the policy, the federal Clean Water Rule of 2015 redefined and expanded the scope of water protection under the Clean Water Act to refer to all water in the United States as opposed to the narrower definition used by some of the Supreme Court that it only applied to navigable waters (Federal Register, 2015). In 2018, President Trump formally suspended this ruling (Davenport, 2018). Because of these different definitions of navigable waters, there is some confusion over which water is *surface water* and therefore eligible for regulation under this act.

While this distinction may not seem relevant to social work practice, wetlands protect other land from flooding. When property is built on wetlands, it is more likely to flood. In addition, the barrier of the wetlands is not available for other property. This can cause people to be dislocated and tends to harm the low- to middle-income families who do not have financial reserves. Since the savings rate for **median** American household is about $11,500, meaning half of households have less and half have more (Elkins, 2018), it is obvious that many households cannot financially endure the financial challenge of being dislocated. Regulation in this area of the environment can affect many communities within which social workers practice.

Median: The midpoint in a group of numbers. Median income, for example, is the point where half of the people whose income is measured have higher incomes and half have lower incomes.

Pipeline and Native American Water Rights

The Keystone XL pipeline and Dakota Access Pipeline (sometimes called DAPL) are two 1,100 mile projects proposed during the Obama administration for the purpose of carrying crude (unprocessed) oil from the oil wells of Alberta, Canada, and Stanley, North Dakota, to Nebraska. There they are proposed to meet up with the existing Keystone pipeline and carry oil to the U.S. Gulf Coast to be refined and shipped (see Figure 16.1).

In a 2017 *National Geographic* article, Heather Brady documented key expected impacts of these projects. Concerns about the environmental impact of the pipelines related to the pipeline's construction, maintenance, and potential oil spills. These included: (1) endangering animals and their habitats as a result of the pipeline construction and maintenance as well as the impact of a potential oil spill on animal populations: (2) creating more greenhouse gases than traditional methods of oil extraction: and (3) threats to the drinking water of Native Americans and others in neighboring communities. The Standing Rock Sioux Tribe is particularly concerned about drinking water effects, because all their water is downstream of the Dakota Access Pipeline. An additional concern for the Dakota Access Pipeline is that it is close to and has the potential to damage sacred Native American land, particularly in the case of a break or spill. Proponents of the pipeline expansion highlight its expected economic benefits, including property tax revenue for the places the pipeline crosses, creation of 12,000 short-term construction jobs, and 40 permanent jobs (Brady, 2017).

Although no single federal agency has jurisdiction over the entire pipeline, the Army Corps of Engineers was responsible for the environmental assessment of certain portions of the route, particularly relating to river crossings. In 2016, the Standing Rock Sioux Tribe filed a lawsuit against the Army Corps of Engineers for violating their rights and violating the National Environmental Policy Act of 1970. They also accused the workers constructing the pipeline of damaging and removing graves and prayer sites from sacred land (Hersher, 2017). In July of 2017, the federal district court held that the Army Corps of Engineers did not conduct sufficient environmental testing before providing a permit for the pipeline. However, construction and use of the pipeline was not halted. The Army Corps of Engineers conducted further evaluation and changed the location of the pipeline (Hasselman, 2018). In 2016 and 2017, Standing Rock activists were joined by members of 300 other tribes and thousands of activists including military veterans for a months-long stand-off at Standing Rock to prevent the final construction and use of the Dakota pipeline. At least 600 people were arrested during these protests; ultimately many of the cases were dropped because the judge found that the police had not given the protesters notice that they were on private land (NBC News, 2017). As a result of public pressure, President Obama stated,

> I think right now the Army Corps is examining whether there are ways to reroute this pipeline in a way. So we're going to let it play out for several more weeks and determine whether or not this can be resolved in a way that I think is properly attentive to the traditions of the first Americans. (Hersher, 2016)

Four days after President Trump took office, he ordered the U.S. Corp of Engineers to expedite the review and approval process for the section left to be built. The Standing Rock

FIGURE 16.1 ■ Map of the proposed Keystone XL and Dakota Access Pipelines

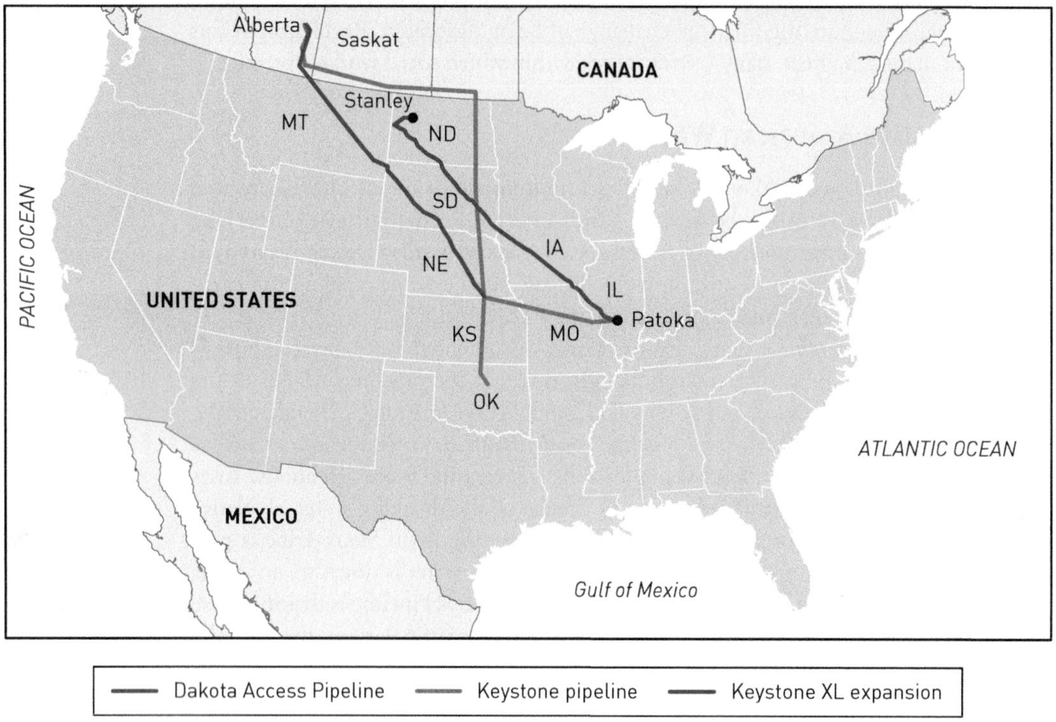

Dakota Access Pipeline — Keystone pipeline — Keystone XL expansion

Source: TransCanada, Energy Transfer Partners

and Cheyenne River Sioux tribes sued the Corp of Engineers to stop construction, but were unsuccessful. The Dakota Access Pipeline became fully operational June 1, 2017 (McCown, 2018). By March of 2018, the Dakota pipeline was transporting 1.18 barrels of oil per day, making North Dakota's oil extraction in the United States second only to Texas and the Gulf of Mexico (McCown, 2018). Ultimately, in August of 2018, the Army Corp of Engineers affirmed their original decision (Hasselman, 2018).

Flint, Michigan

You may already be familiar with the scandal that occurred in Flint, Michigan. The primary industries in Flint and employers of Flint residents were focused around the manufacturing of automobiles. That industry was hit hard by the 2008 recession, and Flint lost significant revenue and population. Eventually, the city was put under the control of an Emergency Manager, authorized under highly controversial state law. City administrators including Emergency Manager Darnell Earley decided to stop getting water from the same source as Detroit and instead get water from a regional pipeline. Until the city could connect to that pipeline, they provided Flint residents with water from the Flint River, starting in April 2014. Earley is accused of making this decision despite knowing that the city's water treatment plant, which had not been used in decades, would not be able to keep the water clean. For 18 months, people in Flint complained that the water looked dirty, smelled bad, and made their children ill. Initially, their concerns were deflected. During this time, the city oversight body told them that their water was fine. The residents of Flint enlisted outside researchers to help them test their water, who proved that the water was heavily polluted and did not meet federal standards. Residents wrote letters, went to community meetings, and demonstrated in front of the city hall (Clark, 2018). In January 2016, they got the federal EPA to intervene, and the EPA allocated $100 million to upgrade Flint's water infrastructure (EPA, 2018a). The situation is slowly improving, but the health effects of the polluted water are still being felt. Because of the delay, many children were poisoned by lead, and both children and adults were exposed to high levels of carcinogenic chemicals. Many children who drank contaminated water during key developmental stages will face lifelong disabilities as a result. Emergency Manager Earley and 15 other administrators have been charged with a multitude of crimes, including involuntary manslaughter, as a result of this crisis.

REFLECTION

FLINT, MICHIGAN

Based on what you have read here and your own research, answer the following questions about the water crisis in Flint.

1. What happened?
2. What are the consequences?
3. Who is affected?
4. Who is (or should be) responsible for solving the problem?
5. What roles can social workers play in addressing this issue at the micro, mezzo, and macro levels?

Water Quality Outside of Flint

Flint, Michigan, is not the only place that has experienced poor water quality and faced difficulty challenging those responsible for the pollution. In Woburn, Massachusetts, in the late 1980s, townspeople came together to engage in a class action lawsuit against a local chemical company that had been polluting the water. They rallied due to the great efforts of a mother whose son was diagnosed with leukemia. After many years, the chemical company was held responsible for the pollution and was required to clean it up and provide monetary compensation to the families who had been harmed. This story was publicized in Jonathan Harr's 1995 bestseller, *A Civil Action*, which was made into a popular movie. This lawsuit and cleanup effort ultimately relied on the CERCLA/Superfund Act described above.

In addition, a recent report (Allaire, Wu, & Lall, 2018) found that health-based water quality concerns are widespread in the United States and effect somewhere between nine and 45 million people annually. This report also found that rural areas as well as low-income and minority communities tended to be more vulnerable to poor water quality. Evidence that poor water quality disproportionately affects low-income and minority communities is supported by the research (Balazs, Morello-Frosch, Hubbard, & Ray, 2011; Stillo & Gibson, 2017). Statewide mechanisms for monitoring water quality are inadequate (Allair et al., 2018) and the cases above demonstrate that local government may also be unable or unwilling to prevent, detect, or address such concerns.

Regulating Toxic Chemicals: Pesticides and DDT/Agent Orange

Agent Orange: A substance that was used to try to kill the foliage to make it easier for anti-American Vietnamese soldiers to hide during the Vietnam War

During the Vietnam War, the U.S. military sprayed a substance called **Agent Orange** to try to kill the foliage that made it easier for anti-American Vietnamese soldiers to hide. The production and distribution of Agent Orange produced a toxic cancer-causing chemical that many Vietnamese and many American soldiers were exposed to. In addition, many military personnel were exposed to Agent Orange in testing and storage areas in the United States (U.S. Department of Veterans Affairs, 2017). The harms caused by soldiers' exposure to Agent Orange led to a greater understanding and concern about how exposure to toxic substances more generally such as DDT, which was used to kill weeds and insects.

In 1976, Congress passed the Toxic Substances Control Act (TSCA) requiring the EPA to regulate and ban chemicals that pose a substantial risk to human health. By 2016, the EPA had used this law in 30 years to ban the use of only nine chemicals (Harrington, 2016). The European Union, in contrast, had by 2017 banned over 1,300 chemicals from cosmetics and personal health care products (*Scientific American*, 2017). The TSCA allows chemicals to be introduced onto the market and removed only when there is evidence of danger to the public (Kollipara, 2015). In contrast to the way we regulate chemicals in the United States, in Europe, chemicals must first be proven to be safe before they can be used, a concept referred to as the **precautionary principle** (Kriebel et al., 2001). When TSCA was passed it is likely that Congress did not predict that they would need to regulate over 62,000 chemicals to determine their risk to human health (Rosenbaum, 2017).

Precautionary principle: A concept, sometimes adopted in policy, according to which something is prohibited unless and until it is proven to be safe

In 2016, the Frank R. Lautenberg Chemical Safety for the 21st Century Act (HR 2576) to amend TSCA (1976) was passed by a bipartisan majority of the House and Senate and signed into law by President Obama. This law improved on the TSCA by changing the EPA's standard from a simple economic cost-benefit analysis to health-based criteria and creating higher standards for vulnerable populations such as pregnant women and children. It also gave the EPA enhanced authority to require testing for new chemicals and mandated safety reviews for new and existing chemicals. From 2016 until spring 2019, the EPA reviewed approximately 2,200 chemicals, far short of the more than 86,000 that have been introduced into the environment since the 1970s (EPA, 2019a, 2019d). However, according to Environmental Defense Fund (Denison, 2018), since President Trump was elected, much of the progress of the Frank Lautenberg Chemical Safety for the 21st Century Act has been halted. For example, three chemicals that the EPA had proposed banning in 2017 have not been banned, and new rules for implementing the TSCA that were heavily supported by the chemical industry and undermine the intent of the law have been added. Further, the EPA is now avoiding comprehensive reviews of new and existing chemicals, and budget cuts have hampered the EPA's ability to enforce existing law (Denison, 2018).

Climate Control

Though politically contested in the United States, the scientific evidence to support climate change is widely accepted throughout the world (Thee-Brenan, 2014). As a result, international efforts have been made to reduce the emission of gases that are believed to lead to global climate change. **Climate change** is the idea that the temperature on the planet is changing as a result of human activity and can therefore be influenced by changing certain human activity such as reducing emissions, reducing deforestation, and reducing our reliance on cattle farming. The intergovernmental panel on climate change, supported by the World Health Organization and the United Nations UN Environment Program, has issued six assessments relying on extensive scientific evidence and concluded that climate change is real and it is happening. Though efforts have been made to reduce carbon emissions to slow the progress of climate change, their success has been limited (IPCC, 2014).

Climate change: The idea that the temperature on the planet is changing as a result of human activity and therefore can be influenced by changing certain human activity such as reducing emissions, reducing deforestation, and reducing our reliance on cattle farming

Lena Dominelli (2011) argues that the social work framework of person-in-environment obligates social workers to understand the science of climate change and to advocate for policy change addressing the effects of climate change as a matter of social justice. Climate change, she argues, will require social workers working on a micro level to help their clients both adapt to changing environments and deal with the aftermath of environmental disasters such as helping climate change refugees who are displaced from the global south. For example, the 1951 Geneva Convention on Refugees makes no mention of climate change refugees, and this needs to be changed if the world is going to be able to deal with the inevitable displacement of people living in low-lying regions that will likely be overcome with water in the not so distant future.

In the past 25 years, there has been growing recognition that many man-made chemicals and behaviors emit pollutants that can and have changed the climate. Because climate change is going on around the planet beyond the boundaries of the countries where pollutants are emitted, international efforts have been made to address it. In 1992, the United Nations (UN) had its first conference, the Framework Convention on Climate Change (UNFCCC), where a loose framework was established to address climate change. As a part of the UNFCCC, countries signed a document agreeing that climate change was real and that there was significant evidence that carbon dioxide emissions were, at least, partially responsible for these changes. Almost all countries signed it in 1992.

In 1997, 149 nations, not including the United States, signed the Kyoto Protocol, pledging to reduce carbon emissions, which are largely seen as a major cause of global warming. Carbon emissions come from burning gasoline in cars, burning coal, gas, and oil to create energy, burning wood in forests (often called clear cutting) to make new fields, and from cow excrement. The Kyoto Protocol was supposed to reduce emissions by almost 30% from 1990–2010. However, by the time it went into effect 8 years later, worldwide emissions had risen due to rising emission in China and the United States. Though the United States was not a signatory to the Kyoto Protocol, China was. This is a good example of how environmental policy changes in some countries can be negated if other countries, particularly large countries, do not participate in the change.

The 2014 Intergovernmental Panel on Climate Change (IPCC) issued a report predicting a global rise in temperatures of between 3 degrees Celsius to 5.8 degrees Celsius by 2100. This will result in rising water levels, unprecedented storms, and a mixing of water from aquifers with salt water making water sources non-potable, declining soil moisture, increasing desertification, and harm to agriculture and livestock sustainability. The IPCC report noted the importance of developing social, institutional, physical, and structural strategies to adapt to and mitigate the impact of global warming. These could include human potential, poverty alleviation, disaster risk management, ecosystem management, and land use.

The Paris Agreement, drafted in 2015, was also designed to combat climate change. By 2018, it had been ratified by 181 countries, including the United States in 2016 (United Nations, 2019). In this agreement, industrialized nations pledged to provide $100,000,000 to non-industrialized countries to finance their efforts to mitigate climate change. In 2017, President Trump announced the U.S. withdrawal from the Paris Agreement (Holtman & Bodner, 2017), making it less likely that the UN will be able to live up to its obligations to less industrialized countries (Urlepainen, 2017). However, some individual U.S. states as well as other nations remain committed to the goals of the Paris Agreement despite the federal government's withdrawal (Holtman & Bodner, 2017; Urlepainen, 2017).

In October of 2018, an UN Intergovernmental Panel on Climate Change report declared that the Paris Agreement did not go far enough to address global warming. It found that the world has approximately 12 years to make sure that global warming does not exceed 1.5 degrees Celsius to avoid major unprecedented long-term environmental changes including the loss of certain ecosystems. The report noted that the standards in the current Paris accord do not go nearly far enough (IPCC, 2018).

Non-regulatory Mechanisms to Address Environmental Hazards

LEED: An international green building certification that indicates that the building construction has made efforts to ensure that the building is energy efficient and made with substances that are less likely to harm people or the environment than those used in typical construction

Environmental problems can be affected through actions of individuals and private companies, not just government decisions. Some private, nonregulatory efforts have been made to address environmental concerns. These include developing conservation land trusts and establishing green companies. Conservation land trusts are, essentially, contracts between owners of land and a government entity or conservation group in which the owner allows limited use of their property to maintain conservation. This may include hunting or hiking paths. Green companies receive private certifications that they are operating in a way that indicates they have made efforts to reduce their carbon footprint, they are using nontoxic chemicals, they are not disturbing old growth forests, and so on. One example of this is the LEED certification for building construction. **LEED** is an international green building certification that indicates that the building construction has made efforts to ensure that the building is energy efficient and made with substances that reduce waste. These materials are less likely to harm people or the environment than those used in typical construction (U.S. Green Building Council, n.d.). Such certification can help guide companies wanting to improve their environmental track records and also makes economic sense in their appeal to conservation-minded consumers.

TABLE 16.1 ■ Summary of U.S. Federal Environmental Laws

Topic	Laws	Oversight Agency	Website
Overall environmental oversight	National Environmental Policy 1969	Office of Federal Activities	https://www.epa.gov/laws-regulations/summary-national-environmental-policy-act
	Comprehensive Environmental Response, Compensation, and Liability Act/Superfund Amendments and Reauthorization Act 1980	Office of Superfund Remediation and Technology Innovation	https://www.epa.gov/laws-regulations/summary-comprehensive-environmental-response-compensation-and-liability-act
	Federal Actions to Address Environmental Justice in Minority Populations and Low-Income Populations 1994	Office of Environmental Justice	https://www.epa.gov/laws-regulations/summary-executive-order-12898-federal-actions-address-environmental-justice
	Protection of Children from Environmental Health Risks and Safety Risks 1997	Office of Children's Health Protection	
Workplace safety	Occupational Safety and Health Act 1970	Occupational Safety and Health Administration The National Institute for Occupational Safety and Health	https://www.epa.gov/laws-regulations/summary-occupational-safety-and-health-act https://www.epa.gov/laws-regulations/summary-executive-order-13045-protection-children-environmental-health-risks-and
Air quality	Clean Air Act 1970	Office of Air and Radiation	https://www.epa.gov/laws-regulations/summary-clean-air-act
	Chemical Safety Information, Site Security and Fuels Regulatory Relief Act 1999	Office of Emergency Management	https://www.epa.gov/laws-regulations/summary-chemical-safety-information-site-security-and-fuels-regulatory-relief-act

Topic	Laws	Oversight Agency	Website
Water quality	Federal Water Pollution Control Act 1948/Clean Water Act 1972	Office of Water	https://www.epa.gov/laws-regulations/summary-clean-water-act
	Safe Drinking Water Act 1974	Office of Ground Water & Drinking Water	https://www.epa.gov/laws-regulations/summary-safe-drinking-water-act
	BEACH Act 2000	Office of Water	https://www.epa.gov/laws-regulations/summary-beach-act
	Shore Protection Act 1988	Office of Water	https://www.epa.gov/laws-regulations/summary-shore-protection-act
Noise pollution	Noise Control Act 1972	State and local governments	https://www.epa.gov/laws-regulations/summary-noise-control-act
Endangered animals	Endangered Species Act 1973	U.S. Fish and Wildlife Service U.S. National Oceanic and Atmospheric Administration National Marine Fisheries Service	https://www.epa.gov/laws-regulations/summary-endangered-species-act
Natural resource conservation	Resource Conservation and Recovery Act 1976	Office of Resource Conservation & Recovery	https://www.epa.gov/laws-regulations/summary-resource-conservation-and-recovery-act
Nuclear waste	Nuclear Waste Policy Act 1982	Office of Air and Radiation	https://www.epa.gov/laws-regulations/summary-nuclear-waste-policy-act
Chemical hazards	Pollution Prevention Act 1990	Office of Pollution and Toxics	https://www.epa.gov/laws-regulations/summary-pollution-prevention-act
	Emergency Planning and Community Right-to-Know Act 1986	Office of Emergency Management	https://www.epa.gov/laws-regulations/summary-emergency-planning-community-right-know-act
Pesticides	Food Quality Protection Act 1996	Environmental Protection Agency	https://www.epa.gov/laws-regulations/summary-food-quality-protection-act
	Federal Food, Drug, and Cosmetic Act 2005	Office of Pesticide Programs	https://www.epa.gov/laws-regulations/summary-federal-food-drug-and-cosmetic-act
Energy policy	Energy Policy Act 2005	Environmental Protection Agency/Office of Underground Storage Tanks	https://www.epa.gov/laws-regulations/summary-energy-policy-act
	Energy Independence and Security Act 2007	Department of Energy	https://www.epa.gov/laws-regulations/summary-energy-independence-and-security-act

POLICY INFORMED BY ALTERNATIVE LENSES

Symbolic interaction theory suggests that people are constantly engaging with the world around them and constructing and negotiating their own realities. Even the names that we give to things affect the way in which these things are perceived (Reck, 1964). Ken Gould and Tammy Lewis (2015) note that because the environment affects everybody, it is a public concern that must be addressed using public strategies and by changing social institutions. In a neoliberal or capitalist system, environmental problems often pit corporations against citizens. As Theodor Geisel, known by his pen name Dr. Seuss, recognized in *The Lorax* (1971), manufacturing often uses natural resources. He describes a sneed as something that can be perceived as either junk or something that no one can live without. This fictional account parallels American (and maybe all) consumerism quite well. When increasing the production of a consumer item relies on the overuse of seemingly unlimited resources, one may find that such resources are not, in fact, unlimited. In addition, manufacturing often produces pollution, which affects the environment of those who reside near and sometimes far from the site of production. Though we have developed some environmental laws in the United States to address these concerns, these laws are limited and further hampered by poor implementation. Those who profit from the manufacture of these goods often lobby against any limitations. If one's main goal is to make a profit, seen as a supreme value in a capitalist economy, environmental protections that require additional tests or safety protection for workers or communities can be seen as inconvenient and expensive. Ultimately, they reduce the profit that one can make.

Environmental justice perspective: A perspective that focuses on the overlap between environmental pollution and the disproportionate impact of environmental hazards on people with lower incomes and people of color

In contrast to a neoliberal perspective, an **environmental justice perspective** focuses on the overlap between environmental pollution and the disproportionate impact of environmental hazards on people living in poverty and people of color. Indeed, in many ways, this perspective overlaps with **critical race theory**, which views policies and practices through the lens of race. Michael Mascarenhas (2015) and Robert Bullard and colleagues (1990, 2007, 2012) have documented the historically disproportionate impact of environmental hazards on people of color. They find that the race of the local population is an independent predictor of how likely hazardous chemicals will be located in a particular place and that African Americans, Latinx, Native Americans, and Asians in the United States are more likely to live in sites affected by hazardous waste.

Free riders: Those who benefit from public goods (such as clean air) without paying when they use, compromise, or destroy them

Executive Order 12898: A federal ruling issued during the Obama administration that required federal agencies to consider environmental justice to rectify policies that disproportionately impacted minority and low-income populations

Green Party: A small U.S. political party whose main goals are to reduce the military infrastructure, reduce or eliminate the use of fossil fuel and become more reliant on renewable energy, create a living wage and make our political system more democratic

From an environmental justice perspective, it is a serious problem that unregulated companies can damage the environment and receive all the profits from whatever they produce or mine without being required to prevent, mitigate, or compensate for environmental hazards they cause. As we have noted several times in this chapter, such harms often disproportionately impact low-income and minority communities and are part of a larger pattern of racist and classist social and economic structures. Damages can include releasing harmful chemicals into the environment as well as leaving pollutants that are the byproducts of extracting or mining minerals from the environment.

An economic perspective on this problem can examine the challenge of companies operating as free riders. **Free riders** are those who benefit from public goods (such as clean air) without paying when they use, compromise, or destroy them. In other words, companies use something publicly available to all and make it less usable for others without shouldering the costs of the damage. In an effort to address environmental (in)justice and the disproportionate exposure of certain populations to pollution, President Clinton's 1994 **Executive Order 12898** required federal agencies to consider environmental justice to rectify policies that disproportionately impacted minority and low-income populations.

Though not one of the United States' major political parties, the U.S. **Green Party's** main goals are to reduce the military infrastructure, reduce or eliminate the use of fossil fuel and become more reliant on renewable energy, create a living wage, and make our political system more democratic. Their platform includes the following statement, illustrating a perspective different from that of other political parties:

> Our houses and buildings, manufacturing processes, and industrial agriculture were all designed with the assumption of an endless supply of cheap and readily available fossil fuels. Pollution and despoiling the land were not part of the thinking. The

Green Party, however, is optimistic about the alternatives that now exist and that could be encouraged through tax policy and the market incentives of fuel efficiency. We also challenge the grip of the oil, automotive, and automobile insurance industries that have managed to block or roll back progress in public mass transit. The gutting of subsidies for the railroads has meant not only fewer passenger routes but also the addition of thousands of large freight trucks on our highways, decreasing public safety and increasing pollution. We are committed to extending the greening of waste management by encouraging the spread of such practices as reduce, return, reuse, and recycle. We strongly oppose the recent attempts to roll back the federal environmental protection laws that safeguard our air, water, and soil. (Green Party US, 2018)

The State of California

While we often look to other countries for different perspectives, the state of California has developed many more restrictive environmental policies than the United States as a whole. As a result, it is sometimes seen as a model for what we could do nationwide. As noted earlier, the Clean Air Act included a carved-out exception for the State of California to enable them to set higher automobile exhaust standards than the national standard. This was possible because California already had a law following a higher standard when the Clean Air Act was passed. California passed this law based on an understanding that given the geography of Los Angeles they were particularly vulnerable to carbon emissions that become trapped in the air and create a dangerous level of smog. Twelve states and the District of Columbia follow California emissions standards (American Council for Energy Efficient Economy, 2018). California was also the first to restrict the use of certain flame-retardant chemicals in furniture (California Technical Bulletin 117, 1975 revised 2014) as well as to require notifications on commercial products, including furniture or beauty products that include known carcinogens (California Proposition 65, 1986). See Table 16.2 for more examples of ways in which California has passed policies which are more stringent and more protective of the environment than is typical in the United States.

TABLE 16.2 ■ List of California Environmental Laws
California Hazardous Substance Account Act, California Health & Safety Code (CH & SC) 25300 to 25395.45
California Underground Storage of Hazardous Substances Act, CH & SC 25280 to 25299.7
California Environmental Quality Act, CH & SC 25570 to 25570.4
California Hazardous Waste Control Act, CH & SC 25100 to 25250.28
California Safe Drinking Water and Toxic Enforcement Act, CH & SC 25249.5 to 25249.13, also known as Proposition 65
Air pollution control laws: CH & SC 39000 to 44474
California Porter-Cologne Water Quality Control Act, California Water Code 13000 to 14958
Toxic Injection Well Control Act, CH & SC 25159.10 to 25159.25
California Used Oil Recycling Act, CH & SC 25250 to 25250.28
California Emergency Planning and Right-to-Know Laws, CH & SC 25500 to 25553

(Continued)

TABLE 16.2 ■ (Continued)

U.S. Environmental Protection Agency (EPA) Identification (ID) numbers: Generators, 22 California Code of Regulations (CCR) 66262.12
The Clean Energy and Pollution Reduction Act of 2015, a.k.a. Senate Bill 350
Divesting from coal: S.B.185
The ivory ban bill: A.B. 96
Marijuana regulation: A.B. 266, A.B. 243 and S.B. 643
Plastic microbeads: A.B. 888
Antibiotic abuse: S.B. 27, S.B. 770, S.B. 361

International Comparisons

Many European consumer protection laws are based on the precautionary principle that was adopted in European Union guidelines, which requires that before any new chemical product is introduced to the market, it must be proven that it will not cause harm to humans or the environment (European Commission, 2000). This contrasts the U.S. model when harm must be proven before a product can be taken off the market or people warned about its potential harm. In addition, in contrast to the United States, which often provides tax subsidies and supports for oil companies, many nations including Costa Rica, Nicaragua, Scotland, Sweden, and Uruguay are investing in renewable energy including wind, solar, and geothermal power with the goal of ultimately eliminating the need for carbon-based power (Climate Reality Project, 2016).

OPPORTUNITIES FOR ADVOCACY

Dominelli (2011) outlines social work skills that could be helpful in addressing climate change: consciousness raising and education around the issue of global warming, lobbying for preventive measures to reduce carbon usage at the local level, and mobilizing communities to engage in environmental sound practices, as well as working with legislators to seek policy change. Zakour (1996) highlights the importance of not only providing clinical services in disaster relief efforts but also coordinating volunteers and addressing social and geographic barriers. Following Hurricane Katrina, social workers were indeed engaged in helping families through "identification, planning, assessment, linkage, monitoring, and advocacy" at the micro and macro level to ensure that the needs of evacuees were being met (Bell, 2008).

Many national and international organizations conduct environmental advocacy, including the Sierra Club, Earth Justice, the Environmental Defense Fund, and the Nature Conservancy. Most cities or states not only have chapters of these environmental groups but also have their own environmental justice organizations. The easiest way to become active in environmental activism is to join forces with existing advocacy organizations. Many participate in letter-writing campaigns directed toward addressing the implementation of policies described above and the need for additional environmental regulations and broad-based demonstrations. In addition, many are engaged in advocacy around specific local level issues such as those that occurred in Flint, Michigan.

Advocacy related to environmental issues requires social workers to ally themselves with organizations that may not be traditional allies such as environmental groups or even hunting groups. For example, Nathan Rott (2018) noted that a reduction in hunting licensing fees, which had traditionally paid for state wildlife agencies, had created allies of hunters and conservationists.

ADVOCACY

WHAT CAN SOCIAL WORKERS DO?

Most social problems can be viewed from multiple viewpoints. Think about one important environmental concern in your state or local community.

1. Describe the issue:
    a. Who are the stakeholders?
    b. What are the key points for each stakeholder?
    c. Compare and contrast their main points. How are their views similar? How are they different?
2. How is each stakeholder trying to create, change, or maintain current policy?
3. Why is this issue important for local, state, and federal communities?
4. What are the roles that social workers play in advocacy for this issue regarding micro, macro, and mezzo systems?

Recent efforts to dismantle environmental protections are often accompanied by significant spending through lobbyists and campaign contributions from industries that will benefit significantly from these efforts. President Trump unsuccessfully proposed defunding the Environmental Justice Office of the EPA, though his administration and Congress have reduced their funding. The Office of Environmental Compliance has dropped from 252 staff members to 182, leaving fewer people available to monitor compliance with environmental regulations. The Trump administration reversed Obama's Executive Order stopping the Dakota Pipeline. Most recently, he placed the head of the Office of Children's Health Protection on administrative leave. The Office of Children's Health Protection was created during the Clinton administration because of a recognition that children are often more vulnerable to pollution than adults, and therefore, stricter standards may be needed for pollutants to which children are exposed. The spokesperson for the EPA declined to give a reason for her leave, but Davenport and Rabin (2018) report that many believe it is, at least in part, because her office refused to reduce regulations that are designed to protect children's health. In addition, she supported an Obama administration rule that farm workers under 18 years old not be exposed to the most toxic chemicals used as insecticides, and the current EPA administrators sought to get rid of that rule (Davenport & Rabin, 2018).

A significant concern around environmental justice is data management and EPA funding. Adjusting for inflation, the budget for the EPA has decreased over time. A report by the nonprofit Environmental Data and Governance Initiative describes broad-based, bipartisan support for the EPA in the 1970s and early 1980s, followed by cost-cutting that hampered the agency beginning in the Reagan years. Because environmental regulation became politicized during the Reagan era, Congress stopped trying to pass new regulations. As a result, court decisions expanded the obligations of the EPA, but workers report there was never sufficient funding to comply with the demands. Further, workers reported that partisans liberally used Freedom of Information Act requests to tie up the EPA so that they had to look for documents rather than pursue compliance with regulations. The report concludes that most of "our interviewees see the new administration as posing the single greatest challenge ever faced by the EPA in its entire half-century of existence," as a result of cost cutting, anti-EPA rhetoric, and lack of agency support (Sellers et al., 2017, p. 39).

Advocacy in the above areas can include involvement in the regulatory process or lobbying members of Congress and the administration. One example of more radical environmental activists call themselves the Valve Turners. They include environmental scientists, lawyers, and writers and are strongly against the use of crude oil, which they believe is not only responsible for global warming but will ultimately destroy the planet. As a result, these activists went onto property owned by the TransCanada Corporation and literally closed valves on the TransPacific pipeline to block the passage of oil between Canada and the United States. Those who closed the valves and their accomplices have been charged with criminal trespass, conspiracy to commit criminal mischief, and reckless endangerment. Emily Johnston, a 51-year-old writer and a member of the Valve Turners was quoted in *The New York Times* saying, "I am not courageous or brave. I'm just more afraid of climate change than I am of prison" (Nijhuis, 2018).

Social Workers and Environmental Action

There are several examples of social workers' involvement in environmental crises. For example, social workers were brought in to help families deal with the emotional after effects of the Chernobyl nuclear power plant explosion in 1996 (Chazin, Hansen, Cohen, & Grishayeva, 2002). Kemp and Palinkas (2015) suggest that social workers can respond to environmental catastrophes by helping with population resettlement and addressing the psychosocial impacts of harm caused to people who have lived through environmental disasters, working as community organizers to develop local capacity to address environmental hazards, and that social workers are well positioned to advocate on behalf of policies to mitigate environmental threats. John Coates and Mel Gray's comprehensive review of social work engagement with the environment in 2011 shows that social workers have been involved in environmental disaster relief and in environmental planning as part of multidisciplinary teams. They also provide a review of the social work literature that addresses environmental issues including climate change, drought, food insecurity, toxic waste exposure, environmental justice where issues or race and poverty overlap with environmental vulnerability, and disaster relief efforts.

In their call to action on environmental justice from an intersectional framework, Bhuyan, Wahab, and Park (2019) ask the profession to consider the following:

> For social work to tackle the call for climate action we will need to (1) broaden our epistemological conceptualization of social justice to include Indigenous and ecological principles of interdependence and responsibility for caring for all our relations (human and nonhuman life); (2) embrace feminist praxis of care that centers connection, mutual empathy, and empowerment (Norton, 2012), and (3) develop a new narrative within social work, where contributing to a low-carbon future can bolster the profession's relevance in an emerging Green economy while transforming the profession's core values of promoting dignity, equality, and respect for all forms of life in a sustainable future. (para. 16)

DISCUSSION
NATURAL DISASTERS

Research the response to a recent environmental or natural disaster, such as Hurricanes Florence, Harvey, Katrina, Maria, or Michael; wildfires in California; Typhoon Mangkhut in the Philippines; the Oaxaca earthquake in Mexico; or earthquakes and tsunamis in Indonesia. You may also want to choose a less well-known environmental disaster that affected your local area.

1. Who responded to the disaster?
2. What role if any did social work have in responding to the disaster?
3. How might social workers engage in policy change to address the consequences of the disaster or try to limit the harm caused by future environmental disasters?

Social work scholar Margaret Alston (2015) identified a number of factors that can be used to assess the social implications of climate change. One is the extent to which problems of social inequality are caused by climate change and are the result of existing inequalities that are exacerbated by climate change. Though those who live in poverty are generally more affected by climate events, climate events such as major storms or environmental disasters have not caused their original vulnerability. Rising population and food insecurity are major environmental problems on their own and will be exacerbated by climate change. Alston suggests that policy has been developed with technocratic solutions designed to reduce the impact of environmental problems rather than to address the social consequences. In light of the global climate change that we will face, we should ask how we address the needs of the people who are affected. Alston notes that this has not yet been done in international treaties or by international governing bodies who study climate control. This is an important area of work to address social injustice, which is well suited to micro, mezzo, and macro level social workers. In other words, social workers have an important role to play in helping address environmental policy harms.

Final Discussion

Now that you have finished reading this chapter, reread the vignette at the beginning. Based on what you have learned, answer the following questions. Point to specific references in the chapter that help you answer these questions. Consider how different theories inform the response to these questions.

1. What are some of the social work concerns that were raised in relation to fracking and its impact on Mary Sue and her community?
2. What do you as a social worker need to know about fracking laws in your own state?
3. What actions might social workers take to help improve the situation at the micro, mezzo, and macro levels?
4. What role might race, class, gender, or other aspects of identity play in this vignette?

GLOSSARY

CHAPTER 1: SOCIAL WORK: A VALUE-BASED PROFESSION IN HISTORICAL CONTEXT

Black Codes: A series of laws and regulations enacted in the post-Civil War South to curtail social, economic, and civil rights of African Americans

Contract with America: Developed by Newt Gingrich, this outlined a vision of reducing taxes and limiting government

(COS): Charity Organization Societies, A movement of early social workers that believed in assessing and meeting social needs through systematized and verifiable process. Generally, COS viewed individual misfortune as due to character flaws or poor choices.

devolution: Shifting authority and responsibility from higher to lower levels of government (e.g., from federal to state or state to local)

Elizabethan Poor Laws: Legislation enacted in England in 1601 that was seen as the beginning of public responsibility for people who were unable to meet their own needs

Great Depression: A period of widespread economic hardship that last approximately 10 years beginning with the stock market crash of 1929

indoor relief: The provision of assistance requiring removal of individuals from their own residence into public institutions such as orphanages, hospitals, or alms houses (in contrast, see **outdoor relief**)

McCarthyism: The anti-Communist panic stoked by Wisconsin Senator Joseph McCarthy that cost the jobs of thousands of suspected Communists or Communist sympathizers and the persecution of many more

Muckrakers: Progressive-era journalists who exposed poor conditions and corruption, often through shocking description, to bring attention to them and inspire reform

The New Deal: A set of federal relief programs enacted by President Franklin Roosevelt in 1932 in response to the Great Depression

outdoor relief: Assistance that allowed people to remain in their own homes (in contrast, see **indoor relief**)

overseers of the poor: Officials who were tasked with administering and supervising aid to people in poverty in England beginning in the 16th century, a practice that was transplanted to parts of the colonial U.S.

principle of less eligibility: The idea that any assistance should either be so meagre, or contingent upon conditions so onerous, as to make it undesirable in comparison to any other options for sustenance

Reaganomics: Named for Ronald Reagan, the belief that regulatory and tax policies favorable to businesses stimulate economic growth, also known as "supply-side" economics, and deregulation of business

Reconstruction: Approximately decade-long period following the Civil War during which the defeated Southern states were rebuilt under supervision of the federal government

Settlement House Movement (SHM): A movement that originated in England and was adopted in many U.S. urban areas with large immigrant populations. Early settlement house workers lived and worked together with people in the communities that they served as partners. It saw poverty and other problems as rooted primarily in systemic problems rather than individual failure.

Social Darwinism: An adaption of Charles Darwin's theory of evolution, Social Darwinism championed techniques such as sterilization to curb social ills. This discredited theory was not grounded in evidence and led to unethical policies such as eugenics.

Star Wars: The popular name for funding for the Strategic Defense Initiative, part of an increase in overall defense spending during a time of decreased spending on social programs

Urbanization: A shift from a primarily rural, farming society to one where the majority of the population resided in cities

The welfare state: The helping functions that governments provide for the social welfare of its populace

The War on Drugs: Coined by Richard Nixon, this term refers to a set of policies enacted and implemented through the Clinton administration.

CHAPTER 2: HOW POLICY IS CREATED AND INFLUENCED

amended: Changed or formally modified

amicus curiae: Meaning "friend of the court," these are authors of legal documents (called amicus briefs) that are filed by those interested in Supreme Court decisions, usually to support the interests of a particular side or outcome.

appeal: In a legal dispute, the procedure to ask a higher court to determine whether a lower court's ruling was correct

appellate court: Also called a court of appeals, which hears appeals of lower courts

censure: Give a formal statement of disapproval by a governing body

clients: As defined by the NASW Code of Ethics, 'Clients' is used inclusively to refer to individuals, families, groups, organizations, and communities."

Conference committee: A committee of the U.S. Congress appointed by the House of Representatives and Senate to resolve disagreements on a particular bill

Executive Branch: The division of the government that carries out laws; at the federal level this includes the president, vice president, Cabinet, and most federal agencies

Federalism: A system of government in which power is divided between the state and federal government in a defined manner in which each level of government has ultimate authority in some areas

Fundamental rights: This is a term that is based on the Constitution and relates to basic rights. Many are included in the Bill of Rights. These rights include freedom of speech, the right not to be incarcerated without a fair hearing, freedom of travel, the right to raise one's children, the right to own property, and the right of privacy.

ideology: Beliefs about society and how it should function

implementation: The process of enacting a piece of policy that has been approved

Judicial Branch: The division of the government that evaluates laws. It includes many courts, including the Supreme Court that can determine laws unconstitutional.

Legislative Branch: The division of the government that makes laws. At the federal level, this branch is made up of Congress, which has two houses, the House of Representatives and the Senate.

Licensure: The process by which the government or other authorized body certifies that a person has the qualifications needed to perform a specific job or task

majority leader: Within a legislative body, the head of the party with the most members

majority party: The political party with more power in a legislative body

markup hearing: The process by which a U.S. congressional committee debates, amends, and rewrites proposed legislation

minority party: The political party with less power in a legislative body

political party: A group of people who share similar political goals and opinions who come together to get candidates elected to office

Ranking Member: The most powerful person on a congressional committee from the party with less power

referendum: A general vote by the electorate on a single question, such as a budget or a ballot question

revenue: Income generated for an organization or government

Speaker of the House: The presiding officer of the U.S. House of Representatives

Unconstitutional: Not in accordance with the U.S. Constitution

CHAPTER 3: PRACTICAL THEORIES FOR UNDERSTANDING AND ANALYZING POLICY

cost-benefit analysis: A process in which the cost and benefits of a policy are weighed against each other and the best possible alternative is seen as the one in which the benefits outweigh the costs

critical race theory (CRT): A race-conscious approach to social policies, practices, and services

economic theory: Theory about how economies, both large (countries) and small (organizations) work. See **micro-** and **macroeconomic** theory for more details

everyday world policy analysis: A method to examine policies by seeking a detailed understanding of how they play out in the lives of ordinary people

feminist theory: Theories based on the assumption that women have been systematically subordinated by patriarchal systems or institutions that privilege men as a group over women as a group

first wave feminism: Early white feminists of the 19th and early 20th century who fought for many causes, including women's suffrage

fiscal policy: Policy that designates how much money a country should spend and how

fourth wave feminism: The resurgent interest in feminism of the early 2000s, driven by diverse groups of young adult feminists, that focuses on sexual harassment and violence, as well as sexuality and gender, and often uses technology and social media

gross domestic product: The total amount of goods and services that are produced by a country

implementation theory: A form of policy analysis that focuses on the stages after policies have been developed

interest group: Group of people who unite to further a common political goal

intersectionality: Refers to people's multiple identities, which can result in compounded oppression as well as different experiences among people who may share some (but not all) identities, like woman, racial minority, immigrant, or low-wage worker

Keynesian economic theory: Suggests that the government should use monetary policy, fiscal policy, and tax policy to ensure economic stability

Macroeconomics: Government policy regarding monetary policy (how much money a country should print), fiscal policy (how much money a country should spend and how), and tax policy (who should pay for the costs associated with government spending). These three areas together help describe how economies work.

Microeconomics: Financial decision making of individuals and institutions such as companies, firms, and nonprofit organizations

monetary policy: How much money a country should print

Neoclassical economics: A theory that holds that as long as there is no intervention of outside forces or government, everyone's focus on their own self-interest will allow those who work the hardest to acquire the most wealth

policy feedback: When the existence of a policy hinders the creation of new policy because of existing constituencies, such as agencies charged with carrying out the initial policy and its beneficiaries, all of whom then have a vested interest in continuing the policy as it is or only making incremental changes

second wave feminism: The central issues of this movement, which began in the early 1960s, were increased opportunities and choices for women, including equality in the workforce, reproductive and sexual freedom, and combating domestic violence.

social construction: The idea that meaning is created through interaction with our environment and existing values, practices, and norms. According to social construction, much of what we understand as truth is determined by our social and cultural milieu.

street level bureaucracy: Frontline social service agencies, like police and child welfare agencies. They are characterized as under-resourced and hierarchical, often charged with internally conflicting mandates and high levels of discretion vis-à-vis the people they serve. Those who work in these agencies are often referred to as street level bureaucrats.

symbolic interaction theory: Suggests that there is no objective "reality" apart from how we describe and think about concepts from our perspective of their reality, which is shaped by the interaction of the individual with others and with society

Systems theory: Suggests that people are influenced by a variety of systems that also influence each other, such as families, culture, and environment

tax policy: Who should pay for the costs associated with government spending

Third wave feminism: A branch of feminism that is focused on intersectionality

CHAPTER 4: FAMILY POLICY

Aid to Dependent Children (ADC): Part of the Social Security Act. The program was created primarily to support widowed mothers so they could remain at home to care for their children.

Biological families: Families into which you are born

Block grants: Federal grants to states in lieu of direct federal support for programs

closed adoptions: Adoptions where birth records are sealed

Domestic adoptions: Adoptions where both the parent/s and child are in the United States

economic theory of marriage: A theory that suggested that spouses (male/female) gained economically from their mutual dependence in marriage and that men's participation in the labor market supported women's domestic work at home (reproduction and child rearing)

families of orientation: Families in which one is raised

families of procreation: Families with whom one chooses to live and procreate

Functional family: Sees families' role as the socialization of children and adolescents, providing emotional and/or financial support to family members and connecting with reproduction

Hague Convention on Protection of Children and Co-operation in Respect of Intercountry Adoption (HCCH, 1993): An international treaty that was designed to protect the welfare of children who are adopted from other countries and to make sure that they are not the victims of kidnapping

In vitro fertilization: A process by which human eggs are fertilized in labs and then, re-implanted into women

Mifepristone or Miliprex: A drug that is used to pharmaceutically induce an abortion

nuclear family: Parents and their children

Structural family: Describes families based on who lives together and often includes some biological relationship

Surrogacy: A process in which a woman's womb is used to carry a baby for another couple or person

Temporary Assistance to Needy Families (TANF): A federal program that provides block grants to states for families in poverty. This program replaced Aid to Families with Dependent Children.

Transactional family: Refers to groups that identify as a family, have emotional connections, shared historical experience, and commitment to a shared future

U.S. Census Bureau: The agency charged with counting U.S. residents

CHAPTER 5: CHILD WELFARE POLICY

Court-appointed special advocate (CASA) (see also *guardian ad litem*): A trained volunteer who is appointed by the court to represent the best interest of the child

disparate treatment: Treating different groups differently, often considered a manifestation of discrimination or prejudice

institutional (policy): Approaches that see intervention or regulation as a regular and appropriate function of government (in contrast, see **residual** policy)

mandatory reporter: A person who by virtue of their profession is obligated to report a suspicion that a child is being abused or neglected

parens patriae: A Latin term describing the state as protector of those who are vulnerable and cannot protect themselves

residual (policy): A policy that seeks only to intervene or meet the needs of individuals in the direct crises (in contrast, see **institutional** policy)

Social casework: Developed by Mary Richmond, social casework was a systematic method focused on interactions with individuals and families

termination of parental rights (TPR): Severs the legal ties between the parent and the child. This means that the child may be legally adopted by another family.

CHAPTER 6: EARLY CHILD CARE AND EDUCATION AND CARE POLICY

cisgender: Describing those whose gender identity matches their assigned gender

Cliff Effect: The abrupt cutting off of eligibility for public benefits due to small increases in income that generally result in recipients being worse off because income increases do not match the loss of benefits

commodification: Giving something a monetary or exchange value. This can refer to labor or products.

custodial care: Describes child care when used primarily as a means to keep children safe and cared for as a substitute for their working parents

day nurseries: Charity-based child care programs of the 19th century that were established to serve families of women who had no choice but to work

double shift: Refers to unacknowledged labor, typically but not always by women, when an individual is primarily responsible for work at home while also working for wages outside the home

maternalist: Perspective which elevates women's roles as primary nurturers and keepers of the home and family

mommy wars: Debates in which value judgments pit the virtue of women who work in the paid labor force against the virtue of women who perform uncompensated labor as primary caretakers for their children and home

opt-out movement: Trend of the 2000s where women who had or could have pursued high-earning successful careers chose to "opt-out" of the paid labor market to perform uncompensated maternal labor

productive labor: Labor that results in goods that have a market value in that they can be bought and sold (in contrast, see **reproductive labor**)

reproductive labor: Work that is necessary but has no commercial value (in contrast, see **productive labor**)

War on Poverty: A set of programs and policy initiatives created by President Lyndon B. Johnson to combat poverty in the United States

CHAPTER 7: EDUCATION POLICY, KINDERGARTEN THROUGH HIGH SCHOOL

adequate yearly progress: Grade-level performance on statewide annual tests based on federal or state standards related to No Child Left Behind and its newer version, Every Student Succeeds

Assimilation: Adjusting to the surrounding cultural context. This is often associated with losing one's original cultural identity and practices and may include losing native languages.

Charter school: Independent schools that are publicly financed but may not be held to legal and union requirements of local public schools. Many are not regulated by a central school board.

Collective bargaining: A technique used, generally by unions, where the union bargains for an entire group of members rather than individuals to make a group contract with an employer

Desegregation: An end to separating people by race in schools or other public accommodation

free appropriate public education:the legal standard for educating children with disabilities in publicly funded schools. The education must be "reasonably calculated to enable a child to receive meaningful educational benefit" (Board of Education of Hendrick Hudson School District v. Rowley, 1982)

Individual Education Plan (IEP): A plan, mandated by the Individuals with Disabilities Education Act for special education students, which identifies the student's disability and needs. It also includes an explanation of how these needs will be addressed including what services will be provided, by whom, how often, and the extent to which the student will be educated with nondisabled peers.

National Assessment for Educational Progress: A national testing tool used to assess student performance

resegregation: Reintroducing segregation where it may have been reduced or previously ended. This is often done through policies that do not explicitly support segregation but their impact results in segregation.

segregation: Separating groups of people by race, religion, ethnicity, or gender

suspect class: The Supreme Court has held that laws that affect one of these groups should be held to a higher standard of review. Suspect classes include race, religion, alienage, and national origin.

Title IX: Ensures all students have the right to be free of discrimination based on gender

Unions: Organized membership groups of workers that advocate for fair wages and better working conditions for employees as a group

CHAPTER 8: HIGHER EDUCATION POLICY

adjunct faculty: Part-time faculty without the job-security protections of tenure, often given contracts one semester at a time

affirmative action: Favoring individuals who belong to groups that have faced historical discrimination

color-blind: Systems that make decisions without regard to race

completion rates: The measure of students who finish the degree they start

contingent faculty: Faculty without significant job security, including those who are full time without the protections of tenure and those who teach part time on a semester-by-semester basis

DREAMer: A person who has lived in the U.S. without official authorization since coming to the country as a minor who may be eligible for a special immigration status under federal legislation

Higher education: Or postsecondary education; the range of options for schooling beyond high school

Historically Black College and University: A college or university that was originally founded to educate students of African American descent

land-grant institution: A college or university designated by a state to receive the benefits of the Land Grant Acts

omnibus bill: A piece of legislation that combines several proposals together

retention rate: The measure of students who stay at the same college from their first year to their second year

tenure: A relatively permanent post, often as a teacher or professor

tribal college: Educational institutions controlled and operated by Native American tribes

CHAPTER 9: WORK AND EMPLOYMENT POLICY

Civil Rights Division: The U.S. Department of Justice arm charged with oversight of the Civil Rights Act that has the authority to investigate and bring forward cases of discrimination

Current Population Survey: A survey carried out by the U.S. Census Bureau

entitlement program: A benefit that government is obligated to provide

Equal Employment Opportunity Commission (EEOC): The federal agency that can investigate and help resolve complaints when the agency determines that discrimination has occurred

gig economy: Newer employment areas that are characterized by temporary employment and decreasing employer commitment to their employees

Great Recession: An economic downturn in the U.S. and global markets, lasting from 2007 through 2009, that especially impacted the real estate and banking industries, which originated with a crisis in the mortgage industry (loans secured by property, often someone's home)

Living wage: The hourly wage that is considered sufficient to meet a worker's needs

minimum wage: The minimum hourly wage that workers must be paid by law

National Labor Relations Board (NLRB): The federal agency housed in the U.S. Department of Labor that is charged with protecting workers' individual and collective rights

Occupational Safety and Health Administration (OSHA): The federal agency housed in the U.S. Department of Labor that sets, provides education about, and enforces regulations regarding workplace safety in government and private employment

shift work: Work that is often carried out during atypical and changing hours, often a feature of low-wage employment

social safety net: The basic set of government programs that mitigates economic risks

Social Security Administration (SSA): The federal agency charged with administering policies and programs under the Social Security Act

whistleblower: An employee who alerts OSHA to safety and health violations under OSHA or other statutes. These individuals are entitled to certain protections against retaliation.

CHAPTER 10: POLICY FOR OLDER ADULTS

coinsurance: The portion of payment for a service such as a doctor's visit that the beneficiary must pay

cost-of-living adjustment: Adjustments that are made to benefits to ensure that they retain their value

dependency ratio: The ratio of those who provide support to those who receive support

disparity: Inequality; differences in outcomes between different populations or groups

Cumulative disadvantage: a term that refers to the compounding nature of disadvantage that accrues across the life course.

homophily: The tendency for people to live and associate with people like themselves

interdependence: A concept expressing the mutual and reciprocal reliance of people and communities

life expectancy: The median age of death for a particular group

longevity dividend: the social and economic benefits of healthy aging essentially by using preventative medicine

sandwich generation: A term describing the cohort of people who simultaneously provide care and support to both older and younger family members, such as parents of young children who also provide care to their own aging relatives

SOGI: An acronym often used as shorthand for sexual orientation and gender identity

substitutive benefit: Benefits that are designed to replace something of equal or similar value

CHAPTER 11: HEALTH POLICY

behavioral health: The field related to the promotion of well-being through assessment, diagnosis, and treatment and prevention of mental illness, substance use, and other addictions

capitalism: A belief system that privileges private ownership of goods and property for profit, rather than ownership by the state. Capitalism also sees individualism and competition as drivers of economic growth and overall prosperity.

decriminalization: The process of redefining a behavior or activity that has been designated as illegal so that it is no longer a criminal offense, even if it is not legal

Diagnostic and Statistical Manual of Mental Disorders: The handbook used as the authoritative guide to the diagnosis of mental disorders

electronic benefit transfer system (EBT): Technology that allows money to be automatically placed on an encoded payment card that can be used to pay for goods or services

essential health benefits: Those procedures and services that must be covered by insurance according to the Affordable Care Act

eugenics: Procedures that are designed to "improve" the human population by increasing desirable characteristics and decreasing undesirable characteristics, primarily through manipulation of reproduction (e.g., sterilization)

harm reduction: Strategies and policies that aim to minimize negative health, social, and legal impacts associated with drug use in a nonjudgmental manner

health insurance: A type of insurance coverage that pays for certain health-related expenses incurred by the insured

health: A state of complete physical, mental, and social well-being and not merely the absence of disease or infirmity

human rights: Rights inherent to all human beings, regardless of race, sex, nationality, ethnicity, language, religion, or any other status

managed care: A system of health decision making by a competitive system of private actors

medication-assisted treatment (MAT): Treatment for substance use that combines behavioral therapy and medications

mental health: A person's condition with regard to their psychological and emotional well being

postpartum: The time following childbirth

Prohibition: Efforts and movements to criminalize the use of substances such as alcohol or other drugs; often refers to the movement in the United States between 1929 and 1933 to prevent the making and sale of alcohol

reimbursement rates: Payments that health care providers receive in exchange for services rendered to patients

single-payer health care: Access to the full continuum of physical and mental health services for all people regardless of age, race, ethnicity, religion, gender or gender expression, sexual orientation, cognitive or physical functioning, socioeconomic or immigration status, or geographic location

social determinants of health: The conditions in which people are born, grow, live, work, and age

underinsured: Individuals or families who have access to some health care that does not fully meet their needs

universal health care: Health system that provides quality medical services to all regardless of their ability to pay

CHAPTER 12: DISABILITY POLICY

activity limitations: Difficulties an individual may have executing activities, generally focused on activities of daily living

activity: Execution of a task or action by an individual

eugenics sterilization: Sterilization carried out against people with disabilities in an effort to rid humans of "bad genes"

Impairments: Problems in body function or structure resulting in an inability to do something that people are generally expected to be able to do

injunctive relief: A court order that requires someone to stop engaging in a particular behavior

non-apparent disabilities: Disabilities that cannot necessarily be seen by others and encompass a wide range of diagnoses including dyslexia, Crohn's Disease, chronic pain, mental illness, and attention-deficit/hyperactivity disorder

participation restrictions: Problems individuals may experience in involvement in life situations

Person-centered planning: An approach that involves putting people in the center of their support planning by looking at goals, barriers to achieving them, and the services that are needed to overcome those barriers

Punitive damages: Court order designed to punish the accused (so that they have greater motivation to follow the law) rather than just make up for the harm that was caused

Ratification: The action of a state that binds it to a treaty

relativist: An approach in which societal expectations of what one should be doing are defined in part in relation to what others are doing

Self-directed services: Services that provide the option for people to select staff, services, organizations, and scheduling of services that they believe works best for them

shell shock: A clinical and colloquial term used to describe what is now generally diagnosed as posttraumatic stress

social model of disability: An approach that views the environment rather than any particular individual attribute or functioning as a limiting factor

Universal design: The idea that education or workplace structures can be designed in a way that is optimal for everyone so that there is less need for adaptation to account for individual needs; this also encompasses the idea that accommodations for some can be helpful for everyone.

Vocational programs: Programs designed to help people either enter or return to the workforce, sometimes referred to as *Vocational Rehabilitation* programs

CHAPTER 13: CRIMINAL JUSTICE

Broken Windows Theory: A theory that claims visible signs of social disorder (such as vandalism or littering) in a particular area encourage more widespread criminal activity in that same area

collateral consequences: Legal and regulatory sanctions and restrictions that limit or prohibit people with criminal records from accessing employment, occupational licensing, housing, voting, education, and other opportunities

gerrymandering: Manipulation of voting districts by a more powerful political party seeking to secure or strengthen a majority by drawing voting maps around different population groups

innocence projects: Organizations or programs devoted to overturning wrongful convictions

juvenile delinquency: Criminal offenses that are committed by minors and status offenses

legal financial obligations (LFOs): Fines and fees beyond what is set out as punishment for a crime and can include restitution, court costs, criminal fines, and fees assessed for supervision or monitoring

mass incarceration: Describes the extremely high rates of incarceration in the United States, both historically and in comparison to other countries

neoliberalism: An orientation toward government characterized by the belief that market-or business-oriented approaches are more effective and less costly than government-run programs, and therefore, includes a preference for minimizing government involvement. It focuses on individual behavior rather than system factors as causes of success or failure programs based on this theory tend to create interventions that focus on individual behavioral changes.

net-widening: A term used to reflect the expansion of the criminal justice system to include more people or behaviors due to programmatic, policy, or implementation changes

over-policing under-policing paradox: The paradox that marginalized communities or groups are both the targets of more surveillance and enforcement and experience a dearth of protection and safety services

Privatization: The outsourcing of government functions to the private for-profit or nonprofit sector, often with financial incentives and reduced oversight

progressive fines: Fines that are calculated to have a relatively equitable impact by, for example, considering a person's income bracket

Regressive fines: Fines that have a disparate impact on people with fewer economic resources

residual powers: Powers that are not explicitly granted to the federal government in the U.S. Constitution and are therefore considered to be within authority of state governments

restorative justice: A theory of justice, drawing inspiration from indigenous practices, that emphasizes repairing the community when a harm is committed through a collaborative process that includes recognition of the harm. Solutions based on restorative justice often include reparations, reconciliations, and reintegration.

school-to-prison pipeline: The collection of policies and practices in schools that lead to greater likelihood of criminal justice involvement

status offense: A behavior that is prohibited for minors but otherwise legal, such as violations of curfews, running away, truancy, possessing alcohol, or ungovernability

Therapeutic Jurisprudence: A term that describes the therapeutic and anti-therapeutic consequences of encounters with the criminal justice system. Therapeutic jurisprudence proponents seek to minimize the anti-therapeutic aspects of criminal justice involvement and maximize its therapeutic potential.

wrongful conviction: When an innocent person is convicted of a crime (see **innocence projects**)

zero tolerance: A term referring to policies that prohibit waiver or reduction of consequences for offenses

CHAPTER 14: HOUSING AND HOMELESSNESS POLICY

chronic homelessness: Long-term homelessness

***de facto* segregation:** Segregation in fact, meaning the existence of segregation even where policy does not explicitly segregate

***de jure* segregation:** Segregation caused by laws

deinstitutionalize: Discharge individuals from institutions; deinstitutionalization refers to a policy strategy designed to release individuals with mental illness from institutional care.

episodic homelessness: Homelessness that is experienced in recurring cycles that are relatively short

homelessness: A state of housing for individuals and families who lack a fixed, regular, and adequate nighttime residence; will imminently lose their primary nighttime residence; unaccompanied youth and families with children and youth; and individuals and families who are fleeing, or are attempting to flee, domestic violence, dating violence, sexual assault, stalking, or other dangerous or life-threatening conditions

integration: A situation in which people live together or near others who are racially and ethnically different from them

Point-in-Time (PIT) Count: Annual count of sheltered and non-sheltered people experiencing homelessness

predatory loans: Types of subprime loans with higher interest and fees than is required, abusive terms, and conditions that fail to take into account the borrower's ability to repay. These loans violate fair lending laws by targeting women, minorities, and communities of color.

redlining: The practice of refusing a loan or insurance to someone because they live in an area deemed to be a poor financial risk that results in significant segregation

rent control: A system where the government uses price controls to keep the cost of rent down for some rental units

reparations: Payments of money to those who have experienced past wrongs

sheltered (homelessness): Individuals or families residing in homeless programs such as emergency shelters, transitional living programs, and rapid rehousing

structural racism: A system in which institutions and policies within our nation disadvantage nonwhites in ways that are often compounding and cumulative

subprime loans: Loans that are designed for borrowers with risky credit who may be unable to obtain loans from mainstream lenders

survival sex: Sex that is exchanged for shelter or other basic necessities

tenements: A room or rooms within a house or block of apartments in which people often lived in overcrowded and unsanitary conditions

transitional homelessness: Short-term homelessness

unsheltered or street (homelessness): individuals or families sleeping outside, in places not meant for human habitation, such as parks, public transportation stations, the street, and wooded areas

urban camping: Sleeping outside in an undesignated area

vagabond: Derogatory term used to describe a person who is experiencing homelessness

wealth: Assets held by individuals and families, including homes and equity in a home, minus any debt they carry

CHAPTER 15: IMMIGRATION POLICY

anchor baby: A political term used for a child who is born in the United States to parents who are not U.S. citizens

Bracero Program: A program from the 1940s that enabled Mexican immigrants to legally enter the United States to work on farms

chain migration: Describes what occurs when one person comes to the United States and brings family members who, in turn, bring other relatives

coyote: A person who smuggles people across the U.S. borders

documented resident: Someone who has been issued papers by the U.S. federal immigration authorities allowing them to reside and sometimes work in the United States

guest workers: Immigrants who are given short visas to work in seasonal labor

H-2B visa: A work visa for nonagricultural workers

ingroups: Those in the majority or accepted by the majority

Operation Wetback: A U.S. immigration program in 1954 where military tactics were used to forcibly remove Mexican immigrants, some of whom were naturalized citizens, often to unfamiliar parts of in Mexico

outgroups: Minorities or unfavored populations

refugee: As defined by the U.S. Code, is someone who leaves their native country and "has a well-founded fear of persecution on account of race, religion, nationality, membership in a particular social group, or political opinion"

remittances: Monies that immigrants send to people in their countries of origin

sanctuary: A loose term with important symbolic value referring to proposed city and state laws to limit cooperation with federal immigration authorities in various ways

Temporary Protected Status (TPS): A U.S. immigration status that enables people from countries that had experienced a major natural disaster or war-torn countries to temporarily live and work in the United States

U visas: Visas that provide temporary immigration benefits

undocumented resident: Immigrants who reside in the United States without legal documentation or status

xenophobia: Fear of and prejudice against people from other countries

CHAPTER 16: ENVIRONMENTAL POLICY

Agent Orange: A substance that was used to try to kill the foliage to make it easier for anti-American Vietnamese soldiers to hide during the Vietnam War

Climate change: The idea that the temperature on the planet is changing as a result of human activity and therefore can be influenced by changing certain human activity such as reducing emissions, reducing deforestation, and reducing our reliance on cattle farming

DDT: A once widely used pesticide with significant harmful health side effects that has been outlawed in the United States since the early 1970s

environmental justice perspective: A perspective that focuses on the overlap between environmental pollution and the disproportionate impact of environmental hazards on people with lower incomes and people of color

Executive Order 12898: A federal ruling issued during the Obama administration that required federal agencies to consider environmental justice to rectify policies that disproportionately impacted minority and low-income populations

fracking: The process of extracting fossil fuels, primarily oil and natural gas, from shale or rocks buried deep in the ground

free riders: Those who benefit from public goods (such as clean air) without paying when they use, compromise, or destroy them

Green Party: A small U.S. political party whose main goals are to reduce the military infrastructure, reduce or eliminate the use of fossil fuel and become more reliant on renewable energy, create a living wage and make our political system more democratic

LEED: An international green building certification that indicates that the building construction has made efforts to ensure that the building is energy efficient and made with substances that are less likely to harm people or the environment than those used in typical construction

median: The midpoint in a group of numbers. Median income, for example, is the point where half of the people whose income is measured have higher incomes and half have lower incomes.

precautionary principle: A concept, sometimes adopted in policy, according to which something is prohibited unless and until it is proven to be safe

REFERENCES

CHAPTER 1

Abramovitz, M. (1983). Everyone is on welfare: 'The role of redistribution in social policy' revisited. *Social Work, 28*(6), 440–445.

Adams, P. (2004). Classroom assessment and social welfare policy: Addressing challenges to teaching and learning. *Journal of Social Work Education, 40*(1), 124–142.

Addams, J. (1909). Immigrants: Report of the Committee. Retrieved from https://digital.janeaddams.ramapo.edu/items/show/4919

Addams, J. (1911). *Democracy and social ethics*. New York, NY: Macmillan.

Alexander, M. (2010). *The new Jim Crow: Mass incarceration in the age of colorblindness*. New York, NY: The New Press.

Association of Centers for the Study of Congress. (n.d.). Elementary and Secondary Education Act of 1965. Retrieved from http://acsc.lib.udel.edu/exhibits/show/legislation/esea

Banks, S. (2010). Integrity in professional life: Issues of conduct, commitment and capacity. *The British Journal of Social Work, 40*(7), 2168–2184.

Baylson, M. (2017). Victim or criminal Street-level prostitutes and the criminal justice system. In K. Hail-Jares, C. Shdaimah, & C. Leon (Eds.), *Challenging perspectives on street-based sex work* (pp. 136–151). Philadelphia, PA: Temple University Press.

Beckor, D. (2005). *The myth of empowerment: Women and the therapeutic culture in America*. New York NY: New York University Press.

Bloy, M. (2002). Elizabethan Poor Laws. *Victorian Web*. Retrieved from http://www.victorianweb.org/history/poorlaw/elizpl.html

Boyer, P. (1992). *Urban masses and moral order in America, 1820–1920*. Boston, MA: Harvard University Press.

Breckenridge, J., & James, K. (2010). Educating social work students in multifaceted interventions for trauma. *Social Work Education, 29*(3), 259–275.

Brieland, D. (1990). The Hull-House tradition and the contemporary social worker: Was Jane Addams really a social worker? *Social Work, 35*(2), 134–138.

British Association of Social Workers. (2002). Code of Ethics [online].Retrievedfromhttp://www.basw.co.uk/Default.aspx?tabid¼64

Brown, M. K. (1999). *Race, money, and the American welfare state*. Ithaca, NY: Cornell University.

Canadian Association of Social Workers. (2005). Code of Ethics 2005. Retrieved from https://www.casw-acts.ca/sites/default/files/attachements/casw_code_of_ethics.pdf

Carney, J. (2017, Dec. 2). CBO: Senate tax bill increases deficit by $1.4 trillion. *The Hill*. Retrieved from https://www.casw-acts .ca/sites/default/files/attachements/casw_code_of_ethics.pdf

Centers for Disease Control and Prevention. (1998). Current trends mortality attributable to HIV Infection/AIDS—United States, 1981–1990. *Mortality and Morbidity Report Weekly*. Retrieved from https://www.cdc.gov/mmwr/preview/mmwrhtml/00001880.htm

Chafe, W. H. (1986). *The unfinished journey: America since World War II*. New York, NY: Oxford University Press.

Chen, M. (2013). From windows to gateways on the lower east side: The Henry Street Settlement from the Progressive Era to the Great Society. *Historian, 75*(4), 760–780.

Cirelli, K. (2014, May 14). Bill Clinton fires back at critics of his financial regulatory policies. *The Hill*. Retrieved from http://thehill.com/policy/finance/206099-clinton-fires-back-at-critics-of-financial-regulatory-policies

Cloward, R. A., & Piven, F. F. (1971/1993). *Regulating the poor: The functions of public welfare*. New York, NY: Vintage Books.

CNN.com. (2002). Bush signs $190 billion farm bill. Retrieved from http://edition.cnn.com/2002/ALLPOLITICS/05/13/farm.bill/

Cohen, W. (1991). *At freedom's edge: Black mobility and the southern white quest for racial control, 1861–1915*. Baton Rouge LA: Louisiana State University Press.

Columbia University Archives. (n.d.). Human Service Employees Registration and Voter Education Fund

(Human SERVE) records, 1982–2000. Retrieved from http://www.columbia.edu/cu/lweb/archival/collections/ldpd_5018097/

Council on Social Work Education. (2015). 2015 Education Policy and Accreditation Standards. Retrieved from https://www.cswe.org/getattachment/Accreditation/Accreditation-Process/2015-EPAS/2015EPAS_Web_FINAL.pdf.aspx

Crow, R. T., & Kindelsperger, K. W. (1975). The PhD or the DSW? *Journal of Education for Social Work, 11*(3), 38–43.

Darwin, C. R. (1869). *On the origin of species by means of natural selection, or the preservation of favoured races in the struggle for life* (5th ed.). London, UK: John Murray. Retrieved from ttp://darwin-online.org.uk/content/frameset?itemID=F387&viewtype=text&pageseq=1

Day, P. J. (2006). *A new history of social welfare* (5th ed.). Boston, MA: Allyn & Bacon.

Degler, C. N. (1991). *In search of human nature: The decline and revival of Darwinism in American social thought*. New York, NY: Oxford University Press.

Demone, H. W., & Gibelman, M. (1984). Reaganomics: Its impact on the voluntary not-for-profit sector. *Social Work, 29*(5), 421–427.

Dempsey, D. (2008). The path to social justice is through economics and politics. *Journal of Policy Practice, 72*(2–3), 94–105.

Ehrenreich, J. H. (1985). *The altruistic imagination: A history of social work and social policy in the United States*. Ithaca, NY: Cornell University Press.

Flexner, A. (1915). Is social work a profession? *Social Welfare History Project*. Retrieved from http://socialwelfare.library.vcu.edu/social-work/is-social-work-a-profession-1915/

Foner, E. (2012). *Who owns history? Rethinking the past in a changing world*. New York, NY: Hill & Wang.

Franklin, J. H. (1993). The Emancipation Proclamation: An act of justice. *Prologue, 25*(2). Retrieved from https://www.archives.gov/publications/prologue/1993/summer/emancipation-proclamation.html

Giles, R., Gould, S., Hart, C., & Swancott, J. (2007). Clinical priorities: strengthening social work practice in health. *Australian Social Work, 60*(2), 147–165.

Great Britain Poor Law Commissioners. (1834). Report from His Majesty's commissioners for inquiring into the administration and practical operation of the Poor Laws (Vol. *2728*). *Victorian Web*. Retrieved from http://www.victorianweb.org/history/poorlaw/workplan.html

Gregg, G. (2017). George W. Bush: Impact and legacy. Retrieved from https://millercenter.org/president/gwbush/impact-and-legacy

Hansan, J. E. (2011). Poor relief in early America. Retrieved from https://socialwelfare.library.vcu.edu/programs/poor-relief-early-amer/

Herndon, R. W. (2012). Poor women and the Boston almshouse in the early republic. *Journal of the Early Republic, 32*(3), 349–381. doi:10.1353/jer.2012.0064

Huey, P. R. (2001). The almshouse in Dutch and English colonial North America and its precedent in the Old World: Historical and archaeological evidence. *International Journal of Historical Archaeology, 5*(2), 123–154.

Hugman, R. (2009). But is it social work? Some reflections on mistaken identities. *The British Journal of Social Work, 39*(6), 1138–1153.

Influencing Social Policy. (n.d.). About. Retrieved from http://influencingsocialpolicy.org/about/

International Federation of Social Workers. (2018). Global social work statement of ethical principles. Retrieved from https://www.ifsw.org/global-social-work-statement-of-ethical-principles/

Jansson, B. (2012). *The reluctant welfare state* (7th ed.). Belmont, CA: Brooks/Cole.

Katz, M. B. (2013). *The undeserving poor: America's enduring confrontation with poverty. Fully updated and revised* (2nd ed.). New York, NY: Oxford University Press.

Khazan, O. (2014, May 12). How welfare reform left single moms behind. *The Atlantic*. Retrieved from https://www.theatlantic.com/business/archive/2014/05/how-welfare-reform-left-single-moms-behind/361964/

Knight, L. W. (2005). *Citizen: Jane Addams and the struggle for democracy*. Chicago, IL: University of Chicago Press.

Korematsu v. United States, 323 U.S. 214 (1944).

Krieger, J. (1987). Social policy in the age of Reagan and Thatcher. *Socialist Register, 23*(23), 177–198.

Kristofer, A. (2003). Race and restriction: Anti-Asian immigration pressures in the Pacific North-west of America during the Progressive Era, 1885–1924. *History, 88*(289), 53–73.

Kurzman, P. A. (1970). Poor relief in medieval England: The forgotten chapter in the history of social welfare. *Child Welfare, 49*(9), 495–501.

Lane,J.B.,Jacob A.(1973).Riisandscientificphilanthropyduring the Progressive Era. *Social Service Review, 47*(1), 32–48.

Lane, S. R., Humphreys, N. A., Graham, E., Matthews, N., & Moriarty, J. (2007). Voter registration: Empowering clients through agency-based voter registration. *Journal of Policy Practice, 6*(4), 79–94. doi:10.1300/J508v06n04_06

Lay, A., & McGuire, L. (2010). Building a lens for critical reflection and reflexivity in social work education. *Social Work Education, 29*(5), 539–550.

Madson, N. H. (2012). The legacy of ACT UP's policies and actions from 1987–1994. *National Lawyers Guild Review, 69*(1), 45–64.

Martin, M. E. (2012). Philosophical and religious influences on social welfare policy in the United States: The ongoing effect of reformed theology and Social Darwinism on attitudes toward the poor and social welfare policy and practice. *Journal of Social Work, 12*(1), 51–64.

Martin, W., & Tichi, C. (2016). *The Gilded Age and Progressive Era: A historical exploration of literature*. Santa Barbara, CA: Greenwood.

McDonald, C., & Marsten, G. (2008). Motivating the unemployed? Attitudes at the front line. *Australian Social Work, 61*(4), 315–326.

McFadden, J. J. (2014). Disciplining the "Frankenstein of pauperism": The early years of charity organization case recording, 1877–1907. *Social Service Review, 88* (3), 469–492.

The Names Project Foundation. (2018). The AIDS memorial quilt. Retrieved from http://www.aidsquilt.org/about/the-aids-memorial-quilt

National Archives. (2016). African American records: Freedman's Bureau. Retrieved from https://www.archives.gov/research/african-americans/freedmens-bureau

National Association of Social Workers. (2017). Read the Code of Ethics. Retrieved from https://www.socialworkers.org/About/Ethics/Code-of-Ethics/Code-of-Ethics-English

National Park Service. (n.d.). The Civil War. Retrieved from https://www.nps.gov/civilwar/facts.htm

Nelson, M. (2017). Barack Obama: Domestic affairs. Retrieved from https://millercenter.org/president/obama/domestic-affairs

O'Connor, B. (2004). *A political history of the American welfare system: When ideas have consequences*. Lanham, MD. Rowman & Littlefield Publishers, Inc.

Office of the United States Trade Representative. (n.d.). North America Free Trade Agreement (NAFTA). Retrieved from https://ustr.gov/trade-agreements/free-trade-agreements/north-american-free-trade-agreement-nafta

Orloff, A. S. (1998). The political origins of America's belated welfare state. In M. Weir, A. S. Orloff, & T. Skocpol (Eds.), *The politics of social policy in the United States* (pp. 37–80). Princeton, NJ: Princeton University Press.

Palley, E., & Shdaimah, C. (2014). *In our hands: The struggle for U.S. child care policy.* New York NY: New York University Press.

Park, M. (2017, January 10). Trump administration ended protected status for 250,000 Salvadorans. These immigrants might be next. *CNN News*. Retrieved from http://www.cnn.com/2018/01/09/politics/temporary-protected-status-countries/index.html

Park, Y. (2008). Facilitating injustice: Tracing the role of social workers in the World War II internment of Japanese Americans. *Social Service Review, 82*(3), 447–483.

Piven, F. F., & Cloward, R. A. (1982). *The new class war: Reagan's attack on the welfare state and its consequences*. New York, NY: Pantheon.

Reagan, R. W. (1981). Speech on 1/20/1981. Retrieved from https://www.youtube.com/watch?v=XObcP69dhCg

Reamer, F. G. (1998). The evolution of social work ethics. *Social Work, 43*(6), 488–500.

Reamer, F. G., & Shardlow, S. M. (2009). Ethical codes of practice in the US and UK: One profession, two standards. *Journal of Social Work Values & Ethics, 6*(2), [online]. Retrieved from http://www.jswvearchives.com/content/view/120/68/

Reisch, M., & Andrews, J. (2001). *The road not taken: A history of radical social work in the United States*. New York, NY: Routledge.

Richmond, M. E. (1901). Charitable cooperation. In I. C. Barrows (Ed.), *Proceedings of the National Conference of Charities and Corrections* (pp. 298–313). Boston, MA: Elles.

Richmond, M. E. (1917). *Social diagnosis*. New York, NY: Russell Sage Foundation.

Riis, J. A. (1890/1967). *How the other half lives: Studies of the tenements of New York*. New York, NY: Scribner.

Riley, R. L. (2017). Bill Clinton: Impact and legacy. Retrieved from https://millercenter.org/president/clinton/impact-and-legacy

Riordan, W. L. (1995). *Plunkitt of Tammany Hall: A series of very plain talks on very practical politics*. New York, NY: Penguin.

Ryan, W. (1976). *Blaming the victim*. New York, NY: Vintage Books.

Schram, S. (1995). *Words of welfare: The poverty of social science and the social science of poverty*. Minneapolis, MN: University of Minnesota.

Shankar, J., Martin, J., & McDonald, C. (2009). Emerging areas of practice for mental health social workers: Education and employment. *Australian Social Work, 62*(1), 28–44.

Shdaimah, C. S., & McCoyd, J.L.M. (2012). Social work sense and sensibility: A framework for teaching an integrated perspective. *Social Work Education, 31*(1), 22–35.

Shdaimah, C. S., Stahl, R., & Schram, S. F. (2009). When you can see the sky through the roof: Homeownership looking from the bottom up. In E. Schatz (Ed.), *Political ethnography*: What immersion contributes to the study of power (pp. 255–274). Chicago, IL: Chicago University Press.

Sinclair, U. (2012/1906). *The jungle*. Mineola, NY: Dover.

Skocpol, T. (1992). *Protecting soldiers and mothers: The political origins of social policy in the United States*. Cambridge, MA: Belknap Press of Harvard University Press.

Slessarev, H. (1988). Racial tensions and institutional support: Social programs during a period of retrenchment. In M. Weir, A. S. Orloff, & T. Skocpol (Eds.), *The politics of social policy in the United States* (pp. 357–380). Princeton, NJ: Princeton University Press.

Southard, S. (2015). What U.S. citizens weren't told about the atomic bombing of Japan. *Los Angeles Times*. Retrieved from http://beta.latimes.com/opinion/op-ed/la-oe-0809-southard-atomic-bomb-survivors-20150806-story.html

Specht, H., & Courtney, M. E. (1994). *Unfaithful angels: How social work has abandoned its mission*. New York, NY: Free Press.

Stepney, P. (2009). English social work at the crossroads: A critical view. *Australian Social Work*, *62*(1), 10–27.

Strier, R., & Binyamin, S. (2014). Introducing anti-oppressive social work practices in public services: Rhetoric to practice. *The British Journal of Social Work*, *44*(8), 2095–2112,

Stuart, P. H. (2013). Social work profession: History. In *Encyclopedia of Social Work*. Retrieved from https://oxfordre.com/social-work/view/10.1093/acrefore/9780199975839.001.0001/acrefore-9780199975839-e-623 doi:10.1093/acrefore/9780199975839.013.623

Sullivan, E., & Tackett, M. (2017, December 22). In signing sweeping tax bill, Trump questions whether he is getting enough credit. *The New York Times*. Retrieved from https://www.nytimes.com/2017/12/22/us/politics/trump-tax-bill.html

Trattner, W. I. (1999). *From poor law to welfare state: A history of social welfare in America* (6th ed.). New York, NY: The Free Press.

U.S. Department of Education. (2009). Race to the top. Retrieved from https://www2.ed.gov/programs/racetothetop/factsheet.html

U.S. Department of Labor. (2013). FMLA is working. Retrieved from https://www.dol.gov/whd/fmla/survey/

United Nations. (2017). The Paris Agreement. Retrieved from http://unfccc.int/paris_agreement/items/9485.php

Vitale, A. (2017). *The end of policing*. Brooklyn, NY: Verso Press.

Waugh, J. A. (2001). "Give this man work!": Josephine Shaw Lowell, the Charity Organization Society of the City of New York, and the Depression of 1893. *Social Science History*, *25*(2), 217–246.

Weber, M. (1992/1930). *The Protestant ethic and the spirit of capitalism*. New York, NY: Routledge.

Weiss-Gal, I. (2008). The person-in-environment approach: Professional ideology and practice of social workers in Israel. *Social Work*, *53*(1), 65–75.

Zimbalist, S. E. (1977). *Historic themes and landmarks in social welfare research*. New York, NY: Harper and Row.

Zubrzycki, J., & McArthur, M. (2004). Pairing social work students for policy practice: An Australian example. *Social Work Education*, *23*(4), 451–464.

CHAPTER 2

Association of Social Work Boards. (n.d.). About licensing and regulation. Retrieved from https://www.aswb.org/licensees/about-licensing-and-regulation/

Ballotpedia. (2017). Teresa Benitez Thompson. Retrieved from https://ballotpedia.org/Teresa_Benitez-Thompson

Brady, P. S. (1972). The slave trade and sectionalism in South Carolina, 1787–1808. *The Journal of Southern History*, *38*(4), 601–620.

Congressional Social Work Caucus. (n.d.). Social workers in Congress. Retrieved from http://crispinc.org/social-workers-in-congress/

Elect Teresa. (2017a). About. Retrieved from http://www.electteresa.com/

Elect Teresa. (2017b). Issues. Retrieved from http://www.electteresa.com/index.php/issues

Elving, R. (2018, March 10). The zombie amendments to the Constitution you've probably never heard of. *NPR*. Retrieved from https://www.npr.org/2018/03/10/591758259/the-zombie-amendments-to-the-constitution-youve-probably-never-heard-of

Feldman, S. M. (2012). *Neoconservatives and the Supreme Court: Law, power, and democracy*. New York, NY: New York University Press.

Fischer, F. (2009). *Democracy and expertise: Reorienting policy inquiry*. Oxford, UK: Oxford University Press.

Fisher, A. (2014). What is a political social worker anyway? *SWHelper*. Retrieved from https://www.socialworkhelper.com/2014/06/25/political-social-worker-anyway/

Galligan, B. (2007). Federalism. In G. Ritzer (Ed.), *The Blackwell Encyclopedia of Sociology*. Hoboken, NJ: Blackwell. doi:10.1002/9781405165518.wbeosf030

Germain, C. B., & Gitterman, A. (1996). *The life model of social work practice: Advances in theory & practice* (2nd ed.). New York, NY: Columbia University Press.

Gibelman, M. (1999). The search for identity: Defining social work—past, present, future. *Social Work, 44*(4), 298–310.

Gillon, S. M. (2000). *That's not what we meant to do: Reform and its unintended consequences in twentieth century America.* New York, NY: W.W. Norton.

Henry, P. (1788). *Federal v. consolidated government.* Retrieved from http://press-pubs.uchicago.edu/founders/documents/v1ch8s38.html

Jefferson, T. (1789). From Thomas Jefferson to Francis Hopkinson, 13 March 1789. Retrieved from https://founders.archives.gov/documents/Jefferson/01-14-02-0402

Karls, J. M., & Wandrei, M. E. (1994). *PIE manual, person-in-environment system: The PIE classification system for social functioning problems.* Washington, DC: NASW Press.

Kerson, T. S. (2002). *Boundary spanning: An ecological reinterpretation of social work practice in health and mental health systems.* New York, NY: Columbia University Press.

Kondrat, M. E. (2002). Actor-centered social work: Revisioning "person-in-environment" through a critical theory lens. *Social Work, 47*(4), 435–448.

Lane, S. R. (2011). Political content in social work education as reported by elected social workers. *Journal of Social Work Education, 47*(1), 53–72.

Lane, S. R., & Humphreys, N. A. (2011). Social workers in politics: A national survey of social work candidates and elected officials. *Journal of Policy Practice, 10*(3), 225–244.

Lewis, M., & Widerquist, K. (2002). *Economics for social workers.* New York, NY: Columbia University Press.

Madison, J. (1787). Federalist No. 10. Retrieved from https://www.congress.gov/resources/display/content/The+Federalist+Papers#TheFederalistPapers 10

Miranda, L. M. (2015). *Hamilton: An American musical* [MP3]. New York, NY: Atlantic Records.

National Archives. (2017a). Constitution of the United States: A history. Retrieved from https://www.archives.gov/founding-docs/more-perfect-union

National Archives. (2017b). The Constitution: How did it happen? Retrieved from https://www.archives.gov/founding-docs/constitution/how-did-it-happen

National Archives. (2017c). The Declaration of Independence: How did it happen? Retrieved from https://www.archives.gov/founding-docs/declaration/how-did-it-happen

National Archives. (2017d). Observing Constitution Day. Retrieved from https://www.archives.gov/education/lessons/constitution-day/ratification.html

National Association of Social Workers (n.d.). Social workers in state and local elected office. Retrieved from https://www.socialworkers.org/Advocacy/Political-Action-for-Candidate-Election-PACE/Social-Workers-in-State-and-Local-Office

National Association of Social Workers. (2017). Read the Code of Ethics. Retrieved from https://www.socialworkers.org/About/Ethics/Code-of-Ethics/Code-of-Ethics-English

Olsen, H. (2017). *The working class Republican: Ronald Reagan and the return of blue-collar conservatism.* New York, NY: HarperCollins.

Pettijohn, S. L., Boris, E. T., DeVita, C. J., & Fuffe, S. D. (2013). Nonprofit-government contracts and grants: Findings from the 2013 National Survey. Washington, DC: Urban Institute. Retrieved from https://www.urban.org/research/publication/nonprofit-government-contracts-and-grants-findings-2013-national-survey/view/full_report

Pew Research Center. (2014). Beyond red vs. blue: The political typology. Retrieved from http://www.people-press.org/2014/06/26/the-political-typology-beyond-red-vs-blue/

Pew Research Center. (2015). A deep dive into party affiliation. Retrieved from http://www.people-press.org/2015/04/07/a-deep-dive-into-party-affiliation/

Pritzker, S., & Burwell, C. (2016). Promoting election-related policy practice among social work students. *Journal of Social Work Education, 52*(4), 434–447.

Pritzker, S., & Garza, G. (2017). *Sanders, Clinton, Trump: Social work students' political engagement in 2016.* Paper presented at the Policy Conference 2.0, St. Louis, MO.

Rabin, R.C. (2019, June 14). Eager to limit exemptions to vaccination, states face staunch resistance. *The New York Times.* Retrieved from https://www.nytimes.com/2019/06/14/health/vaccine-exemption-health.html

Rosenwald, M. (2006). Exploring the political diversity of social workers. *Social Work Research, 30*(2), 121–126.

Silbey, J. (2010). American political parties: History, voters, critical elections, and party systems. In L. Maisel, J. Berry, G. Edwards, & J. Silbey (Eds.), *The Oxford Handbook of American Political Parties and Interest Groups* (pp. 97–120). New York, NY: Oxford University Press.

Supreme Court Historical Society. (n.d.-a). The Jay Court, 1789–1795. Retrieved from http://supremecourthistory.org/timeline_court_jay.html

Supreme Court Historical Society. (n.d.-b). The Marshall Court, 1801–1835. Retrieved from http://supremecourthistory.org/timeline_court_marshall.html

Washington, G. (1796). Washington's farewell address 1796. Retrieved from http://avalon.law.yale.edu/18th_century/washing.asp

CHAPTER 3

Aliferis, L. (2016, January 21). Childhood vaccination rates climb in California. *NPR*. Retrieved from http://www.npr.org/sections/health-shots/2016/01/21/461395411/childhood-vaccination-rates-climb-in-california

Baumgardner, J. (2011). *F'em! Goo goo, gaga, and some thoughts on balls.* Berkeley, CA: Seal Press.

Berger, P., & Luckman, T. (1966). *The social construction of reality.* London, UK: Penguin Books.

Berry, J. (2007). Nonprofit organizations as interest groups: The politics of passivity. In A. Cigler & B. Loomis (Eds.), *Interest group politics* (7th ed.). Washington, DC: CQ Press.

Birkland, T. (2016). *An introduction to the policy process* (4th ed.). New York, NY: Routledge.

Blumer, H. (1971). Social problems as collective behavior. *Social Problems, 18*(3), 298–306. doi:10.2307/799797

Brodkin, E. Z. (2012). Reflections on street-level bureaucracy: Past, present, and future. *Public Administration Review, 72*(6), 940–949.

Bronfenbrenner, U. (1981). *The ecology of human development.* Boston, MA: Harvard University Press.

Centers for Disease Control and Prevention. (2017a). Possible side effects from vaccines. Retrieved from https://www.cdc.gov/vaccines/vac-gen/side-effects.htm

Centers for Disease Control and Prevention (2017b). U.S. Public Health Service Syphilis Study at Tuskegee. Retrieved from https://www.cdc.gov/tuskegee/timeline.htm

Cigler, A., & Loomis, B. (2007). *Interest group politics* (7th ed.). Washington, DC: CQ Press.

Cleaver, K. (1997). The antidemocratic power of whiteness. In R. Delgado & J. Stefancic (Eds.), *Critical white studies* (pp. 157–163). Philadelphia, PA: Temple University Press.

Cobb, R., & Elder, D. (1971). The politics of agenda-building: An alternative perspective for modern democratic theory. *Journal of Politics, 33*(4), 892–915.

Cochrane, K. (2013). *All the rebel women: The rise of the fourth wave of feminism.* London, UK: Guardian Books.

Colgrove, J. (2006). *State of immunity: The politics of vaccination in twentieth-century America.* Berkley, CA: University of California Press.

Collins, P. H. (2005). *Black sexual politics: African-Americans, gender, and new racism.* New York, NY: Routledge.

Collins, P. H., & Anderson, M. (1992). *Race, class and gender: An anthology.* Belmont, CA: Wadsworth.

Covington, S. (2001). In the midst of plenty: Foundation funding of child advocacy organizations in the 1990s. In C. J. De Vita & R. Mosher-Williams (Eds.), *Who speaks for America's children? The role of child advocates in public policy* (pp. 39–80). Washington, DC: Urban Institute Press.

Crenshaw, K. (1989). Demarginalizing the intersection of race and sex: A black feminist critique of antidiscrimination doctrine, feminist theory and antiracist politics. *University of Chicago Legal Forum, 1*(8), 139–167.

Delgado, R., & Stefancic, J. (2001). *Critical race theory: An introduction.* New York, NY: New York University Press.

Friedan, B. (1963). *The feminine mystique.* New York, NY: W.W. Norton.

Habermas, J. (1996). *Between facts and norms: Contributions to a discourse theory of law and democracy.* Boston, MA: MIT Press.

Hawkesworth, M. (2006). *Feminist inquiry: From political conviction to methodological innovation.* New Brunswick, NJ: Rutgers University Press.

Hill, M., & Hupe, P. (2014). *Implementing public policy* (3rd ed.). London, UK: Sage.

Hooks, b. (1984). *Feminist theory: from the margin to the center.* Boston, MA: South End Press.

Keynes, J. M. (1936). *The general theory of employment, interest, and money.* London, UK: Macmillan.

Kuttner, R. (2002, July 15). Philanthropy and movements. *American Prospect*, 2–3. Retrieved from http://prospect.org/article/comment-philanthropy-and-movements

Lewis, M., & Widerquist, K. (2002). *Economics for social workers.* New York, NY: Columbia University Press.

Lipsky, M. (1980; 2010). *Street level bureaucracy: Dilemmas of the individual in public service.* New York, NY: Russell Sage.

Lowi, T. (1979). *The end of liberalism* (2nd ed.). New York, NY: Norton.

Madison, J. (1787). Federalist Paper 10. Retrieved from http://www.let.rug.nl/usa/documents/1786-1800/the-federalist-papers/the-federalist-10.php

Marx, K. (1859). *A contribution to the critique of political economy.* Moscow, Russia: Progress Publishers.

Mills, C. W. (2000). *The sociological imagination* (40th anniversary edition). New York, NY: Oxford Press.

Naples, N. (2003). *Feminism and method: Ethnography, discourse analysis, and activist research*. New York, NY: Routledge.

National Institute on Drug Abuse. (2012). *Principles of drug addiction treatment: A research-based guide* (3rd ed.). Washington, DC: National Institutes of Health. Retrieved from https://www.drugabuse.gov/publications/principles-drug-addiction-treatment-research-based-guide-third-edition/frequently-asked-questions/drug-addiction-treatment-worth-its-cost

National Vaccine Information Center. (2017). State law & vaccine requirements. Retrieved from http://www.nvic.org/vaccine-laws/state-vaccine-requirements.aspx

Palley, E. (2003). The role of the courts in the development and implementation of the Individuals with Disabilities Education Act. *Social Service Review, 77*(4), 605–618.

Palley, E. (2004). Balancing student mental health and discipline: A case study of the Individuals with Disabilities Education Act (IDEA). *Social Service Review, 78*(2), 243–266.

Palley, E., & Shdaimah, C. (2014). *In our hands: The struggle for U.S. child care policy*. New York, NY: New York University Press.

Pierson, P. (1993). Review: When effect becomes cause: Policy feedback and political change. *World Politics, 45*(4), 595–628.

Pressman, J. L., & Wildavsky, A. (1984). *Implementation* (3rd ed.). Berkley, CA: University of California Press.

Rabin, R.C. (2019, June 14). Eager to limit exemptions to vaccination, states face staunch resistance. *The New York Times*. Retrieved from https://www.nytimes.com/2019/06/14/health/vaccine-exemption-health.html

Rampton, M. (2015). Four waves of feminism. Retrieved from https://www.pacificu.edu/about/media/four-waves-feminism

Salisbury, R. (1984). Interest representation and the dominance of institutions. *American Political Science Review, 78*(1), 64–77.

Schattschneider, E. E. (1976). *The semisovereign people*. Hinsdale, IL: Dryden Press.

Shdaimah, C., Stahl, R., & Schram, S. (2011). *Change research: A case study on collaborative methods for social workers and advocates*. New York, NY: Columbia University Press.

Stone, D. (2012). *Policy paradox: The art of political decision making* (3rd ed.). New York, NY: W.W. Norton.

Tran, V. (2018). Asian Americans are falling through the cracks in data representation and social services [Blog post]. Retrieved from https://www.urban.org/urban-wire/asian-americans-are-falling-through-cracks-data-representation-and-social-services

Truman, D. (1951). *The government process*. New York, NY: Knopf.

United States Senate. (n.d.). Direct election of senators. Retrieved from https://www.senate.gov/artandhistory/history/common/briefing/Direct_Election_Senators.htm

Wallace, R. A., & Wolf, A. (1995). *Contemporary sociological theory: Continuing the classical tradition* (4th ed.). Englewood Cliffs, NJ: Prentice Hall.

Wolff, R. D., & Resnick, S. A. (2012). *Contending economic theories: Neoclassical, Keynesian and Marxism*. Cambridge, MA: MIT Press.

Woman's Rights Convention. (1848). Declaration of Sentiments and Resolutions. Retrieved from http://ecssba.rutgers.edu/docs/seneca.html

Young, I. M. (1990). *Justice and the politics of difference*. Princeton, NJ: Princeton University Press.

CHAPTER 4

American Psychological Association, Task Force on Mental Health and Abortion. (2008). *Report of the Task Force on Mental Health and Abortion*. Washington, DC: Author. Retrieved from http://www.apa.org/pi/wpo/mental-health-abortion-report.pdf

Bakalar, N. (2017, July 3). U.S. fertility rate reaches a record low. *The New York Times*. Retrieved from https://www.nytimes.com/2017/07/03/health/united-states-fertility-rate.html

Becker, G. (1981). *A treatise on the family*. Cambridge, MA: Harvard University Press.

Boucai, M. (2105). Glorious precedents: When gay marriage was radical. *Yale Journal of Law & the Humanities, 27*(1), 1–82. Retrieved from http://digitalcommons.law.yale.edu/yjlh/vol27/iss1/1

Brodzinsky, D. (2012). Adoption by lesbians and gay men: A national survey of adoption agency policies and practice. In D. Brodzinsky & A. Pertman (Eds.), *Adoptions by lesbians and gay men: A new dimension in family diversity* (pp. 62–83). Oxford, UK: Oxford University Press.

Center for Reproductive Rights. (n.d.). The world's abortion laws 2019. Retrieved from http://worldabortionlaws.com/map/

Centers for Disease Control and Prevention. (2017). 2015 assisted reproductive technology report. Washington, DC: Author. Retrieved from https://www.cdc.gov/art/pdf/2015-report/ART-2015-National-Summary-Report.pdf

Chambers, D. L., & Polikoff, N. D. (1999). Family law and gay and lesbian family issues in the twentieth century. *Family Law, 33*(3), 523–542. Retrieved from http://repository.law.umich.edu/articles

Council of Economic Advisors, Office of the President. (2014). *The economics of paid and unpaid leave.* Washington, DC: Author. Retrieved from https://obamawhitehouse.archives.gov/sites/default/files/docs/leave_report_final.pdf

Daugherty, J., & Copen, C. (2016). Trends in attitudes about marriage, childbearing, and sexual behavior in the United States, 2002, 2006–2010, and 2011–2013. *National health statistics reports; no 92.* Hyattsville, MD: National Center for Health Statistics. Retrieved from https://www.cdc.gov/nchs/data/nhsr/nhsr092.pdf

Dotterweich, D., & McKinney, M. (2000). National attitudes regarding gender bias in child custody cases. *Family Court Review, 38*(2), 208–223.

Edin, K., & Kefalas, M. (2005). *Promises I can keep: Why poor women put motherhood before marriage.* Berkeley, CA: University of California Press.

Elliot, D. (2018, Feb. 27). Same-sex marriage flashpoint: Alabama considers quitting the marriage business. *NPR.* Retrieved from https://www.npr.org/2018/02/27/588834254/same-sex-marriage-flashpoint-alabama-considers-getting-out-of-the-marriage-busin

European Union. (2003). Working conditions: Working time directive. Retrieved from http://ec.europa.eu/social/main.jsp?catId=706&langId=en&intPageId=205

Family Law Quarterly. (2012). *Chart 4: Grounds for divorce and residency requirements.* Washington, DC: American Bar Association. Retrieved from https://www.americanbar.org/content/dam/aba/publications/family_law_quarterly/vol45/4win12_chart4_divorce.authcheckdam.pdf

The Family and Medical Leave Act of 1993. 29 CFR 825.

Fields, J., & Casper, L. (2000). *America's families and living arrangements.* Washington, DC: U.S. Census Bureau. Retrieved from https://www.census.gov/prod/2001pubs/p20-537.pdf

Flexibility, Efficiency, and Modernization of Child Support Enforcement Programs. (2016, effective 2017). 81 FR 93492, 34 CFR 301-305, 2016. Retrieved from https://www.reginfo.gov/public/do/eAgendaViewRule?pubId=201704&RIN=0970-AC50)

Floyd, I. (2017). *TANF cash benefits have fallen by more than 20 percent in most states and continue to erode.* Washington, DC: Center on Budget and Policy Priorities. Retrieved from https://www.cbpp.org/research/family-income-support/tanf-cash-benefits-have-fallen-by-more-than-20-percent-in-most-states

Focus on the Family (n.d.). Scriptural basis for definition of "marriage" and "family." Retrieved from https://www.focusonthefamily.com/family-q-and-a/relationships-and-marriage/scriptural-basis-for-definition-of-marriage-and-family

Frank, W. (2014). *Law and the gay rights story: The long search for equal justice in a divided democracy.* Rutgers, NJ: Rutgers University Press.

Gault, B. Hartmann, H., Hegewisch, A., Milli, J., & Reichlin, L. (2014). *Paid parental leave in the United States.* Washington, DC: Institute for Women's Policy Research. Retrieved from https://iwpr.org/publications/paid-parental-leave-in-the-united-states-what-the-data-tell-us-about-access-usage-and-economic-and-health-benefits/

Glick, J. E., Bean, F. D., & Van Hook, J. V. (1997). Immigration and changing patterns of extended family household structure in the United States: 1970–1990. *Journal of Marriage and the Family, 59*(1), 177–191.

Guttmacher Institute. (2018). An overview of abortion laws. Retrieved from https://www.guttmacher.org/state-policy/explore/overview-abortion-laws

HCCH. (1993). 33: Convention of 29 May 1993 on Protection of Children and Co-operation in Respect of Intercountry Adoption. Retrieved from https://www.hcch.net/en/instruments/conventions/full-text/?cid=69

Jones, J. (2017). In U.S., 10.2% of LGBT adults now married to same-sex spouse. *Gallup.* Retrieved from https://news.gallup.com/poll/212702/lgbt-adults-married-sex-spouse.aspx

Kahn, B. Z. (2013). *The democratization of invention: Patents and copyrights in American economic development, 1790–1920.* Cambridge, UK: Cambridge University Press.

Kim, J., Spangler, T. L., & Gutter, M. S. (2016). Extended families: Support, socialization, and stress. *Family and Consumer Research Journal, 45*(1), 104–118. http://dx.doi.org/10.1111/fcsr.12187

Livingston, G. (2018a, January 18). They're waiting longer, but U.S. women today more likely to have children than a decade ago. *Pew Research Center.* Retrieved from http://www.pewsocialtrends.org/2018/01/18/theyre-waiting-longer-but-u-s-women-today-more-likely-to-have-children-than-a-decade-ago/

Livingston, G. (2018b, April 25). The changing profile of unmarried parents: A growing share are living with a partner. *Pew Research Center.* Retrieved from https://www.pewsocialtrends.org/2018/04/25/the-changing-profile-of-unmarried-parents/

Livingston, G. (2018c, May 4). More than a million Millennials are becoming moms each year. *Pew Research Center.* Retrieved from https://www.pewresearch.org/fact-tank/2018/05/04/

more-than-a-million-millennials-are-becoming-moms-each-year/

Lofquist, D. (2011). *Same sex couple households: American Community Survey.* Washington, DC: U.S. Census Bureau. Retrieved from https://www.census.gov/content/dam/Census/library/publications/2011/acs/acsbr10-03.pdf

Maroto, M., & Aylsworth, L. (2017). Assessing the relationship between gender, household structure, and net worth in the United States. *Journal of Family Economic Issues, 38*(4), 556–571. http://dx.doi.org/10.1007/s10834-017-9521-z

Martin, J. A., Hamilton, B., Osterman, M., Driscoll, A., & Drake, P. (2018). Births: Final data for 2017. *National Vital Statistics Report, 67*(8). Retrieved from https://www.cdc.gov/nchs/data/nvsr/nvsr67/nvsr67_08-508.pdf

Miller, L. R. (2016). Definition of family. In C. L. Shehan (Ed.), *The Wiley Blackwell Encyclopedia of Family Studies.* Hoboken, NJ: Wiley.

Mintz, S., & Kellogg, S. (1988). *Domestic revolution: A social history of American family life.* New York, NY: Free Press.

Murdock, G. P. (1949). *Social structure.* New York, NY: MacMillan Company. Retrieved from https://archive.org/stream/socialstructure00murd#page/n5/mode/2up

NAC & AARP. (2009). *Caregiving in the U.S. 2009: A focused look at caregivers of children.* Retrieved from http://www.caregiving.org/data/Report_Caregivers_of_Children_11-12-09.pdf

NAC & AARP. (2015). *Caregiving in the U.S.: Research report.* Retrieved from https://www.aarp.org/content/dam/aarp/ppi/2015/caregiving-in-the-united-states-2015-report-revised.pdf

Nash, E. (2019). A surge in bans on abortion as early as six weeks, before most people know they are pregnant. *Guttmacher Institute.* Retrieved from https://www.guttmacher.org/article/2019/03/surge-bans-abortion-early-six-weeks-most-people-know-they-are-pregnant

National Association of Social Workers. (2017). Code of ethics. Retrieved from https://www.socialworkers.org/About/Ethics/Code-of-Ethics

National Conference of State Legislators. (2016). State family and medical leave laws. Retrieved from http://www.ncsl.org/research/labor-and-employment/state-family-and-medical-leave-laws.aspx#1

National Women's Law Center. (2018). State paid family and medical leave insurance laws. Retrieved from http://www.nationalpartnership.org/research-library/work-family/paid-leave/state-paid-family-leave-laws.pdf

Office of Child Support Enforcement. (2016). Flexibility, efficiency, and modernization in child support enforcement programs. *Federal Register.* Retrieved from https://www.federalregister.gov/documents/2016/12/20/2016-29598/flexibility-efficiency-and-modernization-in-child-support-enforcement-programs

Oppenheimer, V. K. (2000). The continuing importance of men's economic position in marriage formation. In L. Waite (Ed.), *The ties that bind* (pp. 283–301). New York, NY: Aldine de Gruyer.

Parker, K., & Livingston, G. (2017). *6 facts about American fathers.* Retrieved from http://www.pewresearch.org/fact-tank/2017/06/15/fathers-day-facts/

Parsons, T. (1943). The kinship system of the contemporary United States. *American Anthropologist, 45,* 22–38. doi:10.1525/aa.1943.45.1.02a00030

Peck, E. (2019, June 3). Connecticut passes most generous paid family leave law in the U.S. *HuffPost.* Retrieved from https://www.huffpost.com/entry/connecticut-paid-family-leave-law_n_5cf5418de4b0e346ce82308e

Pew Research Center. (2015). *Parenting in America.* Social & Demographic Trends. Retrieved from https://www.pewsocialtrends.org/2015/12/17/1-the-american-family-today/

Planned Parenthood. (2016). Mifepristone: Expanding women's options for early abortion in the United States. Retrieved from https://www.plannedparenthood.org/files/4014/6012/8629/Mifepristone.pdf

Polikoff, N. D. (2009). Equality and justice for lesbian and gay families and relationships. *Rutgers Law Review, 61*(3), 529–565. Retrieved from http://digitalcommons.wcl.american.edu/facsch_lawrev

Raley, R. K., Sweeney, M. M., & Wondra, D. (2015). The growing racial and ethnic divide in U.S. marriage patterns. *The Future of Children / Center for the Future of Children, the David and Lucile Packard Foundation, 25*(2), 89–109.

Schenk, R. (2019, May 30). I was an anti-abortion crusader. Now I support *Roe v. Wade. The New York Times, Opinion.* Retrieved from https://www.nytimes.com/2019/05/30/opinion/abortion-schenck.html

Scott, E. S., & Emery, R. E. (2014). Gender politics and child custody: The puzzling persistence of the best-interests standard. *Law and Contemporary Problems, 77,* 69–108. Retrieved from https://scholarship.law.duke.edu/cgi/viewcontent.cgi?article=4388&context=lcp

Shdaimah, C. S., & Palley, E. (2018). Elusive support for U.S. child care. *Community, Work, & Family, 21*(1), 53–69.

Slater, L., & Finck, K. (2012). *Social work practice and the law.* New York, NY: Springer.

Social Security Administration. (1935). Social Security Act of 1935. Retrieved from https://www.ssa.gov/history/35actxi.html

Social Security Administration. (2017). How Social Security can help you when a family member dies. Retrieved from https://www.ssa.gov/pubs/EN-05-10008.pdf

Stone,L.(2018,February.15).Americanwomenarehavingfewer children than they'd like. *The New York Times.* Retrieved from https://www.nytimes.com/2018/02/13/upshot/american-fertility-is-falling-short-of-what-women-want.html

Tavernise, S. (2016). New F.D.A. guidelines ease access to abortion pill. *The New York Times.* Retrieved from https://www.nytimes.com/2016/03/31/health/abortion-pill-mifeprex-ru-486-fda.html

Taylor, L. (2019, March. 19). Switzerland ranked as best country for women's rights, according to the OECD. *World Economic Forum.* Retrieved from https://www.weforum.org/agenda/2019/03/switzerland-ranked-as-best-country-for-womens-rights-oecd/

U.S. Census Bureau. (2015). Current Population Survey: Subject definitions. Retrieved from https://www.census.gov/programs-surveys/cps/technical-documentation/subject-definitions.html#familyU.S.

U.S. Census Bureau. (2016, November 17). *The majority of children live with two parents, Census Bureau reports [Press release].* Retrieved from https://www.census.gov/newsroom/press-releases/2016/cb16-192.html

U.S. Census Bureau. (2017a). Figure CH-2.3.4: Percent of children under 18 who live with their mother only. Retrieved from https://www.census.gov/content/dam/Census/library/visualizations/time-series/demo/families-and-households/ch-2-3-4.pdf

U.S. Census Bureau. (2017b). Historical families tables. Retrieved from https://www.census.gov/data/tables/time-series/demo/families/families.html

U.S. Census Bureau. (2018a). CH-1. Living arrangements of children under 18 years old: 1960 to present. Retrieved from https://www.census.gov/data/tables/time-series/demo/families/children.html

U.S. Census Bureau. (2018b). Figure CH-2.3.4 Percent of children under 18 who live with their mother only. Retrieved from https://www.census.gov/content/dam/Census/library/visualizations/time-series/demo/families-and-households/ch-2-3-4.pdf

U.S. Census Bureau. (2018, November 14). *U.S. Census Bureau releases 2018 families and living arrangements tables [Press release].* Retrieved from https://www.census.gov/newsroom/press-releases/2018/families.html

U.S. Congress, Office of Technology Assessment. (1988). *Artificial insemination: Practice in the United States: Summary of a 1987 survey*—Background paper, OTA-13P-BA-48. Washington, DC: U.S. Government Printing Office. Retrieved from https://www.princeton.edu/~ota/disk2/1988/8804/8804.PDF

Violence Against Women Act of 1994, Pub. L. No. 103-322, Title IV, 108 Stat.

Williams Institute. (2019). Same sex couples: Data and demographics. Retrieved from https://williamsinstitute.law.ucla.edu/visualization/lgbt-stats/?topic=SS#densi

Williams, T., & Binder, A. (2019, May 14). Lawmakers vote to effectively ban abortion in Alabama. *The New York Times.* Retrieved from https://www.nytimes.com/2019/05/14/us/abortion-law-alabama.html

CHAPTER 5

Adoption and Safe Families Act of 1997, PL 105-89.

Adoptive Couple v. Baby Girl. (2013). U.S. LEXIS 4916.

Alston, P. (2018). *United Nations Special Rapporteur on Extreme Poverty and Human Rights on his mission to the United States of America.* Retrieved from https://digitallibrary.un.org/record/1629536?ln=en

Annie E. Casey Foundation. (2016). KIDS COUNT Network brainstorms racial equity strategies. [Blog post]. https://digitallibrary.un.org/record/1629536?ln=en Retrieved from http://www.aecf.org/blog/kids-count-network-brainstorms-racial-equity-strategies/

Annie E. Casey Foundation. (2019). Kids Count Data Center and Data Book: What we do. Retrieved from https://www.aecf.org/work/kids-count/kids-count-data-center/

Anyon, Y. (2011). Reducing racial disparities and disproportionalities in the child welfare system: Policy perspectives about how to serve the best interests of African American youth. *Children and Youth Services Review, 33*(2), 242–253.

Boyd, R. (2014). African American disproportionality and disparity in child welfare: Toward a comprehensive conceptual framework. *Children and Youth Services Review, 37,* 15–27.

Brace, C. L. (1872). *The dangerous classes of New York and twenty years' work among them.* New York, NY: Wynkoop & Hallenbeck.

Branson-Potts, H. (2016, March 13). Santa Clarita foster parents appeal to state Supreme Court in tribal custody battle. *Los Angeles Times.* Retrieved from http://www.latimes.com/

local/lanow/la-me-ln-native-american-santa-clarita-foster-20160321-story.html

Bureau of Indian Affairs. (2018). Indian Child Welfare Act (ICWA). Retrieved from https://www.bia.gov/bia/ois/dhs/icwa.

Children's Bureau/ACYF/HHS. (2015). *Mandatory reporters of child abuse and neglect: State statutes current through August 2015.* Washington, DC: Child Welfare Information Gateway. Retrieved from https://www.childwelfare.gov/pubPDFs/manda.pdf

Children's Bureau/ACYF/HHS. (2016a). *Child maltreatment, 2016.* Washington, DC: Child Welfare Information Gateway. Retrieved from https://www.acf.hhs.gov/sites/default/files/cb/cm2016.pdf

Children's Bureau/ACYF/HHS. (2016b). *Understanding child welfare and the courts: Fact sheet for families.* Washington, DC: Child Welfare Information Gateway. Retrieved from https://www.childwelfare.gov/pubPDFs/cwandcourts.pdf

Children's Bureau/ACYF/HHS. (2016c). Number of children in foster care increases for third consecutive year. *Children's Bureau Express, 17*(8). Retrieved from https://cbexpress.acf.hhs.gov/index.cfm?event=website.viewArticles&issueid=181&articleid=4855

Children's Bureau/ACYF/HHS. (2018). The Indian Child Welfare Act: A primer for child welfare professionals. *Child Welfare Information Gateway.* Retrieved from https://www.childwelfare.gov/pubPDFs/icwa.pdf

Cohen-Schlanger, M., Fitzpatrick, A., Hulchanski, J. D., & Raphael, D. (1995). Housing as a factor in admissions of children to temporary care: A survey. *Child Welfare, 74*(3), 547–563.

Cook, J. F. (1995). A history of placing-out: The orphan trains. *Child Welfare, 74*(1), 181–197.

Creagh, D. (2012). The baby trains: Catholic foster care and western migration, 1873–1929. *Journal of Social History, 46*(1), 197–218. doi:10.1093/jsh/shs023

Crofoot, T. L., & Harris, M. S. (2012). An Indian Child Welfare perspective on disproportionality in child welfare. *Children and Youth Services Review, 34*(9), 1667–1674.

Duarte, C., & Summers, A. (2013). A three-pronged approach to addressing racial disproportionality and disparities in child welfare: The Santa Clara County example of leadership, collaboration and data-driven decisions. *Child & Adolescent Social Work Journal, 30*(1), 1–19.

Eamon, M. K., & Kopels, S. (2004). For reasons of poverty: Court challenges to child welfare practices and mandated programs. *Children and Youth Services Review, 26*(9), 821–836.

Freisthler, B., Merritt, D. H., & LaScala, E. A. (2006). Understanding the ecology of child maltreatment: A review of the literature and directions for future research. *Child Maltreatment, 11*(3), 263–280.

Garner, S. (1993). The Indian Child Welfare Act: A review. *Wicazo Sa Review, 9*(1), 47–51.

Global Coalition to End Child Poverty. (2017). Child-sensitive social protection. Retrieved from http://www.endchildhoodpoverty.org/publications-feed/2017/11/1/9v61mcxy3mw336oilgamomko1p12it

Gordon, L. (1994). *Pitied but not entitled: Single mothers and the history of welfare, 1890–1935.* Boston, MA: Harvard University Press.

Harburger, D. S., & White, R. A. (2004). Reunifying families, cutting costs: Housing–child welfare partnerships for permanent supportive housing. *Child Welfare League of America, 83*(5), 493–528.

Holt, M. I. (1992). *The orphan trains: Placing out in America.* Lincoln: University of Nebraska Press.

Jacobs, M. D. (2014). *A generation removed: The fostering and adoption of indigenous children in the postwar world.* Lincoln, NE: University of Nebraska Press.

Johnson, T. (1999). The state and the American Indian: Who gets the Indian child? *Wicazo Sa Review, 14*(1), 197–214.

Joint Center for Housing Studies (2018). *The state of the nation's housing.* Cambridge, MA: Harvard University. Retrieved from http://www.jchs.harvard.edu/sites/default/files/Harvard_JCHS_State_of_the_Nations_Housing_2018.pdf

Jones, B. J. (1995). The Indian Child Welfare Act: The need for a separate law. *Compleat Lawyer, 12*(4), 18–23.

Kelly, J. (2018, February 6). Family First Act, major foster care finance reform bill, included in House's initial spending deal. *Chronicle of Social Change.* Retrieved from https://chronicleofsocialchange.org/finance-reform/family-first-act-included-in-houses-initial-spending-deal

Letchworth, W. P. (1894). The removal of children from almshouses in the state of New York. *In National Conference on Social Welfare. Official proceedings of the annual meeting: 1894*, 132–136. Retrieved from https://quod.lib.umich.edu/n/ncosw/ach8650.1894.001/156?page=root;rgn=full+text;size=100;view=image;q1=Letchworth

Lindsey, D. (2004). *The welfare of children* (2nd ed.). New York, NY: Oxford University Press.

MacEachron, A., Gustavsson, N., Cross, S., & Lewis, A. (1996). The effectiveness of the Indian Child Welfare Act of 1978. *Social Service Review, 13*(3), 451–463.

Markel, H., & M. D. (2009, December 14). Case shined first light on abuse in children. *The New York Times.* Retrieved from https://www.nytimes.com/2009/12/15/health/15abus.html

McCarthy, P. (2018, February 12). Family First Prevention Services Act will change the lives of children in foster care. Retrieved from http://www.aecf.org/blog/family-first-prevention-services-act-will-change-the-lives-of-children-in-f/

National CASA Foundation. (2019). Advocate for children. Retrieved from https://casaforchildren.org/advocate-for-children/be-a-casa-volunteer/

National Insurance Institute of Israel. (n.d.). Children. Retrieved from https://www.btl.gov.il/English%20Homepage/Benefits/Children/Pages/default.aspx

New York Society for the Prevention of Cruelty to Children. (2017). About. Retrieved from https://www.nyspcc.org/about-the-new-york-society-for-the-prevention-of-cruelty-to-children/

Oliver, J. T. (2014, February 3). Adoptions should consider the black children and black families. *The New York Times*. Retrieved from https://www.nytimes.com/roomfordebate/2014/02/02/in-adoption-does-race-matter/adoptions-should-consider-black-children-and-black-families

Organisation for Economic Co-operation and Development (2009). *Doing better for children*. Retrieved from www.oecd.org/els/social/childwellbeing.

Radel, L., Baldwin, M., Crouse, G., Ghertner, R., & Waters, A. (2018, March 7). *Substance use, the opioid epidemic, and child welfare system: Key findings from a mixed methods study*. Washington, DC: U.S. Department of Health and Human Services, Office of the Assistant Secretary for Planning and Evaluation. Retrieved from https://aspe.hhs.gov/system/files/pdf/258836/SubstanceUseChildWelfareOverview.pdf.

Ramey, J. B. (2012). "I dream of them almost every night": Working-class fathers and orphanages in Pittsburgh, 1878–1929. *Journal of Family History, 37*(1), 36–54.

Reich, J. A. (2005). *Fixing families: Parents, power, and the child welfare system*. New York, NY: Routledge.

Reynolds, B.C. (1939). Re-thinking social case work. Retrieved from https://babel.hathitrust.org/cgi/pt?id=wu.89098714728;view=1up;seq=3

Richmond, M. E. (1922). *What is social case work? An introductory description*. New York, NY: Russell Sage Foundation.

Roberts, D. (2002). *Shattered bonds: The color of child welfare*. New York, NY: Basic Books.

Robinson, B. A. (2018). Child welfare systems and LGBTQ youth homelessness: Gender segregation, instability, and intersectionality. *Child Welfare, 96*(2), 29–45.

Rothman, D. J. (1971). *The discovery of the asylum: Social order and disorder in the New Republic*. Boston, MA and Toronto, ON: Little, Brown and Company.

Schneider, D., & Macey, S. M. (2002). Foundlings, asylums, almshouses and orphanages: Early roots of child protection. *Middle States Geographer, 35*, 92–100.

Shakeshaft, E. (2018). *Legislating race: The Indian Child Welfare Act, the Multiethnic Placement Act & the Interethnic Adoptions Provisions*. Paper presented at the Annual Meetings of the Law and Society Association, Toronto, Canada.

Shdaimah, C (2009). "CPS is not a housing agency"; Housing is a CPS problem: Towards a definition and typology of housing problems in child welfare cases. *Children and Youth Services Review, 31*(2), 211–218.

Summers, A., & Wood, S. (2014). *Measuring compliance with the Indian Child Welfare Act: An assessment toolkit*. Reno, NV: National Council of Juvenile and Family Court Judges.

U.S. Department of Health & Human Services. Administration for Children and Families Administration on Children, Youth and Families, Children's Bureau. (2010). The Child Abuse Prevention and Maltreatment Act of 2010. Retrieved from https://www.acf.hhs.gov/sites/default/files/cb/capta2010.pdf

U.S. Department of Health and Human Services, Administration for Children and Families, Administration on Children, Youth and Families, Children's Bureau. (2017). *The AFCARS report*. Retrieved from https://www.acf.hhs.gov/sites/default/files/cb/afcarsreport24.pdf

Van Leeuwen, J. M., Boyle, S., Salomonsen-Sautel, S., Baker, D. N., Garcia, J. T., Hoffman, A., & Hopfer, C. J. (2006). Lesbian, gay, and bisexual homeless youth: An eight-city public health perspective. *Child Welfare, 85*(2), 151–170.

Wilson, B. D. M., Cooper, K., Kastanis, A., & Nezhad, S. (2014). *Sexual and gender minority youth in foster care: Assessing disproportionality and disparities in Los Angeles*. Los Angeles, CA: Williams Institute.

CHAPTER 6

Acemoglu, D., Autor, D. H., & Lyle, D. (2004). Women, war and wages: The effect of female labor supply on the wage structure at midcentury. *Journal of Political Economy, 112*(3), 497–551.

Amott, T. L., & Matthaei, J. A. (1996). *Race, gender, and work: A multi-cultural economic history of women in the United States*. Boston, MA: South End Press.

Barnett, W. S., Friedman-Krauss, A. H., Weisenfeld, G. G., Horowitz, M., Kasmin, R., & Squires, J. H. (2017). *The state of preschool 2016: State preschool yearbook*. New Brunswick, NJ: National Institute for Early Education Research.

Board of Education of the Hendrick Hudson Central School District v. Amy Rowley, 458 U.S. 176 (1982).

Bureau of Labor Statistics. (2011). Women in the labor force 1970-2009. Retrieved from https://www.bls.gov/opub/ted/2011/ted_20110105.htm

Bureau of Labor Statistics. (2019, April 18). *Employment characteristics of families summary [Press release]*. Retrieved from https://www.bls.gov/news.release/famee.nr0.htm

Center on the Developing Child at Harvard University (2016). From best practices to breakthrough impacts: A science-based approach to building a more promising future for young children and families. Retrieved from https://developingchild.harvard.edu/resources/from-best-practices-to-breakthrough-impacts/

Child Care Aware of America. (2017). Senate introduces bipartisan bill to reform child care tax credit. Retrieved from http://usa.childcareaware.org/2017/01/senators-introduce-bi-partisan-legislation-to-reform-child-care-tax-credits/

Clapp, C. (2016). The smart economics of Norway's parental leave, and why the U.S. should consider it. *The Washington Post*. Retrieved from https://www.washingtonpost.com/news/parenting/wp/2016/01/11/the-smart-economics-of-norways-parental-leave/?utm_term=.3e5498ab6e7c

Clemetson, L. (2006). Work vs. family, complicated by race. *The New York Times*. Retrieved from http://search.ebscohost.com/login.aspx?direct=true&db=aph&AN=28241206&site=ehost-live

Cohen, N. L. (2013). Why America never had universal child care. *New Republic*. Retrieved from https://newrepublic.com/article/113009/child-care-america-was-very-close-universal-day-care

Cohen, S. S. (2001). *Championing child care*. New York, NY: Columbia University Press.

David, T., & Powell, S. (2015). Introduction: Challenging ideas. In T. David & S. Powell (Eds.), *The Routledge International Handbook of Philosophies and Theories of Early Childhood Education and Care*. New York, NY: Routledge.

Diffey, L., Parker, E., & Atchison. (2017). *State pre-K funding 2016–17 fiscal year: Trends and opportunities*. Denver, CO: Education Commission of the States. Retrieved from https://www.ecs.org/ec-content/uploads/State-Pre-K-Funding-2016-17-Fiscal-Year-Trends-and-opportunities-1.pdf

Dinner, D. (2010). The universal childcare debate: Rights mobilization, social policy, and dynamics of feminist activism, 1966–1974. *Law and History Review, 28*, 577–628.

Early Education and Care Consortium. (2017). Federal legislative updates. Retrieved from http://www.ececonsortium.org/federal-action-center/federal-legislation/

England, P., & Folbre, N. (1999). The cost of caring. *The ANNALS of the American Academy of Political and Social Science, 561*(1), 39–51. https://doi.org/10.1177/000271629956100103

Federici, S. (2012). *Revolution at point zero: Housework, reproduction, and the feminist struggle*. Oakland, CA: PM Press.

Fineman, M. A. (1995). *The neutered mother, the sexual family, and other twentieth century tragedies*. New York, NY: Routledge.

First Five Years Fund. (2017). *Innovative financing for early childhood education: Recommendations from the Early Childhood Education Action Tank*. Retrieved from https://savethechildrenactionnetwork.org/wp-content/uploads/2017/01/action-tank-white-paper.pdf

Giardiello, P. (2015). Maria Montessori. In T. David & S. Powell (Eds.), *The Routledge International Handbook of Philosophies and Theories of Early Childhood Education and Care*. New York, NY: Routledge.

Goertz, G., & Mazur, A.G. (2008). *Politics, gender, and concepts: Theory and methodology*. New York, NY: Cambridge University Press.

Government Accounting Office. (2002). *Child care: States have undertaken a variety of quality improvement initiatives, but evaluations of effectiveness are needed*. Retrieved from http://www.gao.gov/news.items/do2897.pdf

Grant, J., Hoorens, S., Sivadasan, S., van het Loo, M., DaVanzo, J., Hale, L., Gibson, S., & Butz, W. (2004). *Low fertility and population ageing: Causes, consequences, and policy options*. Santa Monica, CA: RAND. Retrieved from https://www.rand.org/pubs/monographs/MG206.html

Harris, N. (2008). Radical activism and accidental philanthropy: The impact of first wave feminist activism on the later construction of child care policies in Australia and the United States of America. *Women's Studies International Forum, 31*(1), 42–52. doi:10.1016/j.wsif.2007.11.004

Heckman, J. J., Grunewald, R., & Reynolds, A. (2006). The dollars and cents of investing early: Cost-benefit analysis in early child care and education. *Zero to Three, 26*, 10–17.

Ho, S. (2017, Sept. 16). Childcare choices limited to those working outside 9–5. *CBS Newshour*. Retrieved from http://www.pbs.org/newshour/rundown/child-care-choices-limited-working-outside-9-5/

Hurd Smith, B. (n.d.). Pauline Agassiz Shaw. Retrieved from http://bwht.org/pauline-agassiz-shaw/

Individuals with Disabilities Education Act. (2006). 34 CFR 300.8

Internal Revenue Service. (2019). Topic 602—Child and dependent care credit. Retrieved from https://www.irs.gov/taxtopics/tc602

Kamerman, S., & Kahn, A. (2001). Child and family policies in the United States at the opening of the twenty-first century. *Social Policy & Administration, 35*(1), 69–84.

Katner, D. R. (2010). Delinquency and daycare. *Harvard Law & Policy Review, 4*, 49–72.

Klein, A. G. (1992). *Debate over child care, 1969–1990: A sociohistorical analysis*. Albany, NY: State University of New York Press.

Knight, L. W. (2005). *Citizen: Jane Addams and the struggle for democracy.* Chicago, IL: University of Chicago Press.

Lynch, K. E. (2014). *The Child Care and Development Block Grant: Background and funding.* Retrieved from http://greenbook.waysandmeans.house.gov/sites/greenbook.waysandmeans.house.gov/files/RL30785_gb.pdf

Michel, S. (1999). *Children's interest/mothers' rights: The shaping of America's child care policy.* New Haven, CT: Yale University Press.

Michel, S., & Peng, I. (2017). *Gender, migration, and the work of care: Multi-scalar approach to the Pacific Rim.* New York, NY: Palgrave-MacMillan.

Morgan, K. J., & Zippel, K. (2003). Paid to care: The origins and effects of care leave policies in Western Europe. *Social Politics, 10*(1), 49–85.

Mulligan, D. M., Brimhall, D., West, J., & Chapman, C. (2005). *Child care and early arrangements of infants, toddlers, and preschoolers: 2001 (NCES 2006-039).* Washington, DC: U.S. Department of Education, Institute of Education Sciences, National Center for Education Statistics.

National Conference of State Legislators. (2019). Early education and child care tracking database 2008–2018. Retrieved from http://www.ncsl.org/research/human-services/child-care-and-early-education-legislation-databas.aspx

National Institute of Child Health and Human Development. (2006). *The NICHD study of early child care and youth development.* Retrieved from https://www.nichd.nih.gov/publications/pubs/documents/seccyd_06.pdf

National Scientific Council on the Developing Child. (2004). *Young children develop in an environment of relationships. Working Paper No. 1.* Retrieved from https://developingchild.harvard.edu/resources/wp1/

National Survey of Early Care and Education Project Team (2015). *Fact sheet: Provision of early care and education during non-standard hours (OPRE Report No. 2015-44).* Washington, DC: U.S. Department of Health and Human Services, Office of Planning, Research and Evaluation, Administration for Children and Families. Retrieved from http://www.acf.hhs.gov/programs/opre/resource/fact-sheet-provision-of-early-care-and-education-non-standard-hours

National Women's Law Center. (2015). State child care and dependent care tax provisions. Retrieved from https://nwlc.org/resources/state-child-care-and-dependent-care-tax-provisions/

Nixon, R. (1971). "Veto of the Economic Opportunity Amendments of 1971," December 9, 1971. *American Presidency Project.* Retrieved from http://www.presidency.ucsb.edu/ws/?pid=3251

Oden, S., Schweinhart, L. J., Weikart, D. P., Marcus, S. M., & Xie, Y. (2000). *Into adulthood: A study of the effects of Head Start.* Harpers Ferry, WV: Voyager Books.

U.S. Department of Health and Human Services, Office of Child Care. (n.d.). About. Retrieved from https://childcareta.acf.hhs.gov/licensing/about

U.S. Department of Health and Human Services, Office of Child Care. (2017). Child care and development fund reauthorization. Retrieved from https://www.acf.hhs.gov/occ/ccdf-reauthorization

Open States. (2019). HB 19-1194: School discipline for preschool through second grade. Retrieved from http://leg.colorado.gov/sites/default/files/2019a_1194_signed.pdf

Palley, E., & Shdaimah, C. (2014). *In our hands: The struggle for U.S. child care policy.* New York, NY: New York University.

Parker, L. O. (2005). *I'm every woman: Remixed stories of marriage, motherhood, and work.* New York, NY: HarperCollins.

Pew Center on the States. (2011). *Transforming public education: Pathway to a pre-K–12 future.* Retrieved from http://www.pewtrusts.org/~/media/legacy/uploadedfiles/pcs_assets/2011/pewprektransformingpubliceducationpdf.pdf

Pomper, K., Blank, H., Campbell, N. D., & Schulman, K. (2004). *Be all that you can be: Lessons from the military to improve our nation's child care system. 2004 follow up.* Washington, DC: National Women's Law Center. Retrieved from https://nwlc.org/wp-content/uploads/2015/08/BeAllThatWeCanBe_2004FollowUp.pdf

Rose, E. (1999). *A mother's job.* New York, NY: Oxford University Press.

Schilder, D., Kimura, S., Elliott, K., & Curenton, S. (2011). Perspectives on the impact of pre-K expansion: Factors to consider and lessons from New York and Ohio. Preschool Policy Brief. Issue 21. Retrieved from http://nieer.org/wp-content/uploads/2016/08/22.pdf

Schweitzer, M. M. (1980). World War II and labor force participation rates. *Journal of Economic History, 15*(1), 89–95.

Self, R. O. (2012). *All in the family: The realignment of American democracy since the 1960s.* New York, NY: Hill and Wang.

Shapiro, J., & Applegate, J. S. (2002). Child care as a relational context for early development: Research in neurobiology and emerging roles for social work. *Children and Adolescent Social Work Journal, 19*(2), 97–114

Shdaimah, C. S., Palley, E., & Miller, A. (2018). Voices of child care providers: An exploratory study of the impact of policy changes. *International Journal of Child Care and Education Policy, 12*(4). https://doi.org/10.1186/s40723-018-0043-4

Sheridan, T. (2015). *Head Start: Where does the federal investment go?* Washington, DC: National Head Start Association. Retrieved from https://www.nhsa.org/head-start-101

Spaights, E., & Whitaker, A. (1995). Black women in the workforce: A new look at an old problem. *Journal of Black Studies, 25*(3), 283–296.

Spain, D. (2001). *How women saved the city.* Minneapolis, MN: University of Minnesota Press.

Steinfels, M (1973). *Who's minding the children? The history and politics of day care in America.* New York, NY: Simon and Schuster.

Stolfutz, E. (n.d.). Child care: The federal role during World War II. Retrieved from Congressional Research Service website http://congressionalresearch.com/RS20615/document.php

Bureau of Labor Statistics. (2017). *Employment characteristics of family survey [Press release]. Labor Statistics.* Retrieved from https://www.bls.gov/news.release/famee.nr0.htm

Vinovskis, M. A. (2005). *The birth of Head Start: Preschool education policies in the Kennedy and Johnson administrations.* Chicago, IL: University of Chicago Press.

Vinovskis, M. A. (2015). Using knowledge of the past to improve education today: U.S. education history and policy-making. *Paedagogica Historica, 51*(1–2), 3–44.

Vucic, N. (2013, June 11). It's time to fix child care—Reauthorization bill introduced in Senate. [Blog post]. Retrieved from http://policyblog.usa.childcareaware.org/2013/06/11/reauthorization-bill-introduced-in-senate/

Waldfogel, J. (1998). Understanding the "family gap" in pay for women with children. *Journal of Economic Perspectives, 12*(1), 137 156.

Whitebook, M., McLean, C., & Austin, L. J. (2016). *Early childhood workforce index*, 2016. Berkeley, CA: Center for the Study of Child Care Employment, University of California, Berkeley. Retrieved from http://files.eric.ed.gov/fulltext/ED568873.pdf

Williams, J. C., Manvell, J., & Bornsten, S. (2007). *"Opt out" or pushed out?: How the press covers work/family conflict: The untold story of women leaving the workforce.* San Francisco, CA: Center for WorkLife Law, Hastings College of the Law. Retrieved from http://worklifelaw.org/pubs/OptOutPushedOut.pdf

Wishart, D. (2011). Native American gender roles. In *Encyclopedia of the Great Plains.* Retrieved from http://plainshumanities.unl.edu/encyclopedia/doc/egp.gen.026

Yoshikawa, H., Weiland, C., Brooks-Gunn, J., Burchinal, M., Espinosa, L., Gormley, W. T., Ludwig, J., Magnuson, K., Phillips, D., & Zaslow, M (2013). *Investing in our future: The evidence base on preschool.* Washington, DC: Society for Research in Child Development. Retrieved from https://www.fcd-us.org/the-evidence-base-on-preschool/

Young, I. M. (1990). *Justice and the politics of difference.* Princeton, NJ: Princeton University Press.

Zigler, E., & Muenchow, S. (1992). *The inside story of America's most successful educational experiment.* New York, NY: Basic Books.

CHAPTER 7

Antikainen, A., & Luukkainen, A. (n.d.). Twenty-five years of educational reform initiatives in Finland. Retrieved from http://www.oppi.uef.fi/~anti/publ/uudet/twenty_five_years.pdf

Atkins, J. D. C. (1887). Barbarous dialects should be blotted out. Reprinted in Crawford, J. (1992). *Language loyalties: A source book on the Official English controversy.* Chicago, IL: University of Chicago Press.

Baker, B., Farrie, D., Johnson, M., Luhm, T., & Sciarra, D. (2017). *Is school funding fair: A national report card. Sixth edition. January 2017.* Retrieved from https://drive.google.com/file/d/0BxtYmwryVI00VDhjRGlDOUh3VE0/view

Bear, C. (2008). American Indian boarding schools haunt many. *NPR.* Retrieved from http://www.npr.org/templates/story/story.php?storyId=16516865

Board of Education of Hendrick Hudson School District v. Rowley, 458 U.S. 176 (1982).

Board of Education of Independent School District 92 of Pottawatomie County v. Lindsay Earls, 536 U.S. 822 (2002).

Brinson, D., Boast, L., Hassel, B. C., & Kingsland, N. (2012). *New Orleans-style education reform: A guide for cities—lessons learned 2004–2010.* Chapel Hill, NY: Public Impact.

Brown v. Board of Education, 347 U.S. 483 (1954).

Brown-Martin, G., & Tavakolian, N. (2015). *Learning reimagined.* London, UK: Bloomsbury Academic.

Budde, R. (1996). The evolution of the charter concept. *Phi Delta Kappan, 78*(1), 72.

Buras, K. L. (2013). 'We're not going nowhere': Race, urban space, and the struggle for King Elementary School in New Orleans. *Critical Studies in Education*, *54*(1), 19–32.

Buzuvis, E. (2013). "On the basis of sex": Using Title IX to protect transgender students from discrimination in education. *Wisconsin Journal of Law, Gender, and Society*, *28*(3), 219–243.

Cedar Rapids Community School District v. Garret F., 526 U.S. 66 (1999).

Center for Racial Justice Innovation. (2006). Public schools in the United States: Some history. Retrieved from https://www.raceforward.org/research/reports/public-schools-united-states-some-history

Common Core State Standards Initiative. (n.d.). Standards in your state. Retrieved from http://www.corestandards.org/standards-in-your-state/

DeWitt, L. (2011). Wilbur J. Cohen (June 13, 1913–May 17, 1987)—Government official, educator, social welfare expert. Retrieved from http://socialwelfare.library.vcu.edu/people/cohen-wilbur-j/

Driscoll, J. P. (2001). Charter schools. *Georgetown Journal on Poverty Law & Policy*, *8*(2), 505. Retrieved from http://survey.hshsl.umaryland.edu/?url=http://search.ebscohost.com/login.aspx?direct=true&db=buh&AN=5436062&site=eds-live

Education Commission of the States. (2016). Civic education policies: Curriculum frameworks include civics or citizenship education. Retrieved from http://ecs.force.com/mbdata/MBQuest2RTANW?Rep=CIP1603S

Education Commission of the States. (2017). State summative assessments 2016–2017: All data points. Retrieved from http://ecs.force.com/mbdata/mbquest5E?rep=SUM1606

Education Commission of the States. (2018). 50-state comparison. Retrieved from http://ecs.force.com/mbdata/mbquestNB2C?rep=CS1701

The Elementary and Secondary Education Act of 1965 (ESEA). P.L. 89-10

Equality Act. (2017). SB No. 1006. Retrieved from https://www.congress.gov/bill/115th-congress/senate-bill/1006

Every Student Succeeds. (2015). 20 U.S.C. ch. 28 § 1001 et seq. 20 U.S.C. ch. 70

The Family Educational Rights and Privacy Act (FERPA). (1974). 20 U.S.C. § 1232g; 34 CFR Part 99

Felton, E. (2017, September 6). The Department of Justice is overseeing the resegregation of American Schools. *The Nation*. Retrieved from https://www.thenation.com/article/the-department-of-justice-is-overseeing-the-resegregation-of-american-schools/

Fla. Dep't of Educ. v. Glasser, 622 So. 2d 944, 947 (1993).

Frankenberg, E., Kotok, F., Schafft, K., Mann, B. (2017). Exploring school choice and the consequences for student racial segregation within Pennsylvania's charter school transfers. *Education Policy Analysis Archives*, *25*(22).

Gawlik, M. A. (2016). The U.S. charter school landscape: Extant literature, gaps in research, and implications for the U.S. educational system. *Global Education Review*, *3*(2), 50–83.

Gershoff, E., & Font, S. (2016). Corporal punishment in U.S. public schools: Prevalence, disparities in use, and status in state and federal policy. *Social Policy Report*, *30*, 1.

Goss v. Lopez, 419 U.S. 565 (1975).

Graham, P. A. (1995). Assimilation, adjustment, and access: An antiquarian view of American education. In D. Ravitch & M. Vinovskis (Eds.), *Learning from the Past*. Baltimore, MD: Johns Hopkins University Press.

Gross-Loh, C. (2014). Finnish education chief: 'We created a school system based on equality.' *The Atlantic*. Retrieved from https://www.theatlantic.com/education/archive/2014/03/finnish-education-chief-we-created-a-school-system-based-on-equality/284427/

Gupta, A. (2015). Using postcolonial theory to critically re-frame the child development narrative. In T. David & S. Powell (Eds.), *The Routledge International Handbook of Philosophies and Theories of Early Childhood Education and Care*. New York, NY: Routledge.

Hancock, L. (2011). Why are Finland's schools successful? *Smithsonian Magazine*, *1*(7). Retrieved from https://www.smithsonianmag.com/innovation/why-are-finlands-schools-successful-49859555/

Harris, D., & Larsen, M. F. (2016). *The effects of the New Orleans post-Katrina school reforms on student academic outcomes*. New Orleans, LA: Tulane University, Education Research Alliance for New Orleans. Retrieved from https://education-researchalliancenola.org/publications/what-effect-did-the-post-katrina-school-reforms-have-on-student-outcomes

Harris, E. A. (2016, September 7). Judge, citing inequality, orders Connecticut to overhaul its school system. *The New York Times*. Retrieved from https://www.nytimes.com/2016/09/08/nyregion/connecticut-public-schools-inequality-judge-orders.html?mcubz=1

Hillman, B. S. (2008). Is there a place for religious charter schools? *Yale Law Journal*, *118*(3), 554–599.

Irving v. Tatro, 468 US 883 (1984).

Jefferson, T. (1814). Letter from Thomas Jefferson to Peter Carr (September 7, 1814). In *Encyclopedia Virginia*. Retrieved from https://www.encyclopediavirginia.org/Letter_from_Thomas_Jefferson_to_Peter_Carr_September_7_1814

Kahlenberg, R. (2008, March). The charter school idea turns 20: A history of evolution and role reversals. *EdWeek*. Retrieved from http://www.edweek.org/ew/articles/2008/03/26/29kahlenberg_ep.h27.html

Klein, A. (2015). No Child Left Behind: An overview. *EdWeek*. Retrieved from http://www.edweek.org/ew/section/multimedia/no-child-left-behind-overview-definition-summary.html

Kolderie, T. (2005). Ray Budde and the origins of the charter concept. Retrieved from https://www.educationevolving.org/files/Ray-Budde-Origins-Of-Chartering.pdf

Koski, W. S. (2003). Of fuzzy standards and institutional constraints: A re-examination of the jurisprudential history of educational finance reform litigation. *Santa Clara Law Review, 43*(4), 1185–1298.

Kozol, J. (2005). *The shame of the nation*. New York, NY: Three Rivers Press.

Madigan, J. (2009). The education of girls and women in the United States: A historical perspective. *Advances in Gender and Education, 1*, 11-13. Retrieved from www.mcrcad.org/Web_Madigan.pdf

Massachusetts Court System. (n.d.). Old Deluder Satan Law of 1647. Retrieved from http://www.mass.gov/courts/docs/lawlib/docs/deludersatan.pdf

Millard, M. (2015). State funding mechanisms for English language learners. Retrieved from https://www.ecs.org/clearinghouse/01/16/94/11694.pdf

Millard, M., & Aragon, S. (2015). State funding for students with disabilities. Retrieved from https://www.ecs.org/clearinghouse/01/19/47/11947.pdf

Minnesota Legislative Reference Library, Staff. (July, 2017). Minnesota issues resource guides: Charter schools. Retrieved from https://www.leg.state.mn.us/lrl/guides/guides?issue=charter

Moe, T. M. (2011). *Special interest: The rise of teachers unions and America's public schools*. Washington, DC: Brookings Institute Press.

Nathan, R. P., & Gais, T. L. (2001). Is devolution working? Federal and state roles in welfare. *The Brookings Review, 19*(3), 25–29.

National Center for Education Statistics. (2017). Arts education policies by state, 2017. Retrieved from https://nces.ed.gov/programs/statereform/tab2_18.asp

National Center on Education and the Economy. (2017). Finland: System and school organization. Retrieved from http://ncee.org/what-we-do/center-on-international-education-benchmarking/top-performing-countries/finland-overview/finland-system-and-school-organization/

National Commission on Excellence in Education (1983). A nation at risk. Retrieved from https://www2.ed.gov/pubs/NatAtRisk/risk.html

National Council on Teacher Quality. (2015). *2015 State teacher policy yearbook: National summary*. Washington, DC: Author. Retrieved from http://www.nctq.org/dmsView/2015_State_Teacher_Policy_Yearbook_National_Summary_NCTQ_Report

National Women's History Museum. (n.d.). National Women's History Museum presents: The history of women and education. Retrieved from https://www.nwhm.org/online-exhibits/education/Timeline.htm

New Jersey v. T.L.O., 469 U.S. 325 (1985).

Orfield, G. Ee, J. Frankenberg, E., & Siegel-Hawley, G. (2016). "Brown" at 62: School segregation by race, poverty and state. Retrieved from https://eric.ed.gov/?q=segregation&ft=on&id=ED565900

Organisation of Economic Co-Operation and Development. (2013). Education policy outlook Finland. Retrieved from http://www.oecd.org/edu/EDUCATION%20POLICY%20OUTLOOK%20FINLAND_EN.pdf

Organisation of Economic Co-Operation and Development. (2015). Education policy outlook 2015: Making reforms happen. Retrieved from http://www.oecd.org/edu/highlightsfinland.htm

Osgood, R. L. (2008). *The history of special education: A struggle for equality in American public schools*. Westport, CT: Praeger.

Partanen, A. (2011). What Americans keep ignoring about Finland's school success. *The Atlantic, 29*. Retrieved from https://www.theatlantic.com/national/archive/2011/12/what-americans-keep-ignoring-about-finlands-school-success/250564/

Peak, C. (2019, January 22). School suspensions drop, but still unequal. *New Haven Independent*. Retrieved from https://www.newhavenindependent.org/index.php/archives/entry/school_suspension_disparity/

Plessy v. Ferguson, 163 U.S. 537 (1896).

Prothero, A. (2016). Charter schools aren't good for blacks, civil rights groups say. *EdWeek*. Retrieved from http://www

.edweek.org/ew/articles/2016/08/31/charter-schools-arent-good-for-blacks-civil.html

Prucha, F. P. (1973). *Americanizing the American Indians.* Cambridge, MA: Harvard University.

Rhodes, J. (2012). *An education in politics.* Cornell, NY: Cornell University Press.

San Antonio Indep. Sch. Dist. v. Rodriguez, 411 U.S. 1 (1973).

Sanchez, C. (2017). Just what IS a charter school anyway? *NPR.* Retrieved from http://www.npr.org/sections/ed/2017/03/01/511446388/just-what-is-a-charter-school-anyway.

Smole, D. P. (2005). *Funding for public charter school facilities: Federal policy under the ESEA.* Retrieved from http://www.oswego.edu/~ruddy/Educational%20Policy/CRS%20Reports/Charter%20School-Funding.pdf

Stout. v. Board of Education of Jefferson County, U.S. Dt. Ct, S. Dt. (1971).

Strauss, V. (2017, March). What the public isn't told about high-performing charter schools in Arizona. *The Washington Post.* Retrieved from https://www.washingtonpost.com/news/answer-sheet/wp/2017/03/30/what-the-public-doesnt-know-about-high-performing-charter-schools-in-arizona/?utm_term=.c4941e59dc54

Tiede, R. (2016). IDEA school funding bills are in detention. *Politifact.* Retrieved from http://www.politifact.com/truth-o-meter/promises/obameter/promise/89/fully-fund-the-individuals-with-disabilities-educa/

Turner, C. (2016). School vouchers 101: What they are, how they work—and do they work? *NPR.* Retrieved from https://www.npr.org/sections/ed/2016/12/07/504451460/school-choice-101-what-it-is-how-it-works-and-does-it-work

U.S. Department of Education. (2009). Guidance on standards, assessments, and accountability. Retrieved from https://www2.ed.gov/policy/elsec/guid/standardsassessment/guidance_pg5.html

U.S. Department of Education. (2010). An overview of the U.S. Department of Education. Retrieved from https://www2.ed.gov/about/overview/focus/what_pg2.html

U.S. Department of Education. (2015). Fiscal year 2016 budget summary and background information. Retrieved from http://www2.ed.gov/about/overview/budget/budget16/summary/16summary.pdf

U.S. Department of Education. (n.d.a). Every Student Succeeds Act (ESSA). Retrieved from https://www.ed.gov/essa?src=rn

U.S. Department of Education. (n.d.b). Laws and guidance. Retrieved from https://www2.ed.gov/policy/landing.jhtml

U.S. Department of Health and Human Services. (1972). A common thread of service: A history of the Department of Health, Education, and Welfare. Retrieved from https://aspe.hhs.gov/report/common-thread-service/history-department-health-education-and-welfare

Veronia School District v. Acton, 515 US 646 (1995).

Vieux, A. (2014). Do not count them out just yet: Assessing the impact of religious conservatives on charter school regulations. *Social Science Quarterly, 95*(2), 411–424.

Ward v. Flood, 48 Cal. 36 (1874).

Weinberg, L. D. (2009). Religious charter schools: Gaining ground yet still undefined. *Journal of Research on Christian Education, 18*(3), 290–302.

Wilbur Joseph Cohen obituary. (1987, May 19). *The Washington Post,* p. A19.

CHAPTER 8

American Association of State Colleges and Universities. (2018). Top 10 higher education state policy issues for 2018. Retrieved from http://www.aascu.org/policy/publications/policy-matters/Top10Issues2018.pdf

American Association of University Professors. (2017). Trends in the academic labor force, 1975–2015. Retrieved from https://www.aaup.org/sites/default/files/Academic_Labor_Force_Trends_1975-2015.pdf

American Council on Education. (2018). Renewing the Higher Education Act: Resources for students and institutions. Retrieved from https://www.acenet.edu/Pages/Renewing-the-Higher-Education-Act.aspx

American Immigration Council. (2012). Who and where the DREAMers are, revised estimates: A demographic profile of immigrants who might benefit from the Obama Administration's Deferred Action Initiative. Retrieved from https://www.americanimmigrationcouncil.org/research/who-and-where-dreamers-are-revised-estimates

American Indian Higher Education Consortium. (n.d.). About AIHEC. Retrieved from http://www.aihec.org/who-we-are/index.htm#

Anderson, N. (2018, October 15). Harvard admissions trial opens with university accused of bias against Asian Americans. *The Washington Post.* Retrieved from https://www.washingtonpost.com/education/2018/10/15/harvard-admissions-goes-trial-university-faces-claim-bias-against-asian-americans/

Barr, B. (2014). Identifying and addressing the mental health needs of online students in higher education. *Online Journal of Distance Learning Administration, 17*(2). Retrieved from https://eric.ed.gov/?id=EJ1036730

Bendlin, S. S. (2015). Cocktails on campus: Are libations a liability? *Suffolk University Law Review, 48*, 67–108.

Bourdon, J. L., Moore, A. A., Long, E. C., Kendler, K. S., & Dick, D. M. (2018). The relationship between on-campus service utilization and common mental health concerns in undergraduate college students. *Psychological Services*. https://doi.org/10.1037/ser0000296.supp

GI Bill extended to Korea veterans (1952). In CQ almanac 1952 (7th ed.). Washington, DC: CQ Press. Retrieved from https://library.cqpress.com/cqalmanac/document.php?id=cqal52-1378844

Center for the Analysis of Postsecondary Education and Employment. (2018). For-profit colleges by the numbers. Retrieved from https://capseecenter.org/research/by-the-numbers/for-profit-college-infographic/

Cheyney University of Pennsylvania. (n.d.). About CU. Retrieved from https://www.cheyney.edu/about-cheyney-university/

Columbia School of Social Work. (n.d.). About. Retrieved from https://socialwork.columbia.edu/about/historical-timeline/

Community College Research Center. (n.d.). Community college FAQs. Retrieved from https://ccrc.tc.columbia.edu/Community-College-FAQs.html

Council on Social Work Education. (2017). 2017 statistics on social work education in the United States: Summary of the CSWE Annual Survey of Social Work Programs. Retrieved from https://www.cswe.org/CMSPages/GetFile.aspx?guid=44f2c1de-65bc-41fb-be38-f05a5abae96d

Data Quality Campaign. (2016). Student data privacy legislation: A summary of 2016 state legislation. Retrieved from https://2pido73em67o3eytaq1cp8au-wpengine.netdna-ssl.com/wp-content/uploads/2016/09/DQC-Legislative-summary-09302016.pdf

DeMatteo, D., Galloway, M., Arnold, S., & Patel, U. (2015). Sexual assault on college campuses: A 50-state survey of criminal sexual assault statutes and their relevance to campus sexual assault. *Psychology, Public Policy, and Law, 21*(3), 227–238. doi:10.1037/law0000055

Dorn, C. (2017). "Literary institutions are founded and endowed for the common good": The liberal professions in New England. In *For the Common Good: A New History of Higher Education in America* (pp. 15–29). Ithaca, NY: Cornell University Press. Retrieved from http://www.jstor.org/stable/10.7591/j.ctt1qv5qvw.5

Dortch, A. (2018). *The Post-9/11 GI Bill: A primer.* Retrieved from Congressional Research Service website https://fas.org/sgp/crs/misc/R42755.pdf

Drury, R. L. (2003). Community colleges in America: A historical perspective. *Inquiry, 8*(1), n1.

Fain, P. (2014, September 4). Gambling on the lottery. *Inside Higher Ed.* Retrieved from https://www.insidehighered.com/news/2014/09/04/report-unintended-consequences-lottery-based-scholarships-and-how-fix-them

Federal Register. (2014). Violence Against Women Act. Retrieved from https://www.federalregister.gov/documents/2014/10/20/2014-24284/violence-against-women-act

Flaherty, C. (2018, October 26). Grad students' 'Fight for $15.' *Inside Higher Ed.* Retrieved from https://www.insidehighered.com/news/2018/10/26/graduate-student-assistants-campuses-across-us-are-pushing-15-hour-what-they-call

Frawley, J., Larkin, S., & Smith, J. A. (Eds.). (2017). *Indigenous pathways, transitions and participation in higher education: From policy to practice*. Singapore: Springer.

Gallaudet University. (n.d.). History of Gallaudet University. Retrieved from https://www.gallaudet.edu/about/history-and-traditions

Gross, J. P. (2015, November 2). Introduction: Reauthorization: An opportunity for substantive change in how students pay for college. *Journal of Student Financial Aid, 45*(3), 1–6.

Hannah, S. B. (1996). The Higher Education Act of 1992: Skills, constraints, and the politics of higher education. *Journal of Higher Education, 67*(5), 498–527. doi:10.2307/2943866

Harvard University. (n.d.). History. Retrieved from https://www.harvard.edu/about-harvard/harvard-glance/history

Higher Ed Jobs. (2018). Higher education employment report, Q1 2018. Retrieved from https://www.higheredjobs.com/documents/HEJ_Employment_Report_2018_Q1.pdf

Institute for Women's Policy Research. (2018). Understanding the new college majority: The demographic and financial characteristics of independent students and their post-secondary outcomes. Retrieved from https://iwpr.org/wp-content/uploads/2018/02/C462_Understanding-the-New-College-Majority_final.pdf

Johnson, D. (1986, March. 4). Yale's limit on Jewish enrollment lasted until the early 1960's: book says. *The New York Times.* Retrieved from https://www.nytimes.com/1986/03/04/nyregion/yale-s-limit-on-jewish-enrollment-lasted-until-early-1960-s-book-says.html

Jones, M. (2018, April 10). After Virginia Tech shooting, gun violence still claims victims on college campuses. *Collegiate Times.* Retrieved from http://www.collegiatetimes.com/news/after-virginia-tech-shooting-gun-violence-still-claims-victims-on/article_4c27a5f2-3a98-11e8-9165-4f568030151b.html

Kessler R. C., Berglund P., Demler, O., Jin, R., Merikangas, K. R., & Walters, E. E. (2005). Lifetime prevalence and age-of-onset distributions of *DSM-IV* disorders in the National

Comorbidity Survey Replication. *Archives of General Psychiatry, 62*(6), 593–602. doi:10.1001/archpsyc.62.6.593

Kohlbrenner, B. (1961). Religion and higher education: An historical perspective. *History of Education Quarterly, 1*(2), 45–56. doi:10.2307/367639

Lederman, D. (2018, January 5). Who is studying online (and where). *Inside Higher Ed*. Retrieved from https://www.insidehighered.com/digital-learning/article/2018/01/05/new-us-data-show-continued-growth-college-students-studying

Library of Congress. (n.d.). Primary documents in American history: Morrill Act. Retrieved from https://www.loc.gov/rr/program/bib/ourdocs/morrill.html

Lincoln University. (n.d.). About. Retrieved from https://www.lincoln.edu/about

Mattila, J. P. (1978). G.I. Bill benefits and enrollments: How did Vietnam veterans fare? *Social Science Quarterly, 59*(3), 535–545.

McKensie, L. (2018, April 23). The 100K club. *Inside Higher Ed*. Retrieved from https://www.insidehighered.com/news/2018/04/23/nonprofits-poised-unseat-u-phoenix-largest-online-university

National Center for Education Statistics. (2016). Table 306.10: Total fall enrollment in degree-granting postsecondary institutions, by level of enrollment, sex, attendance status, and race/ethnicity of student: Selected years, 1976 through 2016. Retrieved from https://nces.ed.gov/programs/digest/d17/tables/dt17_306.10.asp?current=yes

National Center for Education Statistics. (2018a). Fast facts: College crime. Retrieved from https://nces.ed.gov/fastfacts/display.asp?id=804

National Center for Education Statistics. (2018b). Undergraduate retention and graduation rates. Retrieved from https://nces.ed.gov/programs/coe/indicator_ctr.asp

National Conference of State Legislatures. (2018). Guns on campus: An overview. Retrieved from http://www.ncsl.org/research/education/guns-on-campus-overview.aspx

National Immigration Law Center. (2017). Dream Act 2017: Summary and answers to frequently asked questions. Retrieved from https://www.nilc.org/issues/immigration-reform-and-executive-actions/dream-act-2017-summary-and-faq/

National Immigration Law Center. (2018). Status of current DACA legislation. Retrieved from https://www.nilc.org/issues/daca/status-current-daca-litigation/

National Student Clearinghouse Research Center. (2018). Snapshot report: First-year persistence and retention. Retrieved from https://nscresearchcenter.org/wp-content/uploads/SnapshotReport33.pdf

Organisation for Economic Cooperation and Development. (2018). Education at a glance 2018: OECD indicators. Paris, France: Authors. https://doi.org/10.1787/eag-2018-en

PennAHEAD. (n.d.). College promise programs. Retrieved from http://ahead-penn.org/creating-knowledge/college-promise

Pew Charitable Trusts. (2015). Federal and state funding of higher education. Retrieved from https://www.pewtrusts.org/-/media/assets/2015/06/federal_state_funding_higher_education_final.pdf

Phillips, K. (2017, October 31). University of Utah student shot and killed in 'senseless, random act of violence,' officials say. *The Washington Post*. Retrieved from https://www.washingtonpost.com/news/grade-point/wp/2017/10/31/university-of-utah-student-shot-and-killed-in-senseless-random-act-of-violence-officials-say/?utm_term=.5be375514997

U.S. Department of Education, Student Privacy Policy Office. (n.d.). Student privacy 101: Student privacy at the U.S. Department of Education. Retrieved from https://studentprivacy.ed.gov/?src=fpco

Rosenboom, L., & Blagg, K. (2018, January). Disconnected from higher education: How geography and internet speed limit access to higher education. Retrieved from https://www.urban.org/sites/default/files/publication/96191/disconnected_from_higher_education_1.pdf

Salem College. (n.d.). About Salem. Retrieved from https://www.salem.edu/about

Saulny, S., & Davey, M. (2008, February 15). Gunman slays 6 at N. Illinois University. *The New York Times*. Retrieved from https://www.nytimes.com/2008/02/15/us/15shoot.html

Schreiber, E. (1973). Opposition to the Vietnam War among American university students and faculty. *British Journal of Sociology, 24*(3), 288–302. doi:10.2307/588233

Senate Committee on Labor and Public Welfare. (1969). *Indian education: A national tragedy—A national challenge. 1969 Report of the Committee on Labor and Public Welfare, United States Senate, made by its Special Subcommittee on Indian Education*. Washington, DC: Congress.

Sloan, J. J., Fisher, B. S., & Cullen, F. T. (1997). Assessing the Student Right-to-Know and Campus Security Act of 1990: An analysis of the victim reporting practices of college and university students. *Crime & Delinquency, 43*(2), 148–168.

Steinberg, S. (1971, Sep.). How Jewish quotas began. *Commentary*. Retrieved from https://www.commentarymagazine.com/articles/how-jewish-quotas-began/

Strohush, V., & Wanner, J. (2015). College degree for everyone? *Advances in Economic Research, 21*(3), 261–273.

Student Aid Alliance. (n.d.). Save student aid! Retrieved from https://studentaidalliance.org/

Tennessee Promise. (n.d.). About. Retrieved from http://tnpromise.gov/about.shtml

Tierney, W. G. (2011). Too big to fail: The role of for-profit colleges and universities in American higher education. *Change: The Magazine of Higher Learning, 43*(6), 27–32.

Turner J. C., Leno E. V., & Keller A. (2013). Causes of mortality among American college students: A pilot study. *Journal of College Student Psychotherapy, 27*(1), 31–42. doi:10.1080/87568225.2013.739022.

U.S. Department of Education, Office of Civil Rights. (1991). Historically Black Colleges and Universities and higher education desegregation. Retrieved from https://www2.ed.gov/about/offices/list/ocr/docs/hq9511.html

U.S. Department of Education. (2017). Campus security. Retrieved from https://www2.ed.gov/admins/lead/safety/campus.html

U.S. Department of Education. (n.d.). The database of accredited postsecondary institutions and programs. Retrieved from https://ope.ed.gov/accreditation/

U.S. Department of Health and Human Services. (1972). A common thread of service: A history of the Department of Health, Education, and Welfare. Retrieved from https://aspe.hhs.gov/report/common-thread-service/history-department-health-education-and-welfare

The College of William & Mary. (n.d.). History & traditions. Retrieved from https://www.wm.edu/about/history/index.php

Wire, S. D. (2017, September 17). The Dream Act came out of California 16 years ago. It's still the bill Democrats want to be a model for DACA's replacement. *Los Angeles Times*. Retrieved from http://www.latimes.com/politics/la-pol-ca-dreamers-california-daca-20170917-story.html

Yosso, T. J., Parker, L., Solórzano, D. G., & Lynn, M. (2004). Chapter 1: From Jim Crow to affirmative action and back again: A critical race discussion of racialized rationales and access to higher education. *Review of Research in Education, 28*(1), 1–25. https://doi.org/10.3102/0091732X028001001

CHAPTER 9

Baldwin v. Foxx, No. 0120133080, 2015 WL 4397641 (E.E.O.C. July 15, 2015). Retrieved from https://www.eeoc.gov/decisions/0120133080.pdf

Bassett, J. (1997). The Pullman Strike of 1894. *OAH Magazine of History, 11*(2), 34–41.

Bernstein, J. (2002). The living wage movement: Viewpoints. [Commentary]. Retrieved from https://www.epi.org/publication/webfeatures_viewpoints_lw_movement/

Boyer, P. (1978). *Urban masses and moral order in America 1820–1920*. Cambridge, MA: Harvard University Press.

Bradley, D. H. (2017). *The federal minimum wage: In brief.* Retrieved from Congressional Research Service website https://fas.org/sgp/crs/misc/R43089.pdf

Bradley, D. H. (2018). *State minimum wages: An overview.* Retrieved from Congressional Research Service website https://fas.org/sgp/crs/misc/R43792.pdf

Bureau of Labor Statistics. (2015). How the government measures unemployment. Retrieved from https://www.bls.gov/cps/cps_htgm.htm

Bureau of Labor Statistics. (2017). Characteristics of minimum wage workers, 2016. Retrieved from https://www.bls.gov/opub/reports/minimum-wage/2016/home.htm

Bureau of Labor Statistics. (2018a). Employment, hours, and earnings from the Current Employment Statistics Survey (National). Retrieved from https://www.bls.gov/ces/

Bureau of Labor Statistics. (2018b). Labor force characteristics. Retrieved from https://www.bls.gov/cps/lfcharacteristics.htm#discouraged

Carson, J. L., & Kleinerman, B.A. (2002). A switch in time saves nine: Institutions, strategic actors, and FDR's court-packing plan. *Public Choice, 113*(304), 301–324.

Civil Rights Act of 1964, Pub. L. 88-352, 78 Stat. 241 (1964).

Dahlberg, S. L. (2012). "Doe not forget me": Richard Frethorne, indentured servitude, and the English Poor Law of 1601. *Early American Literature, 47*(1), 1–30.

DeSilver, D. (2017). 5 facts about the minimum wage. Retrieved from http://www.pewresearch.org/fact-tank/2017/01/04/5-facts-about-the-minimum-wage/

Devinatz, V. (2013). Organizing workfare workers as contingent employees: Lessons from the New York City 'Work Experience Program' Worker Unionization Campaign, 199–1997. *Employee Responsibilities & Rights Journal, 25*(1), 1–21.

DeWitt, L. (1996). Research note #1: Origins of the three-legged stool metaphor for Social Security. Retrieved from https://www.ssa.gov/history/stool.html

DiNitto, D. M. (2011). *Social welfare: Politics and public policy* (7th ed.). Boston, MA: Allyn & Bacon.

Directive 2003/88/EC of the European Parliament and of the Council of 4 November 2003 Concerning Certain Aspects of the Organisation of Working Time. Retrieved from http://eur-lex.europa.eu/legal-content/EN/TXT/PDF/?uri=CELEX:32003L0088&from=EN

Equal Employment Opportunity Commission. (n.d.a). Filing a charge. Retrieved from https://www.eeoc.gov/employees/charge.cfm

Equal Employment Opportunity Commission. (n.d.b). Pre 1965: Events leading to the creation of the EEOC. Retrieved from https://www.eeoc.gov/eeoc/history/35th/pre1965/index.html

European Commission. (2017). Report on the implementation by Member States of Directive 2003/88/EC concerning certain aspects of the organisation of working time. Retrieved from https://eur-lex.europa.eu/legal-content/EN/TXT/PDF/?uri=CELEX:52017DC0254&from=EN

European Commission. (n.d.). Working conditions: Working Time Directive. Retrieved from http://ec.europa.eu/social/main.jsp?catId=706&langId=en&intPageId=205

Fowler, T., & Smith, A. (2015). *Survey of US economists on a $15 federal minimum wage*. Durham, NH: Survey Center University of New Hampshire.

Freeman, R. (2005). Fighting for other folks' wages: The logic and illogic of living wage campaigns. *Industrial Relations, 44*(1), 14–31.

Ginsburg, H. L., Ayers, B., & Zaccone, J. (2018). Employment statistics: Let's tell the whole story. Retrieved from https://njfac.org/index.php/us4/

Glasmier, A. (2018). Living wage calculation for San Francisco County, California. Retrieved from http://livingwage.mit.edu/counties/06075

Goldberg, C. (2001). Harvard sit-in over pay ends with deal to re-examine policies. *The New York Times*. p. A19. Retrieved from https://www.nytimes.com/2001/05/09/us/harvard-sit-in-over-pay-ends-with-deal-to-re-examine-policies.html

Golden, L. (2016). *Still falling short on hours and pay: Part-time work becoming new normal*. Washington, DC: Economic Policy Institute. Retrieved from https://ssrn.com/abstract=2881673 or http://dx.doi.org/10.2139/ssrn.2881673

Graden, D. T. (2016). The United States and the transatlantic slave trade to the Americas, 1776–1867. *American Historical Review, 123*(1), 192–193.

Green, H. (2012). *The company town: The industrial Edens and satanic mills that shaped the American economy*. New York, NY: Basic Books.

Grossman, J. (1978). Fair Labor Standards Act of 1938: Maximum struggle for a minimum wage. *Monthly Labor Review, 101*(6), 22–30.

Grossman, J. (2015). Fair Labor Standards Act of 1938: Maximum struggle for a minimum wage. Retrieved from https://www.dol.gov/general/aboutdol/history/flsa1938

Hegewisch, A., Childers, C., & Hartmann, H. (2019). *Women, automation, and the future of work*. Washington, DC: Institute for Women's Policy Research. Retrieved from https://iwpr.org/publications/women-automation-future-of-work/

Henly, J. R., & Lambert, S. J. (2014). Unpredictable work timing in retail jobs: Implications for employee work-life conflict. *International Labor Relations Review, 67*(3), 986–1016.

Hewlett, S. A., & Sumberg, K. (2011). The cost of closeted employees. *Harvard Business Review*. Retrieved from https://hbr.org/2011/07/the-cost-of-closeted-employees

Internal Revenue Service. (2018a). Choosing a retirement plan: 403(b) Tax-sheltered annuity plan. Retrieved from https://www.irs.gov/retirement-plans/choosing-a-retirement-plan-403b-tax-sheltered-annuity-plan

Internal Revenue Service. (2018b). 401(k) plans. Retrieved from https://www.irs.gov/retirement-plans/401k-plans

Internal Revenue Service. (2019). IRC 403(b) tax-sheltered annuity plans. Retrieved from https://www.irs.gov/retirement-plans/irc-403b-tax-sheltered-annuity-plans

Jennings, J., & Nagel, J. C. (2019). *Federal workforce statistics sources: OPM and OMB*. Retrieved from Congressional Research Service website https://fas.org/sgp/crs/misc/R43590.pdf

Kantor, J. (2014, August 13). Working anything but 9 to 5. The *New York Times*. Retrieved from https://www.nytimes.com/interactive/2014/08/13/us/starbucks-workers-scheduling-hours.html

Karin, M. (2009). Time off for military families: An emerging case study in a time of war . . . and the tipping point for future laws supporting work-life balance? *Rutgers Law Record, 33*, 46–64.

Katzenelson, I. (2005). *When affirmative action was white: An untold history of racial inequity in twentieth-century America*. New York, NY: W.W. Norton.

Kennedy, J. F. (1963). Radio and television report to the American people on civil rights, June 11, 1963. Retrieved from https://www.jfklibrary.org/Research/Research-Aids/JFK-Speeches/Civil-Rights-Radio-and-Television-Report_19630611.aspx

Keyes, A. (2010). Civil rights activist Dorothy Height dies. *NPR*. Retrieved from https://www.npr.org/templates/story/story.php?storyId=126128076

Khatib, M. (2017, January 26). *Jeremy Rifkin - The end of work* [Video file]. Retrieved from https://www.youtube.com/watch?v=c-PYIfGd9hM

Lambert, S. J., Fugiel, P. J., & Henly, J. R. (2014). *Schedule unpredictability among early career workers in the US labor market: A national snapshot*. Chicago, IL: University of Chicago, *EINet Employment Instability, Family Well-being, and Social Policy Network*. Retrieved from https://ssa.uchicago.edu/sites/default/files/uploads/lambert.fugiel.henly_.precarious_work_schedules.august2014_0.pdf.

Ledbetter v. Goodyear Tire & Rubber Company, 550 U.S. 618 (2007).

Lefrançois, M., Messing, K., & Saint-Charles, J. (2017). Time control, job execution and information access: Work/family strategies in the context of low-wage work and 24/7 schedules. *Community, Work & Family, 20*(5), 600–622.

Li, Z. (2019). *The Social Security retirement age*. Retrieved from Congressional Research Service website https://fas.org/sgp/crs/misc/R44670.pdf

Library of Congress. (n.d.). Slavery and indentured servitude. Retrieved from https://memory.loc.gov/ammem/awhhtml/awlaw3/slavery.html

Lurie, H. L. (1934). The New Deal program: Summary and appraisal. *The Annals of the American Academy of Political and Social Science, 176*, 172–183.

Martin, S. B. (2009). FMLA protection recently expanded to military families: Qualifying exigency and servicemember family leave. *Compensation and Benefits Review, 41*, 43–51.

Mayer, G., Collins, B., & Bradley, D. (2013). *The Fair Labor Standards Act (FLSA): An overview*. Washington, DC: Congressional Research Service.

McConnell, S. L. B. (2014). WPA for today: Can the US afford economic recovery? *Journal of Economic Issues, 48*(2), 541–550.

McEvoy, A. F. (1995). The Triangle Shirtwaist Factory fire of 1911: Social change, industrial accidents, and the evolution of common-sense causality. *Law and Social Inquiry 20*(2), 621–654.

McGeehan, P. (2015, July 23). New York plans $15 an hour minimum wage for fast food workers. *The New York Times*. Retrieved from https://www.nytimes.com/2015/07/23/nyregion/new-york-minimum-wage-fast-food-workers.html

Mejia, T. (2015, March 19). Facts about women and the minimum wage. Retrieved from https://blog.dol.gov/2015/03/19/facts-about-women-and-the-minimum-wage

Minter, S. (2019, May 2). Three LGBTQ job discrimination cases could have wider consequences for everyone. *Los Angeles Times*. Retrieved from https://www.latimes.com/opinion/op-ed/la-oe-minter-supreme-court-cases-lgbt-gay-job-discrimination-20190502-story.html

National Conference of State Legislatures. (2019). State minimum wages: 2019 minimum wages by states. Retrieved from http://www.ncsl.org/research/labor-and-employment/state-minimum-wage-chart.aspx

National Labor Relations Board. (2015). National Labor Relations Act. Retrieved from https://www.nlrb.gov/resources/national-labor-relations-act

National Labor Relations Board. (n.d.-a). The NLRB process. Retrieved from https://www.nlrb.gov/resources/nlrb-process

National Labor Relations Board. (n.d.-b). Our history. Retrieved from https://www.nlrb.gov/who-we-are/our-history

National Women's Law Center. (2013). Lilly Ledbetter Fair Pay Act. Retrieved from https://nwlc.org/resources/lilly-ledbetter-fair-pay-act/

New York City Government. (n.d.). Fair Work Week Law: Information and assistance. Retrieved from http://www1.nyc.gov/nyc-resources/service/7344/fair-workweek-law-information-and-assistance

Opfer, C. (2018, October 24). DOJ: Businesses can discriminate against transgender workers. *Bloomberg Law*. Retrieved from https://news.bloomberglaw.com/daily-labor-report/doj-businesses-can-discriminate-against-transgender-workers-1

Out & Equal. (2019). 2017 Workplace equality fact sheet. Retrieved from http://outandequal.org/2017-workplace-equality-fact-sheet/

Palley, E., & Shdaimah, C.S. (2014). *In our hands: The struggle for U.S. child care policy*. New York, NY: New York University Press.

Pavetti, L. (2016). Work requirements don't cut poverty, evidence shows. *Center for Budget and Policy Priorities*. Retrieved from https://www.cbpp.org/research/poverty-and-inequality/work-requirements-dont-cut-poverty-evidence-shows

PBS Learning Media. (n.d.). Civil rights: Community organizing. Retrieved from https://cptv.pbslearningmedia.org/collection/people comorg/

Pew Charitable Trusts. (2016). Employer-sponsored retirement plan access, uptake, and savings: Workers report barriers and opportunities. Retrieved from http://www.pewtrusts.org/~/media/assets/2016/09/employersponsoredretirementplanaccessuptakeandsavings.pdf

Pomper, K., Blank, H., Campbell, N. D., & Schulman, K. (2004). *Be all that you can be: lessons from the military for improving our nation's child care system*. Washington, DC: National Women's Law Center. Retrieved from http://www.nwlc.org/sites/default/files/pdfs/BeAllThatWeCanBe_2004FollowUp.pdf

Reading, D. C. (1973). New Deal activity and the states, 1933 to 1939. *Journal of Economic History, 33*(4), 792–810.

Reiss, M. (2019, May 25). Gov. Lamont signs $15 an hour minimum wage bill. *NBC Connecticut*. Retrieved from https://www.nbcconnecticut.com/news/local/Gov-Lamont-Expected-to-Sign-15-an-Hour-Minimum-Wage-Bill-510423241.html

Romig, K. (2018). *Social Security lifts more Americans above poverty than any other program*. Washington, DC: Center for Budget and Policy Priorities. Retrieved from https://www.cbpp.org/research/social-security/social-security-keeps-22-million-americans-out-of-poverty-a-state-by-state

Samuel, H. D. (2000). Troubled passage: The labor movement and the Fair Labor Standards Act. *Monthly Labor Review, 123*(12), 32–37.

Sangupta, I., Reno, V., & Burton, J. F. (2007). *Workers' compensation: Benefits, coverage, and costs*. Washington, DC: National Academy of Social Insurance. Retrieved from https://www.nasi.org/sites/default/files/research/NASI_Workers_Comp_2005_Full_Report.pdf

Scanlon, E., & Harding, S. (2005). Social work and labor unions: Historical and contemporary alliances. *Journal of Community Practice, 31*(1), 9–30.

Schwartz, B. F. (1984). *The Civil Works Administration, 1984–1984: The business of emergency employment in the New Deal*. Princeton, NJ: Princeton University Press.

Skocpol, T. (1992). *Protecting soldiers and mothers: The political origins of social policy in the United States*. Boston, MA: Harvard University Press.

Social Security Administration, Office of the Chief Actuary. (2019a). Summary of provisions that would change the social security program. Retrieved from https://www.ssa.gov/OACT/solvency/provisions/summary.pdf

Social Security Administration, Office of the Chief Actuary. (2019b). The 2019 annual report of the Board of Trustees of the Federal Old-Age and Survivors Insurance and Federal Disability Insurance Trust Funds. Retrieved from https://www.ssa.gov/oact/TR/2019/tr2019.pdf

Social Security Administration. (2017). Understanding the benefits. Retrieved from https://www.ssa.gov/pubs/EN-05-10024.pdf

Social Security Administration. (2018). Retirement benefits. Retrieved from https://www.ssa.gov/pubs/EN-05-10035.pdf

Tomlins, C. (2010). *Freedom bound: Law, labor, and civic identity in colonizing English America 1580–1865*. Cambridge, UK: Cambridge University Press.

U.S. Department of Justice, Civil Rights Division. (n.d.). Information and technical assistance on the Americans with Disabilities Act. Retrieved from https://www.ada.gov/ada_title_I.htm

U.S. Department of Labor, Employment and Training Administration. (2016a). The Workforce Innovation and Opportunity Act final rules: A detailed look. Retrieved from https://www.doleta.gov/WIOA/Docs/Final-Rules-A-Detailed-Look-Fact-Sheet.pdf

U.S. Department of Labor, Employment and Training Administration. (2016b). The Workforce Innovation and Opportunity Act final rules: WIOA works for America. Retrieved from https://www.doleta.gov/wioa/Docs/WIOA_Factsheets.pdf.

U.S. Department of Labor Employment and Training Administration. (n.d.). About us. Retrieved from https://www.doleta.gov/etainfo/mission.cfm

U.S. Department of Labor. (n.d.-a). About OSHA. Retrieved from https://www.osha.gov/about.html

U.S. Department of Labor. (n.d.-b). Age discrimination. Retrieved from https://www.dol.gov/general/topic/discrimination/agedisc#lawregs

U.S. Department of Labor. (n.d.-c). Subminimum wage. Retrieved from https://www.dol.gov/

U.S. Department of Labor. (n.d.-d). Types of retirement plans. Retrieved from https://www.dol.gov/general/topic/retirement/typesofplans

U.S. Department of Labor. (n.d.-e). Workers' compensation. Retrieved from https://www.dol.gov/general/topic/workcomp

U.S. Postal Service. (2018). Number of postal employees since 1926. Retrieved from https://about.usps.com/who-we-are/postal-history/employee-since-1926.pdf

Vedder, R., & Gallaway, L. (2002). The minimum wage and poverty among full-time workers. *Journal of Labor Research, 23*(1), 41–49.

Veghte, B. W. (2013). Social Security: Past, present, and future. In M. Reisch (Ed.), *Social policy and social justice* (pp. 308–345). Thousand Oaks, CA: Sage.

Vroman, W., Maag, E., O'Leary, C., & Woodbury, S. (2017). *A comparative analysis of unemployment insurance financing methods*. Washington DC: The Urban Institute. Retrieved from https://www.dol.gov/asp/evaluation/completed-studies/A-Comparative-Analysis-of-Unemployment-Insurance-Financing-Methods-Final-Report.pdf

U.S. Department of Labor, Wage and Hour Division. (2015). History of changes to the minimum wage law. Retrieved from https://www.dol.gov/whd/minwage/coverage.htm

U.S. Department of Labor, Wage and Hour Division. (2016). Handy reference guide to the Fair Labor Standards Act. Retrieved from https://www.dol.gov/whd/regs/compliance/hrg.htm

Whittaker, W. G. (2004). *Child labor in America: History, policy, and legislative issues*. Hauppauge, NY: Nova Science.

Zellman, G. L., Gates, S. M., Moini, J. S., & Suttorp, M. (2009). Meeting family and military needs through military child care. *Armed Forces & Society, 35*(3), 437–459.

CHAPTER 10

Acciai, F., & Firebaugh, G. (2017). Why did life expectancy decline in the United States in 2015? A gender-specific analysis. *Social Science & Medicine, 190*, 174–180.

American Association of Retired Persons. (n.d.-a). About AARP: What guides us. Retrieved from https://www.aarp.org/about-aarp/company/what-guides-us/

American Association of Retired Persons. (n.d.-b). Ethel Percy Andrus: The extraordinary woman who changed America. Retrieved from https://www.aarp.org/about-aarp/history/ethel-percy-andrus-biography/

Beard, R., & Williamson, J.B. (2011). Social policy and the internal dynamics of the senior rights movement. *Journal of Aging Studies 25*, 22–33

Bureau of Labor Statistics. (2019, March 21). *Employment situation of veterans–2018 [Press release]*. Retrieved from https://www.bls.gov/news.release/pdf/vet.pdf

Cahill, S. (2017, December 4). If they don't count us, we don't count. *Public Health Post*. Retrieved from https://www.publichealthpost.org/research/if-they-dont-count-us-we-dont-count/

Centers for Medicare & Medicaid Services. (2019). CMS fast facts. Retrieved from https://www.cms.gov/fastfacts/

Centers for Medicare & Medicaid Services. (n.d.). How is Medicare funded? Retrieved from https://www.medicare.gov/about-us/how-is-medicare-funded.

Clark, G., & Rouse, S. (2018). Providing mental health care for the complex older veteran: Implications for social work practice. *Health & Social Work, 43*(1), 7–14.

Cravey, T., & Mitra, A. (2011). Demographics of the sandwich generation by race and ethnicity in the United States. *Journal of Socio-Economics, 40*(3), 306–311.

Cubanski, J., & Neuman, T. (2017). The facts on Medicare spending and financing. Retrieved from https://www.kff.org/medicare/issue-brief/the-facts-on-medicare-spending-and-financing/

DaSilva, B. (2015). Social Security helps millions of elderly Americans [Blog post]. Retrieved from https://www.cbpp.org/blog/social-security-helps-millions-of-elderly-americans

Davitt, J. K., & Baik, S. (in press). Reducing extreme economic inequality. In *Gerontological Social Work and the Grand Challenges: Focusing on Policy and Practice*. New York, NY: Springer Publishing

Davitt, J. K., Lehning, A. J., Scharlach, A., & Greenfield, E. A. (2015). Sociopolitical and cultural context of emerging community-based models in aging: The Village Initiative. *Public Policy & Aging Report, 25*(1), 15–19.

Davitt, J. K., Madigan, E. A., Rantz, M., & Skemp, L. (2016). Aging in community: Developing a more holistic approach to enhance older adults' well-being. *Research in Gerontological Nursing, 9*(1), 6–13.

Day, C. L. (2017). *AARP: America's largest interest group and its impact*. Denver, CO: Praeger.

Demos, J. (1986). *Past, present, and personal: The family and the life course in American history*. New York, NY: Oxford University Press.

Dewitt, L. (1996). Origins of the three-legged stool metaphor for Social Security. Retrieved from https://www.ssa.gov/history/stool.html

Dunn, B., & Wamsley, B. (2018). Grandfamilies: Characteristics and needs of grandparents raising grandchildren. *Journal of Extension, 56*(5). Retrieved from https://joe.org/joe/2018september/rb2.php

Evans, K. L., Millsteed, J., Richmond, J. E., Falkmer, M., Falkmer, T., & Girdler, S. J. (2016). Working sandwich generation women utilize strategies within and between roles to achieve role balance. *PLoS One, 11*(6), e0157469. doi:10.1371/journal.pone.0157469

Fabbre, V. (2017). Queer aging: Implications for social work practice with lesbian, gay, bisexual, transgender, and queer older adults. *Social Work, 62*(1), 73–76.

Fischer, D. H. (1977). *Growing old in America*. New York, NY: Oxford University Press.

Fitzgerald, K. G., & Caro, F. G. (2014). An overview of age-friendly cities and communities around the world. *Journal of Aging & Social Policy, 26*(1–2), 1–18.

Fredriksen-Goldsen, K. I., Hoy-Ellis, C. P., Goldsen, J., Emlet, C. A., & Hooyman, N. R. (2014). Creating a vision for the future: Key competencies and strategies for culturally competent practice with lesbian, gay, bisexual, and transgender (LGBT) older adults in the health and human services. *Journal of Gerontological Social Work, 57*(2–4), 80–107.

Friedman, S. M., Mulhausen, P., Cleveland, M. L., Coll, P. P., Daniel, K. M., Hayward, A. D., . . . White, H. K. (2019). Healthy aging: American Geriatrics Society white paper executive summary. *Journal of American Geriatrics Society, 67*, 17–20.

Fuller-Thomson, E., Minkler, M., & Driver, D. (1997). A profile of grandparents raising grandchildren in the United States. *Gerontologist, 37*(3), 406–411.

Gerard, J. M., Landry-Meyer, L., & Roe, J. G. (2006). Grandparents raising grandchildren: The role of social support in coping with caregiving challenges. *International Journal of Aging and Human Development, 62*(4), 359–383.

Giarrusso, R., Silverstein, M., & Feng, D. (2000). Psychological costs and benefits of raising grandchildren: Evidence from a national survey of grandparents. In C. B. Cox (Ed.), *To grandmother's house we go and stay: Perspectives on custodial grandparents* (pp. 71–90). New York, NY: Springer.

Gould, C. E., Huh, J. W. T., Brunskill, S. R., McConnell, K., & Tenover, J. L. (2015). Disability and treatment outcomes for anxiety and depression in older veterans. *Clinical Gerontologist, 38*(4), 268–282.

Greenfield, E., Scharlach, A., Lehning, A., Davitt, J., & Graham, C. (2013). A tale of two community initiatives for promoting aging in place: Similarities and differences in the national implementation of NORC programs and villages. *Gerontologist, 53*(6), 928–938.

Greenlee, K. (2017). Why I am opposed to the elimination of the sexual orientation question by the Administration for Community Living. *American Journal of Public Health, 107*(8), 1211–1212.

Halinski, M., Duxbury, L, & Higgins, C. (2018). Working while caring for mom, dad, and junior too: Exploring the impact of employees' caregiving situation on demands, control, and perceived stress. *Journal of Family Issues, 39*(12), 3248–3275.

Hillier, S. M., & Barrow, G. M. (2011). *Aging, the individual, and society* (9th ed.). Belmont, CA: Wadsworth.

Housing Assistance Council. (2016). *Aging veterans in the United States*. Retrieved from http://www.ruralhome.org/storage/documents/publications/rrreports/rrr-aging-veterans.pdf.

Hudson, R. B. (2016). Cumulative advantage and disadvantage: Across the life course, across generations. *Public Policy & Aging Report, 26*(2), 39–41,

Hudson, R., & Gonyea, J. (2012). Baby Boomers and the shifting political construction of old age. *The Gerontologist, 52*, 272–282.

Hughes, M. E., Waite, L. J., LaPierre, T. A., & Luo, Y. (2007). All in the family: The impact of caring for grandchildren on grandparents' health. *Journals of Gerontology Series B: Psychological Sciences & Social Sciences, 62*(2), S108–S119.

Intergenerational Family Services. (2018). Kinship care in the opioid epidemic: The overlooked caregivers of the overlooked victims. Retrieved from https://policylab.chop.edu/blog/kinship-care-opioid-epidemic-overlooked-caregivers-overlooked-victims.

Jendrek, M. P. (1994). Grandparents who parent their grandchildren: Circumstances and decisions. *The Gerontologist, 34*, 206–216.

Jermane Bond, M., & Herman, A. A. (2016). Lagging life expectancy for black men: A public health imperative. *American Journal of Public Health, 106*(7), 1167–1169.

Kaiser Family Foundation. (2017, November 22). An overview of Medicare. Retrieved from https://www.kff.org/medicare/issue-brief/an-overview-of-medicare/

Kelley, S. J., Whitley, D., Sipe, T. A., & Yorker, B. C. (2000). Psychological distress in grandmother kinship care providers: The role of resources, social support, and physical health. *Child Abuse and Neglect, 24*, 311–321.

Kim, K., Lehning, A. J., & Sacco, P. (2018). Analyzing the problem: Disparities in behavioral health care for older adults. In C. Moniz & S. Gorin (Eds.), *Mental health policy: Policy practice for social work*. New York, NY: Taylor & Francis.

Knochel, K. (2010). Marriage, civil unions, or reciprocal beneficiary agreements: What best protects older LGBT people? *Journal of Gay & Lesbian Social Services, 22*(1–2), 22–39.

Kuerbis, A., Sacco, P., Blazer, D. G., & Moore, A. A. (2014). Substance abuse among older adults. *Clinics in Geriatric Medicine, 30*(3), 629–654.

Lee, J. S., Frongillo, E. A., & Olson, C. M. (2005). Understanding targeting from the perspective of program providers in the elderly nutrition program. *Journal of Nutrition for the Elderly, 24*(3), 25–45.

Lee, J. S., Sinnett, S., Bengle, R., Johnson, M. A., & Brown, A. (2011). Unmet needs for the Older Americans Act Nutrition Program. *Journal of Applied Gerontology, 30*(5), 587–606.

Levinson, D. L. (1986). A conception of adult development. *American Psychologist, 41*(1), 3–13.

Lyons, C. L. (2018, August 3). Loneliness and social isolation. *CQ Researcher, 28*, 657–680. Retrieved from http://library.cqpress.com/

Mackenzie, C. (2013). The importance of relational autonomy and capabilities for an ethics of vulnerability. In C. Mackenzie, W. Rogers, & S. Dodds, *Vulnerability: New essays in ethics and feminist philosophy* (pp. 33–59). New York, NY: Oxford University Press.

Marmor, T. R. (2017). *The politics of Medicare*. New York, NY: Routledge.

Miller, D. A. (1981). The 'sandwich' generation: Adult children of the aging. *Social Work, 26*(5), 419–423.

Morabia, A. (2017). AJPH dossier on the erasure of the sexual orientation question from the National Survey of Older Americans Act Participants. *American Journal of Public Health, 107*(8), 1203–1204.

Myles, J. (1988). Postwar capitalism and the extension of Social Security into a retirement wage. In M. Weir, A. S. Orloff, & T. Skocpol (Eds.), *The politics of social policy in the United States* (pp. 265–292). Princeton, NJ: Princeton University Press.

National Association of Social Workers. (2017). Code of ethics. Retrieved from https://www.socialworkers.org/About/Ethics/Code-of-Ethics/Code-of-Ethics-English

National Center for Veterans Analysis and Statistics. (2016). Profile of veterans: 2014. Retrieved from https://www.va.gov/vetdata/docs/SpecialReports/Profile_of_veterans_2013.pdf.

National Resource Center on LGBT Aging. (n.d.). Home. Retrieved from https://www.lgbtagingcenter.org/

Organisation for Economic Cooperation and Development. (2019). *Net pension replacement rates (indicator).* doi:10.1787/4b03f028-en (Accessed on 15 August 2019)

Paz, A., Doron, I., & Tur-Sinai, A. (2018). Gender, aging, and the economics of "active aging": Setting a new research agenda. *Journal of Women & Aging, 30*(3), 184–203.

Peterson, T. L. (2018). Grandparents raising grandchildren in the African American community. *Generations, 42*(3), 30–36.

Ports, K. A., Barnack-Tavlaris, J. L., Syme, M. L., Perera, R. A., & Lafata, J. E. (2014). Sexual health discussions with older adult patients during periodic health exams. *The Journal of Sexual Medicine, 11*(4), 901–908.

Proctor, C. M. (2018, 19 October). Largest associations in Greater D.C. *Business Journals*. Retrieved from https://www.bizjournals.com/washington/subscriber-only/2018/10/19/largest-associations-in-greater-dc.html

Quadagno, J. (1988). From Old-Age Assistance to Supplemental Security Income: The political economy of relief in the South, 1935–1972. In M. Weir, A. S. Orloff, & T. Skocpol (Eds.), *The politics of social policy in the United States* (pp. 235–264). Princeton, NJ: Princeton University Press.

Radel, L., Baldwin, M., Crouse, G., Ghertner, R., & Waters, A. (2018). Substance use, the opioid epidemic, and the child welfare system: Key findings from a mixed methods study. Retrieved from https://aspe.hhs.gov/system/files/pdf/258836/SubstanceUseChildWelfareOverview.pdf

Remig, K., & Sherman, A. (2016). *Social Security keeps 22 million Americans out of poverty: A state-by-state analysis.* Washington, DC: Center for Budget and Policy Priorities. Retrieved from https://www.cbpp.org/research/social-security/social-security-keeps-22-million-americans-out-of-poverty-a-state-by-state

SAGE. (2018). Our story. Retrieved from https://www.sageusa.org/about-us/our-story/

Sands, R. G., & Goldberg-Glen, R. S. (2000). Factors associated with stress among grandparents raising their grandchildren. *Family Relations, 49*, 97–105.

Sanjek, R. (2009). *Gray Panthers*. Philadelphia, PA: University of Pennsylvania Press.

Sanjek, R. (2010). Sustaining a social movement: Gray Panther ideology and tactics. *Journal Aging, Humanities, and the Arts, 4*, 133–144.

Sherwood, R. J., Shimel, H., Stolz, P., & Sherwood, D. (2003). The aging veteran: Re-emergence of trauma issues. *Journal of Gerontological Social Work, 40*(4), 73–86.

Silverstein, M., & Marenco, A. (2001). How Americans enact the grandparent role across the family life course. *Journal of Family Issues, 22*(4), 493–522.

Skocpol, T. (1992). *Protecting soldiers and mothers: The political origins of social policy in the United States.* Boston, MA: Belknap Press of Harvard University Press.

Social Security Administration. (2018). Retirement benefits. Retrieved from https://www.ssa.gov/pubs/EN-05-10035.pdf

Social Security Administration. (n.d.-a). Cost-of-living Adjustment (COLA) information. Retrieved from https://www.ssa.gov/cola/

Social Security Administration. (n.d.-b). President Lyndon B. Johnson. Retrieved from https://www.ssa.gov/history/lbjstmts.html

Solway E., Clark S., Singer D., Kirch M., & Malani P. (2018). Let's talk about sex. Ann Arbor, MI: University of Michigan, Institute for Healthcare Policy & Innovation. Retrieved from http://hdl.handle.net/2027.42/143212

Stone, D. A. (1984). *The disabled state*. London, UK: MacMillan.

Sullivan, J. L., Eisenstein, R., Price, T., Solimeo, S., & Shay, K. (2018). Implementation of the geriatric Patient-Aligned Care Team Model in the Veterans Health Administration (VA). *Journal of the American Board of Family Medicine: JABFM, 31*(3), 456–465.

Trivedi, A. N., Grebla, R. C., Wright, S. M., & Washington, D. L. (2011). Despite improved quality of care in the Veterans Affairs health system, racial disparity persists for important clinical outcomes. *Health Affairs 30*(4), 707–715.

U.S. Census Bureau. (2018, March 13). *Older people projected to outnumber children for the first time in U.S. history.* [Press release] Retrieved from https://www.census.gov/newsroom/press-releases/2018/cb18-41-population-projections.html

U.S. Department of Health and Human Services, Administration for Community Living. (n.d.). Older Americans Act. Retrieved from https://acl.gov/about-acl/authorizing-statutes/older-americans-act

U.S. Department of Veterans Affairs. (2017a). Veterans and military service organizations and state directors of veterans affairs. Retrieved from https://www.va.gov/vso/VSO-Directory.pdf

U.S. Department of Veterans Affairs. (2017b). Veterans: VA benefits for elderly veterans. Retrieved from https://www.benefits.va.gov/persona/veteran-elderly.asp

U.S. Department of Veterans Affairs. (n.d.). Geriatrics and extended care. Retrieved from https://www.va.gov/geriatrics/

Vespa, J. (2018). The graying of America: More older adults than kids by 2035. Retrieved from https://www.census.gov/library/stories/2018/03/graying-america.html

Wiltz, T. (2016, November 2). Why more grandparents are raising children. *Stateline: Pew Charitable Trusts.* Retrieved from https://www.pewtrusts.org/en/research-and-analysis/blogs/stateline/2016/11/02/why-more-grandparents-are-raising-children

Zodikoff, B. D. (2006). Community services for lesbian, gay, bisexual and transgender older adults. In B. Berkman (Ed.), *Handbook of Social Work in Health and Aging* (pp. 569–575). New York, NY: Oxford University Press.

CHAPTER 11

Allen, G. (2018). Cost of U.S. opioid epidemic since 2001 is $1 trillion and climbing. *NPR.* Retrieved from https://www.npr.org/sections/health-shots/2018/02/13/585199746/cost-of-u-s-opioid-epidemic-since-2001-is-1-trillion-and-climbing

Aron-Dine, A., Chaudhry, R., & Broaddus, M. (2018, April 11). Many working people could lose health coverage due to Medicaid work requirements. Retrieved from https://www.cbpp.org/research/health/many-working-people-could-lose-health-coverage-due-to-medicaid-work-requirements

Benen, S. (2017, October 2). GOP senator: Health care is 'a privilege,' not a right. *MSNBC.* Retrieved from http://www.msnbc.com/rachel-maddow-show/gop-senator-health-care-coverage-privilege-not-right

Blendon, R., & Benson, J. M. (2001). American's views on health policy: A fifty-year historical perspective. *Health Affairs, 20*(2). https://doi.org/10.1377/hlthaff.20.2.33

Blumel, M., & Busse, R. (2016). The German health care system, 2015. In E. Mossialos, M. Wenzl, R. Osborn, & D. Sarnak (Eds.), *2015 international profiles of health care systems.* Retrieved from http://web90.opencloud.dssdi.ugm.ac.id/wp-content/uploads/sites/644/2016/11/Countries_-Comparison.pdf

Bozorgmehr, K., & Razum, O. (2015, July 22). Effect of restricting access to health care on health expenditures among asylum-seekers and refugees: A quasi-experimental Study in Germany, 1994–2013. *PLoS One, 10*(7): e0131483. https://doi.org/10.1371/journal.pone.0131483

Butterfield, A. K., Rocha, C. J., & Butterfield, W. H. (2010). *The dynamics of family policy: Analysis and advocacy.* Chicago, IL: Lyceum Books.

Carroll, A. E., & Frakt, A. (2017, September 18). The best health care system in the world: Which one would you pick? *The New York Times.* Retrieved from https://www.nytimes.com/interactive/2017/09/18/upshot/best-health-care-system-country-bracket.html

Center on Budget and Policy Priorities. (2018). A quick guide to SNAP eligibility and benefits. Retrieved from https://www.cbpp.org/research/food-assistance/a-quick-guide-to-snap-eligibility-and-benefits

Centers for Medicare & Medicaid Services. (2018). CMS fast facts. Retrieved from https://www.cms.gov/fastfacts/

Chen, J., Vargas-Bustamante, A., Mortensen, K., & Ortega, A.N. (2016). Racial and ethnic disparities in health care access and utilization under the Affordable Care Act. *Medical Care, 54*(2), 140–146. doi:10.1097/MLR.0000000000000467

Cohen, R. A., Martinez, M. E., & Zammitti, E. P. (2018). Health insurance coverage: Early release of estimates from the National Health Interview Survey, January–March 2018. Retrieved from https://www.cdc.gov/nchs/data/nhis/earlyrelease/Insur201808.pdf

Cooper, D. G. (1987). Save the babies: The passage of a federally supported maternal and infant health act. *UCLA Historical Journal, 8*(2), 25–39. Retrieved from https://cloudfront.escholarship.org/dist/prd/content/qt21w4634t/qt21w4634t.pdf

Council of Economic Advisers. (2017). The underestimated cost of the opioid crisis. Retrieved from https://www.whitehouse.gov/sites/whitehouse.gov/files/images/The%20Underestimated%20Cost%20of%20the%20Opioid%20Crisis.pdf

Cubanski, J., & Neuman, T. (2017). The facts on Medicare spending and financing. Retrieved from https://www.kff

.org/medicare/issue-brief/the-facts-on-medicare-spending-and-financing/

Daschle, T., & Nather, D. (2010). *Getting it done: How Obama and Congress finally broke the stalemate to make way for health care reform*. New York, NY: Thomas Dunne Books, St. Martin's Press.

Florida Department of Children and Families. (n.d.). Licensure and regulation. Retrieved from http://myflfamilies.com/service-programs/substance-abuse/licensure-regulation2

Frayer, L. (2017, April 18). In Portugal, drug use is treated as a medical issue, Not a crime. *NPR*. Retrieved from https://www.npr.org/sections/parallels/2017/04/18/524380027/in-portugal-drug-use-is-treated-as-a-medical-issue-not-a-crime

Gratzer, D. (2006). The cure: How capitalism can save American health care [Remarks]. Retrieved from https://www.heritage.org/health-care-reform/report/the-cure-how-capitalism-can-save-american-health-care

Greenwald, G. (2009, April 2). *Drug decriminalization in Portugal: Lessons for creating fair and successful drug policies*. Washington, DC: *CATO Institute* Retrieved from https://www.cato.org/publications/white-paper/drug-decriminalization-portugal-lessons-creating-fair-successful-drug-policies

Haffajee, R. L., & Mello, M. M. (2017). Drug companies' liability for the opioid epidemic. *New England Journal of Medicine, 377*, 2301–2305. doi:10.1056/NEJMp1710756

Hawk, K. F., Vaca, F. E., & D'Onofrio, G. (2015). Reducing fatal opioid overdose: Prevention, treatment and harm reduction strategies. *The Yale Journal of Biology and Medicine, 88*(3), 235–245.

Healthcare.gov. (n.d.). What Marketplace health insurance plans cover. Retrieved from https://www.healthcare.gov/coverage/what-marketplace-plans-cover/

Healthy People 2020. (n.d.). About Healthy People. Retrieved from https://www.healthypeople.gov/2020/About-Healthy-People

Henninger, A., & Sung, H-E. (2014). History of substance abuse treatment. In G. Bruinsma & D. Weisburd (Eds.), *Encyclopedia of Criminology and Criminal Justice*. New York, NY: Springer.

Hoffman, C. (2009). National health insurance: A brief history of reform efforts in the U.S. Retrieved from https://kaiserfamilyfoundation.files.wordpress.com/2013/01/7871.pdf

Hoffman, K. M., Trawalter, S., Axt, J. R., & Oliver, M. N. (2016). Racial bias in pain assessment and treatment beliefs about biological differences between blacks and whites. *Proceedings of the National Academy of Sciences of the United States of America, 113*(16), 4296–4301. doi:10.1073/pnas.1516047113

Indiana Historical Bureau. (n.d.). 1907 Indiana Eugenics Law. Retrieved from https://www.in.gov/history/markers/524.htm

Jordan, M. (2017, July 1). The unexpected political power of dentists. *The Washington Post*. Retrieved from https://www.washingtonpost.com/politics/the-unexpected-political-power-of-dentists/2017/07/01/ee946d56-54f3-11e7-a204-ad706461fa4f_story.html?noredirect=on&utm_term=.7b8aca6225a1

Kaiser Family Foundation. (2017, November 22). An overview of Medicare. Retrieved from https://www.kff.org/medicare/issue-brief/an-overview-of-medicare/

Kim, T. K., & Lane, S. R. (2013). Government health expenditure and public health outcomes. *American International Journal of Contemporary Research, 3*(9), 1–13.

Mann, J. M., Gostin, L., Gruskin, G., Brennan, T., Lazzarini, Z., & Fineberg, H. V. (1994). Health and human rights. *Health and Human Rights, 1*(1), 6–23.

Martin, N., & Montagne, R. (2017, December 7.). Black mothers keep dying after giving birth. Shalon Irving's story explains why. *NPR and ProPublica*. Retrieved from https://www.npr.org/2017/12/07/568948782/black-mothers-keep-dying-after-giving-birth-shalon-irvings-story-explains-why

McCausland, P., & Connor, T. (2018). OxyContin maker Purdue to stop promoting opioids in light of epidemic. *NBC*. Retrieved from https://www.nbcnews.com/storyline/americas-heroin-epidemic/oxycontin-maker-purdue-stop-promoting-opioids-light-epidemic-n846726

McFadden, C., Breslauer, B., & Connor, T. (2018, January 23). Can Commissioner Scott Gottlieb undo FDA missteps in opioid crisis? *NBC*. Retrieved from https://www.nbcnews.com/storyline/americas-heroin-epidemic/can-commissioner-scott-gottlieb-undo-fda-missteps-opioid-crisis-n838636

Moghe, S. (2016). Opioid history: From 'wonder drug' to abuse epidemic. *CNN*. Retrieved from https://www.cnn.com/2016/05/12/health/opioid-addiction-history/index.html

National Association of Social Workers. (2018). *Social work speaks* (11th ed.). Washington, DC: Author.

National Association of Social Workers. (n.d.). Behavioral health. Retrieved from https://www.socialworkers.org/Practice/Behavioral-Health

National Federation of Independent Business et al. v. Sebelius, Secretary of Health and Human Services, et al. 567 U.S. (2012). Retrieved from http://www.supremecourt.gov/opinions/11pdf/11-393c3a2.pdf

National WIC Association. (n.d.). WIC program overview and history. Retrieved from https://www.nwica.org/overview-and-history

New York State Office of Mental Health. (n.d.). Pilgrim Psychiatric Center. Retrieved from https://www.omh.ny.gov omhweb/facilities/pgpc/

Nissen, S. E. (2017). Conflicts of interest and professional medical associations: Progress and remaining challenges. *Journal of the American Medical Association, 317*(17), 1737–1738. doi:10.1001/jama.2017.2516

Novella, E. (2010). Mental health care in the aftermath of deinstitutionalization: A retrospective and prospective view. *Health Care Analysis, 18*, 222–238.

Organisation for Economic Cooperation and Development. (2017). *Health at a glance 2017: OECD indicators*. Paris, France: Author. http://dx.doi.org/10.1787/health_glance-2017-en

Organisation for Economic Cooperation and Development. (2018). *Health spending (indicator)*. Paris, France: Author. doi:10.1787/8643de7e-en

Paradise, J. (2015). Medicaid moving forward. Retrieved from https://www.kff.org/health-reform/issue-brief/medicaid-moving-forward/

PBS NewsHour. (2017, December 20). *The GOP tax bill deals a blow to the Affordable Care Act. Here's how* [Video file]. Retrieved from https://www.pbs.org/newshour/show/the-gop-tax-bill-deals-a-blow-to-the-affordable-care-act-heres-how

Perlin, J. B., Kolodner, R. M., & Roswell, R. H. (2004). The Veterans Health Administration: Quality, value, accountability, and information as transforming strategies for patient-centered care. *American Journal of Managed Care, 10*(11), 828–836.

Robinson, J. C., & Casalino, L. P. (1996). Vertical integration and organizational networks in managed care. *Health Affairs, 15*(10), 7–22. https://doi.org/10.1377/hlthaff.15.1.7

Rodriguez, M. A., & García, R. (2013). First, do no harm: The US sexually transmitted disease experiments in Guatemala. *American Journal of Public Health, 103*(12), 2122–2126. doi:10.2105/AJPH.2013.301520

Ross, J. S. (2002). The Committee on the Costs of Medical Care and the history of health insurance in the United States. *Einstein Quarterly Journal of Biology and Medicine, 19*, 129–134.

Rudowitz, R., & Valentine, A. (2017). Medicaid enrollment and spending growth: FY 2017 & 2018. Retrieved from https://www.kff.org/medicaid/issue-brief/medicaid-enrollment-spending-growth-fy-2017-2018/

Skloot, R. (2010). *The immortal life of Henrietta Lacks*. New York, NY: Crown.

Food and Nutrition Service. (2019, August 2). SNAP Data Tables. Retrieved from https://www.fns.usda.gov/pd/supplemental-nutrition-assistance-program-snap

Social Security Administration. (n.d.). President Lyndon B. Johnson. Retrieved from https://www.ssa.gov/history/lbjstmts.html

U.S. Department of Veterans Affairs. (n.d.). *Veterans Health Administration*. Retrieved from https://www.va.gov/directory/guide/division.asp?dnum=1

U.S. National Library of Medicine. (n.d.). Diseases of the mind: Highlights of American psychiatry through 1900. Retrieved from https://www.nlm.nih.gov/hmd/diseases/index.html

United Nations. (1948). Universal Declaration of Human Rights. Retrieved from http://www.un.org/en/universal-declaration-human-rights/

Vandiver, V. L. (2013). Managed care. In *Encyclopedia of Social Work*. Retrieved from https://oxfordre.com/socialwork/view/10.1093/acrefore/9780199975839.001.0001/acrefore-9780199975839-e-623 doi:10.1093/acrefore/9780199975839.013.623

Vanidestine, T. (2018). Conceptualizing "race" and racism in health disparities discourse: A critical discourse analysis. *Journal of Sociological Research, 9*(2), 1–21.

Warne, D., & Frizell, L. B. (2014). American Indian health policy: Historical trends and contemporary issues. *American Journal of Public Health, 104*(Suppl. 3), S263–S267. doi:10.2105/AJPH.2013.301682

The Washington Post. (2010). *Landmark: The inside story of America's new health-care law—The Affordable Care Act—and what it means for us all*. New York, NY: Perseus Books.

Wasserman, J., Flannery, N. A., & Clair, J. M. (2007). Raising the ivory tower: The production of knowledge and distrust of medicine among African Americans. *Journal of Medical Ethics, 33*, 177–180.

Webster, P. C. (2012). Oxycodone class lawsuit filed. *Canadian Medical Association Journal, 184*(7), E345–E346. https://doi.org/10.1503/cmaj.109-4158

Witters, D. (2019). U.S. uninsured rate rises to four-year high. Gallup National Health and Well-Being Index. *Gallup*. Retrieved from https://news.gallup.com/poll/246134/uninsured-rate-rises-four-year-high.aspx

World Health Organization. (1948). Constitution of WHO-Principles. Retrieved from http://www.who.int/about/mission/en/

World Health Organization. (n.d.). Social determinants of health. Retrieved from http://www.who.int/social_determinants/sdh_definition/en/

CHAPTER 12

The Arc. (n.d.). History of the Arc: History of name changes. Retrieved from https://www.thearc.org/who-we-are/history/name-change

Barnes v. Gorman, 536 U.S. 181 (2002).

Baynton, C. (2011). 'These pushful days': Time and disability in the age of eugenics. *Health and History, 13*(2), 43–64. Retrieved from http://www.jstor.org/stable/10.5401/healthhist.13.2.0043

Bird, K., Foster, M., & Ganz-Glass, E. (2014). *New opportunities to improve economic and career success of low-income youth and adults: Key provisions of the Workforce Innovation and Opportunity Act (WIOA)*. Washington, DC: Center for Law and Social Policy. Retrieved from https://www.clasp.org/sites/default/files/public/resources-and-publications/publication-1/KeyProvisionsofWIOA-Final.pdf

Board of Education of Hendrick Hudson Central School District v. Rowley, 458 U.S. 176 (1982).

Board of Trustees of the University of Alabama v. Garrett, 121 S. Ct. 955 (S. Ct., Feb. 21, 2001).

Brown, L. (2019). Identity first language. Retrieved from https://autisticadvocacy.org/about-asan/identity-first-language/

Buck v. Bell, 274 U.S. 200 (1927).

Chevron U.S.A., Inc. v. Echazabal, 536 U.S. 73 (2002).

Coco, A. P. (2010). Diseased, maimed, and mutilated: Categorizations of disability and an ugly law in late 19th century Chicago. *Journal of Social History, 44*(1), 23–37. http://dx.doi.org/10.1353/jsh.2010.0025

Collier, R. (2012). Person-first language: Noble intent but to what effect? *Canadian Medical Association Journal, 184*(18), 1977–1980. http://dx.doi.org/10.1503/cmaj.109-4319

Commonwealth Fund. (2019). New challenges to the Affordable Care Act. Retrieved from https://www.commonwealthfund.org/trending/new-challenges-affordable-care-act

Dag Hammarskjöld Library. (2018). What is the difference between signing, ratification and accession of UN treaties? Retrieved from http://ask.un.org/faq/14594.

Davis, A. (2005). Invisible disability. *Ethics, 116*(1), 153–213. Retrieved from http://www.jstor.org/stable/10.1086/453151

Day, P. J. (2006). *A new history of social welfare* (5th ed.). Boston, MA: Allyn and Bacon.

Diegelmann, K. M., & Test, D. W. (2018). Effects of a self-monitoring checklist as a component of the self-directed IEP. *Education and Training in Autism and Developmental Disabilities, 53*(1), 73–83.

Disability Rights Advocates. (2019). Federal court issues landmark civil rights ruling likely to lead to more elevators in the New York City Subway. Retrieved from https://dralegal.org/press/federal-court-issues-landmark-civil-rights-ruling-likely-to-lead-to-more-elevators-in-the-new-york-city-subway/

Equal Employment Opportunity Commission. (2018). Filing a charge of discrimination. Retrieved from https://www.eeoc.gov/employees/charge.cfm

Gernsbacher, N., Raimond, A., Balinghasav, N. T., & Boston, J. S. (2016). "Special needs" is an ineffective euphemism. *Cognitive Research: Principles and Implications, 1*(29). doi:10.1186/s41235-016-0025-4

Institute on Disability/UCED. (2017). 2017 disability statistics annual report. Retrieved from https://disabilitycompendium.org/sites/default/files/user-uploads/AnnualReport_2017_FINAL.pdf

Ladau, E. (n.d.). 4 disability euphemisms that need to bite the dust. [Blog post]. Retrieved from http://cdrnys.org/blog/disability-dialogue/the-disability-dialogue-4-disability-euphemisms-that-need-to-bite-the-dust/

Losen, D., & Gillespie, J. (2012). *Opportunities suspended: The disparate impact of disciplinary exclusion from school*. Los Angeles, CA: The University of California, Los Angeles, The Civil Rights Project. Retrieved from https://files.eric.ed.gov/fulltext/ED534178.pdf

Mangan, T. (2018, January. 2018). Trump touts repeal of key part in 'disastrous Obamacare'—the individual mandate. *CNBC*. Retrieved from https://www.cnbc.com/2018/01/30/trump-touts-repeal-of-obamacare-individual-mandate.html

Medicaid (n.d.). Medicaid innovation accelerator program. Retrieved from https://www.medicaid.gov/state-resource-center/innovation-accelerator-program/index.html

Mitra, S. (2006). The capability approach and disability. *Journal of Disability Policy Studies, 16*(4), 236–247.

Nagi, S. (1976). An epidemiology of disability among adults in the United States. *Milbank Memorial Fund Quarterly. Health and Society, 54*(4), 439–467. http://dx.doi.org/10.2307/3349677

National Center for Educational Statistics. (2018). *The condition of education: Children and youth with disabilities*. Washington, DC: Author. Retrieved from https://nces.ed.gov/programs/coe/indicator_cgg.asp

National Council on Disability. (2016). The impact of the Affordable Care Act on people with disabilities: A 2015 status report. Retrieved from https://www.ncd.gov/sites/default/files/NCD_ACA_Report02_508.pdf

National Council on Disability. (n.d.). Origins of self-directed services. Retrieved from https://www.ncd.gov/policy/chapter-2-origins-self-directed-services

NAV. (2017). Rules of calculating disability benefit. Retrieved from Norwegian Labour and Welfare Administration https://www.nav.no/en/Home/Benefits+and+services/Relatert+informasjon/rules-of-calculating-disability-benefit

Neuhaus, R., & Smith, C. (2014). Equality under the law: Then and now. *GPSolo, 31*(6), 46–51. Retrieved from: https://www.americanbar.org/content/dam/aba/publications/gp_solo_magazine/november_december_2014/gpsm_v031n06_14nov_dec.authcheckdam.pdf

O'Brien, G. (2011). Eugenics, genetics, and the minority group model of disabilities: Implications for social work advocacy. *Social Work, 56*(4), 347–354.

Olmstead v. L.C., 527 U.S. 581 (1999).

Prince, M. J. (2017). Persons with invisible disabilities and workplace accommodation: Findings from a scoping literature review. *Journal of Vocational Rehabilitation 46*, 75–86. http://dx.doi.org/10.3233/JVR-160844

Scotch, R. (1984). *From good will to civil rights: transforming federal disability policy*. Philadelphia, PA: Temple University Press.

Scotch, R. (2001). *From good will to civil rights: Transforming federal disability policy*. Philadelphia, PA: Temple University Press.

Sesenbrenner, J. (2017). *Congressman Sensenbrenner introduces the Disability Integration Act in the House of Representatives*. Washington, DC: Federal Information & News Dispatch, Inc.

Shapiro, J. P. (1994). *No pity: People with disabilities forcing a new civil rights era*. New York, NY: Times Books.

Skocpol, T. (1992). *Protecting soldiers and mothers: The political origins of social policy in the United States*. Boston, MA: Harvard University Press.

Social Security Administration. (2016). Social Security programs throughout the world: Europe. Retrieved from https://www.ssa.gov/policy/docs/progdesc/ssptw/2016-2017/europe/norway.html

Social Security Administration. (2018). Benefits for children with disabilities. Retrieved from https://www.ssa.gov/pubs/EN-05-10026.pdf

Social Security Administration. (n.d.-a). Historical background and development of Social Security. Retrieved from https://www.ssa.gov/history/briefhistory3.html

Social Security Administration. (n.d.-b). Plan to Achieve Self Support: PASS. Retrieved from https://www.ssa.gov/disability research/wi/pass.htm

Social Security Office of Policy. (2005/2006). Addressing the challenges facing SSA's disability programs. *Social Security Bulletin, 66*(3). Retrieved from https://www.ssa.gov/policy/docs/ssb/v66n3/v66n3p29.html

Spaulding, S. (2015). *The Workforce Innovation and Opportunity Act and child care for low income parents: Opportunities and challenges under the new law.* Washington, DC: The Urban Institute. Retrieved from https://www.urban.org/sites/default/files/publication/64706/2000309-the-workforce-innovation.pdf

Stanhope, V., Ingoglia, C., Schmelter, B., & Marcus, S. C. (2013). Impact of person-centered planning and collaborative documentation on treatment adherence. *Psychiatric Services, 64*(1), 76–79.

Sutton et al. v. United Airlines, Inc., 527 U.S. 471 (1999).

Switzer, J. V. (2003). *Disabled rights: American disability policy and the fight for equal rights*. Washington, DC: Georgetown University Press.

Taylor, D. (2018). *Americans with disabilities: 2014 household economic studies*. Washington, DC: U.S. Census Bureau. Retrieved from https://www.census.gov/content/dam/Census/library/publications/2018/demo/p70-152.pdf

Tennessee v. Lane, 541 U.S. 509 (2004).

Toyota Motor Manufacturing, Kentucky, Inc. v. Williams, 534 U.S. 184 (2002).

U.S. Airways, Inc. v. Barnett, 535 U.S. 391 (2002).

U.S. Census Bureau (2016). American Community Survey. Annual Disability Statistics Compendium. Retrieved from https://disabilitycompendium.org/compendium/annual-statistics-2016

U.S. Department of Education, Office of Special Education Programs, Individuals with Disabilities Education Act (IDEA). (2017). *Digest of Education Statistics 2017, Table 204.50* [Database]. Retrieved from https://nces.ed.gov/programs/digest/d17/tables/dt17_204.50.asp""

Administration for Community Living. (2018). State protection and advocacy systems. Retrieved from https://www.acl.gov/programs/aging-and-disability-networks/state-protection-advocacy-systems

Bureau of Labor Statistics. (2019, February 26). *Persons with a disability: Labor force characteristics* [Press release]. Retrieved from https://www.bls.gov/news.release/pdf/disabl.pdf

U.S. Department of Veterans Affairs. (2018). History. Retrieved from https://www.va.gov/about_va/vahistory.asp

U.S. Equal Employment Opportunity Commission. (2002). Enforcement guidance: Reasonable accommodation and undue hardship under the Americans with Disabilities Act. Retrieved from https://www.eeoc.gov/policy/docs/accommodation.html

United Cerebral Palsy. (2016). The case for inclusion 2016 report. Retrieved from http://cfi.ucp.org/wp-content/uploads/2014/03/Case-for-Inclusion-2016-FINAL.pdf

United Nations. (2006). Convention on the Rights of Persons with Disabilities: Article 4. Retrieved from https://www.un.org/development/desa/disabilities/convention-on-the-rights-of-persons-with-disabilities/article-4-general-obligations.html

Vitale, A. S. (2018). *The end of policing*. London, UK: Verso.

World Health Organization. (2002). *Toward a common language for functioning, disability and health: ICF; The International Classification of Functioning, Disability and Health*. Geneva, Switzerland: World Health Organization. Retrieved from http://www.who.int/classifications/icf/icfbeginnersguide.pdf?ua=1

World Policy Analysis Center at UCLA Fielding School of Public Health. (2016, December 2). *Putting fundamental rights of persons with disabilities on the map* [Press release]. Retrieved from https://ph.ucla.edu/news/press-release/2016/nov/putting-fundamental-rights-persons-disabilities-map

Yee, S. (2015). The Affordable Care Act and people with disabilities. *GP Solo, 32*(2). Retrieved from https://www.americanbar.org/publications/gp_solo/2015/march-april/the_affordable_care_act_and_people_disabilities.html

Zhou, L. (2019, July 10). The latest legal challenge to the Affordable Care Act, explained. *VOX Media*. Retrieved from https://www.vox.com/policy-and-politics/2019/7/9/20686224/affordable-care-act-constitutional-lawsuit-fifth-circuit-court-texas-district-court

CHAPTER 13

ACLU Washington. (n.d.). *Questions and answers about legal financial obligations (LFOs)*. Retrieved from https://www.aclu-wa.org/questions-and-answers-about-legal-financial-obligations-lfos

Alexander, M. (2012). *The New Jim Crow: Mass incarceration in the age of colorblindness*. New York, NY: New Press.

American Public Health Association. (2013). *Solitary confinement as a public health issue: Policy statement*. Retrieved from https://www.apha.org/policies-and-advocacy/public-health-policy-statements/policy-database/2014/07/14/13/30/solitary-confinement-as-a-public-health-issue

American Public Health Association. (2018). *Addressing law enforcement as a public health issue*. Retrieved from https://www.apha.org/policies-and-advocacy/public-health-policy-statements/policy-database/2019/01/29/law-enforcement-violence

Avery, B., & Hernandez, P. (2018). Ban the box: U.S. cities, counties, and states adopt fair hiring policies. Retrieved from https://www.nelp.org/publication/ban-the-box-fair-chance-hiring-state-and-local-guide/

Beate, V. (2017). Revisiting broken windows: The role of neighborhood and individual characteristics in reaction to disorder cues. *Sociological Science, 4*(22), 528–551.

Benson, E. (2003). Rehabilitate or punish? *Monitor on Psychology, 34*(6), 46. Retrieved from https://www.apa.org/monitor/julaug03/rehab.aspx

Bentham, J. (1798). Proposal for a new and less expensive mode for employing and reforming convicts. In J. Bowring (Ed.), *The works of Jeremy Bentham, Vol. 11* (Memoirs of Bentham part II and analytical index) [1843]. Retrieved from http://oll.libertyfund.org/titles/bentham-the-works-of-jeremy-bentham-vol-11-memoirs-of-bentham-part-ii-and-analytical-index

Bernard, E. H. (1998). Reflecting on the subject: A critique of the social influence conception of deterrence, the broken windows theory, and order-maintenance policing New York style. *Michigan Law Review, 97*(2), 291–389.

Bessler, J. D. (2009). Revisiting Beccaria's vision: The Enlightenment, America's death penalty, and the abolition movement. *Northwestern Journal of Law & Social Policy, 4*(2), 195–328.

Boldt, R. C. (2010). The 'tomahawk' and the 'healing balm': Drug treatment courts in theory and practice. *University of Maryland Law Journal of Race, Religion, Gender and Class, 10*(1), 45–71.

Bowler, A. E., Lilley, T. G., & Leon, C. S. (2016), Reform or remand? Race, nativity, and the immigrant family in the history of prostitution. In A. Sarat (Ed.), *Special Issue: Problematizing Prostitution: Critical Research and Scholarship* (*Studies in Law, Politics and Society Vol. 71*, pp. 63–91). Bingley, UK: Emerald Group.

Brickner, M., & Diaz, S. (2011). Prisons for profit: Incarceration for sale. *Human Rights Magazine, 38*. Retrieved from https://www.americanbar.org/groups/crsj/publications/human_rights_magazine_home/human_rights_vol38_2011/human_rights_summer11/prisons_for_profit_incarceration_for_sale/

Bureau of Justice Statistics. (2015). Prisoners in 2015. Retrieved from https://www.bjs.gov/content/pub/pdf/p15.pdf

Bureau of Justice Statistics. (2016). National sources of law enforcement employment data. Retrieved from https://www.bjs.gov/content/pub/pdf/nsleed.pdf

Bureau of Justice Statistics. (2018). Reentry trends in the U.S. Retrieved from https://www.bjs.gov/content/reentry/releases.cfm

Burkhardt, B. C. (2014). Private prisons in public discourse: Measuring moral legitimacy. *Sociological Focus, 47*(4), 279–298.

Butler, J. (1896). British convicts shipped to American colonies. *American Historical Review, 2*(1), 12–33.

Chesney-Lind, M., & Pasko, L. (Eds.). (2013). *The female offender: Girls, women, and crime*. Thousand Oaks, CA: Sage.

Chilkoti, A. (2017, July 15). States keep saying yes to marijuana use. Now comes the federal no. *The New York Times*. Retrieved from https://www.nytimes.com/2017/07/15/us/politics/marijuana-laws-state-federal.html

Christian, S. (2009). Children of incarcerated parents. Retrieved from https://www.ncsl.org/documents/cyf/childrenofincarceratedparents.pdf

Clarke, J. G., & Simon, R. E. (2013). Shackling and separation: Motherhood in prison. *AMA Journal of Ethics*. Retrieved from https://journalofethics.ama-assn.org/article/shackling-and-separation-motherhood-prison/2013-09

Cox, J. A. (2003). Bilboes, brands, and branks: Colonial crimes and punishments. *Colonial Williamsburg Journal*. Retrieved from http://www.history.org/foundation/journal/spring03/branks.cfm

Csicsek, A. (2011). Spiro T. Agnew and the burning of Baltimore. In J. I Elfenbein, T. I. Hollowak, & E. M. Nix (Eds.), *Baltimore '68: Riots and rebirth in an American city* (pp. 70–85). Philadelphia, PA: Temple University Press.

Daniel, A. (2006). Preventing suicide in prison: A collaborative responsibility of administrative, custodial, and clinical staff. *Journal of the American Academy of Psychiatry and Law, 34*(2), 165–75.

Davis, E., & Snell, T. L. (2018). Capital punishment, 2016. Retrieved from https://www.bjs.gov/content/pub/pdf/cp16sb.pdf

Drywater-Whitekiller, V. (2014). Family group conferencing: An indigenous practice approach to compliance with the Indian Child Welfare Act. *Journal of Public Child Welfare, 8*(3), 260–278.

Fleury-Steiner, B. D. (2004). *Jurors' stories of death: How America's death penalty invests in inequality*. Ann Arbor, MI: University of Michigan Press.

Foucault, M. (1995). *Discipline & punish: The birth of the prison*. New York, NY: Vintage Books.

Friedman, L. M. (2005). *A history of American law* (3rd ed.). New York, NY: Touchstone.

Fuller, D. A., Lamb, H. R, Biasotti, M., & Snook, J. (2015). *Overlooked in the undercounted: The role of mental illness in fatal law enforcement encounters*. Arlington, VA: Treatment Advocacy Center. Retrieved from https://www.treatmentadvocacycenter.org/storage/documents/overlooked-in-the-undercounted.pdf

Giwa, S. (2018). Community policing in racialized communities: A potential role for police social work. *Journal of Human Behavior in the Social Environment, 28*(6), 710–730.

Godsey, M. (2017). *Blind injustice: A former prosecutor exposes, CA the psychology and politics of wrongful convictions*. Oakland: University of California Press.

Gould, J. B., & Leo, R. A. (2010). One hundred years later: Wrongful convictions after a century of research. *Journal of Criminal Law & Criminology, 100*(3), 825–868.

Grand Challenges for Social Work. (n.d.). Promote smart decarceration. Retrieved from http://grandchallengesforsocialwork.org/grand-challenges-initiative/12-challenges/promote-smart-decarceration/

Greenberg, Z. (2017, April 20). In jail, pads and tampons as bargaining chips. *The New York Times*. Retrieved from https://www.nytimes.com/2017/04/20/nyregion/pads-tampons-new-york-womens-prisons.html

Greene, J. (2016). Broken Windows Theory. *In Salem Press Encyclopedia*. Salem, MA: Salem Press.

Gross, S. R., Posely, M., & Stevens, K. (2017). *Race and wrongful convictions in the United States*. Irvine, CA: National Registry of Exonerations. Newkirk Center for Science and Society. Retrieved from http://www.law.umich.edu/special/exoneration/Documents/Race_and_Wrongful_Convictions.pdf

Gumz, E. J., & Grant, C. L. (2009). Restorative justice: A systematic review of the social work literature. *Families in Society, 90*(1), 119–126.

Hadden, S. (2001). *Slave patrols: Law and violence in Virginia and the Carolinas*. Boston, MA: Harvard University Press.

Hansan, J. E. (n.d.). Charity Organization Societies (1877–1893). Retrieved from http://socialwelfare.library.vcu.edu/eras/civil-war-reconstruction/charity-organization-societies-1877-1893/

Harcourt, B. E. (1998). Reflecting on the subject: A critique of the social influence conception of deterrence, the Broken

Windows Theory, and Order-Maintenance Policing New York style. *Michigan Law Review, 97,* 291–389.

Harris, A. (2016). *A pound of flesh: Monetary sanctions as punishment for the poor.* New York, NY: Russell Sage Foundation.

Hernández, C. C. G. (2017). What is crimmigration law? *Insights on Law and Society, 17*(2). Retrieved from https://www.americanbar.org/publications/insights-on-law-and-society/2017/spring2017/what-is-crimmigration-law.html

In re Gault, 387 U.S. 1 (1967).

Juvenile Law Center. (n.d.). Youth in the justice system: An overview. Retrieved from https://jlc.org/youth-justice-system-overview

Kajstura, A., & Immarigeon, R. (n.d.). States of women's incarceration: The global context. Retrieved from https://www.prisonpolicy.org/global/women/

Leon, C. S., & Shdaimah, C. S. (forthcoming). "We'll take the tough ones"—expertise in multi-door justice: A case study of prostitution diversion. *New Criminal Law Review, 22.*

Levoy, J. (2015, January 23). The underpolicing of black America; Despite controversies like Ferguson, police are better at stopping African-Americans at random than at halting an epidemic of murder. *The Wall Street Journal.* Retrieved from https://www.wsj.com/articles/the-underpolicing-of-black-america-1422049080

Looney, A., & Turner, N. (2018). *Work and opportunity before and after incarceration.* Washington, DC: The Brookings Institute. Retrieved from https://www.brookings.edu/wp-content/uploads/2018/03/es_20180314_looneyincarceration_final.pdf

Losen, D., Hewitt, D., & Toldson, I. (2014). Eliminating excessive and unfair exclusionary discipline in schools' policy recommendations for reducing disparities. Bloomington, IN: The Equity Project at Indiana University, Center for Evaluation and Education Policy. Retrieved from http://www.indiana.edu/~atlantic/wp-content/uploads/2015/01/Disparity_Policy_010915.pdf

Lukemeyer, A., & McCorkle, R. C. (2006). Privatization of prisons: Impact on prison conditions. *The American Review of Public Administration, 36*(2), 189–206

Mallett, C. A. (2016). The school-to-prison pipeline: A critical review of the punitive paradigm shift. *Child & Adolescent Social Work Journal, 33*(1), 15–24.

Mallett, C. A. (2017). The school-to-prison pipeline: Disproportionate impact on vulnerable children and adolescents. *Education & Urban Society, 49*(6), 563–592.

Martin, E. (2017). Hidden consequences: The impact of incarceration on dependent children. *NIJ Journal, 278.* Retrieved from https://www.nij.gov/journals/278/Pages/impact-of-incarceration-on-dependent-children.aspx

Martin, K., Sykes, B. L., Shannon, S., Edwards, F., & Harris, A. (2018). Monetary sanctions: Legal financial obligations in US systems of justice. *Annual Review of Criminology, 1*(1), 471–495.

Massoglia, M., Remster, B., & King, R. D. (2011). Stigma or separation? Understanding the incarceration-divorce relationship. *Social Forces, 90,* 133–155.

McCarter, S. (2017). The school-to-prison pipeline: A primer for social workers. *Social Work, 62*(1), 53–61.

McCoy, C. (2003). The politics of problem solving: An overview of the origins and developments of therapeutic courts. *American Criminal Law Review, 40,* 1517–2003.

McKee, A. J. (2017). Broken windows theory. *In Encyclopedia Britannica.* Retrieved from https://www.britannica.com/topic/broken-windows-theory

Metzner, J., & Fellner, J. (2010). Solitary confinement and mental illness in U.S. prisons: A challenge for medical ethics. *Journal of the American Academy of Psychiatry and the Law, 38*(1), 104–108. Retrieved from http://jaapl.org/content/38/1/104

Miller, L. M. (2016). *The myth of mob rule: Violent crime & democratic politics.* New York, NY: Oxford University Press.

Miranda v. Arizona, 384 U.S. 436 (1966).

Morgan, G. (n.d.). North America - Cast away: Criminal transportation. Retrieved from http://convictvoyages.org/expert-essays/north-america

Morgan, G., & Rushton, P. (2004). *Eighteenth century criminal transportation: The formation of the criminal Atlantic.* New York, NY: Palgrave Macmillan.

Morin, R., & Stepler, R. (2016). The racial confidence gap in police performance. Retrieved from http://www.pewsocialtrends.org/2016/09/29/the-racial-confidence-gap-in-police-performance/

Moses, M. C. (2006). Does parental incarceration increase a child's risk for foster care placement? *NIJ Journal, 255.* Retrieved from https://www.nij.gov/journals/255/pages/parental_incarceration.aspx

Mower, L., & Mahoney, E. (2019, April 24). House passes Amendment 4 bill requiring felons to pay up before they can vote. *Miami Herald.* Retrieved from https://www.miamiherald.com/news/politics-government/state-politics/article229619604.html

National Association of Social Workers. (2017). Code of ethics. Retrieved from https://www.socialworkers.org/About/Ethics/Code-of-Ethics/Code-of-Ethics-English

National Alliance on Mental Illness. (2019). Crisis intervention team (CITS) programs. Retrieved from https://www.nami.org/Get-Involved/Law-Enforcement-and-Mental-Health

National Commission on Correctional Health Care. (2016). Solitary confinement (isolation). Retrieved from https://www.ncchc.org/solitary-confinement.

National Drug Court Resource Center. (2016). List of incentives and sanctions. Retrieved from http://www.ndcrc.org/content/list-incentives-and-sanctions

National Institutes of Justice. (2016). Race, trust, and police legitimacy. Retrieved from https://nij.gov/topics/law-enforcement/legitimacy/Pages/welcome.aspx

National Inventory of Collateral Consequences of Conviction. (2019). Welcome to the NICCC. Received from https://niccc.csgjusticecenter.org/

NonprofitVoterEngagementNetwork.(n.d.).AbouttheCensus: Prison inmates, redistricting, and the 2010 Census. Retrieved from https://www.prisonpolicy.org/scans/Counting-Prison-Inmates.pdf

Organisation for Economic Cooperation and Development. (2016). *Society at a glance 2016: OECD social indicators.* Paris, France:Author. https://doi.org/10.1787/soc_glance-2016-29-en

Office of Juvenile Justice and Delinquency Prevention. (2015). Status offenders. Retrieved from https://www.ojjdp.gov/mpg/litreviews/Status_Offenders.pdf

Orr, C. H., Hall, J. W., Reimer, N. L., Malet, E A., O'Dowd, K., & Frazer, A. C. (2009). *America's problem solving courts: The criminal costs for treatment and the case for reform.* Washington, DC: National Association of Criminal Defense Lawyers. Retrieved from http://www.nacdl.org/criminaldefense.aspx?id=20191

Oshinsky, D. M. (1997). *Worse than slavery: Parchman farm and the ordeal of Jim Crow justice.* New York, NY: Free Press.

Pasko, L. (2017). Beyond confinement: The regulation of girl offenders' bodies, sexual choices, and behavior. *Women & Criminal Justice, 27* (1), 4–20.

Patterson, G. T. (2013). Prisoner reentry: A public health or public safety issue for social work practice? *Social Work in Public Health, 28*(2), 129–141.

Pfaff, J. (2017). *Locked in: The true causes of mass incarceration and how to achieve reform.* New York, NY: Basic Books.

Potter, G. (2013). The history of policing in the United States, Part I. Retrieved from https://plsonline.eku.edu/insidelook/history-policing-united-states-part-1

Prison Policy Initiative. (2015, July 9). Prisons of Poverty: Uncovering the pre-incarceration incomes of the imprisoned. Retrieved from https://www.prisonpolicy.org/reports/income.html

Ritchie, A. J., & Jones-Brown, D. (2017). Policing race, gender, and sex: A review of law enforcement policies. *Women & Criminal Justice, 27*(1), 21–50.

Rothman, D. J. (1980). *Conscience and convenience: The asylum and its alternatives in Progressive America.* Boston, MA: Little, Brown and Company.

Saar, M. S., Epstein, R., Rosenthal, L., & Vafa, Y. (2015). *The sexual abuse to prison pipeline: The girls' story.* Washington, DC: Human Rights Project for Girls.

San Francisco Ordinance No. 131-18, 2018. Retrieved from https://sfbos.org/sites/default/files/o0131-18.pdf

Schept, J., Wall, T., & Brisman, A. (2014). Building, staffing, and insulating: An architecture of criminological complicity in the school-to-prison pipeline. *Social Justice, 4*(138), 96–115.

Schierenbeck, A. (2018, March 15). A billionaire and a nurse shouldn't pay the same fine for speeding. *The New York Times.* Retrieved from https://www.nytimes.com/2018/03/15/opinion/flat-fines-wealthy-poor.html

Schlossman, S., & Wallach, S. (1978). The crime of precocious sexuality: Female juvenile delinquency in the Progressive Era. *Harvard Educational Review, 48* (10), 65–69.

Schnittker, J., & John, A. (2007). Enduring stigma: The long-term effects of incarceration on health. *Journal of Health Social Behavior, 48*, 115–130.

Schram, S. F. (2000). *After welfare: The culture of postindustrial social policy.* New York, NY: New York University Press.

The Sentencing Project. (2018). Fact sheet: Incarcerated women and girls, 1980–2016. Retrieved from https://www.sentencingproject.org/publications/incarcerated-women-and-girls/

Shdaimah, C. S., & Bailey-Kloch, M. (2014). "Can you help me with that instead of putting me in jail?': Participant perspectives on Baltimore City's Specialized Prostitution Diversion Program. *Justice System Journal, 35*(3), 287–300.

Shdaimah, C. S., Kaufman, B. R., Bright, C. L., & Flower, S. M. (2014). Neighborhood assessment of prostitution as a pressing social problem and appropriate responses: Results from a community survey. *Criminal Justice Policy Review, 25*(3), 275–297.

Shineman, V. (2018). Restoring rights, restoring trust: Evidence that reversing felon disenfranchisement penalties increases both trust and cooperation with government. Retrieved from https://rubenson.org/wp-content/uploads/2018/09/shineman-tpbw18.pdf

Siegel, R., & Ozug, M. (2016, February 18). From a life time to life on the outside [Radio Program]. *NPR*. Retrieved from https://www.npr.org/2016/02/18/467057603/from-a-life-term-to-life-on-the-outside-when-aging-felons-are-freed

Simon, J. (2007). *Governing through crime: How the war on crime transformed American democracy and created a culture of fear.* New York, NY: Oxford University Press.

Social Workers Against Solitary Confinement. (2018). A call to end health workers' participation in the practice of solitary confinement! Retrieved from http://www.socialworkersasc.org/sign-our-move-on-petition/

Social Workers Against Solitary Confinement. (n.d.). Home. Retrieved from https://www.socialworkersasc.org/

Spohn, C. (2017). Race and sentencing disparity. In E. Luna (Ed.), *Reforming criminal justice: A report of the Academy for Justice on bridging the gap between scholarship and reform* (Vol. *4*, pp. 169–186). Phoenix, AZ: Arizona State University.

Strangio, C. (2017). Project ROSE: A case study on diversion, sex work, and constitutionality. In K. Hail-Jares, C. Shdaimah, & C. Leon (Eds.), *New perspectives on street-based sex work* (pp. 282–291). Philadelphia, PA: Temple University Press.

Strecher, V. G. (1988). Stimuli of police education: Wickersham and LBJ's (Lyndon B. Johnson) commission. *Justice Professional*, *3*(2), 298–317.

Tanenhaus, D. S. (2004). *Juvenile justice in the making.* New York, NY: Oxford University Press.

Turney, K., & Haskins, A. R. (2014). Falling behind? Children's early grade retention after paternal incarceration. *Sociology of Education*, *87*(4), 241–258.

U.S. Commission on Civil Rights. (2018). Police use of force: An examination of modern policing practices. Retrieved from https://www.usccr.gov/pubs/2018/11-15-Police-Force.pdf

U.S. Department of Justice, Civil Rights Division. (2015). Investigation of the Ferguson Police Department. Retrieved from https://www.justice.gov/sites/default/files/opa/press-releases/attachments/2015/03/04/ferguson_police_department_report.pdf

U.S. Department of Justice, Civil Rights Division. (2016). Investigation of the Baltimore City Police Department. Retrieved from https://www.justice.gov/crt/file/883296/download

Uggen, C., Larson, R., & Shannon, S. (2016). 6 million lost voters: State-level estimates of felony voter disenfranchisement. Retrieved from https://www.sentencingproject.org/publications/6-million-lost-voters-state-level-estimates-felony-disenfranchisement-2016/

Van Wormer, K., & Bednar, S. (2002). Working with male batterers: A restorative–strengths perspective. *Families in Society: The Journal of Contemporary Human Services*, *83*(5), 557–565.

Vaver, A. (2013). *Bound with an iron chain: The untold story of how the British transported 50,000 convicts to colonial America.* Westborough, MA: Pickpocket.

Vera Institute of Justice. (2019a). Arrest trends. Retrieved from https://arresttrends.vera.org/

Vera Institute of Justice. (2019b). The burden of mental illness behind bars. Retrieved from https://www.vera.org/the-human-toll-of-jail/inside-the-massive-jail-that-doubles-as-chicagos-largest-mental-health-facility/the-burden-of-mental-illness-behind-bars

Vitale, A. S. (2008). *City of disorder: How the quality of life campaign transformed New York politics.* New York, NY: New York University Press.

Vitale, A. S. (2017). *The end of policing.* New York, NY: Verso Press.

Wahab, S., & Panichelli, M. (2013). Ethical and human rights issues in coercive interventions with sex workers. *Affilia: Journal of Women and Social Work*, *28*(4), 344–349,

Walker, S. (1997). Records of the Wickersham Commission on Law Observance and Enforcement Part 1: Records of the Committee on Official Lawlessness. Retrieved from http://www.lexisnexis.com/documents/academic/upa_cis/1965_WickershamCommPt1.pdf

Washington State Superior Courts. (2018). WA State Superior Courts: 2018 Reference guide on legal financial obligations (LFOs). Retrieved from https://www.courts.wa.gov/content/manuals/Superior%20Court%20LFOs.pdf

Weir, K. (2012). Alone in the hole: Psychologists probe the mental health effects of solitary confinement. *Monitor on Psychology*, *43*(5), 54. Retrieved from https://www.apa.org/monitor/2012/05/solitary

Welsh, B. C., Braga, A., & Bruinsma, G. (2015). Reimagining broken windows: From theory to policy. *Journal of Research in Crime & Delinquency*, *52*(4), 447–463.

Wildeman, C. (2016). Incarceration and population health in wealthy democracies. *Criminology*, *54*(2), 360–382.

Winick, B. J., & Wexler, D. B. (2003). *Judging in a therapeutic key: Therapeutic jurisprudence and the courts.* Durham, NC: Carolina Academic Press.

Wolf, R. V. (2007). Principles of problem-solving justice. *Center for Court Innovation*. Retrieved from http://www.courtinnovation.org/sites/default/files/Principles.pdf

Zehr, H. (1990). *Changing lenses: A new focus for crime and justice*. Harrisonburg, VA: Herald Press.

CHAPTER 14

Abelson, E. S. (2003). "Women who have no men to work for them": Gender and homelessness in the Great Depression, 1930–1934. *Feminist Studies, 29*(1), 105–127.

Barrows, I. C. (1895). Proceedings of the National Conference of Charities and Corrections. Retrieved from https://books.google.com/books?id=RM0pAAAAYAAJ

Bass, D. (1992). *Helping vulnerable youths: Runaway and homeless adolescents in the United States.* Washington, DC: National Association of Social Workers.

Calmore, J. O. (1997). Race/ism lost and found: The Fair Housing Act at thirty. *University of Miami Law Review, 52*, 1067–1130.

"The Civil Rights Cases, 109 U.S. 3 (1883)." (n.d.). Oyez. Retrieved from https://www.oyez.org/cases/1850-1900/109us3

Commission on Equity and Opportunity. (2019). Hope for success: Returning home. Retrieved from https://www.cceh.org/wp-content/uploads/2019/02/CEO-Report-Hope-for-Success-Returning-Home.pdf

Crouse, J. M. (1986). *The homeless transient in the Great Depression: New York state, 1929–1941.* Albany, NY: SUNY Press.

Federal Housing Administration. (1936). Underwriting manual: Underwriting analysis under title II, section 203 of the National Housing Act. Retrieved from https://babel.hathitrust.org/cgi/pt?id=mdp.39015018409246

Federal Register. (2011). Homeless Emergency Assistance and Rapid Transition to Housing: Defining "homeless." Retrieved from https://www.hudexchange.info/resources/documents/HEARTH_HomelessDefinition_FinalRule.pdf

Feldman, S. (1983). Out of the hospital, onto the streets: the overselling of benevolence. *Hastings Center Report, 13*(3), 5–7.

Gollaher, D. L. (1993). Dorothea Dix and the English origins of the American asylum movement. *Canadian Review of American Studies, 23*(3), 149–176.

Greene, J. M., Ringwalt, C. L., & Iachan, R. (1997). Shelters for runaway and homeless youths: Capacity and occupancy. *Child Welfare, 76*(4), 549–561.

Greene, S., Turner, M. A., & Gourevitch, R. (2017, August 29). Racial residential segregation and neighborhood disparities. Retrieved from https://www.mobilitypartnership.org/publications/racial-residential-segregation-and-neighborhood-disparities

Haber, M. G., & Toro, P. A. (2004). Homelessness among families, children, and adolescents: An ecological–developmental perspective. *Clinical Child and Family Psychology Review, 7*(3), 123–164.

Hopper, K. (1991). A poor apart: The distancing of homeless men in New York's history. *Social Research, 58*(1), 107–132.

Ingber, S. (2019, Feb. 27). Oregon set to pass the first statewide rent control bill. *NPR.* Retrieved from https://www.npr.org/2019/02/27/698509957/oregon-set-to-pass-the-first-statewide-rent-control-bill

Jenkins, B. (2009). Rent control: Do economists agree? *Economic Journal Watch, 6*(1), 73–112. Retrieved from https://econjwatch.org/File+download/238/2009-01-jenkins-reach_concl.pdf?mimetype=pdf

Johnson, R. A. (2010). African Americans and homelessness: Moving through history. *Journal of Black Studies, 40*(4), 583–605.

Kingsley, G. T. (2017). *Trends in housing problems and federal housing assistance.* Washington, DC: Urban Institute. Retrieved from https://www.urban.org/sites/default/files/publication/94146/trends-in-housing-problems-and-federal-housing-assistance.pdf

Kuhn, R., & Culhane, D. P. (1998). Applying cluster analysis to test a typology of homelessness by pattern of shelter utilization: Results from the analysis of administrative data. *American Journal of Community Psychology, 26*(2), 207–232.

Lamb, H. R. (1994). Reform of mental health laws: Not repeating the mistakes made in the United States. *Psychiatry and Clinical Neurosciences, 48*, 105–110.

Lazo, A. (2019, Feb 28). Oregon governor signs first statewide rent control measure. *The Wall Street Journal.* Retrieved from https://www.wsj.com/articles/oregon-governor-set-to-sign-first-statewide-rent-control-measure-11551365696

Lubove, R. (1963). *The progressives and the slums: Tenement house reform in New York City, 1890–1917.* Pittsburgh, PA: University of Pittsburgh Press.

McClendon, J., & Lane, S. R. (2014). Homeless people. In A. Gitterman (Ed.), *Handbook of social work practice with vulnerable and resilient populations* (3rd ed., pp. 345–365). New York, NY: Columbia University Press.

McKinney-Vento Act sec. 725(2); 42 U.S.C. 11435(2).

Megan, K. (2018, July 20). Homeless and in college: 17.5 percent of CSCU students surveyed have no permanent home. *Hartford Courant.* Retrieved from https://www.courant.com/education/hc-homeless-college-students-20180717-story.html

Miller, A., Unick, J., & Harburger, D. S. (2017). *Maryland Youth Count 2017: A report on the findings from Youth REACH MD's second survey of unaccompanied youth & young adults experiencing homelessness.* Baltimore: The Institute for Innovation & Implementation, University of Maryland School of Social Work.

National Alliance to End Homelessness. (2017). FY 2018 appropriations: HUD's homeless assistance grants. Retrieved from http://endhomelessness.org/wp-content/uploads/2017/07/McKinney-Vento-HAG-One-Pager.pdf

National Coalition for the Homeless. (2006). A dream denied: The criminalization of homelessness in U.S. cities. Retrieved from https://nationalhomeless.org/wp-content/uploads/2014/06/CrimzReport2006.pdf

National Coalition for the Homeless. (2009). Mental illness and homelessness. Retrieved from https://www.nationalhomeless.org/factsheets/Mental_Illness.pdf

National Coalition for the Homeless. (2018). Vulnerable to hate: A survey of bias-motivated violence against people experiencing homelessness in 2016–2017. Retrieved from https://nationalhomeless.org/wp-content/uploads/2019/01/hate-crimes-2016-17-final_for-web2.pdf

National Community Reinvestment Coalition. (2002). Anti predatory lending toolkit. Retrieved from http://www.housingrights.com/pdfs/Predlend/Toolkit_w_covers.pdf

National Community Reinvestment Coalition. (2018, December 18). HOLC "redlining" maps: The persistent structure of segregation and economic inequality. Retrieved from https://ncrc.org/holc/

National Housing Law Project. (2017). Sources of income discrimination. Retrieved from https://www.nhlp.org/resources/source-of-income-discrimination-2/

National Low Income Housing Coalition. (2012). Who lives in federally assisted housing? Retrieved from https://nlihc.org/sites/default/files/HousingSpotlight2-2.pdf

National Multifamily Housing Council. (2018). Rent control laws by state. Retrieved from https://www.nmhc.org/research-insight/analysis-and-guidance/rent-control-laws-by-state/

Owens, D. (2017, February 20). Veteran congressman still pushing for reparations in a divided America. *NBC News*. Retrieved from https://www.nbcnews.com/news/nbcblk/rep-john-conyers-still-pushing-reparations-divided-america-n723151

Padgett, D. K., Gulcur, L., & Tsemberis, S. (2006). Housing First services for people who are homeless with co-occurring serious mental illness and substance abuse. *Research on Social Work Practice, 16*(1), 74–83.

Pew Research Center. (2014). Wealth inequality has widened along racial, ethnic lines since end of Great Recession. Retrieved from http://www.pewresearch.org/fact-tank/2014/12/12/racial-wealth-gaps-great-recession/

Reynolds, M. T. (1893). *The housing of the poor in American cities: The prize essay of the American Economic Association for 1892* (Vol. *8*, No. 2–3). Baltimore, MD: American Economic Association.

Rice, D. (2016). Chart book: Cuts in federal assistance have exacerbated families struggle to afford housing. Washington, DC: Center for Budget and Policy Priorities. Retrieved from https://www.cbpp.org/research/housing/chart-book-cuts-in-federal-assistance-have-exacerbated-families-struggles-to-afford#section01

Riis, J. A. (1890/1967). *How the other half lives: Studies of the tenements of New York*. New York, NY: Scribner.

Robertson, C. T., Egelhof, R., & Hoke, M. (2008). Get sick, get out: The medical causes for home mortgage foreclosures. *Health Matrix, 18*, 65–105.

Robertson, M. J., & Toro, P. A. (1999, August). Homeless youth: Research, intervention, and policy. Retrieved from https://aspe.hhs.gov/system/files/pdf/167051/6817.pdf#page=75

Rothstein, R. (2017). *The color of law: A forgotten history of how our government segregated America*. New York, NY: Liveright.

Squires, G. D. (Ed.). (2017). *The fight for fair housing: Causes, consequences, and future implications of the 1968 Federal Fair Housing Act*. New York, NY: Routledge.

U.S. Commission on Civil Rights. (1973). Understanding fair housing. Retrieved from https://www2.law.umaryland.edu/marshall/usccr/documents/cr11042.pdf

U.S. Department of Housing and Urban Development. (2011). The 2010 Annual Homeless Assessment Report to Congress. Retrieved from https://www.hudexchange.info/resources/documents/2010HomelessAssessmentReport.pdf

U.S. Department of Housing and Urban Development. (2018a). Homeownership: The American dream. Retrieved from https://www.huduser.gov/portal/pdredge/pdr-edge-frm-asst-sec-081318.html

U.S. Department of Housing and Urban Development. (2018b). The 2018 Annual Homeless Assessment Report (AHAR) to Congress. Retrieved from https://www.hudexchange.info/resources/documents/2018-AHAR-Part-1.pdf

U.S. Department of Housing and Urban Development. (n.d.-a). Continuum of Care (CoC) Program. Retrieved from https://www.hudexchange.info/programs/coc/

U.S. Department of Housing and Urban Development. (n.d.-b). Federal partner participation. Retrieved from https://www.hudexchange.info/hmis/federal-partner-participation/

U.S. Department of Housing and Urban Development. (n.d.-c). Homeless Emergency Assistance and Rapid Transition to Housing Act. Retrieved from https://www.hudexchange.info/homelessness-assistance/hearth-act/

U.S. Department of Housing and Urban Development. (n.d.-d). Section 202 Supportive Housing for the Elderly Program. Retrieved from https://www.hud.gov/program_offices/housing/mfh/progdesc/eld202

U.S. Interagency Council on Homelessness. (2018). Supportive housing. Retrieved from https://www.usich.gov/solutions/housing/supportive-housing/

United States House of Representatives. (n.d.). Historical highlights: The Civil Rights Act of 1875. Retrieved from https://history.house.gov/Historical-Highlights/1851-1900/The-Civil-Rights-Act-of-1875/

Wardrip, K., Pelletiere, D., & Crowley, S. (2005). Out of reach 2005. Retrieved from https://nlihc.org/oor/2005

Wu, G. (2018, December 31). A Bay Area New Year's resolution: Fixing the homelessness crisis. *San Francisco Chronicle*. Retrieved from https://www.sfchronicle.com/bayarea/article/A-Bay-Area-New-Year-s-resolution-fixing-the-13500968.php#photo-11848186

Youth.gov. (n.d.a). Federal definitions. Retrieved from https://youth.gov/youth-topics/runaway-and-homeless-youth/federal-definitions

Youth.gov. (n.d.b). Federal programs. Retrieved from https://youth.gov/youth-topics/runaway-and-homeless-youth/federal-programs

CHAPTER 15

Abramsky, S. (2019, Jan. 25). Why does Trump want to terminate Temporary Protected Status? *The Nation*. Retrieved from https://www.thenation.com/article/tps-immigration-trump-family-separation/

Adamy, J., & Overberg, P. (2018, June 21). Growth in retiring baby boomers strains U.S. Entitlement Programs: Census projections see a rapid increase in retiree-age Americans, putting pressure on Social Security. *The Wall Street Journal*. Retrieved from https://www.wsj.com/articles/retiring-baby-boomers-leave-the-u-s-with-fewer-workers-to-support-the-elderly-1529553660

Altschuler, D. (2011). The Dreamers movement comes of age. *Dissent*. Retrieved from https://www.dissentmagazine.org/online_articles/the-dreamers-movement-comes-of-age

American Immigration Council. (2018). An overview of U.S. refugee law and policy. Retrieved from https://www.americanimmigrationcouncil.org/research/overview-us-refugee-law-and-policy

Amuedo-Dorantes, C., & Antman, F. (2016). Can authorization reduce poverty among undocumented immigrants? Evidence from the Deferred Action for Childhood Arrivals program. *Economics Letters, 147*, 1–4.

Balderrama, F., & Rodriguez, R. (1995). *Decades of betrayal: Mexican repatriation in the 1930s*. Albuquerque, NM: University of New Mexico Press.

Berkowitz, D., Huizer, L., & Smith, R. (2017). Protecting injured immigrant workers from retaliation. Retrieved from https://www.nelp.org/publication/protecting-injured-immigrant-workers-from-retaliation/

Blau, J., & Frezzo, M. (Eds.). (2012). *Sociology for a new Century Series: Sociology and human rights: A bill of rights for the twenty-first century*. Thousand Oaks, CA: SAGE Publications, Inc. doi:10.4135/9781483349121

Borjas, G. (2016). Yes, immigration hurts American workers: The candidates tell drastically different stories about immigration. They're both skipping half the truth. *Politico Magazine*. Retrieved from https://www.politico.com/magazine/story/2016/09/trump-clinton-immigration-economy-unemployment-jobs-214216

Brodkin, K. (1998). *How Jews became white folk and what that says about race in America*. New Brunswick, NJ: Rutgers University Press.

Bump, P. (2018, Oct 22). Welcome to the fear election (for the third election in a row). *The Washington Post*. Retrieved from https://www.washingtonpost.com/politics/2018/10/22/welcome-fear-election-third-election-row/?utm_term=.3c5c94296784

Cassidy, J. (2018, June 22). Why the United States needs more immigrants. *The New Yorker*. Retrieved from https://www.newyorker.com/news/our-columnists/why-the-united-states-needs-more-immigrants

Chamber of Commerce v. Whiting, 563 U.S. 582 (2011). Retrieved from https://www.supremecourt.gov/opinions/10pdf/09-115.pdf

Chaudry, A., Capps, R., Pedroza, J., Castañeda, R. M., Santos, R., & Scott, M. (2010). *Facing our future: Children in the aftermath of immigration enforcement*. Washington, DC: Urban Institute.

Cohn, I. (2015). How U.S. immigration laws and rules have changed through history. Retrieved from http://www.pewresearch.org/fact-tank/2015/09/30/how-u-s-immigration-laws-and-rules-have-changed-through-history/

DeSipio, L., & de la Garcia, R. (2015). *U.S. Immigration in the twenty-first century: Making Americans, remaking America*. New York, NY: Routledge.

Dickerson, C. (2019, Mar. 5). Border at 'breaking point' as more than 76,000 unauthorized migrants cross in a month. *The New York Times*. Retrieved from https://www.nytimes.com/2019/03/05/us/border-crossing-increase.html

Dreier, H. (2018). How a crackdown on MS-13 caught up innocent high school students. *The New York Times*. Retrieved from https://www.nytimes.com/2018/12/27/magazine/ms13-deportation-ice.html

Duara, N. (2016, Sept. 15). Arizona's once-feared immigration law, SB 1070, loses most of its power in settlement. *Los Angeles Times*. Retrieved from http://www.latimes.com/nation/la-na-arizona-law-20160915-snap-story.html

E.D. v. Sharkey, No. 18-1688 (3d Cir. 2019).

Fernandez, M., Dickerson, C., & Villegas, P. (2019, July 4). The price of Trump's migrant deterrence strategy: New chaos on the border. *The New York Times*. Retrieved from https://www.nytimes.com/2019/01/04/us/mexico-wall-policy-trump.html

Foner, N. (2006). *In a new land: A comparative view of immigration*. New York, NY: New York University Press.

Garcia, A., & Franchim, S. (2013). 10 facts you need to know about immigrant women (2013 update). Retrieved from https://www.americanprogress.org/issues/immigration/news/2013/03/08/55794/10-facts-you-need-to-know-about-immigrant-women-2013-update/

Garrison, J., Bensinger, K., & Singer-Vine, J. (2015). The new American slavery: Invited to the U.S., foreign workers find a nightmare. *BuzzFeed*. Retrieved from https://www.buzzfeednews.com/article/jessicagarrison/the-new-american-slavery-invited-to-the-us-foreign-workers-f

Griffith, B., & Vaughan, J. (2019). *Maps: Sanctuary cities, counties, and states*. Washington, DC: Center for Immigration Studies. Retrieved from https://cis.org/Map-Sanctuary-Cities-Counties-and-States

Huennekens, J. (2018). Impact of H-2B guestworkers in 2018. Retrieved from https://cis.org/Report/Impact-H2B-Guestworkers-2018

Human Rights Watch. (2018). In the freezer: Abusive conditions for women and children in US immigration holding cells. Retrieved from https://www.hrw.org/report/2018/02/28/freezer/abusive-conditions-women-and-children-us-immigration-holding-cells#

Ignatiev, N. (1995). *How the Irish became white*. New York, NY: Routledge.

Immigration and Nationality Act, USC 101(a)(42)(A), 2013. Retrieved from https://www.uscis.gov/ilink/docView/SLB/HTML/SLB/act.html

International Organization on Migration (2018). Migrant deaths remain high despite sharp fall in US-Mexico border crossings in 2017. Retrieved from https://www.iom.int/news/migrant-deaths-remain-high-despite-sharp-fall-us-mexico-border-crossings-2017

Kerwin, D. (2014). Creating a more responsive and seamless refugee protection system: The scope, promise, and limitations of US temporary protection programs. *Journal of Migration and Human Security, 2*(1), 4–72.

Krogstadt, J. M., & Radford, J. (2017). Key facts about immigration. Retrieved from http://www.pewresearch.org/fact-tank/2017/01/30/key-facts-about-refugees-to-the-u-s/

Legal Arizona Workers Act. (2007). HB 2799. Retrieved from https://www.azleg.gov/search/oop/qfullhit.asp?CiWebHitsFile=/legtext/48leg/1r/bills/hb2779c.htm&CiRestriction=2779&CiBeginHilite=%3Cb%3E&CiEndHilite=%3C/b%3E&CiHiliteType=Full

Levin, S. (2017, March 30). Immigration crackdown enables worker exploitation, labor department staff say. *The Guardian*. Retrieved from https://www.theguardian.com/us-news/2017/mar/30/undocumented-workers-deportation-fears-trump-administration-department-labor

López, G., Bialik, J., & Radford, J. (2018, Nov. 30). *Key findings about U.S. immigrants*. Washington, DC: Pew Research Center. Retrieved from http://www.pewresearch.org/fact-tank/2018/11/30/key-findings-about-u-s-immigrants/

López, G., Ruiz, N. G., & Patten, E. (2017). *Key facts about Asian Americans, a diverse and growing population*. Washington, DC: Pew Research Center. Retrieved from https://www.pewresearch.org/fact-tank/2017/09/08/key-facts-about-asian-americans/

López, V., & Park, S. (2018). ICE detention center says it's not responsible for staff's sexual abuse of detainees. [Blog post]. Retrieved from https://www.aclu.org/blog/immigrants-rights/immigrants-rights-and-detention/ice-detention-center-says-its-not-responsible

Luden, J. (2006). 1965 immigration law changed face of America. *NPR*. Retrieved from https://www.npr.org/templates/story/story.php?storyId=5391395

Lyons, K., Levin, S., Glenzam J., & Holpuch, A. (2018, July 9). Why were families being separated at the southern US border? *The Guardian*. Retrieved from https://www.theguardian.com/us-news/live/2018/jun/20/tender-age-trump-children-separations-detention-shelters-latest-news-updates-live

Messick, M., & Bergeron, C. (2014). Temporary Protected Status in the United States: A grant of humanitarian relief that is less than permanent. Retrieved from https://www.migrationpolicy.org/article/temporary-protected-status-united-states-grant-humanitarian-relief-less-permanent

National Academies of Sciences, Engineering, and Medicine. (2017). *The economic and fiscal consequences of immigration.* Washington, DC: The National Academies Press. Retrieved from https://www.nap.edu/download/23550

National Association of Social Workers. (2018, May 30). *NASW says plan to separate undocumented immigrant children from their parents is malicious and unconscionable.* [Press release] Retrieved from https://www.socialworkers.org/news/news-releases/id/1654/nasw-says-plan-to-separate-undocumented-immigrant-children-from-their-parents-is-malicious-and-unconscionable

National Conference of State Legislators. (2019). Report on state immigration laws 2018. Retrieved from http://www.ncsl.org/research/immigration/report-on-state-immigration-laws.aspx

National Immigration Law Center. (2018). Status of current DACA litigation. Retrieved from https://www.nilc.org/issues/daca/status-current-daca-litigation/

Olson, L. (2008). *Immigrant students in our public schools* (10th ed.). New York, NY: New Press.

Raff, J. (2018). Some immigrant parents fear losing their children forever. *The Atlantic*. Retrieved from https://www.theatlantic.com/politics/archive/2018/10/immigrant-parents-fear-losing-their-children-forever/573331/

Sarlin, B. (2013, December. 16). How America's harshest immigration law failed. *MSNBC*. Retrieved from http://www.msnbc.com/msnbc/undocumented-workers-immigration-alabama

Savage, C., & Pear, R. (2019, February. 18). 16 states sue to stop Trump's use of emergency powers to build border wall. *The New York Times.* Retrieved from https://www.nytimes.com/2019/02/18/us/politics/national-emergency-lawsuits-trump.html

Shetty, S. (2019). Most dangerous journey: What Central Americans face when they try to cross the border. Retrieved from https://www.amnestyusa.org/most-dangerous-journey-what-central-american-migrants-face-when-they-try-to-cross-the-border/

Slobe, E. (2018, Oct. 8). DOJ blocked from restricting federal grants to 'sanctuary cities.' *The Jurist*. Retrieved from https://www.jurist.org/news/2018/10/doj-blocked-from-restricting-federal-grants-to-sanctuary-cities/

Taxin, A. (2018). Immigrant children describe treatment in detention centers. *AP News*. Retrieved from https://www.apnews.com/1a8db84a88a940049558b4c450dccc8a

U.S. Border Patrol. (2017). U.S. Border Patrol monthly apprehensions (FY 2000–FY 2017). Retrieved from https://www.cbp.gov/sites/default/files/assets/documents/2017-Dec/BP%20Total%20Monthly%20Apps%20by%20Sector%20and%20Area%2C%20FY2000-FY2017.pdf

U.S. Census Bureau. (2018). Quick facts: Arizona. Retrieved from https://www.census.gov/quickfacts/fact/table/az/PST045217.

U.S. Citizenship and Immigration Services. (2012). Overview of INS history. Retrieved from https://www.uscis.gov/sites/default/files/USCIS/History%20and%20Genealogy/Our%20History/INS%20History/INSHistory.pdf

U.S. Citizenship and Immigration Services. (2017). Number of form I-821D, consideration of deferred action for childhood arrivals, by fiscal year, quarter, intake, biometrics and case status fiscal year 2012–2017. Retrieved from https://www.uscis.gov/sites/default/files/USCIS/Resources/Reports%20and%20Studies/Immigration%20Forms%20Data/All%20Form%20Types/DACA/daca_performancedata_fy2017_qtr2.pdf

U.S. Citizenship and Immigration Services. (2018). Renew your DACA. Retrieved from https://www.uscis.gov/archive/renew-your-daca

U.S. Citizenship and Immigration Services. (2019). Deferred Action for Childhood Arrivals: Response to January 2018 preliminary injunction. Retrieved from https://www.uscis.gov/humanitarian/deferred-action-childhood-arrivals-response-january-2018-preliminary-injunction

U.S. Department of Homeland Security. (2018). FY 2018: Budget in brief. Retrieved from .https://www.dhs.gov/sites/default/files/publications/DHS%20FY18%20BIB%20Final.pdf

U.S. Department of Homeland Security. (n.d.-a). Paths to U.S. citizenship. Retrieved from https://www.uscis.gov/us-citizenship/citizenship-through-naturalization/path-us-citizenship

U.S. Department of Homeland Security. (n.d.-b). Permanent workers. Retrieved from https://www.uscis.gov/working-united-states/permanent-workers

U.S. Department of Justice. (2017). Department of Justice reviewing letters from ten potential sanctuary jurisdictions. Retrieved from https://www.justice.gov/opa/pr/department-justice-reviewing-letters-ten-potential-sanctuary-jurisdictions

U.S. Department of State. (n.d.-a). Family-based immigrant visas. Retrieved from https://travel.state.gov/content/travel/en/us-visas/immigrate/family-immigration/family-based-immigrant-visas.html#1

U.S. Department of State. (n.d.-b). The Immigration Act of 1924 (The Johnson-Reed Act). Retrieved from https://history.state.gov/milestones/1921-1936/immigration-act

U.S. Holocaust Memorial Museum. (n.d.). The United States and the Holocaust. Retrieved from https://encyclopedia.ushmm.org/content/en/article/the-united-states-and-the-holocaust

United Nations. (1948, December. 10). The Declaration on Human Rights. Retrieved from http://www.un.org/en/universal-declaration-human-rights/

Venkataramani, A. S., Shah, S. J., O'Brien, R., Kawachi, I., & Tsai, A. (2017). Health consequences of the U.S. Deferred Action for Childhood Arrivals (DACA) immigration programme: A quasi-experimental study. *Lancet Public Health, 2*: e175–81. Retrieved from https://www.thelancet.com/action/showPdf?pii=S2468-2667%2817%2930047-6

Vitale, A. (2017). *The end of policing.* New York, NY: Verso Press.

Warren, R., & Kerwin, D. (2017). The 2,000 mile wall in search of a purpose: Since 2007 visa overstays have outnumbered undocumented border crossers by a half million. *Journal on Migration and Human Security, 5*(1), 124–136. Retrieved from http://cmsny.org/publications/jmhs-visa-overstays-border-wall/

World Bank Group. (2016). Migration and development: A role for the World Bank Group. Retrieved from http://documents.worldbank.org/curated/en/690381472677671445/Migration-and-development-a-role-for-the-World-Bank-Group

Zayas, L., & Bradlee, M. (2014). Exiling children, creating orphans: When immigration policies hurt citizens. *Social Work, 52*(2), 167–175.

CHAPTER 16

Allaire, M., Wu, H., & Lall, U. (2018). National trends in drinking water quality violations. *Proceedings of the National Academy of Sciences, 115*(9), 2078–2083.

Alston, M. (2015). Social work, climate change and global cooperation. *International Social Work, 58*(3), 355–363. https://doi.org/10.1177/0020872814556824

American Council for Energy Efficient Economy. (2018). Tailpipe emissions standards. Retrieved from https://database.aceee.org/state/tailpipe-emission-standards

Balazs, C., Morello-Frosch, R., Hubbard, A., & Ray, I. (2011). Social disparities in nitrate: Contaminated drinking water in California's San Joaquin Valley. *Environmental Health Perspectives, 119*(9), 1272–1278.

Bell, H. (2008). Case management with displaced survivors of Hurricane Katrina: A case study of one host community. *Journal of Social Service Research, 34*(3), 15–27.

Berger, R., & Kelly, J. (1993). Social work in the ecological crisis. *Social Work, 38*, 521–526.

Bhuyan, R., Wahab, S., & Park, Y. (2019). A green new deal for social work. *Affilia, 34*(3), 289–294. https://doi.org/10.1177/0886109919861700

Brady, H. (2017). 4 key impacts of the Keystone XL and Dakota Access Pipelines. *National Geographic.* Retrieved from https://news.nationalgeographic.com/2017/01/impact-keystone-dakota-access-pipeline-environment-global-warming-oil-health/

Bullard, R. (1990). *Dumping in Dixie: Race, class and environmental quality.* Boulder, CO: Westview Press.

Bullard, R., & Wright, B. (2012). *The wrong complexion for protection: How the government response to disaster endangers African American communities.* New York, NY: New York University Press.

Bullard, R., Mohai, P., Saha, R., & Wright, B. (2007). *Toxic waste and race at twenty, 1987–2007. A report prepared for the United Church of Christ Justice & Witness Ministries.* Cleveland, OH: The United Church of Christ. Retrieved from https://www.nrdc.org/sites/default/files/toxic-wastes-and-race-at-twenty-1987-2007.pdf

California Proposition 65, 1986. Retrieved from https://oehha.ca.gov/proposition-65/law/proposition-65-law-and-regulations

California Technical Bulletin 117, 1975 revised 2014. Retrieved from https://bhgs.dca.ca.gov/about_us/tb117_2013.pdf

Carson, R. (1962;/2002). *Silent spring.* New York, NY: Houghton Mifflin.

Chazin, R., Hanson, M., Cohen, C., & Grishayeva, I. (2002). Sharing knowledge and skills: Learning from training school-based practitioners in Ukraine. *Journal of Teaching in Social Work, 22*(3/4), 89–101.

Clark, A. (2018, July 3). 'Nothing to worry about. The water is fine': How Flint poisoned its people. *The Guardian.* Retrieved from https://www.theguardian.com/news/2018/jul/03/nothing-to-worry-about-the-water-is-fine-how-flint-michigan-poisoned-its-people

Climate Reality Project. (2016). Follow the leader: How 11 countries are shifting to renewable energy. Retrieved from https://www.climaterealityproject.org/blog/follow-leader-how-11-countries-are-shifting-renewable-energy

Coates, J., & Gray, M. (2011). The environment and social work: An overview and introduction. *International Journal of Social Welfare, 21*(3), 230–238. https://doi.org/10.1111/j.1468-2397.2011.00851.x

Corburn, J., Osleeb, J., & Porter, M. (2006). Urban asthma and the neighbourhood environment in New York City. *Health & Place, 12*(2), 167–179.

Davenport, C. (2018, January 31). E.P.A. blocks Obama-era clean water rule. *The New York Times*. Retrieved from https://www.nytimes.com/2018/01/31/climate/trump-water-wotus.html

Davenport, C., & Rabin, R. C. (2018, September 26). E.P.A. places the head of its Office of Children's Health on leave. *The New York Times*. Retrieved from https://www.nytimes.com/2018/09/26/climate/epa-etzel-children-health-program.html

Denison, R. (2018). 5 ways chemical safety is eroding under Trump. [Blog post]. Retrieved from https://www.edf.org/blog/2018/05/01/5-ways-chemical-safety-eroding-under-trump

Dominelli, L. (2011). Climate change: Social workers' roles and contributions to policy debates and interventions. *International Journal of Social Welfare, 20*(4), 430–438. Retrieved from https://onlinelibrary.wiley.com/doi/abs/10.1111/j.1468-2397.2011.00795.x

Egelko, B. (2018, August 2). Trump attack on California's emission standards faces legal battle. *San Francisco Chronicle*. Retrieved from https://www.sfchronicle.com/news/article/Trump-attack-of-Ca-s-emission-standards-faces-13128243.php

Elkins, K. (2018, September. 28). Here's how much money Americans have in savings at every income level. *CNN*. Retrieved from https://www.cnbc.com/2018/09/27/heres-how-much-money-americans-have-in-savings-at-every-income-level.html

Environmental Protection Agency. (1999). 25 years of the Safe Drinking Water Act: History and trends. Retrieved from https://www.hsdl.org/?abstract&did=449348

Environmental Protection Agency. (2017). Evolution of the Clean Air Act. Retrieved from https://www.epa.gov/clean-air-act-overview/evolution-clean-air-act

Environmental Protection Agency. (2018a). Flint drinking water response: EPA continues to oversee state and city action to protect public health. Retrieved from https://www.epa.gov/flint

Environmental Protection Agency. (2018b). Superfund CERCLA Overview. Retrieved from https://www.epa.gov/superfund/superfund-cercla-overview

Environmental Protection Agency. (2019, February 19). *EPA releases first major update to chemicals list in 40 years* [Press release]. Retrieved from https://www.epa.gov/newsreleases/epa-releases-first-major-update-chemicals-list-40-years

Environmental Protection Agency. (2019b). History of the Resource Conservation and Recovery Act. Retrieved from https://www.epa.gov/rcra/history-resource-conservation-and-recovery-act-rcra

Environmental Protection Agency. (2019c). Private drinking water wells. Retrieved from https://www.epa.gov/privatewells

Environmental Protection Agency. (2019d). Statistics for the New Chemicals Review Program under TSCA. Retrieved from https://www.epa.gov/reviewing-new-chemicals-under-toxic-substances-control-act-tsca/statistics-new-chemicals-review

European Commission. (2000). Communication from the Commission on the precautionary principle. Retrieved from https://eur-lex.europa.eu/legal-content/EN/TXT/?uri=celex%3A52000DC0001

Federal Register. (2015, August. 28). Clean Water Rule of 2015. 40 CFR 23. Retrieved from https://www.federalregister.gov/documents/2015/06/29/2015-13435/clean-water-rule-definition-of-waters-of-the-united-states

Friedman, L. (2019, May 19). E.P.A. plans to get thousands of pollution deaths off the books by changing its math. *The New York Times*. Retrieved from https://www.nytimes.com/2019/05/20/climate/epa-air-pollution-deaths.html

Geisel, T. (1971). *The Lorax*. New York, NY: Random House.

Gould, K., & Lewis, T. (2015). *Twenty lessons in environmental sociology* (2nd ed.). New York, NY: Oxford University Press.

Green Party US. (2018). Ecological sustainability. Retrieved from http://www.gp.org/ecological_sustainability_2016

Harr, J. (1995). *A civil action*. New York, NY: Random House.

Hasselman, J. (2018). *On the U.S. Army Corps' Aug. 31 decision on the Dakota Access Pipeline*. Washington, DC: Earth Justice. Retrieved from https://earthjustice.org/features/inside-the-legal-case-dapl-update

Healy, J. (2018, November 3). Rural America's own private Flint: Polluted water too dangerous to drink. *The New York Times*. Retrieved from https://www.nytimes.com/2018/11/03/us/water-contaminated-rural-america.html

Hersher, R. (2016, November. 2). Obama: Army Corps examining possible rerouting of Dakota Access Pipeline. *NPR*. Retrieved from https://www.npr.org/sections/thetwo-way/2016/11/02/500363689/obama-army-corps-examining-possible-rerouting-of-dakota-access-pipeline

Hersher, R. (2017, February 22). Key moments in the Dakota Access Pipeline fight. *NPR*. Retrieved from https://www.npr.org/sections/thetwo-way/2017/02/22/514988040/key-moments-in-the-dakota-access-pipeline-fight

Hirji, Z., & Song, L. (2016). The fracking boom: State by state. *Inside Climate News*. Retrieved from https://insideclimatenews.org/news/20150120/map-fracking-boom-state-state

Hoff, M. D., & McNutt, J. G. (1994). *The global environmental crisis: Implications for social welfare and social work*. Marlborough, UK: Averbury.

Holtman, N., & Bodner, P. (2017). *Trump tried to kill the Paris Agreement but the effect has been the opposite*. Washington, DC: Brookings Institute. Retrieved from https://www.brookings.edu/blog/planetpolicy/2018/06/01/trump-tried-to-kill-the-paris-agreement-but-the-effect-has-been-the-opposite/

Intergovernmental Panel on Climate Change. (2014). Climate Change 2014: Synthesis report. Contribution of working groups I, II and III to the fifth assessment report of the Intergovernmental Panel on Climate Change [Core writing team, R. K. Pachauri & L. A. Meyer (Eds.)]. Geneva, Switzerland: IPCC. Retrieved from http://www.ipcc.ch/report/ar5/

Intergovernmental Panel on Climate Change. (2018, October 8). *Press release: Summary for policymakers of IPCC Special Report on Global Warming of 1.5°C approved by governments* [Press release]. Retrieved from http://www.ipcc.ch/news_and_events/pr_181008_P48_spm.shtml

Kemp, S., & Palinkas, L. (2015). Strengthening the social response to the human impacts of environmental change (Working paper no. 5). Retrieved from https://aaswsw.org/wp-content/uploads/2015/03/Social-Work-and-Global-Environmental-Change-3.24.15.pdf

Kollipara, P. (2015, March. 19). The bizarre way the U.S. regulates chemicals—letting them on the market first, then maybe studying them. *The Washington Post*. Retrieved from https://www.washingtonpost.com/news/energy-environment/wp/2015/03/19/our-broken-congresss-latest-effort-to-fix-our-broken-toxic-chemicals-law/?utm_term=.74e06d693072

Kriebel, D., Tickner, J., Epstein, P., Lemons, J., Levins, R., Loechler, E. L., . . . Stoto, M. (2001). The precautionary principle in environmental science. *Environmental Health Perspectives, 109*(9), 871–876.

Lewis, J. (1985). The birth of EPA. *EPA Journal, 11*, 6.

Mai-Duc, C. (2015). The 1969 Santa Barbara oil spill that changed oil and gas exploration forever. *Los Angeles Times*. Retrieved from http://www.latimes.com/local/lanow/la-me-ln-santa-barbara-oil-spill-1969-20150520-htmlstory.html

Mascarenhas, M. (2015). Environmental inequality and environmental justice. In K. Gould & T. Lewis (Eds.), *Twenty lessons in environmental sociology*. Oxford, UK: Oxford University Press.

Massachusetts v. Environmental Protection Agency, 549 U.S. 497 (2007).

McCown, B. (2018, June 4). What ever happened to the Dakota Access Pipeline? *Forbes Magazine*. Retrieved from https://www.forbes.com/sites/brighammccown/2018/06/04/what-ever-happened-to-the-dakota-access-pipeline/#1de0c3bd4055

McKinnon, J. (2008). Exploring the nexus between social work and the environment. *Australian Social Work., 61*(3), 256–268.

Morris, C. (2017, September 16). Hurricane alert: 40 percent of small businesses never recover from a disaster. *CNBC*. Retrieved from https://www.cnbc.com/2017/09/16/hurricane-watch-40-percent-of-small-businesses-dont-reopen-after-a-disaster.html

Morris, J., Song, L., & Hasemyer, D. (2014). Big oil, bad air: Fracking the Eagle Ford Shale of South Texas. Retrieved from https://eagleford.publicintegrity.org/

National Forest Management Act of 1976. P.O. 94-588, 90 Stat. 2949, as amended; 16 U.S.C. Retrieved from https://www.fs.fed.us/emc/nfma/includes/NFMA1976.pdf

National Oceanic and Atmospheric Administration. (2018). About the National Coastal Zone Management Program. Retrieved from https://coast.noaa.gov/czm/about/

NBC News. (2017, April 23). Authorities drop 33 cases against Dakota Access protesters. Retrieved from https://www.nbcnews.com/storyline/dakota-pipeline-protests/authorities-drop-33-cases-against-dakota-access-protesters-n749806

Nijhuis, M. (2018, February 18). The Valve Turners. *The New York Times*. Retrieved from https://www.nytimes.com/2018/02/13/magazine/afraid-climate-change-prison-valve-turners-global-warming.html

Office of Environmental Health Hazard Assessment. (2018). Proposition 65. Retrieved from https://oehha.ca.gov/proposition-65

Office of Health and Safety Administration. (2018). Directives. Retrieved from https://www.osha.gov/enforcement/directives/directivenumber/CPL

Pennsylvania General Assembly. (2012). Title 58 Sec 3218. Retrieved from http://blogs.law.widener.edu/envirolawcenter/files/2013/12/Act13of20121.pdf

Praglin, L. (2007). Ida Cannon, Ethel Cohen, and early medical social work in Boston: The foundations of a model of culturally competent social service. *Social Service Review, 81*(1), 27–45.

Rapanos v. United States, 547 U.S. 715 (2006).

Reck, A. (1964). *Selected writings: George Herbert Mead.* Chicago, IL: University of Chicago Press.

Rodgers, P. (1990). EPA history: The Clean Air Act of 1970. Retrieved from https://archive.epa.gov/epa/aboutepa/epa-history-clean-air-act-1970.html

Rosenbaum, W. (2017). *Environmental politics and policy* (10th ed.). Washington, DC: CQ Press.

Rott, N. (2018, March 20). Decline in hunters threatens how U.S. pays for conservation. *NPR.* Retrieved from https://www.npr.org/2018/03/20/593001800/decline-in-hunters-threatens-how-u-s-pays-for-conservation

Scientific American. (2017). The FDA needs more power to regulate toxic chemicals in cosmetics. Retrieved from https://www.scientificamerican.com/article/the-fda-needs-more-power-to-regulate-toxic-chemicals-in-cosmetics/

Sellers, C., Dillon, L., Ohayon, J. L., Shapiro, N., Sullivan, M., Amoss, C., . . . Wylie, S. (2017). The EPA under siege: Trump's assault in history and testimony. Retrieved from https://envirodata-gov.org/wp-content/uploads/2017/06/Part-1-EPA-Under-Siege.pdf

Soine, L. (1987). Expanding the environment in social work: The case for including environmental hazards content. *Journal of Social Work Education, 23*(2), 40–46.

Stillo, F., & Gibson, J. M. (2017). Exposure to contaminated drinking water and health disparities in North Carolina. *American Journal of Public Health, 107*(1), 180–185.

Thee-Brenan, M. (2014). Americans are outliers in views on climate change. *The New York Times.* Retrieved from https://www.nytimes.com/2014/05/07/upshot/americans-are-outliers-in-views-on-climate-change.html

U.S. Department of Veterans Affairs. (2017). Exposure to Agent Orange by location. Retrieved from https://www.publichealth.va.gov/exposures/agentorange/locations/index.asp

U.S. Green Building Council. (n.d.). LEED is green building. Retrieved from https://new.usgbc.org/leed

United Nations. (2019). Paris Agreement: Status of ratification. Retrieved from https://unfccc.int/process/the-paris-agreement/status-of-ratification

Urlepainen, J. (2017, November 21). Trump's withdrawal from the Paris agreement means other countries will spend less to fight climate change. *The Washington Post.* Retrieved https://www.washingtonpost.com/news/monkey-cage/wp/2017/11/21/trumps-noncooperation-threatens-climate-finance-under-the-paris-agreement/

Warner, B., & Shapiro, J. (2013). Fractured, fragmented federalism: A study in fracking regulatory policy. *Publius: The Journal of Federalism, 43*(3), 474–496. https://doi.org/10.1093/publius/pjt014

Zakour, M. J. (1996). Geographic and social distance during emergencies: A path model of interorganizational links. *Social Work Research, 20*(1), 19–30.

INDEX